DUE DATE	RETURN DATE	DUE DATE	RETURN DATE
APR 1 4 1989	APR 1 4 1989		
MAY 5 1989			
APR 1 9 1989			
AUG 2 1 1991			
AUG 0 7 1991			

TUTORIAL:

GALLIUM ARSENIDE COMPUTER DESIGN

V. M. MILUTINOVIĆ AND DAVID A. FURA

COMPUTER SOCIETY OF THE IEEE ORDER NUMBER 795
LIBRARY OF CONGRESS NUMBER 87-72829
IEEE CATALOG NUMBER EH0266-7
ISBN 0-8186-0795-5
SAN 264-620X

 THE COMPUTER SOCIETY
OF THE IEEE

IEEE THE INSTITUTE OF ELECTRICAL AND ELECTRONICS ENGINEERS, INC.

IEEE
**COMPUTER
SOCIETY
PRESS**

TUTORIAL:

GALLIUM ARSENIDE COMPUTER DESIGN

V. M. MILUTINOVIĆ AND DAVID A. FURA

COMPUTER SOCIETY OF THE IEEE ORDER NUMBER 795
LIBRARY OF CONGRESS NUMBER 87-72829
IEEE CATALOG NUMBER EHO266-7
ISBN 0-8186-0795-5
SAN 264-620X

 THE COMPUTER SOCIETY
OF THE IEEE

IEEE   THE INSTITUTE OF ELECTRICAL AND ELECTRONICS ENGINEERS, INC.

IEEE
COMPUTER
SOCIETY
PRESS

Published by Computer Society Press of the IEEE
1730 Massachusetts Avenue, N.W.
Washington, D.C. 20036-1903

Cover designed by Jack I. Ballestero

Computer Society of the IEEE Order Number 795
Library of Congress Number 87-72829
IEEE Catalog Number EH0266-7
ISBN 0-8186-0795-5 (Paper)
ISBN 0-8186-4795-7 (Microfiche)
SAN 264-620X

Order from: Computer Society of the IEEE   IEEE Service Center   Computer Society of the IEEE
Terminal Annex   445 Hoes Lane   13, Avenue de l'Aquilon
Post Office Box 4699   P.O. Box 1331   B-1200 Brussels
Los Angeles, CA 90080   Piscataway, NJ 08855-1331   BELGIUM

 THE INSTITUTE OF ELECTRICAL AND ELECTRONICS ENGINEERS, INC.

IEEE

Preface

The past 10 years have been a time of remarkable growth for gallium arsenide (GaAs) technology. Even in its immature youth, GaAs was hailed as a potentially important material for future computer implementations. Although still far from full maturity, GaAs technology is reaching the advanced sophistication predicted by early researchers, and its role in computer system design requires a thorough evaluation. For what applications is GaAs well suited and for which computer design approaches will the strengths of this new technology be best exploited? To best utilize the increasingly capable GaAs integrated circuits of the foreseeable future, these questions must begin to be addressed today.

This tutorial is presented as a tool for computer designers in both academia and industry. It provides a thorough description of GaAs technology, detailing both its advantages and disadvantages. Several computer design approaches are shown to emerge from the characteristics of this technology. Example GaAs designs are also shown, ranging from individual IC's to multi-chip computer systems. This tutorial is intended for use in universities for advanced courses in computer design and computer architecture and in industry by computer researchers, implementers, and managers interested in keeping abreast of modern integrated circuit technology and modern computer design.

This tutorial is a self-contained presentation of GaAs computer design fundamentals. Chapter 1 provides an overview of the principal GaAs material and device properties that influence computer design. Chapter 2 presents the important GaAs devices and examples of their incorporation into advanced integrated circuits. Chapter 3 presents computer system applications and design concepts that are most appropriate for this new technology. Chapter 4 demonstrates the great interest in GaAs technology expressed through several advanced GaAs system designs. Chapter 5 concludes this tutorial with the description of experiments undertaken to support the design of a GaAs microprocessor, and also with a description of the related microprocessor architecture.

Table of Contents

Chapter 1: GaAs Technology Properties

This chapter overviews the fundamental characteristics of gallium arsenide (GaAs) technology. Several of these properties give GaAs advantages over silicon for computer implementation. For the same power consumption, GaAs transistors are roughly one half an order of magnitude faster than silicon transistors. GaAs is also considered to be generally more resistant to both radiation and temperature threats. Finally, GaAs has optical properties that may permit optical interconnections in future digital systems.

Unfortunately, GaAs currently has its share of problems, too. The poor quality of GaAs wafers leads to either very poor yields or else to physically small GaAs chips and, hence, to low levels of integration. Cost problems also exist because of the expensiveness of GaAs material, the need to use gold interconnects instead of aluminum, and the more frequent breakage of GaAs wafers owing to their brittleness. Poor noise margins and a large sensitivity to fan-in and fan-out, although considered temporary problems, also exist in GaAs. Packaging problems are more severe for GaAs: Crosstalk, ringing, and conductor length mismatches must be addressed. Finally, the testing of high-speed GaAs circuits requires advances in test equipment.

The properties of GaAs technology are very important from the point of view of a computer designer. These properties directly affect computer design through their influence on parameters such as gate delay, on-chip gate count, and the ratio of off-chip to on-chip memory access times. In an indirect way, they influence computer design because they determine which application environments are likely to see the use of GaAs technology.

In his paper "Radiation Effects in GaAs Integrated Circuits: A Comparison with Silicon," Simons describes the radiation-resistance properties of GaAs and compares them to those of silicon. In his study of four radiation threats, he finds that GaAs has a clear advantage for one, but that its capability against a second is not clear. This paper shows that GaAs is generally better able to tolerate radiation than is silicon, but that the GaAs advantage is derived from the device designs used and is only indirectly dependent upon material properties.

Miyazawa and Ishii, in their paper "Dislocations as the Origin of Threshold Voltage Scatterings for GaAs MESFET on LEC-Grown Semi-Insulating GaAs Substrate," illustrate the effect that GaAs material quality has on some GaAs circuits. They report that crystal dislocations near certain types of GaAs transistors cause wide variations in transistor threshold voltages. This paper establishes a clear need for improved GaAs material in order to implement large working chips with high yield. Alternatively, it suggests a motivation for using only small chips or else implementing some form of fault tolerance to increase yield.

In his article entitled "Limitations on the Performance of Field-Effect Devices for Logic Applications," Cooper presents fundamental limits on the performance of field effect transistor (FET) devices. He examines four considerations that directly influence performance and shows that silicon device performance will become limited before GaAs device performance will. This important result indicates that the role of GaAs technology will be an increasingly prominent one as future improvements are made in integrated circuit technology.

RADIATION EFFECTS IN GaAs INTEGRATED CIRCUITS:
A COMPARISON WITH SILICON

Mayrant Simons

Research Triangle Institute

Research Triangle Park, NC 27709

ABSTRACT

This paper reviews the hardness capability of contemporary GaAs devices and logic circuits in terms of the four major nuclear and space radiation threat categories--neutron effects, total dose effects, dose rate effects, and single particle phenomena. The basic interaction mechanisms for each threat area are briefly described, with emphasis given to potential problem areas and to fundamental differences between gallium arsenide and silicon. Existing and projected hardness levels characteristic of GaAs devices are compared with corresponding levels for silicon LSI technologies.

INTRODUCTION

There is considerable interest in the radiation hardness capability of contemporary GaAs integrated circuits since their performance properties make them attractive candidates for future military and space systems applications. Contemporary GaAs IC technology is based principally on the MESFET or JFET structure which is fabricated in epitaxially grown layers or implanted directly into the semi-insulating GaAs substrate material. Among the more popular logic families are SDFL and BFL, which employ depletion mode MESFETs, and DCFL, which is based on the EFET. GaAs linear ICs are limited mainly to monolithic microwave amplifiers. Although the library of available radiation response data for GaAs ICs is relatively small in comparison with the large silicon data base, enough has been published to enable a general characterization of the present technology. Existing GaAs IC data are based principally on tests of discrete FETs and logic gates of SSI complexity, some monolithic microwave amplifiers, and, more recently, several MSI level digital circuits.

It should be noted that, in general, the task of maintaining a particular hardness level becomes more difficult and requires tighter parameter control as circuit complexity increases toward the LSI and VLSI levels and the number of devices that must remain functional on a single chip increases.

In considering the effects of nuclear and space radiation on semiconductor circuits, it is convenient to separate the effects into four categories that can be treated independently (neglecting syner-gistic effects that may occur when simultaneously approaching failure levels from two or more threats). The four categories are:

1. Neutron Effects - permanent damage resulting from cumulative neutron exposure; units are in n/cm^2.

2. Total Dose Effects - permanent damage arising from cumulative ionizing radiation exposure to X-rays, gammas, electrons, or protons; units are in rads (material).

3. Dose Rate or Photocurrent Effects - transient upset, soft error, or latchup phenomena resulting from the ionizing dose rate usually associated with a gamma pulse; permanent damage (burnout) may occur at very high intensities; units are in rads (mat)/s.

4. Single Event Upset (SEU) Phenomena - soft errors (and maybe latchup) arising from α-particles, protons, or heavy ions incident on an individual cell or logic element; device susceptibility expressed as an upset cross section or particle fluence per upset/bit.

In the following sections, the basic interaction mechanisms associated with each of these threats are summarized and approximate failure thresholds for contemporary GaAs ICs are established from a review of available test data. These values are then compared with corresponding levels characteristic of the major silicon LSI technologies.

NEUTRON EFFECTS

High energy (E > 10 keV) neutrons originating from a nuclear event or reactor interact with a semiconductor through elastic collisions with atoms in the crystal lattice. The resulting atomic displacements from the equilibrium lattice sites produce defect centers in the semiconductor bandgap that can affect majority carrier concentration and mobility and minority carrier generation and recombination lifetimes. Gallium arsenide and silicon are affected in much the same manner by displacement damage. Since traps are introduced near midgap, p- and n-type material in both semiconductors are compensated by neutron exposure and, at very high fluences, tend to become intrinsic. Carrier re-

Reprinted from *Proceedings of the GaAs IC Symposium*, 1983, pages 124-128.
Copyright © 1983 by The Institute of Electrical and Electronics Engineers, Inc.

moval rates depend on a number of factors (such as carrier type and concentration, temperature, etc.) but are on the order of 10 cm^{-1} for GaAs and Si (1). Majority carrier mobility and minority carrier lifetimes also decrease in GaAs and Si as additional ionized scattering centers and generation/recombination centers are introduced by atomic displacements.

Minority carrier devices suffer mainly from gain degradation and increased leakage currents resulting from lifetime reduction while majority carrier device parameters are affected primarily by reductions in carrier concentration and mobility. Since the onset of significant minority carrier lifetime changes typically occur at lower fluences than do changes in majority carrier concentration and mobility, FET technologies (whether Si or GaAs) are inherently more resistant to neutron irradiation than bipolar technologies. The principal FET parameters that are affected by displacement damage are the maximum channel current (I_{DSS}), the maximum transconductance (g_{max}), the pinchoff voltage (V_p), and the cutoff frequency (f_c). All decrease monotonically with increasing neutron exposure (2).

Neutron test data reported for discrete GaAs JFETs (3) and MESFETs (4) show that the onset of parameter degradation occurs in the 10^{14} to 10^{15} n/cm^2 range; however, at an optimum channel doping level of 10^{17} cm^{-3}, changes were small after 10^{15} n/cm^2 (2,4). GaAs MSI logic devices based on either JFET or MESFET technologies should thus be capable of operating up to about 10^{15} n/cm^2 without suffering failure or significant performance degradation. However, as these technologies mature, failure thresholds for MSI devices are projected to extend into the 10^{15} to 10^{16} n/cm^2 regime. Linear devices, on the other hand, can be expected to be somewhat less tolerant as indicated by data showing increased noise figure in GaAs MESFET microwave amplifiers beginning at 10^{14} n/cm^2 (5). Significantly lower failure thresholds have been reported for GaAs CCDs which, like Si CCDs, suffer unacceptably large increases in transfer inefficiency between 10^{12} and 10^{13} n/cm^2 as a result of the introduction of shallow trapping levels (6).

For the reason previously mentioned, both GaAs FET and Si MOS ICs are characterized by a higher neutron tolerance than Si bipolar circuits. This is reflected in the comparison of neutron damage thresholds for GaAs and Si (7,8) IC technologies depicted in Figure 1.

TOTAL DOSE EFFECTS

The most dramatic difference in the radiation tolerances of GaAs and Si devices occur in their sensitivities to cumulative ionizing radiation exposure. In silicon devices, ionizing radiation produces a positive space charge in SiO_2 insulating layers and interface states at the SiO_2-Si interfaces. MOS technologies are particularly sensitive to this "surface damage" and ultimately fail because of gate threshold voltage shifts or increased leakage currents. However, since thermally grown SiO_2 is an integral part of the silicon planar process, bipolar ICs are also sensitive to surface damage phenomena (leakage channel formation, gain degradation, etc.), although they are usually characterized by higher failure thresholds than MOS devices. (Various hardening techniques have greatly improved the tolerances of bipolar and MOS technologies to total dose effects.)

Since unpassivated GaAs surfaces exhibit good stability and are generally insensitive to slowly accumulated total dose effects, JFET and MESFET technologies that employ no dielectric isolation or surface passivation should be almost immune to surface damage problems. However, since dielectric passivation is used in some planar GaAs FET fabrication processes (9), the potential for surface problems in such devices cannot be completely dismissed; obviously, any sensitivity to total dose effects would be determined by the properties of the passivation material and its proximity to active device regions. (The total dose susceptibility of GaAs MISFET devices would also be governed by the properties of the gate dielectric.)

While surface damage does not now appear to pose a major threat to contemporary GaAs ICs, GaAs devices do not have unlimited tolerance to cumulative ionizing radiation exposure. At high doses displacement damage becomes the limiting mechanism (as in the case of neutrons).

Co 60 radiation test data taken on discrete EJFET devices have shown that relatively small changes in threshold voltage and mobility occur at 10^8 rad (GaAs), provided the channel doping level is about 10^{17} cm^{-3}; however, at a doping level of 10^{16} cm^{-3} significant changes were seen at 10^7 rads (GaAs) (2). A 256-bit EJFET DCFL RAM of MSI complexity has also been reported to remain functional after 5×10^7 rads (GaAs) with only a 10% decrease in power dissipation (10). Small changes in MESFET parameters have been measured up to a level of 8×10^7 rads (Si) (11), and a Schottky diode FET logic (SDFL) circuit (150 gate complexity) was tested up to 10^8 rads while continuing to function and requiring only a small adjustment in the pulldown supply voltage (12). GaAs microwave MESFETs (13) and an MMIC amplifier (14) have also retained functionality up to 10^8 rads or more, although RF gain (13)

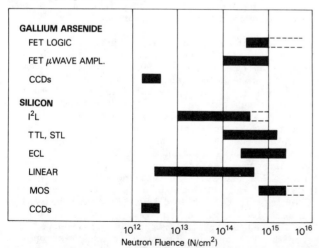

Figure 1. Reported (solid) and Projected (dotted) Displacement Damage Thresholds.

and noise figure (5) begin to degrade between 10^7 and 10^8 rads.

Based on the above data, it is concluded that both digital and linear GaAs ICs fabricated with contemporary FET technologies are capable of operating well into the 10^7 to 10^8 rad regime without suffering significant performance degradation. A comparison of total dose failure thresholds for contemporary GaAs and silicon technologies (7,8) is shown in Figure 2. Although total dose data have not been published on GaAs CCDs, they are expected to tolerate levels well above a megarad, making them appreciably harder than Si CCDs (4×10^4 to 10^6 rads).

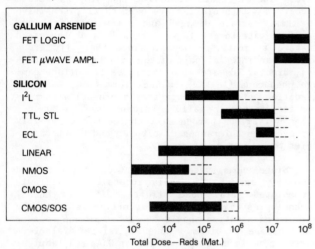

Figure 2. Reported (solid) and Projected (dotted) Total Dose Failure Thresholds.

DOSE RATE EFFECTS

Dose rate or photocurrent effects are produced in ICs as the excess carriers generated by the incident ionizing radiation are collected by p-n junctions. These effects are manifested in a circuit by large current or voltage perturbations whose magnitude and duration depend on the peak dose rate, pulse duration (t), junction area (A), collection volumes, carrier lifetimes (τ), and circuit/device time constants (especially when $> t$). For the simplest case of a p-n junction exposed to a square pulse of dose rate $\dot{\gamma}$ and duration $t \gg \tau_n, \tau_p$, the primary photocurrent is given by

$$I_{pp} = qA(W + L_n + L_p)g_o\dot{\gamma}$$

Here W is the depletion width and g_o is the pair generation constant which is about 7×10^{13} pairs/cm^3-rad for GaAs and 4×10^{13} pairs/cm^3-rad for silicon. Although g_o is slightly higher for GaAs than for Si, GaAs is characterized by much shorter diffusion lengths (L_n, L_p) and carrier lifetimes.

Obviously, photocurrent phenomena become quite complex in ICs where, in addition to primary photocurrents, transistors may contribute larger secondary photocurrents due to current or voltage amplification. The net effect of photocurrent transients in an IC is to disrupt linear circuit operation with large signal swings and produce logic errors in digital devices. Logic errors will appear as transient excursions or upsets in combinational logic elements and soft errors or bit-flips in bistable elements such as latches, registers, and memory cells.

Widespread differences exist in the upset sensitivities of the various silicon technologies and even among different types of devices belonging to the same technology. Variations can also be anticipated among GaAs circuits and logic families. Certain hardening techniques, such as photocurrent compensation, are available to the circuit designer to increase transient upset hardness; however, some of the most effective hardening methods are intimately related to the technology itself and include small device geometries and thin active layers to minimize photocurrent collection volumes and junction areas, dielectric isolation (D.I.) rather than junction isolation, and the use of low lifetime material. In view of these factors, GaAs IC technology would therefore appear relatively attractive in terms of dose rate hardness.

Unfortunately, semi-insulating GaAs substrate material can reduce the dose rate hardness of GaAs ICs by two different mechanisms. The first is via substrate photocurrents that can flow between contact pads or metallization placed directly on chip surfaces. Measurements have shown that such currents can be larger by several orders of magnitude than device photocurrents and, in fact, can dominate circuit response (15); however, it was also found that circuit response could be reduced by an order of magnitude by placing the bonding pads and metal interconnects on an insulating layer. The second substrate response mechanism is charge trapping in the deep levels that are characteristic of the semi-insulating substrate material (16). Conduction in FET structures can be severely affected (even cut off) by the trapped charge which decays with time constants that range from milliseconds to seconds. Recent work has shown though that this backgating-like effect can be appreciably reduced (and perhaps even eliminated) by the use of high quality LEC substrates and/or by various FET structural modifications, such a p-layer implanted beneath the n-channel (17). The effect can also be minimized by operating at high current levels.

Transient response data reported for GaAs digital ICs of MSI complexity have shown a broad range of upset thresholds. SDFL circuits have demonstrated upset thresholds ranging from 1×10^8 to 2×10^{10} rads/s (18), while the EJFET 256-bit RAM functioned without soft errors up to dose rates of 6×10^9 to 1×10^{10} rads (GaAs)/s (10). While these circuit upsets apparently resulted from photocurrent phenomena, disruptions in BFL logic gate and ring oscillator performance for tens of milliseconds have been observed by the author following 1 μsec LINAC exposures at total doses between about 10^2 and 10^3 rads (10^8 to 10^9 rads/s) and after 3 ns FXR pulses at the 100 rad level (3×10^{10} rads/s), all as a result of the backgating problem. Radiation-induced backgating has also been reported in power MESFETs and in a monolithic amplifier operating at X-band (19), although transient-free operation of a microwave MESFET was observed up to a dose rate of 3×10^{10} rad (Si)/s (20).

As indicated by the data above and illustrated in Figure 3, short pulse (< 100 ns) upset thresholds reported for GaAs ICs compare quite favorably with those characteristic of silicon LSI technologies (7,8). Long pulse (> 1 μs) thresholds decrease somewhat for silicon devices (because of the long lifetimes) but should not change appreciably for GaAs devices in the absence of severe "backgating" problems. Moreover, GaAs FET circuits are not susceptible to latchup associated with extraneous 4-layer paths as are many bipolar and CMOS/bulk silicon ICs. With respect to burnout or survivability thresholds (not discussed in this paper), most GaAs and Si ICs should exceed 10^{11} rads/s. Extremely low upset thresholds can be expected for both GaAs and Si CCDs (10^6 to 10^8 rad/s and lower).

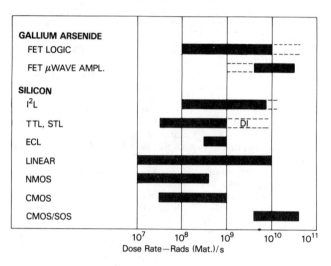

Figure 3.   Reported (solid) and Projected (dotted) Short Pulse Upset Thresholds.

SINGLE EVENT UPSETS

Single event or single particle upset represents a relatively new radiation threat for digital microcircuits and has arisen because of the trend to smaller device dimensions and faster switching speeds (21). The SEU problem involves the introduction of soft errors in the bistable elements that comprise circuit memories, registers, and latches. Single particle upset can occur when the charge collected, Q_{COL}, by a sensitive cell node exceeds the critical charge, Q_{CRIT}, required at the node for cell upset. Obviously, as devices become smaller and faster, the energy and charge associated with a bit of stored data (and hence Q_{CRIT}) decreases. The charge deposited by an incident particle depends on the product of the characteristic energy loss (dE/dx) of the particle and its path length, dl; Q_{COL} will be collected in a fraction of a nanosecond along that part of the path length that extends through the depletion region to the depth of the funnel beneath the depletion region. Charge funneling can increase Q_{COL} in silicon devices by several times that expected from the ionization path in the depletion region alone, and can thereby significantly increase device sensitivity to SEU. Although dielectric isolation and SOS eliminate funneling from the substrate, recent experiments with 5.1 MeV

alpha particles indicate that charge funneling can extend into the semi-insulating GaAs substrate underlying an epilayer device (22).

The radiation environment producing the SEU threat consists of heavy ions from cosmic rays and solar flares and also trapped protons in the radiation belts. Heavy ions produce ionization paths directly in the target material. Protons, on the other hand, do not produce upsets directly but undergo elastic scattering or nuclear reactions with the semiconductor atoms; the heavy recoil neuclei or byproduct alpha particles then produce ionization tracks (23).

There are insufficient experimental data presently available to enable a meaningful assessment of the SEU susceptibility of GaAs technology in general. In fact, the only information published to date describes measurements made on the 256-bit EJFET RAM when exposed to 40 MeV protons (24). The proton upset data point for this device, expressed in terms of an inverse cross section, is shown in Figure 4 along with data taken on several silicon RAMs in the same environment. Not shown in the figure are the results of proton experiments conducted on some other CMOS bulk silicon RAMs and two CMOS/SOS RAMs in which no upsets were observed (25).

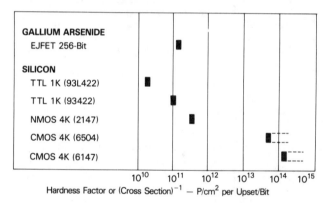

Figure 4.   40 meV Proton Upset Data for Static RAMs (24).

Since no heavy ion upset data are available for GaAs, one can only speculate as to how GaAs RAMs will compare with silicon RAMs in the cosmic ray environment. It is anticipated that in the absence of specific SEU hardening techniques, GaAs devices will be characterized by a range of sensitivities corresponding approximately to those for bulk silicon devices but below the range for CMOS/SOS. Whether or not circuit hardening techniques that can successfully eliminate SEU susceptibility in CMOS RAM cells (26) can be applied to GaAs cells remains to be seen.

SUMMARY

Contemporary GaAs ICs are characterized by a neutron hardness capability exceeding that of most silicon bipolar circuits and comparable to that of MOS circuits; the neutron hardness of GaAs FET logic devices is projected to improve. Gallium arsenide circuits exhibit a clear superiority over silicon

ICs in terms of their total dose susceptibility due to the absence of radiation sensitive dielectric layers such as SiO_2. Transient upset thresholds of GaAs ICs vary widely, corresponding approximately to those of the harder silicon bipolar devices; increased dose rate hardness toward the CMOS/SOS level is expected in some GaAs logic families as the technology improves. The SEU sensitivity of GaAs technology cannot be accurately established from presently available data; the SEU threat is clearly a potential problem area that needs further study.

REFERENCES

(1) Microwave Semiconductor Devices: Fundamentals and Radiation Effects by R.J. Chaffin, John Wiley and Sons, New York, 1973.

(2) R. Zuleeg and K. Lehovec, IEEE Trans. on Nucl. Sci., NS-27, 1343, Oct. 1980.

(3) R. Zuleeg, J.K. Notthoff, and K. Lehovec, IEEE Trans. on Nucl. Sci., NS-24, 2305, Dec. 1977.

(4) R.J. Gutmann and J.M. Borrego, IEEE Trans. on Rel., R-29, 232, Aug. 1980.

(5) J.M. Borrego, R.J. Gutmann, and S.B. Moghe, IEEE Trans. on Nucl. Sci., NS-26, 5092, Dec. 1979.

(6) W.C. Jenkins and J.M. Killiany, Naval Research Lab, Washington, DC, July 1982 (Private Communication).

(7) M. Simons, R.P. Donovan, and J.R. Hauser, AFAL-TR-76-194, Jan. 1977, RTI, Res. Tri. Pk., NC.

(8) D.M. Long, IEEE Trans. on Nucl. Sci., NS-27, 1674, Dec. 1980.

(9) B.M. Welch, Y. Shen, R. Zucca, R.C. Eden, S.I. Long, IEEE Trans. on Elec. Dev., ED-27, 1116, June 1980.

(10) J.K. Notoff, R. Zuleeg, and G.L. Troeger, 1983 IEEE NSRE Conf., Gatlinburg, TN, July 1983.

(11) J.M. Borego, R.J. Gutmann, S.B. Moghe, and M.J. Chudzicbi, IEEE Trans. on Nucl. Sci., NS-25, 1436, Dec. 1978.

(12) E.R. Walton, Rockwell International, Thousand Oaks, Cal., Aug. 1983 (Private Communication).

(13) D.M. Newell, P.T. Ho, R.L. Mencik, and J.R. Pelose, IEEE Trans. on Nucl. Sci., NS-28, 4403, Dec. 1981.

(14) Y. Kadowaki, Y. Mitsui, T. Takebe, O. Ishihara, and M. Nakatani, Technical Digest 1982 GaAs IC Symposium, 82CH17640, 83, Nov. 1982.

(15) R. Zuleeg, J.K. Notthoff, and G.L. Troeger, 1983 IEEE NSRE Conf., Gatlinburg, TN, July 1983.

(16) M. Simons, E.E. King, W.T. Anderson, and H.M. Day, J. Appl. Phys., 52, 6630, Nov. 1981.

(17) W.T. Anderson, M. Simons, E.E. King, H.B. Dietrich, and R.J. Lambert, IEEE Trans. on Nucl. Sci., NS-29, 1533, Dec. 82.

(18) E.R. Walton, W.T. Anderson, R. Zucca, and J.K. Notthoff, 1983 IEEE NSRE Conf., Gatlinburg, TN, July 1983.

(19) W.T. Anderson and S.C. Binary, 1983 IEEE NSRE Conf., Gatlinburg, TN, July 1983.

(20) J G. Castle, Sandia Laboratories, Albuquerque, NM, July 1983 (Private Communication).

(21) For recent papers on SEU see IEEE Trans. on Nucl. Sci., NS-29, 2018-2100, Dec. 1982.

(22) M.A. Hopkins and J.R. Srour, 1983 IEEE NSRE Conf., Gatlinburg, TN, July 1983.

(23) E.L. Petersen, IEEE Trans. on Nucl. Sci., NS-27, 1494, Dec. 1980.

(24) P. Shapiro, A.B. Cambell, J.C. Ritter, R. Zuleeg, and J.K. Notthoff, 1983 IEEE NSRE Conf., Gatlinburg, TN, July 1983.

(25) W.E. Price, D.K. Nichols, and C.J. Malone, 1983 IEEE NSRE Conf., Gatlinburg, TN, July 1983.

(26) S.E. Diehl, A. Ochoa, P.V. Dressendorfer, R. Koga, W.A. Kolasinski, IEEE Trans. on Nucl. Sci., NS-29, 2040, Dec. 1982.

Dislocations as the Origin of Threshold Voltage Scatterings for GaAs MESFET on LEC-Grown Semi-Insulating GaAs Substrate

SHINTARO MIYAZAWA AND YASUNOBU ISHII

Reprinted from *IEEE Transactions on Electron Devices*, Volume ED-31, Number 8, August 1984, pages 1057-1062. Copyright © 1984 by The Institute of Electrical and Electronics Engineers, Inc.

Abstract—This paper describes the extended results on the influence of dislocations in liquid-encapsulated Czochralski (LEC) grown semi-insulating GaAs substrates on threshold voltage of GaAs MESFET's. MESFET's located less than about 50 μm from a dislocation exhibit threshold voltage lower than those far from a dislocation and threshold voltage scatters at less than about 30 μm from a dislocation. The scattering is considered briefly from anisotropy of stress field around dislocations. Particular interest is devoted to the electrical properties around dislocations because of their detrimental influence on the FET threshold voltage.

I. INTRODUCTION

RECENT ADVANCES in GaAs integrated circuits (IC's) have been significant for complexity and performances, and the availability of good semi-insulating (100) GaAs substrates is now making GaAs IC production a reality [1]. Particularly, the liquid-encapsulated Czochralski (LEC) growth of large-sized round-shaped ⟨100⟩ GaAs semi-insulating crystals has facilitated the development of GaAs IC processing, to the extent that device manufacturing activities are possible.

Many reports have extensively pointed out the existence, however, of crystal inhomogeneities in LEC-grown GaAs, in spite of many advantages proposed earlier [2]. Inhomogeneities have been observed by photoluminescence intensity variation [3], [4], leakage current I_L variation [5], bulk resistivity variation [6], [7] for As-grown undoped and/or Cr-doped substrates, and by Hall measurements of Si-implanted layers [8]. Usually, an LEC-grown GaAs crystal includes a high dislocation density, ranging from a low-10^4 cm^{-2} to more than a mid-10^5 cm^{-2} over 2-/ and 3-in diameter (100) wafers, and the dislocation density provides a pronounced W-shaped variation across the wafer. The inhomogeneities reported elsewhere have been collectively correlated to this W-shaped dislocation density variation. On the other hand, in-house grown and commercially available materials with substantially high dislocation density have been applied to digital IC MESFET processing without noticeable effects on yield and performance. Recently, it was demonstrated that the threshold voltage for MESFET was closely correlated to dislocation density distribution in either undoped or Cr-doped semi-insulating LEC GaAs [9], [10].

Manuscript received January 2, 1984; revised March 14, 1984.
The authors are with the Atsugi Electrical Communication Laboratory, Nippon Telegraph and Telephone Public Corporation, 1839, Ono, Atsugi-shi, Kanagawa 243-01, Japan.

More recently, the influence of dislocations on MESFET characteristics fabricated with a direct ion implantation in LEC-grown semi-insulating GaAs substrates has become significant. A direct observation of the dislocation effect on MESFET threshold voltage for the LEC-grown GaAs has been reported, for the first time, by the present authors [11]. Moreover, a scattering of MESFET threshold voltage has been found to be caused by dislocation-clustered network cell [12], commonly existing in the LEC-grown GaAs crystals.

In this paper, more extended study is reported for clarifying the influence of grown-in dislocations on threshold voltage for FET's fabricated in LEC-grown semi-insulating GaAs substrates. The scattering in threshold voltage around dislocations is considered briefly. Particular interest is paid to electrical properties around dislocations because of their detrimental influence on FET threshold voltage.

II. EXPERIMENTS

The semi-insulating (100) substrates used in this study were slightly Cr-doped (0.1 ~ 0.3 wt ppm), LEC-grown 2-in-diameter wafers. The substrates were implanted with ^{28}Si ions at 60 keV acceleration energy and annealed at 800°C for 20 min in flowing N$_2$ with a plasma-CVD SiN cap film. Au/Ge–Ni ohmic metal was deposited and alloyed at about 400°C. By means of a conventional photolithography, a FET channel with a 6-μm source–drain distance and 5-μm gate width, as well as source and drain pads, was mesa etched. Ti/Pt/Au gate metal with a 1-μm gate length was also evaporated through photolithography. This test FET was fabricated at intervals of 200 μm over the whole wafer surface. Fig. 1(a) shows a microphoto of thus-fabricated FET array, and (b) is an enlarged FET channel part.

In order to analyze the influence of dislocations on FET characteristics, the substrates with FET's were chemically etched with molten KOH. Etching at 450°C for 30-60 s allowed sizable dislocation pits and also distinguishable FET channel part. Fig. 2 shows microphotos with magnifications of an etched FET channel part. Even on Au/Ge–Ni ohmic alloyed pads (source and drain), dislocation pits can be readily delineated as is indicated in Fig. 2.

For nondestructive examinations of substrate inhomogeneities, a cathodoluminescence image was taken with the acceleration energy of 35 keV at ambient temperature. The wave-

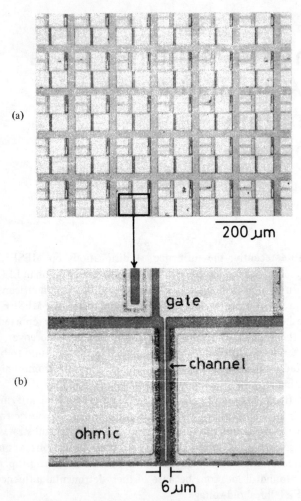

Fig. 1. (a) A test MESFET array fabricated on a substrate by means of conventional photolithography with mesa-etching, and (b) an enlarged FET channel part.

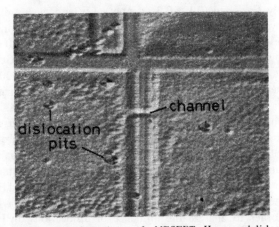

Fig. 2. KOH-etched channel part of a MESFET. Hexagonal dislocation pits are distinguishable.

length of the cathodoluminscence was fixed at around 8700 A through a monochrometer with an S-1 photomultiplier.

III. EXPERIMENTAL RESULTS

Threshold voltage for FET's was automatically measured by means of MAP system [13]. Followed by measuring threshold voltage for more than 1200 FET's lying on a 1 × 50-mm stripe running along the ⟨110⟩ direction on the wafer, the sample was slightly etched with molten KOH so as to reveal dislocation pits. A FET channel part and dislocation pits could be clearly observed simultaneously, as shown in Fig. 2. Etched figures of FET's were then randomly photographed under an optical microscope at an interval of 1 mm. Fig. 3 shows an example of an etched feature for five FET's adjacent to each other, with the threshold voltage V_{th} for each FET and the distance x from the nearest neighbored dislocation pit to an FET channel. Black hexagonal spots are dislocation pits revealed with molten KOH. One can readily notice that the shorter the distance x, the lower the threshold voltage V_{th}. FET's located far from a dislocation pit showed a normally off threshold voltage, while FET's around a dislocation pit exhibited a normally on condition. Therefore, it was meaningful to plot the threshold voltage for FET's against the distance from the nearest neighbored dislocation pit. Fig. 4 shows the plot between FET threshold voltage and the distance. In this case, the mean threshold voltage for measured FET's was +0.126 V. FET's located more than about 50 μm from the dislocation pit exhibited an almost constant threshold voltage, around +0.28 V. Although there were several exceptional points, the threshold voltage V_{th} decreased slightly as the distance shortened from 50 μm to about 30 μm. At less than about 30 μm, the threshold voltage decreased strongly, and saturated at around -0.12 V, though the values were scattering to some extent. The maximum-to-minimum difference in V_{th} was roughly 400 mV. This characteristic dependency was also recognized for another sample [11], where the mean threshold voltage was -0.012 V.

From Fig. 4, one can readily assume that electrical properties at less than about 30 μm were different from those at more than about 30 μm. There have been many reports on dislocations in GaAs. Heinke and Queisser [14] demonstrated a clear isointensity photoluminescence contour map around a dislocation in GaAs with a high spatial definition. They showed the existence of an approximately 20-μm radius reduced luminescent area surrounding a dislocation. Casey [15] and Shaw and Thornton [16] investigated dislocations in n-type GaAs with cathodoluminescence and depicted a 25–100-μm-diameter bright region around dislocations. More recently, Chin *et al.* [17] shows a clear cathodoluminescence image around dislocation cluster in LEC-grown semi-insulating GaAs. Dislocations were surrounded by about 50-μm-wide region where luminescence intensity is 10 percent greater than that of the dislocation-free region due to the redistribution of point defects. All of these results can be explained by the presence of a stable Cottrell atmosphere, by which impurities around the dislocation are gettered into the dislocation core. It seems likely that acceptors are attracted toward the dislocation core and leave a cylindrical acceptor depletion region around the dislocation [14]. This few tens of micrometers-wide bright cathodoluminescence area around a dislocation has been referred sometimes as to be "denuded" of acceptor-like impurities and/or point defects [15], associated with a Cottrell atmosphere. Together with these well-established results on dislocations, the preceding distance of about 30 μm, observed in Fig. 4, is in good agreement with the radius of a "denuded zone" around dislocations.

Fig. 4 depicts evidently that a dislocation influences more or

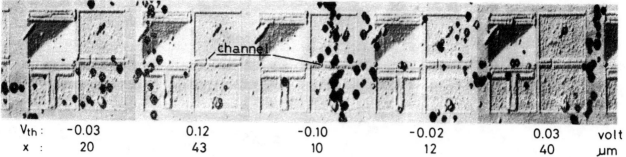

V_{th}:	−0.03	0.12	−0.10	−0.02	0.03	volt
x :	20	43	10	12	40	μm

Fig. 3. An example of KOH-etched FET array. V_{th} is the threshold voltage for each FET, and x is the distance from a channel part to the nearest neighborhood etch pit.

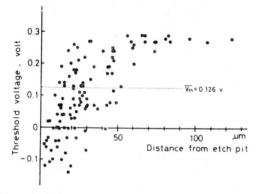

Fig. 4. Plot of FET threshold voltage against the distance from the nearest neighbored dislocation pit.

less strongly FET threshold voltage. This figure is the first evidence for the necessity of dislocation-free GaAs crystals as the substrate for LSI's with high performances.

We will discuss briefly the maximum-to-minimum difference in threshold voltage of 400 mV, attributed to dislocations. The theoretical approximation of threshold voltage V_{th} can be given by the following equation:

$$V_{th} = V_{bi} - \frac{kT}{q} \ln\left(\frac{N_c}{n}\right) - \frac{q}{2\epsilon} n \, d^2$$

where V_{bi} is built-in potential, k is the Boltzmann constant, q is the electronic charge, N_c is the effective density of states in the conduction band, n is the carrier concentration in the implanted active layer, ϵ is the static dielectric constant, and d is the thickness of the active layer implanted at 60 keV, taking into consideration the diffusion of implanted Si ions after annealing. Then, assuming [18] that the differences in built-in Schottky-barrier height and an active layer thickness between positions close to and far from dislocations are less effective on the threshold voltage difference of 400 mV, the maximum-to-minimum difference ΔV_{th} was considered to be attributable to the difference in carrier concentration $\Delta n = 3 \sim 5 \times 10^{16}$ cm^{-3} estimated from the equation.

Previously, the authors have elucidated [8] that sheet carrier concentration in a Si-implanted layer was strongly influenced by dislocation density. In a higher dislocation density area of more than 10^5 cm^{-2}, the sheet carrier concentration was higher by about 2×10^{11} cm^{-2} than that in a lower dislocation density area of about 3×10^4 cm^{-2}. This value agrees roughly with the estimated difference in carrier concentration of 3-5 $\times 10^{16}$

cm^{-3}, taking into consideration that the implanted active layer thickness was 0.12 μm [19] and that the lower the dislocation density, the lower the sheet carrier concentration.

It has been widely established that dislocations would surely be strong nonradiative centers [20]. When dislocations act as a "sink" of nonradiative impurities and/or point defects through the Cottrell effect or dislocation climb motion during or after crystal growth, the region around dislocation of a few tens of micrometers becomes "denuded" of nonradiative centers. Impurities such as Si, Cr, O, and C around dislocations were tentatively analyzed by means of a secondary ion mass spectroscopy (SIMS), but no clear distributions attributable to dislocations were distinguished. Kamejima et al. [21] also reported the segregation of the impurities at clustered dislocations but, with poor spatial resolution, could not detect the dislocation core and surrounding "denuded" zone.

The other possibility contributing to the difference in V_{th} is the distribution of deep-level point defects. The well-known deep level $EL2$ is the dominant level in undoped and lightly Cr-doped ($\sim 5 \times 10^{15}$ to 10^{16} cm^{-3}) materials [22]. It has been demonstrated [23] that the deep-level $EL2$ concentration increases with dislocation density. The difference in $EL2$ concentration was shown to be more than 1×10^{16} cm^{-3} between higher and lower dislocation density regions in an undoped material. This difference is also on the same order of the estimated difference in carrier concentration. In higher dislocation density regions, dislocations are very close to each other, and the "denuded" zone around a dislocation are overlapped to some extent [8]. It is plausible, therefore, that point defects such as the deep-level $EL2$ may be higher in the "denuded" zone of about 30 μm in radius around a dislocation than the area far from a dislocation. Spectulating that $EL2$ concentration decreases far from a dislocation, the activation of the implanted Si ions is enhanced to some extent around a dislocation. As the result, the threshold voltage for FET's located far from a dislocation shows more normally off than that for FET's around a dislocation. Further detailed studies are required for clarifying the speculation.

IV. DISCUSSION

In this section, a relatively large scattering in threshold voltage observed at less than about 30 μm, as shown in Fig. 4, is considered. The scattering is thought to arise from the two following aspects: i) the distance x was simply measured from the nearst neighbored dislocation pit, while the bright cath-

9

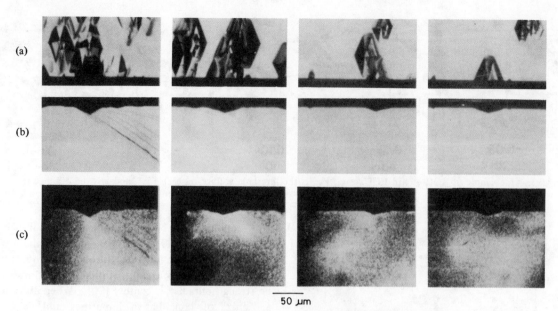

50 μm

Fig. 5. Cathodoluminescence images around dislocation pit grooves.
(a) Etch pits on the (100) face, (b) grooves of dislocation pits corresponding to (a), and (c) cathodoluminescence images around grooves.

odoluminescence area does not always coincide with dislocation pits; ii) crystallographic orientation of a FET channel from a dislocation on the (100) surface was neglected for the distance measurement, because a dislocation usually provides stress field around it.

A. Cathodoluminescence Study Around Dislocations

As was considered above, the distance of 30 μm from a dislocation pit agreed well with a bright cathodoluminescence zone around dislocations reported elsewhere. Then, the cathodoluminescence image around dislocation pits was observed in detailed. An As-grown semi-insulating GaAs (100) wafer was etched with molten KOH so as to reveal dislocation pits, and the (110) cross-sectional view of dislocation pits was afforded by crystal cleavage. The cathodoluminescence image was taken around grooves of dislocation pits appeared on the cleaved (110). Fig. 5 shows typical examples of correspondence between dislocation pits and cathodoluminescence image, where (a) shows etched pits on the (100), (b) shows etch pit grooves on the cleaved (110) corresponding to (a), and (c) shows cathodoluminescence image corresponding to (b). The cleaved face ran almost at the center of dislocation pits. While a bright cathodoluminescence zone was found around clustered dislocation grooves (two left figures), one-to-one correspondence was not always observed for isolated dislocation grooves (two right figures). Taking into consideration that, in general, dislocations are not always perpendicular to the (100) and actual geometry depends on the angle of the emergence of dislocations, the poor one-to-one correspondence is attributable to an irregular "denuded zone" resulted from the inclined angle of dislocations to the (100) surface. Therefore, one possible origin for the scattering might have arisen from that the measurement of the distance was simply carried out two-dimensionally from the nearest neighbored dislocation pit on the (100) surface. It has been well established that there are several kinds of dislocations in GaAs. In LEC-grown GaAs, they can be classified into three types of dislocations [24], i.e., threading dislocations from a seed crystal, grown-in dislocations at the melt–crystal interface during the growth, and stress-induced dislocations during pulling and/or after growth. With KOH etching, it was generally hard to distinguish them from the etch pit shape, because almost all pits appeared on the (100) are hexagonal in shape. Which type of dislocations have an effect on the threshold voltage is not understood at present.

B. Angle Dependence of Threshold Voltage Around Dislocation

From another point of view, it is well known that a dislocation provides a stress field around it. It is probable that stresses may provide redistribution of impurities around a dislocation. Hence, the measured threshold voltage was plotted against the rotation angle around a dislocation pit with the distance as a parameter. The result is shown in Fig. 6, where the distance from a dislocation pit was 5 ± 2, 10 ± 2, 20 ± 2, and 30 ± 2 μm. The mark on the center indicates a hexagonal etch pit shape. Symmetrical distribution was observed for each distance. FET's at 5 ± 2 μm from a dislocation pit showed almost constant threshold voltage independent of the angle from ⟨110⟩ direction. The distance of $x = 5 \pm 2$ μm is very close to dislocation core gettered impurities, where the cathodoluminescence intensity decreased about 5 percent relative to the bright region around it [15], [17]. However, FET's at 10 ± 2 μm exhibited a relatively strong orientation dependency. FET's along the two equivalent ⟨110⟩ directions exhibit a normally off threshold voltage, while those along the ⟨100⟩ direction exhibited a normally on threshold voltage. And, at 20 ± 2 μm from a dislocation pit, threshold voltage for FET's located along the ⟨100⟩ direction shifts to normally off more than those along another orientation. Also, for $x = 30 \pm 2$ μm, the distribution of threshold voltage around the dislocation shows a relatively weak symmetry against the orientation. Steckenborn et al. [25] presented a cathodoluminescence intensity contour map

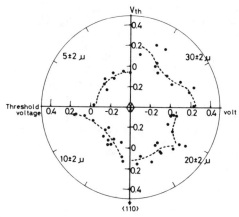

Fig. 6. Orientation dependences of threshold voltage for FET's around the dislocation pit as a function of the distance $x = 5$, 10, 20, and $30 \pm 2 \mu m$ from the pit to a FET channel.

around a dislocation in n^--GaAs ($n \approx 4 \times 10^{16}$ cm^{-3}) with high resolution at 50 K. It was noticed that, at about $20 \pm 5 \mu m$ from the dislocation, a bright cathodoluminescent area could be clearly visualized. Intensity distribution seems to locate in four-fold symmetry around the dislocation, although the crystallographic orientation was not identified. Stress field associated with dislocations may allow redistribution of impurities and/or point defects around dislocations. It can be emphasized, therefore, that FET threshold voltage scattering around a dislocation is assumed to be dependent on the distance and the orientation from dislocations.

There is still a lack of knowledge about fundamental questions such as the mechanism for threshold voltage shift as far from a dislocation discussed before, but it can be stressed that dislocation-free (for example, less than 100 cm^{-2}), semi-insulating GaAs is strongly needed as the substrate for high-performance GaAs LSI developments. On the other hand, the authors have found [26] that the dislocation effect on the threshold voltage was reduced drastically by annealing the substrate or the As-grown ingot for long period, for example more than 10 h at 800°C, prior to the ion implantation. This simple technique is the most useful candidate for utilizing the conventionally grown LEC crystals in application to LSI's substrate with improved homogeneities.

V. CONCLUSION

The influence of dislocations on GaAs MESFET threshold voltage was depicted as a function of the distance from a dislocation pit to a FET channel part for LEC-grown semi-insulating substrates. FET's located less than about $30 \simeq 50$ μm from a dislocation showed a threshold voltage shifted to more normally on than those far from a dislocation. The maximum-to-minimum difference in threshold voltage attributed to a dislocation was roughly 400 mV. This difference was discussed from the viewpoint of carrier concentration estimation, and was speculated to be attributable to a distribution of point defects such as deep-level $EL2$ around dislocations.

It was demonstated that the threshold voltage for FET's located less than about 30 μm from a dislocation scattered to some extent. This scattering was considered to be caused temporarily by the anisotropy of stress field around a dislocation.

Although a definitive correlation between dislocations and MESFET characteristics discussed in this paper is still unreliable, it can be concluded that dislocation-free GaAs crystals of, maybe, less than 100 cm^{-2} are required for future high-performance GaAs LSI development as the substrate for a direct ion implantation. Many efforts are aimed at reducing dislocation density in LEC-grown materials, but it is still significant way to do.

ACKNOWLEDGMENT

The authors would like to express their thanks to Dr. M. Ohmori for his valuable discussion and comment. They also thank S. Shibata for cathodoluminescence experiments, S. Ishida for fabricating test FET's and T. Honda and H. Yamazaki for ion implantation.

REFERENCES

[1] K. Asai, K. Kurumada, M. Hirayama, and M. Ohmori, "1 Kb static RAM using self-aligned FET technology," in *IEEE Int. Solid-State Circuits Conf. Dig. Tech. Papers*, pp. 46–47, Feb. 1983.

[2] F. D. Fairman, R. T. Chen, J. R. Oliver, and D. R. Ch'en, "Growth of high-purity semi-insulating bulk GaAs for integrated-circuit applications," *IEEE Trans. Electron Devices*, vol. ED-28, no. 2, pp. 135–140, Feb. 1981.

[3] M. Tajima and Y. Okada, "Characterization of deep levels in LEC GaAs crystals by the photoluminescence technique," *Physica*, vol. 116B, pp. 404–408, 1983.

[4] K. Kitahara, K. Nakai, and S. Shibatomi, "One-dimensional photoluminescence distribution in semi-insulating GaAs grown by CZ and HB methods," *J. Electrochem. Soc.*, vol. 129, no. 4, pp. 880–883, 1982.

[5] S. Miyazawa, T. Mizutani, and H. Yamazaki, "Leakage current I_L variation correlated with dislocation density in undoped, semi-insulating LEC-GaAs," *Japan. J. Appl. Phys.*, vol. 21, no. 9, pp. L542–L544, 1982.

[6] R. T. Blunt, S. Clark, and D. J. Stirland, "Dislocation density and sheet resistance variations across semi-insulating GaAs wafers," *IEEE Trans. Electron Devices*, vol. ED-29, no. 7, pp. 1039–1045, July, 1982.

[7] I. Grant, D. Rumsby, R. M. Ware, M. R. Brozel, and B. Tuck, "Etch pit density, resistivity and chromium distribution in chromium doped LEC GaAs," in *Semi-insulating III-V Materials*, S. Makaram-Ebeid and B. Tuck, Eds. Siva, 1983, pp. 98–106.

[8] T. Honda, Y. Ishii, S. Miyazawa, H. Yamazaki, and Y. Nanishi, "The influence of dislocation density on the uniformity of electrical properties of Si implanted, semi-insulating LEC-GaAs," *Japan. J. Appl. Phys.*, vol. 22, no. 5, pp. L270–L272, 1983.

[9] Y. Nanishi, S. Ishida, T. Honda, H. Yamazaki, and S. Miyazawa, "Inhomogeneous GaAs FET threshold voltage related to dislocation distribution," *Japan. J. Appl. Phys.*, vol. 21, no. 6, pp. L335–L337, 1982.

[10] Y. Nanishi, S. Ishida, and S. Miyazawa, "Correlation between dislocation distribution and FET performances observed in low Cr doped LEC GaAs," *Japan. J. Appl. Phys.*, vol. 22, no. 1, pp. L54–L56, 1983.

[11] S. Miyazawa, Y. Ishii, and S. Ishida, "Direct observation of dislocation effects on threshold voltage of GaAs field-effect transistor," *Appl. Phys. Lett.*, vol. 43, no. 9, pp. 853–855, 1983.

[12] Y. Ishii, S. Miyazawa, and S. Ishida, "Threshold voltage scattering of GaAs MESFET's fabricated on LEC-grown semi-insulating substrates," *IEEE Trans. Electron Devices*, vol. ED-31, no. 6, pp. 800–804, June 1984.

[13] ——, "Characterization of thin active layer on semi-insulating GaAs by mapping of FET array performances," *IEEE Trans. Electron Device*, pp. 1051–1056, this issue.

[14] W. Heinke and H. J. Queisser, "Photoluminescence at dislocations in GaAs," *Phys. Rev. Lett.*, vol. 33, no. 18, pp. 1082–1084, 1974.

[15] H. C. Casey, Jr., "Investigation of inhomogeneities in GaAs by electron-beam excitation," *J. Electrochem. Soc.*, vol. 114, no. 2, pp. 153–158, 1967.

[16] D. A. Shaw and P. R. Thornton, "Cathodoluminescence studies of laser quality GaAs," *J. Mat. Sci.*, vol. 3, pp. 507–518, 1968.

[17] A. K. Chin, A. R. VonNeida, and R. Caruso, "Spatially resolved cathodoluminescence study of semi-insulating GaAs substrate," *J. Electronchem. Soc.*, vol. 129, no. 10, pp. 2386–2388, 1982.

[18] Y. Hirayama and S. Miyazawa, unpublished.

[19] H. Yamazaki, T. Honda, and S. Miyazawa, "Low-dose Si ion implantation ioto semi-insulating LEC GaAs," *Electron. Lett.*, vol. 17, no. 21, pp. 817–819, 1981.

[20] K. Bohm and B. Fischer, "Photoluminescence at dislocations in GaAs and InP," *J. Appl. Phys.*, vol. 50, no. 8, pp. 5453–5460, 1979.

[21] T. Kamejima, F. Shimura, Y. Matsumoto, H. Watanabe, and J. Matsui, "Role of dislocations in semi-insulation mechanism in undoped LEC GaAs crystal," *Japan. J. Appl. Phys.*, vol. 21, no. 11, pp. L721–L723, 1982.

[22] S. Sriram and M. B. Das, "Characterization of electron traps in ion-implanted GaAs MESFET's on undoped and Cr-doped LEC semi-insulating substrates," *IEEE Trans. Electron Devices*, vol. ED-30, no. 6, pp. 586–592, June 1983.

[23] M. R. Brozel, I. Grant, R. M. Ware, and D. J. Stirland, "Direct observation of the principle deep level (EL2) in undoped semi-insulating GaAs," *Appl. Phys. Lett.*, vol. 42, no. 7, pp. 610–612. 1983.

[24] S. Miyazawa, unpublished.

[25] A. Stenkenborn, H. Munzel, and D. Bimberg, "Cathodoluminescence lifetime pattern of GaAs surface around dislocations," *J. Luminescence*, vols. 24/25, part I, pp. 351–354, 1981.

[26] S. Miyazawa, T. Honda, Y. Ishii, and S. Ishida, "Improvement of crystal homogeneities in liquid-encapsulated Czochralshi grown, semi-insulating GaAs by heat treatment," *Appl. Phys. Lett.*, vol. 44, no. 4, pp. 410–412, 1984.

Reprinted from *Proceedings of the IEEE*, Volume 69, Number 2, February 1981, pages 226-231. Copyright © 1981 by The Institute of Electrical and Electronics Engineers, Inc.

Limitations on the Performance of Field-Effect Devices for Logic Applications

JAMES A. COOPER, JR., MEMBER, IEEE

Abstract—The switching time and power dissipation of field-effect devices in integrated logic circuits are obtained using a simple equivalent circuit. It is seen that performance is determined by four basic parameters: channel length, operating voltage, parasitic capacitance, and saturation drift velocity. The effects limiting the optimization of these parameters are examined. It is found that channel length cannot be reduced below about 0.2 μm in the metal-oxide-semiconductor field-effect transistor (MOSFET) or below about 500 Å in the metal-semiconductor field-effect transistor (MESFET). Operating voltages cannot be reduced below about 750 mV due to subthreshold leakage. In the limit of extremely small sizes, the most promising high-speed devices appear to be MESFET structures in GaAs or InP.

I. INTRODUCTION, SCOPE, AND ASSUMPTIONS

IN the continuing development of digital integrated circuits and in the evolution of these circuits toward higher speeds of operation, it is useful periodically to assess the limits on the performance of the device structures presently known to us in order to judge how much room for improvement remains and at what point in the evolution a radical change in device concepts will become necessary. Several authors have considered the limits on field-effect devices in the past, [1]–[3], but rapid developments in fabrication methods and the emergence of several novel device concepts in recent years suggest the need for a reevaluation of our position and prospects. It is to this end that the present effort is directed.

In this work, we shall be concerned only with unipolar field-effect devices, since in the limit of very small size these devices are expected to give comparable speed and lower power-delay products than bipolar junction transistors [3]–[5]. Within the unipolar class are two basic types of devices, the metal-oxide-semiconductor field-effect transistor (MOSFET) [6]–[10] and the metal–semiconductor field-effect transistor (MESFET) [11], [12]. Typical device structures are illustrated in Fig. 1. We shall consider both MOSFET and MESFET devices, placing primary emphasis on MOSFET devices owing to the early stage of development of MESFET logic [13], [14]. We estimate ultimate limits on performance where such limits can be defined with some degree of confidence, but the main thrust of our discussion will be directed toward practical problems likely to be encountered as high-speed devices evolve, and possible means of dealing with the problems, where such means are known at this time. Thus in most cases we shall be dealing not with *ultimate* limits but rather with *practical* limits. We shall be primarily interested in estimating the factors limiting the speed of integrated circuits fashioned from these devices, and only secondarily interested in minimizing the power dissipation or maximizing the packing density. Of course, power dissipation may place a *de facto* limit on speed in applications where the thermal limit of the package has been reached, a common occurence in LSI circuits designed using static NMOS logic [1],

Manuscript received September 26, 1980.
The author is with Bell Laboratories, Murray Hill, NJ 07974.

EH0266-7/88/0000/0013$01.00 © 1981 IEEE

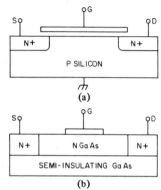

Fig. 1. The MOSFET (a) makes use of an insulating film between the gate electrode and the semiconductor to provide electrical isolation, whereas the MESFET (b) relies on a reverse-biased Shottky barrier diode formed between the gate metal and the semiconductor. For the integrated MESFET, we assume that a semi-insulating substrate provides isolation between adjacent devices; the MOSFET device is self-isolating.

[2], [15]. For this reason, we shall discuss the factors affecting power dissipation and how power dissipation can be minimized without significant degradation in speed. For concreteness, we shall assume room temperature operation unless explicitly noted.

II. MATERIALS LIMITATIONS

The performance of field-effect integrated circuits will ultimately be limited by the physical properties of the materials used in the fabrication. It is useful at the outset to list the materials limitations of interest here:

1) avalanche and Zener breakdown of the semiconductor;
2) electrical quality of insulators (MOSFET only), including passivation characteristics, stability, permittivity, and dielectric breakdown;
3) limiting velocities of carriers;
4) limited electrical conductivity of conductors and doped semiconductors;
5) electromigration in metals, due to high current densities during switching transients;
6) limited thermal conductivity of semiconductors and substrates;
7) random fluctuations of material properties such as doping, layer thickness, fixed charges, etc.

III. AN ELEMENTARY CIRCUIT MODEL AND ITS PERFORMANCE PARAMETERS

For concreteness, it is necessary to consider a specific circuit model which can be considered representative of a wide class of actual circuits. Such a model is shown in Fig. 2. Here we assume a circuit consisting of a field-effect device discharging a load capacitance. This circuit does not include any means of

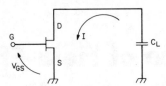

Fig. 2. The operation of field-effect integrated circuits can be modeled by a simple equivalent circuit consisting of a field-effect device discharging its load capacitance.

"pull-up" by which the load capacitance can be initially charged, nor does it include any provision for level-shifting as would be required in fully depletion-mode circuits. Nevertheless, it does represent a broad class of practical circuits, both MOSFET and MESFET, and it allows us to introduce and employ simple performance criteria which lead to conclusions which have general validity. In a later section we shall consider the effects of other circuit configurations. However, it should be emphasized that the speed of our prototype circuit will represent the optimum and that other nonsymmetrical or multistage configurations will result in a decrease in speed.

We now obtain simple expressions for switching delay, power dissipation, and power-delay product for the circuit of Fig. 2. The current in the active device may be written

$$I = WQv \tag{1}$$

where Q is the average mobile charge density in the control region of the device in coulombs per square centimeter, W is the width of the control region, and v is the carrier velocity. In a MOSFET or a MESFET, it is apparent that

$$Q = \left(\frac{C_{IN}}{WL}\right)\frac{(V_{GS} - V_T)}{2} \tag{2}$$

$$v = \mu E = \mu \left(\frac{V_{GS} - V_T}{L}\right) \tag{3}$$

where C_{IN} represents the effective capacitance between the gate electrode and the controlled charge Q, V_{GS} the gate-to-source voltage, V_T the threshold or turn-on voltage, μ the carrier mobility, and E the electric field in the channel, given approximately by the channel voltage drop at pinch off ($V_{GS} - V_T$) divided by the channel length L. Equation (3) strictly applies only for carrier velocities below the saturated drift velocity v_s (typically on the order of 10^7 cm/s; more detailed discussion later) and must be replaced by

$$v = v_s \tag{4}$$

for the limiting cases considered here. Combining (1), (2), and (4) gives

$$I = C_{IN} \frac{(V_{GS} - V_T)v_s}{2L}. \tag{5}$$

Thus we consider the field-effect device to be a constant-current source for the duration of the switching transient (i.e., the current is essentially independent of drain voltage), an approximation which gives reasonably accurate results in practical cases. The load capacitance C_L in Fig. 2 is taken to represent the total capacitance loading the FET, including its own output capacitance C_{OUT}, the parasitic capacitance of the inter-stage interconnect wiring C_W, and the input capacitance of the following stage C_{IN}. Thus, for a fanout of n,

$$C_L = n(C_{IN} + C_W) + C_{OUT}. \tag{6}$$

The time required to discharge the load capacitance from an initial value of V_{DD} to a final value of $V_{DD}/2$ (assuming that the following stage begins switching at $V_{DD}/2$) is

$$T = \frac{C_L V_{DD}}{2I} \tag{7}$$

or, using (5) and (6), and assuming $V_{GS} = V_{DD}$,

$$T = \left[\frac{n(C_{IN} + C_W) + C_{OUT}}{C_{IN}}\right]\left[\frac{V_{DD}}{V_{DD} - V_T}\right]\frac{L}{v_s}. \tag{8}$$

The first term in (8) represents the factor by which the load capacitance exceeds the input capacitance. For a ring-oscillator with fanout of one and small wiring capacitance, the first term can approach unity. However, for integrated circuits used for digital logic, this ratio is typically between four and sixteen. One of the objectives of integrated circuit designers is to reduce this ratio, and a number of techniques have been employed, including the use of insulating substrates ("silicon-on-sapphire" or SOS [16], [17]) to minimize C_W and C_{OUT}. We shall consider this factor in more detail in Section VI. The second factor in (8) represents the inefficiency caused by the requirement for a nonzero threshold voltage V_T. The considerations limiting the reduction of V_T will be discussed in Section V. The third factor in (8) is simply the intrinsic transit time of the device, and represents the fundamental limit on switching time. It should be emphasized here that the variable L represents the length of the control *region* and not simply the control *electrode*. Cases can be cited in which the control region is smaller (e.g., as in double-diffused MOS or DMOS [18]) or larger (e.g., as in the permeable-base transistor or PBT [19], [20]) than the control electrode. The transit time limit can only be approached, never actually reached, owing to the capacitance and voltage prefactors. However, improvements in the intrinsic transit time reflect directly in the switching time through (8). Such improvements might be made by reducing the length of the control region or by using a material with higher saturation velocity.

An important consideration in large-scale integrated circuits is power dissipation. The energy required per switching event or the power–delay product is simply $\frac{1}{2} C_L V_{DD}^2$,

$$PT = \frac{1}{2}[n(C_{IN} + C_W) + C_{OUT}]V_{DD}^2. \tag{9}$$

The power dissipated during the transient is obtained by dividing by the switching time, resulting in

$$P = \frac{1}{2} C_{IN} V_{DD}[V_{DD} - V_T]\frac{v_s}{L}. \tag{10}$$

It is seen that while the delay is only weakly dependent on supply voltage, the power–delay product goes as the square of the supply voltage. For this reason it is desirable to reduce the voltage as much as possible. In addition, it is obviously desirable to reduce lateral dimensions in order to reduce the capacitance terms. Thus, to summarize, it appears from (8)–(10) that there are four basic considerations in estimating the performance limits of field-effect devices in logic circuits.

1) How short can the control region be made?

2) How small can threshold voltage be made? Corresponding to this threshold, what supply voltage V_{DD} should be used?

3) How much can the parasitic output and wiring capacitance be reduced?

14

4) What are the considerations limiting the saturation velocity v_s, and what improvements can be expected in materials other than silicon?

Not all of these four questions can be answered precisely, in part because the limits in some cases are difficult to define and in part because innovation and ingenuity will certainly suggest alternative solutions to those presently envisioned. However, it is our purpose here to suggest reasonable limits based on extrapolations of *current* technology and to identify the points at which such extrapolations will become inadequate.

IV. LIMITATIONS ON MINIMUM CHANNEL LENGTH

Hoeneisen and Mead [1] have considered the factors limiting the reduction of channel length in a MOSFET. They pointed out that as channel length is reduced, the tendency of source and drain depletion regions to touch, or "punchthrough," poses the most severe limitation to minimum channel length. Once the drain depletion region penetrates to the source, the potential barrier at the source is lowered, and an uncontrolled source–drain current will flow. The maximum depletion region width of the drain junction is given by

$$x_d = \left[\frac{2\epsilon_s(\phi_B + V_{DD})}{qN}\right]^{1/2} \tag{11}$$

where ϵ_s is the dielectric constant of the semiconductor, ϕ_B the built-in potential of the junction, q the electronic charge, and N the doping in the channel. Thus it is desirable to reduce the operating voltage and increase the substrate doping in order to avoid punchthrough. However, both actions tend to make it more difficult to invert the channel of the device. Given an arbitrary choice of power supply voltage V_{DD}, one selects the minimum possible oxide thickness (limited by dielectric breakdown), since thinner oxides make it easier to invert the channel. With this oxide thickness, the doping can be increased until the threshold voltage V_T is some desired fraction of V_{DD}, say $V_{DD}/3$. This doping then determines the depletion widths and thus the channel length, as shown in Fig. 3. Hoeneisen and Mead noted that the ultimate limit on MOSFET miniaturization was imposed by the fact that oxides thinner than about 50 Å are susceptible to direct tunneling from the silicon or gate metal completely through the oxide. Thus they conclude that the ultimate MOSFET might operate at 0.7 V, with an oxide thickness of 50 Å, a doping concentration of 4×10^{17} cm^{-3}, and a channel length of 0.15 μm.

We note in passing that the analysis of Hoeneisen and Mead was restricted to a conventional planar MOSFET geometry with a uniformly doped substrate, and it is to be expected that departures from this simple geometry [21] may permit further reductions in channel length beyond the limits envisioned by these authors. However, of the new structures which have been introduced to date (such as DMOS [18], [22] and VMOS [23], [24]), none have demonstrated sufficient gains in performance to offset the added complexity, and none has yet enjoyed widespread commercial acceptance.

In contrast to the MOSFET, the MESFET and similar devices (e.g., the junction field-effect transistor (JFET), [25], [26] the static-induction transistor (SIT) [27], the permeable base transistor (PBT) [19], [20], etc.) do not suffer punchthrough in the conventional sense, since the source, drain, and channel are all of the same conductivity type. However, one must still ensure that the potential barrier at the source is controlled by the gate rather than by the drain. This places a constraint on the

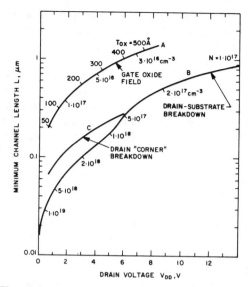

Fig. 3. The minimum channel length of a MOSFET, as calculated by Hoeneisen and Mead [1]. Curve A represents the limit imposed by gate oxide breakdown in the load or "pull-up" transistor, whose gate was assumed held at 2 V_{DD}. Curves B and C represent the limits imposed by semiconductor breakdown, and can be thought of as representing the limit in the case of the MESFET. (Note that for the depletion-mode MESFET, the gate-drain voltage actually reaches 2 V_{DD}.) For curves B and C, the length L indicated in the figure is twice the depletion region width at breakdown.

length of the gate electrode relative to the thickness of the channel. For example, in order to reduce the channel length, it is necessary to increase the channel doping and reduce the channel thickness so that the field from the gate will still control the potential barrier at the source. Reducing the thickness of the channel in a MESFET is analogous to reducing the oxide thickness in a MOSFET. However, since the MESFET has no gate dielectric, the limitation now is breakdown of the semiconductor. As seen in Fig. 3, curves B and C, this constraint is less severe than that of dielectric breakdown in the MOSFET. Thus it appears that very short channel lengths are possible, at least in principle, in the MESFET device—channel lengths perhaps as short as 500 to 1000 Å.

V. LIMITATIONS ON OPERATING VOLTAGE

Equation (8) shows that in order to obtain the minimum switching delay, it is desirable that the operating voltage exceed the threshold voltage by a large amount. On the other hand, equation (9) reminds us that the power-delay product goes up as the square of the operating voltage, suggesting that V_{DD} should be kept small. Although the choice of the ratio V_{DD}/V_T is somewhat arbitrary, for concreteness a value of $V_{DD} = 3 V_T$ will be assumed in what follows. This choice results in a switching time which can never be less than 1.5 times the intrinsic transit time of the device, but it also holds the power dissipation to a reasonable value. Having established a relationship between operating voltage V_{DD} and threshold voltage V_T, we now ask how small V_T can be made.

The minimum practical value of threshold voltage is limited by the obvious need to turn the device off, that is, to reduce the drain current far enough below the ON value so that logic levels in static circuits are not significantly altered and so that charge retention times in dynamic circuits are not unduly reduced. However, cutoff of current is not ideally abrupt at $V_{GS} = V_T$, as would be indicated by the simple expression of (5); rather there exists both in MOSFET's and MESFET's a nonzero subthreshold current which decreases exponentially with gate voltage [28]. For both devices, the subthreshold current may be written

$$I = I_0 \exp\left[q(V_{GS} - V_T)/mkT\right], \quad V_{GS} \le V_T \quad (12)$$

where I_0 is a parameter which may depend upon drain voltage, and m is a constant which depends upon geometry and doping and represents the inefficiency of the gate in controlling channel current. Typical values for m are in the range 1.5 to 3 for both devices. With $m = 2$, the gate-to-source voltage must be brought approximately 4.6 kT/q (or about 120 mV at room temperature) below threshold for each decade reduction in drain current. While the amount of subthreshold current which is tolerable depends on the specific circuit, it is not unreasonable to expect that a practical lower limit on threshold would be around 10 kT/q or 250 mV at room temperature. (It is clear from another consideration that voltages much below 10 kT/q are impractical: since kT represents the mean thermal energy of motion of electrons at temperature T, it is necessary to impress several kT of signal energy on the electron population in order to overcome thermal noise.) With a threshold of at least 250 mV, we conclude that operating voltages cannot be reduced below 500–750 mV at room temperature.

There is another consideration in choosing the minimum value of operating voltage, namely that it be large enough to bring the carriers to their saturated drift velocity in the channel—for lower voltages, the channel current falls as the square of the voltage according to (1)–(3), and the switching time increases linearly as voltage is reduced. For most materials the required electric field for saturation is around 10^4 V/cm, so that for a channel length of 1 μm, V_{DD} should be greater than 2 V; the "minimum" value of 500 mV would only be reached for channel lengths of 0.25 μm or less. We note that the electric field needed to achieve velocity saturation depends upon the mobility of the material. The principal advantage of a high mobility in short channel devices is that it permits velocity saturation to be achieved at lower operating voltages, thus reducing the power–delay product.

Some readers might point out that it is in principle possible to operate entirely in the subthreshold regime, i.e., $V_{DD} < V_T$, using the subthreshold current of the devices to charge and discharge the load capacitances over a very limited voltage swing. However, substitution of (12) into (7) shows that as V_{DD} is reduced below V_T, the current falls exponentially while the logic swing only linearly, with the result that the switching time goes up exponentially with decreasing V_{DD}. This situation obviously does not lead to improved performance.

In present-day MOSFET's, an important limitation arises from impact ionization in the drift region near the drain and the accompanying injection of "hot" electrons (and "hot" holes) into the gate oxide, where they become trapped, resulting in long-term threshold voltage instabilities [29]–[31]. However, impact ionization ceases to be a consideration when the drain bias is less than the semiconductor bandgap potential, since carriers cannot gain sufficient energy from the field to ionize valence electrons. Thus, the low operating voltages predicted here would effectively eliminate the "hot-electron" problem in short-channel MOSFET's.

Finally, we must mention the practical considerations of circuit noise margin and parameter fluctuations due to random processing variations. It is tacitly assumed in the above discussions that internal noise fluctuations placed on the gate by capacitive coupling from adjacent interconnect wires scale down with supply voltage, so that a proportional reduction in noise margins of the logic gate can be tolerated. It was also assumed that process control improved in direct proportion to the reduction in threshold voltage. While the former assumption is probably valid (provided that the ratio of coupling capacitance to gate capacitance remains constant), the latter is much more questionable. This is because of the inherently two-dimensional nature of FET devices, and the fact that for short channel lengths, threshold voltage depends on channel length and drain voltage as well as on channel doping and oxide thickness [21]. The necessity of controlling more parameters as devices are scaled down presents formidable practical problems. However, it should be possible in principle to achieve operating voltages as low as those cited above.

VI. Limitations on the Reduction of Parasitic Capacitance

As can be seen from (8) and (9), the switching time of an elementary logic gate is proportional to the ratio of load capacitance to input capacitance, while the power–delay product is proportional to load capacitance. A straightforward way to reduce these capacitances is to scale all lateral dimensions by the factor k; the capacitances are then reduced by k^2. However, because of strong two-dimensional effects in short-channel MOSFET's, it becomes necessary to increase the channel doping and reduce the oxide thickness as lateral dimensions are reduced, actions which tend to increase on-chip capacitances. Furthermore, as the width of interconnect wires becomes comparable to the field dielectric thickness, fringing fields from the edges of the wires come into play, and the capacitance per unit length tends to go down logarithmically with width rather than linearly. Because of these problems, considerable attention has been paid in recent years to the technology for fabricating field effect integrated circuits on an insulating substrate [16], [17]. The use of an insulating substrate effectively eliminates the capacitance between the drain and ground, and between interconnect wiring and ground. However, the improvement in speed is often not as great as would normally be expected. This is because, as lateral dimensions decrease, the capacitance between adjacent interconnect wires becomes comparable to the capacitance from the wires to ground, so that removing the conducting substrate eventually produces little improvement. Moreover, the switching noise coupled onto a long interconnect line from adjacent lines is more severe on an insulating substrate, since the "damping" capacitance between the interconnect line and ground has been eliminated. For high-speed circuits on insulating substrates, it may become necessary to space adjacent interconnect lines much further apart than the widths of the lines in order to significantly reduce the interelectrode capacitance. This, however, ultimately results in larger chips and longer average interconnect wires, thus partially defeating the intent.

At the present time, it appears likely that on-chip capacitances will scale approximately linearly with lateral dimensions (rather than as k^2) for the case of the high-speed devices considered here. Some additional reductions may be obtained with insulating substrates if conservative device spacings are employed. The switching time will fall approximately linearly (or slightly less than linearly) with lateral dimension through the transit time factor, and the power–delay product will fall in proportion to capacitance. The ultimate limits on capacitance reduction depend upon fabrication techniques rather than upon material limitations, and are difficult to assess at this time.

VII. LIMITATIONS ON VELOCITY

One clearly fundamental limit on device performance arises because of the limited drift velocity reached by electronic carriers at high fields [32], [33]. At low fields, carriers are scattered by ionized impurity atoms and acoustic phonons in the lattice, losing only a small fraction of their total energy in any scattering event. Thus, an increase in average energy supplied by the external electric field results in a proportional increase in carrier drift velocity ($v = \mu E$). For electric fields above about 10^4 V/cm, however, the carriers gain sufficient energy from the field to begin emitting optical phonons. This process allows the carriers to shed a significant fraction of their total energy in each phonon interaction, so that further increases in the applied field fail to increase the average carrier energy, resulting in velocity saturation. High-speed field-effect devices are already experiencing velocity saturation, and future devices will certainly be dominated by this effect, a fact which was incorporated into the development of (5).

The velocity field curves for several semiconductors are shown in Fig. 4. Although some of the III–V materials exhibit higher velocities than silicon, the improvements are slight (i.e., within a factor of two). It is therefore considered unlikely that silicon will be displaced from its current commanding position as a device material for channel lengths above about 0.2 μm. However, for channel lengths in the range of 0.2 μm and below, a new phenomenon, ballistic transport, has to be considered [34]. In this regime, the transit time across the control region may be shorter than the mean time required to emit an optical phonon, with the results that the carrier accelerates throughout its transit without losing energy due to phonon emission, reaching average velocities well in excess of the saturation velocity. These effects were predicted theoretically by Ruch [35] and other workers [36], [37]. Ballistic effects begin to appear at channel lengths of around 0.4 μm in GaAs, but only at lengths of a few hundred angstroms or less in silicon. Hence, it is expected that short-channel MESFET (or MESFET-like) devices in GaAs will ultimately reach performance levels well in excess of those attainable in silicon.

VIII. EFFECT OF DEVIATIONS FROM THE MODEL CONDITIONS

The results which have been obtained so far were based on an elementary circuit model consisting of a field-effect device discharging a (voltage-independent) load capacitor. Real logic circuits must have some provision for recharging the load capacitance once the pull-down device is turned off. Several possibilities exist. The pull-up device may be an active device of complementary conductivity (as in CMOS). In this case, the two devices are never on at the same time, and the pull-up transient may be as fast as the pull-down. More commonly, the pull-up is a device of the same conductivity type biased so that it is always on (as in enhancement-load NMOS or depletion-load NMOS). The pull-up device must then be of much lower conductivity than the pull-down, in order to ensure that the output is pulled near ground when both devices are on. The necessarily lower conductivity slows the pull-up transient considerably, so that the overall propagation delay is degraded. In MESFET logic, the most common mode of operation is to make use of depletion-mode transistors [13] (i.e., transistors which are on at zero applied gate voltage and must be biased negative to turn off). In these circuits, two supply voltages are required, one positive (applied to the drain) and one negative (to turn off the gate). Since the gate swing is negative while the drain swing

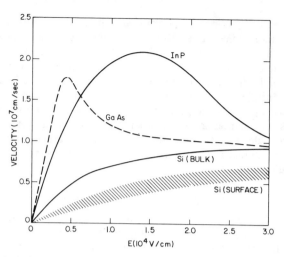

Fig. 4. Velocity-field curves for electrons in several semiconductors at room temperature. The surface curve for silicon represents the range of velocities obtained for various normal electric fields. Transient velocity overshoot effects are not included.

is positive, a level-shifting stage must be included with each logic gate, thereby increasing the switching time above our simple estimates. However, even though the simple model and resulting equations used in this work have to be modified to accurately represent the various actual circuit configurations, nevertheless the conclusions regarding voltage, channel length, capacitance, and saturation velocity remain valid.

An emerging problem area in very small devices is the increasing series resistance of contacts and of source and drain regions. (Such series resistors were not included in our simple equivalent circuit.) In MOSFET's, as devices are scaled down, the source and drain diffusions must be made shallower, and this contributes a significant parasitic resistance to the device, thereby limiting drain current and increasing switching times. The presence of series resistances in source and drain regions can also place an added constraint on operating voltage for both MOSFET's and MESFET's: since a significant fraction of the applied voltage may be dropped across the parasitic resistances, a higher operating voltage may be required to insure that the transistor experiences fields high enough to reach velocity saturation in the channel. This, in turn, leads to a higher power–delay product.

The resistance of polysilicon interconnect lines also begins to pose problems—long polysilicon runners behave like distributed RC transmission lines having time constants that can be an appreciable fraction of the on-chip gate delays. These problems arise because, under uniform scaling, the cross-sectional area of the conductors goes down as the square of the scale factor, while the length only goes linearly with scale factor. The polysilicon problem appears to be close to a solution due to recent work on refractory metal silicides [38], and should not pose a fundamental limitation.

Recently, considerable attention has been given to the possibility of low temperature operations [39]–[41], for example at liquid nitrogen temperatures (77 K). Not only are series resistances lower, but saturation drift velocities are higher at low temperatures [32], [33], owing to increased optical phonon energies. Moreover, since kT/q has been reduced, it should be possible to reduce the threshold voltage and operating voltage below the values needed at room temperature. For example, at 77 K, V_T could be reduced to 70 mV and V_{DD} to around 200 mV. Saturated drift velocity in bulk silicon would be increased by about 30 percent [32], series source and drain resistances decreased by about 25 percent, and the resistances of polysilicon interconnect lines decreased by about 8 percent. In addition, the thermal conductivity of the silicon substrate would be increased by almost 400 percent. The speed of operation would be increased by about 30 percent due to the increase in saturation velocity, but the power dissipation would be reduced by around 90 percent because of the sharply lower voltages. Since internal heating is a major limitation in present-day large-scale integrated circuits, the increased thermal conductivity and reduced power dissipation available at low temperatures would be very attractive.

IX. SUMMARY AND CONCLUSIONS

We have seen that there are four basic parameters affecting the performance of field-effect integrated circuits: 1) the length of the control region, 2) operating voltages, 3) on-chip capacitances, and 4) limiting carrier velocities. The conventional MOSFET will be limited to channel lengths of around 0.2 μm, with operating voltages slightly less than one volt, but MESFET structures are potentially capable of reaching channel lengths of several hundred angstroms, limited by semiconductor breakdown. There is no clear lower limit on the reduction of on-chip capacitances, although fringing fields and interdevice coupling will need to be considered carefully in new designs. The limiting drift velocity is a materials parameter which represents a fundamental limit, at least until ballistic effects begin to occur, a situation which is not likely to be reached in silicon. In the limit of extremely small sizes, the most promising high-speed devices appear to be MESFET structures in GaAs or InP.

REFERENCES

[1] B. Hoeneisen and C. A. Mead, "Fundamental limitations in microelectronics—I. MOS technology," *Solid-State Electron.*, vol. 15, pp. 819–829. Aug. 1972.

[2] R. W. Keyes, "Physical limits in semiconductor electronics," *Science*, vol. 195, pp. 1230–1235, Mar. 18, 1977.

[3] F. M. Klaassen, "Design and performance of micron-size devices," *Solid-State Electron.*, vol. 21, pp. 565–571, March 1978.

[4] B. Hoeneisen and C. A. Mead, "Limitations in microelectronics—II. Bipolar technology," *Solid-State Electron.*, vol. 15, pp. 891–897, Sept. 1972.

[5] P. A. Hart, T. van't Hof, and F. M. Klaassen, "Device down scaling and expected circuit performance," *IEEE Trans. Electron Devices*, vol. ED-26, pp. 42–429, Apr. 1979.

[6] D. Kahng and M. M. Atalla, "Silicon-silicon dioxide field induced surface devices," presented at IRE Solid-State Device Research Conf., Carnegie Inst. Technol., Pittsburgh, PA, 1960.

[7] H. K. J. Ihantola, "Design theory of a surface field-effect transistor," Stanford Electronics Lab., Tech. Rep. 1661-1, 1961.

[8] H. K. J. Ihantola and J. L. Moll, "Design theory of a surface field-effect transistor," *Solid-State Electron.*, vol. 7, pp. 423–430, June 1964.

[9] C. T. Sah, "Characteristics of the metal-oxide semiconductor transistors," *IEEE Trans. Electron Devices*, vol. ED-11, pp. 324–345, July 1964.

[10] S. R. Hofstein and F. P. Heiman, "The silicon insulated-gate field-effect transistor," *Proc. IEEE*, vol. 51, pp. 1190–1202, Sept. 1963.

[11] C. A. Mead, "Schottky barrier gate field-effect transistor," *Proc. IEEE*, vol. 54, pp. 307–308, Feb. 1966.

[12] W. W. Hooper and W. I. Lehrer, "An epitaxial GaAs field-effect transistor," *Proc. IEEE*, vol. 55, pp. 1237–1238, July 1967.

[13] R. C. Eden, B. M. Welch, R. Zucca, and S. I. Lang, "The prospects for ultrahigh-speed VLSI GaAs digital logic," *IEEE Trans. Electron Devices*, vol. ED-26, pp. 299–317, Apr. 1979.

[14] K. Lehovec and R. Zuleeg, "Analysis of GaAs FET's for integrated logic," *IEEE Trans. Electron Devices*, vol. ED-27, pp. 1074–1091, June 1980.

[15] R. W. Keyes, "A figure of merit for IC packaging," *IEEE J. Solid-State Circuits*, vol. SC-13, pp. 265–266, Apr. 1978.

[16] E. J. Boleky, "The performance of complementary MOS transistors on insulating substrates," *RCA Rev.*, vol. 31, pp. 372–395, June 1970.

[17] J. H. Yuan and E. Harari, "Short-channel C-MOS/SOS technology," *IEEE Trans. Electron Devices*, vol. ED-25, pp. 989–995, Aug. 1978.

[18] Y. Tarui, Y. Hayashi, and T. Sekigawa, "Diffusion self-aligned MOST: A new approach for high-speed devices," in *Proc. 1st Conf. Solid-State Devices* (suppl. *J. Japan Soc. Appl. Phys.*, vol. 39, pp. 105–110, 1970).

[19] C. O. Bozler, G. D. Alley, R. A. Murphy, D. C. Flanders, and W. T. Lindley, "Permeable base transistor," in *Proc. 7th Bien. Cornell Conf. Active Microwave Semiconductor Devices*, Aug. 1979.

[20] C. O. Bozler and G. D. Alley, "Fabrication and numerical simulation of the permeable base transistor," *IEEE Trans. Electron Devices*, vol. ED-27, pp. 1128–1141, June 1980.

[21] R. H. Dennard, F. H. Gaensslen, H-N. Yu, V. L. Rideout, E. Bassous, and A. R. Le Blanc, "Design of ion-implanted MOSFET's with very small physical dimensions," *IEEE J. Solid-State Circuits*, vol. SC-9, pp. 256–267, Oct. 1974.

[22] I. Ohkura, O. Tomisawa, M. Ohmori, and T. Nakano, "Electrical characteristics of a DSA MOS transistor with a fine structure," *IEEE Tran. Electron Devices*, vol. ED-26, pp. 430–435, Apr. 1979.

[23] F. E. Holmes and C. A. T. Solama, "VMOS—A new MOS integrated circuit technology," *Solid-State Electron.*, vol. 17, pp. 791–797, Aug. 1974.

[24] T. J. Rodgers and J. D. Meindl, "VMOS: High-speed TTL compatible MOS logic," *IEEE J. Solid-State Circuits*, vol. SC-9, pp. 239–250, Oct. 1974.

[25] W. Shockley, "A unipolar 'field-effect' transistor," *Proc. IRE*, vol. 40, pp. 1365–1376, Nov. 1952.

[26] R. S. C. Cobbold and F. N. Trofimenkoff, "Theory and application of the field-effect transistor," *Proc. Inst. Elec. Eng.*, vol. 111, pp. 1981–1992, Dec. 1964.

[27] J-I. Nishizawa, T. Terosaki, and J. Shibota, "Field-effect transistor versus analog transistor (static induction transistor)," *IEEE Trans. Electron Devices*, vol. ED-22, pp. 185–197, Apr. 1975.

[28] R. R. Troutman and S. N. Chakravarti, "Subthreshold characteristics of insulated-gate field-effect transistors," *IEEE Tran. Circuit Theory*, vol. CT-20, pp. 659–665, Nov. 1973.

[29] J. F. Verwey, "Nonavalanche injection of hot carriers into SiO_2," *J. Appl. Phys.*, vol. 44, pp. 2681–2687, June 1973.

[30] S. A. Abbas and R. C. Dockerty, "Hot carrier instability in IGFETs," *Appl. Phys. Letters*, vol. 27, pp. 147–148, 1 Aug. 1975.

[31] T. H. Ning, P. W. Cook, R. H. Dennard, C. M. Osborn, S. E. Schuster, and H. E. Luhn, "1 μm MOSFET VLSI technology: Part IV, Hot-electron design constraints," *IEEE Trans. Electron Devices*, vol. ED-26, pp. 346–353, Apr. 1979.

[32] C. Jacoboni, C. Canali, G. Ottaviani, and A. A. Quaranta, "A review of some charge transport properties of silicon," *Solid-State Electron*, vol. 20, pp. 77–89, Feb. 1977.

[33] R. W. Coen and R. S. Muller, "Velocity of surface carriers in inversion layers on silicon," *Solid-State Electron.*, vol. 23, pp. 35–40, Jan. 1980.

[34] T. J. Maloney and J. Frey, "Transient and steady-state electron transport properties of GaAs and InP," *J. Appl. Phys.*, vol. 48, pp. 781–787, Feb. 1977.

[35] J. G. Ruch, "Electron dynamics in short channel field-effect transistors," *IEEE Trans. Electron Devices*, vol. ED-19, pp. 652–654, May 1972.

[36] Y-C. Wang and Y-T. Hsieh, "Velocity overshoot effect on a short-gate microwave MESFET," *Int. J. Electron.*, vol. 49, pp. 49–66, Jan. 1979.

[37] T. Wada and J. Frey, "Physical basis of short-channel MESFET operations," *IEEE Trans. Electron Devices*, vol. ED-26, pp. 476–490, Apr. 1979.

[38] P. L. Shah, "Refractory metal gate processes for VLSI applications," *IEEE Trans. Electron Devices*, vol. ED-26, pp. 631–640, Apr. 1979.

[39] A. K. Jonscher, "Semiconductors at cryogenic temperatures," *Proc. IEEE*, vol. 52, pp. 1092–1104, Oct. 1964.

[40] R. W. Keyes, E. P. Harris, and K. L. Kannerth, "The role of low temperatures in the operation of logic circuitry," *Proc. IEEE*, vol. 58, pp. 1914–1932, Dec. 1970.

[41] F. H. Gaensslen, V. L. Rideout, E. J. Walker, and J. J. Walker, "Very small MOSFET's for low temperature operations," *IEEE Trans. Electron Devices*, vol. ED-24, pp. 218–229, Mar. 1977.

Chapter 2: GaAs Devices and Advanced IC Implementations

This chapter surveys gallium arsenide (GaAs) device designs used in digital circuits, and presents advanced integrated circuit implementations to demonstrate the capability of these devices (at the date that this tutorial was developed).

The first paper entitled "High Speed GaAs Integrated Circuits" by Long et al., describes Metal-Semiconductor FETs (MESFETs) and Junction FETs (JFETs). The authors describe the fabrication, device structure, logic circuit implementation, and relative performance characteristics of these devices.

Solomon and Morkoc, in their article "Modulation-Doped GaAs/Al GaAs Heterojunction Field-Effect Transistors (MODFETs), Ultrahigh-Speed Device for Supercomputers," describe Modulation-Doped FETS (MODFETs), also referred to by others as High Electron Mobility Transistors (HEMTs), Selectively Doped Heterojunction Transistors (SDHTs), or Two-Dimensional Electron Gas FETs (TEGFETs). The authors describe the theoretical basis underlying the advantages of modulation doping, MODFET device fabrication and optimization, MODFET circuit implementations, and the relative performance of MODFETs in comparison with other GaAs devices.

In his paper entitled "Heterostructure Bipolar Transistors and Integrated Circuits," Kroemer describes Heterostructure Bipolar Transistors (HBTs). He explains the theoretical advantages of the wide bandgap emitter, upon which HBTs are based; he describes device performance tradeoffs and some device and circuit implementations; and he compares the future of HBTs with that of FET technology.

Hirayama et al. present an advanced integrated circuit implementation that uses MESFETs in their paper entitled "A GaAs 16-Kbit Static RAM Using Dislocation-Free Crystal." The chip is a 16-Kbit static RAM containing more than 100,000 transistors, and represents the highest level of integration achieved at the time of this writing. The authors describe the circuit design, fabrication, and performance characteristics of this chip.

Kobayashi et al., in their paper "A Fully Operational 1-Kbit HEMT Static RAM," present an advanced integrated circuit implementation that uses MODFETs. The chip is a 1-Kbit static RAM containing more than 7000 transistors. Although not describing the highest level of integration achieved thus far (a 4-Kbit version was described earlier in a short paper), the authors here describe in greater detail the fabrication process, circuit design, and performance issues.

Yuan et al., in their paper "A 4K GaAs Bipolar Gate Array," present an advanced integrated circuit implementation that uses HBTs. The chip is a 4K gate array. The authors present some fabrication details and performance characteristics, and they compare the properties of their design with the properties of silicon ECL and GaAs MESFETs.

High Speed GaAs Integrated Circuits

STEVEN I. LONG, SENIOR MEMBER, IEEE, BRYANT M. WELCH, MEMBER, IEEE, RICARDO ZUCCA, SENIOR MEMBER, IEEE, PETER M. ASBECK, MEMBER, IEEE, C-P. LEE, CONILEE G. KIRKPATRICK, SENIOR MEMBER, IEEE, FRANK S. LEE, GEORGE R. KAELIN, MEMBER, IEEE, AND RICHARD C. EDEN, MEMBER, IEEE

Reprinted from *Proceedings of the IEEE*, Volume 70, Number 1, January 1982, pages 35-45. Copyright © 1982 by The Institute of Electrical and Electronics Engineers, Inc.

Invited Paper

Abstract—Much interest has been expressed in the use of GaAs MESFET's for high speed digital integrated circuits (IC's). Propagation delays in the 60- to 90-ps/gate range have been demonstrated by several laboratories on SSI and MSI logic circuits. Recently, large scale digital IC's with over 1000 gates have been demonstrated in GaAs. In this review paper, the device, circuit, and processing approaches presently being explored for high speed GaAs digital circuits are presented. The present performance status of high speed circuits and LSI circuits is reviewed.

I. Introduction

OVER THE PAST DECADE, GaAs Metal-Semiconductor FET's (MESFET's) have been developed and extensively utilized for high-frequency low-noise amplification. The maximum available gain, noise figure, and bandwidth capabilities of analog microwave FET amplifiers have been unequaled by any other semiconductor device in the 2- to 18-GHz range. These amplifiers have been widely utilized in commercial and government systems. Reliability studies on low-noise FET's have proven that these devices are sutiable for most system applications. These discrete GaAs devices have also been shown to be readily manufacturable in large quantities despite their 0.5- and 1.0-μm gate lengths.

More recently, application of GaAs MESFET's for high speed digital circuits has also been emphasized in several laboratories because of the high switching speed and transconductance of these devices. Propagation delays as low as 30 ps/gate at room temperature and 17.5 ps/gate at 77 K have been reported on minimum-area lightly loaded GaAs ring oscillator circuits [1]. Even on more complex circuits, such as MSI binary divider circuits, delays in the 60- to 90-ps/gate range have been obtained in several laboratories using various circuit implementations and processing approaches. As a consequence, frequency dividers have been built in GaAs MESFET logic which function at input frequencies of 5.5 GHz [2].

These promising high speed results have placed emphasis on achieving fabrication methods which result in high density FET logic gate structures with highly uniform device characteristics.

Manuscript received July 8, 1981; revised October 1, 1981.
B. M. Welch, R. Zucca, P. M. Asbeck, C. P. Lee, C. Kirkpatrick, F. S. Lee, and G. R. Kaelin are with Rockwell International Microelectronic Research and Development Center, Thousand Oaks, CA 91360.
S. I. Long was with Rockwell International Microelectronics Research and Development Center, Thousand Oaks, CA 91360. He is now with the University of California, Santa Barbara, CA.
R. C. Eden was with Rockwell International Microelectronics Research and Development Center, Thousand Oaks, CA 91360. He is now with Gigabit Logic, Culver City, CA.

While density was not of importance for the discrete FET, which generally was rather large in area and used relatively high pinchoff voltage active channel layers, it is of importance in an IC because of the desire to maximize yield of functional circuits and to press circuit complexity beyond the small scale region (20 gates). Therefore, planar fabrication methods, similar in concept and apperance to well-established silicon IC approaches, have been developed. The planar approach employs selective ion implantation to localize active devices in the semi-insulating GaAs substrate, and gate densities over 100 000/cm² have been reported on very dense circuit structures [5].

The development of planar fabrication methods and high speed logic gate structures with modest power dissipation (<1 mW/gate) and high density has created interest in the extension of GaAs digital IC's into the large or very large scale of integration range. The achievement of LSI or VLSI is important if very high speed components for signal processors, computers, and memory are to be feasible in GaAs IC's. The high complexity of such systems makes it very desirable to include large numbers of components on a single chip to reduce the large quantity of high speed interconnections. Trends in this direction are also quite evident in silicon IC implemented signal processing and computational hardware [6], [7].

Very recent demonstration of high speed LSI parallel multiplier chips in GaAs MESFET logic [8] has proven that such chip complexities (over 1000 gates) are feasible in a well-controlled IC process. While further development and optimization will certainly provide improved results, the initial observation of 150-ps/gate propagation delays in the 1000 gate 8 bit multiplier structure is quite encouraging. Also, even though the 1000 gate complexity level (about 3000 transistors and 3000 diodes) permits a wide variety of "random" logic circuits or sequential circuits to be developed, memory requirements (fast access RAM) will mandate even greater complexity if memory chips are to be large enough to permit fast processor integration in small volumes (needed to minimize the effect of interconnect delay on system clock speeds).

In this paper, a variety of device, circuit, and fabrication approaches currently being employed for high speed GaAs digital IC's are presented and discussed. The performance of both ring oscillation and frequency divider "benchmark"-type IC's is compared followed by a brief summary of the LSI status of GaAs IC's.

II. GaAs Digital IC Device and Circuit Approaches

The Schottky barrier gate field effect transistor (MESFET) is the main active device used in GaAs IC's. Fig. 1(a) shows a

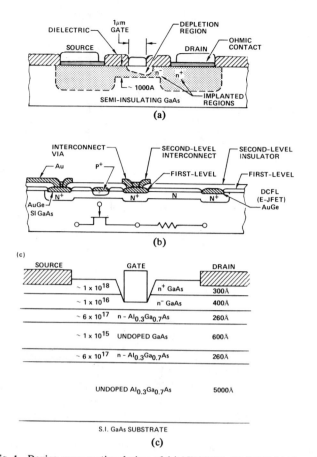

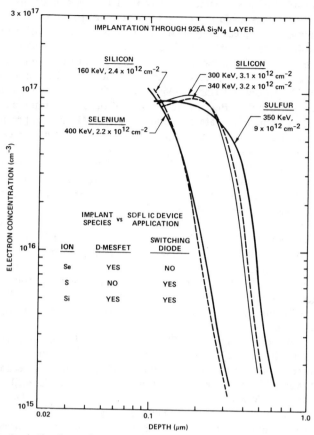

Fig. 1. Device cross-sectional view of (a) MESFET, (b) JFET [11], and (c) modulation-doped [16] device structures.

Fig. 2. Active layer dopant profiles for the n-FET channel Selenium implant and the n+ high-speed switching diode sulfur implant. A silicon implant can also be used for both the n- and n+ regions.

cross-sectional diagram of a typical planar ion-implanted MESFET fabricated by localized implantation into a semi-insulating GaAs substrate. The channel implant species, energy, and dose are chosen so that the peak position and depth of the doping profile (as shown in Fig. 2) result in a device with the desired pinchoff (V_p) voltage. If the device channel is conductive at $V_{gs} = 0$, the pinchoff voltage is negative and a depletion-mode (normally ON) device is obtained. The logic voltage swing can extend from below $-V_p$ to the onset of gate conduction due to the forward-biased gate-source junction. Larger logic swings will produce higher speed circuits for a given device type since $I_{ds} \alpha (V_{gs} - V_p)^2$ when $V_{gs} - V_p < 1.2$ V for GaAs FET's. Therefore, higher I_{ds} per device area will be available with increasing gate bias for charging load capacitances. Further increase of logic voltage will result in velocity saturation limited currents ($I_{ds} \alpha (V_{gs} - V_p)$) and no further improvement in speed should be observed. The speed–power product will, however, be greatly increased by the higher logic voltage swing [9]. Thus a superior approach for higher speed circuit performance would be to increase gm/C_{in} (or the current gain–bandwidth product) of the switching transistor. This can be done by reducing source resistance and gate length through process improvements (or by substitution of a higher performance device type as discussed in [10]).

If the built-in potential of the Schottky gate metal is capable of preventing current flow in the channel at $V_{gs} = 0$, an enhancement-mode (normally OFF) device results. This device requires forward gate bias ($V_{gs} > 0$) to enable flow of I_{ds}. Therefore, the logic voltage swing of an enhancement-mode FET is re-stricted to a narrower range (generally 0 V to 0.7 V, the forward gate conduction voltage for a MESFET) than was the depletion-mode FET device. This restriction results in smaller I_{ds} for a given device area of an enhancement-mode FET than a depletion-mode FET, and therefore, the propagation delay is generally higher and power dissipation lower for GaAs IC's implemented with normally OFF transistors.

JFET devices, using a p+ gate stripe formed by selective ion implantation, have also been successfully employed in GaAs digital IC's [11]. A diagram of a GaAs JFET is illustrated in Fig. 1(b). The JFET is somewhat more difficult to fabricate than a MESFET because of the additional p+ implant process steps and the precise control of the p+ junction depth necessary to control the pinchoff voltage of the device. However, sufficient control has been obtained, at least for SSI circuits. Gate lengths in the 1- to 2-µm range are readily achievable with optical lithography. The greater built-in potential of the p+-n junction provides a higher forward-bias gate conduction limit (approximately 1.1 V) which should provide a significant speed advantage for enhancement-mode JFET's over MESFET's, assuming that source and gate resistances are minimized on this structure [12]. However, the speed performance reported to date on these devices has not yet equaled the MESFET. The larger available logic voltage swing will also be beneficial in increasing noise margins for normally OFF JFET logic over normally OFF MESFET logic.

The choice of a particular type of FET device is associated with a choice of circuit and fabrication approach. The depletion-mode metal-semiconductor (Schottky barrier) FET

(D-MESFET) is the most widely used device, and also is the one that has given the highest performance to date. Circuits employing depletion-mode MESFET's pose the least fabrication problems (see Section III) because Schottky barriers on GaAs are easier to fabricate than p-n junctions, and the larger (typically 1-V) logic swings associated with D-MESFET circuits avoid excessively stringent requirements for FET pinchoff voltage uniformity. Because any regions of the source-drain channel not under the gate are conductive in D-MESFET's, precise gate alignments are not required, nor are special gate recess etch processes or other means to avoid parasitic source and drain resistances necessary. The MESFET fabrication simplicity makes it considerably easier to achieve high yields than with more complex device structures. On the other hand, however, logic gates employing depletion-mode active devices necessarily require some form of voltage level shifting between FET drains and gates to meet turnoff requirements, and usually require two power supplies, imposing some penalty in terms of wafer area utilization. An exception to the two power supply requirements for D-MESFET circuits is the enhancement-depletion logic approach [13] which uses $-0.4\text{-V} < V_p < 0.1\text{-V}$ MESFET's with diode level shifting in single power supply logic circuits.

Enhancement-mode MESFET's (E-MESFET's) offer circuit simplicity because the logic gates require only one power supply, but the permissible voltage swing is rather low because Schottky barrier gates on GaAs cannot be forward biased above 0.6 to 0.8 V without drawing excessive currents. A 0.5-V swing is a desirable goal for the operating range of ultra low power circuits, but very tight control is required in order to fabricate uniform, very thin active layers, so that they are totally depleted at zero gate bias voltage and yet give good device transconductance when the device is turned on. For reasonable noise margins and good dynamic performance, standard deviations of FET pinchoff voltage of the order of 25 mV could be required—a very difficult goal for GaAs FET's.

Implementation of a MOSFET or MISFET (Metal Insulating Semiconductor FET) technology in GaAs would eliminate the logic swing limitation completely, but attaining such devices has proven difficult. Some simple ring oscillators have been fabricated using directly coupled FET logic implemented with buried channel GaAs MOSFET's and resistor loads [14]. However, at this point, stable oxides have not been achieved in such circuits, so that gate threshold voltages shift with respect to the prior input signal history. This limitation has constrained the demonstration of GaAs MOSFET's to ring oscillators and other simple circuits in which the input waveform has a symmetric (50-percent duty cycle) nature, but the performance observed to date does not support MOSFET's in general digital circuit applications. Efforts to improve the state of GaAs oxide technology are continuing, however. The use of InP for MISFET devices may be more promising than GaAs [15].

High mobility FET devices are also being developed for use in GaAs IC's. These devices take advantage of the greatly reduced ionized impurity scattering possible at 77 K in a lightly doped n-GaAs channel when free carriers are introduced through a wide-gap $n^+\text{-Al}_x\text{Ga}_{1-x}\text{As}$ heterojunction as shown in Fig. 1(c). These structures have been referred to as modulation-doped FET's [16] or high electron mobility transistors (HEMT) [17], and electron mobilities of 80 000 cm²/V · s at 77 K have been reported [16]. Such FET's, fabricated with short gate lengths, should achieve high g_m and f_τ with very small logic

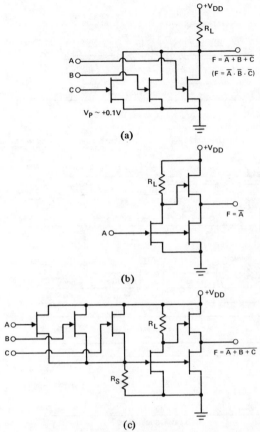

Fig. 3. Enhancement-mode JFET or MESFET circuits [11], [12], [18]. (a) Simple direct-coupled FET logic (DCFL) NOR gate with resistor load. (b) Pseudocomplementary buffered inverter gate. (c) combination of source-follower logic with the circuit of (b) to give a buffered NOR gate. This type of approach has been extended to two-level gates as well.

swings of only 100 mV or so. This would result in extremely low speed–power products. To utilize these devices for LSI GaAs circuits, however, an effective means of fabrication of large numbers of these transistors with nearly identical device characteristics must be developed. At the present time, only discrete transistors have been demonstrated.

Enhancement-Mode Circuit Designs

A number of circuit designs for basic logic gate structures have been proposed or demonstrated utilizing normally OFF FET's in conjunction with resistor or depletion loads and Schottky-barrier level shifting diodes. These have mainly been oriented toward use of the MESFET or JFET as the active switching devices. The following subsection will summarize and review several of these circuit approaches.

The simplest circuit approach, direct-coupled FET logic (DCFL), is illustrated for a 3-input (positive) NOR gate in Fig. 3(a). In this approach, a logic "0" corresponds to a voltage near zero. A logic "1" corresponds to a positive voltage capable of fully turning on the normally OFF FET's, a value usually limited by the onset of gate conduction in the FET; typically on the order of 0.6 V to 1.4 V depending on what technology is used (MESFET, JFET, or HJFET). It has been proposed to place input FET's in series, generating the NAND function [18]. However, the implementation of such design would appear impractical because the on resistance of the conducting FET's would cause larger threshold shifts than could be tolerated with the very low logic swings of E-MESFET logic. (It would probably work with E-JFET's or H-JFET's, however, and should represent no problem with MOSFET's.)

A significant improvement to the DCFL gate shown in Fig. 3(a) would be to substitute for load resistor R_L, an active load current source made with a normally ON (depletion-mode) FET, with its gate tied to the source. Such a nonlinear load would sharpen the transfer characteristic and significantly improve the speed and speed–power products of the circuits (by perhaps a factor of 2). The fabrication of the depletion-mode active load requires a dopant concentration profile different from that of the enhancement-mode devices. Although enhancement-mode demonstration circuits have been fabricated using a single active layer, the multiple localized implantation fabrication technique used for the Schottky-diode FET logic (SDFL) approach (discussed later in this section) could be applied to such enhancement-mode circuits so that depletion-mode active loads could be used. An additional nonlinear load component which shows great promise for enhancement-mode logic circuit is the saturated drift velocity resistor [12], [19] in which the current limiting action is enhanced by the use of a short-channel gateless FET structure. Here, the current is limited by velocity saturation of the channel electrons, and very low saturation voltages should be possible with short source-drain gaps, thus reducing power dissipation.

From a static point of view, the fanout capability of DCFL is excellent since it is determined by the very low gate leakage currents. However, from a dynamic point of view, the switching speeds are reduced by the gate capacitance loadings by a factor of approximately $1/N$ where N is the number of loading gates, as in silicon MOS. In general, the current through the resistor R_L, saturated resistor, or active load is kept fairly low in DCFL in order to reduce static power and improve noise margin by reducing the output "low" voltage of the FET. Consequently, the output risetime under heavy fanout loading conditions is very poor. This can be greatly improved with the pseudocomplementary output buffer configuration of Fig. 3(b), at very little increase in static power dissipation, but this circuit performs only logic inversion [12]. By combining the inverting buffer with a source-follower positive-OR input structure as shown in Fig. 3(c), a general multiple-input NOR gate can be achieved which has excellent fan-in and fan-out drive capabilities at very modest static power levels [18]. Unfortunately, this source-OR/pseudocomplementary inverter gate configuration is also quite complex, requiring 7 FET's and 2 resistors for a 4-input NOR gate, which can be expected to consume considerable chip area and have significant self-capacitance.

Enhancement-Depletion-Mode MESFET Logic

Because of the nonlinear, approximately square-law nature of the FET I_{ds} versus V_{gs} relationship, it is not always necessary to completely turn off the FET (i.e., make V_{gs} more negative than V_p) in order to obtain switching behavior.

Drain dotting of many FET's, as in Fig. 3(a), necessitates turning all of the FET's nearly off so that the sum of all of their drain currents is substantially less than the load current I_L through R_L require to produce an output voltage near the switching threshold of the next driven gate. However, if only a single FET switches the load, it is only necessary to reduce its drain current in the OFF state to a value significantly

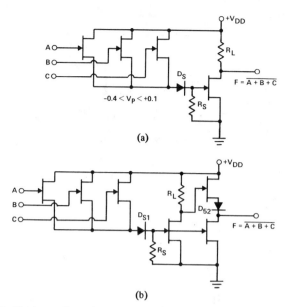

Fig. 4. Single-supply enhancement-mode MESFET NOR gate circuits [13]. (a) Quasi-normally off 3-input NOR gate. (b) 3-input NOR gate with pseudocomplementary buffer; note similarity to Fig. 3(c).

smaller than I_L, while its "ON" current is well above I_L. This can be achieved in depletion-mode MESFET's with reasonably small pinchoff voltages ($V_p \approx -0.4$ V) with zero or slightly positive gate voltages, so that only a single power supply is required. For example, with $V_p = -0.4$ V and $V_{gs}(\text{ON}) = +0.7$ V, $V_{gs}(\text{OFF}) = +0.1$ V, we have $I_{ds}(\text{ON}) = 4.84 \times I_{ds}(\text{OFF})$, an ample margin for switching.

A number of circuit approaches for single supply E-D MESFET logic have been proposed and analyzed [13]. Fig. 4(a) shows the circuit diagram for an elemental 3-input NOR gate in the most promising of these published approaches. This uses source follower logic to obtain the positive OR function, with single diode level shifting and a resistor pulldown R_S to drive the output inverter FET. The analysis in [13] indicates proper gate operation for MESFET pinchoff voltages in the $-0.4 < V_p < +0.1$-V range, which is several times the allowable range width for E-MESFET logic and much more reasonable in terms of practical fabrication control. The supply voltage ($V_{dd} \sim 3$ V) and logic voltage swing ($V_{out} \sim 0.2$ V to 2.4 V) values used are even larger than those used in the SDFL D-MESFET approach, so that very low $P_D \tau_d$ products would not be expected. The gate output of Fig. 4(a) has the same drive problems as that of Fig. 3(a), but this should be improved for heavily loaded gates with the buffer structure of Fig. 4(b). This is, of course, very similar (except for the two voltages shifting diodes) to the enhancement circuit of Fig. 3(c).

At the present time, demonstration circuits containing up to 15 gates have been fabricated using enhancement-mode FET's. MESFET-implemented circuits have exceeded the performance of JFET circuits in both speed and power even through the higher JFET logic swing should provide greater speed as discussed above. Complexity of enhancement-mode circuits has probably been limited by fabrication technology and threshold uniformity. Comparisons of ring oscillators and frequency divider demonstration circuits are made in Section IV.

Depletion-Mode Logic Approaches

Buffered FET logic (BFL) [20] and Schottky Diode FET Logic (SDFL) [21] gate circuit approaches have been exten-

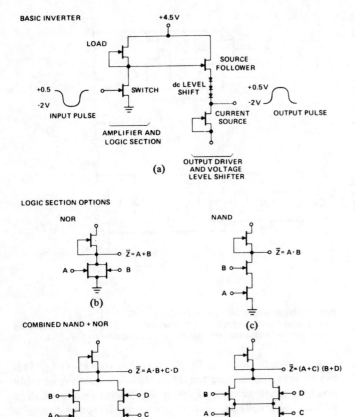

Fig. 5. Basic circuit configurations for buffered FET logic [20]. (a) Basic inverter circuit. (b)–(e) Options for the input section for NOR NAND and combined NAND-NOR functions.

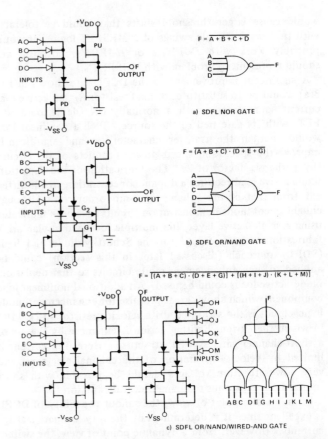

Fig. 6. Comparison of 1- , 2- , and 3-level SDFL gate configurations [22]. All FET's are depletion-mode, typically $-1.5 < V_p < -0.5$ V; unshaded diodes are very small high speed switching Schottky diodes while shaded diodes are larger area, higher capacitance voltage shifting diodes.

sively employed for depletion-mode GaAs IC's. Circuit diagrams for NOR gates formed by these two approaches are presented in Figs. 5 and 6. The BFL circuit employs FET's to perform a NOR (or 2-input NAND for a dual-gate FET) function at the input. The output is driven by a source follower, with level shifting diodes to restore the required logic levels to the +0.7-V (high) to $-V_p$ (low) voltages required by the input FET's. The source-follower output driver yields a gate structure which has relatively low sensitivity to fanout loading and load capacitance. Also no dc output current is required to drive subsequent BFL gate inputs. Fan-in is limited for practical purposes to 3 for a NOR gate by the drain capacitances of the input transistors and the area required by these devices and 2 for the NAND gate because of voltage drop in the series FET's which results in threshold shift.

Nearly all BFL circuits reported to date have utilized relatively high pinchoff voltages (~ 2.5 V) and three level-shift diodes for convenience in fabrication (since epi/implant-mesa approaches provide suitable threshold control for large logic voltage swings) and, therefore, have exhibited high power dissipation per gate (40 mW typical). However, since fabrication methods and pinchoff voltage control have been improved with ion-implanted planar approaches, there is no reason why low pinchoff (~ 1-V) MESFET's and two level-shift diodes should not be employed for advanced BFL gates designs. These modifications should reduce power dissipation to ~5 mW/gate by allowing operation at lower voltage and current levels with relatively little sacrifice in speed and could make BFL circuits a possible candidate for

applications requiring lower LSI complexity (200–500 gates). Demonstration circuits with about 20 gates complexity have been reported in the literature using high pinchoff BFL gates [20]; however, larger BFL circuits (≥200 gates) using low pinchoff FET's are currently in development.

The SDFL circuit approach, shown in Fig. 6, permits high speed operation comparable to the BFL approach, but results in considerable savings in area/gate (600 to 2000 μm^2) and in lower power dissipation (0.2 to 2 mW/gate). SDFL utilizes clusters of small high-performance Schottky diodes to perform the logical positive-OR function on groups of inputs which may then be further processed with the normal FET logic functions (series-NAND, wired-AND, etc.). Fig. 6 shows SDFL gate circuits diagrams for single- , two- , and three-level logic gate configurations [22]. Note that the SDFL gate structure allows virtually unlimited fan-in at the first (positive-OR) logic level (SDFL circuits with up to 8-input NOR gates have been described in publications) [23], but it has the same practical restrictions to a fan-in of 2 at the second (series FET NAND) and third (wired-AND) levels if dynamic performance is to be maintained.

The SDFL circuit approach offers large savings, not only in power, but also in circuit area, over previous D-MESFET approaches. The circuit area savings comes about because of the simplicity of the gate design and replacement of (large) FET's with very small (typically 1 $\mu m \times$ 2 μm) Schottky diodes for most logic functions. The fact that the diodes are 2-terminal devices also significantly reduces the number of vias and over-

24

crossings required in most circuits as compared to the vias and overcrossings needed when 3-terminal FET's are used as the logic elements.

The input logic diodes require a lower carrier concentration, lower sheet resistance implant than the FET channel to optimize their reverse-bias capacitance and series resistance. Thus SDFL circuits require two separate implant steps using localized implantation into selected areas of the substrate.

Fanout of the basic SDFL gate is limited to 3 without buffering or using wider channel widths in the driving gate. However, the propagation delay is not as sensitive to fanout loading as the direct coupled FET logic (or NMOS) approach, since the gate-source capacitance of the switching FET is discharged by the pulldown active load instead of the preceding FET drain current.

III. GaAs Digital IC Fabrication Approaches

In the following section, a review of fabrication methods currently in use on GaAs digital IC's will be presented. These methods are schematically represented in Fig. 7. While the selection of processing techniques to be discussed is by no means exhaustive, it is a representative cross section of approaches suitable for fabrication of FET-based GaAs IC's with gate lengths as short as 1 μm for optical lithography or $\frac{1}{2}$ μm for electron beam or certain types of self-aligned procedures.

Mesa-Implanted D-MESFET

Initial GaAs IC efforts were based on the well-developed depletion-mode GaAs MESFET mesa fabrication technology used in the production of low-noise microwave FET's. Isolation between active devices is accomplished in this approach by etching through the epitaxial or implanted active layer. Basically, as shown in Fig. 7(a), a discrete MESFET fabrication process is used with the addition of a second layer of metal and a dielectric layer for interconnecting the various circuit elements. First layer to second layer metal overcrossings have also been fabricated using plated air-bridges rather than a dielectric. Initial work employing epitaxial techniques for the (~2000-Å) active layers encountered difficulties in achieving the uniformity and reproducibility required for IC's. Subsequently, an implanted layer was substituted for epitaxial layer, with the implantation made into a high resistivity epitaxial buffer layer or directly into the semi-insulating substrate. Both techniques are currently being used in the mesa-implanted D-MESFET fabrication of buffered FET logic (BFL) circuits [20] shown in Fig. 7(a).

While this mesa fabrication approach has the important advantage of process simplicity, it has been, at least in its present form, restricted to applications in which only a single active layer (implanted or epitaxial) is required, i.e., circuits in which only a single type of device needs to be optimized. The density and yield limitations associated with mesa structures may inhibit the extension of this technology to LSI/VLSI. Most of the work using this approach has been directed toward high speed MSI logic, with excellent results achieved using 1-μm contact photolithography [24].

Mesa Epitaxial/Implanted E-MESFET

Enhancement-mode GaAs MESFET devices have also been fabricated on epitaxial layers and isolated by mesa etching. This technique has provided Direct Coupled FET Logic circuits

as shown in Fig. 7(b) [25], [26]. Other similar processes not illustrated [27], [28] have used both epitaxial and ion-implanted layers. Precise thickness control has proven very difficult for GaAs E-MESFET IC's utilizing vapor phase epitaxy. This has necessitated controlled thinning of the epitaxial layer using self-limiting anodization and stripping techniques which do not appear practical for LSI. Workers employing ion-implanted layers [28] appear to omit this step. However, all of these E-MESFET approaches require the use of recessed gate structures. Recessed gates circumvent some of the difficulties associated with the high series resistance surface depletion layers often observed on very thin FET channel layers. A deep implant or thicker epitaxial layer is initially provided (lower sheet resistance), and the Schottky gate is recessed into the GaAs surface by using a chemical etchant or chemical anodization method. This process approach provides improved FET characteristics by lowering source/drain to gate series resistance, but the uniformity, control, and yield of the resulting devices for LSI applications are in serious question. For example, the difficulties encountered in obtaining adequate uniformity using implanted layers and recessed gate structures for E-MESFET devices has led workers to explore innovative, less demanding (in terms of device uniformity) circuit concepts such as quasi-normally OFF MESFET logic [13].

Both contact photolithography [27] and EBL [28] have been employed in the fabrication of L_g = 1-μm circuits of this type. The fabrication of these E-MESFET circuits is quite similar to that of the mesa D-MESFET approach except for the variation shown in Fig. 7(b) which uses the ohmic contact metallization for the first-level interconnects, with the Schottky gate metallization also serving for the second-level interconnects [27].

Self-Aligned Epitaxial D-MESFET

The development of a planar technology in Si IC's marked the turning point which led to rapid progress toward LSI, suggesting that planar development in GaAs will also have a similar impact. Recent work toward the development of structures has led to the fabrication of D-MESFET GaAs IC's shown in Fig. 7(c) [30]. In this fabrication process, the structure can be made planar by replacing the mesa isolation step with selective proton, oxygen, or boron bombardment which renders the underlying epitaxial material semi-insulating. This fabrication method may use epitaxial or implanted layers. However, it is still limited to a single active layer. The quality of the electrical isolation and the long-term reliability in high temperature operation of this high resistivity ion bombarded layer needs to be investigated in greater detail.

Unique to this fabrication approach is the use of a self-aligned FET gate scheme which does not require a Schottky gate masking step. This process requires the use of Al gates since alloyed ohmic contacts are fabricated after the formation of the gates and Al provides a suitable Schottky barrier material capable of withstanding the subsequent 450°C alloying cycle. Since the ohmic contacts are composed to AuGe and the gates are made of Al, a Mo barrier layer is required to separate the Al and Au based metallization systems, adding some complexity to the process and raising some concern regarding the long-term reliability of mixing Al and Au metallizations. Circuits of this type have been fabricated using contact photolithography and have yielded promising results in the lower MSI level of complexity, with reasonable promise of extension to larger circuits [2].

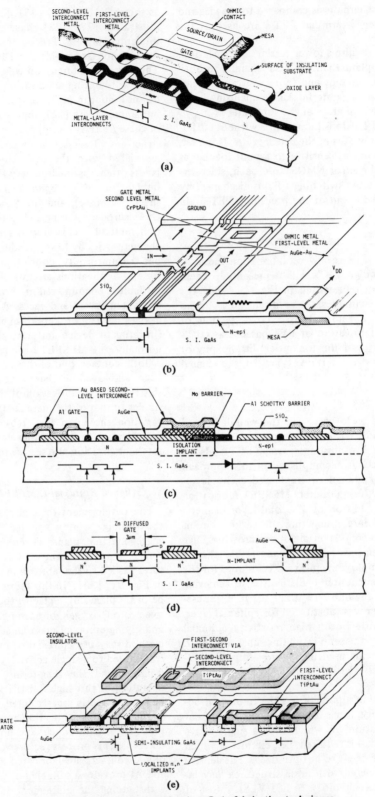

Fig. 7. Schematic representation of various GaAs fabrication techniques.
(a) Mesa implanted *D*-MESFET. (b) Mesa epitaxial *E*-MESFET. (c)
Self-aligned epitaxial *D*-MESFET. (d) Planar implanted *E*-JFET (e)
Planar implanted *D*-MESFET (SDFL).

Planar Implanted E-JFET

A planar enhancement-mode *E*-JFET fabrication technology
[4], [11] currently under development is illustrated in Fig.

7(d). This approach uses a junction FET (JFET) to provide
DCFL circuits with resistor loads. The FET channel and heavily
doped regions under the ohmic contacts are produced by using

26

multiple selective n-type implantation steps and the gate region is fabricated using a p-type implant. Since isolation through mesa is no longer needed, a planar structure is obtained.

The principal interest in the E-JFET is in its larger allowable voltage swing before the onset of gate conduction, although the structure also offers potentially lower parasitic source and drain channel resistances than the E-MESFET. The E-JFET might also offer better control over gate threshold voltage than the E-MESFET in that V_p can be controlled both by the n-implant and by controlling the depth of the p^+/n junction (in a manner similar to controlling the emitter depth of a Si bipolar transistor). This fabrication technology has been used to produce E-JFET devices with gate lengths of 1 μm, using a Mg implant for the p^+ gate. This work is at an earlier stage of development than the D-MESFET or E-MESFET efforts, but some inverter ring oscillator results have been published with gate densities of 200 gates/mm^2 with projected [4], [11] gate densities of 800 gates/mm^2. In principle this appears to be an attractive fabrication and circuit approach for enhancement logic. The main drawback for practical LSI results from the yield limiting additional processing required for JFET's in comparison to D-MESFET's. In particular the additional p^+ implant and subsequent self-aligned gate electrode pose difficult fabrication problems at the 1-μm level and below. Also, it would appear that a depletion-mode active load would be an attractive alternative to the currently used resistor load configuration, leading to additional processing in the form of implants and Schottky barriers. Optimized development of planar JFET logic will possibly require one (or more) additional mask levels than D-MESFET fabrication approaches.

Planar Implanted D-MESFET

The planar implanted D-MESFET GaAs IC fabrication approach is illustrated in Fig. 7(e). Planar circuits are fabricated as in the planar E-JFET approach by using multiple localized ion implants directly into semi-insulating GaAs substrates [5]. Hence, individual devices can be optimized by using different implants, and the unimplanted GaAs substrate directly provides isolation between devices. Very uniform MESFET device parameters have been obtained over 1-in GaAs IC wafers using the direct implant approach. Standard deviations of pinchoff voltage as low as 34 mV have been observed, while 50 to 80 mV is routinely obtained [38]. This fabrication method conveniently complements the Schottky diode-FET logic (SDFL) circuit approach [21], which requires the use of at least two different implantations for optimizing both D-MESFET and high speed Schottky barrier switching diodes. Also, planar devices can generally be located closer together than mesa devices, because space need not be allocated for mesa side walls.

The fabrication process outlined in Fig. 7(e) is much less prone to surface related problems than other approaches because the GaAs substrate is totally protected by dielectric layers throughout the fabrication process; windows are opened in the dielectric only where ohmic contacts, Schottky barriers, or interconnect metallizations are required. One micron features are resolved using reduction projection photolithography in conjunction with liftoff, plasma etching, and ion milling techniques. The metallizations used in these IC's are AuGe for alloyed ohmic contacts and TiPtAu for gates, first- and second-level interconnections. At the present level of development this fabrication technology has demonstrated gate areas as low as 600 μm^2/gate or circuit densities of ~800 gates/mm^2 (includ-

ing interconnects) in test IC's. MSI/LSI circuits with up to 1000 gate complexities have been successfully demonstrated with this fabrication technology with gate densities as high as 350 gates/mm^2. A complete description of this particular planar approach has been previously reported [5].

Electron-Beam Lithography

Direct writing electron-beam lithography (EBL) has been utilized as an alternative to projection optical lithography when submicrometer gate lengths are required. The performance of the GaAs MESFET (current gain–bandwidth product) increases as linewidths below 1 μm are used, and very high speed GaAs IC's, which employ gate lengths in the 0.5- to 0.7-μm range have been demonstrated [2]. Ring oscillators using 0.6 μm × 20 μm normally OFF GaAs MESFET's were fabricated by EBL [29], and propagation delays as low as 30 ps/gate were observed at a power dissipation/gate of 1.9 mW. These same devices also were used in a divide-by-8 circuit with 66-ps/gate equivalent delay.

Another advantage provided by direct-write EBL is the ability to rapidly modify circuit and device designs to optimize circuit performance. Delays associated with photomask procurement are thereby eliminated. The writing rate of all but the most exotic EBL systems is, however, much too slow to be considered for LSI or VLSI circuit fabrication on large substates. Writing rates are also limited by the sensitivity of electron-beam resists. Application of direct-write EBL for LSI circuits will, for the most part, be conditional on the development of higher sensitivity electron resists or EBL systems with faster beam scanning and higher beam intensities.

IV. PERFORMANCE OF GaAs IC's

In the following section, the high speed performance of various GaAs digital IC approaches will be presented and contrasted. This comparison will be based on reported speed and power dissipation of GaAs IC ring oscillators and binary frequency dividers, demonstration circuits which nearly all of the approaches discussed in Sections II and III have successfully fabricated and evaluated. In addition, a brief description of the status of Large Scale Integration in GaAs will be presented, along with a description of the performance of a 1000 gate parallel multiplier circuit implemented in SDFL.

Ring oscillators (RO) are a widely used, simple circuits consisting of chains of an odd number (N) of inverters or logic gates. If the loop gain exceeds 1 then an oscillation is obtained with frequency f. The propagation delay τ_D of the inverters or gates is related to f by $\tau_D = 1/(2fN)$, and the dynamic switching energy $P_D\tau_D$ is also provided by this measurement. The parameters extracted by the ring oscillator techniques represent nearly intrinsic speed and power since capacitive loading due to parasitics are generally minimized by a compact layout and fanout of 1 is usually employed. Since the propagation delay of all logic families increases by varying degrees with fanout and capacitive loading, ring oscillator results are not necessarily representative of the performance to be expected in larger, more realistic logic circuits. In spite of the above limitations, the RO is still a useful evaluator of the intrinsic speed of a circuit-device combination, and at least provides a lower bound on propagation delay and dynamic switching energy.

Table I presents a summary of published ring oscillator data from both enhancement- and depletion-mode approaches employed in several laboratories. Propagation delays as low as 30 ps/gate are shown on a submicron gate length RO (17.5 ps/

TABLE I
RING OSCILLATORS SPEED-POWER PERFORMANCE FOR SEVERAL GaAs IC TECHNOLOGIES

Source	Approach	Gate Length & Gate Width (μm × μm)	Propagation Delay ps	Speed-Power Product pJ	Fanin/Fanout
Hughes [28]	DMESFET/BFL Inverter	0.5 × 50	34	1.4	1/1
H.P. [20]	DMESFET/BFL NOR	1 × 20	86	3.9	2/2
Rockwell	DMESFET/SDFL NOR	1 × 10	120 52	0.040 0.063	2/1 2/1
Thomson CSF[30]	DMESFET/BFL	0.75 × 20	68	2	1/1
FUJITSU [31]	EMESFET/D-LOAD	1.2 × 20	170	0.12	1/1
FUJITSU [32]	SELF ALIGN E/DCFL	1.5 × 30	50	0.287	1/1
N.T.T.[29]	EMESFET/DCFL	0.6 × 20	30* 17.5*	0.057 0.616	1/1 1/1
MCD [12]	EJFET/Pseudo Complementary	1.0 × 10	150	0.06	1/1
Thomson CSF[13]	EMESFET/quasi-normally-off	1.0 × 35	105	0.23	1/1

*Measured at 77°K.

TABLE II
GaAs IC FREQUENCY DIVIDER PERFORMANCE

GaAs IC Technology	Circuit Approach	Theoretical Max. Toggle F.	Measured Max. Toggle F.	Equivalent τ_d	Power Dissipation	$P_D \tau_d$
1 μm D/SDFL Rockwell [23]	D.F.F. ÷ 2 (NOR GATE)	1/5 τ_D	1.9 GHz	105 ps	2.5 mW/gate	0.26 pJ
0.7 μm D/BFL TCSF [30]	D.F.F. ÷ 2	1/5 τ_D	3.0	67	40	2.68
1 μm D/BFL Hughes [33]	D.F.F. ÷ 2	1/5 τ_D	2.2	91	78	7.1
1 μm D/BFL H.P. [20]	NAND/NOR ÷ 2 COM. CLOCK	1/2 τ_D	4.5	111	40	4.4
0.6 μm D/BFL LEP [2]	NAND/NOR ÷ 2 COM. CLOCK	1/2 τ_D	5.5	91	40	3.6
0.6 μm E/DCFL N.T.T. [29]	D.F.F. ÷ 8 (NOR)	1/4 τ_D	3.8	66	1.2	0.079
1.2 μm E/DCFL NEC [34]	COMP. CLOCK ÷ 2 NOR	1/4 τ_D	2.4	100	3.9	0.39

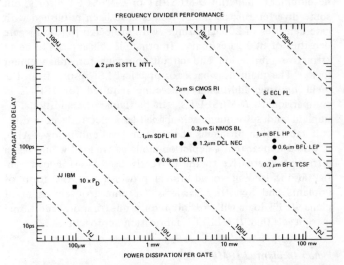

FREQUENCY DIVIDER PERFORMANCE

Fig. 9. Speed-power comparison of a variety of frequency divider approaches corresponding to Table II. At the far left, for reference, is a Josephson Junction divider. Its power dissipation has been scaled by a factor or 10 to account for the inefficient heat dissipation in liquid He.

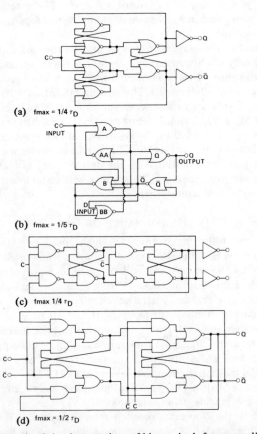

(a) fmax = 1/4 τ_D

(b) fmax = 1/5 τ_D

(c) fmax 1/4 τ_D

(d) fmax = 1/2 τ_D

Fig. 8. Four circuit implementations of binary ripple frequency dividers (divide by 2 circuits) with different theoretical maximum toggle frequencies. These frequencies are expressed as inverse multiples of logic gate propagation delays. (a) 1/4 τ_d D-type single-clocked FF. (b) 1/5 τ_d D-type single-clocked FF. (c) 1/4 τ_d master-slave, complementary-clocked FF, (d) 1/2 τ_d master–slave complementary-clocked FF.

gate at 77 K—a speed rivaling that of the Josephson Junction). However, the interpretation of the Table I data is complex; performance is expected to vary with gate length and width and with other factors, such as source resistance and parasitic capacitance. At gate lengths in the 0.5- to 1.5-μm range, transconductance should increase roughly as $1/L_g$ at small gate biases above threshold (avoiding velocity saturation effects). Thus a shorter gate length device should provide higher current (I_{ds}) at fixed logic swing and load capacitance, and therefore will reduce propagation delay. An increase in gate width (w_g) will directly increase I_{ds} at a given gate bias. While the device

capacitance also increases directly, the ratio of device capacitance to parasitic capacitance increases and thus the propagation delay asymptotically approaches the intrinsic device performance. Therefore, it is very important to only compare data for circuits with the same gate length FET's (and to a lesser extent gate widths) to obtain a meaningful comparison of performance.

The performance of logic circuits such as a binary ripple frequency divider is a more meaningful indicator of the overall performance of a particular circuit and device approach because fan-in, fanout, and capacitance loading are greater in an actual sequential or combinational circuit than in a ring oscillator. Fig. 8 depicts the circuit diagrams of four types of frequency dividers which have been implemented in GaAs. The theoretical maximum toggle frequency of these dividers depends on the number of logic gates which must serially stabilize before the output reaches its correct state. This factor ranges from $2\tau_d$ for a complementary-clocked NAND/NOR implemented flip-flop (Fig. 8(d)) to $5\tau_d$ for the D-type flip-flop shown in Fig. 8(b). Thus equal gate delays will produce 2.5 times higher clock frequencies in the former circuit than in the latter.

Table II and Fig. 9 present a comparison of speed and power of a variety of frequency divider approaches. The propagation delays determined from the dividing frequencies of all the depletion-mode circuits are fairly close to those obtained from ring oscillator evaluation. This indicates that the speed of the

Fig. 10. Photomicrograph of an 8 × 8 multiplier chip. The chip, including bonding pads, covers a 2.7-mm × 2.25-mm area.

logic gate of the depletion-mode circuits is not greatly reduced by fanouts of 2 or 3. The higher toggling frequencies (also at the expense of high power) demonstrated by the HP [20] BFL circuits and the LEP [2] BFL circuits are primarily the consequence of the use of complementary-clocked master–slave flip-flops implemented with NAND/NOR gates. This complementary clock design can also be implemented in SDFL by using the OR/NAND gate discussed in Section II.

With enhancement-mode GaAs FET's, a divide by eight frequency counter (gate length of 0.6 μm) has demonstrated a maximum clock frequency of 3.8 GHz with a power dissipation of 1.2 mW/gate. This corresponds to a gate delay time of 66 ps and a speed–power product of 79 fJ. This is a significant achievement. However, the enhancement-mode FET approach has a basic limitation on the permissible logic voltage swing ~0.6 V, due to the onset of gate conduction. To achieve reasonable LSI/VLSI yields, further improvement in gate threshold voltage control is required. On the other hand, most of the BFL depletion-mode approaches would likely be prohibited from achieving LSI/VLSI complexities due to the relatively high power dissipation required and the lower packing density.

To date, the SDFL approach appears to be the only one meeting the power dissipation, gate density, and fabrication yield required for LSI. In fact, the first GaAs LSI circuits to be reported have utilized the depletion-mode low pinchoff voltage SDFL approach. As shown by the results in Table I and II, the 1-μm SDFL circuits provide a middle ground between the potentially lower power but more difficult to control E/DCFL circuits and the higher power, higher pinchoff voltage, BFL approaches.

The LSI circuit recently demonstrated is a parallel multiplier [8]. This circuit, consisting of NOR gate full adders and half adders in a regular array, forms the binary product of two 8 bit input words. The planar, localized-implant fabrication approach, described in Section III, was used to process the 2.25 × 2.7 chip shown in Fig. 10. This 8 × 8 multiplier, which also contained D-type flip-flop latches every input and output

TABLE III
COMPARISON OF GaAs LSI 8 × 8 BIT PARALLEL MULTIPLIER PERFORMANCE WITH STATE-OF-THE-ART SILICON BIPOLAR CIRCUITS

MPX-8HJ-1	MULTIPLY TIME (NANOSECONDS)	POWER DISSIPATION (WATTS)	MULTIPLY TIME-POWER PRODUCT
RI [1] (GaAs)	5.2 16.8	2.2 0.9	11.4 (Nanosec-Watt) 15.1
MOT [2] MC10901	19	4.4	84
TRW [3] MPX-8HJ-1	45	1.2	54
AMD 25S557	45	1.4	63
MMI 67558	125	1.4	175

(1) Under Development; Material: GaAs
(2) Uses Carry Lookahead
(3) Contains Multiplier Array and Output Latches Only (No Input Latches.)
    Estimated Gate Count = 900

bit, required over 1000 NOR gates (about 3000 FET's and 3000 Schottky diodes) for the complete circuit. This level of complexity would clearly qualify this as an LSI GaAs digital circuit and also the most complex GaAs circuit to be successfully demonstrated to date.

The best performance observed on the 8 bit multiplier corresponds to a propagation delay of 150 ps/gate at a power dissipation of about 2 mW/gate. At this speed, a full 16 bit product would be available every 5.25 ns. Lower power operation 0.6 mW/gate was also possible (using lower pinchoff voltages) at the still respectable multiply time of 16.8 ns. This performance is summarized in Table III and contrasted to the reported performance of state-of-the-art silicon-based multiplier circuits. The two best Si multipliers utilize 2-μm bipolar technology [35], [36]. The best speed of the 1-μm GaAs MESFET IC is about 4 times better than that of the fastest Si 8 bit multiplier [36] employing input bit recording [37] and carry-look-ahead adders. Even faster GaAs multipliers (1.5 to 3 ns) would be expected if these same circuit approaches were to be utilized.

The successful fabrication of the SDFL 8 × 8 multipliers brings the GaAs technology into the realm of LSI while advancing the state-of-the-art for multiplier chips. The propagation delay of 150 ps/gate observed on the 8×8 multiplier is in good agreement with the results of much simpler GaAs SDFL circuits such as ring oscillators and frequency dividers.

This high speed of operation indicates that the extension of the planar SDFL circuit approach to the LSI level of complexity does not result in significant speed degradation. The low power dissipation on the 8×8 multipliers also indicates that the SDFL approach is a suitable candidate for the VLSI range of complexity if further modest reductions in power per gate are achieved.

V. Conclusion

GaAs has matured as a semiconductor material to provide a viable IC technology. Significant advantages in performance over conventional silicon IC's have been demonstrated with the operation of GaAs circuits at high speed and low power. Furthermore, the ability to achieve LSI complexities with GaAs (1000 gates) has also been demonstrated. Further improvements in the performance of GaAs IC's are still possible through the use of heterojunctions in a new generation of devices.

Today, strong development programs exist in the U.S.A., Europe, and Japan, and applications of GaAs logic into systems are anticipated soon. The first applications are expected to take place in the form of MSI circuits utilized at the front end of high speed digital systems. In the near future, further applications of MSI/LSI GaAs circuits are expected in high speed signal processing. A scenario can be envisioned where successful utilization of GaAs IC's will stimulate further development, which will, in turn, encourage further applications.

The potential for long range application of GaAs digital IC's also exists in computer mainframes. A forecast on whether, or when and how this type of application may occur is presently difficult due to the many considerations which determine the choice of an IC technology for a computer mainframe. However, the application of GaAs IC's for this purpose is becoming increasingly feasible with the advance of this high speed technology.

References

[1] T. Mizutani, N. Kato, S. Ishida, K. Osafune, and M. Ohmori, "GaAs gigabit logic circuits using normally-OFF MESFET's," *Electron. Lett.*, vol. 16, pp. 315–316, Apr. 24, 1980.

[2] M. Cathelin, M. Gavant, and M. Rocchi, "A 3.5 GHz single-clocked binary frequency divider on GaAs," *Proc. Inst. Elec. Eng.*, vol. 127, pt. I, no. 5, pp. 270–277, Oct. 1980.

[3] M. Cathelin and G. Durand, "Logic IC's using GaAs FET's in a planar technology," *L'onde Electrique*, vol. 58, pp. 218–221, Mar. 1978.

[4] G. L. Troeger, A. F. Behle, P. E. Friebertshauser, K. L. Hu, and S. H. Watanabe, "Fully ion implanted planar GaAs E-JFET process," *1979 Int. Electron Devices Meeting, Tech. Dig.*, pp. 497–500, Dec. 1979.

[5] B. M. Welch *et al.*, "LSI processing technology for planar GaAs integrated circuits," *IEEE Trans. Electron Dev.*, vol. ED-27, pp. 1116–1123, June 1980.

[6] H. Horikoshi *et al.*, "An example of LSI-oriented logic implementation in a large-scale computer, the HITAC M-200H," *COMPCON Tech. Papers*, pp. 62–65, Spring 1980.

[7] R. J. Blumberg and S. Brenner, "A 1500 gate, random logic, large scale integrated (LSI) masterslice," *IEEE J. Solid-State Circuits*, vol. SC-14, pp. 818–822, Oct. 1979.

[8] F. S. Lee *et al.*, "High speed LSI GaAs digital integrated circuits," GaAs IC Symp. Abstracts, Las Vegas, NV, Nov. 1980.

[9] R. C. Eden *et al.*, "The prospects for ultra-high speed VLSI GaAs digital logic," *IEEE J. Solid-State Circuit*, vol. SC-14, pp. 221–239, Apr. 1979.

[10] H. Kroemer, "Heterostructure bipolar transistor and integrated

[11] R. Zuleeg, J. K. Notthoff, and K. Lehovec, "Femtojoule high-speed planar GaAs E-JFET logic," *IEEE Trans. Electron Devices*, Vol. ED-25, pp. 628–639, June 1978.

[12] K. Lehovec and R. Zuleeg, "Analysis of GaAs FET's integrated logic," *IEEE Trans. Electron Devices*, vol. ED-27, pp. 1074–1091, June 1980.

[13] G. Nuzillat, G. Bert, T. P. Ngu, and M. Gloanec, "Quasi-normally-off MESFET logic for high-performance GaAs IC's," *IEEE Trans. Electron Devices*, vol. ED-27, pp. 1102–1108, June 1980.

[14] N. Yokoyama, T. Mimura, and M. Fukuta, "Planar GaAs MOSFET integrated logic," *IEEE Trans. Electron Devices*, vol. ED-27, pp. 1124–1127, June 1980.

[15] L. Messick, "A dc to 16 GHz Indium Phosphide MISFET," *Solid-State Electron.*, vol. 23, pp. 551–555, 1980.

[16] S. Judaprawira *et al.*, "Modulation doped MBE GaAs/nAl$_x$Ga$_{1-x}$ As MESFET's," *IEEE Electron Device Lett.*, vol. 1, EDL-2, pp. 14–15, Jan. 19, 1981.

[17] T. Mimura, S. Hiyamizu, T. Fujii, and K. Nanbu, "A new field-effect transistor with selectively doped GaAs/n-Al$_x$Ga$_{1-x}$As heterojunctions," *Japan. J. Appl. Phys. Lett.*, vol. 19, no. 5, pp. 225–227, 1980.

[18] J. K. Notthoff and C. H. Vogelsang, "Gate design for DCFL with GaAs E-JFET's," in *Research Abstracts of First Annual Gallium Arsenide Integrated Circuit Symp.*, Lake Tahoe, Sept. 27, 1979, Paper 10.

[19] R. Zuleeg, *Jap. J. Appl. Phys.*, vol. 19, pp. 315–318, 1980.

[20] R. L. VanTuyl, C. Liechti, R. E. Lee, and E. Gowen, "GaAs MESFET logic with 4-GHz clock rate," *IEEE J. Solid-State Circuits*, vol. SC-12, pp. 485–496, Oct. 1977.

[21] R. C. Eden, B. M. Welch, and R. Zucca, "Lower power GaAs digital IC's using Schottky diode-FET logic," *1978 Int. Solid State Circuits Conf. Dig. Tech. Papers*, pp. 68–69, Feb. 1977.

[22] R. C. Eden, F. S. Lee, S. I. Long, B. M. Welch, and R. Zucca, "Multi-level logic gate implementation in GaAs IC's using Schottky diode-FET logic," *1980 Int. Solid State Circuits Conf., Dig. Tech. Papers*, pp. 122–123, Feb. 1980.

[23] S. I. Long, F. S. Lee, R. Zucca, B. M. Welch, and R. C. Eden, "MSI high-speed low-power GaAs IC's using Schottky diode FET logic," *IEEE Trans. Microwave Theory Tech.*, vol. MTT-28, pp. 466–471, May 1980.

[24] C. A. Liechti, "GaAs FET logic," *1976 Int. GaAs Symp., Inst. Phys. Conf. Series 33a*, ch. 5, pp. 227–236, 1977.

[25] H. Ishikawa, H. Kusakawa, K. Suyama, and M. Fukuta, "Normally-off type GaAs MESFET for low-power high-speed logic circuits," *1977 Int. Solid State Circuits Conf., Dig. Tech. Papers*, pp. 200–201, Feb. 1977.

[26] M. Fukuta, K. Suyama, and H. Kusakawa, "Low power GaAs digital integrated circuits with normally off MESFET's," *IEEE Trans. Electron Devices*, vol. ED-25, p. 1340, Nov. 1978.

[27] G. Bert, G. Nuzillat, and C. Arnodo, "Femtojoule logic circuit using normally-off GaAs MESFET's," *Electron. Lett.*, vol. 13, pp. 644–645, Oct. 1977.

[28] R. E. Lundgren, C. F. Krumm, and R. L. Pierson, "Fast enhancement-mode GaAs MESFET logic," presented at 37th Annu. Dev. Research Conf., Boulder, CO., June 25–27, 1979.

[29] T. Mizutani, N. Kato, K. Osafune, and M. Ohmori, "Gigabit logic operation with enhancement mode GaAs MESFET IC's," *IEEE Trans. Electron Devices*, to be published.

[30] G. Nuzillat, F. Damay-Kavala, G. Bert, and C. Arnodo, "Low pinch-off voltage FET logic (LPFL): LSI oriented logic approach using quasinormally off GaAs MESFET's," *Proc. Inst. Elec. Eng.*, vol. 127, pt. 1, no. 5, pp. 287–296, Oct. 1980.

[31] K. Suyama, H. Kusakawa, and M. Fukuta, "Design and performance of GaAs normally-off MESFET integrated circuits," *IEEE Trans. Electron Devices*, vol. ED-27, pp. 1092–1097, June 1980.

[32] N. Yokoyama, T. Mimura, M. Fukuta, and H. Ishikawa, "A self-aligned source/drain planar device for ultrahigh speed GaAs MESFET VLSI's," *1981 Int. Solid State Circuits Conf., Dig. Tech. Papers*, Feb. 1981.

[33] P. T. Greiling, R. E. Lundgren, C. F. Krumm, and R. F. Lohr, Jr., "Why design logic with GaAs and How? MSN, pp. 48–60, Jan. 1980.

[34] F. Katano, T. Furutsuka, and A. Higashisaka, "High speed normally-off GaAs MESFET integrated circuits," *Electron. Lett.*, vol. 17, no. 6, pp. 236–239, Mar. 1981.

[35] TRW MPY8HJ-1, See "Digital processing gets a boost from bipolar LSI multipliers," *EDN Magazine*, vol. 20, pp. 38–43, Nov. 5, 1978.

[36] "Single-chip 8×8 multiplier forms 16-bit product in 19 nsec," *EDN Magazine*, vol. 22, p. 152, Dec. 15, 1980.

[37] "2 bit-by-4 bit parallel binary multipliers," Suppl. to the TTL Data Book, Texas Instruments, Incorporated, 1974.

[38] R. Zucca *et al.*, "Process evaluation test structures and measurement techniques for a planar GaAs IC technology," *IEEE Trans. Electron Devices*, vol. ED-27, pp. 2292–2298, Dec. 1980.

Modulation-Doped GaAs/AlGaAs Heterojunction Field-Effect Transistors (MODFET's), Ultrahigh-Speed Device for Supercomputers

PAUL M. SOLOMON AND HADIS MORKOÇ, SENIOR MEMBER, IEEE

Reprinted from *IEEE Transactions on Electron Devices,* Volume ED-31, Number 8, August 1984, pages 1015-1027. Copyright © 1984 by The Institute of Electrical and Electronics Engineers, Inc.

Abstract—In the past few years, a new transistor has appeared on the scene, made of GaAs and AlGaAs, which now holds the record as the fastest logic switching device, switching at speeds of close to ten trillionths of a second (10 ps). The device evolved from the work on GaAs-AlGaAs superlattices (thin alternating layers of differing materials sharing the same crystalline lattice) pioneered by L. Esaki and R. Tsu at IBM in the late 1960's. They realized that high mobilities in GaAs could be achieved if electrons were transferred from the doped and wider band-gap AlGaAs to an adjacent undoped GaAs layer, a process now called modulation doping. R. Dingle, H. L. Stormer, A. C. Gossard, and W. Wiegmann of AT&T Bell Labs, working independently, were the first to demonstrate high mobilities obtained by modulation doping in 1978, in a GaAs–AlGaAs superlattice. Realizing that such a structure could form the basis for a high-performance field-effect transistor (Bell Labs Patent 4163237, filed on April 24, 1978), researchers at various labs in the United States (Bell Labs, University of Illinois, and Rockwell), Japan (Fujitsu), and France (Thomson CSF) began working on this device. In 1980, the first such device with a reasonable microwave performance was fabricated by the University of Illinois and Rockwell, which they called a modulation-doped FET or MODFET. The same year Fujitsu reported the results obtained in a device with a 400-μm gate which they called the "high electron mobility transistor" or HEMT, in the open literature. Thomson CSF published shortly thereafter calling their realization a "two-dimensional electron gas FET" or TEGFET, and Bell Labs followed, using the name "selectively doped heterojection transistor" or SDHT. These names are all descriptive of various aspects of the device operation as we will discuss in the text. For the sake of internal consistency will call it MODFET, hereafter.

In this paper we review the principals of MODFET operation, factors affecting its performance, optimization of the device, and comparison with other high-performance compound and elemental semiconductor devices. Finally, the remaining problems and future challenges are pointed out.

I. INTRODUCTION

ELECTRON devices with ever-increasing speed are used either as switches or amplifiers. As advanced semiconductor preparation and processing tools become available and are combined with ingenious device synthesis, the frequency of operation and switching speeds are constantly being challenged. In switching devices, such as those used in digital circuits, the current flowing through the devices is used to drive the subse-

Manuscript received February 25, 1984. The work on MODFET's at the University of Illinois was funded by the Air Force Office of Scientific Research.

P. M. Solomon is with the IBM Thomas J. Watson Research Center, Yorktown Heights, NY 10598.

H. Morkoç is with the Department of Electrical Engineering and Coordinated Science Laboratory, University of Illinois, Urbana, IL 61801.

quent stages. The speed with which such a switching operation takes place is primarily determined by how fast the capacitances associated with the device and interconnects can be charged and discharged. It is clear that the interconnect capacitance plays an important role and must be minimized by proper circuit design. This presentation will not deal with the interconnect capacitances per se, but will instead concentrate on the device itself. It must, however, be pointed out that in a large-scale integrated circuit, devices and interconnects must be considered simultaneously.

The switching speed of the device is primarily determined by how fast an input pulse can be transmitted to the output. The transit time through the device, "intrinsic propagation delay," and input and output capacitance charging times are added to give the switching time of the device. This implies that for a fast switching time, the capacitances and the transit time through the devices must be made smaller. The issue of capacitance should be treated in the context of the available current since larger amounts of current, if available, can charge and discharge capacitances faster. The transit time can be made smaller by either reducing the current path length by making the terminals closer together or by increasing the speed at which the carriers travel.

The speed of the carriers, for low electric fields, is given by the product of the mobility and electric field; however, in short-channel field-effect transistors (FET's) electric fields are quite large and the carrier velocity reaches some limiting value. As the device dimensions are pushed to submicrometer range, electron velocities greater than equilibrium values, or "over-shoot," effects can be obtained. Since the current is proportional to the carrier velocity as well as the carrier density, carrier density must be increased if one wants a larger current to charge and discharge the capacitances faster. Since the transport properties of electrons are better than those of holes, we will concentrate on the use of electrons as carriers or n-channel devices.

In conventional metal–semiconductor FET's (MESFET's), the electrons are obtained by incorporating donor impurities which share the same space with electrons and interact with them (Fig. 1). Increased electron concentration, necessary for the high currents required for high speed, also means increased donor concentration which leads to more electron–donor interaction, called ionized impurity scattering. A conclusion that can be drawn from this is that one must pay a price for

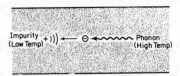

Fig. 1. In bulk semiconductors, the electrons (n-type material) and positively charged donor impurities share the same space. As a result, interaction of electrons and positive ions is inevitable. In small-geometry devices, the thickness of the conducting channel is reduced and the dopant concentration is increased, leading to increased scattering which becomes more dominant at low lattice temperatures. At high lattice temperatures electrons are scattered by the vibrating atoms (phonon scattering) and either gain or lose energy.

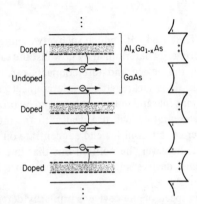

Fig. 2. Multiple-interface AlGaAs GaAs modulation-doped structures where only the center region (shaded) of AlGaAs layers is doped with Si donors. Since the bottom of the conduction band energy in GaAs is smaller than donor energy level in AlGaAs (right-hand side), the electrons diffuse into GaAs layers where they are confined because of the energy barrier. Positive signs indicate the ionized donors and the negative ones represent the transferred electrons. If the parameters are chosen correctly, all of the free electrons will be located in GaAs layers where they show enhanced transport parallel to the heterointerfaces.

large electron concentrations since they are associated with large donor concentrations with their deleterious effects. In fact, the peak velocity of electrons in GaAs goes down from 2.1×10^7 cm/s for pure GaAs down to 1.7×10^7 cm/s for GaAs with 10^{17}-cm^{-3} donors.

In general, as FET's become smaller, thinner channel layers and higher electron concentrations are required. The requirement for large electron concentration without the deleterious effects of donors can be met by novel heterojunctions. A heterojunction composed of AlGaAs and GaAs layers can be structured so that the donors are introduced only into the larger bandgap (AlGaAs) material [1], [2]. The heterojunction lineup is such that the energy of the electrons donated to the AlGaAs layer is higher in the AlGaAs than in the adjacent GaAs (Fig. 2). The electrons originally introduced into the AlGaAs layer then diffuse to the lower energy GaAs layer where they are confined due to the energy barrier at the heterointerface as shown in Fig. 2. This technique of "modulation doping" is a perfect means of introducing electrons into the GaAs layer without the adverse effects of donors.

Having the electrons confined at the heterointerface in a "two-dimensional electron gas" very close to the gate and a perfect interface leads to very high mobilities and large electron velocities at very small values of drain voltage [3]. This in turn leads to extremely fast charging times of capacitors with

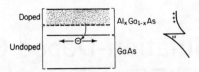

Fig. 3. Single-interface heterostructure used for MODFET's. The structure with AlGaAs grown on top of GaAs, "normal modulation-doped structure," is the one that is used commonly for FET's. The diagram on the right-hand side shows the conduction band edge with respect to distance.

small power consumption. These advantages are enhanced by almost a factor of two when cooled to 77 K, which is conceivable for larger supercomputer systems. Minimum switching speeds of <10 ps per gate should be possible in a few years, corresponding to typical switching delays of <30 ps in a large computer, compared to switching speeds of >500 ps found in the fastest computers today [4]. The principles of operation of MODFET's are similar to that of Si MOSFET and the models developed for MODFET's benefited greatly from Si MOSFET models [5].

With 1-μm gate lengths and using conventional MESFET technology, propagation delay times as low as 12.2 ps at 300 K as measured by ring oscillators (logic inverters connected in a recirculating loop) with a power–delay product of 13.7 fJ have been obtained [6]. Frequency dividers have also been demonstrated at 77 K with operation frequencies of up to 8 GHz [7].

How Modulation Doping Works

These structures are prepared by molecular-beam epitaxy, which is an ultrahigh vacuum semiconductor deposition technique with control on the atomic scale of both the dopants and constituents forming the semiconductor itself [8]. This is achieved by blocking or not blocking the beam flux with a mechanical shutter controlled with computer to allow the formation of alternating heterolayers as thin as about 10 Å each, about 3-4 atomic layers. In the case of modulation-doped structures intended for FET's, single-interface structures with larger layer thicknesses are used (Fig. 3).

The region of the $Al_x Ga_{1-x}$As depleted of electrons forms a positive space charge region which is balanced by the electrons confined at the heterointerface. The resulting electric field perpendicular to the interface reaches values over 10^5 V/cm and causes a severe band bending, particularly in GaAs because the electrons are confined to a space of about 80 Å thick (Fig. 4). The electron energies are increased by their quantum-mechanical confinement, and discrete quantum-electric subbands are formed, each subband corresponding to a discrete state of the electron's perpendicular momentum (or to a discrete number of standing waves in the electron wave function, see the inset of Fig. 4) [9]. Even though the electrons and donors are separated spatially, their close proximity allows an electrostatic interaction called Coulomb scattering. By setting the donors away from the interface, Coulombic scattering by donors can be reduced (Fig. 5). This was demonstrated by the University of Illinois group with a resultant understanding that increased set back leads to enhanced electron mobilities and concomitantly reduced electron transfer [10]. The amount of electron

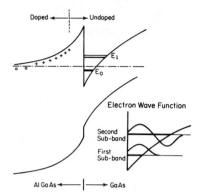

Fig. 4. Energy band diagram of a single-interface modulation-doped structure. Donor impurities are in the AlGaAs layer and set back (between 20 and 500 Å depending on the application) from the interface to reduce Coulombic interaction between the electrons that diffuse into the GaAs and remaining ionized donors in the AlGaAs. The depleted region in the AlGaAs layer is positively charged and is balanced by the electrons in GaAs in equilibrium. The large electric field present in GaAs severely bends the conduction band and forms a quasi-triangular potential leading to quantum electric subband. In MODFET's, the first subband at energy E_0 is filled completely (solid dark line) whereas the second subband at energy E_1 is partially filled (dark and light lines). Inset shows the electron wave functions associated with the first and second subbands.

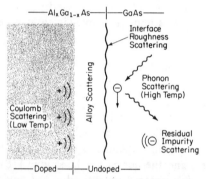

Fig. 5. Scattering mechanisms present in modulation-doped structures. The ionized donor impurities in AlGaAs scatter electrons that diffused to GaAs from AlGaAs through the force of attraction (Coulomb interaction) which is noticeable at cryogenic temperatures. Interaction of electrons with vibrating host atoms in GaAs leads to energy and momentum gain or loss (phonon scattering), which is important when the lattice temperature is high. In inverted modulation-doped structures, the heterointerface is not of high quality, e.g., not atomically smooth and perhaps contaminated with impurities, which causes scattering of the electrons. The overlap of electron wave function with AlGaAs allows interaction with potential perturbation caused by the random distribution of Al Atoms (alloy scattering). This process is very small and may affect the electron mobility only at low temperatures. Finally, unintentionally introduced impurities in GaAs, acceptor type in GaAs grown by MBE, scatter the electrons transferred from AlGaAs, but their effect is reduced substantially because high-mobility electrons can surround the residual acceptors and screen them. This is why 4-K mobilities in modulation-doped structures with about 5×10^{14} cm^{-3} residual ions are more than an order of magnitude larger than those obtained in high-purity bulk GaAs with only about mid 10^{13} cm^{-3} ionized impurities.

transfer is determined by the donor density in AlGaAs, conduction band edge discontinuity and the amount of set back.

Even though electrons and donors are separated at room temperature, electrons interact with the lattice vibrations, "phonons" in GaAs. The phonon scattering limited mobility in GaAs is 8500–9000 cm^2/V · s which sets an upper limit to the

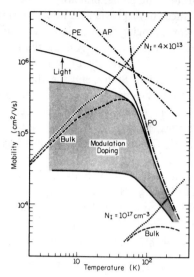

Fig. 6. Electron mobility versus lattice temperature of modulation-doped structures having equivalent electron concentrations larger than 10^{18} cm^{-3} in bulk GaAs. For comparison GaAs with ion concentration of 4×10^{13} cm^{-3} (lowest obtained) is also shown. The mobility of modulation-doped structures is limited by piezoelectric and acoustic phonon scattering at low temperatures and polar optical scattering at high temperatures. Because of large electron gas concentrations needed for MODFET's, both subbands are filled and the undoped layer thickness is small. Low-temperature electron mobilities obtained are about 30 000–60 000 cm^2/V · s. When the undoped layer thickness is increased, the Coulomb scattering and the electron gas concentration drop, leading to mobilities in excess of 10^6 cm^2/V · s at 4 K. With light, the mobility increases even more because of increased Fermi energy and possible neutralization of scattering centers in AlGaAs within about 100 Å of the interface. The mobilities obtained in single-interface structures are generally larger than those in modulation-doped superlattices.

mobility obtainable in modulation-doped structures at 300 K [11]. At low lattice temperature, however, the phonon scattering in both bulk GaAs and modulation-doped structures is reduced. In bulk GaAs, ionized impurity scattering becomes dominant to the point of reducing the 50-K mobility from 3×10^5 cm^2/V · s with $N_I = 4 \times 10^{13}$ cm^{-3} [12] to 5000 cm^2/V · s with $N_I = 10^{17}$ cm^{-3} (Fig. 6).

Background impurities ($\sim 10^{14}$ cm^{-2}) are still present in the bulk GaAs, even in the modulation-doped structures, and these would limit mobilities to about 10^5 cm^2/V · s if it were not for the effect of electrostatic screening of the impurities by the electrons in the 2-D gas layer. In fact mobilities of about 2×10^6 cm^2/V · s have been obtained at low temperatures [13]. Fig. 6 shows the influence of the various electron scattering mechanisms on mobility, and how modulation doping effectively eliminates the previously dominant impurity scattering component. Though of a secondary nature, mechanisms such as alloy scattering and interface roughness scattering do play a role in determining the mobility. Such high mobilities, while indicative of extremely good interfaces are not really essential for devices since the electron velocity is the dominant factor [14]. High mobilities, however, have recently made it possible to observe quantum Hall effects at high magnetic fields. It should be pointed out that basic physics behind the electron gas and its behavior under electric and magnetic fields are to some extent similar to those of Si/SiO$_2$ MOS structures [15].

At the time of this writing many industrial and university

laboratories around the globe, primarily in the United States, Japan, and France, have programs addressing various aspects of MODFET work, ranging from basic understanding through high-speed circuit development. Among the universities, the University of Illinois, University of Minnesota, and Cornell University in the United States, and the University of Tokyo in Japan are currently active in this study. Industrial participants are greater in number and include Bell Laboratories, Honeywell, Hughes, Rockwell, TRW, Hewlett-Packard, Texas Instruments, IBM, General Electric, and Westinghouse of the United States, Fujitsu and Nippon Telephone and Telegraph of Japan, and Thomson CSF of France. Some of the governmental laboratories, e.g., Naval Research Laboratories and Air Force Avionics Laboratories, have some in-house projects underway. It is quite possible that the list is even greater than what has been made available to the authors.

FABRICATION OF MODFET's

The heterojunction structures needed for MODFET's are grown by molecular-beam epitaxy on semi-insulating substrates. First, a nominally 1-μm-thick undoped GaAs layer is grown at a substrate temperature of about 580°C. Gallium flux, which determines the growth rate, is adjusted to yield a growth rate of about 1 μm/h. This rate can be increased if desired to about 5 μm/h by increasing the source temperature. This is followed by the growth of the AlGaAs layer, about 20-60 Å of which is not doped near the heterointerface. The doped AlGaAs layer, about 600 Å thick, may be capped with a doped GaAs layer (200-300 Å thick) or the mole fraction may be graded down to GaAs towards the surface.

Device isolation is in most cases done by chemically etching mesas down to the undoped GaAs layer or to the semi-insulating substrate, or by an isolating implant. The source and drain areas are then defined in positive photoresist and typically AuGe/Ni/Au metallization is evaporated. Following the lift-off, the source-drain metallization is alloyed at or above 400°C for a short time (~1 min) to obtain ohmic contacts. During this process, Ge diffuses down past the heterointerface, thus making contact to the sheet of electrons. In some instances a surface passivation layer of SiO_2 has been used between the terminals.

The gate is then defined and a very small amount of recessing is done by either chemical etching, reactive ion etching, or ion milling. The extent of the recess is dependent upon whether depletion or enhancement mode devices are desired. In depletion mode devices, the remaining doped layer should be just the thickness to be depleted by the gate Schottky barrier. In enhancement mode devices, the remaining doped AlGaAs is much thinner and thus the Schottky barrier depletes the electron gas as well. In test circuits composed of ring oscillators, the switches are of enhancement mode which conduct current when a positive voltage is applied to the gate and the loads are of depletion type. Fig. 7 shows an artistic view of the cross section of a MODFET.

PRINCIPLES OF MODFET OPERATION

A. General Background

The MODFET operation is to some extent analogous to that of the Si/SiO_2 MOSFET. While the basic principles of operation

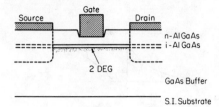

Fig. 7. Cross-sectional view of a MODFET.

are similar, material systems and the details of device physics are different. The most striking difference, however, is the lack of interface states in MODFET structures. In MODFET's the gate metal and the channel are separated by only about 400 Å. This, coupled with the large dielectric constant of $Al_xGa_{1-x}As$ as compared to SiO_2 gives rise to extremely large transconductances. In addition, large electron densities, about 10^{12} cm^{-2}, can be achieved at the interface which leads to high current levels. The effective mass of electrons in GaAs is much smaller than in Si and therefore electron concentrations under consideration raise the Fermi level well up into the conduction band, which is not the case for Si MOSFET's. It is therefore necessary to develop a new model for the MODFET as has been attempted by the Thomson CSF group [16] and by the team at the Universities of Minnesota and Illinois [17]. In order to calculate the current-voltage characteristics of MODFET's, we must first determine the two-dimensional electron gas concentration.

B. Electron Gas Concentration

As indicated earlier, the electrons diffuse from the doped $Al_xGa_{1-x}As$ to the GaAs where they are confined by the energy barrier, Fig. 4, and form a two-dimensional electron gas. This was verified by observing the Shubnikov-de Haas oscillations and their dependence on the angle between the magnetic field and the normal of the sample [18]. The wave vector for such a system is quantized in the direction perpendicular to but not parallel to the interface.

The electric field set up by the charge separation causes a severe band bending in the GaAs layer with a resultant triangular potential barrier where the allowed states are no longer continuous in energy, but discrete. As a result, quantized subbands are formed and a new two-dimensional model is needed to calculate the electron concentration. In most cases the ground subband is filled while the first subband is partially empty. Since the spread in the electron concentration perpendicular to the heterointerface is very small and the density varies, we will refer to the areal density of the electrons from now on.

To determine the electron concentration we must first relate it to the subband energies. The rigorous approach is to solve for the subband energies self-consistently with the solution for the potential derived from the electric charge distribution. This has been done by Stern and co-workers for the silicon-silicon dioxide system in the sixties, and more recently by Ando for the GaAs-AlGaAs system. A workable approximation is to assume that the potential well is perfectly triangular, and that only the ground and first subbands need be considered. Using the experimentally obtained subband populations, adjustments in the parameters can be made to account for the nonconstant electric field and nonparabolic conduction band. Solving Pois-

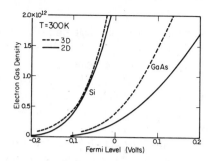

Fig. 8. Variation of the electron gas density with Fermi level as measured from the bottom of the conduction band in GaAs. Since the conduction band density of states in Si is very large, the Fermi level even for the largest sheet carrier concentration, 2×10^{12} cm^{-2}, is still below the conduction band and predictions are reasonably accurate when the problem is treated in a three-dimensional manner and the quantization is neglected. For GaAs, however, the density of states is smaller (or the effective mass is smaller) and the quantization of the electron population at the heterointerface can not be neglected. Models encompassing the two-dimensional (solid lines) nature of the electron population must be utilized.

son's equation in AlGaAs and GaAs layers and using Gauss' law, one can obtain another expression for the sheet electron concentration in terms of structural parameters, e.g., the doping level in AlGaAs, doped and undoped AlGaAs layer thicknesses, and the magnitude of conduction band energy discontinuity or the AlAs mole fraction in AlGaAs.

Analysis of the Fermi level shows that it is a linear function of the sheet carrier concentration n_{so} for $n_{so} \geqslant 5 \times 10^{11}$ cm^{-2}. Taking this into account one can eliminate the iteration process because analytical expressions become available [14], [19]. Another feature that must be considered in the model is the necessity of using the Fermi–Dirac as opposed to the commonly used Maxwell–Boltzmann statistics. This term is particularly important at room temperature because of larger thermal energy and thus larger uncertainty in the position of electrons at the boundary of the depletion region. In the case of Si/SiO$_2$ MOSFET's, three-dimensional analyses work quite well because the Fermi level is not as high; but they fail for MODFET's, as illustrated in Fig. 8 where broken lines take into account the two-dimensionality and the solid lines do not [5].

C. Charge Control and I-V Characteristics

So far we have related the interface charge, which is to carry the current parallel to the heterointerface, to the structural parameters of the heterojunction system. To control and modulate this charge, and therefore the current, a Schottky barrier is placed on the doped AlGaAs layer. The doped AlGaAs is depleted at the heterointerface by electron diffusion into GaAs, but this is limited to about 100 Å for an AlGaAs doping level of about 10^{18} cm^{-3}. It is also depleted from the surface by the Schottky barrier [16], [17]. To avoid conduction through AlGaAs which has inferior transport properties and screening of the channel by the carriers in the AlGaAs, parameters must be chosen such that the two depletion regions just overlap.

In normally on devices the depletion by the gate built-in voltage should be just enough to have the surface depletion extended to the interface depletion. Devices designed for $\sim 10^{12}$ cm^{-2} in the channel and an AlGaAs thickness of ~ 600

Å will be turned off at a gate bias of -1 V. This is the structure used for discrete high-speed analog applications, e.g., microwave low-noise amplifiers, since the power consumption is too high for large-scale integration.

In normally off devices, the thickness of the doped AlGaAs under the gate is smaller and the gate built-in voltage depletes the doped AlGaAs, overcomes the built-in potential at the heterointerface, and depletes the electron gas. No current flows through the device unless a positive gate voltage is applied to the gate. This type of device is used as a switch in high-speed integrated digital circuits because of the associated low power dissipation. The loads may be normally on transistors with the gate shorted to the source, or an ungated "saturated resistor," which has a saturating current characteristic due to the velocity saturation of the carriers.

Away from the cutoff regime, it is quite reasonable to assume that the capacitance under the gate is constant and thus the charge at the interface is linearly proportional to the gate voltage minus the threshold voltage. As threshold voltage is approached, the triangular potential well widens, and the Fermi energy of the electrons is lowered. This change in surface potential with electron concentration subtracts from the change in the applied gate bias, so that a lesser change in potential acts across the AlGaAs layer, reducing the transconductance of the device, and causing the curvature of the gate characteristic near threshold [14], as will be discussed later. This curvature is more pronounced at room temperature, due to the thermal distribution of the electrons; however, some curvature will persist down to the lowest temperatures, due to quantum-mechanical confinement energies. This has profound implications for device operation since it preclues high-speed operation at voltages less than a few tenths of a volt. This means that ultralow power–delay products, similar to those of Josephson junction devices, which operate at a few millivolts only, would not be realized.

Away from cutoff, the charge can be assumed to be linearly proportional to the gate voltage, and in the volocity saturated regime the current will then be linearly proportional to gate voltage and the transconductance will approach a constant (except if the AlGaAs starts conducting). These arguments apply to the velocity saturated MOSFET as well. For the MESFET, in contrast, the transconductance increases with increasing gate biases, since the depletion layer width narrows and modulation of the channel charge increases.

In order to calculate the current–voltage characteristic, one must know the electron velocity as a function of electric field. Since the device dimensions (gate) used are about 1 μm or less, high field effects such as velocity saturation must be considered.

Even though the electrons in MODFET's are located in GaAs and the electron transport in GaAs is well known, there was some confusion in the early days as to what one should expect from MODFET's. There were, in fact, reports, such as the ones from Fujitsu, that this heterojunction structure held promise because of the high mobilities obtained. One should, however, keep in mind that mobilities are measured at extremely small voltages (electric field $\simeq 5$ V/cm). In short-channel MODFET's, the electric field can reach tens of kilovolts per centimeter, making it necessary to understand the high field transport.

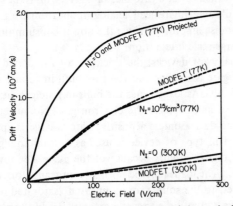

Fig. 9. Velocity versus electric field measured in a single-interface modulation-doped structure at 300 and 77 K. The electron gas concentration at the heterointerface is about 7×10^{11} cm^{-3} and the unintentional background acceptor concentration in GaAs of the MODFET structure is about 10^{14} cm^{-3}. For comparison, calculated velocity field characteristics of bulk GaAs with zero ionized impurity density ($N_I = 0$) at 300 and 77 K and with $N_I = 10^{15}$ cm^{-3} at 77 K are also shown. It is clearly seen that at 300 K, transport properties of the modulation-doped structure with as many electrons as needed for FET's are comparable to the pure GaAs. At 77 K, it is almost comparable to pure GaAs at fields below 300 V/cm and quite comparable at 2 kV/cm and above (estimated from MODFET performance).

Using 400-μm-long conventional Hall bar structures the team at the University of Illinois measured the velocity field characteristics. A dc technique below 300 V/cm and a pulsed technique up to 2 kV/cm were used to measure the current versus field characteristics [20]. Knowing the electron concentration from the same sample by Hall measurements, the electron velocity versus electric field characteristics were calculated on many modulation-doped structures. Above 2 kV/cm the results were not reliable because the electric field was nonuniform as indicated by the voltage between equally spaced voltage probes along the sample.

The velocity versus field characteristics below 300 V/cm for a typical modulation-doped structure is shown in Fig. 9. Also shown are the Monte Carlo calculations performed for lightly doped and ion free bulk GaAs layers [21]. The agreement between the modulation-doped structures and undoped GaAs ($N_I \leq 10^{15}$ cm^{-3}) is striking. The agreement at low temperatures is even better at high fields as determined from the MODFET performance. It is clear that having electrons but not the donors in concentrations of about 10^{12} cm^{-2} in modulation-doped structures does not degrade the velocity. The most important aspects of these results are:

1) A quasisaturation of electron velocities is obtained at fields of about 200 V/cm. This implies that the extremely high electron mobilities obtained at very low electric fields have only a secondary effect on device performance.

2) The higher mobilities at low fields help give the device a low saturation voltage and small on-resistance.

3) Since the properties of the pure GaAs are maintained, electron peak velocities over 2×10^7 and 3×10^7 cm/s at 300 and 77 K, respectively, can be obtained. These values have already been deduced using drain current versus gate voltage characteristics in MODFET's.

It can simply be concluded that modulation-doped structures provide current transport which is needed to charge and discharge capacitances, without degrading the properties of pure GaAs. To get electrons in conventional structures, the donors have to be incorporated, which degrades the velocity. From the velocity considerations only, MODFET's offer about 20 percent improvement at 300 K and about 60 percent at 77 K. However, other factors, e.g., large current, large transconductance, and low source resistance improve the performance of MODFET's in a real circuit far beyond the aforementioned figures.

OPTIMIZATION

In a normally off MODFET, the type used for the switches in a circuit, a positive gate voltage is applied to turn the device on. The maximum gate voltage is limited to the value above which the doped AlGaAs layer begins to conduct. If exceeded, a conduction path through the AlGaAs layer which has much inferior properties is created leading to reduced performance. This parasitic MESFET for typical parameters becomes noticeable above a gate voltage of about +0.6 V which determines the gate logic swing. Using alternate methods to improve this shortcoming should be very useful.

Since the ultimate speed of a switching device is determined by the transconductance divided by the sum of the gate and interconnect capacitances, the larger the transconductance, the better the speed is [5]. MOSFET's already exhibit larger transconductances because of higher electron velocity and, in addition, since the electron gas is located only about 400 Å away from the gate metal, a large concentration of charge can be modulated by small gate voltages. The latter comes at the expense of slightly larger gate capacitance. Considering the interconnect capacitances, any increase in transconductance, even with increased gate capacitance, improves this component of the speed.

The transconductance in MODFET's can be optimized by reducing the AlGaAs layer thickness. This must accompany increased doping in AlGaAs, which in turn is limited to about 10^{18} cm^{-3} by the requirement for a nonleaky Schottky barrier. By decreasing the undoped setback layer thickness, one can not only increase the transconductance, but also the current level (through the increased electron gas concentration). There is, of course, a limit to this process as well because thinner setback layers increase the Coulombic scattering. All things considered, a setback layer thickness of about 20–30 Å appears to be the best at the present time, as shown in Fig. 10. Setback layers less than 20 Å led to much inferior performance. Transconductances of about 225 (275 being the best) and 400 mS/mm gate width have been demonstrated at 300 and 77 K, respectively [3]. The theoretical and experimental current levels of MODFET's also depend strongly on the setback layer thickness as shown in Fig. 11 and on the doping level in AlGaAs [5].

For good switching and amplifier devices, a good saturation low-differential conductance in the current saturation region, and a low saturation voltage are needed. These are attained quite well in MODFET's, particularly at 77 K, as shown in Fig. 12. The increased current level at 77 K is attributed to the enhancement of electron velocity. The rise in current would have been more if it were not for the shift in the threshold

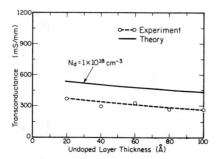

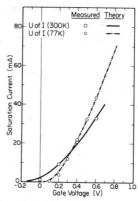

Fig. 10. Since the transconductance is inversely proportional to the gate to electron gas separation, the undoped AlGaAs layer at the heterointerface can influence the transconductance substantially. Considering that the gate to electron gas distance is about 300 Å, an undoped layer thickness of greater than 100 Å can have a dramatic influence on the transconductance. For best results an undoped layer thickness of about 20–40 Å must be used. This imposes stringent requirements on the epitaxial growth process and only molecular-beam epitaxy has so far been able to produce such structures. The circles are the experimental data points while the solid line shows the theory. Below 20 Å, the performance degrades.

Fig. 13. Drain saturation current with respect to gate voltage of a n-off MODFET at 300 and 77 K. The threshold voltage shifts about +0.1 V as the device is cooled to 77 K which is attributed to freeze out of electrons in the AlGaAs and also to traps. As discussed in the text, the drain current, particularly at 77 K, is proportional to the gate voltage away from cutoff. Near cutoff, the quasitriangular potential well widens, no longer confining the electrons, which in turn results in the observed nonlinear behavior.

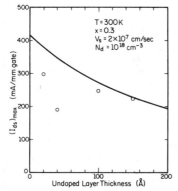

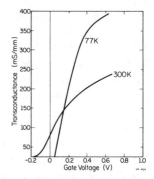

Fig. 11. Maximum drain current is also very sensitive to the undoped AlGaAs layer thickness. For desired large current levels a smaller electron–donor separation is needed to yield a large electron gas concentration. The available data (circles) obtained in n-on MODFET's (University of Illinois) while showing the general trends, should be augmented with more experiments. Maximum current levels of about 300 mA (per millimeter of gate width) at 300 K in n-off MODFET's with a 1-μm gate length is possible. Large current levels obtainable at low voltages lead to fast switching speeds with low power dissipation. Solid line shows the calculated values.

Fig. 14. Transconductance normalized to 1 mm of gate width obtained at 300 and 77 K. The decrease in the rate of increase above a gate bias of +0.7 V at 77 K is observable. This effect is attributed to filling of the second subband and undepleting the doped AlGaAs under the gate, which creates a new conduction path through the inferior quality AlGaAs.

voltage, from about 0 V at 300 K to about ⩾0.1 V at 77 K, which will further be discussed.

Experimental drain saturation current and transconductance as a function of gate voltage are shown in Figs. 13 and 14. Away from threshold and below Schottky turn-on, the drain saturation current is proportional to the gate voltage and the proportionality constant gets larger at 77 K, again because of enhanced electron velocity. The shift in threshold voltage is apparent both in g_m versus V_g and I_{DS} versus V_g characteristics as the device is cooled to 77 K. Using the model developed and the I_{DS} versus V_g characteristics, average electron velocities as high as 2 and 3 × 10^7 cm/s were deduced at 300 and 77 K, respectively.

To summarize optimizing the transistor for use in normally off logic, the main parameters to be determined are the Al concentration in the AlGaAs, and the thickness and doping of the AlGaAs layer.

1) Increasing the Al concentration in the AlGaAs increases both the Schottky-barrier height of the gate, and the heterojunction interface barrier. These permit higher forward gate voltages on the device, reduced hot-carrier injection from the GaAs into the AlGaAs, and permit higher electron concentra-

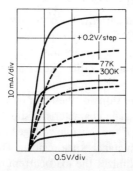

Fig. 12. Drain I-V characteristic of a MODFET with a 300-μm gate width at 300 and 77 K. As indicated, the extrinsic transconductance increases from about 225 (best 275 mS/mm) to 400 mS/mm as the device is cooled to 77 K. The improvement in the drain current observed at 77 K could be much larger if it were not for the positive shift in the threshold voltage. This shift is attributed to electronic defects in AlGaAs and is a subject of current research. (Data are from the University of Illinois).

tions in the channel without conduction in the AlGaAs. The concentration of Al in the AlGaAs should therefore be as high as possible consistent with obtaining low ionization energies for the donors, good ohmic contacts, and minimum traps. In present practice it varies from 25 to 30 percent.

2) Maximum voltages on the gate, limited by Schottky diode leakage or by conduction in the AlGaAs, are about 0.8 V at room temperature and about 1 V at liquid nitrogen temperature. Threshold voltages should be about 0.1 V for good noise margins and tolerances.

3) To maximize transconductance (and dc current, since voltage swings are given) the AlGaAs should be as thin as possible. Thinner AlGaAs implies higher doping to achieve the desired threshold voltage. Doping levels cannot be larger than about 1×10^{18} cm^{-3} because of gate leakage currents.

4) The setback layer should be as narrow as possible without compromising transport properties (20–40 Å) since this gives the minimum total AlGaAs thickness and maximum transconductance consistent with the above limits. Typical parameters for a normally off MODFET to satisfy these criteria would be: Al concentration of 30 percent, AlGaAs thickness of 350 Å, setback thickness of 40 Å, and doping of 1×10^{18} cm^{-3}.

PERFORMANCE AND APPLICATIONS

Interest in the MODFET device was aroused almost immediately after the first working circuits were built by Fujitsu in 1980, by the (then) record-breaking delays of 17 ps attained by ring oscillators operating at liquid nitrogen temperature [22]. These results can be explained on the basis of the higher velocities and transconductance, and lower saturation voltages of the device as evidenced from the experimental characteristics of Fig. 11. These results have been improved since then, both at liquid nitrogen and room temperatures.

In the logic application area, using 1-μm gate technology and ring oscillators (about 25 stages), Fujitsu in 1982 reported a τ_D = 12.8 ps switching time at 77 K (power consumption not given) [22] and Thomson CSF reported 18.4 ps with a power dissipation of P_D = 0.9 mW/stage at 300 K [23]. In late 1982, Bell Labs reported $\tau_D \sim$ 23 ps and $P_D \sim$ 4 mW/stage with 1-μm gate technology [24]. Very recently Rockwell reported a switching speed of 12.2 ps at 300 K with 13.6-fJ/stage power–delay product [6]. Rockwell also reported a switching speed of 27.3 ps with 3.9-fJ/stage power–speed product. The much-improved results of Rockwell can be attributed to the low source resistance, ~0.5 Ω · mm, obtained.

MODFET's have recently progressed from no-function circuits, e.g., ring oscillators, to frequency dividers. Bell Laboratories reported on a type D flip-flop divide-by-two circuit with 1-μm gate technology operating at 3.7 GHz (with 2.4-mW/gate power dissipation and 38-ps/gate propagation delay) at 300 K and 5.9 GHz (with 5.1-mW/gate power dissipation and 18-ps/ gate propagation delay) at 77 K [25]. Fujitsu has also recently reported results on their master–slave direct-coupled flip-flop divide-by-two circuit [7]. At 300 K and with a dc bias of 1.3 V, input signals with frequencies up to 5.5 GHz were divided by two. At 77 K, the frequency of the input signal could be increased to 8.9 GHz before the divide-by-two function was no longer possible. The dissipation per gate was 3 mW and the dc bias voltage was 0.96 V.

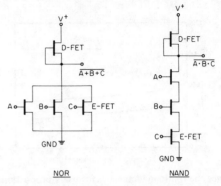

Fig. 15. NOR and NAND gates utilizing enhancement mode drivers (E-FET) and depletion mode loads (D-FET) with gate shorted to source.

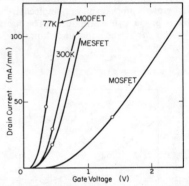

Fig. 16. Saturated drain current versus gate–source voltage for a Si MOSFET, a GaAs MESFET, and a GaAs–AlGaAs MODFET. The MODFET characteristics were measured at temperatures of 300 and 77 K. The MODFET data originated from the University of Illinois, and the MOSFET and MESFET data from the IBM Research Center. The curves were shifted with respect to the voltage axis to simulate operation in a logic inverter with adequate noise margins. The points represent the design load current for that inverter.

All of the preceding circuits have used the simple direct-coupled logic circuit family using enhancement mode drivers and depletion mode loads, or saturated resistor loads. Circuit diagrams of NOR and NAND gates, implemented using direct-coupled logic, are shown in Fig. 15. A simplified delay equation for such a stage is given by

$$\text{delay} = (C_D + C_L) V_L / 2 I_L$$

where I_L is the load current, V_L the logic voltage, C_D the device capacitance, and C_L the load capacitance which includes the wiring capacitance. To achieve high speed we need to develop a high current-to-voltage ratio. Referring to Figs. 13 and 16, this is more than just demanding a high transconductance, which is simply the slope of the drain current versus gate voltage characteristic. The characteristic should also have a sharp knee so that little of the valuable voltage swing is lost traversing the low transconductance knee region. The sharp turn-on of the MODFET maximizes the load current of the NOR gate for a given noise margin and therefore maximizes speed. The maximum transconductance is mainly a function of the saturated carrier velocity, but the sharpness of the knee depends strongly on the lower field part of the velocity versus field characteristic (as well as on the charge control characteristics as mentioned previously) and it is in both of these areas that the MODFET excels. While the MODFET possesses good high-speed characteristics at room temperature, these are enhanced at liquid nitrogren temperature.

Low voltages are the key to low-power operation, since the switching energy of the circuit is proportional to CV^2; however, operation at low power supply voltages would require a very tight control over turn-on characteristics of the device. Good uniformity of threshold voltage has been achieved over distances of a few centimeters, the best number being about a 10-mV standard deviation, achieved by Fujitsu [7], and 14 mV over a $2\frac{1}{2}$-in wafer achieved by Honeywell [26]. This control would be sufficient for enhance–deplete logic, if they could be obtained reproducibly. Shifts in threshold voltage due to trapping in the AlGaAs is a yet unsolved problem with regard to liquid nitrogen operation. Recent results, however, look promising.

The higher mobility and hence low on-resistance of the MODFET make it ideal for circuits where logic is performed by serial connection of devices, as illustrated for a NAND gate in Fig. 15. Another example would be in a static memory, where serial devices are used to couple the cells to the sense amplifier and to decode the sense amplifier. Serial switched logic (pass-transistor logic) has the property of higher speed, higher densities, and lower power than conventional NAND or NOR gates.

The combination of a large transconductance per unit width, with low on-resistance is ideal for off-chip drivers. For instance, a MODFET of only 75-μm width at 77 K, or 150-μm width at 300 K would suffice for an off-chip driver into 50 Ω, and with the addition of the good driving characteristics of the predriver stage, would give good overall performance.

The MODFET at room temperature offers a higher speed than the GaAs MESFET (see next section) but more materials complexity. Certainly the Rockwell results of 12.2 ps are very encouraging, although ring oscillator results can be very misleading since they are usually not designed with adequate noise margins for performing general-purpose logic (about a factor of 2 in performance can be gained by operating the ring oscillator in a "small-signal" mode.) Nevertheless, the first applications for MODFET logic will undoubtedly be at room temperature, and at relatively low levels of integration, where its higher speed compared to a GaAs MESFET will give it an edge in small-signal and logic "front end" applications. Its progress in integration level will depend on improvement of the quality of the epitaxial layers.

While the room temperature applications should nurture the MODFET technology initially, the real leverage for the MODFET, which was early appreciated by Fujitsu, is in large digital systems (e.g., supercomputer) at liquid nitrogen temperature. The improvement in MODFET speeds of greater than 50 percent and power-delay products of greater than a factor of two (if lower voltages are used) are not the only driving forces. As important is the improvement in wire resistance ($\sim$10 times) and reduction of electromigration (a wire failure mechanism) with temperature which greatly improve the allowable wire density on-chip and improve system performance. An additional bonus is the improvement in the thermal conductivity of GaAs ($\sim$10 times) at lower temperatures, allowing for larger power dissipations. The problems of cooling the system

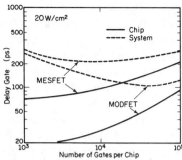

Fig. 17. Fujitsu study showing the projected chip delay and also the average stage delay in a large system, including off-chip delays for both MODFET and MESFET technologies. Power consumption per chip is limited to 20 W/cm². For a given total number of gates the delay associated with the interchip connections decreases or the number of gates per chip is increased. On the other hand, the delay per gate increases as the number of gates per chip is increased because of smaller power dissipation available per gate. The balance of these two competing factors gives rise to an optimum number of gates per chip which is strongly dependent on the individual device performance.

to liquid nitrogen temperature do not seem much more formidable than those already faced by designers in cooling high-performance silicon modules. The advantages will be systems of the future operating at Josephson-like speeds, which will be unattainable by future silicon technology.

The Fujitsu study [22] (see Fig. 17) illustrates the advantage of high speed at low power of the MODFET in a large system. The system delay is comprised of the chip and package delays. As the integration level is increased the on-chip wiring capacitance increases and the power per logic gate is reduced (to stay within chip power constraints) so that the circuit delay increases. The package delay is reduced since the package is used less and less as more of the system fits on a chip, so that the result is a minimum system delay at an optimum level of integration which depends on the speed–power characteristics of the circuit, the power dissipation capability per chip, and the propagation time in the package. The MODFET offers high speed at high integration levels due to two favorable characteristics, its small speed power product and its large current per unit area, which means that smaller area (compared to MOSFET or MESFET) devices can be used to drive on-chip capacitances and to drive off-chip. The problems in achieving high levels of integration will be formidable; yet this is where the large pay-off will be.

While a great majority of the MODFET related research has so far been directed toward logic applications because of distinct advantages over conventional GaAs MESFET's, recently promising results in the area of low-noise amplifiers have become available. Even though this device is being considered for power applications as well, its power handling capabilities are limited by the relatively low breakdown voltage of the gate Schottky barrier. Approaches such as camel gate, which utilizes a p^+-n^+ structure on n-AlGaAs for an increased breakdown voltage will have to be advanced before this device could be a good contender in the power FET area.

In the microwave low-noise FET area, using a 0.55-μm gate technology, researchers at Thomson CSF obtained noise figures of 1.26, 1.7, and 2.25 dB at 10, 12, and 17.5 GHz with associated gains of 12, 10.3, and 6.6 dB, respectively [27]. At cryogenic temperatures, the noise performance is enhanced substantially, well below 0.5 dB. Assigning a hard figure, however, is hampered by the inaccuracy of measurements in that range. Programs are currently being initiated to carefully characterize the noise performance at cryogenic temperatures. If the state-of-the-art source resistance were obtained, almost a two-fold improvement over GaAs MESFET's could be expected.

Three-stage amplifiers for satellite communications operating at 20 GHz were constructed by the Fujitsu group with a 300 K (L_g = 0.5 μm) overall noise figure of 3.9 dB and gain of 30 dB [28]. It must be pointed out that these results by no means represent the ultimate from MODFET's. With further improvements in the source resistance, much lower noise figures can be expected.

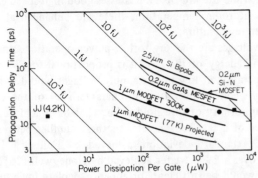

Fig. 18. Delay versus power curve for various technologies obtained in ring oscillators (except for the Josephson junction, where a gate chain was used).

COMPARISON WITH OTHER DEVICES

The MODFET is a field-effect transistor and can conveniently be compared with the GaAs MESFET, and the silicon MOS-FET (NMOS and CMOS) all of which are FET technologies. The key advantage of the MODFET, as we have discussed, is its ability to operate at high currents and at low voltages. A comparison of the MODFET, in this regard, to other devices is shown in Fig. 16, where in all cases the best devices (at dimensions of about 1 μm) reported in the open literature were selected. The maximum transconductances for these devices were 80 mS/mm (MOSFET), 230 mS/mm (MESFET), 270 mS/mm (MODFET, 300 K), and 400 mS/mm (MODFET, 77 K). The curves were all displaced horizontally, from the original data, to match the noise margin requirements for logic gates having a logic swing of 0.5 V (MODFET, 77 K), 0.8 V (MESFET and 300-K MODFET), and 2.5 V (MOSFET). The circuit switching energies vary as the square of the voltage, and will be in the ratio of 1 : 2.6 : 25 for the technologies considered. The MOSFET could operate at smaller voltages with a better delay–power product, but at the lower voltages its transconductance, hence speed, would be drastically reduced. Comparing the devices for a driver application, for the same 50-Ω driver design, the widths of the different devices would be 75 μm (MODFET, 77 K), 150 μm (MODFET, 300 K), 200 μm (MESFET, 300 K), and 400 μm for the MOSFET.

The other factor in determining device performance is capacitance. Parasitic capacitances are less in the GaAs technology due to the semi-insulating substrate. Silicon-on-sapphire circuits share this advantage. Studies have shown, however, that this advantage is much diminished at higher levels of integration. MOSFET's have larger gate–drain overlap capacitance, but this is no longer an important factor in the comparison due to improved device structures. The intrinsic speed capability is given by transconductance capacitance ratio, and this is related to the average drift velocity of the carriers in the channel, for a given device dimension. As deduced from device characteristics, velocities of 0.8-1 × 10⁷ cm/s are characteristic of MOS-FET's, 1.2-1.5 × 10⁷ cm/s of MESFET's, and 2 × 10⁷ cm/s (300 K)-3 × 10⁷ cm/s (77 K) of MODFET's.

The scaling potential of the MODFET, MESFET, and MOS-FET should be comparable, with minimum dimensions in the 0.1-0.2-μm range, before short-channel effects become severe. Vertical dimensions are reduced in coordination with horizontal dimensions, i.e., the AlGaAs thickness for the MODFET,

the channel depth for the MESFET, and the SiO₂ thickness for the MOSFET. Transconductances improve both as a result of the reduced thicknesses and as a result of increased carrier velocities. On the former, the MOSFET is perhaps more extendible than the MODFET, while the AlGaAs thickness of 350 Å is close to the limit set by breakdown, present thicknesses of SiO₂ in the MOSFET of 250 Å can be reduced to 50 Å before encountering a tunneling breakdown limit. On the latter, increases in velocity due to velocity overshoot effects are anticipated in both GaAs MESFET and MODFET's as device dimensions are reduced, but to a much lesser extent in Si MOSFET's.

Performance characteristics of various technologies on the basis of ring oscillator results (except for Josephson, where a gate chain was used) are shown in Fig. 18. Josephson junction circuits have been demonstrated with 13-ps switching times and 0.03-fJ power–delay products [29] (see *IEEE Spectrum*, May 1979). The best 300-K figure of silicon NMOSFET's with a 0.3-μm source–drain spacing is 28-ps delay time with a 40-fJ power-delay product [30]. The fastest GaAs self-aligned gate MESFET ring oscillators exhibit a delay time of 15 ps with a power-delay product of 84 fJ [31]. Silicon bipolar nonthreshold logic (0.5 × 5 μm²) (NTL) circuits have achieved delays of 42 ps at a delay-power product of 20 fJ per gate [32], while the more useful ECL circuits have achieved delays of 96 ps with 96-fJ power-delay product [33], [34]. The GaAs heterojunction bipolar transistor technology, although potentially very fast, has been demonstrated only in I^2L circuits where delays of 200 ps at 2 mW have been obtained [35]. As mentioned previously, these results are rather misleading because the ring oscillators are not usually designed to adequate noise margins, and loading effects are not taken into account. Fig. 19 shows delay estimations for more conservative designs, and in a large-scale integration environment. Excluding the Josephson junction technology, which is very difficult in practice, and requires liquid helium (~4.2 K) which is expensive to maintain and difficult to interface (a much more demanding requirement than liquid nitrogen), only the MODFET combines the advantages of both high speed and low power.

The high-speed market that the MODFET would have to compete in is at present dominated by the Si bipolar transistor at the high-speed low-integration level end, and is increasingly being encroached on by NMOS and especially CMOS at lower

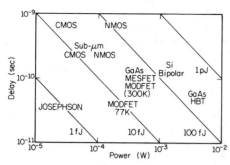

Fig. 19. Delay versus power curve for logic circuits in a large-scale integrated chip taking into account the effect of loading and conservative design for tolerances.

speeds yet much higher levels of integration. The bipolar technology has seen significant improvements, and projections for loaded logic delays are 100 and 50 ps for 1- and 0.5-μm lithographies, respectively. Spectacular improvements in heat removal capability from silicon have recently been demonstrated [36], which should enable the high-power high-speed silicon bipolar circuits to attain higher levels of integration. Bipolar technology, however, is much more complex than FET, including MODFET, technology.

Complimentary MOS has very low power–delay products, since the circuits only dissipate power while switching. The low-voltage advantage of the MODFET at 77 K would more or less balance the switching factor advantage of CMOS, giving these two technologies roughly equal power–delay products; however, the MODFET would still be much faster by about a factor of 10. Because of its technological maturity, the silicon technology may be able to take advantage of smaller channel lengths than the MODFET. Short-channel MOSFET's made (0.15-μm channel lengths by Bell Labs) [37] have a lower transconductance (200 mS/mm) than a 1-μm MODFET. The commercial MOSFET technology is still practiced at dimensions of >1 μm, but the MODFET would have to achieve a rapid learning to compete effectively with silicon. The liquid nitrogen option can be exercised by silicon MOSFET's as well, as shown by IBM researchers where mobilities in MOSFET's increase to 3000 cm^2/V · s. MOSFET peak velocities, even at 77 K are only about 1.2 $\times$ 10^7 cm/s compared with MODFET peak velocities of >3 $\times$ 10^7 cm/s so that the MODFET would retain a speed advantage.

The GaAs MESFET technology has made rapid strides recently, with circuits containing >10 000 devices having been demonstrated. While the MODFET benefits from advances in the GaAs based technology (just as GaAs benefits from advances made in silicon), it still is in a much more primitive state. The applications area of the GaAs MESFET and the MODFET, especially at room temperature, are very similar, placing these technologies in direct competition. The MODFET at room temperature has advantages over the standard GaAs MESFET circuits because of its higher mobility (8000 versus 4000 cm^2/V · s) which gives it a sharper turn-on, higher peak velocities (by about 20 percent) in undoped versus doped GaAs, and also due to its higher turn-on voltage due to the larger barrier height of the (Ga, Al) As compared with GaAs. An area where the MODFET may not be able to compete with the MESFET is in

radiation hardness, in analog with a MOSFET, due to charge generation in the AlGaAs. Short-channel MESFET's will be able to compete at room temperature with MODFET's in terms of speed, but not at liquid-nitrogen temperature.

Other devices are being investigated by various laboratories for high-speed applications. Vertical-type FET's replace control of horizontal dimensions of the channel length for the much easier control of vertical dimension. Examples are the permeable base transistor [38] (a solid-state analog of a vacuum tube), and the vertical FET's [39] which have a heterojunction "ballistic launcher" source, to increase electron velocities. The devices should be faster eventually than the MODFET but at the cost of considerable fabrication complexity. The vertical FET's swap the problems of vertical with horizontal dimensional control and vice-versa; in particular the problem of threshold voltage control is exacerbated since it now depends on the horizontal dimension. As mentioned earlier, another competitor to the MODFET is the heterojunction bipolar transistor. Again, transit times are controlled by vertical dimension (transit times as small as 1.5 ps have been predicted by a Texas Instruments group) [40]. The heterojunction bipolar transistor should achieve performance in the same range as the MODFET, with the inherent good control of turn-on characteristics of bipolar transistors. Like its silicon counterpart, the heterojunction bipolar transistor would suffer from charge storage effects in saturation. This leaves the circuit designer with the choice of ultrahigh speed, but high-power nonsaturating circuits like ECL ($\sim$30 ps) compared with low-power less area-consuming, but slower, I^2L circuits (>100 ps). A compromise choice is Schottky transistor logic, which is faster than I^2L yet has very low power. The fabrication complexity of the heterojunction bipolar transistor versus that of the MODFET bears the same relationship as silicon bipolar versus FET. None of these alternatives has yet demonstrated high-speed operation in logic circuits.

A comparison summary of the various high-speed technologies is shown in Table I. Compared to the other devices, the MODFET has the advantage of high speed and low power, combined with relatively simple processing and a relaxed lithography requirement. Solutions to the difficult materials problems represent the greatest challenge.

Remaining Problems and Projections

Since MODFET's are large-current and small-voltage devices, the saturation voltage and transconductance are very sensitive to the contact resistance. In fact, the higher the transconductance the more severe the effect of the source resistance becomes. In order to fully take advantage of the device potential, it is essential that extremely low contact resistances be obtained. Not only the contact resistance but parasitic resistances such as the source and drain semiconductor access resistance must be minimized. This could be done using the gate as an ion implantation mask to increase the conductance on each side of the gate but has not yet been done, partially because of degradation of the quality of the channel during annealing to activate donors. Currently many laboratories, both university and industrial, are looking into the degradation mechanism occurring during the annealing step. Although preliminary,

TABLE I
Device Comparison Graded 1 (Best) Through 5

	GaAs				Si	
	MODFET	MESFET	Vertical FET	HBT	MOSFET [CMOS]	BJT
Speed	1	3	1	2	5	4
Power delay product	1	2	2	4	1	4
Lithographic requirement	2	3	5	1	4	1
Doping control	4	4	4	1	2	1
Processing complexity	2	1	4	5	3	5
Materials problems	4	3	5	4	1	2

the transient annealing technique looks very promising in this regard.

Modulation-doped structures also suffer from the persistent photoconductivity (PPC) effect below 100 K [41]. This is believed to be the result of donor-induced defects in AlGaAs which once ionized exhibit a repulsion towards capture. Recent results, however, appear to indicate that defect-related processes in GaAs as well can play an important role. As a result, increased carrier concentrations, which persist unless the sample is warmed up, are obtained. The electron mobility too, increases with illumination in samples with low areal carrier density. This is tentatively attributed to perhaps neutralizing some defect centers in the depleted AlGaAs near the hetero-interface which then do not cause as much scattering. This PPC effect has been shown to decrease when the AlGaAs layer is grown at high substrate temperatures. It must be kept in mind that in a few instances almost PPC-free MODFET structures have been obtained.

Although for the most part the heterointerface in MODFET's is almost perfect so that interface states encountered in Si MOSFET's do not occur, in a few instances the AlGaAs layer quality is not good enough because of larger concentration of traps. The drain I–V characteristics of a few MODFET's at 77 K collapsed when the device was stressed with a large drain bias of 3 V. Exciting the device with light or raising the temperature cause the device to return to its normal properties. This is attributed to thermionic emission and trap assisted tunneling of electrons into AlGaAs through the barrier and/or PPC related defects in AlGaAs.

It is obvious that the problems associated with the AlGaAs must be minimized so that their influence on device performance is not noticeable. Realizing the importance of the issue, many researchers are looking into sources and causes of the traps and electronic defects in AlGaAs. MODFET's, in contrast to injection lasers, are the first devices utilizing AlGaAs where charge and defect concentrations of about 10^{11} cm^{-2} give rise to unacceptably large adverse effects on the device performance. There are also efforts to explore device structures that are not very sensitive to at least some of the obstacles discussed earlier.

The question of yield and reliability may, however, take a little longer to resolve. For yield, the processing philosophy with regard to GaAs must change. Instrumentation, care, and environment similar to that used for Si IC's must be implemented.

There is also the question of epi defects either introduced by the epi process or present on substrates. Some of those are morphological defects which not only degrade the semiconductor but also cause processing defects. The present state of the art of molecular-beam epitaxy when used with average GaAs substrates is such that only MSI circuits with some success in terms of yield are possible. Efforts are under way to reduce the morphological defect count on the epi. There are already encouraging results which tend to suggest that by the latter part of the decade the substrate quality, the epi morphological quality, the processing that introduces few defects and thus functional circuits with active elements in the mid to upper thousands may be possible.

Like that of MESFET's, the threshold voltage of MODFET's is very sensitive to the epi properties. For a normally off MODFET, a thickness control to about 2 monolayers ($\sim$5 Å) and doping control and AlAs mole fraction control of about 1 percent are needed to control the threshold voltage within about 10 mV. Controls like this have already, though occasionally, been obtained on wafers with slightly less than 3-in diameter. The repeatability of this technology is one of the questions that is also being addressed.

In summary, it is clear that the MODFET has many of the attributes required for high-speed devices, particularly those of the integrated circuits. Present results with moderate numbers of devices are very encouraging and with more effort even better results are expected. In fact, the heterojunction FET with only 1-μm gate length and 3-μm source–drain spacing has surpassed the performance of other techniques, e.g., conventional GaAs with sub 0.5-μm dimensions as shown in Fig. 18. It should be kept in mind that the delay times shown in Fig. 18 are bound to increase substantially in a real circuit with loaded gates. Nevertheless, the MODFET should be capable of providing functional operations in a large system by about a factor of 10 faster than the current state of the art. With more advanced fabrication technologies, even better performance can be expected.

Acknowledgment

H. Morkoç would like to express his sincere thanks to his graduate students, particularly to T. J. Drummond, for carrying out the research reported here. Contributions by and with Prof. M. S. Shur of the University of Minnesota and his student, K. Lee, were invaluable. The authors would also like to thank Dr. C. P. Lee of Rockwell, Dr. N. T. Linh of Thomson CSF, and Dr. M. Helix of Honeywell for providing the results of their work prior to publication. Discussions with Prof. L. F. Eastman of Cornell University were very fruitful.

REFERENCES

[1] R. Dingle, H. Stormer, A. C. Gossard, and W. Wiegmann, "Electron mobilities in modulation doped semiconductor heterojunction superlattices, *Appl. Phys. Lett.*, vol. 31, pp. 665–667, 1978.

[2] L. Esaki and R. Tsu, "Superlattice and negative conductivity in semiconductors," *IBM Internal Res. Rep.*, RC2418, Mar. 26, 1969.

[3] M. Morkoç and P. M. Solomon, "The HEMT: A superfast transistor," *IEEE Spectrum*, vol. 21, pp. 28–35, Feb. 1984.

[4] P. M. Solomon, "A comparison of semiconductor devices for high speed logic," *Proc. IEEE*, vol. 70, no. 5, pp. 489–509, 1982.

[5] K. Lee, M. S. Shur, T. J. Drummond, S. L. Su, W. G. Lyons, R. Fischer, and H. Morkoç, "Design and analysis of modulation doped (Al, Ga)As/GaAs FET's (MODFET's), *J. Vacuum Sci. Technol.*, vol. JVST B1, pp. 186–189, 1982.

[6] C. P. Lee, D. L. Miller, D. Hou, and R. J. Anderson, "Ultra high speed integrated circuits using GaAs/AlGaAs high electron mobility transistors," *IEEE Trans. Electron Devices*, vol. ED-30, p. 1569, 1983.

[7] K. Nishiuchi, T. Mimura, S. Kuroda, S. Hiyamizu, H. Nishi, and M. Abe, "Device characteristics of short channel high electron mobility transistors (HEMT)," *IEEE Trans. Electron Devices*, vol. ED-30, p. 1569, 1983.

[8] A. Y. Cho and J. R. Arthur, "Molecular beam epitaxy," in *Progress in Solid State Chem.*, vol. 10, 1975, pp. 157–191.

[9] T. Ando, "Self-consistent results for a GaAs/Al_xGaAs_{1-x} heterojunction I. Subband structure and light scattering spectra," *J. Phys. Soc. Japan.*, vol. 51, pp. 3872–3899, 1982.

[10] L. C. Witkowski, T. J. Drummond, C. M. Stanchak, and H. Morkoç, "High electron mobilities in modulation doped AlGaAs/GaAs heterojunctions prepared by MBE," *Appl. Phys. Lett.*, vol. 37, pp. 1033–1035, 1980.

[11] D. L. Rode, "Electron mobility in direct gap semiconductors," *Phys. Rev. B*, vol. 2, pp. 1012–1024, 1970.

[12] G. E. Stillman, C. M. Wolfe, and J. O. Dimmock, "Hall coefficient factor for polar mode scattering in n-type GaAs," *J. Phys. Chem. Solids*, vol. 31, pp. 1199–1204, 1970.

[13] H. Heiblum, private communication.

[14] T. J. Drummond, H. Morkoç, K. Lee, and M. S. Shur, "Model for modulation doped Al_xGaAs_{1-x}/GaAs field effect transistors," *IEEE Electron Device Lett.*, vol. EDL-3, pp. 338–341, 1982.

[15] F. Stern and E. Howard, "Properties of semiconductor surface inversion layers in electric quantum subband limit," *Phys. Rev.*, vol. 163, pp. 816–835, 1967.

[16] D. Delagebeaudeuf and N. T. Linh, "Metal-(n) AlGaAs–GaAs two dimensional gas FET," *IEEE Trans. Electron Devices*, vol. ED-29, pp. 955–960, 1982.

[17] K. Lee, M. S. Shur, T. J. Drummond, and H. Morkoç, "Current voltage and capacitance voltage characteristics of modulation doped field effect transistors," *IEEE Trans. Electron Devices*, vol. ED-30, pp. 207–212, 1983.

[18] H. Stormer, R. Dingle, A. C. Gossard, and W. Wiegmann, "Two-dimensional electron gas at a semiconductor–semiconductor interface," *Solid-State Commun.*, vol. 29, pp. 705–709, 1979.

[19] K. Lee, M. S. Shur, T. J. Drummond, and H. Morkoç, "Two-dimensional electron gas in modulation doped layers," *J. Appl. Phys.*, vol. 54, pp. 2093–2096, 1983.

[20] H. Morkoç, "Current transport in modulation doped (Al, Ga) As/GaAs heterostructure: Applications to high-speed FET's," *IEEE Electron Device Lett.*, vol. EDL-2, pp. 260–261, 1981.

[21] T. J. Drummond, W. Kopp, H. Morkoç, and M. Keever, "Transport in modulation doped structures (Al_xGa_{1-x}As/GaAs): Correlations with Monte Carlo calculations (GaAs)," *Appl. Phys. Lett.*, vol. 41, pp. 277–279, 1982.

[22] M. Abe, T. Mimura, N. Yokoyama, and H. Ishikawa, "New technology towards GaAs LSI/VLSI for computer applications," *IEEE Trans. Electron Devices*, vol. ED-29, pp. 1088–1093, 1982.

[23] N. T. Linh, P. N. Tung, D. Delagebeaudeuf, P. Deslescluse, and M. Laviron, "High speed-low power GaAs/AlGaAs TEGFET integrated circuits," *IEDM Tech. Dig.*, pp. 582–585, Dec. 1982.

[24] J. V. Dilorenzo, R. Dingle, M. Feuer, A. C. Gossard, R. Hendal, J. C. M. Hwang, A. Katalsky, V. G. Keramidas, R. A. Kiehl, and P. O'Connor, "Material and device considerations for selectively doped heterojunction transistors," *IEDM Tech. Dig.*, pp. 578–581, Dec. 1982.

[25] R. A. Kiehl, M. D. Feuer, R. H. Handle, J. C. M. Hwang, V. G. Keramidas, C. L. Allyn, and R. Dingle, "Selectivity doped heterostructure frequency dividers," *IEEE Electron Device Lett.*, vol. EDL-4, pp. 377–379, 1983.

[26] J. Abrokwah, N. C. Cirillo, M. Helix, and M. Longerbone, "Modulation doped FET: Threshold voltage uniformity of a high throughput 3-inch MBE system," presented at 5th Annual MBE Workshop (Georgia Techn.), Oct. 6–7, 1983; and *J. Vacuum Sci. Technol.*, to be published.

[27] N. T. Linh, M. Laviron, P. Delescluse, P. N. Tung, D. Delagebeaudeuf, F. Diamond, and J. Chevrier, "Low-noise performance of two-dimensional electron gas FET's," in *Proc. 9th IEEE Cornell Biennial Conf.*, to be published.

[28] M. Niori, T. Sito, S. Joshin, and T. Mimura, "A 20 GHz HEMT amplifier for satellite communications," presented at IEEE Int. Solid State Circuit Conf., (New York), Feb. 23–25, (see the digests).

[29] W. Anacker, "Computing at 4 degrees Kelvin," *IEEE Spectrum*, pp. 26–37, May 1979.

[30] G. E. Smith, "Fine line MOS technology for high speed integrated circuits," *IEEE Trans. Electron Devices*, vol. ED-39, p. 1564, 1983.

[31] R. Sadler and L. F. Eastman, "High-speed logic and 300 K with self-aligned submicrometer gate GaAs MESFET's," *IEEE Electron Device Lett.*, vol. EDL-24, pp. 215–217, 1983.

[32] T. Sakai, S. Konaka, Y. Kobayashi, M. Suzuki, and Y. Kawai, "Gigabit logic bipolar technology: Advanced super self aligned process technology," *Electron. Letts.*, vol. 19, pp. 283–284, 1983.

[33] T. H. Ning, R. D. Isaac, P. M. Solomon, D. D. Tang, H. N. Yu, G. C. Feth, and S. K. Wiedmann, "Self-aligned bipolar transistors for high-performance low-power VLSI," *IEEE Trans. Electron Devices*, vol. ED-28, pp. 1010–1012, 1981.

[34] C. P. Snapp, "Advanced silicon bipolar technology yields usable monolithic microwave and high speed digital IC's," *Microwave J.*, pp. 93–103, Aug. 1983.

[35] H. T. Yuan, Texas Instruments, private communication.

[36] D. B. Tuckerman and R. F. W. Pease, "High-performance heat sinking for VLSI," *IEEE Electron Device Lett.*, vol. EDL-2, pp. 126–129, 1981.

[37] W. Fichtner, R. K. Watts, D. B. Fraser, R. L. Johnston, and S. M. Sze, "0.15-μm channel length MOSFET'S fabricated using E-beam lithography," *IEEE Electron Device Lett.*, vol. EDL-3, pp. 412–414, 1982.

[38] C. O. Bozler and G. D. Alley, "Fabrication and numerical simulations of the permeable base transistors," *IEEE Trans. Electron Devices*, vol. ED-27, pp. 1128–1141, 1980.

[39] E. Kohn, N. Mishra, and L. F. Eastman, "Short channel effects in 0.5 μm source–drain spaced vertical GaAs FET's: A first experimental investigation," *IEEE Electron Device Lett.*, vol. EDL-4, pp. 125–127, 1983.

[40] W. R. Frensley, private communication.

[41] T. J. Drummond, W. Kopp, R. Fischer, H. Morkoç, R. E. Thorne, and A. Y. Cho, "Photoconductivity effects in extremely high mobility modulation doped (Al, Ga)As/GaAs heterostructures," *J. Appl. Phys.*, vol. 53, pp. 1238–1240, 1982.

Heterostructure Bipolar Transistors and Integrated Circuits

HERBERT KROEMER, FELLOW, IEEE

Reprinted from *Proceedings of the IEEE*, Volume 70, Number 1, January *Invited Paper*
1982, pages 13-25. Copyright © 1982 by The Institute of Electrical and Electronics Engineers, Inc.

Abstract—Two new epitaxial technologies have emerged in recent years (molecular beam epitaxy (MBE) and metal-organic chemical vapor deposition (MOCVD)), which offer the promise of making highly advanced heterostructures routinely available. While many kinds of devices will benefit, the principal and first beneficiary will be bipolar transistors. The underlying central principle is the use of energy gap variations beside electric fields to control the forces acting on electrons and holes, separately and independently of each other. The resulting greater design freedom permits a re-optimization of doping levels and geometries, leading to higher speed devices. Microwave transistors with maximum oscillation frequencies above 100 GHz and digital switching transistors with switching times below 10 ps should become available. An inverted transistor structure with a smaller collector on top and a larger emitter on the bottom becomes possible, with speed advantages over the common "emitter-up" design. Double-heterostructure (DH) transistors with both wide-gap emitters and collectors offer additional advantages. They exhibit better performance under saturated operation. Their emitters and collectors may be interchanged by simply changing biasing conditions, greatly simplifying the architecture of bipolar IC's. Examples of heterostructure implementations of I^2L and ECL are discussed. The present overwhelming dominance of the compound semiconductor device field by FET's is likely to come to an end, with bipolar devices assuming an at least equal role, and very likely a leading one.

"What is claimed is:

1) ...

2) A device as set forth in claim 1 in which one of the separated zones is of a semiconductive material having a wider energy gap than that of the material in the other zones."

Claim 2 of U.S. Patent 2 569 347 to W. Shockley,
Filed 26 June 1948,
Issued 25 September 1951,
Expired 24 September 1968.

I. INTRODUCTION

THIS IS A PAPER about an idea whose time has come: A bipolar transistor with a wide-gap emitter. As the introductory quote shows, the idea is as old as the transistor itself. The great potential advantages of such a design over the conventional homostructure design have long been recognized [1]–[3], but until the early 70's, no technology existed to build practically useful transistors of this kind, even though numerous attempts had been made [3], [4]. The situation started to change with the emergence of liquid-phase epitaxy (LPE) as a technology for III/V-compound semiconductor heterostructures, and in recent years reports on increasingly impressive true three-terminal heterostructure bipolar transistors (HBT's) have appeared at an increasing rate [5]–[14]. In addition, there is also a rapidly growing literature on two-terminal *photo*transistors with wide-gap emitters [15]. Many of the phototransistors employ InP emitters with a lattice-matched (Ga, In) (P,As) base.

Since the mid-70's, two additional very promising heterostructure technologies have appeared: molecular beam epitaxy (MBE) [16] and metal-organic chemical vapor deposition (MOCVD) [17]. Impressive results on MOCVD-grown (Al,Ga)As-GaAs phototransistors have already been published [18]; HBT's grown by MBE have also been achieved [19].

Because of the pre-eminence of silicon in current IC technology, there exists a strong incentive to incorporate wide-gap emitters into Si transistors, in a way compatible with existing Si technology. A possible approach—and the most successful one so far—has been the use of heavily doped "semi-insulating polycrystalline" silicon (SIPOS) as emitter [20], utilizing the wider energy gap of "polycrystalline" (really: amorphous) Si compared to crystalline Si. An alternate approach has been the use of gallium phosphide, which has a room-temperature lattice constant within 0.3 percent of that of Si, grown on Si either by CVD [21] or by MBE [22]. But the results reported for the GaP-Si combination have so far been disappointing.

Finally, the first reports have recently appeared, in which HBT's have been integrated on the same chip with other devices, such as double-heterostructure (DH) lasers [23] or LED's [24].

In view of these recent developments it appears that Shockley's vision is about to become a reality. In fact, one of the purposes of this paper is to show that the possibilities for HBT's go far beyond simply replacing a homojunction emitter by a heterojunction emitter.

To appreciate these possibilities, it is useful first to view the wide-gap emitter as a simple example of a more general *central design principle* of heterostructure devices; it is discussed in Section II of this paper. Discussions of future device possibilities must be based on technological premises; they are discussed in Section III. In Section IV and V the concept and the high-speed benefits of the wide-gap emitter are reviewed, including some recent conceptual developments that do not appear to have been widely appreciated. Section VI discusses the promising concept of an inverted transistor design, in which the collector is made smaller than the emitter and placed on the surface of the structure, similar to I^2L, but using a heterostructure design applicable to all transistors. In Section VII the idea of a single-heterostructure transistor with a wide-gap emitter is generalized to DH transistors with both wide-gap emitters and wide-gap collectors. Such a design appears to

Manuscript received June 30, 1981; revised August 31, 1981. This work was supported in part by the Army Research Office and by the Office of Naval Research.

The author is with the Department of Electrical and Computer Engineering, University of California, Santa Barbara, CA 93106.

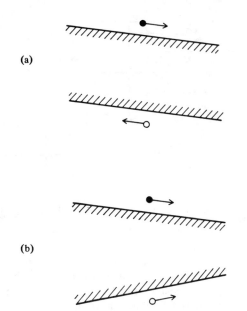

(a)

(b)

Fig. 1. Forces on electrons and holes. In a uniform-gap semiconductor (top) the two forces are equal and opposite to each other, and equal to the electrostatic force $\pm q\vec{E}$. In a graded-gap structure, the forces in electrons and holes may be in the same direction.

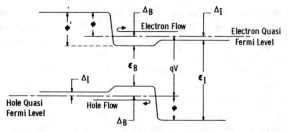

Fig. 2. Energy band diagram of a DH laser, showing the confinement forces driving both electrons and holes towards the active layer, on both sides of the latter. (From [25].)

offer surprisingly large advantages for both microwave and digital devices, and especially for digital IC's. As examples of potential IC advantages, heterostructure modifications of both I^2L and ECL architecture are discussed. Finally, Section VIII offers some speculations on the question of FET's-versus-bipolars, and related questions.

In line with the character of this Special Issue (integrated) digital HBT's are emphasized over (discrete) microwave devices, but not to the point of exclusion of the latter. It would be artificial to attempt a complete separation: Not only was much of the past development of HBT's oriented towards discrete microwave devices, but several of the newer concepts originating in a digital context would improve microwave transistors as well.

II. THE CENTRAL DESIGN PRINCIPLE OF HETEROSTRUCTURE DEVICES

If one looks for a general principle underlying most heterostructure devices, one is led to the following considerations. If one ignores magnetic effects, the forces acting on the electrons and holes in a semiconductor are equal (except for a sign in the case of electrons) to the slopes of the edge of the band in which the carriers reside (Fig. 1). In ideal homostructures the energy gap is constant; hence the slopes of the two band edges are equal, and the forces acting on electrons and holes are necessarily equal in magnitude and opposite in sign. In fact they are equal to the ordinary electrostatic force $\pm q\vec{E}$ on a charge of magnitude $\pm q$ in an electric field $\vec{E}$. In a heterostructure, the energy gap may vary; hence the two band edge slopes and with it the magnitudes of the two forces need not be the same, nor need they be in any simple way related to the electrostatic force exerted by a field $\vec{E}$. In fact, the two slopes may have opposite signs (Fig. 1), implying forces on electrons and holes that act in the same direction, despite their opposite charges.

In effect, heterostructures utilize energy gap variations in addition to electric fields as forces acting on electrons and holes, to control their distribution and flow. This is what I would

like to call the *Central Design Principle* of heterostructure devices. It is a very powerful principle, and one of the purposes of this paper is to give examples that show just how powerful it is.

Although by no means restricted to bipolar devices, the principle is especially powerful when, as in a bipolar transistor, the distribution and flow of *both* electrons and holes must be controlled. By a judicious combination of energy gap variations and electric fields it then becomes possible, within wide limits, to control the forces acting on electrons and holes, *separately and independently of each other*, a design freedom not achievable in homostructures.

The central design principle plays a role in almost all heterostructure devices, and it serves both to unify the ideas underlying different such devices, and as guidance in the development of new device concepts. No device demonstrates the central design principle better than the oldest and so far most important heterostructure device, the DH laser. This point is illustrated in Fig. 2, which shows the energy band structure of the device under lasing conditions, as anticipated (with only slight exaggeration) in the paper in which this device was first proposed [25], and from which Fig. 2 is taken. The drawing shows band edge slopes corresponding to forces that drive *both* electrons and holes towards the inside of the active layer, at *both* edges of the latter. This is the principal reason why the DH laser works, although it is not the only reason. The difference in refractive indices between the inner and outer semiconductors also plays an important role. Such a participation of additional concepts is not uncommon in other heterostructure devices either.

III. THE TECHNOLOGICAL PREMISE

Throughout its history, heterostructure device design has chronically suffered from a technology bottleneck. Even LPE, whatever its merits as a superb laboratory technology, has outside the laboratory been largely limited to devices, such as injection lasers for fiberoptics use, which could simply not be built without heterostructures, but which were needed sufficiently urgently to put up with the limitations of LPE technology. Already for the "ordinary" three-terminal transistor (i.e., excepting phototransistors), the necessary high-performance combination of LPE and lithography was never developed to the point that the resulting heterostructures would reach the speed capability of state-of-the-art Si bipolars, much less reach their own theoretical potential exceeding that of Si.

As a result of the emergence of two new epitaxial technologies in the last few years, the heterostructure technology bottleneck is rapidly disappearing, to the point that the incorporation of heterostructures into most compound semiconductor devices will probably be one of the dominant themes of compound semiconductor technology during the remainder of the present decade.

The two new technologies are MBE [16] and MOCVD [17]. Although differing in many ways, for the purposes of this paper the commonalities of the two technologies are more important than their differences, and there is no need to enter here into the debate as to which of the two technologies will eventually be best for doing what.

Both technologies are capable of growing epitaxial layers with high crystalline perfection and purity, comparable to state-of-the-art results with LPE and halide-CVD. Highly controlled doping levels up to 10^{19} impurities per cm^3 and more can be achieved, and highly controlled changes in doping level are possible during growth without interrupting the latter, and with at most a minor adjustment in growth parameters. The doping may be changed either gradually or abruptly. Because of the comparatively low growth temperatures (especially for MBE), diffusion effects during growth are weak, and with certain dopants much more abrupt doping steps can be achieved than with any other technique, not only when doping is "turned on," but also when it is "turned off."

Most important in our context of heterostructures, it is possible in both technologies to change from one III/V semiconductor to a different (lattice-matched) III/V semiconductor with greater ease than in any other technique. In both techniques, a change in semiconductor and hence in energy gap is not significantly harder to achieve than a change in doping level! In particular, the change can again be accomplished during growth without interruption, either gradually or abruptly and, if abruptly, over extremely short distances.

Finally, in both techniques the growth rates and hence the layer thicknesses can be very precisely controlled. Because the growth rates themselves are low (or can be made low), extremely thin layers can be achieved, to the point that effects due to the finite quantum-mechanical wavelengths of the electrons can be readily generated. It is in the context of the study of such quantum effects that both techniques have demonstrated their so far highest capability level. With both MOCVD and MBE, GaAs-(Al,Ga)As structures with over 100 epitaxial layers have been built [26], [27], and essentially arbitrary numbers appear possible. With MOCVD, layer thicknesses below 50 Å have been achieved, with MBE, below 10 Å. In either case, the capability far exceeds anything needed in the foreseeable future for transistor-like devices.

So far, these are laboratory results, mostly on GaAs-(Al,Ga)As structures. But it is the consensus of those working on the two technologies that much of this performance can be carried over into a production environment, with high yields and at an acceptable cost. Acceptable here means a cost low enough that it will not deter the use of the new technologies in most of those high-performance applications that need the performance potential of heterostructure devices.

An extension of both technologies to lattice-matched III/V-compound heterosystems beyond GaAs-(Al,Ga)As is an all but foregone conclusion, including GaAs-(Ga,In)P, InP-(Ga,In)(P,As), and InAs-(Al,Ga)Sb.

In view of these developments, the following scenario for the III/V-compound heterostructure technology of the 1990's is likely. Epitaxial technologies will be routinely available in which both the doping and the energy gap can be varied almost at will, over distances significantly below 100 Å, and covering

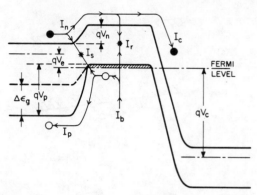

Fig. 3. Band diagram of an n-p-n transistor with a wide-gap emitter, showing the various current components, and the hole-repelling effect of the additional energy gap in the emitter.

a large fraction of their physically possible ranges, by what is essentially a software-controlled operation within a given growth run. The cost of the technology will be sufficiently low to encourage the development of high-performance devices that utilize this capability. The cost will be essentially a fixed cost per growth run, depending on the overall tolerance level but hardly at all on the number of layers and what they contain, similar to the cost of optical lithography, which has largely a fixed cost per masking step, almost independent of what is on the mask (at a given tolerance level). In particular, there will be only a negligible cost increment associated with using a heterojunction over using a homojunction (or no junction at all), and hence there will be only a negligible economic incentive *not* to use a heterojunction.

What *will* be expensive, just as with masking, are multiple growth runs, in which the growth is interrupted and the wafer removed from the growth system for intermediate processing, with the growth to be resumed afterwards. Hence there will be a strong incentive to accomplish the desired device structure with the minimum number of growth runs, no matter how complicated the individual run might become.

The above scenario is the technological premise of the remainder of this paper. Although presented here in the context of bipolar transistors and IC's, this scenario, as well as the central design principle of Section II, obviously go far beyond these specific devices. Together, the two concepts might form the starting point for a fascinating speculation about the future of semiconductor devices beyond simple bipolar structures. However, such a discussion would go beyond the scope of this paper as well as of this Special Issue.

IV. THE WIDE-GAP EMITTER

A. Basic Theory

The basic theory behind a wide-gap emitter is simple [1]. Consider the energy band structure of an n-p-n transistor, as in Fig. 3. In drawing the band edges as smooth monotonic curves we are implicitly assuming that the emitter junction has been graded sufficiently to obliterate any band edge discontinuities or even any nonmonotonic variations of the conduction band edge. We will return to this point later. There are the following injection-related dc currents flowing in such a transistor:
 a) A current I_n of electrons injected from the emitter into the base;
 b) A current I_p of holes injected from the base into the emitter;
 c) A current I_s due to electron–hole recombination within

the forward biased emitter-base space charge layer.

d) A small part of I_r of the electron injection current I_n is lost due to bulk recombination.

The current contribution I_n is the principal current on which the device operation depends; the contributions I_p, I_s, and I_r are strictly nuisance currents, as are the capacitive currents (not shown in Fig. 3) that accompany any voltage changes. We have neglected any currents created by electron–hole pair generation in the collector depletion layer or the collector body.

Expressed in terms of these physical current contributions, the net currents at the three terminals are:

Emitter current: $\quad I_e = I_n + I_p + I_s \qquad$ (1a)

Collector current: $\quad I_c = I_n - I_r \qquad$ (1b)

Base current: $\quad I_b = I_p + I_r + I_s. \qquad$ (1c)

A figure of merit for such a transistor is the ratio

$$\beta = \frac{I_c}{I_b} = \frac{I_n - I_r}{I_p + I_r + I_s} < \frac{I_n}{I_p} \equiv \beta_{\max}. \qquad (2)$$

Here, $\beta_{\max}$ is the highest possible value of β, in the limit of negligible recombination currents. It is the improvement of $\beta_{\max}$ to which the wide-gap emitter idea addresses itself.

To estimate $\beta_{\max}$ we assume that emitter and base are uniformly doped with the doping levels N_e and P_b. We denote with qV_n and qV_p the (not necessarily equal) heights of the potential energy barriers for electrons and holes, between emitter and base. We may then write the electron and hole injection current densities in the form

$$J_n = N_e v_{nb} \exp\left(-qV_n/kT\right) \qquad (3a)$$

$$J_p = P_b v_{pe} \exp\left(-qV_p/kT\right). \qquad (3b)$$

Here v_{nb} and v_{pe} are the mean speeds, due to the combined effects of drift and diffusion, of electrons at the emitter-end of the base, and of holes at the base-end of the emitter.

In writing (3a, b) with simple Boltzmann factors, we have implicitly assumed that both emitter and base are nondegenerate. In a homojunction transistor the emitter might be degenerate; in a heterojunction transistor the base might be degenerate, as is in fact assumed in Fig. 3. This requires small corrections either in (3a) for the homojunction case, or (3b) for the heterojunction case, which we neglect here for simplicity. We have also neglected correction factors allowing for the differences in the effective densities of states of the semiconductors.

We are interested here only in the ratio of the two currents. If the energy gap of the emitter is larger than that of the base by $\Delta\epsilon_g$, we have

$$q(V_p - V_n) = \Delta\epsilon_g \qquad (4a)$$

and we obtain

$$\frac{I_n}{I_p} = \beta_{\max} = \frac{N_e}{P_b} \frac{v_{nb}}{v_{pe}} \exp\left(\Delta\epsilon_g/kT\right). \qquad (5a)$$

For a good transistor, a value $\beta_{\max} \gtrsim 100$ is desirable.

Of the three factors in (5), the ratio v_{nb}/v_{pe} is least subject to manipulation. As a rule

$$5 < v_{nb}/v_{pe} < 50. \qquad (6)$$

To obtain $\beta_{\max} \gtrsim 100$ it is therefore necessary that either

$$N_e \gg P_b \qquad (7)$$

or that $\Delta\epsilon_g$ is at least a few-times kT.

Energy gap differences that are many-times kT are readily obtainable. As a result, very high values of I_n/I_p can be achieved *almost regardless of the doping ratio*. This does not mean that arbitrarily high β's can be obtained. It simply means that the hole injection current I_p becomes a negligible part of the base current compared to the two recombination currents: $I_b \cong I_s + I_r$. To have a useful transistor, we must still have $I_r \ll I_n$. If we approximate I_e by I_n, we obtain

$$\beta = \frac{I_n}{I_r + I_s}. \qquad (8)$$

Based on the evidence from high-β HBT's that have been reported $(\beta \geq 10^3)$,[1] the emitter–base hetero-interface can be made sufficiently defect-free to keep the interface recombination current I_s below $10^{-3} I_n$, at least at sufficiently high current levels I_n. At the same time, the base doping in a properly designed heterostructure transistor will be very high, and hence the minority carrier lifetime correspondingly low, to the point that the bulk recombination current I_r, rather than the interface recombination current I_s will dominate, in contrast to the situation in many homojunction transistors. We therefore neglect I_s beside I_r.

The bulk recombination current density may be written

$$J_r = \gamma n_e(0) w_b/\tau. \qquad (9)$$

Here $n_e(0)$ is the injected electron concentration at the emitter end of the base, w_b is the base width, and τ the average electron lifetime in the base. The factor γ is a factor between 0.5 and 1.0, indicating by how much the average electron concentration differs from the electron concentration at the emitter end. If we insert (3a) and (9) into (8), and neglect I_s, we obtain

$$\beta \cong \frac{1}{\gamma} \frac{v_{nb}\tau}{w_b}. \qquad (10)$$

This depends on the base doping only through the effect of the base doping on the lifetime. For heavy base doping levels the lifetimes may be short indeed.[2] Nevertheless, even for very short lifetimes, high β's should be achievable in transistors with a sufficiently thin base region, which is the case of dominant interest in any event. As an example, assume $w_b \cong 1000$ Å $= 10^{-5}$ cm. In such a transistor the electron velocity is likely to approach values close to bulk limited drift velocities $v_{nb} \cong 10^7$ cm $\cdot$ s^{-1}. Even for a lifetime as short as 10^{-9} s, this would lead to $\beta \cong 10^3$, a value that should satisfy even the most stringent demands. Evidently, no serious problems from reduced minority carrier lifetimes arise unless the latter drop to the vicinity of 10^{-10} s or lower, at least not for plausible base widths not exceeding 1000 Å.

Much of the remainder of this paper will deal with the tradeoffs made possible when high β-values can be obtained without a high emitter-to-base doping ratio. Before turning to these tradeoffs, it is instructive to return to (5) and to apply it to

[1] See, e.g., [7], [8], [9], [14], [18]. Even higher values have been found in some phototransistors. See [15] for further references.
[2] For GaAs, injection laser experience suggests lifetimes between 10^{-10} and 10^{-9} s for degenerate doping levels, slightly longer for nondegenerate doping.

energy gap variations in the conventional silicon transistor. The energy gap of Si, like that of the other semiconductors, is not strictly constant, but decreases slightly at the high doping levels that are desirable in the emitters of a homojunction transistor. As a result, a Si transistor is not strictly a uniform-gap transistor; it is itself a heterojunction transistor, but with a small yet highly undesirable *negative* value of $\Delta\epsilon_g$. The best available data, taken on actual transistor structures [28], indicate a gap shrinkage beginning at a doping level $N_d \sim 10^{17}$ cm^{-3}, and reducing the gap approximately logarithmically with doping level, reaching a gap shrinkage between 75 and 80 meV $(>3kT)$ at $N_d \sim 10^{19}$ cm^{-3}. According to (5), an emitter gap shrinkage of $3kT$ reduces the ratio I_n/I_p by a factor $e^{-3} \sim 1/20$. The overall effect at this doping level is the same as if the emitter were doped only to 5×10^{17} cm^{-3}, without gap shrinkage. To obtain β-values larger than the ratio v_{nb}/v_{pe} (<50), the base region must be even less heavily doped than this value, which is far below what is metallurgically possible, and far below what would be desirable in the interest of almost all other performance characteristics, especially base resistance. Increasing the emitter doping beyond 10^{19} cm^{-3} improves β only very slowly, roughly proportionally to $N_e^{0.33}$. By pushing everything to the limit, state-of-the-art microwave transistors with P_b-values (averaged over the base region) of about 1×10^{18} cm^{-3} have been achieved [29]. But this is still far below what would be desirable.

Evidently, the conventional Si bipolar transistor behaves far less well than the naive uniform-gap textbook model would predict. In fact, the energy gap shrinkage and its consequences represent one of the dominant performance limitations of the device.

B. Graded Versus Abrupt Emitter Junctions

In Fig. 3, and in the discussion accompanying it, we had assumed that the emitter/base junction is compositionally graded, so as to yield smoothly and monotonically varying band edges. Such graded transitions are easily achieved, but unless the appropriate measures are taken to do so, the modern epitaxial technologies tend to produce abrupt transistors in which band edge discontinuities are present. As a rule, the conduction band on the wider gap side lies energetically above that on the narrower gap side. Applied to the wide-gap emitter in a transistor, this leads to the "spike-and-notch" energy band diagram shown in Fig. 4(a). Because the emitter-to-base doping ratio in an HBT tends to be low, most of the electrostatic potential drop will occur on the less heavily doped emitter side, and the potential spike will project above the conduction band in the neutral portion of the base, leading to a potential barrier of net height $\Delta\epsilon_B$. Such a barrier has both advantages and disadvantages, and a brief discussion is in order.

Consider first the potential notch accompanying the barrier on the base side. Such a notch will collect injected electrons, and therefore enhance recombination losses, a highly undesirable effect. Because of the low emitter-to-base doping ratio expected in an HBT, the notch will be quite shallow, with a depth given approximately by

$$\Delta\epsilon_N = (P_e/N_b)\, q V_n \qquad (11)$$

which will typically be of the order 5 meV $\ll kT$. Nevertheless, because of the danger of interface recombination defects, it would be desirable to eliminate the notch altogether, and perhaps even replace it by a slightly repulsive potential, as

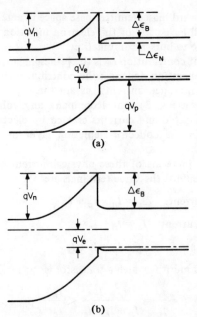

Fig. 4. Band structure of an abrupt wide-gap emitter, showing the spike barrier and the accompanying electron trapping notch in the conduction band structure. The notch can be removed (b) by the incorporation of a planar acceptor doping sheet into the heterojunction.

shown in Fig. 4(b). This is easily accomplished by incorporating a very thin sheet with a very high acceptor concentration right at the interface. Typical required sheet doping concentrations will be of the order 10^{11} acceptors per *square* centimeter. The feasibility of such "planar doping" sheets has been demonstrated [30], at least with MBE, and there is little doubt that it can be accomplished by MOCVD as well.

As to the barrier itself, one minor drawback of its existence is the accompanying increase of the order $\Delta\epsilon_B/q$, in required emitter voltage to yield a given current density. More severe is the (related) drawback that the potential barrier $\Delta\epsilon_B$ drastically reduces the ratio J_n/J_p, from the value in (5), by a factor exp $(-\Delta\epsilon_B/kT)$. Instead of (4a), we now have

$$q(V_p - V_n) = \Delta\epsilon_g - \Delta\epsilon_B \cong \Delta\epsilon_V. \qquad (4b)$$

The last equality results if the notch depth is small compared to kT, in which case $\Delta\epsilon_B = \Delta\epsilon_C$. Here $\Delta\epsilon_C$ and $\Delta\epsilon_V$ represent the conduction and valence band discontinuities. Instead of (5a), we obtain

$$\frac{I_n}{I_p} = \beta_{max} = \frac{N_e}{P_b}\frac{v_{nb}}{v_{pe}} \exp\left(\Delta\epsilon_V/kT\right). \qquad (5b)$$

If the valence band discontinuity is sufficiently large, a major improvement remains. Unfortunately, in the system of largest current interest, the (Al,Ga)As/GaAs system, the valence band discontinuity is quite small, $\Delta\epsilon_V = 0.15\, \Delta\epsilon_g$ [31], and the reduction of the spike by grading is probably essential. A detailed discussion of the detrimental effects of the spike is found in a paper by Marty et al. [10].

The above drawbacks of the extra potential barrier accompanying an abrupt emitter/base junction are partially compensated by the fact that such a barrier would inject the electrons into the base region with a substantial kinetic energy, and hence with a very high velocity $(\sim 10^8$ cm/s). Because of the directional dependence of the polar optical phonon scattering that is the dominant scattering process in III/V-compounds, several collisions are required before the electrons have lost their high forward velocity. The result should be a highly efficient and very fast near-ballistic electron transport through the base. Such ballistic transport effects have been of great interest recently, and although their discussion has been largely in an FET context [32], [33], much of this discussion applies as well (or even more) to bipolar transistors with an emitter junction barrier that represents, in effect, a ballistic launching ramp.

Exactly what the balance between drawbacks and benefits will be for the abrupt emitter/base junction versus the graded one, remains to be seen. But it appears likely that ballistic effects will find their way into future transistors specifically designed around them.

An extreme case of high-energy electron injection into the base was discussed some time ago by Kroemer [34], in the form of a so-called *Auger transistor*. If the conduction band discontinuity $\Delta\epsilon_C$ becomes larger than the energy gap in the base, the electron injection may lead to Auger multiplication of electrons, and hence to a transistor with true current amplification in a grounded-base configuration $\alpha > 1$. Such a transistor might be of interest for power switching applications at very high microwave speeds. It remains to be seen what will come of this idea.

V. Speed Tradeoffs

A. The Emitter Capacitance Tradeoff

High beta-values above, say, 100 are of limited interest by themselves, except perhaps in phototransistors. The principal benefit of a wide-gap emitter is therefore not the ability to achieve high β-values, but the freedom to change doping levels in emitter and base without significant constraints by injection efficiency consideration, and thereby to re-optimize the transistor at a higher performance level.

We start our discussion with the choice of emitter doping. A wide-gap emitter permits a drop in emitter doping by several orders of magnitude without a deterioration of β, a prediction [1] that has been confirmed experimentally in almost all HBT's built. Now it is well known that the junction capacitance of a highly unsymmetrically doped p-n junction depends only on the doping level of the less heavily doped side. Suppose the base doping is initially kept fixed. If the emitter doping is now dropped below the base doping, the emitter capacitance of the transistor then depends principally on the emitter doping and drops with a decrease of the latter, roughly as

$$C_e \propto N_e^{1/2}. \tag{12}$$

Evidently, by dropping the emitter doping sufficiently far below the (initial) base doping a large reduction in emitter capacitance can be obtained [1], and this reduction remains if the base doping is subsequently increased. The result is an improvement in speed, but this effect is usually small, because the emitter capacitance is only one of several capacitances. The true significance of the reduction of the capacitance per unit area lies in two different facts. First, it permits an increase in the capacitive emitter area in the inverted transistor design discussed later, without increase in total emitter capacitance. Second, in HBT's for small-signal microwave amplification, a reduction in emitter capacitance will reduce the noise significantly [35].

Obviously, the doping in the emitter cannot be lowered arbitrarily far. Even if achievable crystal purities permitted it, the emitter series resistance would eventually become excessive, at least for a thick emitter body. However, under the technological scenario envisaged earlier, the weakly doped part of the emitter can always be kept very thin (say, a few-times 10^{-5} cm) to permit a drop in emitter capacitance per unit area by at least a factor 10 before emitter series resistance effects become serious.

A minor advantage of reduced emitter doping, mentioned by Milnes and Feucht [3], might be that the resulting emitters would have a significant reverse breakdown voltage. It is not clear how much of an advantage this would be.

B. The Base Resistance Tradeoff: Microwave Transistors

The most important single change made possible by a wide-gap emitter is a drastic increase in base doping, limited only by technological constraints and by the need to keep the minority lifetime in the base significantly above 10^{-10} s. The principal benefit is a major reduction in base resistance, which, in turn, increases the speed significantly [2]. A second benefit is a major improvement in overall transistor performance at high current densities [1], [3]-[5], including specifically an improvement in the speed-versus-power tradeoffs of microwave transistors.

Because we are principally interested in low-power speed aspects, we concentrate here on the effect of base resistance reduction. This effect is somewhat different in microwave transistors and in switching transistors.

For microwave transistors, Ladd and Feucht [2] have given a very detailed analysis, using the maximum oscillation frequency f_{max} as the figure of merit. It may be written in the form

$$f_{max} = \frac{1}{2}(f_t f_c)^{1/2} \tag{13}$$

where f_t has its familiar meaning as the frequency at which the current gain is reduced to unity, and f_c is the frequency equivalent of the RC time constant of the combination base resistance–collector capacitance,

$$f_c = 1/(2\pi R_b C_c). \tag{14}$$

Evidently, a reduction in R_b causes an increase in f_c and with it a smaller increase in f_{max}.

Ladd and Feucht's work was done in the late 60's and they give numerical values only for the "best" system known at the time, a GaAs emitter on a Ge base, of a construction previously demonstrated by Jadus and Feucht [36]. Because of severe limitations inherent in the then-available technology, the *external* base resistance (between the emitter edge and the base contact) could not be significantly decreased, and as a result, Ladd and Feucht concluded that only a negligible improvement in frequency could be achieved with the then-existing technology. If, however, the external base resistance problem could be solved, maximum oscillation frequencies f_{max} around 100 GHz would be achievable. Similarly high values can be predicted for other heterosystems such as (Al,Ga)As-on-GaAs or GaP-on-Si [37], [38]. There is little point in quoting more exact values, becaue the predictions depend noticeably on both technological and operating parameters whose choice would be applications-dependent. To pursue these matters in detail would lead us too far away from our principal interest in digital switching transistors.

C. The Base Resistance Tradeoff: Digital Switching Transistors

The quantity of interest in digital switching transistors is not the maximum frequency of oscillation but the (somewhat vaguely defined) switching time. Although one would expect that any structural measures that improve the maximum oscillation frequency will also improve the switching speed, there is no simple one-to-one relationship between the two. The modes of operation are just too different. For example, in microwave transistors a high output power is usually of interest, while in highly integrated digital switching transistors the opposite is the case.

A comparison is further complicated by the fact that switching time depends on the circuit, and no standard measure for switching time, comparable to the frequencies f_t and f_{max} for oscillatory operation, has been agreed upon. Probably the best measure of switching time applicable to HBT's is the estimate by Dumke, Woodall, and Rideout (DWR) [5], who estimate the switching time as

$$\tau_s = \frac{5}{2} R_b C_c + \frac{R_b}{R_L} \tau_b + (3C_c + C_L) R_L. \qquad (15)$$

Here R_b is the base resistance, C_c the collector capacitance, and τ_b the base transit time, while R_L and C_L are load resistance and capacitance of the circuit. The result (15) is based on Ashar's analysis [39] of a two-transistor circuit, modified by Dumke. Dumke's modification simply consists of the following [40]. The load resistance must be large enough to develop a potential change equal to the necessary emitter swing ΔV on the next stage. Therefore, $R_L = \Delta V/I = R_E$, where I is the current that is switched to. Making the appropriate substitutions in Ashar's expression yields (15). Dumke *et al.* apply (15) to estimate the switching time of a hypothetical (Al,Ga) As-on-GaAs transistor with the following parameters. Base width: 1200 Å; base doping: 3×10^{18} cm^{-3}; base and emitter stripe widths: 2.5 μm, separated by 0.5-μm gaps; collector doping: 3×10^{16} cm^{-3}; load resistance: 50 Ω; load capacitance: negligible compared to collector capacitance. These values lead to the following values for the three terms in (15): 8.3 ps, 1.4 ps, and 8.3 ps, combining into an overall switching time of ~18 ps. The authors state that this is "roughly a factor of 5 or 8 faster than that which might be realized from the current post alloy diffused Ge or double diffused Si technologies respectively." Today, nearly 10 years later, post-alloy diffused Ge technology is all but forgotten (it never made it into IC's), and much of the then-predicted advantage over Si remains.

Just as in the case of Ladd and Feucht's estimate of f_{max}, much of the improvement is due to the reduction in base resistance that is associated with the high base doping possible in an HBT. In fact, two of the three terms in (15) depend linearly on R_b rather than with the square root as does f_{max}. This means that as long as those terms dominate τ_s, a reduction of R_b is even more effective in a digital switching transistor than in a microwave transistor. Only after the base resistance reduction has been carried so far that the $R_L C_L$ term dominates, does a further reduction in R_b lead to no further benefit. The hypothetical device analyzed by DWR lies at the borderline between the two regimes.

The specific numerical values quoted above should be viewed as approximations. To obtain an expression as simple as (15), Ashar and Dumke had to make numerous simplifications, just as the expression (13) for f_{max} is based on gross simplifications. The importance of the Ashar–Dumke result (15) is that it indicates the relative significance of the most important transistor parameters. A more detailed analysis is certainly needed, in particular, one that investigates the extent to which the various approximations made in deriving (15) remain applicable in HBT's that have been drastically modified from conventional design.

The assumption of different structural transistor parameters would, of course, have led to different values of τ_s. But the values assumed by DWR were quite reasonable in 1972; they are easily within the range of today's technology, and hence conservative. Further reductions in τ_s to below 10 ps appear readily achievable.

One possibility for improvement is to strive for a lower load resistance than the ad hoc value of 50 Ω assumed by DWR. One sees readily from (15) that the switching time goes through a minimum for

$$R_L = [R_b \tau_b/(3C_c + C_L)]^{1/2} \qquad (16)$$

for which (15) reduces the

$$\tau_s = \frac{5}{2} R_b C_c + 2[(3C_c + C_L) R_b \tau_b]^{1/2}. \qquad (17)$$

For the structural values assumed in DWR one would need $R_L \cong 21$ Ω, which would yield $\tau_s \cong 15$ ps. The improvement is not large, and the low load resistance might not be easy to achieve [40]. A much larger improvement would result from a reduction of the collector capacitance, obtained by inverting the transistor. This possibility will be discussed later.

D. The External Base Resistance Problem

In their detailed analysis of the (microwave) performance potential of HBT's, Ladd and Feucht go to great lengths to discuss the special problem posed by the highly detrimental external portion of the base resistance. Because their considerations also apply to digital switching transistors, and because they appear not to have been fully appreciated by subsequent workers on heterostructure bipolar transistors [41], it appears proper to re-emphasize the problem raised by Ladd and Feucht here, and to offer a remedy.

In all real transistors only part of the base resistance lies underneath the emitter, part lies between the edge of the emitter and the base contact. Usually, the outer region of the base is appreciably thicker than the inner region, and the near-surface portion of the outer base is more heavily doped than the remainder (Fig. 5(a)). This design minimizes the outer base resistance. If one wishes to obtain the postulated advantages of a wide-gap emitter, it is essential that the outer base resistance is not permitted to dominate the overall base resistance. This is easier said than done. For example, suppose that technological changes associated with the change from a (diffused or implanted) homojunction emitter to a heterojunction emitter, forced a change in geometry from that in Fig. 5(a) to that in Fig. 5(b) with a thin outer base. This is in fact the geometry used in the HBT's reported in the literature, except for the transistors reported by Ankri *et al.* [11], [14] and by Katz *et al.* [23]. Even though the doping level in the

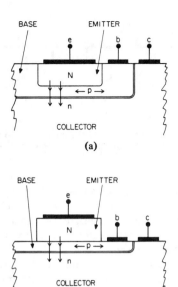

(a)

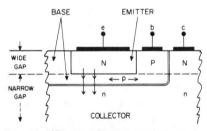

(b)

Fig. 5. In homojunction transistors of current technology (a), the base region is usually much thicker and more heavily doped outside the emitter than between the emitter and collector, reducing the external base resistance. This desirable feature would be lost in heterostructure transistors with the emitter island design shown in (b). To appreciate this point fully, recall that in actual structures the horizontal dimensions greatly exceed the vertical ones. In this drawing (and in Fig. 6) the vertical dimensions have been greatly exaggerated relative to the horizontal ones.

Fig. 6. Desirable emitter structure in which the p-n junction does not follow the planar hetero-interface, but is pulled up towards the surface.

outer base may have been increased, the beneficial effect of this change would be at least partially compensated by the reduction in thickness of the outer base. In unfavorable cases the outer base resistance might even have increased. Ladd and Feucht fully recognized the importance of this problem. They wrote "... *it is clear that the advantages of the low base resistance of the heterojunction devices will only be exploited if suitable geometries can be developed.*"

It is now important to realize that the wide-gap emitter configuration contains a built-in design possibility to keep the outer base resistance low [37], [38], [41], [42]. The design is shown in Fig. 6. Rather than constructing the wide-gap emitter as an island riding by itself on the top of a uniformly thin narrow-gap base layer, the wide-gap semiconductor may be extended beyond the emitter edge, forming part of the outer base region, with the emitter-base p-n junction pulled away from the heteroboundary and towards the surface. Such a configuration should be easily achievable by first growing the top wide-gap layer with the same relatively low n-type doping as the emitter, and then converting the region outside the emitter to heavy p-type doping by diffusion or ion implantation.

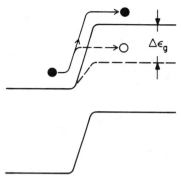

Fig. 7. Blocking of injection of electrons into the wide-gap portion of the base region in Fig. 6, due to the extra repulsive force generated by the wider energy gap.

In such a design the portion of the emitter that lies within the wide-gap region carries only a negligible current, compared to the wide–narrow portion. The reason for this is illustrated in Fig. 7. For injection into the wide-gap p-region, the electrons would have to climb a barrier that is higher by the energy gap difference $\Delta\epsilon_g$. But this reduces the injection current density by the same factor $\exp(-\Delta\epsilon_g/kT)$ that also reduces the hole injection into the wide-gap emitter.

This possibility does not appear to have been as widely recognized as it deserves; it *has* been used in the devices reported by Ankri *et al.* [11], [14], and by Katz *et al.* [23]. In both cases diffusion was used to convert the wide-gap portion of the base region to p-type.

VI. THE "INVERTED" TRANSISTOR

Since the first days of the alloy transistor, bipolar transistors have been built with a larger collector than emitter area, in the interest of efficient charge collection. In planar technology, the two junctions are necessarily of different area. The need for efficient charge collection then enforces the familiar configuration with the collector at the bottom and the emitter at the top. The exception to this rule is, of course, integrated injection logic (I^2L), where other considerations override this rule—at a price. I will say more about I^2L below. But apart from the I^2L exception, the "emitter-up rule" is so pervasive that it has become hard to imagine that a useful transistor could be built with the inverse order.

Now we have just seen that with a wide-gap emitter the emitter junction can be designed in such a way that part of the emitter-base junction does not inject carriers. Evidently, with such a design the need for efficient carrier collection can be met even with an emitter larger than the collector, IF those portions of the emitter-base junction that are not immediately opposite to a part of the collector-base junction are inactivated by pulling them onto the high-gap side of the hetero-interface. Once this is done, the transistor might just as well be "flipped," with the emitter on the substrate side and the collector on top, as shown in Fig. 8. The inverted configuration has several advantages, to the point that it might very well turn out the "canonical" configuration of future heterostructure bipolar transistor design [43].

The principal (but not the only) advantage of the inverted transistor is that it permits the use of a significantly smaller collector area, with an appropriately smaller collector capacitance. The consequences for the high-speed performance are obvious. Modern high speed transistors, both digital and (inter-

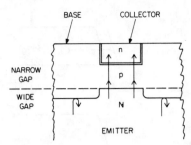

Fig. 8. Inverted "collector-up" transistor structure in which the emitter has a larger area than the collector, but the external portions of the emitter do not contribute to the injection, because there the p-n junction has been pulled into the wide-gap portion of the structure.

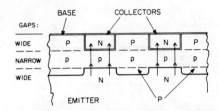

Fig. 9. A DH implementation of I^2L, combining wide-gap collectors with noninjecting emitter regions between the collectors.

digitated) microwave transistors, typically have a collector area close to three-times the active (emitter) area. Inverting the structure thus permits a reduction of the collector capacitance by close to a factor of 3. For example, in the hypothetical switching transistor analyzed by Dumke *et al.*[5], the collector area was 3.4-times the emitter area. If, in that device, one reduces the collector area by a factor $\frac{1}{3}$ and leaves all other quantities unchanged, the two dominant terms in (15) are reduced by the same factor, and the switching time is reduced from ~ 18 ps to ~ 7 ps. Similar improvements would occur in micowave power transistors.

However, some care is in order: Because now the total emitter area is larger than the active area, the emitter junction capacitance will increase, at least compared to a heterostructure transistor of conventional emitter-up configuration. But, as we saw earlier, the emitter junction capacitance per unit area of a heterojunction transistor can in any event be made significantly less than for a homojunction transistor. Hence, compared to the latter, a net reduction in emitter capacitance may result even in the face of a larger (inactive) emitter area.

A second advantage of the inverted configuration is the possibility of a major reduction of the large lead inductance in series with the emitter that is present in the conventional emitter-up configuration. Again an improvement in high-frequency properties will result.

A third advantage of an inverted transistor configuration, for digital switching transistors, will emerge later.

Technologically, the inverted structure should be achievable in essentially the same way as the pulled-up emitter junction: By first growing the top layer lightly n-type doped throughout, and then converting the region outside the collector to heavy p-doping by diffusion or ion implantation. Obviously, the collector layer must be chosen thick enough to support the intended collector bias voltage. Converting part of the surface inside the collector region to n^+ might be desirable.

VII. DH TRANSISTORS

A. Introduction: The Wide-Gap Collector

A reading of Shockley's patent quoted at the beginning of this paper leaves no doubt that the "*one. . . zone . . . having a wider energy gap than. . . the other zones*" is the emitter of the transistor. The question was soon raised whether there might also be advantages to a wide-gap collector [1]; but only the trivial and insignificant advantage of a reduction in the reverse-biased collector saturation was recognized.

This assessment must be revised in the light of the anticipated technological scenario discussed in Section III of this paper,

and particularly in the light of the increased interest in highly integrated digital switching transistors. It appears that there are in fact several excellent reasons urging a wide-gap collector design, to the point that DH transistors with a wide-gap collector might very well be the rule rather than the exception for future bipolar transistor designs.

I give in this Section three examples that illustrate advantages to be gained by such a design. They fall into three groups:

a) Suppression of hole injection from base into collector in digital switching transistors under conditions of saturation;
b) Emitter/collector interchangeability in IC's;
c) Separate optimization of base and collector, especially in microwave power transistors.

The presentation does not attempt to give a complete and systematic critical evaluation of all aspects of DH transistor design. Its purpose is to initiate a discussion, not to end it.

B. Suppression of Hole Injection into the Collector under Saturated Conditions

In many digital logic families the collectors of the transistors are forward-biased during part of the logic cycle. If the base region is more heavily doped than the collector, as would normally be desirable, a copious injection of holes from the base into the collector takes place, which increases dissipation and slows down the switching speed. In a heterostructure technology, this highly deleterious phenomenon is easily suppressed the same way hole injection into the emitter is suppressed: By making the collector a wide-gap collector [38]. Such a design is an attractive alternative to the Schottky clamp in Schottky-TTL. Just as the wide-gap emitter, the wide-gap collector should be fairly lightly doped, in the interest of a low collector capacitance, and the base should remain heavily doped, in the interest of low base resistance. This choice of relative doping levels remains both possible and desirable in the inverted I^2L configuration, rather than calling for a weakly doped base to suppress collector injection, with its high base resistance penalty. In fact, in a recent paper [42], Kroemer has proposed a DH implementation of I^2L, which combines this idea with the idea of a selectively injecting emitter, discussed earlier. The structure is shown in Fig. 9. It avoids both the electron injection into those portions of the base where such injection is undesirable because of the absence of a collector opposite to the emitter, and the injection of holes into either collector or emitter. Even electrons spilling over at the edge of the active portion of the base region would not be able to penetrate into the upper part of the inactive portion of the base, because they would be repelled by the heterobarrier in the conduction band at the p–P interface. Because of the essentially complete suppression of parasitic charge storage, combined with greatly reduced *RC*-time constant effects due to the reduced base resistance, such an implementation of I^2L can be expected to have a much higher speed than the notoriously

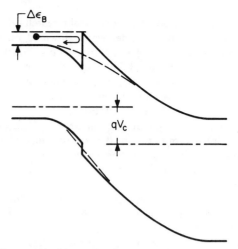

Fig. 10. Electron blocking action for low reverse bias at an abrupt p-n heterojunction collector. The blocking action can be prevented by grading the heterojunction, as indicated by the broken line.

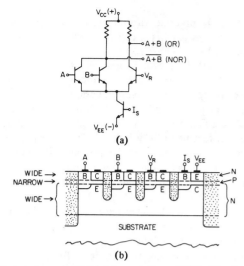

Fig. 11. Input stage of a DH implementation of ECL. The four transistors shown are implemented by three inverted and one noninverted transistor of identical structure, differing only in biasing. The dotted regions are isolation regions, prepared by proton bombardment or equivalent techniques.

slow homostructure implementations of I^2L, without increasing the highly desirable low dissipation levels of I^2L. Unfortunately, no quantitative estimates of the expected performance improvement have so far been published, but the possible improvements appear to be large.[3]

The referenced paper [42] also shows that the pnp horizontal transistor that serves as a current source in I^2L is easily incorporated into a DH design. It emerges as a rather peculiar structure that is basically a homostructure transistor with heterostructure sidewalls, which confine the current and improve the performance of the device.

There is one important restriction in the use of wide-gap collectors, which must not be overlooked. It is important that the free collection of electrons by the reverse-biased collector not be impeded by any heterobarrier due to a conduction band discontinuity (Fig. 10). Such barriers are easily eliminated by grading the heterostructure [44], [45].

C. Emitter/Collector Interchangeability

The advantages of a DH design for bipolar transistors are not restricted to the suppression of hole injection into the collector in saturating logic. A different advantage lies in the possibility of designing transistors in which the role of emitter and collector can be interchanged by simply changing the biasing conditions, while retaining the advantages of a wide-gap emitter regardless of which of the two terminal n-regions is used as the emitter. To achieve this freedom, the transistor need not be geometrically symmetrical: In the inverted structure shown earlier in Fig. 8, in which the active portion of the lower p-n junction covered the same area as the upper p-n junction; either the upper junction or the lower junction could be used as the emitter. While this might be no more than a mildly esoteric advantage in a discrete transistor, it offers a major new option in the architecture of digital IC's, be they of the saturating or nonsaturating variety: The DH design makes it possible, within a common three-layer n-p-n epitaxial layer structure, to integrate high-performance wide-gap emitter transistors having the conventional emitter-up configuration, with similar transistors

---

[3] I have been informed by an anonymous reviewer that K. T. Alavi, in an unpublished M.S. thesis (M.I.T., 1980) has estimated that "over a 10-fold improvement in speed–power product can be anticipated." I did not have access to this work.

having the I^2L-like inverted emitter-down configuration discussed previously.

The full power of this new option can probably not be appreciated without an example. The input stage of emitter-coupled logic (ECL), a nonsaturating logic family, serves admirably. Fig. 11(a) gives the basic circuit diagram of the parts of interest here. The top three transistors serve as a differential switch that compares the voltage levels of two logic signals A and B with a reference voltage V_R. The bottom transistor serves essentially as a constant-current source. (In some simpler versions of ECL it is replaced by a resistor.)

Evidently, the configuration calls for tying together the emitters of three transistors with the collector of a fourth. In a DH design, this integration is achieved easily, without sacrificing a high transistor performance, by implementing the top three transistors as inverted transistors, and the current supply transistor as a conventional emitter-up transistor, as shown in Fig. 11(b). The emitters of the three top transistors and the collector of the bottom transistor come together in a buried n-layer on top of the substrate. All four transistors are structurally identical; they differ merely in their biasing. Those readers who are familiar with ECL and its notorious integration difficulties will undoubtedly recognize the great integration advantages offered by what I would like to call HECL, for Heterostructure ECL.

A complete discussion of various other heterostructure modifications of ECL is intended for another place; the purpose of the present discussion was merely to demonstrate the central idea of the interchangeability of emitter and collector in a DH IC design.

D. Separate Optimization of Base and Collector

Except for the interrelated needs of a high mobility and a high saturated drift velocity for the electrons, the semiconductor properties desired for the base of a transistor are quite different from those for the collector and for the base/collector depletion layer. This is especially true in microwave power transistors. Evidently the different needs of base and collector regions can, at least in principle, be optimized best by selecting different materials in the two regions, that is, by a heterostructure collector. In practice, this tends to mean a semiconductor with a wider energy gap in the collector and in the base/collector layer, compared to the base region.

Again, an example is called for to illustrate this idea. Consider the question as to the semiconductor combination offering the highest speed in a room-temperature microwave power transistor. One can argue that the fastest possible such transistor would be a GaAs-Ge-GaAs transistor [46] —IF such a transistor could in fact be built, which is by no means certain.

The reason for the choice of Ge as the ideal semiconductor for the base region is its high hole mobility, unexcelled by any other group-IV or III/V-compound semiconductor. Also, Ge is easily doped very heavily p-type. Taken together, the two properties assure a much lower base resistance than any other known useable semiconductor.

Admittedly, Ge has a lower electron mobility than several III/V compounds one might consider. But in a microwave power transistor with its necessarily fairly thick collector depletion layer (in the interest of a high breakdown voltage and a low collector capacitance) the transit time through the base is only a minor speed limitation compared to that through the collector depletion layer. Hence the beneficial effects of the high hole mobility in a Ge base layer are much larger than the detrimental effects of the lower electron mobility compared to, say, GaAs. On the other hand, Ge is hardly a desirable semiconductor for the collector and the base/collector depletion layer: Apart from a somewhat low saturated electron drift velocity ($v_s \cong 5 \times 10^6$ cm/s) and a high dielectric constant ($\epsilon \cong 16$), its low energy gap would lead to a low breakdown field and high thermally generated currents. Here a wider gap semiconductor is needed. Lattice-matching considerations suggest GaAs, which would be near-ideal in any event. One might be inclined to argue that the narrow gap of Ge also rules Ge out as a base region material of acceptably low thermal current generation rate. However, this is not the case: In a practical GaAs-Ge-GaAs transistor the Ge base region would be so thin and so heavily p-type doped that the thermal generation of electrons in the base would not contribute an unacceptably high collector saturating current.

Unfortunately, it is not at all clear whether or not GaAs-Ge-GaAs transistors with an acceptably low density of interface defects can be grown. Our own work at UCSB with the MBE growth of GaAs on Ge, and GaP on Si, has shown that the defect-free growth of a polar semiconductor such as GaAs on a nonpolar substrate such as Ge faces a number of quite fundamental difficulties, which have so far not been surmounted, and which may, in fact, be insurmountable [47].

However, none of the experimental uncertainties affect the principal point of our discussion here: The desirability of different semiconductors for base and collector, implying a heterostructure collector, is likely to be the rule rather than the exception in the technology of the future.

VIII. Some Speculations About the Future of Compound Semiconductor Devices

A. Bipolar Transistors versus FET's

If one ignores injection lasers and other optoelectronic devices, today's compound semiconductor device world is a pure FET world with essentially no bipolar inhabitants. A paper that predicts what amounts to a bipolar revolution in this FET world cannot simply ignore FET's. This is true even more once one realizes that the same technologies that promise to revolutionize bipolar transistors will also improve FET's

[48]. In fact, very active and successful research into heterostructure FET's is already under way. However, on balance, heterostructures can be expected to benefit bipolar devices much more than they benefit FET's, and if so, this will naturally tend to shift the balance between the devices much more towards bipolars than past developments might suggest. There are several reasons for these expectations:

a) As was pointed out already in Section II, the Central Design Principle permits one to control the flow of electrons and holes separately and independently of each other. This makes heterostructures a very major advantage in bipolar devices (including lasers) in which there are in fact both kinds of carriers present. It does little for an FET, although a related benefit is obtained in FET's through the concept of modulation doping [49].

b) Every device has a dimension in the direction of current flow that controls the speed of the device. In FET's (other than VMOS) the current flow is parallel to the surface, and the critical control dimension is established by fine-line lithography. In a bipolar transistor, the speed-determining part of the current path is perpendicular to the surface (and to the epilayers), and to the first order, speed is governed by the layer thicknesses. Because vertical layer thicknesses can be easily made much smaller than horizontal lithography dimensions, there is, for given horizontal dimensions, an inherently higher speed potential in bipolar structures than in FET's. The two qualifiers "to the first order" and "for given horizontal dimensions" are important, though: Small horizontal dimensions are still needed to minimize speed-limiting *second-order* effects caused by horizontal resistive voltage drops in the thin base layers. These second-order effects are actually reduced in HBT's, due to the much higher base doping levels, and they are not as severe as the first-order limiting effects of the horizontal dimensions in FET's. But in any event, there is nothing in bipolar technologies that would require or even suggest the use of larger horizontal dimensions than in FET's. The same fine-line lithography technologies that are used for FET's, can and will be used for bipolar devices. The capability offered by the new epitaxial technologies is an *additional* capability, not an alternate.

c) Once sufficiently small dimensions have been achieved, "ballistic" effects become important [32], [33], and they are in fact extensively studied, so far predominantly in an FET context. On the whole, ballistic effects improve device performance by minimizing electron scattering. To obtain this benefit, two conditions must be satisfied. First, the electrons must be accelerated very quickly [32]. The most effective way to do this is by launching the electrons with a high kinetic energy from the conduction band discontinuity in a heterostructure, as discussed earlier. This is much more effective than acceleration by an ordinary nonuniform electric field, the rate of nonuniformity of which is limited by Debye-length considerations. Second, the path along which ballistic effects are to be utilized, must be short, at most a few thousand Angstrom units long. Evidently, both the abrupt launching and the short current paths call for a current flow perpendicular to the epitaxial layers rather than parallel to them, once again favoring the geometry of bipolar designs.

d) All digital switching transistors have a critical bias voltage (often called turn-on voltage), in the vicinity of which the switching action takes place. For high-performance digital IC's, especially VLSI circuits, it is important that this critical voltage be as reproducible as possible, not only across the chip in a single VLSI circuit, but also from wafer to wafer. This reproducibility is easier to achieve in bipolar transistors than in FET's. In bipolar transistors the turn-on voltage is almost fixed for a fixed energy gap of the semiconductor in the base region. It depends logarithmically on the base doping and, apart from temperature, on hardly anything else. Hence it is easy to keep stable. One might say with little exaggeration that it is close to being a natural constant. The turn-on voltage in an FET is, by contrast, purely "man-made," depending at least linearly on both the electron concentration in the channel and the channel thicknesses. To achieve reproducible turn-on voltages, at least two separate quantities must be controlled tightly. Considering that processing differences tend to be very important in IC technology, this particular difference between bipolars and FET's might well turn out to be as important as the more fundamental differences, strongly favoring bipolars [50].

The above arguments suggest strongly that bipolar devices will play a much larger role in the future that they have in the past, eventually assuming a leading role ahead of FET's. Exactly where the border between the two technologies will be, is something too hazardous to predict.

B. A Change in Technological Philosophy?

We have witnessed, since about 1964, a steady growth in III/V-compound semiconductor devices, principally GaAs devices. The driving force behind this development has been the high performance of such devices, not attainable with mainstream Si devices. If we ignore once again lasers and other optoelectronic devices, and restrict ourselves to purely electronic amplifying and switching devices, high performance has been largely synonymous with high speed, made possible by the high electron mobility of GaAs, and by the availability of semi-insulating GaAs as a substrate. However, not even the most ardent advocate of GaAs ever claimed that GaAs was used because it had an attractive technology. We used GaAs despite its technology, not because of it, and the threat was never far away that Si devices, with their much simpler and more highly developed technology, would catch up with GaAs performance, the fundamental advantages of GaAs notwithstanding.

It is exactly this imbalance between fundamental promise and technological weakness that is being removed by the new epitaxial technologies. If the technological scenario postulated in Section III of this paper is even remotely correct, it means nothing less but that the great future strength of III/V-compounds lies precisely in their new technology, which permits an unprecedented complexity and diversity in epitaxial structures, going far beyond anything available in Si technology! This new technological strength is thus emerging as more important than the older fundamental strengths of high mobilities and semi-insulating substrates. It is a remarkable reversal of priorities indeed.

None of this means even remotely that III/V compounds will replace Si. They will not do so any more than aluminum, magnesium, and titanium replaced steel. The analogy of Si to steel is due to M. Lepselter, who called Si technology "the new steel" [51], to bring out the similarity in the role of Si in the new industrial revolution of our own days, to the role of steel in the industrial revolution of the early-19th century. I would like to carry this excellent analogy a bit further. Just as the *structural* metallurgy of the 19th century found it necessary eventually to go beyond steel, to aluminum, magnesium, titanium, and others taking their place beside steel, so the *electronic* metallurgy of our own age is going beyond Si, to the III/V-compounds and probably further, to take their own place beside Si.

We continue to build locomotives, ships, and automobiles from steel, but if it is airplanes and spacecraft we want, we need the other metals besides. And, of course, it took us a while to go from locomotives to spacecraft. The analogy to semiconductors is too obvious to require elaboration; only the time scale will be compressed.

All along the way from steel to titanium there were those who argued that the next step, while perhaps possible, was one for which no foreseeable need existed: All foreseeable needs of man could presumably be met by improvements of the technologies already in hand. Well, this too has not changed.

ACKNOWLEDGMENT

The work of this paper has greatly benefited from uncounted discussions, over several years, with numerous individuals. Foremost amongst them were R. C. Eden, D. G. Chen, and S. I. Long, all (at the time) at the Rockwell Electronics Research Center. Others at Rockwell to whom I am indebted for discussions are J. S. Harris, R. Zucca, D. L. Miller, and P. Asbeck. I am grateful to W. P. Dumke (IBM) for a copy of his unpublished work on the switching time of bipolar transistors, which clarified many questions I had about that difficult problem. The final version of the paper benefitted from intense discussions with Prof. H. Beneking (Aachen) and from comments made by two anonymous reviewers.

REFERENCES

[1] H. Kroemer, "Theory of a wide-gap emitter for transistors," *Proc. IRE*, vol. 45, no. 11, pp. 1535–1537, Nov. 1957.
[2] G. O. Ladd and D. L. Feucht, "Performance potential of high-frequency heterojunction transistors," *IEEE Trans. Electron Devices*, vol. 17, pp. 413–420, May 1970.
[3] For a review see A. G. Milnes and D. L. Feucht, *Heterojunctions and Metal-Semiconductor Junctions.* New York: Academic, 1972. (See especially ch. 3.)
[4] For additional references see B. L. Sharma and R. K. Purohit, *Semiconductor Heterojunctions.* Elmsford, NY: Pergamon, 1974. (See especially sect. 7.6.)
[5] W. P. Dumke, J. M. Woodall, and V. L. Rideout, "GaAs-GaAlAs heterojunction transistor for high frequency operation," *Solid-State Electron.*, vol. 15, no. 12, pp. 1339–1334, Dec. 1972.
[6] a) M. Konagai and K. Takahashi, "Formation of GaAs-(GaAl)As heterojunction transistors by liquid phase epitaxy," *Elect. Eng. Japan*, vol. 94, no. 4, 1974;
b) ——, "(GaAl)As-GaAs heterojunction transistors with high injection efficiency," *J. Appl. Phys.*, vol. 46, no. 5, pp. 2120–2124, May 1975.
[7] B. W. Clark, H. G. B. Hicks, I. G. A. Davies, and J. S. Heeks, "A (GaAl)As-GaAs heterojunction structure for studying the role of cathode contacts on transferred electron devices," *Gallium Arsenide and Related Compounds 1974* (Deauville), Inst. Phys. Conf. Ser., vol. 24, 1975, pp. 373–375.
[8] M. Konagai, K. Katsukawa, and K. Takahashi, "(GaAl)As/GaAs heterojunction phototransistors with high current gain," *J. Appl. Phys.*, vol. 48, no. 10, pp. 4389–4394, Oct. 1977.
[9] P. W. Ross, H. G. B. Hicks, J. Froom, L. G. Davies, F. J. Probert, and J. E. Carroll, "Heterojunction transistors with enhanced gain," *Electron Eng.*, vol. 49, no. 589, pp. 36–38, Mar. 1977.
[10] A. Marty, G. Rey, and J. P. Bailbe, "Electrical behavior of an n-p-n GaAlAs/GaAs heterojunction transistor," *Solid-State Electron.*, vol. 22, no. 6, pp. 549–557, June 1979.
[11] D. Ankri and A. Scavennec, "Design and evaluation of a planar GaAlAs-GaAs bipolar transistor," *Electron. Lett.*, vol. 16, no. 1, pp. 41–47, Jan. 1980.
[12] J-P. Bailbe, A. Marty, P. H. Hiep, and G. E. Rey, "Design and fabrication of high-speed GaAlAs/GaAs heterojunction transistors," *IEEE Trans. Electron Devices*, vol. ED-27, pp. 1160–1164, June 1980.
[13] H. Beneking and L. M. Su, "GaAlAs/GaAs heterojunction microwave bipolar transistor," *Electron. Lett.*, vol. 17, no. 8, pp. 301–302, Apr. 1981.

[14] D. Ankri, A. Scavennec, C. Besombes, C. Courbet, F. Heliot, and J. Riou, "High frequency low current GaAlAs-GaAs bipolar transistor," presented at Dev. Res. Conf., Santa Barbara, June 1981, unpublished.

[15] For an up-to-date account, containing essentially complete earlier references, see three of the most recent papers on the subject:
a) M. Tobe, Y. Amemiya, S. Sakai, and M. Umeno, "High-sensitivity InGaAsP/InP phototransistors," *Appl. Phys. Lett.*, vol. 37, no. 1, pp. 73–75, July 1980;
b) M. N. Svilans, N. Grote, and H. Benking, "Sensitive GaAlAs/GaAs wide-gap emitter phototransistors for high current applications," *IEEE Electron Devices Lett.*, vol. ED-11, pp. 247–249, Dec. 1980;
c) J. C. Campbell, A. G. Dentai, C. A. Burrus, Jr., and J. F. Ferguson, "InP/InGaAs heterojunction phototransistors," *IEEE J. Quant. Electron.*, vol. QE-17, pp. 264–269, Feb. 1981.

[16] For two reviews see:
a) A. Y. Cho and J. R. Arthur, "Molecular beam epitaxy," *Prog. Solid State Chem.*, vol. 10, pt. 3, pp. 157–191, 1975;
b) K. Ploog, "Molecular beam epitaxy of III-V compounds," in *Crystals: Growth, Properties, and Applications*, H. C. Freyhardt, Ed. New York: Springer-Verlag, 1980, vol. 3, pp. 73–162.

[17] For a review with complete references to earlier work, see: R.D. Dupuis, L. A. Moudy, and P. D. Dapkus "Preparation and properties of Ga$_{1-x}$Al$_x$As-GaAs heterojunctions grown by metal-organic chemical vapor deposition," *Gallium Arsenide and Related Compounds 1978* (St. Louis), Inst. Phys. Conf. Ser., vol. 45, pp. 1–9, 1979.

[18] R. A. Milano, T. H. Windhorn, E. R. Anderson, G. E. Stillman, R. D. Dupuis, and P. D. Dapkus, "Al$_{0.5}$Ga$_{0.5}$As-GaAs heterojunction phototransistors grown by metalorganic chemical vapor deposition," *Appl. Phys. Lett.*, vol. 39, no. 9, pp. 562–564, May 1979.

[19] D. L. Miller, personal communication.

[20] a) T. Matsushita, N. Oh-uchi, H. Hayashi, and H. Yamoto, "A silicon heterojunction transistor," *Appl. Phys. Lett.*, vol. 35, no. 7, pp. 549–550, Oct. 1979;
b) N. Oh-uchi, H. Hayashi, H. Yamoto, and T. Matsushita, "A new silicon heterojunction transistor using the doped SIPOS," *IEDM Dig.*, pp. 522–524, Dec. 1979;
c) T. Matsushita, H. Hayashi, N. Oh-uchi, and H. Yamamoto, "A SIPOS-Si heterojunction transistor," *Japan. J. Appl. Phys.*, vol. 20, suppl. 20-1, pp. 75–81, Jan. 1981 (Proc. 12th Conf. Solid-State Devices, Tokyo, Aug. 1980).

[21] T. Katoda and M. Kishi, "Heteroepitaxial growth of gallium phosphide on silicon," *J. Electron Mat.*, vol. 9, no. 4, pp. 783–796, Apr. 1980.

[22] S. L. Wright and H. Kroemer, to be published.

[23] J. Katz, N. Bar-Chaim, P. C. Chen, S. Margalit, I. Ury, D. Wilt, M. Yust, and A. Yariv, "A monolithic integration of GaAs/GaAlAs bipolar transistor and heterostructure laser," *Appl. Phys. Lett.*, vol. 37, no. 2, pp. 211–213, July 1980.

[24] H. Beneking, N. Grote, and M. N. Svilans, "Monolithic GaAlAs/GaAs infrared-to-visible wavelength converter with optical power amplification," *IEEE Trans. Electron Devices*, vol. ED-28, pp. 404–407, Apr. 1981.

[25] H. Kroemer, "A proposed class of heterojunction injection lasers," *Proc. IEEE*, vol. 51, pp. 1782–1783, Dec. 1963.

[26] See, e.g., J. J. Coleman, P. D. Dapkus, N. Holonyak, Jr., and W. D. Laidig, "Device-quality epitaxial AlAs by metalorganic-chemical vapor deposition," *Appl. Phys. Lett.*, vol. 38, no. 11, pp. 894–896, June 1981. This paper quotes only structures containing about 80 layers; much larger numbers have been achieved in unpublished work (personal communication).

[27] For two recent reviews see:
a) L. L. Chang and L. Esaki, "Semiconductor superlattices by MBE and their characterization," *Prog. Cryst. Growth Charact.*, vol. 2, no. 1, pp. 3–12, 1979;
b) A. C. Gossard, "Molecular beam epitaxy of superlattices in thin films," in *Thin Films: Preparation and Properties*, K. N. Tu and R. Rosenberg, Eds. New York: Academic, to be published.

[28] J. S. Slotboom and H. C. de Graaf, "Measurement of bandgap narrowing in Si bipolar transistors," *Solid-State Electron.*, vol. 19, no. 10, pp. 857–862, Oct. 1976.

[29] See, e.g.,
a) J. A. Archer, "Design and performance of small-signal microwave transistors," *Solid-State Electron.*, vol. 15, no. 3, pp. 249–258, Mar. 1972.
b) J. M. Gladstone, P. T. Chen, P. Wang, and S. Kakihana, "Computer aided design and fabrication of an X-band oscillator transistor," Int. Electron Devices Meeting (IEDM) 1973, *IEDM Dig.*, pp. 384–386, Dec. 1973.
c) T. W. Sigmon, "Characteristics of high performance microwave transistors fabricated by ion implantation," Int. Electron Devices Meeting (IEDM) 1973, *IEDM Dig.*, pp. 387–389, Dec. 1973.

[30] C.E.C. Wood, G. Metze, J. Berry, and L. F. Eastman, "Complex free-carrier profile synthesis by atomic-plane doping of MBE GaAs," *J. Appl. Phys.*, vol. 51, no. 1, pp. 383–387, Jan. 1980.

[31] R. Dingle, "Confined carrier quantum states in ultrathin semiconductor heterostructures," *Festkörperprobleme/Advances in Solid State Physics*, vol. 15, pp. 21–48, 1975.

[32] For a review, see H. Kroemer, "Hot electron relaxation effects in devices," *Solid-State Electron.*, vol. 21, no. 1, pp. 61–67, Jan. 1978.

[33] M. S. Shur and L. F. Eastman, "Ballistic and near ballistic transport in GaAs," *IEEE Electron Devices Lett.*, vol. EDL-1, pp. 147–148, Aug. 1980.

[34] H. Kroemer, "Heterojunction device concepts," U.S. Air Force Tech. Rep. AFAL-TR-65-243, Oct. 1965, unpublished. A published description is found in Milnes and Feucht [3], pp. 28–29.

[35] R. E. Yeats, personal communications.

[36] D. K. Jadus and D. L. Feucht, "The realization of a GaAs-Ge wide band gap emitter transistor," *IEEE Trans. Electron Devices*, vol. 16, pp. 102–107, Jan. 1969.

[37] H. Kroemer, Dev. Res. Conf. 1978, Santa Barbara; see *IEEE Trans. Electron Devices*, vol. ED-25, p. 1339, Nov. 1978.

[38] ——, *Bull. Amer. Phys. Soc.*, vol. 24, p. 230, Mar. 1979.

[39] K. G. Ashar, "The method of estimating delay in switching circuits and the figure of merit of a switching transistor," *IEEE Trans. Electron Devices*, vol. ED-11, pp. 497–506, Nov. 1964.

[40] W. P. Dumke, personal communication, unpublished.

[41] The concept at issue here *has* been widely discussed in the DH laser literature. See, e.g., W. Susaki, H. Namizaki, H. Kan, and A. Ito, "A new geometry double-heterostructure injection laser for room-temperature continuous operation: Junction-stripe-geometry DH lasers," *J. Appl. Phys.*, vol. 44, no. 6, pp. 2893–2894, June 1973.

[42] H. Kroemer, "Heterostructures for everything—device principle of the 1980's?," *Japan. J. Appl. Phys.*, vol. 20, suppl. 20-1, pp. 9–13, Jan. 1981 (Proc. 12th Conf. Solid-State Devices, Tokyo, Aug. 1980).

[43] Inverted transistors (with a Schottky collector) with a wide-gap emitter, but without the idea of inactivating the "uncovered" part of the emitter area, have already been reported: H. Beneking, N. Grote, W. Roth, L. M. Su, and M. N. Svilans, "Realization of a bipolar GaAs/GaAlAs Schottky-collector transistor," *Gallium Arsenide and Related Compounds 1980* (Vienna), Inst. Phys. Conf. Ser., vol. 56, pp. 385–392, 1981.

[44] W. G. Oldham and A. G. Milnes, "n-n semiconductor heterojunctions," *Solid-State Electron.*, vol. 6, no. 2, pp. 121–132, Mar./Apr. 1963.

[45] D. T. Cheung, S. Y. Chiang, and G. L. Pearson, "A simplified model for graded-gap heterojunctions," *Solid-State Electron.*, vol. 18, no. 3, pp. 263–266, Mar. 1975.

[46] Some of the ideas on this subject were independently developed by Dr. Daniel G. Chen, to whom I owe several detailed discussions on this subject.

[47] For a discussion of those problems, see H. Kroemer, K. J. Polasko, and S. C. Wright, "On the (110) orientation as the preferred orientation for the molecular beam epitaxial growth of GaAs on Ge, GaP on Si, and similar zincblende-on-diamond systems," *Appl. Phys. Lett.*, vol. 36, no. 9, pp. 763–765, May 1980.— Unfortunately, even the switch to the (110) orientation has not solved the problems satisfactorily.

[48] See, e.g., D. Boccon-Gibod, J-P. André, P. Baudet, and J-P. Hallais, "The use of GaAs-(Ga, Al)As heterostructures for FET devices," *IEEE Trans. Electron Devices*, vol. ED-27, pp. 1141–1147, June 1980.

[49] See, e.g., S. Judaprawira, W. I. Wang, P. C. Chao, C.E.C. Wood, D. W. Woodard, and L. F. Eastman, "Modulation-doped MBE GaAs/n-Al$_x$Ga$_{1-x}$As MESFETs," *IEEE Electron Devices Lett.*, vol. EDL-2, pp. 14–15, Jan. 1981.

[50] The importance of this advantage of bipolar devices was first pointed out to me by Dr. R. C. Eden.

[51] M. Lepselter, "Integrated circuits—the new steel," Int. Electron Dev. Meeting (IEDM) 1974, *IEDM Dig.*, Dec. 1974.

Reprinted from *IEEE Transactions on Electron Devices*, Volume ED-33, Number 1, January 1986, pages 104-110. Copyright © 1986 by The Institute of Electrical and Electronics Engineers, Inc.

A GaAs 16-kbit Static RAM Using Dislocation-Free Crystal

MASAHIRO HIRAYAMA, MEMBER, IEEE, MINORU TOGASHI, NAOKI KATO, MASAMITSU SUZUKI, YUTAKA MATSUOKA, AND YASUHIRO KAWASAKI

Abstract—A GaAs 16-kbit static RAM was developed using high-density integration technology and high-uniformity crystal. Highly integrated SAINT FET's with 1.0-μm gate length and 1.5-μm interconnection lines were formed by self-alignment and fine photolithography. Highly uniform crystal with less than 20-mV threshold scattering was obtained from an In-doped dislocation-free LEC with a 2-in diameter. An address access time of 4.1 ns was obtained with an associated power dissipation of 1.46 W.

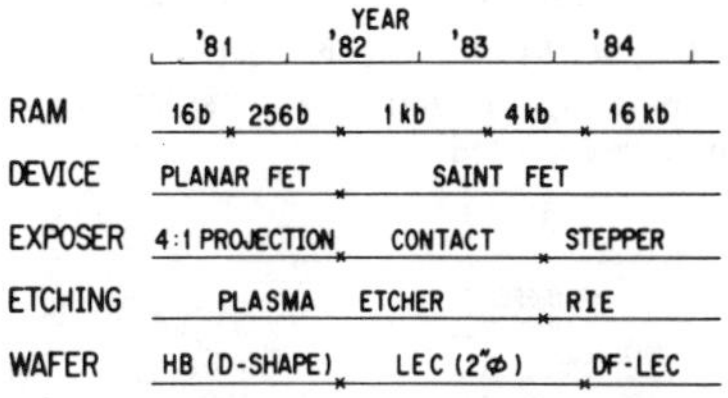

Fig. 1. GaAs RAM development history at the Electrical Communication Laboratories, NTT. Integration scale increased 1000 times in four years.

I. INTRODUCTION

ULTRAHIGH-SPEED digital LSI's are in demand for super computers, digital signal processors, digital switching systems, and digital transmission systems. The LSI operation speed is determined by the combined effect of the device intrinsic delay time and the interconnection delay time. GaAs MESFET's have a very short delay time about 10 ps [1]. A GaAs semi-insulating substrate has the advantage of lower interconnection line capacitance.

GaAs LSI technology first found wide-spread application in 1980, 10 years later than for silicon LSI's. It had the disadvantages of being a compound crystal material and having to develop a new fabrication process and device structure. The mass-production of 2–3-in-diameter wafer materials was realized using the LEC method. The highly uniform substrates have been realized by using high-quality In-doped dislocation-free crystals (etch pit density:EPD less than 300 cm^{-2}). Since low-temperature processes were required for GaAs processing, plasma-enhanced CVD or etching was used. Fine photolithographic patterning has been established using a 10:1 projection aligner and reactive ion etcher (RIE). High g_m MESFET's were realized by using self-aligned implantation for n$^+$ layer technology (SAINT) [2].

A GaAs 16-kbit static RAM consisting of more than 10^5 FET's was successfully realized using the latest GaAs technologies mentioned above. The history of our development is shown in Fig. 1 [3]–[8]. Circuit design technology was also developed for a high-accuracy FET circuit model [9].

In this paper, we will describe a 16-kbit static RAM circuit design, its fabrication process, and its results using dislocation-free crystal. The address access time obtained was 4.1 ns as a measurement result. Silicon bipolar 16-kbit static RAM's were reported with an address access time of 15–16 ns [10], [11].

II. RAM CIRCUIT DESIGN

The 16-kbit RAM's target performance was a 2-ns address access time with power dissipation of about 2 W. A feature of the DCFL circuit is high-speed operation with low power consumption. The DCFL circuit was mainly used for a RAM whose word organization was 4096 words × 4 bits. An attainable set of device parameters for 16-kbit RAM design was given by SAINT FET with 1-μm gate length.

A. Circuit Construction

The features of the 16-kbit RAM circuit design are high speed and reliable operation. The RAM circuit construction is shown in Fig. 2. Conventional six-transistor-type memory cells were adapted for the RAM. Normally-on-type transfer gate FET's were adapted, and these have low resistances when they are addressed. Therefore, memory cell signals can transmit to bit lines in a shorter time and have smaller voltage drops. In addition, the on-resistance of the normally-on FET's has a smaller scattering than that of normally-off FET's.

FET gate widths for memory cells are determined to be 12 μm for drivers, 2 μm for loads, and 4 μm for transfer gates in order to achieve the access time goal with stable RAM operation.

Source follower circuits with D-FET's and a diode were designed to drive the normally-on transfer gates. This word line driver has two advantages compared with the DCFL type. 1) It can provide larger drive current, and 2) there is no dc gate current flow through the transfer gate FET's, since the source follower settled at a high level output of 0.6 V.

Manuscript received April 8, 1985; August 6, 1985.

The authors are with the Atsugi Electrical Communication Laboratories, Nippon Telegraph and Telephone Corporation, 3-1, Morinosato Wakamiya, Atsugi-shi, Kanagawa 243, Japan.

IEEE Log Number 8405972.

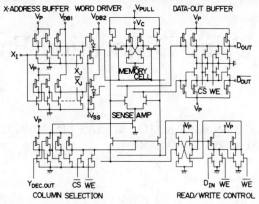

X-ADDRESS BUFFER   WORD DRIVER   V_PULL   DATA-OUT BUFFER

Fig. 2. GaAs 16-kbit RAM circuit construction. Mainly E/D DCFL circuits are used. Some super buffers for address buffer and source followers for word line drivers are used.

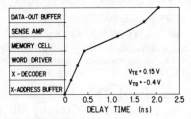

Fig. 3. The simulated address access time of GaAs static RAM using mostly E/D DCFL circuits.

A super buffer circuit was adapted for an input address buffer with completely complementary outputs, and the problem of double word line selection was automatically suppressed.

A bit line pull-up with E-FET's was also applied to the 16-kbit RAM to obtain high speed operation. The pull-up voltage near the sense amplifier threshold was controllable by tuning the supply voltage V_{PULL} as shown in Fig. 2. The sense amplifier consisted of an E/D DCFL inverter amplifier with a series gate for column selection. A data out buffer was designed using a 3-input NOR gate and an E/D DCFL inverter amplifier with 400-μm/200-μm gate width.

B. Circuit Simulation Result

The simulated delay time in the 16-kbit static RAM is shown in Fig. 3. A READ access delay time of 2.06 ns was attainable with an associated power dissipation of 2.2 W. Memory cell and sense amplifier delay times accounted for about 65 percent of all delay time. The simulated result was obtained using threshold voltage and dc supply voltage conditions as follows: $V_{TE} = 0.15$ V, $V_{TD} = -0.4$ V, $V_C = V_p = 1$ V, $V_{DB1} = 2$ V, $V_{SS} = -1$ V, and $V_{PULL} = 0.9$ V.

The access time did not vary for V_{TE} in the range of 0.15 to 0.25 V. The estimated threshold voltage scattering was up to 15 mV for 16-kbit RAM full bit operation.

C. RAM Chip Design

The memory cell array was divided into two blocks to reduce the word line voltage drop. The FET gates were aligned in one direction to avoid the threshold voltage scattering due to crystal orientation dependence.

A 42.0 μm $\times$ 32.5 μm memory cell consisting of 6 transistors was designed that was one third the area of 4-kbit RAM [7]. A memory-chip integrated 102 028 FET's and 256 diodes was formed in an 7.2 mm $\times$ 6.2 mm area. A process test element group (TEG) for FET, ohmic contact, and interconnection line were also designed on the same mask.

III. Fabrication Technology

The LSI process requires high yield, high reproducibility, and high uniformity. In the 16-kbit RAM, high yield was obtained by the use of a 10:1 stepper. This greatly reduces the lithographic defects. High reproducibility was achieved with SAINT and the metal embedding interconnection process. High slice uniformity was realized by the development of a dislocation-free crystal.

A. Device Process

The SAINT FET was adapted for the 16-kbit static RAM, as it was for the 1- and 4-kbit RAM's. The SAINT process has excellent reproducibility because of its rational process sequence. The basic process of the SAINT is shown in Fig. 4. The most effective patterning is the slight and straight under-cutting of the underlying resist by highly accurate dry etching. Ion implantation for the n$^+$ layer was made at an energy of 200 keV with the dosage of 4×10^{13} cm^{-2} through 1500-Å-thick SiN film.

Some features of SAINT FET's have to be compared with those of refractory metal-gate self-alignment FET's. 1)The distance between the n$^+$ layer and the gate metal is precisely controllable with the appropriate photoresist under-cutting before n$^+$ layer implantation. This structure can suppress the increase of gate capacitance which deteriorates the propagation delay time and improve gate breakdown voltage. 2)Any gate material is applicable for the SAINT FET. In this process, a dummy gate made of photoresist is used and is lifted off after SiO$_2$ deposition. The inverted pattern of SiO$_2$ determines the gate region. After ohmic contact formation, the gate area is opened with self-alignment and deposited with gate material. Many choices of gate materials are allowable, for example, Ti/Pt/Au, Al, and even amorphous silicon which has a barrier height of 1 V [12]. 3)The under-cutting of the bottom resist makes that effective gate length smaller than the line width of the top layer photoresist. For a top layer resist line width of 1.0 μm, the final gate length is about 0.5 μm [13].

An SEM photomicrograph of a completed FET with a fine pattern rule is shown in Fig. 5. The channel region was implanted at an energy of 67 keV with a dosage of 0.9–1.2 $\times 10^{12}$ cm^{-2}. The FET gate whose metal is Au/Pt/Ti has a 1.0-μm gate length and 2.0 μm metal length. The SAINT FET with 1.0-μm gate length showed a g_m of 150–170 mS/mm at a V_{TE} of 0.15–0.25 V.

B. Interconnection Process

Interconnection line formation is an important as FET fabrication in the development of LSI's. The 16-kbit RAM

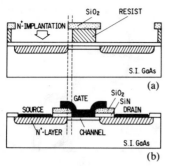

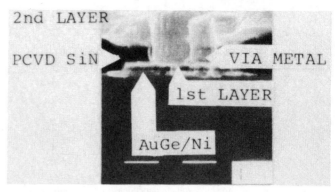

Fig. 4. (a) Fundamental process explanation figure for SAINT and (b) the cross sectional view of the completed SAINT FET.

Fig. 7. SEM photomicrograph for the first level metal via hole/metal and the second level metal interconnections.

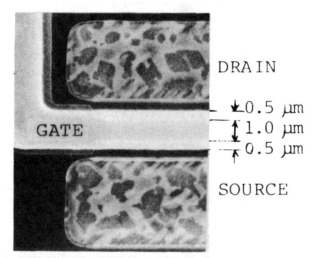

DRAIN

↓ 0.5 μm
↕ 1.0 μm
↑ 0.5 μm

GATE

SOURCE

Fig. 5. SAINT FET SEM photomicrograph fabricated by fine photolithography using a stepper.

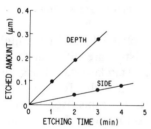

Fig. 6. Plasma enchanced CVD SiN film etching performance by RIE equipment.

line/space is 1.5 μm/1.5 μm for the first-level metal and 3 μm/3 μm for the second-level metal. The via hole size on the mask was designed to be 1.5 μm square. The process sequence was the same as that for 1- and 4-kbit RAM's published previously. RIE was needed for this work of 1.5-μm lithography because of the inhomogeneous etching characteristics.

The RIE etching performance for plasma-enhanced CVD deposition SiN film is shown in Fig. 6. The etch-rate ratio amount for depth versus lateral direction is 4.5. This ratio is appropriate for the dielectric-assisted lift-off process. The condition was applied to the first-level metal line formation with a dielectric thickness of 0.3 μm and via-metal formation with a thickness of 0.5 μm.

A cross-sectional view of the interconnection with the first-level metal on a ohmic contact, via metal, and the second-level metal is shown in Fig. 7 as a SEM photomicrograph. The first level and via metals were embedded in plasma CVD SiN film by the dielectric-assisted lift-off process mentioned above. After the second-level interconnection formation, the second-level metal located on a cylindrical via metal seems to be one with the via metal. The measurement results for the contact resistance between the first- and second-level lines through the vial metal were 0.26 Ω for a 1.5-μm-square mask pattern. The resistance scattering was only 0.005 Ω of standard deviation because of stepper photolithography and normal direction metal evaporation. The second-level metal was patterned by ion milling as in 1- and 4-kbit RAM's.

IV. DISLOCATION-FREE CRYSTAL APPLICATION

One of the most significant problems in the development of GaAs LSI was that the FET characteristics on a wafer depend on the crystal defects of the semi-insulating GaAs substrates. Dislocation densities in low Cr-doped LEC-grown crystal are generally more than 10^4 cm^{-2}. The FET threshold voltage changes with its relative location to dislocations [14]. Therefore, dislocation-free (DF) crystal is desirable for achieving high uniformity in GaAs LSI's. In 1984, when 16-kbit RAM fabrication first started, a DF (EPD:less then 300 cm^{-2}) LEC was developed.

A. Threshold Voltage Control

The first data needed for LSI development using DF LEC's are the FET threshold voltage dependence on the ion-implanted dosage. ^{29}Si$^+$ was used for the study and implanted at 67 keV for the channel layer. FET threshold voltages for implantation dosages from 0.9 to 1.2 $\times$ 10^{12} cm^{-2} are shown in Fig. 8. The data for DF LEC's are within a distribution area of that for conventional LEC's that were simultaneously used for the same test. The Threshold-voltage-controllable range is within 100 mV for E-FET's and 150 mV for D-FET's.

B. Uniformity of DF Crystal

FET threshold voltage scattering for DF and conventional LEC's is shown in Fig. 9 (a) and (b). The DF wafer shows very small threshold scattering for E-FET's and D-FET's as shown in Fig. 9(a). The standard deviation for

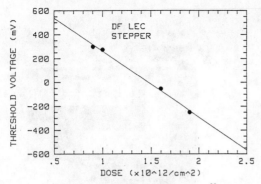

Fig. 8. SAINT FET threshold voltage dependence on $^{29}Si^+$ dosage at 67-keV implantation.

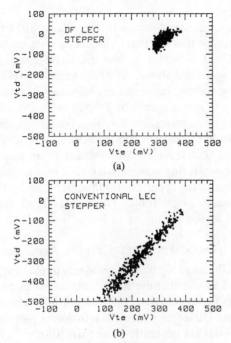

(a)

(b)

Fig. 9. Threshold voltage corelations between E-FET and D-FET for (a) DF LEC and (b) conventional LEC.

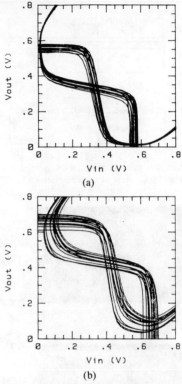

(a)

(b)

Fig. 10. E/D DCFL inverter transfer characteristics for (a) DF LEC and (b) conventional LEC.

E-FET's is 20 mV on a 2-in full wafer. In the case of conventional LEC's, the standard deviation is 54 mV as shown in Fig. 9(b). The scattering on DF crystal is one third the value as compared with that of conventional LEC's. Measured FET's have a 1-μm gate length and were fabricated by the SAINT process using a stepper. The stepper exposes each chip individually, and therefore keeps higher uniformity than that of a contact mask aligner. A threshold scattering deviation of 10 mV was reduced by using the stepper. A 20-mV threshold deviation on a wafer is sufficient for the 16-kbit RAM because there is less than 10-mV deviation in chip area.

Evaluation of the crystals was made using DCFL inverters. The transfer characteristics of the E/D DCFL inverter were measured and the plotted output voltage V_{OUT} versus input voltage V_{IN}, is shown in Fig. 10(a) for a DF LEC and Fig. 10(b) for a conventional LEC. V_{OUT} is clamped by the input Schottky gate of the next stage. The inverter switching voltage standard deviations for DF and conventional crystal are 14 and 17 mV, respectively.

The 3-mV difference in switching voltage scatterings between the two kinds of crystal is much smaller than the 34-mV difference in the FET threshold voltage scatterings. This implies that the threshold voltages for E- and D-FET's on the inverters are strongly correlated as shown in Fig. 9(b).

The logic low voltage V_L and logic high voltage V_H in transfer characteristics are different for DF and conventional LEC's. The standard deviations for V_L and V_H are 10 and nearly 0 mV for DF LEC's, and 17 and 14 mV for conventional LEC's, respectively. The nearly zero V_L scattering is a direct result of the excellent crystalline uniformity in the DF LEC wafer. This low scattering of V_L assures reliable operation in GaAs DCFL LSI's.

As mentioned above, very high uniformity in the DF LEC was demonstrated by measurements of threshold voltage and transfer characteristics. Electron mobility and SAINT FET transconductance for DF LEC's were no different from those for conventional LEC's.

V. THE REALIZED RAM AND ITS PERFORMANCE

The 16-kbit static RAM was synthesized using a reasonable pattern layout, a find photolighographic and reproducible fabrication process, and DF wafer application.

A. Memory Chip

A realized memory cell photomicrograph is shown in Fig. 11. All FET gates are aligned vertically. Two driver FET's with the widest gate (12 μm) are at the center of the memory cell and are located under the second-level metal for the ground. The ground line is completely iso-

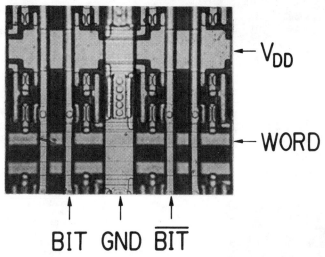

Fig. 11. 16-kbit static memory cell photomicrograph.

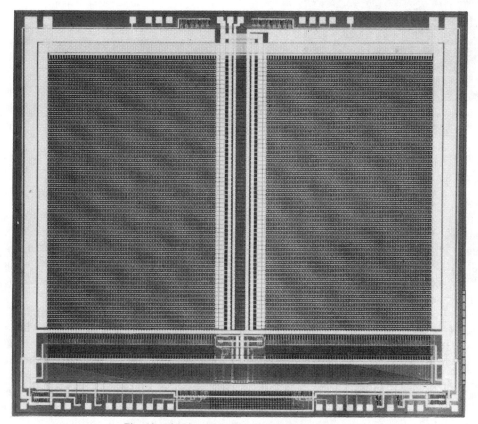

Fig. 12. 16-kbit static memory chip photomicrograph.

lated from the gate metal which sits on a SiO_2/SiN step. The dc supply line and word line in a cell are oriented horizontally using the first-level metal. Bit lines and the ground line are arranged vertically with the second-level pattern. A ground line width of 10 μm was determined to limit ground level voltage to less than 50 mV.

A photomicrograph of the 16-kbit RAM chip is shown in Fig. 12. The memory cell array is divided into two parts as described above. The X-address buffer is located on the top of the chip. Data out buffers for 4-bit parallel output are arranged at the bottom of the chip.

B. Dynamic Performance

The SAINT FET delay time using a DF LEC is shown in Fig. 13. The delay time for 6 wafers was measured using unloaded ring oscillator. Each point in the figure shows the average delay time for a wafer. The supply voltage was 1 V for the measurements. A 0.5-V logic swing was confirmed from transfer characteristic measurements. A 100-ps delay time was achieved with a load curent of 115 μA. A 10-percent speed-up was recognized for the SAINT FET by the gate MIS capacitance reduction with fine alignment of the stepper.

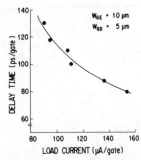

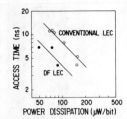

Fig. 15. The measured result difference between DF LEC and conventional LEC.

Fig. 13. Ring oscillator propagation delay time for E/D DCFL inverter.

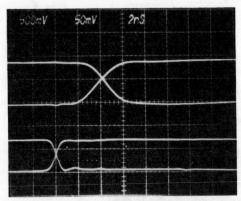

Fig. 14. X-address access time measurement results for 16-kbit RAM. Upper and lower waves are address input and data output, respectively.

TABLE I
SUMMARY OF GaAs 16-kbit STATIC RAM DATA

ORGANIZATION	4096 x 4
CIRCUIT	E/D DCFL + SF
DEVICE	SAINT FET
GATE LENGTH	1 µm
LINE/SPACE	1.5 µm/1.5 µm
VIA-HOLE	1.5 µm x 1.5 µm
CELL SIZE	41.0 µm x 32.5 µm
CHIP SIZE	7.2 mm x 6.2 mm
ACCESS TIME	4.1 ns
POWER DISSIPATION	1.46 W

The completed RAM wafer was functionally probed with a 40-MHz memory tester. The dc supply voltages for each wafer were set around the designed value for optimum operation conditions. High-performance chips were selected based on the measurement result and assembled in 40 p-i-n flat packages for the pulse measurement. We are also able to measure the RAM access time on the wafer by using a specially ordered probe card with a coaxial probe for a gigabit per second pulse test.

A minimum address access time of 4.1 ns with dissipation power of 1.46 W was obtained using the packaged measurement system, as shown in Fig. 14. Monitored FET threshold voltages on this chip were 0.186 V for the E-FET and −0.393 V for the D-FET. Standard deviations for these FET's were 9 mV for the E-FET and 14 mV for the D-FET. Typical access time was about twice that of the minimum. The main reason that this access time distribution occurs is thought to be related to the change of the switching voltage in inverter-type sense amplifier due to the E-FET threshold voltage deviation.

An interesting result for RAM performance with DF and conventional LEC's is shown in Fig. 15. The minimum address access time for both crystals was 4.1 ns, but the power dissipation for the two circuits differed by 1.7 times. These results were probably caused by the difference in FET uniformity. DF LEC's have such a high uniformity that the circuit operation margin can be small compared with that of conventional LEC's.

The WRITE and READ RAM operations were also confirmed for many chips. The minimum WRITE pulse width was less than 2 ns, which was limited by the pulser used

in the measurement system. A marching test, a kind of RAM test pattern, was made for 16-kbit RAM chips. Only 33 bits out of 16 384 bits failed in the DF wafer chip. All bits of the 4-kbit RAM located on the same wafer were operational [15]. Using state-of-the-art technology we can extrapolate a 16-kbit chip yield of about 1 percent. This result is approximately consistent with a previous estimation [16]. If the defect density is reduced to 10 cm^{-2}, we can obtain a 16-kbit chip yield of about 10 percent.

VI. CONCLUSION

A GaAs 16-kbit static RAM was fabricated using DF crystal. A resulting summary of the RAM chip is shown in Table I. Essential technologies which lead to 16-kbit RAM operation are high-speed circuit design, fine photolithography and RIE etching technologies, and DF LEC application.

The difference between simulated and measured access time was revealed through analysis for parasitic capacitance surrounding FET source and drain, and interconnection cross points. The revised simulated access time with these parasitics included is 4.6 ns.

The 16-kbit static RAM 10^5 FET scale LSI realization proved the SAINT process to have a very good reproducibility and a very high uniformity.

ACKNOWLEDGMENT

The authors would like to thank K. Yamasaki, Y. Ishii, and H. Yamazaki for their processing, and M. Idda and M. Ino for their help in design and testing. They also wish to thank Dr. M. Ohmori, Dr. M. Fujimoto and, Dr. T. Ikegami for their helpful comments and encouragement.

REFERENCES

[1] K. Yamasaki, N. Kato, and M. Hirayama, "Below 10 ps/gate operation with buried p-layer SAINT FET's," *Electron. Lett.*, vol. 20, no. 25, pp. 1029–1031, Dec. 1984.
[2] K. Yamasaki, K. Asai, and K. Kurumada, "GaAs LSI-directed MESFET's with self-aligned implantation for N$^+$ layer technology

(SAINT)," *IEEE Trans. Electron Devices*, vol. ED-29, no. 11, pp. 1772–1777, Nov. 1982.

[3] K. Asai, M. Ino, K. Kurumada, Y. Kawasaki, and M. Ohomori, "GaAs E/D FET technology for application to static RAM's," *Inst. Phys. Conf. Ser. No. 63*, ch. 11, pp. 533–538; also presented at the Int. Symp. GaAs and Related Compound, Oiso, Japan, Dec. 1981.

[4] K. Ohwada, M. Ino, T. Mizutani, and K. Asai, "GaAs 256-bit static RAM," *Electron. Lett.*, vol. 18, no. 7, pp. 299–300, Apr. 1982.

[5] M. Ino, M. Hirayama, K. Ohwada, and K. Kurumada, "GaAs 1 kb Static RAM with MESFET DCFL," in *Proc. GaAs IC Symp.*, pp. 2–5, Nov. 1982.

[6] K. Asai, K. Kurumada, M. Hirayama, and M. Ohmori, "1 kb static RAM using self-aligned FET technology," in *ISSCC Dig. Tech. Papers*, pp. 46–47, Feb. 1983.

[7] M. Hirayama, M. Ino, Y. Matsuoka, and M. Suzuki, "A GaAs 4 kb SRAM with direct coupled FET logic," in *ISSCC Dig. Tech. Papers*, pp. 46–47, Feb. 1984.

[8] Y. Ishii, M. Ino, M. Idda, M. Hirayama, and M. Ohmori, "Processing technologies for GaAs memory LSI's," *GaAs IC Symp. Tech. Dig.*, pp. 121–124, Oct. 1984.

[9] T. Takada, Y. Yokoyama, M. Idda, and T. Sudo, "A MESFET Variable-capacitance model for GaAs integrated circuit simulation," *IEEE Trans. Microwave Theory Tech.*, vol. MTT-30, no. 5, pp. 719–724, May 1982.

[10] Y. Kato, M. Odaka, and K. Ogiue, "A 16 ns 16 kb bipolar RAM," in *ISSCC Dig. Tech. Papers*, pp. 106–107, Feb. 1983.

[11] K. Toyoda, M. Tanaka, H. Isogai, C. Ono, Y. Kawabe, and H. Goto, "A 15 ns 16 kb ECL RAM with PNP load cell," in *ISSCC Dig. Tech. Papers*, pp. 108–109, Feb. 1983.

[12] M. Suzuki, K. Murase, and M. Hirayama, "A large logic swing and high speed DCFL with GaAs MASFET's," in *Extended Abstract 16th (Int.) Conf. Solid State Devices and Materials* (Kobe, Japan), pp. 387–390, 1984.

[13] *Microwave and Millimeter-Wave Monolithic Circuits Symp. Dig. Tech. Papers*, pp. 22–26, 1985.

[14] H. Yamazaki, T. Honda, S. Ishida, and Y. Kawasaki, "Improvement of field effect transistor threshold voltage uniformity by using very low dislocation density liquid encapsulated Czochralski-grown GaAs," *Appl. Phys. Lett.*, vol. 45, no. 10, pp. 1109–1111, Nov. 1984.

[15] M. Idda, H. Yamazaki, N. Kato, and M. Ohmori, "A 2 ns GaAs 4 kb SRAM using a Dislocation Free LEC Crystal," in *Late News Abstract 16th (Int.) Conf. Solid State Devices and Materials* (Kobe, Japan), pp. 30–31, 1984.

[16] C. A. Liechti, "GaAs IC technology—Impact on the semiconductor industry," in *IEDM Tech. Dig.*, pp. 13–18, Dec. 1984.

*

Masahiro Hirayama (M'85) was born in Hokkaido, Japan, in 1942. He received the B.S. and M.S. degrees in electronic engineering from Hokkaido University, Sapporo Japan, in 1966 and 1968, respectively.

Since joining the NTT Musashino Electrical Communication Laboratories, Tokyo, Japan, in 1968, he has been engaged in the research and development of millimeter and submillimeter wave frequency converters and integrated circuits. He recently worked on GaAs 1- and 4-kbit RAM circuit design, and is responsible for GaAs highly integrated LSI's including 16-kbit RAM fabrication process and for submicrometer FET technology as a team leader. He is now a Senior Staff Engineer at the NTT Atsugi Electrical Communication Laboratories.

Mr. Hirayama is a member of the Institute of Electronics and Communication Engineers of Japan and the Japan Society of Applied Physics.

*

Minoru Togashi was born in Miyagi, Japan, on October 2, 1955. He received the B.S. and M.S. degrees in electronics engineering from Tohoku University, Sendai, Japan, in 1979 and 1981, respectively.

He joined the Musashino Electrical Communication Laboratories, NTT, Tokyo, in 1981. Since then, he has been engaged in research and development work on GaAs IC design. He is currently an Engineer at the NTT Atsugi Laboratories.

Mr. Togashi is a member of the Institute of the Electronics and communication Engineers of Japan.

Naoki Kato was born in Aichi Prefecture, Japan, on July 11, 1949. He received the B.S. degree in applied physics from Waseda University and the M.S. degree from Tokyo Metropolitan University.

He joined the Musashino Electrical Communication Laboratory, Nippon Telegraph and Telephone Corporation, in 1976. He moved to the Atsugi Electrical Communication Laboratory in 1983. Since joining NTT, he has been engaged in the development of GaAs MESFET's, GaAs digital IC's, and micro-lithography. He is currently engaged in GaAs LSI processing.

Mr. Kato is a member of the Institute of Electronics and communication Engineers of Japan and the Japan Society of Applied Physics.

*

Masamitsu Suzuki was born in Chiba, Japan, on April 9, 1951. He received the B.S. and M.S. degrees in electronic engineering from the University of Electro-Communications, Tokyo, Japan, in 1974 and 1976, respectively.

Since joining the Electrical Communication Laboratory, Nippon Telegraph and Telephone Public Corporation, Tokyo, in 1976, he has been engaged in research work on GaAs MESFET's and IC's. He is now a Staff Engineer at the Atsugi Electrical Communication Laboratory, NTT, Kanagawa, Japan.

Mr. Suzuki is a member of the Institute of Electronics and Communication Engineers of Japan and the Japan Society of Applied Physics.

*

Yutaka Matsuoka was born in Gunma, Japan, on March 9, 1952. He received the B.S. and M.S. degrees in physics from the Tokyo Institute of Technology, Tokyo, Japan, in 1974 and 1976, respectively.

In 1976, he joined the Musashino Electrical Communication Laboratory, Nippon Telegraph and Telephone Public Corporation, Tokyo, Japan. He worked in electrical evaluation of silicon and GaAs crystals. Since 1982, he has been engaged in the development of GaAs LSI's. He is now a Staff Engineer at the NTT Atsugi Electrical Communication Laboratories.

Mr. Mastuoka is a member of the Institute of Electronics and Communication Engineers of Japan and the Japan Society of Applied Physics.

*

Yasuhiro Kawasaki was born in Shizuoka, Japan, on November 30, 1940. He received the B.S. and M.S. degrees in electronics engineering from Shizuoka University, Japan, in 1964 and 1966, respectively.

He joined the Electrical Communication Laboratory, Nippon Telegraph and Telephone Public Corporation, Tokyo, Japan, in 1966. He was worked on the research and development of Gunn diodes, ion implantation, and its application to IMPATT diodes and GaAs LSI's. He is currently a senior staff engineer at the Atsugi Electrical Communication Laboratory, NTT, Japan.

Mr. Kawasaki is a member of the Institute of Electronics and Communication Engineers of Japan and the Japan Society of Applied Physics.

Reprinted from *IEEE Transactions on Electron Devices*, Volume ED-33,
Number 5, May 1986, pages 548-553. Copyright © 1986 by The Institute
of Electrical and Electronics Engineers, Inc.

A Fully Operational 1-kbit HEMT Static RAM

NAOKI KOBAYASHI, SEISHI NOTOMI, MASAHISA SUZUKI, TAKUMA TSUCHIYA, KOICHI
NISHIUCHI, MEMBER, IEEE, KOUICHIRO ODANI, AKIHIRO SHIBATOMI, MEMBER, IEEE,
TAKASHI MIMURA, MEMBER, IEEE, AND MASAYUKI ABE, MEMBER, IEEE

Abstract—In this paper we describe the current status of materials
and fabrication technologies, and optimal design of a memory cell, and
the performance of fully functional 1-kbit HEMT SRAM's. The surface defect density on MBE-grown wafers has been reduced to less than
100 cm^{-2} by improving MBE technology. Standard deviations of
threshold voltages are 6.7 and 11.8 mV for enhancement-type and de-
pletion-type HEMT's, respectively, measured in a 10 mm × 10 mm
area. These deviations are sufficiently small for DCFL circuits. Memory cell design parameters have been optimized by circuit simulation,
where the effects of variations in threshold voltages are taken into account. Full function of 1-kbit SRAM's has been confirmed by marching
tests and partial galloping tests. The RAM chips have also shown excellent uniformity in access time. The difference between maximum
and average values on the RAM chip is 4 percent.

I. INTRODUCTION

HIGH ELECTRON mobility transistors (HEMT's) are
promising for very high-speed LSI's [1]–[3] as demonstrated with 1- and 4-kbit SRAM's in previous papers
[4], [5]. Currently, it has become important to establish
HEMT LSI technology to realize fully functional LSI circuits.

As reported in previous papers [5], [6], an intensive
effort is required to improve materials and fabrication
technology. A low density of surface defects on MBE-
grown wafers and high uniformity of device parameters
are necessary to obtain fully functional chips. Variations
in threshold voltages must be sufficiently less than logic
swings in LSI circuits. The logic swing in DCFL circuits,
adopted in HEMT LSI's, is smaller than that found in
normally-ON type logic circuits; however, DCFL circuits
have the advantages of simple circuit configuration and
low power dissipation [7]. Therefore, a DCFL circuit is
preferable for the design of SRAM's if high uniformity of
threshold voltages can be obtained.

Optimal design of a memory cell is also important. Stable memory operation depends greatly on the memory cell
stability, which is affected by variations in threshold voltages. It is necessary to take this effect into account for
memory cell design.

This paper reports the current status of materials and

fabrication technologies to achieve low surface defect
density and highly uniform device parameters, and also
discusses circuit design consideration for static RAM's,
mainly memory cell stability, and the performance of fully
functional 1-kbit SRAM's.

II. MATERIALS

An important problem in MBE technology is to reduce
surface defect (oval defect) density. If there are defects in
the gate region, the drain current cannot be pinched off.
We have reduced the defect density to less than 100 cm^{-2}
by using wet-chemical and Ar$^+$ plasma dry etching of
GaAs substrates before epitaxial growth and by optimizing growth conditions. Assuming a defect density of 100
cm^{-2}, the number of defects in the total gate area of the
chip is calculated to be less than 0.31 for 1-kbit and 0.96
for 4-kbit HEMT SRAM's.

Another important problem is to reduce variations in
device parameters. We have developed the MBE growth
conditions for highly uniform epitaxial layers. As shown
in Fig. 1, the thickness variations ($\Delta t/t$) and the carrier
concentration variations ($\Delta n/n$) are less than ±1 percent
within 60 mm.

III. THE FABRICATION PROCESS

We have obtained excellent uniformity in threshold
voltages for both enhancement-type (E-HEMT's) and de-
pletion-type HEMT's (D-HEMT's) by using a self-ter-
minating selective dry-etching technology. This technology is based on the large difference in the etching rate
between GaAs and AlGaAs, and is very suitable for
HEMT's because the excellent uniformity of MBE-grown
epitaxial layers guarantees uniformity of the threshold
voltages.

Fig. 2 shows etching characteristics, using CCl_2F_2 +
He gas, of GaAs (60-nm-thick)–AlGaAs heterojunction
material. A high-selectivity ratio of more than 260 is
achieved, with the etching rate of AlGaAs as low as 2 nm/
min and that of GaAs about 520 nm/min at 140 V in self-
generated bias voltage.

Fig. 3 shows threshold voltages at 300 K versus thickness of the cap layer and the AlGaAs layer between surface and heterointerface. The basic epilayer structure
consists of a 600-nm undoped GaAs layer, a 30-nm
$Al_{0.3}Ga_{0.7}As$ layer doped to 2×10^{18} cm^{-3} with Si, and
a 70-nm GaAs cap layer. They are successively grown on
a semi-insulating GaAs substrate by MBE. A very thin

Manuscript received October 7, 1985; revised January 7, 1986. The
present research effort is part of the National Research and Development
Program on "Scientific Computing System," conducted under a program
set by the Agency of Industrial Science and Technology, Ministry of In-
ternational Trade and Industry.
The authors are with Fujitsu Laboratories, Ltd., Fujitsu Limited, 10-1
Morinosato-Wakamiya, Atsugi 243-01, Japan.
IEEE Log Number 8607885.

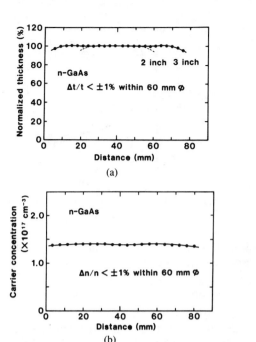

(a)

(b)

Fig. 1. n-GaAs (a) thickness and (b) carrier concentration variations on a 3-in ϕ wafer.

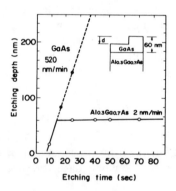

Fig. 2. Characteristics of selective dry etching.

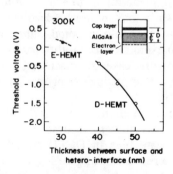

Fig. 3. Threshold voltages of HEMT's with new epi-structure.

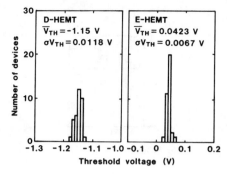

Fig. 4. Histogram of threshold voltages of HEMT's with 1.2-μm gate lengths.

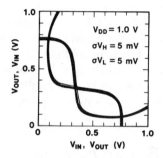

Fig. 5. Superimposed transfer curves of 20 HEMT DCFL inverters on a 2-in ϕ wafer.

Fig. 4 shows histograms of threshold voltages of HEMT's with gate lengths of 1.2 μm, measured on a 10 mm $\times$ 10 mm area at room temperature. The standard deviations are 6.7 mV for E-HEMT's and 11.8 mV for D-HEMT's, about $\frac{1}{2}$ of those for GaAs MESFET's. Moreover, for transconductance, a standard deviation of 3 percent has been obtained for E-HEMT's, having an average value of 180 mS/mm.

Fig. 5 shows superimposed transfer curves of 20 HEMT E/D type DCFL inverters on a 2-in ϕ wafer, measured at a supply voltage of 1.0 V at room temperature. Standard deviations of 5 mV are obtained for both the high and low logic levels. These deviations are less than 1 percent of the logic swing, which is approximately 0.7 V. Therefore, the high uniformity of the device parameters satisfies the requirements for stable operation in a DCFL circuit.

IV. Circuit Design

A. Memory Cell Stability

The 1-kbit SRAM has the same circuit configuration as reported in a previous paper [4]. There are two requirements for the design of HEMT SRAM's; that is, high-speed performance and high memory density. Because the memory density depends entirely on a memory cell size, the cell size should be small enough although the cell may have a contribution to the dynamic performance. To achieve high-speed performance, it is better to increase the driving ability of the peripheral circuits. Therefore, the driver devices have very wide gates in the peripheral circuits of HEMT SRAM's. A threshold voltage of 0.15 V is adopted for E-HEMT's to guarantee high-speed per-

AlGaAs layer, embedded in the cap layer, acts as an etching stopper against the selective dry etching in the gate recess process. Selective dry etching is carried out to remove the cap layer and expose the top surface of the thin AlGaAs stopper for D-HEMT's. To fabricate E-HEMT's, nonselective wet-chemical etching is carried out to remove the stopper before the selective dry etching. When the temperature is lowered from 300 to 77 K, threshold voltages shift to positive by around 0.1 V.

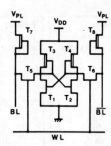

Fig. 6. Schematic of the memory cell.

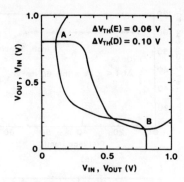

Fig. 7. Simulated dc characteristics of a memory cell in the worst case for $I_A/I_D = I_{PL}/I_D = 0.5$.

formance and sufficient noise margin in the peripheral circuits. The threshold voltage for D-HEMT's is -1.00 V.

Stable memory operation depends greatly on memory cell stability, which means that the input data are surely written and that the stored data are retained until the next WRITE operation. It is impossible to obtain fully functional SRAM's without considering cell stability. Because cell stability may be affected by variations in device parameters, detailed circuit analysis for optimal cell design must take this effect into account.

B. Memory Cell Design Parameters

Fig. 6 shows a schematic of the memory cell, which is a usual flip-flop circuit, consisting of 6 HEMT's. The current ratios I_A/I_D, I_{PL}/I_D, and I_D/I_L are cell-design parameters. I_D is the drain current of the drivers T_1 and T_2, and I_L is the drain current of the cell loads T_3 and T_4. I_A is the drain current of the access transistors T_5 and T_6, and I_{PL} is the drain current of the bit-line-pull-up loads T_7 and T_8. I_D and I_A are measured at $V_{DS} = 1$ V and $V_{GS} = 0.8$ V, and I_L and I_{PL} at $V_{DS} = 1$ V and $V_{GS} = 0$ V.

I_A/I_D and I_{PL}/I_D have greater effect on cell stability. The READ error may be caused by the transient current from the high-voltage storage node to the low-voltage bit line when the cell is selected. If I_A/I_D is larger and I_{PL}/I_D is smaller, the data destruction becomes more likely because the voltage drop at the storage node becomes larger. The WRITE condition is the opposite of the READ condition. The WRITE error may be caused by an insufficient voltage drop at the storage node in the WRITE operation. If I_A/I_D is smaller and I_{PL}/I_D is larger, it becomes harder to write in the cell. It is necessary to optimize these parameters by circuit simulation, taking into account the effects of variations in threshold voltages.

The current ratio of the cell inverter I_D/I_L has less effect on cell stability because the bit lines are pulled up. Although the cell noise margin decreases with the I_D/I_L ratio for $I_D/I_L < 5$, the margin is less dependent on the ratio for $I_D/I_L > 5$. This ratio also concerns power dissipation in a memory cell. Although a larger ratio is preferable for lower power dissipation, it is difficult to realize a very large ratio because the gate width of the load becomes very narrow and the gate length becomes very long. Based on these, I_D/I_L is chosen to be 10.

In the 1-kbit chips actually fabricated, the gate of the bit-line-pull-up load is not connected with the source, but connected to a pad. The gate bias can be controlled by an external voltage source.

C. Circuit Simulation

To investigate the effect of the variation in threshold voltages, we executed worst case simulation as follows. For a given variation ΔV_{TH}, we consider the worst case of many possible configurations in threshold voltages of the 8 HEMT's (T_1–T_8). That is, a threshold voltage of each HEMT is shifted by $+$ or $-\Delta V_{TH}$ to maximize the difference in the noise margin between two stable states in the cell. The threshold voltage shifts used in the worst case simulation are as follows. A shift by $+\Delta V_{TH}$ is for T_1, T_4, T_6, and T_8, and a shift by $-\Delta V_{TH}$ for T_2, T_3, T_5, and T_7.

Fig. 7 shows the simulated dc characteristics of the memory cell for $I_A/I_D = I_{PL}/I_D = 0.5$ in the worst case, with a variation of 0.06 V for E-HEMT's, and 0.10 V for D-HEMT's. As shown in the figure, the difference in the noise margin between the states, A and B, is maximized. A corresponds to the worst case for writing, and B for reading.

By the worst case simulation discussed above, we can obtain cell design conditions to achieve a fully functional chip if actual variations in threshold voltages are within a shift of $\pm\Delta V_{TH}$. It should be noted that transient analysis is necessary to examine cell stability for both reading and writing in the worst case. As discussed before, the transient currents act in an important role in the READ and WRITE operations.

We performed the circuit simulation with the SPICE II JFET model. This model can describe HEMT dc characteristics for gate bias in DCFL circuits. The device model parameters, for 1-μm gate length and 50-μm gate width at room temperature, are as follows: $\beta = 16$ mA/V^2, $\lambda = 0.1$, $R_S = R_D = 15$ Ω, $C_{GS} = 150$ fF, $C_{GD} = 15$ fF, $I_S = 1.4 \times 10^{-17}$ A.

D. Optimization of the Parameters

Two simulation results are shown in Fig. 8. For E-HEMT's, Fig. 8(a) is for a variation of 0.03 V and (b) for 0.06 V. For D-HEMT's, Fig. 8(a) is for a variation of 0.05 V and (b) for 0.10 V. The stable operating region and the error regions are shown in the figure. The WRITE error boundary is calculated for a WRITE-enable pulse

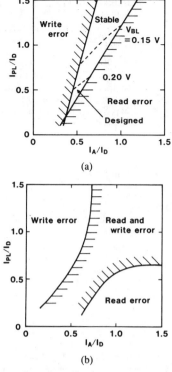

(a)

(b)

Fig. 8. Stable operating and error regions for (a) $\Delta V_{TH}(E) = 0.03$ V and $\Delta V_{TH}(D) = 0.05$ V, and (b) $\Delta V_{TH}(E) = 0.06$ V and $\Delta V_{TH}(D) = 0.10$ V. The broken lines show the cell design parameters where logic swings on the bit lines, V_{BL}, are 0.15 and 0.20 V.

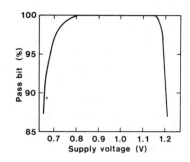

Fig. 9. Normalized pass-bit number for several supply voltages.

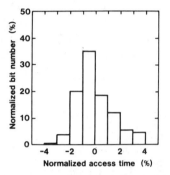

Fig. 10. Histogram of normalized X-address access time.

width of 500 ps. The stable operating region is significantly narrow in the case shown in Fig. 8(a), and disappears in the case shown in Fig. 8(b). These results indicate that the variation in threshold voltage affects the cell stability considerably. As discussed before, high uniformity of threshold voltages has been obtained for HEMT's. Three times the standard deviation for E-HEMT's is 20 mV, and for D-HEMT's is 35 mV, which is less than ΔV_{TH} in the case of Fig. 8(a). It can be considered that the measured variations in threshold voltages are within ΔV_{TH} in the case of Fig. 8(a). Therefore, the cell design conditions to achieve fully functional chips are found to be satisfied in the case shown in Fig. 8(a).

The logic swing on the bit lines also should be considered to optimize the design parameters because the logic swing depends on I_A/I_D and I_{PL}/I_D. The broken lines in the figure show the design parameters where logic swings on the bit lines V_{BL} are 0.15 and 0.20 V. The logic swing on the bit lines must be at least 0.2 V for driving the sensing amplifiers. Based on these, the optimal design parameters I_A/I_D and I_{PL}/I_D have been chosen to be 0.5.

V. PERFORMANCE OF 1-kbit SRAM's

We have confirmed that the 1-kbit SRAM's are fully functional by marching tests with a 1-kHz clock at room temperature. The high-level voltage of input signals was 0.7 V, and the low-level voltage was 0 V. The tests were executed on wafers. The chip size was 3.0 mm × 2.9 mm, consisting of 7244 HEMT's, and 100 chips were fabricated on a wafer. Fig. 9 shows the normalized pass bit number for several supply voltages. The chip passed the marching test for supply voltages between 0.8 and 1.15 V.

The marching test is not sufficient for detecting interference between memory cells. An additional test (partial galloping test) was performed to detect the interference. We examined the interference between a test cell, which was selected in a cell array, and any other cells in the READ cycle. Several test cells were selected on each chip. This test was similar to a galloping test, although all the combinations of cells were not tested. The chips which passed the marching test also passed this additional test.

The SRAM's have also shown excellent uniformity in access time. Fig. 10 shows a histogram of the normalized X-address access time for 512 pairs of adjacent cells, measured at room temperature. The difference between maximum and average values is only 4 percent, which is much smaller than that for GaAs MESFET SRAM's. The average value is 9 ns, not fast, because the load current in the whole circuit is about $\frac{1}{3}$ of the designed value. It has been demonstrated, however, that the access time can be as fast as 0.9 ns at 77 K if the load current is just the designed value [4]. The access time scattering is caused by variations in load current. Even if the access time becomes faster, the normalized scattering is constant because the relative variation in load current is considered to be constant.

VI. SUMMARY

HEMT LSI technology to achieve fully functional chips is presented. Highly uniform MBE-grown wafers and selective dry-etching technology enable excellent control of the device parameters. The standard deviations of threshold voltages are 6.7 mV for E-HEMT's and 11.8 mV for

D-HEMT's. Surface defect densities have been reduced to less than 100 cm^{-2}. The cell design parameters have been optimized by worst case simulation, taking into account the effects of variations in threshold voltage. I_A/I_D and I_{PL}/I_D are chosen to be 0.5. Fully functional 1-kbit SRAM's with excellent uniformity in access time have been fabricated. These indicate that HEMT technology is promising for application to high-speed LSI's, and that higher density HEMT static RAM's can be projected.

ACKNOWLEDGMENT

The authors wish to thank Dr. T. Misugi and M. Kobayashi for their encouragement and support, and also wish to thank K. Kondo and M. Nakayama for their support in materials and fabrication.

REFERENCES

[1] T. Mimura, S. Hiyamizu, T. Fujii, and K. Nanbu, "A new field-effect transistor with selectively doped GaAs/n-AlGaAs heterojunctions," *Japan J. Appl. Phys.*, vol. 19, pp. L225–L227, 1980.
[2] T. Mimura, K. Joshin, S. Hiyamizu, K. Hikosaka, and M. Abe, "High electron mobility transistor logic," *Japan J. Appl. Phys.* vol. 20, pp. L598–L600, 1981.
[3] K. Nishiuchi, T. Mimura, S. Kuroda, S. Hiyamizu, H. Nishi, and M. Abe, "Device characteristics of short channel high electron mobility transistor (HEMT)," in *Proc. Device Res. Conf.* (Vermont), IIA-8, June 1983.
[4] K. Nishiuchi, N. Kobayashi, S. Kuroda, S. Notomi, T. Mimura, M. Abe, and M. Kobayashi, "A subnanosecond HEMT 1 Kb static RAM," in *ISSCC Dig. Tech. Papers*, pp. 48–49, 314, 1984.
[5] S. Kuroda, T. Mimura, M. Suzuki, N. Kobayashi, K. Nishiuchi, A. Shibatomi, and M. Abe, "New device structure for 4 Kb HEMT SRAM," in *GaAS IC Symp. Tech. Dig.*, pp. 125–128, 1984.
[6] A. Shibatomi, J. Saito, M. Abe, T. Mimura, K. Nishiuchi, and M. Kobayashi, "Material and device considerations for HEMT LSI," in *IEDM Tech. Dig.*, pp. 340–343, 1984.
[7] R. C. Eden, B. M. Welch, R. Zucca, and S. I. Long, "The prospects for ultrahigh-speed VLSI GaAs digital logic," *IEEE J. Solid-State Circuits*, vol. SC-14, pp. 221–239, 1979.

*

Naoki Kobayashi was born in Nagano Prefecture, Japan, on September 22, 1952. He received the B.S. and M.S. degrees in solid-state physics from Tohoku University, Sendai, Japan, in 1976 and 1978, respectively.

Since joining the Compound Semiconductor Devices Laboratory, Fujitsu Laboratories Ltd., in 1982, he has been engaged in the research and development of HEMT LSI circuits.

Mr. Kobayashi is a member of the Institute of Electronics and Communication Engineers of Japan.

*

Seishi Notomi was born in Kumamoto, Japan, on December 20, 1958. He received the B.S. and M.S. degrees in applied physics from the University of Tokyo, Tokyo, Japan, in 1981 and 1983, respectively.

In 1983, he joined the Compound Semiconductor Devices Laboratory, Fujitsu Laboratories Ltd., Atsugi, Japan, where he has been engaged in the development of HEMT LSI devices.

Mr. Notomi is a member of the Institute of Electronics and Communication Engineers of Japan and the Physical Society of Japan.

Masahisa Suzuki was born in Tokyo, Japan, on March 31, 1959. He received the B.S. and M.S. degrees in electrical engineering from Keio University, Tokyo, Japan, in 1981 and 1983, respectively.

In 1983, he joined the Compound Semiconductor Devices Laboratory, Fujitsu Laboratories Ltd., Atsugi, Japan, where he has been engaged in the development of HEMT LSI devices.

Mr. Suzuki is a member of the Japan Society of Applied Physics.

*

Takuma Tsuchiya was born in Sendai, Japan, on June 13, 1960. He received the B.S. degree in physics from the Tokyo Institute of Technology, Tokyo, Japan, in 1984.

In 1984, he joined the Compound Semiconductor Devices Laboratory, Fujitsu Laboratories Ltd., Atsugi, Japan, where he has been engaged in the development of HEMT LSI devices.

Mr. Tsuchiya is a member of the Institute of Electronics and Communication Engineers of Japan.

*

Koichi Nishiuchi (M'80) was born in Hyogo, Japan, on December 7, 1944. He received the B.S. degree in electronical engineering from the Himeji Institute of Technology, Himeji, Japan, in 1969 and the M.S. degree in electronical engineering from Kyoto University, Kyoto, Japan, in 1971.

In 1971, he joined Fujitsu Laboratories Ltd., Kawasaki, Japan, where he was originally engaged in the development of high-frequency bipolar transistors. Later, he was engaged in research and development of short-channel MOS devices, high-speed MOS logic circuits, and MOS LSI's. Recently, he has been engaged in research on high-speed compound semiconductor LSI's using high electron mobility transistors.

Mr. Nishiuchi is a member of the Institute of Electronics and Communication Engineers of Japan.

*

Kouichiro Odani was born in Osaka, Japan, on September 27, 1943. He graduated from the Tsu Institute of Technology in 1962.

He then joined the Kobe Industries Company, which later merged with Fujitsu Ltd. Since joining the company, he has been working in the field of semiconductor devices, including Si RF power transistors, IC's, GaAs FET's and HEMT LSI's.

Mr. Odani is a member of the Japan Society of Applied Physics.

*

Akihiro Shibatomi (M'83) was born in Kobe, Japan, on January 18, 1942. He received the B.S. degree in physics from Kanazawa University, Kanazawa, in 1965 and the Ph.D. degree in electrical engineering from Osaka University, Osaka, Japan, in 1983.

In 1965, he joined the Kobe Industries Company, which later merged with Fujitsu Ltd. He has worked in research and development of microwave tubes. In 1970, he was responsible for research and development of VPE and GaAs microwave devices at Fujitsu Laboratories, Ltd., Kawasaki. Since 1976, he has been engaged in research and development of GaAs IC (MESFET, HEMT, HBT, and RHET). He is currently a Deputy Manager of the Compound Semiconductor Devices Laboratory of the Semiconductor Division.

Dr. Shibatomi is a member of the Institute of Electrical and Communication Engineers of Japan and the Japan Society of Applied Physics.

*

Takashi Mimura (M'73) was born on December 14, 1944. He received the B.S. degree in physics from Kwanseigakuin University in 1967, Nishinomiya, Japan, and the M.E. and Ph.D. degrees in solid-state physics from Osaka University, Osaka, Japan, in 1970 and 1982, respectively.

In 1970, he joined Fujitsu Ltd., Kobe, Japan, where he had worked on research and development of silicon and gallium arsenide microwave devices, including planar analog transistors. In 1975 he transferred to the Fujitsu Laboratories, Ltd., Atsugi, Japan, where he has been engaged in the research and development of compound semiconductor high-speed devices, including high electron mobility transistors (HEMT's).

Dr. Mimura received the prize of the Minister of Science and Techniques in Japan for the invention of a HEMT in 1981. He also received an outstanding contributed paper award from the Japan Society of Applied Physics in 1982 and the Achievement Award from the Institute of Electronics and Communication Engineers of Japan in 1983.

*

Masayuki Abe (S'70–M'74) was born in Fukushima, Japan, on January 7, 1941. He received the B.E., M.E., and Ph.D. degrees in electrical engineering from Osaka University, Osaka, Japan, in 1967, 1969, and 1973, respectively.

His research has included high electric-field transport in semiconductors, especially dynamic characteristics of hot electrons in GaAs. In 1973, he joined Fujitsu Laboratories Ltd., Kawasaki, Japan, where he was engaged in Gunn-effect logic devices and Monte Carlo simulation of Gunn-domain dynamics. From 1975 to 1980, he was engaged in developing thick-window high-radiance GaAlAs and InGaAsP LED's for fiber-optical communications. Since 1980, he has engaged in developing high-speed GaAs MESFET and HEMT LSI's. He is currently Section Manager of the Compound Semiconductor Devices Laboratory, Fujitsu Laboratories Ltd., Atsugi.

Dr. Abe received the Paper Award of the Laser Society of Japan for "GaAlAs Monolithic Lensed LED" in 1980. He has served as Overseas Advisor for the IEEE GaAs IC Symposium (1983–1985). He is a member of the Institute of Electronics and Communication Engineers of Japan and the Japan Society of Applied Physics.

SESSION VII: SEMI-CUSTOM ARRAYS

WPM 7.4: A 4K GaAs Bipolar Gate Array*

Han-Tzong Yuan, Joseph B. Delaney, Hung-Dah Shin, Liem T. Tran

Texas Instruments Central Research Laboratory

Dallas, TX

SEVERAL IC TECHNOLOGIES are applied to the development of high speed gate arrays. Among the most notable are silicon ECL[1], GaAs super buffer logic[2], and GaAs E-MESFET logic[3]. They are all reported to have achieved subnanosecond switching. Their success, however, is not universally accepted because of unsolved problems related to operating temperature, noise margin and gate packing density. GaAs bipolar IC technology is considered an attractive solution to these problems, but its development has been marked by the difficulty of preparing starting materials, the need of mesa isolation and the lack of a self-aligned emitter process. To circumvent some of the problems a gate-array technology using heterojunction inverted transistor integrated logic (HI^{2}L) was under development since 1980 and its progress was reported previously[4,5].

In the latest 4K gate array design the basic gate was merged into a stick type of tank transistor that measured $10 \times 36\mu m^2$. The layout of the fanout = 4 gate is shown in Figure 1. This is different from the previous 1K gate array design in that the switching transistor and the output Schottky diodes are separated into two isolated moats. Stacking the Schottky diodes on top of the collector has the advantage of minimizing the series resistance of the Schottky diodes, hence improving the noise margin, particurarly, at logic low level. A $8 \times 8\mu m^2$ square pitch was also adopted for the first and second-level interconnections. This made autorouting more amenable, easing the bottleneck in CAD assist design. To improve the utility of the gate array further, WSi$_x$ thin film was applied for the fabrication of the load resistors. This allows the circuit designer to adjust the resistor value without altering the transistor structure as was the case before. The gate arrays were fabricated on N+ GaAs substrate with Molecular Beam Epitaxy

(MBE) grown AlGaAs emitter and GaAs base and collector. Instead of using all grown junctions, however, the P-type base and the extended P+ base contacts were furnished by beryllium implant. Current gains obtained from the inverted GaAs heterojunction bipolar transistor are typically ranging from 15 to 40.

Figure 2 shows a micrograph of the experimental 4K gate array. The bar size, including the process test stripe, is $5.8 \times 58mm^2$. It has 126 I/O signal pads and 8 power supply pads. The array consists of 14 columns with 288 fanout = 4 gates in each column. In Figure 2 the gate array was wired into 14 identical 32-bit shift registers; each occupies one column and each has its own input, output and clock. The design was used to examine the fabrication yield. In the best bar we have measured, there were 10 good 32-shift registers out of 14 available circuits. Table 1 lists all other important design parameters of this gate array.

The propagation delay measured from a 15 stage fanout = 4 ring oscillator is shown in Figure 3. It is worth pointing out that the logic gate can function over a power range from 0.1 to 10mW, and even at high power, no saturation effect is noticeable. This indicates that the switching characteristics are mostly controlled by the emitter junction capacitance, which has a value of 0.6pF for the present gate design. With a more refined process, for example, using self-aligned Schottky contacts, it is possible to scale down the size of the transistor and reduce the junction capacitance by at least a factor of 2. Such reduction will lead to the realization of 100ps propagation delay at a power consumption no more than 4mW per gate. Figure 4 shows the measured results of the logic gate operating over −100 to +150°C. The slight increase in propagation delay with a corresponding power reduction is a reflection of the P-N junction turn-on voltage, which has a coefficient of 2mV/°C. Other than this the logic circuit is expected to operate at even higher than 150°C*.

Table 2 compares the performance of HI^{2}L gate array to other high-speed technologies. The features of the HI^{2}L technology are high gate packing density, excellent noise margin that allows the circuit to operate from −100°C to +200°C, and the ability to tailor speed power over a wide range by simply adjusting the load resistors.

*This project was supported by the Defense Advanced Research Project Agency and monitored by the Office of Naval Research under Contract No. N00014-84-C-0476.

[1] Horiguchi, S., Suzuki, M., Ichino, H., Konaka, S., Sakai, T., "An 80ps 2500-Gate Bipolar Macrocell Array", *ISSCC DIGEST OF TECHNICAL PAPERS*, p. 198-199; Feb., 1985.

[2] Nakamura, H., Tanaka, K., Tsunotani, M., Kawakami, Y., Akiyama, M., Kaminishi, K., "A 390ps 1000-Gate Array using GaAs Super-Buffer FET Logic", *ISSCC DIGEST OF TECHNICAL PAPERS*, p. 204-205; Feb., 1985.

[3] Toyoda, N., Uchitomi, N., Kitaura, Y., Mochizuki, Y., Kanazawa, K., Terada, T., Ikawa, Y., Hojo, J., "A 42ps 2K-Gate GaAs Gate Array", *ISSCC DIGEST OF TECHNICAL PAPERS*, p. 206-207; Feb., 1985.

[4] Yuan, H.T., "GaAs Bipolar Gate Array Technology", *GaAs IC Symposium Technical Digest*, p. 100; Nov., 1982.

[5] Yuan, H.T., McLevige, W.V., Shih, H.D. and Hearn, A.S., "GaAs Heterojunction Bipolar 1K Gate Array", *ISSCC DIGEST OF TECHNICAL PAPERS*, p. 42-43; Feb., 1984.

[6] Doerbeck, F.H., Duncan, W.V., McLevige, W.V., Yuan, H.T., "Fabrication and High Temperature Characteristics of Ion-Implanted GaAs Bipolar Transistors and Ring-Oscillators", *IEEE Trans. on Indust. Electron*, Vol. IE-29, p. 136; 1982.

USABLE LOGIC GATES	4032
GATE PROPAGATION DELAY	1.25 ns (at 0.2 mW/GATE) 0.40 ns (at 1.0 mW/GATE)
FAN-OUT	4
I/O SIGNAL PADS	160
POWER SUPPLY PADS	8
DRIVE CAPABILITY	50 ohm/ECL COMPATIBLE
POWER DISSIPATION	2.5 W (LOW POWER) 5.5 W (HIGH SPEED)
OPERATING TEMPERATURE	-100°C to + 200°C

TABLE 1—Design parameters of GaAs bipolar 4K gate array.

Reprinted from *Proceedings of the 1986 IEEE International Solid-State Circuits Conference*, 1986, pages 74-75, 312. Copyright © 1986 by The Institute of Electrical and Electronics Engineers, Inc.

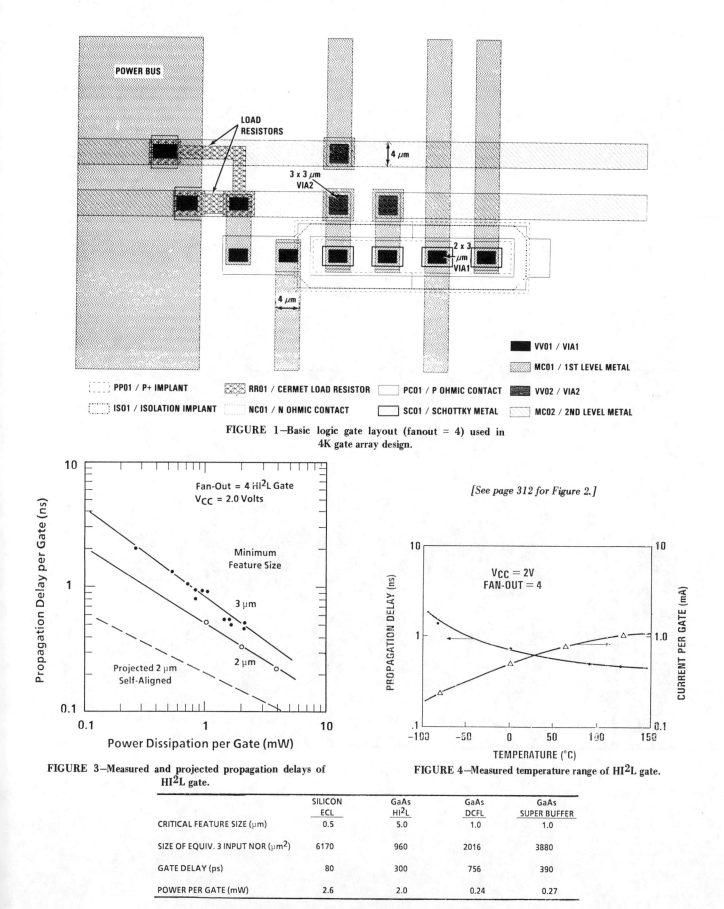

FIGURE 1—Basic logic gate layout (fanout = 4) used in
4K gate array design.

Legend:
- VV01 / VIA1
- MC01 / 1ST LEVEL METAL
- PP01 / P+ IMPLANT
- RR01 / CERMET LOAD RESISTOR
- PC01 / P OHMIC CONTACT
- VV02 / VIA2
- ISO1 / ISOLATION IMPLANT
- NC01 / N OHMIC CONTACT
- SC01 / SCHOTTKY METAL
- MC02 / 2ND LEVEL METAL

FIGURE 3—Measured and projected propagation delays of
HI²L gate.

[See page 312 for Figure 2.]

FIGURE 4—Measured temperature range of HI²L gate.

	SILICON ECL	GaAs HI²L	GaAs DCFL	GaAs SUPER BUFFER
CRITICAL FEATURE SIZE (μm)	0.5	5.0	1.0	1.0
SIZE OF EQUIV. 3 INPUT NOR (μm²)	6170	960	2016	3880
GATE DELAY (ps)	80	300	756	390
POWER PER GATE (mW)	2.6	2.0	0.24	0.27

TABLE 2—Technology comparisons of high-speed gate array.

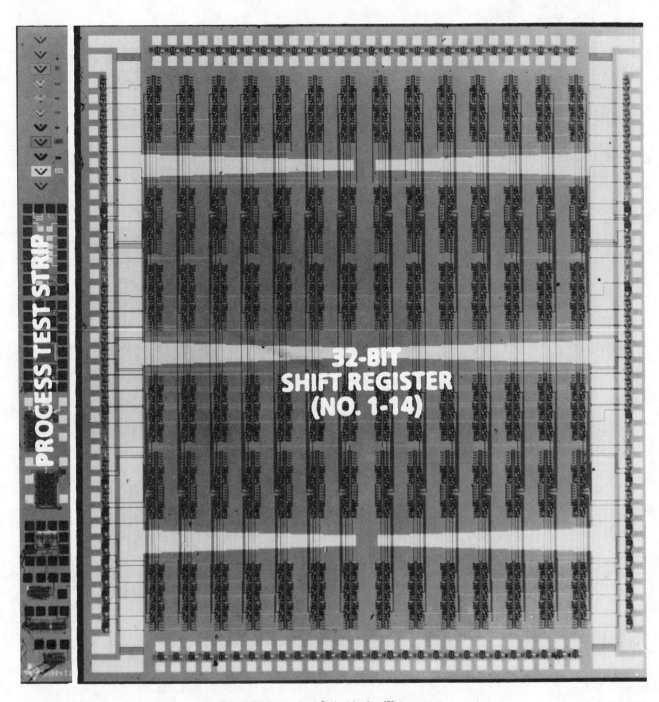

FIGURE 2—Micrograph of GaAs bipolar 4K gate array.

Chapter 3: GaAs Computer Design Concepts

This chapter surveys computer design considerations and approaches that result directly from gallium arsenide (GaAs) technology properties or indirectly through GaAs application environments.

The GaAs computer system design discipline is an immature one (as of this writing, no single-chip GaAs microprocessors are commercially available). However, as is evident from the first two chapters of this tutorial, a large body of useful GaAs knowledge is available to guide computer designers. One approach to GaAs computer design is to project the manner in which GaAs technology will influence higher-level architectural issues and then to make appropriate design decisions. In fact, the papers in this chapter generally adopt such a method.

GaAs technology can be viewed in two ways. First, GaAs may be considered slightly faster than silicon (ECL) but considerably less power hungry and, hence, able to achieve much higher levels of integration. Alternatively, GaAs may be viewed as considerably faster than silicon (MOS) but able to achieve much lower levels of integration owing to increased power requirements. Depending on one's view of this situation, GaAs computer design may have two different interpretations.

Many computer designers see GaAs as a replacement for silicon ECL in random logic designs on the PC (printed circuit) board level. Because the problems associated with using a high-speed technology have already been addressed by these designers, the conversion to GaAs is relatively nontraumatic. As a result, this area is very poorly represented in the open literature and in this tutorial. This is not meant to imply that it is an unimportant area, however. In fact, many commercial vendors already supply SSI and MSI GaAs parts for use by the supercomputer industry and others (e.g., Cray-3).

Many computer designers view GaAs (in LSI and VLSI implementations) as a vehicle for implementation of microprocessors and large memories. For these people, GaAs technology poses some very interesting problems that are described, along with useful design approaches, in this chapter.

Milutinović, in the first paper entitled "Guest Editor's Introduction: GaAs Microprocessor Technology," introduces and overviews GaAs computer design. He begins by listing the advantages and disadvantages that GaAs has in a comparison with silicon. He finishes by briefly describing how GaAs characteristics impact computer design.

In "System Level Comparison of High Speed Technologies," Gheewala compares the performance of various GaAs and silicon technologies in three computer configurations: scientific computers, large mainframe computers, and reduced instruction set computers (RISCs). A significant result is that while GaAs performs better than silicon in all three configurations, the greatest performance improvement is observed for RISC implementations. Although there are good arguments in favor of the results of this analysis, it will be very interesting to observe whether they are indeed present in practice when real systems become available.

Karp and Roosild's paper entitled "Darpa, SDI, and GaAs" outlines the history of digital GaAs technology and details the involvement of the U.S. government in the development of this technology. They point out the importance of GaAs in the government's need for low-power, radiation-hard computers for signal processing tasks in space vehicles. This paper demonstrates the very prominent role that the U.S. government played in the drive toward GaAs microprocessor-based computer systems.

Gilbert et al., in their paper entitled "Signal Processors Based upon GaAs ICs: The Need for a Wholistic Design Approach" survey the area of GaAs computer design for signal processing applications, but much of the discussion is appropriate for GaAs design in general. They describe appropriate application areas for GaAs; they present desirable architectural constructs for GaAs; and they discuss system packaging, inter-chip communication, and testing for GaAs systems. This paper effectively argues for a "wholistic" design approach, one that integrates architecture design with heretofore independent areas such as packaging, or cooling.

In "An Introduction to GaAs Microprocessor Architecture for VLSI," Milutinović, Fura, and Helbig survey the area of GaAs microprocessor design. They examine the characteristics of GaAs technology and determine the resulting impact on microprocessor design. They outline design considerations and recommendations for several microprocessor subunits, including the instruction pipeline, register file, execution unit, and instruction format. This paper effectively demonstrates a somewhat different approach required for GaAs microprocessor design than is required for silicon.

Milutinović et al., in the sixth paper entitled "Issues of Importance in Designing GaAs Microcomputer Systems," overview design concerns involved in computer systems based on a single-chip GaAs microprocessor. They present design considerations and suggestions for issues such as the memory system, arithmetic and I/O coprocessors, and system packaging. They also describe two systems under development, one based on an 8-bit microprocessor and the other on a 32-bit microprocessor. This paper is among the first to present results obtained from working hardware for a GaAs microprocessor-based system.

Milutinović et al., in the paper entitled "Architecture/Compiler Synergism in GaAs Computer Systems," examine the role that compiler technology is expected to play in GaAs microprocessor performance. They explain how advanced compilation techniques can improve significantly GaAs system performance. They discuss compiler algorithms to enhance hardware mechanisms such as the control logic, the memory system, and the arithmetic hardware, and present some performance results from the compiler developed for RCA Corporation's 32-bit GaAs microprocessor.

Gheewala and MacMillan's paper entitled "High-Speed GaAs Logic Systems Require Special Packaging" describes packaging problems and approaches associated with high-speed GaAs systems and presents a list of criteria to use in evaluating packaging and printed circuit board material alternatives. They describe existing methods and conclude that revolutionary rather than evolutionary improvement is needed in this area.

Goodman et al., in their paper entitled "Optical Interconnections for VLSI Systems," discuss the impact that optical interconnects may have in future high-speed systems. Although not restricted to GaAs-based systems, optics are potentially very important here because GaAs system performance depends very heavily on inter-chip communication cost and because, as is discussed in Chapter 1, GaAs efficiently transmits and receives optical information whereas silicon does not. The authors begin by describing integrated circuit technology and interconnect limitations, and they illustrate classes of algorithms whose performance greatly depends upon interconnection capability. They also describe some applications for optical interconnects. This paper effectively demonstrates the enormous potential that optical methods hold for improving the performance of future high-speed systems. The desirability of GaAs technology for future high-speed systems is underlined.

In "Analysis of Crosstalk in Very High-Speed LSI/VLSI's Using a Coupled Multiconductor MIS Microstrip Line Model," Seki and Hasegawa analyze crosstalk in very high-speed LSI/VLSI chips using a coupled multiconductor metal-insulator-semiconductor microstrip line model. They study the effect of line length, spacing, substrate thickness, and gate output impedance and show that lumped circuit models are inadequate at clock periods below 200-300 ps, conclude that crosstalk studies require transmission line models, and propose a shielded multilevel interconnect scheme to reduce crosstalk.

Gheewala, in the last paper entitled "Requirements and Interim Solutions for High-Speed Testing of GaAs ICs," identifies test system requirements for high-speed testing of GaAs ICs and proposes interim solutions for use until future test systems become available. He proposes that until high-speed circuits and novel test-fixture techniques become available, techniques such as D.C. testing, reliance on such parameters as ring-oscillator speeds, and novel on-chip test techniques may be used.

Guest Editor's Introduction

Reprinted from *Computer*, October 1986, pages 10-13. Copyright © 1986 by The Institute of Electrical and Electronics Engineers, Inc.

GaAs Microprocessor Technology

GaAs will never totally replace silicon; it will be used in selected aerospace, defense, and supercomputing applications. The extent of its usage is open to question.

Veljko Milutinović, Purdue University

Gallium arsenide (GaAs) technology has finally, during its third "reincarnation," reached the VLSI level of complexity.

Actually, early work on GaAs ICs started at about the same time as early work on silicon ICs. A number of technology-related problems, however, soon caused researchers to give up on GaAs, and silicon became dominant. Some important advantages of GaAs over silicon motivated the research community to try to turn back to GaAs several times during the past two decades. These "comebacks" did not succeed until the early 1980's.

A comparison of GaAs and silicon technologies

Although a number of different GaAs IC families exist, it is possible to draw some general conclusions about the advantages of GaAs technology over silicon technology:

• Currently, for the same power consumption, GaAs is about half an order of magnitude faster than emitter-coupled logic (ECL), the fastest silicon family. (This statement applies to integration levels and fabrication processes that can be depended on for production purposes. Data from laboratory experiments can be misleading if based on conditions that are not applicable to a reliable production environment.) Many researchers predict that the speed advantage of GaAs will increase over the coming years, although some researchers are skeptical about this.

• GaAs is more radiation-hard than silicon. At this time, however, the difference is difficult to quantify. On one hand, there is an indication of huge differences (several orders of magnitude). On the other hand, some recent measurements from an experimental microprocessor design show barely any difference with respect to radiation hardness. [1]

• GaAs is tolerant of temperature variations. Its operating range is from about -200°C to about +200°C. With respect to capability for accommodating a wide temperature range, the advantage of GaAs is definite.

• Also, GaAs is better suited to the efficient integration of electronic and optic

EH0266-7/88/0000/0075$01.00 © 1986 IEEE

75

components. The usefulness of GaAs for this type of integration is still under investigation, and if developed to the appropriate level, it may have a major impact on the area of system design in general.

Basic disadvantages of GaAs technology, as compared with silicon technology, are as follows:

• GaAs wafers presently exhibit a larger "density of dislocations" (that is, a larger number of irregularities per unit of area). Consequently, GaAs chips (1) have to be smaller in VLSI area, (2) have a smaller transistor count, and (3) have a worse yield. Of course, VLSI area can be traded off against production yield to some extent. Fabrication projections for 1987[2-4] put the transistor count for GaAs ICs below 30K. However, the *absolute* limits are higher. Recently, Japanese researchers announced a GaAs memory chip with 102,300 transistors.[5] It is believed that this integration level was achieved by serious sacrifices in the yield, and under special laboratory conditions.

In conclusion, the current integration level of GaAs is about one order of magnitude below that of silicon, and is expected to stay that way, although both technologies will improve.

• At the present time, GaAs substrates are about two orders of magnitude more expensive than silicon substrates. GaAs is intolerant of aluminum, and gold interconnects have to be used. Moreover, GaAs is brittle; wafers can be damaged easily during the fabrication of integrated circuits. However, many problems related to materials are considered temporary in nature, and one prediction states that the steady-state cost will be about one order of magnitude greater for GaAs than for silicon.[6]

• The noise margin at present is not as good as in silicon. It is often necessary to trade off chip area for higher reliability. Some GaAs IC families also exhibit a sensitivity to increased fan-in and fan-out. These problems are also considered temporary.

• Companies are currently reporting problems with the testing of designs for high-speed GaAs ICs. Testing facilities that are fast enough are simply not yet available. This situation is expected to improve.

Table 1 summarizes the most important performance-related facts. These facts reveal more about possible applications of GaAs technology. GaAs will never totally replace silicon, but will be used in selected aerospace, defense, and supercomputing applications. The extent of its usage is open to question; the "competition" between GaAs and silicon is an on-going one.

Considerations for designing GaAs microprocessors

Now that GaAs has reached the VLSI level of complexity, how should one design a GaAs microprocessor? One company that was involved in the design of both a 32-bit microprocessor for GaAs technology (namely a direct-coupled FET logic enhancement/depletion-mode metal semiconductor field-effect transistor, or DCFL E/D-MESFET) and a 32-bit microprocessor for silicon technology (in this case, complementary metal oxide semiconductor/silicon on sapphire, or CMOS/SOS) released the following data:

The technology speed ratio (i.e., the gate speed ratio) of the GaAs and silicon devices was about 6:1. However, the ratio of processor speeds (for compiled HLL code) was only about 3:1 in favor of GaAs. The situation was even worse in the area of coprocessor design. For the arithmetic coprocessor, the speed ratio was only 2:1 in favor of GaAs.[1]

The conclusion is clear—something has to be done in the area of microprocessor architecture and microprocessor design. This special issue explores the problem, which is difficult and represents a real challenge for the research community.

Is GaAs a "different animal" to work with than silicon? To answer this question, it is necessary to identify the basic technology differences of relevance for microprocessor architecture and design. GaAs is characterized by

• small on-chip VLSI area and transistor count, as well as
• high ratio of off-chip to on-chip delays.

Secondary and—one hopes—temporary differences that are limited to cer-

GaAs DRAM cell research is underway at Purdue

Future GaAs VLSI architectures will require large quantities of fast, high-density memory. To date, the only memory elements available to GaAs system designers have been six-transistor static RAMs (SRAMs), which require considerable chip area and continuously consume power.

However, researchers at Purdue University, under NSF sponsorship, are developing one-transistor dynamic random access memory (DRAM) cells for use in GaAs ICs. Like the test DRAM cell shown at right, they are designed with AlGaAs/GaAs heterojunction field-effect transistor technology (variously known as MODFET, HEMT, or HIGFET technology).

DRAMs made with this technology store electrons or holes in localized potential wells at the AlGaAs/GaAs heterojunction interface. Since the stored carriers tend to escape because of thermionic emission, the stored data is volatile (or "dynamic") and requires periodic refresh, just as silicon DRAMs do. However, since system cycle times in the AlGaAs/GaAs heterojunction field-effect transistor technology will be measured in nanoseconds, DRAMs in this technology will be feasible if storage times of a few hundred milliseconds or longer can be achieved.

Recent results obtained by J. A. Cooper, M. R. Melloch, and Q.-D. Qian at

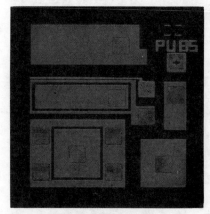

A test DRAM cell developed for use in GaAs ICs. (Test cell supplied by Purdue University. Photo taken by Melgar Commercial Photographers.)

Purdue with cells similar to the one shown have demonstrated storage times of 75 seconds at 175°K, 500 minutes at 140°K, and 220 hours at 77°K (the temperature of liquid nitrogen). These storage times are sufficient for DRAM operation at cryogenic temperatures, where MODFET circuits perform best.

The Office of Naval Research is also supporting work at Purdue on DRAM cells that operate efficiently at room temperature (300°K) and above. This work may soon fill a very important gap in GaAs IC technology.

James A. Cooper
Purdue University

Table 1. Performance comparisons of GaAs and silicon ICs.

	GaAs*1 (1μDCFL E/D-MESFET)*4	Silicon*2 (2μECL)*4	Silicon*3 (1.25μCMOS)*4	Silicon*2 (2μCMOS)*4	Silicon*2 (2μNMOS)*4
Complexity					
Transistor count per chip	20K to 30K	30K to 45K (TR or R)*4	300K	175K	200K to 300K
Chip area	Yield- and power-dependent	Yield- and power-dependent	Yield- and power-dependent	Yield- and power-dependent	Yield- and power-dependent
Speed					
Gate delay (for minimum values of fan-in and fan-out	50 ps to 150 ps	150 ps to 250 ps	500 ps to 750 ps	800 ps to 1 ns	1 ns to 3 ns
On-chip memory access (32 by 32)	0.5 ns to 2 ns	2 ns to 3 ns	5 ns to 10 ns	10 ns to 20 ns	20 ns to 40 ns
Off-chip/on-package memory access (256 by 32)	4 ns to 6 ns	6 ns to 10 ns	20 ns to 30 ns	30 ns to 40 ns	40 ns to 60 ns
Off-chip/off-package memory access	10 ns to 40 ns	20 ns to 60 ns	40 ns to 80 ns	60 ns to 100 ns	100 ns to 200 ns
IC Design					
Transistors per gate	1 + (fan-in)	3 + (fan-in)	2∗(fan-in)	2∗(fan-in)	1 + (fan-in)
Transistors per memory cell					
Static	6	6	5-6	5-6	6
Dynamic	1	N/A	N/A	N/A	1
Fan-in (typical transistor size)	2 to 3 (NOR)	8	5	5	5
Fan-out (typical transistor size)	3 to 4 (NOR)	10 to 20	5	5	5
Gate delay increase for each additional fan-out (relative to gate delay with fan-out = 1)	25% to 45%	5%	20% to 30%	20% to 30%	20% to 30%

*1. Information supplied by TriQuint.
*2. Information supplied by Fairchild.
*3. Information supplied by Toshiba.
*4. Abbreviations used in this table: "DCFL E/D-MESFET," for direct-coupled FET logic enhancement/depletion-mode metal semiconductor field-effect transistor; "ECL," for emitter-coupled logic; "CMOS," for complementary metal-oxide semiconductor; "NMOS," for N-type metal-oxide semiconductor; "TR," for transistor; "R," for resistor.

tain GaAs IC families should also be taken into consideration:

- higher dependency of gate delay on fan-in and fan-out, and
- nonexistence of some register-transfer-level and lower level components, such as the pass transistor, tri-state buffer, and so on.

Small on-chip "real estate" does not necessarily impact architecture and design adversely. The impact is strong only if penalties for going off-chip are relatively high, which is the case in GaAs. Therefore, a careful partitioning of system functions across chip boundaries is extremely important. The single-chip reduced instruction set computer (RISC) type of design is probably the only viable alternative among possible approaches to GaAs CPU design.[7] For a silicon environment, one might argue for a complex instruction set computer (CISC) approach or a RISC approach; in a GaAs environment there is no such choice.

RISC design strategy, however, has to be considerably modified for GaAs. First, in GaAs there is no place for an on-chip cache memory. If memory pipelining is chosen, it is much deeper than in silicon, and code optimization algorithms developed in a silicon environment for overcoming timing and sequencing hazards in pipelined architectures are of little use in a GaAs environment. Some researchers, moreover, advocate an approach in which traditional hardware functions (like various types of interlocks, bypass buses, cache control mechanisms, and so on) are migrated into software. This approach is contrary to the silicon design environment trend during the past decade. According to this so-called "synergism methodology,[2]" the "real estate" released by hardware-to-software migration should be invested in architecture constructs (like large register files) that have been proven efficient in technologies with large penalties for going off-chip.

Finally, differences related to fan-in/fan-out and nonexistence of certain register-transfer-level (RTL) and related elements can impact low-level design solutions.

In this issue

Important research in the area of GaAs microprocessor design and architecture went into DARPA's recent effort to build a 32-bit GaAs microprocessor.[8] Most of the contributions in this special issue of *Computer* were generated as part of that program.

The article by Sherman Karp and Sven Roosild of DARPA was invited specifically for this special issue to acknowledge the important role of DARPA during the past two decades in the areas of GaAs technology and GaAs microprocessor design. The focus of the article is on the activities that preceded and enabled the realization of the old dream, a 32-bit microprocessor in GaAs technology.

Lawrence Larson, Joseph Jensen, and Paul Greiling, all of Hughes Research Laboratories, present an overview of

GaAs IC technology. Their article was included to provide the background necessary for an understanding of the field in general, and the articles that follow theirs in particular.

In their article, Barry Gilbert, Barbara Naused, Daniel Schwab, and Rick Thompson summarize the results of DARPA-sponsored efforts in GaAs system design. The emphasis is on signal-processing architectures and their implementations.

The article by myself, Alex Silbey, David Fura, Kevin Keirn, and Mark Bettinger of Purdue University, and Walter Helbig, William Heagerty, Richard Zieger, Bob Schellack, and Walter Curtice of RCA Corporation, discusses various design issues of interest for GaAs microprocessor systems. Its focus is on RCA's effort to develop an 8-bit CPU and a 32-bit CPU in DCFL E/D-MESFET GaAs technology.

Terrence Rasset, Roger Niederland, John Lane, and William Geideman of McDonnell Douglas Astronautics Company describe an effort to build a 32-bit CPU with enhancement-mode JFET GaAs technology. Numerous design decisions are discussed and explained.

In their article, Eric Fox, Kenneth Kiefer, Robert Vangen, and Shaun Whalen of Control Data Corporation (CDC) describe the design and architecture of a 32-bit CPU to be produced jointly by Texas Instruments and CDC. This CPU is based on bipolar GaAs technology.

This special issue, I believe, will have an impact on the further development of the field. Unfortunately, because of space limitations, some excellent contributions could not be included. They are scheduled to appear in future issues of *Computer*. Below, I briefly address their contents:

Douglas Fouts, John Johnson, Steven Butner, and Stephen Long of the University of California at Santa Barbara describe the system architecture of a GaAs 1 GHz tester for digital ICs.

The article by J. McDonald, H. Greub, R. Steinvorth, and A. Bergendahl of Rensselaer Polytechnic Institute concentrates on interconnection issues in wafer-scale integration for GaAs technology. (In this article, the authors propose a RISC-type architecture that is well suited for the GaAs design environment.)

In their article, Theodore Lehr and Robert Wedig of Carnegie Mellon University describe a RISC-type architecture that is oriented to the production-system environment and is well suited for implementation in GaAs technology.

Michael Morgan of Magnavox Corporation describes an architecture that is oriented to the Lisp language and is well suited for implementation in GaAs technology. The architecture is referred to as GAELIC (Gallium Arsenide Experimental Lisp IC).

Further information

Obviously, there are a number of questions that have yet to be answered. Among important sources of new ideas and results, the reader is referred to conference proceedings from the IEEE GaAs IC Symposia and the IEEE/ACM Hawaii International Conferences on System Sciences (information about these proceedings is available from the IEEE Service Center in Piscataway, N.J.) and to proceedings from the IEEE ICCD Conferences (information about these proceedings is available from the IEEE-CS West Coast Office in Los Alamitos, Calif.).

Other important sources are the specialized journals, such as *IEEE Transactions on Computers, IEEE Micro,* and *IEEE Design & Test of Computers.* □

Acknowledgments

This special issue could not have been realized without the help that came from various sources.

Much of the empirical research on GaAs architecture was based on an Endot Corporation software package, N.2, and the related functional description language, ISP'; these were recently donated to several universities. Much of the research on the VLSI design level was based on in-house software packages, such as RCA's CADDAS with the related hardware description language (HDL); the basic parts of the CADDAS package were recently donated to some universities. Both donations (N.2 and CADDAS) enabled the university environment to catch up quickly in the new field of GaAs microprocessor design. Therefore, new contributions from both industrial and academic environments can be expected soon.

The enthusiasm and prompt response of the reviewers deserves a very special acknowledgment. Much of the technical quality of this special issue can be attributed to their dedicated work. Their names will be included in a list of all reviewers for *Computer* magazine that is scheduled for publication in an upcoming issue.

On the IEEE-CS side, *Computer* Editor-in-Chief Michael Mulder and *Computer* Editorial Board member Wing Toy assisted in improving the final form of this special issue.

Finally, colleagues of mine at Purdue University, Robert Pierret and Mark and Sarah Yoder, provided invaluable comments and suggestions for my Guest Editor's Introduction.

References

1. W. Helbig, "RISC vs. CISC, GaAs vs. Silicon, and Hardware vs. Software,"
invited lecture, Joint Chapter Meeting of the IEEE Microwave Theory and Techniques/IEEE Electron Devices societies, Princeton, New Jersey, Jan. 1986.
2. V. Milutinović et al., "Design Issues in GaAs Microcomputer Systems," *Computer,* Vol. 19, No. 10, Oct. 1986 (this issue).
3. T. L. Rasset et al., "A 32-bit RISC Implemented in Enhancement-Mode JFET GaAs," *Computer,* Vol. 19, No. 10, Oct. 1986 (this issue).
4. E. R. Fox et al., "Reduced Instruction Set Architecture for a GaAs Microprocessor System," *Computer,* Vol. 19, No. 10, Oct. 1986 (this issue).
5. Y. Ishii et al., "Processing Technologies for GaAs Memory LSIs," *Proc. GaAs IC Symposium,* Oct. 1984, pp. 121-124.
6. M. R. Namordi, "Advances in GaAs Technology," invited lecture, Purdue University, West Lafayette, Indiana, Oct. 1984.
7. V. Milutinović, D. Fura, and W. Helbig, "An Introduction to GaAs Microprocessor Architecture for VLSI," *Computer,* Vol. 19, No. 3, Mar. 1986, pp. 30-42.
8. C. Barney, "DARPA Eyes 100-MIPS GaAs Chip for Star Wars," *Electronics Week,* Vol. 58, No. 20, May 20, 1985, pp. 22-23.

Veljko Milutinović is on the faculty of the School of Electrical Engineering, Purdue University. He has published over 60 technical papers and two original books and has edited four books. He is the editor of the IEEE Press *Tutorial on Advanced Microprocessors and High-Level Language Computer Architecture* and the coeditor of the IEEE Press Tutorial on *Advanced Computer Architecture.* His current interests include VLSI computer architecture for GaAs, high-level language computer architecture, and artificial intelligence computer architecture. He has consulted for Fairchild, Intel, Honeywell, NASA, RCA, and other companies. He was involved in the industrial implementation of a 32-bit VLSI microprocessor in GaAs technology, with responsibilities in the microarchitecture domain.

Milutinović received the PhD degree from the University of Belgrade, Belgrade, Yugoslavia.

Readers may direct questions concerning this special issue to Veljko Milutinović, Purdue University, School of Electrical Engineering, West Lafayette, IN 47907.

SYSTEM LEVEL COMPARISON OF HIGH SPEED TECHNOLOGIES

Tushar R. Gheewala

Gigabit Logic, 1908 Oak Terrace Lane, Newbury Park, CA 91320

ABSTRACT

The performance of Silicon, GaAs MESFET, HEMT and the Josephson technologies are compared at packaged, system levels. The comparative analysis indicates that at system level the 1μm GaAs MESFET technology offers a roughly 1.5x performance advantage over super-self-aligned-deep-trench 1μm ECL while using similar packaging technology. The 1μm HEMT technology, at 77K temperature promises roughly a 3x performance advantage over 1μm ECL, when armed with a 2x superior package. The 2.5μm Josephson technology at 4K temperature is judged to be about 2x faster than ECL - faster than GaAs MESFET but slower than HEMT. Finally, the performance of RISC like computers based on VLSI chip sets is estimated for CMOS and GaAs MESFET technologies. It is shown that with the speeds and densities achievable from the GaAs MESFET technology the performance of a VLSI microcomputer will be comparable to that of LSI mainframe computers.

I. INTRODUCTION

Design of a high-performance computer requires a careful match between its architecture, the speed and integration levels of the circuit technology and the packaging technology. In this paper we will compare the system level performance of various contending high-speed circuit technologies for a set of different computer architectures and while defining the requirements for the necessary packaging techniques. The contending high-speed circuit techniques we have selected are:

1) 1μm super-self-aligned, deep-groove-isolated bipolar ECL [1];
2) 1μm, Enhancement-Depletion mode GaAs MESFET [2];
3) 1μm, 77K HEMT [3] and
4) 2.5μm, 4K Josephson technology [4]

(2.5μm minimum dimension was selected for Josephson technology instead of 1.0μm because of its need for very tight line width controls.) We will also consider 1μm CMOS technology as a condidate for high-performance VLSI microcomputers.

The three architectures used to compare the different technologies are:

1. scientific computers,
2. large mainframe computers, and
3. reduced instruction set computers (RISC).

For each of the above architectures a representative critical path is selected to estimate the computer cycle time.

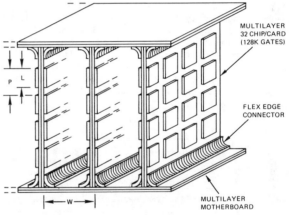

Fig 1

The general packaging approach is a card-on-board arrangement indicated in Fig. 1 [5]. Each card contains 32 surface mounted single-chip modules. This will provide sufficient circuits to implement a complete functional unit such as cache or instruction fetch and decode logic on a single card, minimizing the communications bandwidth between cards. In case of the VLSI microcomputer, a single card would contain the entire processor chip set and a cache. Refering back to the Fig. 1, single chip module size L, pitch P, card spacing W and the materials and wiring densities of the card and the motherboard are determined by the following considerations:

chip size
cooling requirements
stub lengths
series inductance
thermal mismatch, etc.

Reprinted from *Proceedings of the IEEE International Conference on Computer Design: VLSI in Computers*, 1984, pages 245-250. Copyright © 1984 by The Institute of Electrical and Electronics Engineers, Inc.

In the following sections we will review the performance of the circuit technologies, establish package characteristics, look at the critical paths and then finally compare the performance.

II. CIRCUIT TECHNOLOGY

The characteristics of the four competing high-speed technologies are listed in Table 1. The loaded gate delay corresponds to an average fan-in and fan-out of three. The minimum ring oscillator delays are the best published results, whereas the rest of the numbers in Table 1 are estimates made by the author on the basis of published data. The off-chip driver delay estimates are based on the package dimensions and materials described in the next section. The substantially higher power dissipation of ECL chips results in lower packaging density for ECL chips as compared to GaAs chips, resulting in longer driver delays. The HEMT driver delay estimate is based on a direct ´flip-chip´ (or C_4) interconnection of HEMT IC chips on a multilayer substrate, resulting in high packaging densities, similar to those reported for the IBM 3081 Thermal Conduction Modules (TCM) [6]. The Josephson driver circuit delays are also based on a ´flip-chip´ mounting of Josephson ICs on a silicon substrate with multilevel metallization [5]. However, the driver delays in this case are substantially degraded due to the low impedence of the transmission lines used for signal transmission, which amplifies the inductive load delays, L/Z_0. The gate array density per chip is estimated on the basis of the device sizes as well as on the processing capabilities in similar phases of development.

In addition, for VLSI micro-computer designs, one of the following two scenarios is considered: a 1µm CMOS technology with 1.5nS gate delay and up to 20K gates per chip capability, assumed to be available in 1986 and second, at a later date in 1990, a 1µm GaAs MESFET technology with 300ps gate delay and 10K gates per chip capability.

III. PACKAGING TECHNOLOGY

Refering to Fig 1, a three level packaging hierarchy is judged adequate for ECL and GaAs MESFET technologies: chip-on-module, module-on-card and card-on-board. Direct chip-on-card packaging with flip-chip technique would eliminate the delay through the chip module. However, this approach has one major drawback, in that only multi-layer ceramic (MLC) cards can be used for this application due to the need for a good match between the thermal expansions of the chip and the card. Because of the higher dielectric constant of ceramic and the higher skin losses in Tugnsten or Molybdenum metallizations used with the multi-layer ceramic boards, this approach is judged to have no significant performance advantage over the chip-to-module-to-card approach where the card is made from low-dielectric constant materials such as polyimide or Teflon [7]. The region between the cards is used for heat removal. The medium for heat removal differs for each technology. For GaAs it would be air, for ECL it would be chilled water running through conduits in thermal contact with the chips, liquid Nitrogen for HEMT and liquid Helium for Josephson technology.

The electrical requirements on the packaging technology are listed in Table 2. The stub lengths and the discontinuity limits in the table are designed so as to produce less than 20% ringing in the signal lines.

TECHNOLOGY	1µm self-aligned ECL	1µm GaAs MESFET (E/D)	1µm GaAs HEMT	2.5µm Josephson
OPERATING TEMPERATURE	300K	300K	77K	4K
VOLTAGE SWING (V)	0.6	0.6	0.2	1mV
MINIMUM RING OSC. DELAY (ps)	115	50	13	9
LOADED GATE DELAY (ps)	200	150	50	35
POWER DISSIPATION/GATE (mW)	6	0.5	0.1	0.002
OFF-CHIP DRIVER DELAY (ps)	400	300	200	200
4K RAM ACCESS TIME (ns)	3.0	1.5	0.5	1.0
GATE ARRAY DENSITY	4K	4K	4K	1K

TABLE 1.   PROJECTED PERFORMANCE OF HIGH-SPEED TECHNOLOGIES

TECHNOLOGY	1µm ECL or GaAs MESFET	1µm HEMT	2.5µm Josephson
CHIP-TO-MODULE CONNECTIONS	WIREBONDS OR TAB	SOLDER BUMP (C_4)	SOLDER BUMP (C_4)
CARD AND BOARD DIELECTRICS	POLYIMIDE, CERAMIC or TEFLON	POLYIMIDE on CERAMIC	SiO ON SILICON
SIGNAL CONDUCTORS	COPPER or TUNGSTEN	COPPER and TUNGSTEN	LEAD or NIOBIUM
POWER REGULATION/ BY-PASS CAPACITORS	OFF-CHIP	ON-CHIP	ON-CHIP
OFF-CHIP TRANSMISSION LINES IMPEDANCE(Ω)	50-100	50-100	10-15
MINIMUM OFF-CHIP RISE AND FALL TIMES (ps)	150	75	50
MAXIMUM PACKAGE DISCONTINUITIES (e.g. PINS, VIAS, etc.)	4nH 0.5pF	1nH 0.25pF	0.15nH 1.25pF
MAXIMUM STUB LENGTH (e_R= 4)	8mm	4mm ALLOWED	STUBS NOT

TABLE 2.   REQUIRED ELECTRICAL PROPERITES OF PACKAGES
FOR VERY HIGH SPEED TECHNOLOGIES

	BIPOLAR ECL	GaAs MESFET	GaAs HEMT	JOSEPHSON TECHNOLOGY
GATE DENSITY	4K	4K	4K	1K
CHIP SIZE	.300"x.300"	.200"x.200"	0.200"x0.200"	0.250"x0.250"
NUMBER of I/Os	300	250	300	250
L	0.750"	0.600"	0.300"	0.250"
P	1.000"	0.750"	0.400"	0.300"
W	1.200"	0.700"	0.300"	0.150"

TABLE III.   PHYSICAL DIMENSIONS OF CARD-ON-BOARD
PACKAGES FOR HIGH-SPEED TECHNOLOGIES.

The Josephson technology package is based on a direct chip-on-card technique, utilizing a silicon card for thermal expansion match with the Si substrate of the ICs down to 4K temperature. It uses SiO insulator and superconducting signal lines. As mentioned earlier, the series inductance of card-to-board connectors ($\approx$300 pH) is a crucial limiting factor of this package.

To extract the maximum performance from the HEMT technology, we require direct chip-to-card interconnect technique on a low dielectric constant material card with low resistance metallization and with good thermal expansion match to 77K. No adequate solution to these requirements can at present be found among the existing packaging materials. For now, we must use multilayer ceramic card to package HEMT circuits - resulting in a degraded driver performance of 200ps delay, as indicated earlier in Table 1.

The physical dimensions of the package for the different high-speed technologies are derived on the basis of above considerations and listed in Table 3.

IV. PERFORMANCE COMPARISON

a. Scientific Computers

One of the critical paths in any scientific computers is the addition of two large numbers. Based on a Carry Look Ahead / Carry Save Adder (CLA/CSA) architecture for the Arithmatic and Logic Unit (ALU) we can estimate the length of this critical path in different technologies using the following simple formula:

$$t_{cyc} = 6 \text{ Gate Delay} + N \text{ Chip Crossing delay} + \text{Latch} + \text{Clock Skew}$$

Where N, the number of chip crossings, depends on the circuit integration level on the chip. For the 4K gates/chip integration level we have allowed for the bipolar, GaAs and HEMT technologies, three chip crossings is a very reasonable assumption. For the Josephson technology with a lower level of integration 4 chip crossings are estimated to be necessary. The results are compared in Fig. 2. The large amount of latch and clock skew delay for the Josephson technology is caused by the so called punch-through phenomena which restricts the rise and fall times of the clock to 0.7nS. The number of megaflops per second are derived from the following formula:

$$\text{Megaflops} = \frac{3}{t_{cyc(ns)}}$$

which assumes that there are three parallel computational processes in the scientific computer.

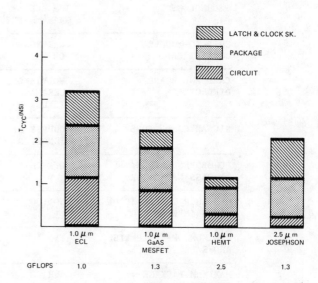

Fig.2 Projected Performance of Scientific Computers.

b. Large Mainframe Computers

Cache access is very often a critical path in the determination of the cycletime of a large mainframe computer. We estimate this delay as follows:

$$t_{cycle} = 10 \text{ Gate Delays} + \text{Memory Access} + 3 \text{ Chip Crossing} + 1 \text{ Card Crossing} + \text{Latch} + \text{Clock Skew}$$

and the number of Million Instructions Per Second (MIPS) is give by

$$\text{MIPS} = \frac{1}{4 \, t_{cyc(ns)}}$$

Allowing on average four cycles to execute a single instruction.

Once again, for the Josephson technology we include one additional chip crossing because of its lower circuit density. The performances of large mainframe computers for the four high-speed technologies are compared in Fig. 3.

c. VLSI Micro-Computer

The VLSI micro-computer relies on very large scale integration to compress the entire processor into a single chip. The architectures of such computers, because of density limitations are not highly pipelined. The cycletime in this case is derived using the following equation:

$$t_{cyc} = 20 \text{ Gate delays} + \text{Register File Access} + \text{Latch} + \text{Clock Skew}$$

LARGE BUSINESS COMPUTER

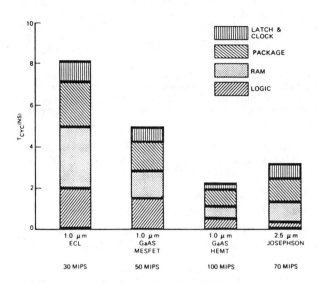

Fig.3 Projected Performance of Large Mainframe Computers.

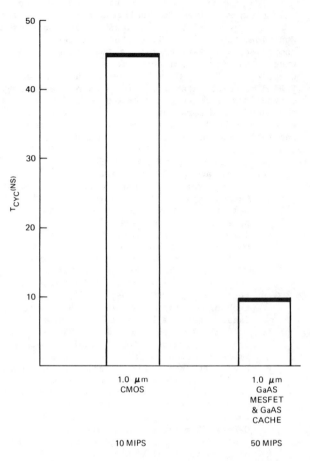

Fig.4 Projected Performance of VLSI micro-computers.

Note that no chip crossing delay is included because of the single chip implementation of the entire instruction execution path. Only two technologies are judged capable of such integration levels: CMOS and GaAs MESFET. The 1µm ECL technology consumes too much power to be suitable for this application. We estimate that at 6 mW per gate power dissipation and at 10,000 gates per chip integration level necessary for VLSI implementation of micro-computers, the 60 W per chip power dissipation is impractical for most applications of VLSI computers such as desktop computers. Lower power logic families of the bipolar technology such as TTL, STL, $I^2 L$ have shown no performance, density or power advantage over CMOS and are therefore of little interest. The HEMT technology was not considered for the micro-computer applications because of its need for liquid Nitrogen cooling.

The performance of the VLSI micro-computers based on CMOS and GaAs MESFET technology are compared in Fig. 4. The equivalent million instructions per second (MIPS) were estimated assuming a reduced instruction set computer (RISC) architecture that requires on the average about two cycles per instruction. For the GaAs micro-computer a 10ns GaAs cache is necessary to sustain such a high level of performance.

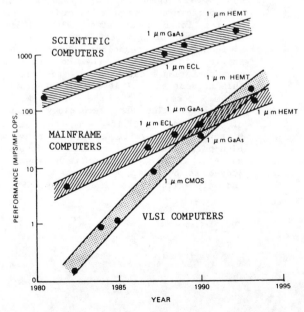

Fig.5 Performance Trends (Right)

V. DISCUSSIONS AND SUMMARY

We have compared the sytem level performance of competing high-performance circuit technologies. These technologies are 1μm bipolar ECL, 1μm GaAs MESFET, 1μm HEMT, 2.5μm Josephson Junction and 1μm CMOS technologies. The comparison was carried out on the basis of three widely varying architectures: 1) scientific computers; 2) large mainframe computers; and 3) VLSI micro-computers. For each technology appropriate packaging technology was defined and the physical dimensions and the packaging delays were determined. On the basis of this analysis the following conclusions can be drawn:

1. The 1.0μm GaAs MESFET technology is judged to be about 1.5x superior to 1.0μm super-self-aligned, deep-trench, bipolar technology. Since a large part of this performance advantage can be traced to the superior speed of GaAs cache memory, it is likely that the GaAs MESFET technology will be first introduced in the computers in the form of high-speed cache memory.

2. The 77K, HEMT techology is judged to be roughly 3x superior to the 1.0μm ECL technology. The 4K, 2.5μm Josephson technology is estimated to be about 2x faster than the 1.0μm ECL technology.

3. 1.0μm CMOS and GaAs MESFET technologies are suitable for VLSI chip-set implementation of micro-computers. With high-performance RISC architectures these VLSI micro-computers are capable of performance that is competitive with that of large mainframe computers - at a much lower cost. We estimate here that a 1μm GaAs VLSI micro-computer with a GaAs cache would be capable of generating 50 MIPS performance level.(Fig.5).

4. On the basis of the above analysis we can conclude that the CMOS technology will dominate the low cost computer area. The GaAs MESFET technology will dominate the cost-performance computer domain because of its lower power dissipation, higher density and higher performance than the silicon bipolar technology. It will make initial inroads into the computers as high-performance cache memory and dominate this segment as VLSI levels of integration become possible in the GaAs MESFET technology. The HEMT technology because of high cost and its need for liquid Nitrogen cooling will be limited to very-high-performance scientific computer market. The Josephson technology is judged to be lower performance than HEMT and only slightly superior to GaAs MESFET.

REFERENCES

[1] T. Sakai, et. al., "HighSpeed Bipolar IC´s Using Super Self-Aligned Process Technology", Proceedings, 12th Conference of the Solid-State Devices, Tokyo, 1980.; also, D.D. Tang, et. al., "1-25μm Deep-Groove-Isolated Self-Aligned ECL Circuits", Proceedings, ISSCC, p. 242, Feb. 1982.

[2] Y. Yamasaki, et. al., "GaAs LSI-Directed MESFETs with Self-Aligned Implantation for N+-Layer Technology (SAINT)". IEEE Trans. on Electron Dev., Vol. ED-29, No. 11, p. 1772, Nov. 1982.

[3] T. Mimura, et. al., "High Electron Mobility Transistor Logic," Japanese Jour. Appl. Phys., Vol. 20, p. L598, Aug. 1981.

[4] T. Gheewala, "The Josephson Technology", IEEE Proc., Vol. 70, No.1, p. 26-34, Jan. 1982.

[5] M. Ketchen, et. al., "A Josephson Technology System Level Experiment", IEEE Electron Dev. Lett., Oct. 1981.

[6] A. J. Blodgett and D.R. Barbour, "Thermal Conduction Module: A High-Performance Multi-layer Ceramic Package", IBM Jour. Res. Develop., Vol. 26, No.1, p. 30, Jan. 1982.

Reprinted from *Computer*, October 1986, pages 17-19. Copyright © 1986 by The Institute of Electrical and Electronics Engineers, Inc.

DARPA, SDI, and GaAs

A 1K-bit GaAs complementary static RAM. (Photo courtesy McDonnell Douglas Microelectronics Center.)

Sherman Karp and Sven Roosild

Defense Advanced Research Projects Agency

DARPA and the SDI support the development of GaAs technology because of its vital military applications. It has great potential for high-speed signal processing, low power dissipation, and high radiation resistance.

When silicon replaced germanium in the early 1960's as the semiconductor of choice for solid state devices, it converted the entire industry in just a few years because of two important characteristics. First, silicon has a higher energy bandgap, which permits silicon-based devices to operate over a wider temperature range (a feature especially important to the military). Second, and more important, silicon has a native oxide that provided for improved stability and planar, rather than mesa, type devices. Planar technology soon spawned integrated circuits. The integrated circuit in turn brought on the electronics revolution, allowing the complexity of circuits to increase by a factor of two every year (Moore's Law) and bringing us from single transistors to megabit memory chips.

Characteristics of GaAs

As a semiconductor, gallium arsenide has one of the characteristics that proved so important to the rapid development of silicon technology. GaAs has an even higher bandgap, allowing operation over an even wider temperature range. However, instead of a native oxide, GaAs provides a semi-insulating substrate, which neither silicon nor germanium possess. This semi-insulating substrate is ideal for an all-ion-implanted planar device technology.

Furthermore, despite the absence of a native oxide, the GaAs surface is stabilized by surface defect states (rather than passivated by a native oxide). This benefits

the development of GaAs radiation-hardened circuits, of vital interest to many military systems, since radiation-induced charging of native or deposited insulators will not cause shifts in device characteristics as it does in silicon devices.

Unfortunately, the surface properties of GaAs impede commercial production of high-complexity, low-cost chips: The lack of passivation eliminates the possibility of the MOS-type circuits that form the basis for the widest segment of present day silicon VLSI.

Early efforts

In the early 1960's a lot of effort went into developing bipolar transistors in GaAs. These efforts were frustrated by the low lifetime of minority carriers in this direct-bandgap semiconductor, the difficulties of introducing dopants by diffusion, and the thermal conversion (becoming electrically conductive after heat treatments) of the semi-insulating substrates. Real progress in GaAs-based circuits began when the principal cause of thermal conversion—even slight crystal growth on the gallium-rich side of the binary phase diagram—was uncovered. Ion implantation replaced diffusion as the means for introducing dopants, and metal-semiconductor FETs (MESFETs) and junction field-effect transistors (JFETs) emerged as devices suitable for building ICs in GaAs, being majority carrier devices for which the short lifetime of GaAs is not a difficulty.

Once a workable IC fabrication technology became available, additional impetus to the development of a GaAs-based semiconductor technology came from the high electron mobility inherent to GaAs, which translates into improved speed and power. This advantage of GaAs plus its inherent radiation hardness made it a natural for military research. Realizing this, in the mid-1970's the Defense Sciences Office (DSO) of DARPA started a technology-based program to develop GaAs digital circuits.

At about the same time, the Strategic Technology Office (STO) in DARPA was investigating spaceborne signal processing for a broad range of military missions. STO concluded that a need existed for radiation resistant, low power, highly reliable, and programmable signal processing systems. They initiated the advanced onboard signal processor (AOSP) program to develop a suitable architecture. One of the goals of this program was the fabrication of an AOSP brassboard. After careful investigation, the best candidate technology was found to be GaAs.

GaAs chip manufacture

The first ingredient of reliable electronic systems is a reduced total chip count. Studies showed that a minimum of a 16K-bit static RAM was necessary, with a strong desire for a 64K-bit SRAM. Additionally, a large configurable gate array (6000 gates) was necessary. Considering that the most complex GaAs chip successfully fabricated at that time (1980) was a laboratory-fabricated 8-by-8 multiplier composed of 1008 gates, the task ahead looked formidable and extremely risky—just the type of technical challenge for which DARPA was created.

In 1982, DSO and STO joined forces to start development of an all-GaAs prototype of the AOSP. Both complexity and yield of GaAs ICs had to increase by orders of magnitude simultaneously. Only by phenomenally increasing yield could a sufficient number of memory and gate array chips of the desired complexity be produced to realize the GaAs AOSP prototype. Clearly, it was necessary to emulate the same learning curve improvement in yield and complexity that had propelled silicon technology to the VLSI era—and in a shorter time. Fortunately, much of the methodology and equipment used by the silicon industry transfers to GaAs circuit fabrication with minor changes. Lines processing a minimum of 100 three-inch wafers a week were contractually required, based on surveys of the silicon industry showing that such a throughput is the minimum necessary to ensure a reasonable yield of complex chips.

The first pilot line program began in 1983, the next in 1985, and a third is planned for late 1986 or early 1987. In addition to developing the chips for the AOSP, these pilot lines will provide the foundation for military and commercial uses of digital circuits in advanced computers, instrumentation, and communication systems.

GaAs specifications

In setting the specifications for components manufactured on the GaAs pilot line, it was necessary to keep in mind the primary concerns for spaceborne systems: weight and power. Consequently, not raw speed but millions of instructions per second per unit of power, or MIPS per watt, became the critical figure. Despite pressure from the contractors, DARPA maintained this commitment and set the specification of the SRAM at one microwatt per bit for static power with a 10 ns access time. Similarly, for the gate arrays the requirements were 400 μW for a D-flip-flop toggling at 50 MHz. These low power goals require operation at low threshold voltages with extremely tight control on uniformity to achieve adequate noise margins. An IC fabrication process developed for these requirements can always be relaxed to accommodate the higher drive needs of fast circuits. The reverse, however, would not necessarily be true. (Furthermore, an increase of two in frequency often requires an order of magnitude increase in power.)

Because of the multiplicity of GaAs pilot lines being developed under the auspices of DARPA contracts and the resulting legacy for military use, it was recognized that some mechanism would be required to allow defense contractors not intimately familiar with these lines to exploit their manufacturing potential. Each pilot line uses a different GaAs chip technology. Since each technology possesses different strengths, the capability to fabricate the same chip design(s) in more than one of these technologies could aid system optimization. In the commercial silicon VLSI world, in general, the design of each IC must be targeted from the outset for a particular chip technology (2-micron CMOS, 1.25-micron NMOS, ECL, etc.). To refabricate the same chip design in a different silicon chip technology, nearly the entire design process must be repeated. To minimize this problem across the several GaAs pilot lines and technologies, DARPA has sponsored the development at the Mayo Foundation of a comprehensive computer aided design package, which allows the design of technology-independent chips in a straightforward manner.

CAD of GaAs

Hosted on Digital Equipment Corporation VAX computers, this large CAD software system dramatically reduces the amount of redesign effort required to change from one GaAs technology to another. Every integrated circuit, or in fact the entire processor system, is designed initially using a generic library of gate array and standard cell functional components.

The CAD system also supports a number of technology-specific libraries of functional components. Every functional component, or macro, in every technology library has a corresponding macro component in the generic library. This matching between generic and technology-specific functional components permits an entire chip or system design to be retargeted from its initial generic form into a technology-specific form, then laid out on the specific ICs for the selected GaAs technology. The retargeting process can be fully automatic, fully manual, or a combination of both, depending upon desired chip packing density (efficiency) and desired turnaround time. Simply by selecting different technology-specific libraries, the same generic design can be retargeted for any one or more of the emerging GaAs technologies. Also, at least one silicon technology will be targeted so that functionality can be tested for minimum cost.

A GaAs microprocessor

In the spring of 1984 it was decided that, in addition to the gate array and the RAM, a custom GaAs microprocessor was needed as an engine to drive the AOSP. While it is possible to construct a microprocessor from gate arrays, performance would clearly suffer. The need for a 32-bit machine added a further complication. At the time, a 10K-bit custom chip was considered the outer limit of complexity achievable in the program's timeframe. Moreover, an interest in high performance resulted in a desire to build the microprocessor on a single chip. An exhaustive search was made of the known microprocessor architectures. The only single-chip design that met all the requirements outlined above was a DARPA-developed reduced instruction set computer (RISC) design at Stanford called Microprocessor without Interlocked Pipeline Stages (MIPS).

In the fall of 1984, three Phase I contracts were competitively awarded to TI, RCA, and McDonnell-Douglas to start the construction of a single chip, all GaAs, MIPS microprocessor with a 200-MHz clock frequency. In the fall of 1985, two of the three contractors, TI and McDonnell-Douglas, were selected to fully develop the MIPS microprocessor with a floating-point coprocessor and the necessary bus and memory interface chips.

As part of the Phase I effort, each of the contractors has undertaken to produce portions of the final design, constituting 2000 to 3000 gates. None of these parts are as yet working, but these efforts will continue into Phase II. Completion of the GaAs MIPS microprocessor is scheduled for late 1987. Current projections for the microprocessor performance are 50 ns for a floating-point multiply. To obtain these speeds, a small (1K word) cache memory with a 1 ns access time will be needed. Thus, the final design will include working chips for both fast and slow memory access, as well as chips for bus and sensor interfaces. Both contractor designs will use the same core instruction set, to which several software compilers (Pascal, Ada, and C) and translators (1750a and 68000) have already been targeted.

These two contractors will also design a vector coprocessor to support the MIPS processing system. The only requirement for this vector processor is that it run the Macro Function Assembly Language (MFAL) currently used in the development of the AOSP software. This will allow an orderly transition of the planned AOSP demonstration onto the GaAs brassboard. Since careful consideration was given to using the MFAL language initially, this is considered a plus for ease of programming. Other languages will also be accommodated.

GaAs and the SDI

The Strategic Defense Initiative was formed in 1984. DARPA's GaAs Pilot Program was shifted to SDI as a fundamental part of the radiation-resistant space signal processor program. By mutual consent, DARPA has continued to manage the GaAs program for the SDI Organization. The SDI office has in turn staunchly supported both GaAs and the AOSP. The all-GaAs AOSP system is currently scheduled for completion in 1990 as one of the major technology milestones in the SDI program. Although the specifications have not been set, it is likely that this system will operate at processing rates up to several GFlops and occupy no more than half a standard rack.

Having identified radiation-hard, low power circuitry as a unique niche for digital technology, and having identified the AOSP architecture for implementation with these circuits, we have every reason to expect that GaAs-based digital semiconductor technology will become firmly established by the end of this DARPA/SDIO program. □

Sherman Karp is a consultant whose interests include communications and signal processing. As a principal scientist in the Strategic Technology Office of DARPA, his contributions included the Blue/Green Satellite-to-Submarine communications system, the DOD GaAs digital technology, and the miniaturized GPS receiver and associated systems. He won the Scientist of the Year award at NOSC in 1976.

Karp received a BS in 1960 and an MS in 1962 from MIT, and a PhD in 1967 from USC, all in electrical engineering.

Sven A. Roosild is assistant director for electronic sciences in the Defense Sciences Office of DARPA. While program manager, he initiated the DARPA low power, radiation hard GaAs LSI pilot line programs. His interests include high energy ion implantation technology, radiation hardening of semiconductor devices, solid state analog signal processing components, and infrared imaging.

Roosild received a BA in engineering and applied physics from Harvard in 1960 and an MA in physics from Boston University in 1966.

Readers may write to Roosild at the Electronic Sciences Division, 1400 Wilson Blvd., Arlington, VA 22209-2308.

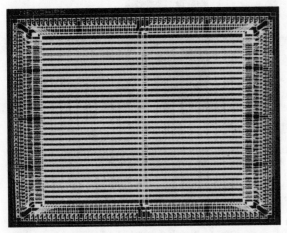

The floorplan of the Honeywell 5183, a 5500-equivalent-gate GaAs gate array developed by Honeywell, Inc., Rockwell International, and the Mayo Foundation. (Photo courtesy of the Mayo Foundation.)

Reprinted from *Computer*, October 1986, pages 29-43. Copyright © 1986 by The Institute of Electrical and Electronics Engineers, Inc.

Signal Processors Based Upon GaAs ICs:

The Need for a Wholistic Design Approach

Barry K. Gilbert, Barbara A. Naused, Daniel J. Schwab, and Rick L. Thompson

Mayo Foundation

Recasting traditional signal-processor architectures at the memory-layout, logic-design, arithmetic-implementation, and system-architecture levels will permit fuller use of GaAs technology.

Advances in the development of digital GaAs ICs have progressed to the point that designers of signal and data processors and of analog conversion modules can begin to discern the systems applications for which they are best suited. The high electron mobilities of GaAs transistors result in very fast electron transit times across their active regions and hence generate the potential for extremely short gate propagation delays.[1] So-called first-generation GaAs gates using FET structures (both depletion-mode MESFETs, or D-MESFETs, and enhancement-mode junction FETs, or EJFETs) similar to those fabricated in silicon have exhibited switching delays as low as 100 ps at 1-3 mW power dissipation. First-generation GaAs components that have been manufactured at reasonable yield levels are currently in the 1000-2000 gate range, with components of 5000-6000 gate density presently in development and demonstration.[2,3]

More advanced GaAs transistor technologies are also undergoing development that rely upon enhancement- and depletion-mode GaAs FET devices working together (so-called E/D MESFET structures); these devices have demonstrated 52-ps switching delays at 0.55 mW power dissipation.[4] In addition, an even more sophisticated second generation of GaAs transistors is being studied, i.e., a hetero-junction structure combining alternate layers of GaAs and GaAlAs, in which the effective electron mobility of the device can be five times greater than in the first-generation GaAs transistor. Switching delays for the resulting gates have been reported[5] as low as 5.8 ps at 77° Kelvin and 10.2 ps at 25° centigrade. These heterojunction FET structures are referred to as High Electron Mobility Transistors (HEMTs), Modulation-Doped FETs (MODFETs), or Selectively Doped Heterojunction Transistors (SDHTs). Heterojunction GaAs bipolar transistor (HBT) equivalents of silicon bipolar and silicon IIL bipolar transistors have also been developed, with both demonstrating considerable promise as well.[6,7]

As illustrated by the previous comments, the natural operational regime of GaAs digital ICs appears to be in high bandwidth, high clock rate signal and array processing, and in supporting disciplines such as wide bandwidth short burst data recording. Optimum exploitation of the high gate speeds typical of GaAs devices will require a different approach to processor architectures than for silicon VLSI. As will be emphasized later, the number of gate delays that occur on each IC should be maximized, thereby minimizing the system performance loss caused by the interchip connections. A reconsideration of architectural issues will become even more crucial when second-generation heterojunction transistors (e.g., the HEMT structures) can be used[5] to fabricate gates with propagation delays as low as 10-50 ps. The best mechanisms for exploiting such outstanding transistor performance for logic, arithmetic, and memory must be ascertained, and the architectural designs for entire systems will have to be reconsidered as well.[8] In the following sections we will discuss these issues for logic and for arithmetic, and then for memory components; we will also comment on the manner in which these elements may be configured in large processor systems.

The remainder of this article will expand upon the problem of designing processor systems in GaAs through the discussion of an additional set of topics that, until recently, have been of particular concern, not to the computer architect, but to the computer fabricator. In the past, processor architects employing silicon have been able to neglect many important implementation and fabrication issues, in the certain knowledge that these issues would be addressed at a later time in the system evolution by individuals experienced in IC packaging, system cooling, intraprocessor communications, and power handling. One of the most important lessons to have emerged from GaAs is that these heretofore mundane issues have, with the advent of high system clock rates, become inseparable from the architectural design itself, and can represent the difference between success in implementing the processor and total project failure. These ancillary areas are now very central to processor design and quite closely interdigitated with one another, and yet are very little understood by traditional designers of signal processors. Only the adoption of a wholistic approach to the design of high clock rate signal processors will result in the type of robust high performance systems of which GaAs is capable.

Signal processing applications requiring digital GaAs

With the prior comments in mind, there is a growing consensus among many design engineers that the majority of near-term applications for digital GaAs ICs will include: high-speed acquisition and perhaps storage of very wide bandwidth pulsed, pseudo-random, or continuous stream data; real-time radar signal processing and signature analysis; electronic countermeasures; data encryption; spread spectrum communications; error detection and correction of wideband data flowing through noisy channels (thereby

in effect improving the signal to noise ratio of the channel); and in communications interfaces between electronic signal processors and fiber-optic data channels. As but a single example of this large class of problems for which digital GaAs appears extremely well suited, a very serious requirement exists in the US military community to be able to characterize accurately the onset of occurrence, duration, and other characteristics of radiated electromagnetic energy, e.g., radar pulses, impinging upon a vehicle such as an aircraft. Receiving antennas and RF amplifiers mounted on the vehicle can receive the energy, increase its amplitude, and convert its frequency to lower values. If the time course of the electromagnetic pulse is to be characterized, the pulse must be sampled, or digitized, by very high-speed analog-to-digital (A/D) converters, and the digitized values stored in a small scratch pad memory, from which they can be read at more leisurely rates by a digital computer, or transmitted to the inputs of a high speed D/A converter. Such a combined A/D converter and scratch pad memory, which is referred to as a Digital RF Memory (DRFM), is described more completely in reference 9. To the present, these devices have been manufactured with silicon components, and hence have been limited to sampling rates of a few hundred megahertz and sampling resolutions of 4-6 bits. The DRFMs are of such importance that the military customers for these processors have been willing to employ silicon-based DRFMs even though their performance is considered less than optimal. Thus, there is considerable interest in the expansion of their capabilities, initially through the judicious use of GaAs and silicon components in combination, and eventually, through the design and fabrication of units based entirely upon GaAs. An example of the performance achievable with GaAs-based DRFMs will be presented later in this article.

Interdependence of algorithms, architectures, and device technologies

As an extension of these comments, it should be noted that nearly a generation of architecture research for general-purpose computers, and especially for digital signal processors, has demonstrated that there is a close relationship between the type of algorithm requiring implementation, the processor architecture with which such a design is implemented, and the transistor technology building blocks from which the architecture is constructed. Recent research regarding the optimum use of

silicon VLSI has assumed the availability of a large number of gates on each IC, while downplaying the utility or even the effects of gate speed. Hence, VLSI circuit designers have been motivated to employ highly parallel signal processor architectures, and have placed less emphasis on structures that exploit gate speed. Only recently has the Very High Speed Integrated Circuits (VHSIC) Program, sponsored by the US Department of Defense, placed more emphasis on speed requirements for large silicon components.

Conversely, a different class of signal processor architectures is best suited to implementation in GaAs, in particular those designs that retain all operands on each IC for the maximum duration. Specific examples of such layouts include iterative and recursive algorithms executed on-chip at high clock rates, systolic arrays,[10] and the so-called element-per-pixel approaches as embodied in the GAP processor developed in the United States and the CLIP machines developed in the United Kingdom.[11] During the past few years, these types of iterative and array structured algorithms have received increased attention from architectural theoreticians, and are now being studied under the generic title of "cellular automata," as described in reference 12. In general, structures that are deeply pipelined and (by inference) require a minimum of decision branching appear to be the best architectures for GaAs ICs.

It is noteworthy that even when silicon VLSI can handle the majority of a signal processing task, GaAs may still be profitably employed at the "front end" of a signal processor in either of two special instances, which are often intermingled. First, the processor may be confronted with a single stream of digital data at rates of 0.1-2 gigasamples/second, usually generated by very wideband image sensors or detectors. In these cases, a single high-speed data stream must be partitioned into a set of lower rate, parallel substreams, which in turn can be further processed by silicon devices operating at much slower clock rates. The necessity for high clock rates in these "front end" units is sometimes compounded because as many as 10-20 microcycles of the processor may be required to preprocess each incoming data sample; an input data rate of 10^8 samples/second might thus demand a system clock rate as high as 2×10^9 Hz.

As noted above, the high bandwidth signal processing environment does appear to be the most natural vehicle for digital GaAs in the near to intermediate term, since signal processor architectures can often be deeply pipelined and thus can exploit high system clock rates. However, although mainframe and supercomputer architectures execute more decision

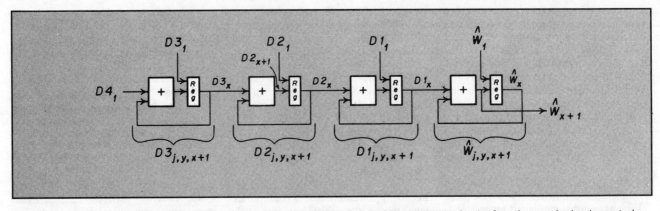

Figure 1. A fourth-degree recursion suitable for hardware implementation in GaAs digital logic; the function can be implemented either in fixed-precision or floating-point arithmetic. This implementation recirculates the partially processed data operands "on-chip" before releasing the final values, and the computational structure is very simple; both features are ideal for the gate characteristics of GaAs (see text).

branches and are usually less deeply pipelined than signal processors, it should be possible to modify traditional data processor architectures to exploit the high speeds of GaAs. It might not even be necessary or desirable to fabricate an entire mainframe with GaAs components; specific locations might be identified in the architecture, e.g., in the instruction pipes or in the cache memories of large machines, where a large benefit may be derived from the use of a relatively small number of GaAs components. It is even possible that entire supercomputer mainframes may eventually be fabricated from GaAs components. One well known US vendor of supercomputers, Cray Research, is in fact conducting a substantial GaAs research effort for its Cray III machine; apparently this vendor has been able to identify ways to modify its architecture to exploit the best features of GaAs.

The on-chip architectures employed for logic and memory components must be completely reconsidered to maximize their throughput while minimizing the amount of system performance dissipated in the intercomponent and on-chip propagation delays.[8] Simple logic, e.g., 8:1 multiplexers with two or three levels of gates, will not make efficient use of the GaAs transistor capability, particularly with the advent of the second-generation heterojunction transistors. Designers will feel compelled to maximize the number of gate stages traversed by the data operands. One effective method of increasing the number of gate stages on-chip is through iterative implementations of signal processing algorithms commonly fabricated as parallel designs. A serial implementation can often be identified by rewriting the signal processing equations in a bit-expanded form, and then operating on the least significant bits of the data operands, followed recursively or iteratively by operations on the

next most significant bits, etc.; an example of this type of approach appears in reference 13).

Not infrequently it is possible to recast a problem into a completely different form, which itself can be implemented as a recursion or iteration. An example of this type of approach is the evaluation of polynomials that are being used as auxiliary equations to generate constants or parameters in a more complex system of equations. Specifically, the equation:

$$Y_i = (A_n)X_i^n + (A_{n-1})X_i^{n-1} + ... + (A_1)X_i + A_0$$

could be evaluated by performing all of the indicated multiplications and additions for all values of A_i and X_i, or else the right-hand side of the equation could be factored according to Horner's rule to decrease the number of multiplications that must be performed. However, it has been known since the eighteenth century that a polynomial of any given degree can be replaced exactly by a recursion of the same degree, in which case no multiplications need be performed at all. The recursion for a fourth degree polynomial may be written as:

$$Y(X_{i+1}) = W(X_i) + D1(X_i)$$
$$D1(X_{i+1}) = D1(X_i) + D2(X_i)$$
$$D2(X_{i+1}) = D2(X_i) + D3(X_i)$$
$$D3(X_{i+1}) = D3(X_i) + D4$$

where $Y(1)$, $D1(1)$, $D2(1)$, and $D3(1)$ are initial values, and D4 is a constant. Extending the approach one step further, the recursion in turn has a straightforward equivalent in hardware, as indicated in Figure 1, which illustrates the implementation for this particular recursion. A hardware embodiment of this type of algorithmic form is a natural structure for digital GaAs because of its simplicity, the relatively large number of machine cycles during which a given data operand would recirculate within the hardware, and the flowthrough nature of the resulting struc-

ture (whether implemented in fixed-precision or floating-point arithmetic). This particular method, which is described in greater detail in reference 14, has applications in synthetic aperture radar and synthetic focus sonar, and in any high-speed signal-processing application in which the evaluation of auxiliary equations must be performed to generate internal constants or parameters for a larger algorithmic process.

Of the wide variety of approaches at the disposal of the designer to tailor architectures for the features of GaAs logic gates, some, such as those described above, can be employed to implement common functions such as fixed precision multiplication, to calculate inner products or matrix products, or to conduct special operations such as recursions. As such, they may be employed as sections of full-scale signal processors but do not impact the global designs of these processors. However, some approaches affect the entire concept and architecture of a signal processor, as well as the detailed implementations of arithmetic operations. Examples of these techniques will be presented later, in conjunction with a discussion of global architectural issues.

Memory components

Both signal and data processors require large amounts of high-speed memory; for many signal-processing algorithms, e.g., in-place computation of the Fast Fourier Transform, memory speed is often the dominant element in overall system performance. Two types of memories must be developed for these processors: (1) extremely fast cycle time (1-3 ns) static random access memories (SRAMs) and read-only memories (ROMs) to support GaAs microprogram control units and high-speed caches (see, e.g., reference 15); and (2) somewhat slower (4-10 ns), larger

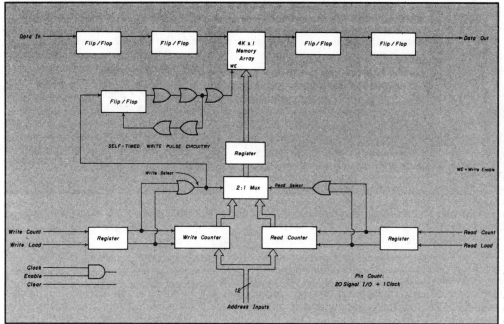

Figure 2. Pipelined implementation of a 4K × 1-bit GaAs SRAM uses self-timed write pulse circuitry and incorporates read and write counter/registers that allow presetting of initial addresses with on-chip address generation for stream read/write operations. This structure also implements interleaved read/write operations and random addressing. This architecture minimizes delivering addresses at high speed during every clock cycle; the only high-speed signal required by the memory is the clock.

memories, either SRAMs or dynamic random access memories (DRAMs) for local memory.

Although GaAs SRAMs and DRAMs exhibiting cycle times longer than approximately 5-7 ns can use conventional silicon memory component design approaches, novel configurations will be needed for memories to operate with cycle times of 4 ns or less, particularly in the peripheries of these memory chips. This situation arises because the long propagation delays typical even of small printed circuit boards make it extremely difficult to exploit conventional SRAM or ROM designs. In a conventional memory component design, address lines, chip select, and read/write signals

(1) must be applied to their lines, settle, and propagate into the memory array;

(2) must activate the memory array, and (in the case of a read operation) extract the desired bit and provide it as output data; and

(3) the retrieved data must propagate on the output lines to other portions of the processor, where it is latched into intermediate data registers.

At least 0.5-1.0 ns is required in the best case for the wavefronts to propagate to their destinations and for the input lines to settle; similar constraints exist at the outputs of the memory. A 1-ns cycle time employing "silicon memory" designs would allow less than 200 ps for each of these steps, which is unlikely to be readily achieved even in GaAs, since infeasibly short wavefront risetimes and line settling times would be required.

There is, however, a straightforward solution for this constraint. Since micro-

program sequencers, arithmetic and logic units (ALUs), cache memories, and in fact entire signal processors tend to use pipelined architectures, the same type of pipelining can be introduced into the SRAM or ROM components themselves. The inclusion of output registers within the memory components would eliminate the necessity for the pipeline instruction register in a microprogram control unit, and pipeline registers in other portions of the systems as well, thereby improving performance and decreasing system complexity (that is, total chip count, though not necessarily total system gate count). An improved design for a 1- to 3-ns memory would employ on-chip pipeline registers in the address, chip-select, data-in, and data-out paths (Figure 2).

A pipelined 1-ns cycle time SRAM might require three clock cycles to fetch a given item of data: the first cycle to set up the address and chip enable lines and latch these into the on-chip pipeline registers under the control of an externally applied clock pulse, the second to fetch the data item from the memory array and place it in the on-chip output register, and the third cycle to read these values from the output register. By allowing a full 1-ns duration for each substep in the memory read or write operation, the effective distance between the memory and its source/destination hardware can be as much as 7-12 inches. Note that if this type of design approach is employed, one of the inputs to each memory chip will be a clock signal; that is, the memory will become a synchronous rather than an asynchronous component. In an additional refinement of the memory chip design, the write pulse required to write a data bit into the memory

array could also be generated within the component, since the rising edge of this pulse must always occur a fixed duration after the rising edge of the clock pulse. Generation of the write pulse on the memory component itself would again decrease the number of high-speed signals transmitted on the memory board.

The foregoing description of memory access pipelining concepts still leaves a major issue unresolved. Memory components must be provided with an updated address just prior to each read or write cycle. For a memory component operating at speeds of 500 MHz or greater, the magnitude of the task of generating and distributing this stream of addresses across a page of memory is so daunting that the creation of a workable system design appears problematic at best. A small amount of additional setup time could be gained by providing two sets of address input lines, and generating consecutive addresses in different sets of hardware; an address multiplexer on the memory chip would then select in an interleaved manner between the two address input paths for the addresses supplied to the memory array.

Alternately, because the designs of most such processors are heavily pipelined, successive rather than random addresses are read from or written into their memories; instructions tend to be read in long, non-branched sequences, while the data operands are often long vectors or large matrices with regular address sequences. Thus, an attractive substitute for off-chip address generation is the incorporation of two presettable up/down counters on each memory component, the first to control read sequences, and the second to control write sequences. Initial addresses may be preset into the counters at moderate speeds; during high-speed operation, only a clock signal and a single read/write control line need be provided to the chip at full operating rates, thereby allowing reads and writes to be interleaved at full speed (Figure 2). The memory chip write pulse could also be generated on-chip, as noted earlier.

A further enhancement of the design of the memory component would also support occasional reads and writes on random locations within memory, which could be interleaved with the stream reads and writes at full speed, though not during two or more successive memory cycles. Designs of this type have been investigated in our laboratory, and have been found to be applicable to a broad range of high-speed memory requirements. It is of considerable interest in this context that at least one merchant vendor of digital GaAs components, Gigabit Logic, plans to offer several SRAM components of various sizes and access times that do employ on-chip pipelining in the data input and data output paths, and that perform on-chip generation of the memory write pulses. [16] Further, McDonnell Douglas Microelectronics Center is fabricating an experimental, extremely low power 4K × 1-bit radiation-hardened synchronous SRAM that also includes pipeline registers on the data and address inputs, and on the data output; a 16K SRAM also under development by McDonnell Douglas is also a possible candidate for on-chip write pulse generation logic. These devices do not, however, currently support on-chip generation of the addresses for a stream read or stream write operation; it is to be expected that these additional functions will be added as the GaAs SRAM technology matures.

As a final comment regarding memory performance, it should be noted that even the eventual introduction of second-generation GaAs heterojunction transistors capable of supporting even faster memory access times will not assist the systems designer. For example, a 4K-bit × 1, 100-ps memory could not be used at its full speed, since off-chip signal lines could not conduct the signal from its source to its destination in less than 0.5-1.0 ns. However, the number of bits in each memory chip could increase markedly while retaining very fast memory cycle times in the 1- to 2-ns range. Clearly, several of these issues of speed performance versus interconnect length could be resolved by incorporating all memory bits into the same components containing, for example, the microsequencer function, since only on-chip propagation of data from the memory to its point of utilization

would be required. However, there will be a continuing demand for high performance off-chip memory; it is to these requirements that the foregoing comments have been addressed.

Microprocessor architectures attractive for implementation in GaAs

In 1982, the Mayo Foundation was assigned by the Strategic Technology Office of the Defense Advanced Research Projects Agency (DARPA/STO) the task of identifying a machine architecture that could be implemented as at most a few custom ICs, but fabricated in GaAs rather than in silicon. In an attempt to minimize the development time for a microprocessor initially targeted for implementation in GaAs, silicon microprocessor architectures available at that time were reviewed for the possibility that one or more of them could be implemented in GaAs. Although a microprocessor could, of course, have been designed de novo specifically for GaAs, this approach was deemed unattractive unless plentiful software support could have been guaranteed. The possible use of an existing architecture added another constraint to the GaAs microprocessor selection effort; the design and layout of the selected microprocessor were required to be nonproprietary, readily available, and well documented.

Microprocessor designers have capitalized on the availability of large numbers of gates on VLSI chips to create relatively powerful architectures based upon structural parallelism and a rich set of assembly language instruction types; the instructions are often implemented in microcode, and the chip incorporates a microprogram sequencer and a microinstruction ROM. Because of the architectural complexity of these processors, and the desire of the designers to minimize power dissipation, the microcycle clock rates of these processors have been constrained to the range of 2-25 MHz. If high clock rate is of no consequence to the application for which these processors are intended, the use of rich instruction sets and parallel architectures is a reasonable method of achieving high computational capability.

Because GaAs digital IC fabrication technology is still relatively immature, the device densities of semicustom and custom components are currently considerably less than in silicon. As a result, one major constraint placed on the design of a microprocessor to be implemented in GaAs was that it would have to contain less than 10,000 equivalent gates, allowing its placement on a single custom chip that could be

fabricated with acceptable yields by the end of the 1980's. Additional constraints included a 32-bit architecture, a 24- or even a 32-bit address bus to support at least 16M bytes of direct memory access, an efficient input/output (I/O) and interrupt handler, a high instruction execution rate, and the capability of floating-point operation, in software if not in hardware.

Several commercial or aerospace industry architectures that were examined but rejected on the basis of one or more of the criteria described above were the National Semiconductor 16032, the Texas Instruments 9900 series, the Motorola 68010, and the Intel iAPX 432. For all of these microprocessor architectures, the principal drawback was their large device counts, which were well in excess of 10,000 gates.

A microprocessor architectural approach that appeared to fit the constraints for a GaAs microprocessor more closely was represented by the family of reduced instruction set computers (RISCs). (See the article by Fox et al. in this issue for an overview of the use of RISC architecture in the GaAs microprocessors.) All of the generic RISC architectures have several features in common:

(1) a small number of simplified instructions;
(2) a fixed instruction format (all instructions are the same size and structure);
(3) hardwired rather than microcode control;
(4) single-cycle execution for most instructions; and
(5) a load/store architecture (i.e., in which only the load and store instructions access memory, while other instructions operate on registers).

The Stanford MIPS architecture was selected to serve as a baseline for the development of a 32-bit microprocessor implemented in GaAs. Three contractors, RCA, Inc., McDonnell Douglas, and Texas Instruments completed an architecture study phase in the fall of 1985, and two of these teams are presently involved in a two year project to fabricate two 32-bit GaAs microprocessors, an effort made feasible by the simplicity of the original MIPS architecture. The goal for this GaAs version of MIPS is a custom microprocessor chip of not more than 10,000 gates, a 200-MHz clock rate, and a 100 million instruction per second execution rate. A floating point coprocessor chip, also of 10,000 gate size (or less), will accompany the main processor when high-speed floating-point operations are required.

A collaborative effort among research teams at Stanford University, Carnegie Mellon University, the Mayo Foundation, Sperry Univac, Control Data Corpora-

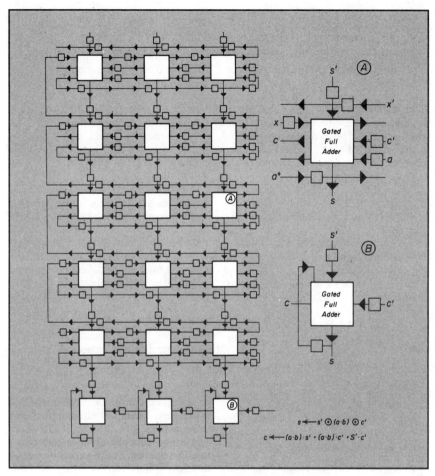

Figure 3. Implementation of a typical signal processor function, a convolver-correlator, using bit-level modular systolic arrays. Complexities of the basic functions are low (pipelined full adder is 25 gates) and all connections are single-source, single destination, and nearest neighbor; such a structure is ideal for implementation as a high-clock-rate GaAs IC. (Source: *Gallium Arsenide Technology*, 1985. Used by the courtesy of Howard W. Sams & Company, publisher.)

tion, General Electric, RCA, Inc., McDonnell Douglas, Texas Instruments, and representatives of DARPA have developed a single DOD-standard MIPS Instruction Set Architecture (ISA) document (which, with a total of 69 unique instructions, differs significantly from and improves considerably upon the 1981 version of the Stanford MIPS instruction set). The GaAs microprocessor development teams are in fact designing their processors to execute this standardized ISA. The successful creation of a standard ISA document (see reference 17) for the DOD version of the MIPS processor (now referred to as the "DOD-standard MIPS" machine) allows for flexibility at the hardware design level. In addition, the new DOD-standard MIPS ISA is currently being used as the baseline document upon which three high-level language compilers, Pascal, LISP, and ADA, are being prepared for the MIPS processors.

The original goal of the computer evaluation project conducted at the Mayo Foundation was the identification of a 32-bit microprocessor architecture that could execute at high speed, but could also be fabricated on a single GaAs chip (excluding the floating-point coprocessor) in the near future. The DOD-standard MIPS ISA meets this goal; a GaAs implementation of this new ISA should remain viable for many years, both as a stand-alone computer and as an embedded engine inside high complexity fully GaAs data and signal processors.

Architectural approaches at the system level

It was noted earlier that the special behavioral characteristics of GaAs transistors and gates must be accounted for in the design of memory, logic, and arithmetic; if designs for these functions are carried over directly from silicon VLSI, full advantage from the high speed of the GaAs transistors cannot usually be achieved. Similarly, when we wish to develop an architecture for an entire processor, we must again account for the peculiarities of GaAs transistors and gates, and the high clock and edge rates at which they function best, if a near-optimum design is to emerge. This requirement for a wholistic approach to the design of processors is not particularly necessary for implementations in silicon, but is mandatory if any of the GaAs technologies are to be employed. For example, system designs in which the data can flow continuously and uniformly between ICs that are nearest neighbors of one another, across the logic boards from one edge to the opposite edge of the same board, and between nearest-neighbor logic boards will result in minimum data path lengths and hence the fastest overall throughput. Such an approach to the layout of the ICs and their substrates will also result in minimum-complexity, lower cost logic boards and chip packages; the ability to employ only two or three signal layers rather than 10 signal layers in a multilayer printed circuit board has implications for cost control and performance improvements in these substrates. Because almost all interconnects between GaAs components behave as transmission lines and must be terminated with resistor networks that dissipate considerable power, [18] it is desirable to minimize the number of unique interconnects on a logic board or between logic boards, and to operate all such lines at the maximum possible bit rates (up to 1-2 gigabits/second/line in some cases). These constraints on chip-to-chip interconnection also have a major effect on the types of architectures that are best suited to GaAs implementation. Other equally critical issues, to be noted later, include the need to consider closely the types of intraprocessor communications structures (e.g., buses versus any of the various data exchange networks) that may be feasible to implement in GaAs chips operating at high clock rates. In the following discussion of overall global architectures that may be best suited to implementation in GaAs, the aforementioned topics must always be kept clearly in mind.

At the system architectural level, certain types of multiprocessors appear promising for implementation in GaAs because of their modularity, the amount of work performed in each node of the multiprocessor, the iterative nature of the algorithm executed in each node, or the flow-through nature of the processor architecture itself. Recently, these disparate approaches have been categorized as examples of a common architectural type referred to as "cellular automata"; these studies are attempting to develop concepts that will place such structures on a firm mathematical foundation.[12] An additional feature of several of these new architectural concepts that renders them well matched to the characteristics of GaAs components is their ability to be partitioned among numerous ICs, each of which then requires a minimum of input/output lines operating at maximum bit rates. Fortunately, the characteristics of GaAs off-chip driver transistors allow very high bit stream rates.

It may be instructive to present as an example of these architectural approaches a group of algorithms originally derived from the systolic array concept proposed by Kung and coworkers.[10] R. A. Evans and coworkers at the Royal Signals and Radar Establishment (RSRE) in the United Kingdom have generated an entire set of signal-processing algorithms for fixed-precision operand streams that execute all processing using modular bit-level systolic arrays, rather than the word-serial approaches first proposed by Kung.[10] Operations that can be performed in this bit-decomposed manner include scalar, vector-matrix, and matrix-matrix multiplication, (and hence) linear transforms, convolution/correlation (see Figure 3), and eigenvalue/eigenvector extractions.[19-20]

In these bit-decomposed algorithms, the arithmetic primitive functions are each rather small (5-200 gates), are connected to one another only by nearest neighbor links, and can be pipelined at the bit level in both the horizontal and vertical directions on a single IC. The small number of cell types (typically 1-bit full and half adders, registers, and small multiplexer/demultiplexers; see Figure 3) and their regularity of interconnection will permit a straightforward conversion of these algorithms into GaAs ICs using any of several attractive chip design strategies (see following discussion). Maximum computation will thus be performed on-chip in the environment of a moderate-sized processor "engine" operating at high clock rates, for which GaAs appears best suited. Further, these realizations appear to be extensible in vector length by cascading identical chips, while the number of high-speed off-chip signals is constrained to an absolute minimum. For example, in one silicon CMOS-based design test case conducted by Evans and coworkers, a bit-decomposed systolic array convolver/correlator for 8-bit two's-complement operands required only 13 external pins per chip, including clock, power, ground, and data lines, and up to 1024 chips could be cascaded using only nearest neighbor connections.[20]

It is of interest that the advantage of the bit-decomposed algorithm approach was originally considered by Evans and co-workers to be an improvement in the "mappability" of systolic array functions onto silicon VLSI. Initial examinations conducted at the Mayo Foundation indicate that the same benefits apply to mappings onto first- and second-generation GaAs components as well, though for quite different reasons. The RSRE group believed that the bit-level structures provided a straightforward way to cover the entire surface of a very dense VLSI component with large amounts of useful logic but with a minimum of design effort, since the same blocks could be replicated as often as desired with simple step-and-repeat operations of their chip layout software; further, a minimum of chip real estate would be devoted to interconnects. For GaAs, however, the advantages of these structures are:

- their small size and hence the ease of simulating them completely at high clock rates;
- the fact that all connections between cells are nearest neighbor and hence very short;
- that all connections are "single source, single destination," thereby decreasing the capacitive loads on the drive transistors;
- the pipelined nature of even the smallest segment of the design, thereby allowing the use of very high system clock rates; and
- their miniscule requirement for off-chip interconnects.

Intraprocessor communication problems

As the system clock rates of processors increase, a variety of physical constraints conspire to nullify many of the time-tested architectural solutions to such tasks as data communication between subsections of a large processor. One of the most troublesome of these "solutions gone awry" is the difficulty at clock rates above 50-100 MHz of employing wire-based busses to transmit instructions and intermediate data between portions of a signal processor, or to communicate with the external environment by the same mechanism. Earlier comments implied that making busses narrower, while sending the data at higher bit rates over the remaining lines, would minimize problems; nonetheless, a wire-based bus requires the connection of several drive transistors and several receiving gates to the same wire, which causes harmful transient electrical disturbances to occur on the individual bit lines of the bus. High-speed silicon ECL and GaAs components generate off-chip electrical wavefronts of 100-500 ps; these wavefronts are fast enough to contain frequency components as high as 5-10 GHz, thereby exciting the interconnects as if they were transmission lines. In turn, every source and every destination gate on a bus inevitably creates a focus for the generation of "reflections" of these fast wavefronts; the reflections in turn travel to and fro on the individual bit lines of the bus, thereby distorting and destroying the square shape of the original digital data pulses and degrading the AC noise margins of the signals.[18]

Although methods of damping these reflections are available, none is perfect and all become less than satisfactory as the data rates on the bus line rise above 100 megabits/second. At bit rates greater than a few hundred megahertz, alternative approaches must be identified. One method investigated in this laboratory that may work well up to data rates of 700-1000 megabits/second/line is a scheme that converts each single-bit line in the bus into a two-wire, fully differential structure, as diagrammed in two versions in Figure 4. We have been able to demonstrate that many of the signal contaminants that have been observed on differential data lines are so-called common mode phenomena; that is, the same wavefront distortions appear on both "legs" of a differential data line in synchrony with one another, and hence can be removed almost completely by a differential line receiver with good common mode signal rejection characteristics.[18] Extending this finding. we have proposed a design for a differential bus transceiver that does allow multiple signal sources and destinations to be connected to a common "wire" while maintaining high signal transmission rates; this approach preserves the architectural simplicity of bus interconnections inside a high clock rate processor.

If the differential bus approach cannot be made to perform satisfactorily, there is then no choice but to revert to communications structures that use only single sources and single destinations to obviate ringing and reflections on the data lines.[18] However, since the need to route data and instructions between different sections of a processor still remains, some alternate architectural approach must be devised. One such method may be conceptualized as a hub-and-spoke structure,[21] in which every node feeds a set of source lines to and receives a set of destination lines from a central IC or group of circuits; the function implemented within these centrally located chips is a word-wide multiplexer in series with a word-wide output selector, with the two functions separately controllable. Whichever node gains control of this "bus" sets the multiplex function to accept data from the controlling node, and sets the output selector to route data to one

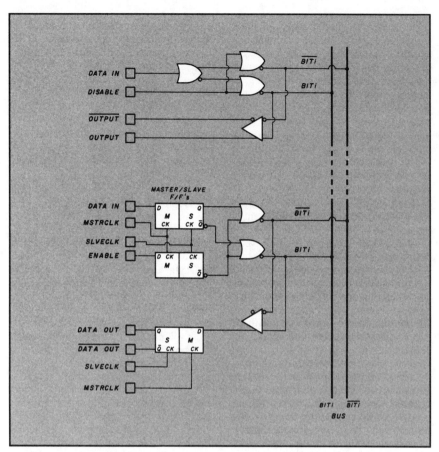

Figure 4. Two versions of a differential transceiver for use in very high data bandwidth bus architectures. Upper transceiver is not pipelined, while lower transceiver is pipelined to buffer out bus line delays in the highest speed systems. The differential structure suppresses signal reflections typical of single-wire busses because these reflections tend to be common mode, and hence are cancelled by the common mode rejection features of the line receivers in each signal transceiver.

or more of the destination nodes. By routing the data in this manner, the single-source, single-or-multiple-destination structure of the hub-and-spoke network minimizes reflections and allows single wire-per-bit data to flow at high speeds, while preserving the topology if not the geography of a bus design. Because long wait times are not required to permit the wavefront reflections to die away, as would be necessary on a conventional bus running at high speed, a hub-and-spoke communications path can operate as fast as or faster than can the bus, even including the additional gate delays through the multiplexer/demultiplexer component(s).

The reader may question why such low level issues have been raised in a discussion of architectures for high-speed GaAs circuits. Note that the use of differential bus structures will have a formidable impact on pin availability on every IC involved with intraprocessor communications, on the internal designs of these circuits, and hence on the partitioning of the entire processor. Similarly, the replacement of a con-

ventional bus with a hub-and-spoke architecture would have a major impact on the mechanisms implemented to resolve "bus" contention, on the firmware developed for the system, and even on the ways in which application programs are executed on the processor. Again, this discussion is but one more example of the way in which the high clock rate nature of GaAs ICs can cause major ripple effects that propagate to the highest architectural levels of a processor design; the would-be GaAs systems designer must become aware of these new problems very early, lest he or she be surprised at a later stage of a new processor design.

Design methodology for GaAs components

Three generic design philosophies are available for the development of high-performance GaAs ICs. The first and best known of these is custom chip design. Throughout the early developmental phases of GaAs digital ICs, custom design

has been relied upon heavily to produce the most compact, highest speed, or lowest power components with the best possible fabrication yields; the penalties (as always with custom designs) have been high design costs and lengthy turnaround times. In the rapid turnaround design and fabrication environment typical of many processor design cycles and virtually all military/aerospace design projects, custom design may thus be unacceptable for GaAs ICs except for memory components or microprocessors (such as the DARPA-RISC project described earlier, which *will* result in a custom chip implementation); the design costs in both manpower and computer time are too high, and the design cycles too long, for ICs that may be manufactured in relatively small quantities.

An intermediate approach to rapid turnaround design of ICs is the configurable gate array, in which an array of active "islands" or cells, each composed of a small number of unconnected transistors, resistors, and/or diodes, are created in the lower layers of an IC. The elements of each island can be connected to one another during the final metal layer processes to form any one of a half dozen or more simple gate types, or more complex functions referred to as "macros." This type of active island or cell structure is quite versatile because the desired gate type can always be made available precisely where it is needed on the IC for maximum layout efficiency. Since the active islands are in turn connected to one another to form even more complex functions with only two or three layers of metal lines and one or two via layers on the upper surface of the array,[2] some types of wafers can be fabricated and stockpiled against the time that they are needed.

Because the total "customization" required for gate arrays requires only the final few layers on the array, chip turnaround from initial design to available parts can be a matter of weeks (provided that the appropriate computer-aided design software packages are available to support the rapid fabrication process). There is at present a strong interest in the provision of a rapid turnaround configurable gate array capability for GaAs digital ICs, which would allow the inclusion of GaAs components in demonstration processors without heavy commitments to custom designs; the lower levels of chip integration and speed performance caused by the rather loose gate packing density of configurable gate arrays will be counterbalanced by the availability of a quick-response chip design capacity in this new material. Considerable development in this regard for GaAs depletion-mode and enhancement-/depletion-mode MESFET gates is presently under way in the research laboratories of several defense contractors.[2,4] Under DARPA sponsorship or with corporate funds, four aerospace corporations, Honeywell, Inc., Rockwell International, Texas Instruments, and McDonnell Douglas, have designed and are now fabricating prototype configurable gate arrays in the size range of approximately 1800-6000 gates,[22-23] with 8000- to 10,000-gate structures appearing feasible by the end of the decade. Finally, at least one civilian-sector company, Tri-Quint, Inc., is developing GaAs configurable gate arrays using GaAs enhancement-/depletion-mode MESFET transistors.[4]

The second possibility for semicustom chip design, and the best way to achieve maximum speed performance short of a custom chip design, is the use of so-called standard height cells, or simply standard cells. In this approach, functional building blocks, or macros, of 5- to 200-gate complexity are custom designed to the transistor level and heavily simulated to verify and guarantee their performance. The macros are carefully selected for their wide applicability to numerous signal processing problems and their ease of configuration in a variety of ways as building blocks to assemble much more complex functions. The individual standard cells are essentially custom designs at all mask levels, but because their layout and function remain constant over time, the individual mask layers for each cell can be stored in a library on computer disk and recalled for repeated use. A number of standard cells are laid out on the chip, with "customized" interconnects designed to coordinate the cells into a complete functional entity. Since logical and analog simulations can be performed with extreme rigor on the custom cells, ultimately this approach provides a very low risk, rapid turnaround method of achieving ICs with high levels of performance. The standard cell approach will eventually be very attractive for the rapid implementation of signal processors exploiting GaAs ICs, in large measure because of the regularity of logic and arithmetic functions employed in signal processors.

The development of design techniques for GaAs-configurable gate arrays is more advanced than for GaAs standard cells, and there are valid technical reasons why this has occurred. The design and verification through computer simulation of the small number of cell types in a gate array is a relatively straightforward and inexpensive task, allowing the fabricators of GaAs circuits to justify this initial cost. If the fabrication process and/or the chip layout change, usually less than a dozen cells, each of one- or two-gate complexity, need be redesigned and resimulated. Conversely, each standard cell is essentially a rather complex custom-designed logical function; every transistor in the function is uniquely specified for its particular task. Thus, every standard cell must be completely simulated, then fabricated and tested, before it can be added to the library of available functions. This process is consumptive of both computer and human effort, and hence is very expensive. If the fabrication technology changes after the functional library has been established, all of the library elements may become nonoperative and may have to be completely redesigned. Because the silicon fabrication technology is currently evolving less rapidly than in the past, the commitment to standard cell libraries is often considered an acceptable risk. In GaAs, however, a stable set of fabrication technologies has only recently begun to evolve; for example, the method of growing GaAs ingots has changed markedly at least three times since 1980 (with an additional modification now in prospect), each time with impacts on the remainder of the IC fabrication processes using these ingots. As a result of these uncertainties, most fabricators of GaAs devices are only now becoming willing to develop and exploit standard cell design and fabrication approaches. However, as the GaAs technology matures, it is expected that greater reliance will be placed upon standard cell libraries, which will yield much more performance than gate arrays but with much less design effort than fully custom components. At least two commercial suppliers of GaAs devices, Gigabit Logic and TriQuint, Inc., have begun to use or investigate the standard cell approach; additional merchant vendors of GaAs digital devices will almost certainly follow suit during the next two years. Finally, AT&T uses small standard cell functions in the layout of GaAs ICs that it fabricates for internal consumption.

Each of the three approaches to the design and fabrication of GaAs ICs has both advantages and deficiencies; as noted earlier, because of the intimate relationships between chip design and system design, the system architect must become familiar with the trade-offs among these various approaches to IC implementation, as well as the trade-offs between the GaAs technologies themselves irrespective of the implementation approach.

Built-in self-test issues for high-speed GaAs ICs

An additional issue, previously the purview of the IC designer, which must now be accounted for by the would-be designer of GaAs processor architectures, is that of operational testing of both the individual ICs and the entire processor once fabricated. Silicon designers, confronted with complexity levels of individual chips exceeding 50,000 gates, as well as the increasing expense of chip testers, are working diligently to identify mechanisms for chips to assess their own performance; by including self-test functions in the very core of the chip design, a higher percentage of the deeply buried gates in the design can be verified. Further, the removal of the financial burden of sophisticated computer controlled testers would in turn decrease the cost of the individual devices. Thus, cost issues are significant drivers in the development of on-chip test logic for silicon devices; however, the testing of these devices could in principle be conducted with externally generated test programs on a modern tester.

Digital GaAs ICs will also require on-chip self-test capabilities; here again, however, the reasons and motivations are somewhat different from those of silicon. Chip complexity is not the issue; GaAs devices will not achieve the 50,000-gate level for some years, and will initially be sufficiently costly that the cost burden of external testing may even be a low percentage of the purchase price of the device. The most critical reason for on-chip test functions in GaAs is that even the lowest clock rate GaAs gate arrays currently in development will operate at 50-MHz clock rates, which are only now being achieved by the most sophisticated commercial IC testers; the next generation of large gate arrays will operate at 200 MHz, while LSI-complexity second-generation standard cell chips can be expected to operate at gigahertz rates. The fastest GaAs devices, though of low complexity, already operate at clock rates above 1 GHz, and may achieve 5- to 8-GHz operation by the end of the decade. Because of its higher purchase cost, GaAs is likely to be used in many applications in which brute-force speed performance is of paramount concern. In such cases, the ability to verify that a chip operates at 10 MHz or even 50 MHz will simply be unacceptable to the ultimate users of the device; if it cannot be guaranteed that each chip will function at its rated speed, the performance of the total system will be in serious doubt. Since commercial IC testers will thus always remain behind the speed capabilities of the devices, the chips must be designed to verify their own performance at full operating speed. Finally, even if the individual chips could be verified at full speed by external testing, once they are incorporated into a system, the same problem arises: system test hardware capable of operating at high speeds is expensive and requires highly trained technical staff in short supply, and the equipment will always be slower than the GaAs-based systems to be tested.

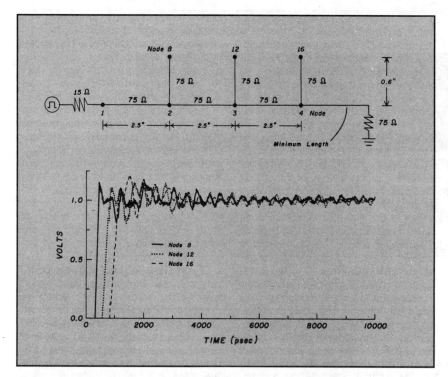

Figure 5. Computer-simulated behavior of a single-source, multiple-destination transmission line logic string connecting digital ICs when exposed to 200-ps risetime pulsed signals. This type of interconnect, the so-called shunt-terminated line, has been used successfully to connect silicon ECL logic circuits (with risetimes of 0.6-2 ns) for more than two decades. However, as risetimes decrease below 200 ps, anomalous ringing occurs because the wider bandwidths of the faster signals reflect repeatedly from the signal string branch points, and from the open circuit stubs at the destination chips (at nodes 8, 12, and 16), creating voltage transients that persist for several nanoseconds. Alternate interconnect approaches common in microwave circuit layouts must be employed to stabilize the interchip signal waveforms.

Fortunately, it is not out of the question to include on-chip test circuits that give a high percentage of gate coverage and that can operate at full chip speeds. Several of the self-test schemes developed for silicon, such as Built-In Logic Block Organization (BILBO), LSSD, Scan-Path, and others (for a comprehensive review of these methods, see reference 24) can make a major contribution to on-chip testing at the full intended clock rate of the component. Although published reviews of on-chip self-test approaches state that optimally at least 20 percent of the chip real estate should be reserved for these functions, small or even "large" GaAs chips may not have a sufficient number of gates to permit such a high percentage commitment of real estate to the self-test function. However, even a commitment of 3 to 5 percent of the available real estate may be sufficient to ensure high confidence in the full speed functionality of the IC; for example, the inclusion of a serial shift-out capability in instruction and data pipeline registers at critical locations in the chip design can be used to examine the states of the chip after each clock cycle or after several clock cycles. Although all gates may not be verified with only 3 to 5 percent

on-chip test hardware, coverages above 50 to 75 percent may be achievable in this manner. Finally, it is noteworthy that these same test schemes can, with sufficient prior planning in the design phases of the system, also be configured to allow each chip to retest itself even after incorporation into the processor and to report on its health to a "health manager" function. Here again it should be noted that the design planning for the ICs can no longer be separated from the design planning for the system; the system architect must understand and plan for the problems and constraints of the chip specialist, and conversely.

Packaging and interconnect technology issues for high-frequency GaAs digital ICs

As noted on several earlier occasions, the class of problems best solved with GaAs digital ICs will exploit the ability of these components to operate at system clock rates of 100 MHz and greater with

on-chip gate delays of 10-100 ps and off-chip risetimes of 100-250 ps. Since the early days of high-speed silicon ECL components, it has been common practice to employ transmission line interconnects, in combination with resistor termination networks, whenever it was desired to transmit signals between chips whose off-chip risetimes were 2 ns or less in duration; GaAs risetimes are now at least eight times faster than that of early 1970's vintage ECL. Thus, the absolutely mandatory requirement for a controlled impedance circuit board interconnect environment for signals with such extremely short risetimes implies that all aspects of the chip encapsulant and circuit board design be mutually complementary. Both the chip encapsulation and the logic board substrate must be designed to preserve the transmission line environment, from the interfaces between the encapsulant leads and the logic board at least to the perimeter of the die-well inside the chip encapsulant, if not directly to the chip itself. As will be described below, the chip packages and the interconnections on the circuit boards must be treated as high frequency passive analog electrical components connected in series with all of the inputs and outputs of all of the chips in a processor system.

The absence of controlled impedance interconnects in GaAs digital systems will in most cases result in multiple signal reflections that degrade waveform conformations for many nanoseconds, as illustrated in the simulation of Figure 5. This simulation depicts the magnitude and duration of ringing on a *properly terminated* signal string, as might be found on a typical logic board. Presently available chip encapsulants do not provide a suitable electrical environment, and must be redesigned to do so. The stresses that these new high-speed devices will exert on the packaging technology are considerably more severe than those generated by the high-density, low-speed silicon devices.

Example of a high-clock-rate processor: Digital RF Memory

It may be instructive to describe one such very high clock rate system presently under development in our laboratory in order to illustrate the problems in system design, layout, and packaging, which are the principal topics of discussion of this presentation. A Digital RF Memory is essentially an A/D converter generating 2-, 4-, or 6-bit samples of an analog signal at rates of hundreds of megahertz or greater, a serial-to-parallel converter that packs several samples together into a wider word (thereby decreasing the data rate), a

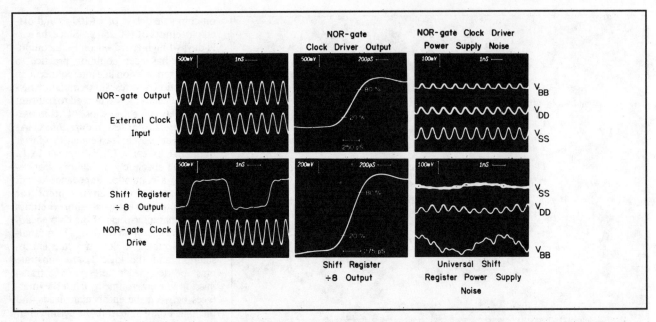

Figure 6. Waveform measurements from selected locations within the high-frequency GaAs front end subsystem of a Digital RF Memory operating at 1.14 GHz. The 250-ps signal risetimes (upper middle panel) did not cause undue amounts of overshoot and ringing on the signal lines (two lower leftmost panels). Sheet resistance and inductance in the power and ground planes, which are the current return paths for the signal strings, were minimized (upper and lower rightmost panels) by providing multiple return paths through the use of 12 power/ground planes in the circuit board, although some residual noise on the power planes may be observed. All such issues must be dealt with at the outset of system design if processors are to operate properly at clock rates above 1 GHz.

read/write scratch pad memory in which the data may be stored temporarily, and a parallel-to-serial converter that speeds up the data rate and feeds the digital inputs of a D/A converter.[9] Since only the very front end and very back end of the system need operate at the highest speeds, it is common practice to treat those sections separately from, for example, the large memory, which can operate at clock rates perhaps 1/8 or 1/16 those of the highest speed sections of the system. In the DRFM fabricated at the Mayo Foundation, the memory section was assembled with commercial ECL components and operated at 125-MHz clock rates. At that frequency, multiple destination gates in the system could be driven from a single source gate; straightforward transmission line termination approaches could be used; the chip carriers and logic boards did not themselves present overly difficult design problems; off-chip signal risetimes were not less than 600 ps; the highest analog frequency components of these signals did not exceed 1-2 GHz; and the signal waveshapes were of good conformation and essentially free of reflections and crosstalk.

It was a much more difficult, though ultimately feasible, task to achieve correct operation in the sections of the system that operated at 1-GHz clock rates; the waveforms of Figure 6 indicate that good signal quality was attained after a number of potentially serious issues were correctly ac-

counted for. Even the slightest mismatches of transmission line characteristics could have caused serious ringing and reflections, which in turn would have destroyed waveform conformations and decreased the signal/noise ratio of the subsystem. All interconnects had to be properly located and treated as transmission lines to prevent the radiation of energy and the pickup of crosstalk signals. The chip carrier packages employed in the project contributed small amounts of unwanted parasitic inductances and capacitances that, if not properly addressed, could have resulted in local oscillations on the signal lines. Studies indicated that, if not accounted for, sheet inductances in the power and ground planes of the circuit board could have seriously impeded the flow of high-frequency AC return path currents, thereby causing instantaneous voltage fluctuations on the power planes at various locations on the circuit board. To minimize this problem, special multilayer circuit boards were designed that contained 12 power/ground planes to provide multiple shunt paths for the flow of high-frequency return-path currents; in addition, every chip location was liberally supplied with RF decoupling capacitors. Finally, the highest speed signal lines were not permitted to have more than two destinations, thereby decreasing the severity of wavefront reflections and increasing the effective speed of the interconnects. To achieve this goal, logical chip

output bits were replicated in several instances. A very considerable effort was expended in the creation of a processor architecture that supported a flowthrough path for the highest speed data as it emerged from the A/D converter and as it entered the D/A converter. In this system, a flowthrough design could be achieved; in other architectures, the designer may not be as fortunate.

This experiment underscored the importance of:

• flowthrough designs and extremely short interconnect lengths for at least the highest speed data and clock paths;

• the careful selection of logical and physical input and output signals on each chip;

• a coordinated system layout concept, in which every IC part type was carefully designed to function at full speed with all the others;

• the execution of computer simulations and timing verifications of all of the individual part types separately and operating together;

• the use of high-frequency models for the GaAs gates and transistors that accurately represent the AC behavior of the actual structures; and finally,

• for the need, in most cases, to develop much higher quality packaging at the chip carrier and circuit board levels than has been available heretofore.

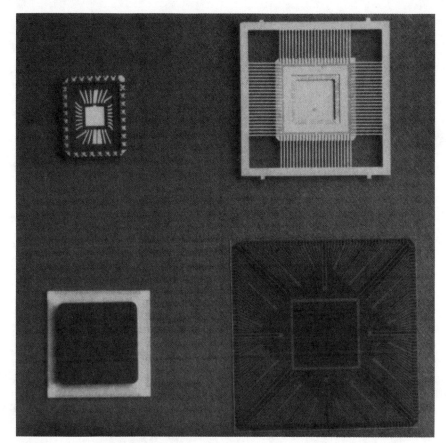

Figure 7. Four generations of controlled-impedance chip carriers designed at Mayo Foundation for GaAs chips. All have 50-ohm or 75-ohm signal leads, dedicated leads and/or internal ground/power planes for ripple-free power delivery, and locations for microwave decoupling capacitors. Clockwise from upper left: a 28-lead, 400 × 500-mil cofired alumina leadless carrier with contacts on 50-mil centers (1981); an 88-contact (64 signal, 24 power/ground) 500 × 500-mil cofired alumina leaded/leadless chip carrier with 20-mil center contacts (1984); a 216-lead (192 signal, 24 power/ground) 1200 × 1200-mil alumina leadless carrier with 20-mil center contacts, shown in film format (1986); a 216-contact (192 signal, 24 power/ground) 650 × 650-mil thin-film-on-BeO leadless minicarrier with 10-mil center contacts (1986). The minicarrier includes 192 thin-film resistor terminators. Note the 8:1 increases in interconnect density between oldest and newest designs; carrier size has remained roughly constant.

It must be reiterated that the design and fabrication of a system that will operate correctly at 1- to 2-GHz system clock rates is extremely difficult. The issues discussed herein are sufficiently complex and intertwined that appropriate solutions for them must be developed by both the system architect and the chip designer working together; otherwise, the final product can be nearly guaranteed not to work as intended, or perhaps at all.

The foregoing discussion of the problems encountered in one example high-clock-rate processor project is intended to forewarn the systems designer of the numerous issues with which he or she will be confronted. The remainder of this presentation will address several of the most critical packaging and component interconnect issues in greater detail, under the assumption that the GaAs ICs will experience clock rates above 100 MHz, will have moderate pin counts (24-200), and will generate short risetimes (less than 500 ps).

Intercomponent connection problems

Chip-to-chip interconnect delays must be minimized even when on-chip designs employ multiple gate stages or implement iterative algorithms. Although it has been noted in several published papers that a deliberate degradation of the off-chip risetimes would minimize the interconnect problem, overall system performance would also be reduced. Computer simulations of the combined wire delay and risetime effects for a given interconnect length and logic board dielectric constant have demonstrated that risetimes as low as 100-200 ps result in a substantial reduction

Figure 8. Frequency domain performance of two chip carrier packages designed to encapsulate high-clock-rate GaAs digital ICs. The plots display voltage standing wave ratio (VSWR) as a function of frequency. VSWR values of less than 2 represent the range of satisfactory performance; the polyimide package is usable to signal bandwidths of 6-8 GHz, while the alumina package is usable to 3 GHz. The packages must be conceptualized as analog microwave elements connected in series with the digital ICs that they contain. These analog microwave effects must be accounted for in the planning of the layout and partitioning of high-clock-rate signal processors fabricated with GaAs devices.

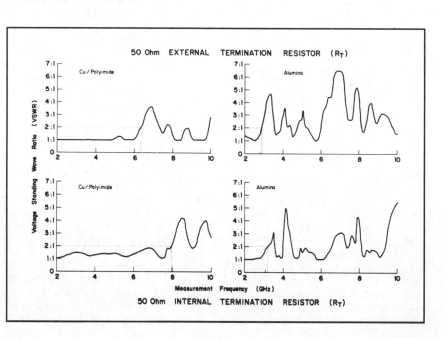

in effective interconnect length. For example, for a logic board dielectric constant of 2.3, a change in the designs of off-chip drive transistors that has the effect of altering the signal risetime from 1 ns to 200 ps is equivalent to a saving of 6.2 inches of interconnect in every logic net on the circuit board. [18] However, even assuming terminated transmission line interconnects, each off-chip drive transistor and its associated line terminator will dissipate 20-80 mW, which in a high I/O count IC can result in unacceptably large on-chip power dissipation. To minimize this problem, two separate but complementary concepts might be explored. First, significant reductions in power dissipation in the chip periphery may be achieved by employing either bit-serial or nibble-serial intercomponent communications. The data operands may be reassembled on-chip to full width over several system clock cycles, or the operands themselves may be processed bit or nibble-serially using iterative algorithms or bit-decomposed algorithms, as described earlier and discussed in references 19 and 20.

Alternately, a re-examination of off-chip electrical transmission protocols might yield an approach with sufficiently high noise margin at lower logic voltage swings, thus decreasing the power dissipated both in the driver transistor and in its line terminator. While silicon TTL components use a 3- to 5-V logic swing, silicon ECL has successfully employed 800-mV logic amplitudes. Provided that the AC noise margin is sufficiently high for the logic family, small-amplitude logic swings can be used without concern for system robustness. Logic swings as low as 500-600 mV appear feasible in a few of the GaAs technologies with inherently high AC noise margins, and are actively being explored through design and computer simulation studies by Mayo Foundation and McDonnell Douglas Microelectronics Center for the GaAs EJFET technology.

If a critical data signal or the clock signal on a circuit board must be kept free of contamination, it is sometimes necessary to transmit the signal differentially from its principal source to its principal destination, receive the signal with a differential line receiver, and then retransmit the signal for short distances as a single ended signal. In the case of critical clock waveforms, the additional precaution is taken of feeding the signal into the center of the board, then using several tiers of differential distribution, with a final conversion to a single ended waveform that is fed to only a few components each at numerous locations around the logic board. As noted earlier, the number of destination gates driven by each source gate must be constrained to four or even less; furthermore, because of high-frequency ringing

phenomena, conventional single wire bus-type interconnect structures may not work at all. Either the busses will have to be removed from the architectural design entirely, or a fully differential data path may have to be employed along with special differential line transceiver components to drive onto and receive from the bus or, as a final resort, a hub-and-spoke data distribution network may be required, as described earlier.

Design issues for chip carrier packages and logic boards for GaAs components operating above 100 MHz

The electrical characteristics of the chip carriers used to package GaAs ICs can substantially limit the effective performance available from the highest speed versions of these chips. In general, the DC resistance of the signal leads in the encapsulation is of little consequence, since DC resistance values less than half an ohm are the rule. At high frequencies, however, signal lead parasitic inductive and capacitive reactances are the primary causes of degradation in high-speed chip performance. Although the circuit board interconnects must be designed as transmission lines whenever signal risetimes are less than 1-2 ns, the shunt capacitances measured at the inputs of the encapsulant signal leads always degrade the performance of the board interconnects by creating a local decrease in transmission line impedance. Chip packages connected to a transmission line usually create a local decrease in line impedance, which causes wavefront reflections to propagate to and fro along the signal string. Such reflections are always in the direction of the logic threshold (defined as the "negative" direction), and hence decrease signal noise margins to some extent. If the shunt capacitances are large enough, their effects can be detected even in silicon ECL systems operating at 100-150 MHz.

At frequencies above 100 MHz, the signal paths in the chip carriers, the chip wire bonds, and the circuit board traces must be included in the simulations of subsystem performance; further, these simulations must be conducted both in the digital timing domain and also in the analog electrical sense to completely model the behavior of these elements. Topics previously considered to be the responsibility of the radio frequency (RF) analog microwave specialist in the design of monolithic microwave integrated circuits (MMICs) are now rapidly becoming the concern of the digital systems designer as well. New versions of chip carrier pack-

ages intended for GaAs circuits are designed to provide a shielded cavity, transmission line interconnect environment for the ICs, and are simulated using microwave simulation programs. The chip packages should be fabricated with two or more layers of internal ground and power supply planes much like those found in a multilayer printed circuit board, with integral thin film termination resistors, and with integral RF decoupling capacitors to control voltage fluctuations on the internal power supply planes of the carrier. For each successive generation of packages, the carriers must become smaller, with tighter interlead spacing, finer metal line geometries, and improved crosstalk control. Figure 7 depicts several successive generations of these carriers designed at Mayo Foundation for digital GaAs ICs; see the legend for further details. The as-fabricated packages are tested on analog vector network analyzers; the most critical package operating parameters are considered to be voltage standing wave ratio (VSWR), and RF crosstalk (see, for example, Figure 8).

Great care should be also used in the design of logic boards for high-clock-rate GaAs circuits. Test coupons containing examples of various types of interconnects are designed, laid out, and fabricated in the same materials from which the final circuit boards will be manufactured. The coupons are then also tested using analog microwave equipment, and the test results are compared with those derived from the computer models. Disparities between the measured and simulated data are resolved; thereafter, the simulation results are used as design guides during logic board layout. In the near future, the operating parameters of every interconnect in an as-laid-out logic board will be verified by computer simulation to ensure satisfactory high-frequency performance, including VSWR, forward and backward crosstalk, and wavefront reflections (see Figures 5 and 8).

As the clock rates of GaAs-based processors increase beyond 2 GHz, a major change must occur in the traditional method of packaging digital ICs. No matter how carefully designed, single chip or even multichip carriers will extract too great a performance penalty from the ICs; impedance mismatches at the chip carrier/logic board interface will always be difficult to prevent completely, and unavoidable time delays will occur as the signal propagates into and out of the carrier. Ultimately, methods must be identified to bond the chips directly to the logic board substrate; the boards themselves will have to support at least two levels of interconnects of transmission line quality, with lines on 4-8 mil centers to match the contact pad spacing on the chips them-

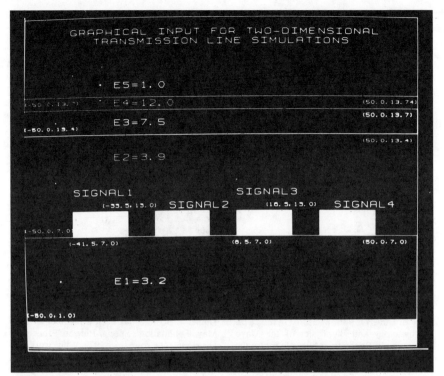

Figure 9. Computer terminal display from a CAD software tool that allows a design engineer to simulate electromagnetic and transmission line behavior of complex metal-dielectric sandwiches; these sandwiches, shown in cross section, are typical of multilayer circuit boards and advanced chip carriers. The designer specifies locations of signal and ground conductors, ground and power planes, and the dimensions of the structures and the dielectric constants of the insulating layers, employing color coding throughout the diagram. The diagram is then parsed in a postprocessing step to extract necessary parameters for electromagnetic simulation. Results are overlaid on the graphical input, including line impedance, mutual and self-inductances and capacitances, and forward and backward crosstalk values.

narrow fields. The design of a GaAs processor that works properly at full speed must be a well-integrated team effort involving representatives from all of these disciplines. The failure to establish and nurture a strong team-oriented effort, with all contributors sharing a working knowledge of the responsibilities of the other team members, is virtually a guarantee of poor performance of the ultimate product, and even of complete collapse of the entire project. This article has attempted to illustrate several of the more crucial areas of concern; however, there is much more to be learned by all workers in this field before the new set of GaAs technologies is completely reduced to practice. □

Acknowledgments

This research was supported in part by contracts MDA903-84-C-0324 and F29601-84-C-0016 from the Defense Advanced Research Projects Agency. The author wishes to thank L. Krueger, S. Karwoski, S. Zahn, D. Endry, C. Treder, G-W. Pan, M. Samson, C. Bates, J. Ryan, B. Shamblin, and T. Volkman, all of the Mayo Foundation, for invaluable technical assistance; S. Roosild and S. Karp, of Defense Advanced Research Projects Agency; J. Kesperis, of the US Army LABCOM, for advice, encouragement, and helpful discussions; T. Webb and J. Spangler, of McDonnell Douglas Microelectronics Center, for fabrication of the 216 pad experimental chip carrier mockup shown in Figure 7; and E. Doherty and S. Richardson, of the Mayo Foundation, for preparation of text and figures.

selves. Wire, ribbon, or tape automated bonds (TABs) will form the electrical connections between the chips and the logic boards. The technology for these substrates will undoubtedly be exotic; however, less sophisticated approaches are unlikely to allow signal processors to operate at the clock rates of which the GaAs components themselves will be capable.

Finally, it must be noted that the accuracy and flexibility of the computer codes employed for the modeling of the high-frequency electrical environment of chips, chip packages, and logic boards must be significantly improved. Computer simulations based on the century-old telegrapher's equations and on relaxation methods must be replaced by the much more powerful theoretical methods that have been developed for both two- and three-dimensional metal/dielectric structures during the past decade (see, e.g., reference 25); these methods are more flexible and accurate, and execute faster on a computer than the older approaches. Based on the method discussed in reference 25, we have developed both two- and

three-dimensional computer codes that can simulate the electromagnetic behavior of multilayer IC packages and logic boards, thereby providing chip and package designers with valuable data that aids in the design of these structures. By providing graphically oriented interfaces between the simulation codes and the designers, a user-friendly environment is created that allows the designer to experiment rapidly with various combinations and dimensions of conductors and dielectric sandwich structures until an optimum design is achieved (Figure 9).

The design of high-performance signal processors with GaAs ICs must be a multidisciplinary task, at a level of integration uncommon and probably unnecessary for silicon-based systems. No longer will the system designer be able to concentrate on the architecture of a processor with the certain knowledge that chip design and simulation, packaging and interconnection layouts, circuit board design, and a host of other central issues will be "cleaned up" by specialists in these

References

1. S. Long et al., "High-Speed GaAs Integrated Circuits," *Proc. IEEE,* Vol. 70, No. 1, Jan. 1982, pp. 35-45.

2. R. N. Deming et al., "A Gallium Arsenide Configurable Cell Array Using Buffered FET Logic," *IEEE J. Solid State Circuits,* Vol. SC-19, No. 5, Oct. 1984, pp. 728-738.

3. W. Yuan et al., "GaAs Heterojunction Bipolar 1K Gate Array," *Proc. IEEE 1984 Int'l Solid-State Circuits Conf.,* pp. 42-43.

4. A. Rode, T. Flegel, and G. LaRue, "A High Yield GaAs Gate Array Technology and Applications," *1983 IEEE Gallium Arsenide IC Symp.,* pp. 178-181. IEEE Publ. #83CH1876-2.

5. S. S. Pei, N. Shah, and C. Tu, "Bell Labs Transistor Sets a Speed Record," *Science,* Vol. 231, No. 4736, Jan. 24, 1986, p. 340.

6. T. Ohshima et al., "A Self-Aligned GaAs/AlGaAs Heterojunction Bipolar Transistor With V-Groove Isolated Planar Structure," *Proc. IEEE 1985 Gallium Arsenide Integrated Circuit Symp.,* pp. 53-56. IEEE Publ. #85CH2182-4.

7. H. Yuan, "GaAs Bipolar Gate Array Technology," *Proc. IEEE 1982 Gallium*

Arsenide IC Symp., pp. 100-103. IEEE Publ. #82CH1764-0.

8. R. O. Grandin, W. Porod, and D. K. Ferry, "Delay Time and Signal Propagation in Large-Scale Integrated Circuits," *IEEE J. Solid State Circuits,* Vol. SC-19, No. 2, Apr. 1984, pp. 262-263.

9. B. K. Gilbert et al., "Design and Fabrication of a Digital RF Memory Using Custom Designed Integrated Circuits," *Proc. IEEE GaAs IC Symp.,* 1985, pp. 173-176. IEEE Publ. #85CH2182-4.

10. H. T. Kung, "Why Systolic Architectures?," *Computer,* Vol. 15, No. 1, Jan. 1982, pp. 37-46.

11. T. J. Fountain, "The Development of the CLIP7 Image Processing System," *Pattern Recognition Letters,* Vol. 1, pp. 331-339.

12. K. Preston and M. J. B. Duff, *Modern Cellular Automata, Theory and Applications,* Plenum Press, New York, 1984. ISBN O-306-41737-5.

13. E. E. Swartzlander, Jr., B. K. Gilbert, and I. S. Reed, "Inner Product Computers," *IEEE Trans. Computers,* Vol. C-27, No. 1, Jan. 1978, pp. 21-31.

14. B. K. Gilbert et al., "Rapid Execution of Fan Beam Image Reconstruction Algorithms Using Efficient Computational Techniques and Special-Purpose Processors," *IEEE Trans. Biomedical Engineering,* Vol. BME-28, No. 2, Feb. 1981, pp. 98-116.

15. A. Kazuyoshi, K. Kurumada, M. Hirayoma, and M. Ohmori, "GaAs 1 K-Bit Static RAM With Self-Aligned FET Technology," *IEEE J. Solid-State Circuits,* Vol. SC-19 , No. 2, Apr. 1984, pp. 260-262.

16. R. Eden, "Capacitor-Diode FET Logic (CDFL) Circuit Approach for GaAs D-MESFET ICs," *Proc. 1984 IEEE GaAs IC Symp.,* pp. 11-14. IEEE #84CH2065-1.

17. T. Gross, *Core Set of Assembly Language Instructions for MIPS-based Microprocessors,* Version 3.0, April 2, 1986.

18. B. K. Gilbert, "Packaging and Interconnection of GaAs Digital Integrated Circuits" in N. G. Einspruch and W. R. Wisseman (eds.), *VLSI Electronics Microstructure Science,* 1985, Academic Press, New York, Vol. 11, pp. 289-331.

19. J. V. McCanny and J. G. McWhirter, "Implementation of Signal Processing Functions Using 1-Bit Systolic Arrays," *Electronics Letters,* Vol. 18, No. 6, March 1982, pp. 241-243.

20. J. G. McWhirter et al., "Multibit Convolution Using a Bit Level Systolic Array," *IEEE Trans. Circuits and Systems,* Vol. CAS-32, No. 1, Jan. 1985, pp. 95-99.

21. B. K. Gilbert et al.,"A Real-Time Hardware System For Digital Processing of Wideband Video Images," *IEEE Trans. Computers,* Vol. C-25, No. 11, Nov. 1976, pp. 1089-1100.

22. T. T. Vu et al., "Low-Power Logic Circuits and 2K Gate Array Using GaAs Self-Aligned MESFETs," *IEEE J. Solid State Circuits.* To be published.

23. G. L. Troeger and J. K. Notthoff, "A Radiation-Hard Low-Power GaAs Static RAM Using E-JFET DCFL," *Proc. IEEE 1983 Gallium Arsenide IC Symp.,* pp. 78-81. IEEE Publ. #83CH1876-2.

24. T. W. Williams, "Design for Testability—A Survey," *Proc. IEEE,* Vol. 71, No. 1, Jan. 1983, pp. 98-112.

25. C. Wei et al., "Multiconductor Transmission Lines in Multilayered Dielectric Media," *IEEE Trans. Microwave Theory and Techniques,* Vol. MTT-32, No. 4, Apr., 1984, pp. 439-449.

Barry K. Gilbert is a staff scientist in the Dept. of Physiology and Biophysics of the Mayo Foundation in Rochester, Minn. He is also the director of the Special- Purpose Processor Development Group at the Mayo Foundation.

His research interests include the development of algorithms for the real-time analysis of wide bandwidth image and signal data; the design of specialized signal-processing computers to execute these tasks; the development of CAD tools to allow the timely design of high-complexity digital signal processors; and the advancement of high- performance IC technologies, such as GaAs, that can be used to assemble very-high-performance signal processors.

Gilbert received his PhD degree in physiology and biophysics from the University of Minnesota.

Daniel J. Schwab has been a member of the Mayo Foundation's Special-Purpose Processor Development Group since 1979. While working for the group, he has specialized in the layout, fabrication, and testing of high-speed digital processors that incorporate high-speed subnanosecond emitter-coupled logic, gallium arsenide digital ICs, and conventional TTL logic.

Schwab attended the Mankato Vocational-Technical School from 1974 to 1976, where he specialized in instrumentation and control technology. He is presently completing his BS degree in electrical engineering at the University of Minnesota, Minneapolis.

Barbara A. Naused joined the Mayo Foundation's Special-Purpose Processor Development Group in 1981; she has experience with signal processor architecture systems and GaAs IC circuit design. She has conducted comparative reviews of microprocessor architectures, and worked on their hardware and software designs.

She is completing a master's degree in electronics engineering from the University of Minnesota.

Rick L. Thompson joined the Special-Purpose Processor Development Group in late 1984, after graduating from Purdue University with a BS degree in electrical engineering technology, with subspecialties in analog and digital systems. He has designed a number of GaAs IC circuits of up to 6000-gate complexity, and has worked extensively with CAD software for GaAs processors.

Prior to beginning work on his BS degree, Thompson spent four years in the US Air Force in Germany as a telecommunications control specialist.

Readers may write to Gilbert at the Medical Science Bldg., Mayo Clinic, Rochester, MN 55905.

Reprinted from *Computer*, March 1986, pages 30-42. Copyright © 1986 by
The Institute of Electrical and Electronics Engineers, Inc.

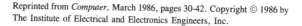

An Introduction to GaAs Microprocessor Architecture for VLSI

Veljko Milutinovic and David Fura, Purdue University

Walter Helbig, RCA

The implementation of GaAs processors is now feasible with their VLSI capability, their higher speed, and their greater tolerance of environmental variations.

Gallium arsenide, or GaAs, technology has recently shown rapid increases in maturity. In particular, the advances made in digital chip complexity have been enormous. This progress is especially evident in two types of chips: static RAMs and gate arrays. In 1983, static RAMs containing 1K bits were announced. One year later both a 4K-bit and a 16K-bit version were presented. Gate arrays have advanced from a 1000-gate design presented in 1984 to a 2000-gate design announced in 1985. With this enormous progress underway, it is now appropriate to consider the use of this new technology in the implementation of high-performance processors.

GaAs technology generates high levels of enthusiasm primarily because of two advantages it enjoys over silicon: higher speed and greater resistance to adverse environmental conditions.

GaAs gates switch faster than silicon transistor-transistor logic, or TTL, gates by nearly an order of magnitude. These switching speeds are even faster than those attained by the fastest silicon emitter-coupled logic, or ECL, but at power levels an order of magnitude lower.[1] For this reason, GaAs is seen to have applications in computer design within several computationally intensive areas. In fact, it has been reported that the Cray-3 will contain GaAs parts.

GaAs also enjoys greater resistance to radiation and temperature variations than does silicon. GaAs successfully operates in radiation levels of 10 to 100 million rads. Its operating temperature range extends from −200 to 200°C. Consequently, GaAs has created great excitement in the military and aerospace markets.

Unfortunately, GaAs is also characterized by some undesirable properties. Two significant areas where GaAs is inferior to silicon are cost and transistor count capability.

The higher cost of GaAs chips is largely the result of the higher cost of the GaAs material itself and the lower yield (typically 1 to 2 percent for VLSI in 1985) of GaAs chips. GaAs material is more expensive than silicon since gallium is relatively rare, whereas silicon is abundant. Also, since GaAs is a compound, additional processing is required to create it from its elements and to verify its composition. The lower GaAs yield is also due to multiple influences. First, although improvements are being made in this area, GaAs is characterized by a higher density of dislocations than silicon. Second, in order to achieve working devices with adequate noise margins, very fine control of circuit parameters is required, and this is not yet easily achieved. Finally, the high brittleness of the GaAs substrate (the gallium arsenide material itself) contributes to its high cost because of increased breakage of the finished product. Currently, GaAs chips are roughly two orders of magnitude more expensive than their silicon

This research, conducted at the Purdue University School of Electrical Engineering, has been sponsored by and conducted in collaboration with the RCA Advanced Technology Laboratories.

counterparts; however, this difference should narrow to possibly one order of magnitude by the end of this decade.

Transistor count limitations of GaAs are attributed to both yield and power considerations. The relatively low yield of GaAs chips forces designers to consider chips with a smaller area (therefore lower transistor count) in order to get more chips on each wafer. When operating at the same speeds as silicon gates, GaAs gates require less power. However, GaAs gates do consume considerably more power than slower silicon MOS gates. Because of the thermal management problem this creates, fast GaAs chips cannot match the transistor count potential of silicon chips.

It is believed that these four GaAs-silicon differences are not of a temporary nature, but instead result from inherent differences between GaAs and silicon materials. Conclusions that are based on these four fundamental characteristics will remain valid even as GaAs technology matures.

Because of these GaAs-silicon differences, it is not sufficient merely to copy existing silicon designs into GaAs in order to obtain optimal GaAs performance. The GaAs environment presents the computer architecture designer with a new set of challenges. However, the rewards of successfully exploiting this new environment are substantial. With the high speeds that characterize GaAs and the recent introduction of GaAs chips with VLSI levels of integration (> 10,000 transistors), we are presently on the verge of achieving, with a single-chip processor, speeds for scalar operations typical of present-day supercomputers.

To explore the use of GaAs as a technology for high-speed processor design, an examination of GaAs technology and the identification of those of its characteristics that influence processor design should be made, as should where these characteristics differ from those found in silicon. This information is needed in order to discuss the trade-offs present in GaAs processor design. Design approaches that appear well-suited to this environment may then be presented.

Technology and IC design

To illustrate which GaAs device and logic families have shown the greatest potential

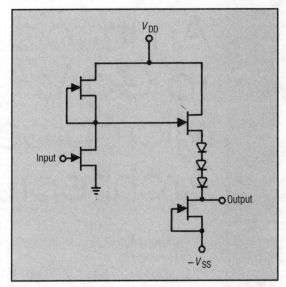

Figure 1. BFL D-MESFET inverter.

for near-term processor implementation it is best to select one family as representative GaAs technology and then present the characteristics that are relevant for processor design. These characteristics, when compared with those of silicon NMOS, will illuminate those traits of GaAs that introduce architectural design considerations different from those found with using silicon.

GaAs device families. Several different device families have been studied for GaAs implementation. However, because of the superior maturity of the metal semiconductor field effect transistor, or MESFET, device family, we will use it in all our comparisons with silicon. Some other devices show greater potential than MESFETs but just aren't expected to achieve VLSI complexity soon. These other devices include heterojunction bipolar transistors, or HJBTs, and modulation doped FETs, or MODFETs, also known as high electron mobility transistors or HEMTs.

GaAs MESFET logic families. MESFET logic circuits have been built in GaAs using both depletion-mode transistor drivers, or D-MESFETs, and enhancement-mode transistor drivers, or E-MESFETs. These two transistor designs have a number of important differences. D-MESFETs are better in that they are generally faster, have better noise immunity, are less sensitive to increases in fan-in and fan-out, and have fewer fabrication problems than E-MESFETs. However, D-MESFETs require two power supplies and extra logic to provide

voltage level shifting—neither of which is needed by E-MESFETs. D-MESFETs also require more power than E-MESFETs and use a more complex circuit design, which results in higher area requirements. [2]

There currently exist three principal GaAs MESFET logic families. They are Buffered FET Logic, or BFL, and Schottky Diode FET Logic, or SDFL, of the D-MESFET family, and Direct Coupled FET Logic, or DCFL, of the E-MESFET family. [3]

The earliest work in GaAs digital circuits was done with BFL D-MESFETs. This family is generally characterized by fast switching speeds and high power requirements. Early work produced BFL logic gates with propagation delays of 34 ps and a power dissipation of 41.0 mW per gate. More recently, however, there have been efforts to reduce the power requirements with the introduction of low-power, or lp, BFL circuits. An lp-BFL design for a 4-bit ripple-carry-adder containing about 40 gates with gate delays of 250 ps at 6.0 mW per gate has been presented. The highest integration obtained with BFL gates to date appears to be a 32-bit adder containing 420 gates with gate delays of 230 ps at 0.8 mW per gate. [4] An example of a BFL D-MESFET inverter is shown in Figure 1.

SDFL D-MESFET gates were proposed as an alternative to BFL logic gates. SDFL gates generally require less power and area than BFL gates. Consequently, this family has received considerable interest for LSI circuit applications. One of the first LSI

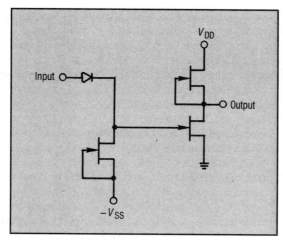

Figure 2.
SDFL D-MESFET
inverter.

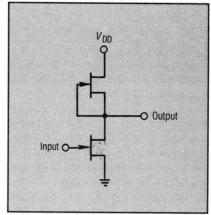

Figure 3. DCFL E/D-MESFET inverter.

GaAs applications was an 8×8-bit multiplier containing 1008 gates using SDFL logic. Gate delays were 150 ps and power dissipation was approximately 1.5 mW per gate. Recently an SDFL RAM-per-gate array chip has been presented. The chip contains 432 SDFL cells, 32 interface cells, and 64 bits of RAM totaling approximately 3000 FETs and 5000 diodes. The gate delays are 150 ps and power dissipation is 1.5 mW per gate. Simulations of low-power versions of this design indicate that gate delays of 300 ps at power levels below 0.2 mW per gate are possible. An example of an SDFL D-MESFET inverter is shown in Figure 2.

E-MESFETs were long considered to be more suitable for VLSI implementation than D-MESFETs because of lower power requirements and simpler circuit design. However, it has been only recently that advances in fabrication have allowed E-MESFETs to reach the VLSI level of complexity. A number of recent designs have been introduced using the DCFL E/D MESFET (enhancement-mode driver with depletion-mode load) approach. A 16×16-bit parallel multiplier containing 3000 gates with gate delays of 160 ps at 0.3 mW per gate has been reported. A gate array containing 2000 gates has been designed with a gate delay below 100 ps and a power dissipation of 0.4 mW per gate. The highest reported level of integration achieved to date with a GaAs process is a DCFL $16K \times 1K$ SRAM containing 102,300 FETs with an access time of 4.1 ns and power dissipation of 2.5 W. An example of a DCFL E/D-MESFET inverter is shown in Figure 3.

Characteristics of GaAs MESFET designs. Table 1 contains the published performance characteristics of some GaAs MESFET designs. As this table indicates

and the above discussion implies, it is clear that GaAs will soon provide a suitable vehicle for processor implementation. Currently the most promising MESFET solution is provided by the DCFL E/D-MESFET approach, based on its low power requirements. The presentation of a 102,300-FET chip certainly helps demonstrate the merits of DCFL. Currently, the major drawback to this approach is its fabrication complexity and resulting low yield and high cost. However, based on the present rate of fabrication technology improvement, the implementation of microprocessors in GaAs should be feasible within two or three years. Therefore, it is crucial that we now begin to understand the GaAs environment, and determine how the characteristics of GaAs will influence processor architecture design in that environment.

GaAs-silicon comparison. A GaAs-silicon comparison can be made using GaAs circuits based on the DCFL E/D-MESFET logic family.

Table 2 compares several characteristics of GaAs and silicon processes that are important for computer architecture design and optimization. Significant GaAs-silicon differences can be observed in the following areas: (1) transistor count, (2) on-chip gate delay, (3) the ratio of off-chip to on-chip memory access time, and (4) gate fan-in and fan-out.

Transistor count limitations were once primarily dictated by the poor yield of large GaAs chips. Recently, however, power dissipation has taken a more dominant role. If on-chip power requirements significantly exceed 2 W, special packaging techniques are required in order to remove heat from

Table 1. Performance characteristics of GaAs MESFETs.

Unit	Speed, ns	Power	Device count
Arithmetic			
32-bit adder (BFL)	2.9 total	1.2 W total	2.5K
8×8-bit multiplier (SDFL)	5.2 total	2.2 W total	6.0K
16×16-bit multiplier (DCFL)	10.5 total	1.0 W total	10K
Control			
Gate array/SRAM (SDFL)	0.15/gate	3.0 W total	8.0K
1000-gate gate array (DCFL)	0.10/gate	0.4 W total	3.0K
2000-gate gate array (DCFL)	0.08/gate	0.4 W total	8.2K
Memory			
1K-bit SRAM (DCFL)	2.0 total	0.5 W total	7.1K
4K-bit SRAM (DCFL)	4.1 total	2.5 W total	102.3K

the chip. With current GaAs processes characterized by power dissipations of 0.2 mW per gate, a 2-W chip will contain about only 30K transistors. In the silicon environment, the Motorola 68020 with a transistor count of close to 200K and power of 2 W is commercially available.

Small on-chip gate delays give GaAs an essential edge over silicon for high-performance digital systems. These speed advantages are derived from inherent properties of GaAs, such as higher electron mobility and lower parasitic capacitances. For this reason, GaAs will remain a potentially faster technology than silicon.

Unfortunately, the speed advantage that GaAs enjoys over silicon for the on-chip environment is reduced considerably for the off-chip environment because of propagation delays. Such sources of off-chip delay as capacitive loading and speed-of-light limitations (about 0.5 ns per foot propagation delay) affect GaAs and silicon equally. However, as these delays increase, they dominate the switching delays in GaAs and reduce the inherent GaAs advantage. Techniques utilized by microwave engineers are commonly used to help minimize these delays. Also, new interchip connection schemes are being investigated.[5] However, the ratio of off-chip to on-chip delays is still considerably higher than that found within silicon.

Low fan-in and fan-out of GaAs gates, although not believed to be a permanent characteristic, nevertheless currently introduce constraints not found in silicon. Gate fan-out can be generally be increased by using larger transistors, as is done in silicon. However, low gate fan-in is a serious problem, particularly for NAND gates. This is because an increase in the number of inputs to a NAND gate reduces the noise margin, and noise margins are very small in GaAs devices to begin with.

In addition, varying degrees of difficulty have been reported in the implementation of read only memories, or ROMs, tristate buffers, and pass transistors.

In conclusion, the differences between GaAs and silicon are substantial.

GaAs processor design

To discuss processor design in the GaAs environment it is best to present the characteristics of GaAs that heavily in-

fluence processor design and to outline techniques for overcoming some of the problems posed by GaAs. Such individual design issues as the choice of processor configuration, pipeline structure, register file, execution unit, and instruction set figure importantly in such a discussion.

Implications of GaAs characteristics on computer architecture design. Several of the characteristics of GaAs enumerated previously have a large influence on computer architecture design. As already indicated, these characteristics are a low transistor count, a high ratio of off-chip memory access delay to on-chip datapath delay, low gate fan-in and fan-out, and low yield.

A processor implemented in GaAs is limited to fewer transistors than if implemented in silicon; therefore, a premium is placed on simple designs in the GaAs environment. This has a large effect on the processor design philosophy in general, as well as on the design of the individual sections of the processor.

The advantage that GaAs enjoys over silicon for on-chip switching speed is, unfortunately, not accompanied by an equal ad-

vantage in off-chip memory access time. Thus a GaAs processor will generally have a very high ratio of off-chip memory access delay to on-chip datapath delay. The fundamental problem caused by this high ratio is that the information (instructions and data) requirement of a GaAs processor may not be satisfied, and lower-than-expected performance will result. Careful design techniques are needed so that the advantage in gate switching speed that GaAs enjoys can be maximally exploited, even though the off-chip to off-package speed advantage is much lower.

There are two approaches to solving the GaAs information bandwidth problem. The first one is to reduce the processor's requirements for off-chip information. This can be accomplished by either increasing the size of on-chip memory or by increasing the length of time that information is used by the on-chip execution unit. The second one is to increase the rate of information flow. There are two ways of accomplishing this. First, the information content of each transfer can be increased, either by increasing the number of bits per transfer or by reducing the redundancy in the information transferred. Reducing instructions falls in

Table 2. Performance comparison of typical GaAs (DCFL E/D MESFET) and silicon (NMOS) and silicon (CMO/SOS).

	GaAs	Silicon NMOS	Silicon CMOS/SOS
Complexity			
Transistor count/chip	20-30K	300-450K	75-175K
Chip area (max.)	40,000 sq. mils	90,000 sq. mils.	120,000 sq. mils
Speed			
Gate delay	50-150 ps	1-3 ns	1-1.25 ns
On-chip memory access	0.5-2.0 ns	10-20 ns	10-20 ns
Off-chip/on-package memory access	4-10 ns	40-80 ns	20-40 ns
Off-chip/off-package memory access*	20-80 ns	100-200 ns	100-200 ns
IC design			
Transistors/single gate	1+fan-in	1+fan-in	2×fan-in
Transistors/memory cell			
Static	6	6	6
Dynamic	1	1	—
Fan-in (max.)	5	5	5
Fan-out (max.)	3-5	10-20	10-20
Gate delay increase for each additional fan-out relative to gate delay with fan-out = 1	25-40%	25-40%	10-20%

*Subject to change.

106

> In general, multichip GaAs processor configurations are less desirable than configurations containing only one chip.

the latter category. The second approach is to increase the effective transfer rate. This may be accomplished through sophisticated off-chip memory design techniques.

The lower on-chip fan-in and fan-out of GaAs circuits has important consequences for circuit design within the processor, especially within the execution unit. We will show the effects of this GaAs characteristic later in this section.

Lower GaAs yield encourages the computer architect to consider including features to improve this yield.

Choice of processor configuration. Several types of processor configurations have been used in the silicon environment. The Cray-1 was implemented with SSI, MSI, and LSI parts. The Univac 1100/60 was implemented using bit-slice parts. The Xerox PARC Dorado processor contains multiple VLSI chips. Several processors are available as a single VLSI chip, including the Intel iAPX 286.

In general, multichip GaAs processor configurations are less desirable than configurations containing only one chip. This is because the large amount of interchip communication typical for multichip configurations greatly diminishes the inherent GaAs switching speed advantage. A single-chip processor configuration minimizes this interchip communication and, therefore, offers the best potential performance.

Single-chip processor design methodology. Low transistor count severely limits the types of architecture we can consider for GaAs implementation of a single-chip processor. Today we cannot implement a GaAs design requiring considerably more than 30K transistors. Therefore, we must carefully examine what trade-offs may be necessary in adding certain hardware

features in a GaAs processor. Every transistor must be justified.

Fortunately, a product of modern design philosophy that is compatible with the close scrutiny of all design options has already been introduced: Reduced Instruction Set Computers, or RISCs. Examples of RISCs include the University of California at Berkeley RISC I & II, or UCB-RISC, and the Stanford University MIPS, or SU-MIPS,[7] with transistor counts of 41K and 25K, respectively. In contrast, some Complex Instruction Set Computers, or CISCs, contain over 100K transistors, such as the Motorola MC68020 and HP-FOCUS, with approximately 190K and 450K transistors, respectively. We wish to make an important distinction between the term *RISC*, which represents either the reduced instruction set philosophy or any processor design based on this philosophy, and *UCB-RISC*, which is a specific processor design based on the RISC philosophy.

The RISC design philosophy has been stated as follows:

1. First identify the machine instructions most frequently used by the target application.
2. Optimize the datapath and timing for these frequent instructions only.
3. Incorporate other frequent instructions into the instruction set only if they fit into the already elaborated VLSI scheme.[8]

Implicit in the RISC design philosophy is a constant examination of hardware/software trade-offs. A function is included in hardware only if justified by an acceptable increase in expected performance. Functions that are not directly supported by hardware must then be synthesized by the compiler out of more primitive functions.

Current silicon RISCs are characterized by several common traits. As their name implies, they have simplified instruction sets. The number of different instructions is low, instructions are of fixed length and execute in a single cycle, register-to-register operations are used, and data memory is accessed via loads and stores. Because of the simplicity of their instruction sets, RISCs use hardwired control logic instead of microcode. The control logic of the UCB-RISC requires only 10 percent of the total chip area, compared to the 68 percent required by the control logic of the MC68000. RISC designers try to move as much work as possible from execution time to compile time. In fact, the capabilities of a sophisti-

cated optimizing compiler are included in the architectural design trade-off analysis. The result is that RISCs are better targets for optimizing compilers and, consequently, execute programs written in high-level languages faster.

Performance comparisons between some RISCs and CISCs have been presented in reference 9, where it is shown that RISCs execute high-level language programs considerably faster. There are those who remain unconvinced of the superiority of RISCs, however, especially when system-level issues are considered. Examples of some strong counterarguments are presented in reference 10.

In the silicon environment the RISC-CISC debate rages on. However, in the GaAs environment there is no such dilemma. Because of the limited transistor count of a single-chip GaAs processor, the RISC philosophy is clearly the most appropriate approach.

Pipeline design and optimization in a GaAs environment. Pipeline design consideration for GaAs processors can be approached by describing a principal goal of pipelining. Example pipelines used in silicon processors and a demonstration of why these may be inappropriate for a GaAs implementation are integral parts of such an approach. The optimal design of a GaAs processor pipeline influences the design of the execution unit, register file, instruction set, and off-chip memory system.

Pipelining is frequently used in silicon processors to improve performance. This performance gain is primarily achieved through increased utilization of the processor's datapath. We define the datapath time as the time the processor takes to fetch the operand(s) from the register file, to propagate them through the execution unit, to write the result back into the register file, and to perform optional bus precharging. The goal of pipelining in the GaAs environment is the same as in the silicon environment. However, full datapath utilization is much harder to achieve in a GaAs processor because the ratio of instruction memory access time to datapath time is much higher. The reasons for this high ratio are evident from Table 2 and are

1. The ratio of off-chip memory access delay to both on-chip memory access delay and ALU delay is much higher in the GaAs environment than in the silicon environment.

2. The lower transistor count of GaAs chips precludes the use of an on-chip cache for memory access speedup.

In Table 3 we present typical ratios of the instruction memory access time to the datapath time for both GaAs and silicon. We assume that in all four of these cases an instruction cache is used. For reasons noted above, the ratios for GaAs are considerably higher than for silicon.

As Table 3 shows, in the silicon environment the instruction fetch delay is generally equal to or less than the datapath delay. This has a direct effect on the type of pipelines that are implemented in the silicon environment. In Figures 4 and 5 we show two such pipelines, which are from silicon RISCs: the UCB-RISC and the SU-MIPS, respectively.

In the GaAs environment, on the other hand, the instruction fetch delay is generally much greater than the datapath delay. If a silicon pipeline is used directly in a GaAs environment, severe datapath underutilization will occur. As an example, in Figure 6 we show the UCB-RISC pipeline implemented in a GaAs environment with an instruction fetch-to-datapath ratio of 3.

The reason for the ineffectiveness of silicon pipelines in a GaAs environment is apparent from the data in Table 2. As already indicated, although the GaAs on-chip switching speed is nearly 10 times faster than in silicon, the off-chip/off-package memory access delay is improved only by a much smaller amount. A critical design problem for computer architects is to exploit the much superior switching speed of GaAs, even though the GaAs off-chip/off-package memory access speed improvement is much lower.

The GaAs pipeline design problem is again primarily one of finding methods to ensure that the instruction bandwidth satisfies the processor's datapath requirements. Two such methods exist. One is to increase the instruction information bandwidth. Another is to increase the length of time the datapath is used in order to match the instruction fetch delay, hopefully in a way that yields benefits.

Increasing the instruction information bandwidth can be accomplished in several ways. The methods that we present here have implications on the off-chip memory system, processor pin count, and the instruction format.

One method is to include more levels in the instruction memory hierarchy than is typically found in memory systems for silicon processors. For a given hierarchical memory system, the difference in access times (in terms of instruction cycles) between the various levels will be greater for a GaAs processor than for a silicon processor. With such large differences, the addition of more levels will greatly reduce the average memory access time.

Another method is to use a pipelined memory system. This has been used on such high-performance silicon computers as the Amdahl 470V/6. The pipeline illustrated in Figure 7 reflects this approach.

A third method is to use an interleaved memory system. This technique has been used on such silicon computers as the IBM 3033. Here, multiple words are read from a relatively slow, but large memory into a faster, smaller memory, or possibly even into the processor.

The final method we will consider for increasing the effective instruction fetch rate is to fetch multiple instructions. This technique has been used in the silicon environment as well, in the SU-MIPS, although there are indications that the benefits of this approach were not great. In the GaAs environment, however, multiple-instruction fetches are potentially more valuable. Pipe-

lines produced by this method resemble that in Figure 8. Multiple instruction fetching introduces requirements for increased package pin count, compact instruction formats, or both.

Table 3. Memory access to datapath delay ratios for silicon and GaAs.

Technology	Access type	Typical ratio
Silicon	On-chip	0.3—0.6
Silicon	Off-chip	0.8—1.2
GaAs	Off-chip/on package	1.6—3.2
GaAs	Off-chip/off-package	4.0—8.0

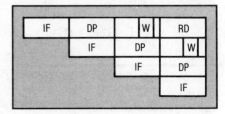

Figure 4. Pipeline structure used in the UCB-RISC. IF—Instruction Fetch Cycle; DP—Datapath Cycle; W—Register Write; RD—Data Load Cycle.

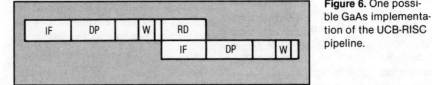

Figure 5. Pipeline structure used in SU-MIPS.

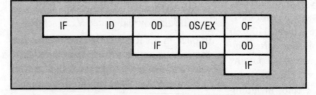

Figure 6. One possible GaAs implementation of the UCB-RISC pipeline.

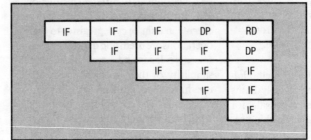

Figure 7. Example pipeline with a pipelined memory.

Key to cycles:
IF—Instruction Fetch
ID—Instruction Decode
OD—Operand Decode
DP—Datapath
OS/EX—Operand Store/Execute
W—Register Write
OF—Operand Fetch
RD—Data Load

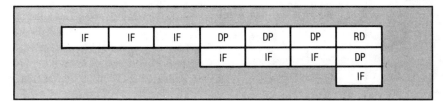

Figure 8. Example pipeline with instruction packing. IF—Instruction Fetch Cycles; DP—Datapath Cycles; RD—Data Load Cycle.

If the above methods cannot provide a sufficiently close match between the instruction fetch and datapath times, then increasing the time the datapath is used may yield some important benefits.

One method of increasing datapath delay is to remove resources, (transistors, chip area, etc.) from datapath functions and to reallocate them elsewhere. This is in keeping with the RISC philosophy in that hardware resources should be allocated only where they will provide benefits. The adder is one example of a datapath element where this technique may be used.

Another method is to use the execution unit more than once for each instruction fetch. Of course, this works only for complex operations that may be synthesized from multiple primitive operations, and it is also contrary to the design of many silicon RISCs. However, this technique may increase the average datapath utilization substantially. Another benefit of using multiple-cycle instructions is that application programs are more compact. An experimental GaAs processor design that uses this approach is the VM architecture.

Still another is to include within the execution unit the hardware to directly execute a complex operation. The comments made concerning the previous method apply here as well. An on-chip, off-datapath, bit-serial multiplier is one example of an application of this method.

Register file design and optimization in the GaAs environment. Registers provide a greater performance enhancement for GaAs processors than for silicon processors. Although there are some problems associated with register files, certain register file configurations can combat these problems. Moreover, using register file fault-tolerance techniques can also increase the yield of GaAs processors.

Performance enhancement of register files for GaAs processors. The benefits of a large on-chip register file for silicon processor performance enchancement have been well documented. Several of these benefits, presented reference 11, are even more important in the GaAs environment in the following ways:

1. Since the ratio of off-chip memory access delay to register access delay is larger for a GaAs processor, the improvement that registers provide in reduced operand access delay is more substantial.

2. The reduction in instruction size that results from shorter operand addresses is also more important for GaAs processors. This is because compact programs increase the effectiveness of the instruction cache and other elements of the memory hierarchy.

3. Since GaAs processors will likely have load/store architectures, accessing a value in the register file eliminates the execution of a load/store instruction. Not only are fewer load/store instructions executed, but they also need not be stored in instruction memory, again reducing the program size.

In conclusion, in a silicon environment, allocating leftover transistors to the register file may be acceptable. However, in a GaAs environment, because of the more severe performance penalties in accessing off-chip data, register file design is one of the most important design considerations. A large and well-designed register file is critical for superior performance in the GaAs environment.

Register cell design. Several register cell designs have been used in silicon processors. For high-performance designs, register cells with multiple read and/or write ports are commonly used. In Figures 9 and 10 are shown the register cells used in the SU-MIPS and HP-FOCUS respectively. Although these two register cells are fairly complex, they both allow two reads or two writes to be performed in parallel.

In the GaAs environment, simpler register cell designs are generally more appropriate because the off-chip instruction fetch time may exceed the datapath time, anyway. There is no performance loss in slowing the register access as long as the total datapath delay is less than the effective instruction fetch delay. Another reason for simple cell design is that in the transistor-scarce GaAs environment the chip resources not needed for register cells may be profitably used elsewhere.

An example of a register cell that deserves strong consideration for a GaAs implementation is shown in Figure 11. This cell was used in the UCB-RISC register file. Two reads may be performed in parallel, but the access speed is not as good as that in complex cells. Even though two buses are required, this cell design still requires far fewer chip resources than complex cells.

Thus the register cell that might be the most suitable for GaAs—one with only a single read bus—is one that sees increasingly less use in the silicon environment. If two operands are to be read from this type of cell, they must be fetched serially. This increases the time loss of this segment of the datapath, but even this will most likely not be the performance bottleneck (usually the adder carry chain is anyway). On the other hand, the area saved by eliminating the read bus may be profitably used for other purposes, especially in increasing the number of registers in the register file. There are indications that this approach yields benefits in the GaAs environment. This register cell is shown in Figure 12.

Register file configurations. Most modern silicon processors contain a monolithic (single window) register file containing 16 or 32 registers, for example, the National NS32032. There are a few exceptions, however, such as the UCB-RISC with 138 registers divided into eight windows. Perhaps a movement toward large, multiple-window register files for high-level language support is underway; however, currently single-window register files with 16 or 32 registers dominate the silicon environment.

There are, however, two disturbing characteristics of single-window register files that take increased importance in the GaAs environment. First, on context switches, data generally must be transferred between the register file and off-chip memory. Second, very few registers need to be allocated for subroutine variables and formal parameters in well-structured programs. Thus

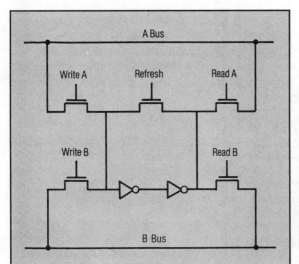

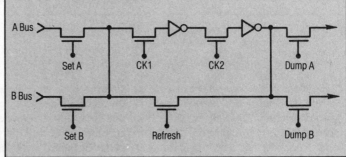

Figure 9. Register cell used in the SU-MIPS.

Figure 10. Register cell used in the HP-FOCUS.

the average register file utilization tends to be low. In the GaAs environment, which penalizes off-chip communication so severely, a more sophsicated register management policy is highly desirable.

With a single-window configuration, the main method of reducing the information bandwidth requirements during context switches is through sophisticated compilation techniques. What is required is the ability to preserve values in registers across procedure boundaries. One method of achieving this is through the use of "in-line procedures." With this technique the compiler replaces the machine code that implements the procedure call with the machine code of the called procedure itself. However, this technique is generally limited to very small procedures or to those called only once, otherwise large increases in program size are incurred. A substantial reduction in context switching overhead appears to be beyond the current state-of-the-art compiler technology.

It is because of the inherent limitations of single-window register files for reducing context switching overhead and register file underutilization that multiple-window techniques are promising alternatives for GaAs processors. In a multiple-window scheme, the register file is partitioned into windows and each window may be allocated to a separate procedure. On a context switch, instead of saving and restoring the register file, a new window is "made active," perhaps by moving a pointer as in the UCB-RISC. The only time that values need to be transferred is on an "overflow" or "underflow." An overflow occurs when

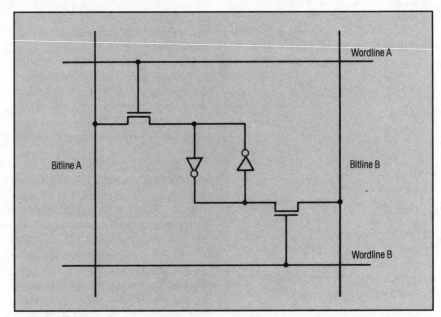

Figure 11. Register cell used in the UCB-RISC.

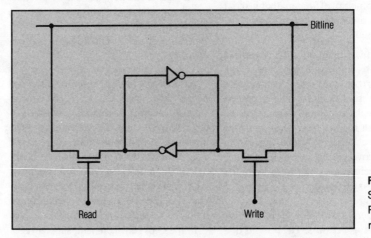

Figure 12. Single Read bus register cell.

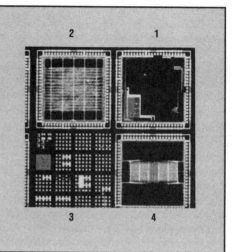
all the windows are full and a procedure call is required. As underflow occurs on returns when the values of the returned procedure were previously stored to off-chip memory because of an overflow.

The multiple-window schemes studied for silicon implementation are characterized by a large number of registers.[12] However, the large area and transistor requirements of these schemes make them unsuitable for GaAs. This warrants examining two schemes that have been presented for silicon: a multiple-window scheme with variable-size windows and a multiple-window scheme with background-mode loading and storing. Both attempt to achieve the performance level of a large register file with a much smaller register file.

The multiple-window scheme with variable-size windows is worthy of strong consideration for GaAs implementation because of its ability to achieve 100 percent register file utilization. Well-structured application programs have many procedures that contain few local scalars. With the ability to allocate exactly enough registers for each procedure, small register files can contain several windows.

The multiple-window scheme with background-mode loading and storing is also a candidate for futher study. This scheme utilizes a very effective technique for combating high communication costs—communication is performed in parallel with computation. This technique allows a register file with few windows to perform as well as a register file with many more by reducing the frequency of overflows and underflows. This is achieved through selective preloading and prestoring of variables through one window of the register file, while another window is used for normal computations.

The selection of an appropriate register file configuration is, of course, dependent upon the application environment as well as technology. Multiple-window schemes perform best when procedures contain few local variables and formal parameters. They also do well when the "locality of nesting depth" is low, so that overflows and underflows aren't too frequent.

Multiple-window register files deserve much more attention in the GaAs environment than they currently seem to be getting from silicon designers. Their major advantage is their ability to reduce off-chip communication, which is a more serious problem in the GaAs environment. The implementation cost of a multiple-window scheme is higher, however. The effect is felt in possibly increased datapath delay, which is not as disastrous as in silicon, and increased transistor count, which is even more so. The variable-size window and background load/store approaches rate serious considerations. However, their advantages must be weighed against their contribution to hardware complexity. A careful study of design trade-offs is necessary to determine the appropriate configuration.

Fault tolerance for yield improvement. Fault-tolerant design features incorporated into the register file may provide important increases in the yield of GaAs processors. In a GaAs processor with fault-tolerance capabilities, a fault in a register cell will not disable the entire chip. The approach depends on the register file configuration. One approach is a single window register file; the other, a multiple window register file. Of course, many traditional approaches to fault tolerance can be applied to the GaAs environment as well.

In a single-window register file configuration, fault tolerance may be implemented through compilation techniques. The basic approach is to let the compiler locate only variables in registers that are known to be good. One disadvantage is that the smaller register file size will result in decreased performance. Also, a program compiled for one machine may not work on another. However, for dedicated applications this may not be an unreasonable approach.

In a multiple-window register file configuration, fault tolerance may be added with little runtime overhead. Initially, a self-test program is required to detect the presence of a bad register cell and to store the register cell somewhere within the processor. During execution, whenever the window pointer is moved, the register cell status is checked. If the new window contains a bad cell, then the window pointer is moved again.

The appropriateness of this approach depends on several factors. First, the runtime overhead involved with fault checking must be acceptable. Also, the loss of performance due to the reduced number of register windows must not be too severe. The hardware cost must be acceptable as well. A thorough analysis should be performed in order to determine the appropriateness of fault tolerance for yield improvement in GaAs processors.

Execution unit design and optimization in the GaAs environment. There are some particularly important GaAs properties that influence the goals of execution unit design. Execution unit design involves three major execution unit components: the adder, the multiplier/divider, and the shifter.

Execution unit design philosphy. The two prominent GaAs characteristics that have a direct influence on execution unit design are the high off-chip memory access delay and the low transistor count of GaAs chips. As a result, the goal of execution unit design in GaAs is not to utilize large amounts of chip resources to speed up primitive operations, as is often done in silicon designs. One reason is that chip resources are scarce. Also, because off-chip communications will likely be the performance bottleneck, speeding up the execution of primitive operations may yield no benefit anyway.

There are two promising approaches to execution unit design in the GaAs environment. The first is to decrease the resources allocated to execution unit members even if this slows down the execution of primitive operations. This will cause no loss in execution speed as long as off-chip communication costs remain dominant. The resources saved may then be used elsewhere, perhaps to increase the size of on-chip memory, as already pointed out. The second approach is to increase the resources dedicated to the execution unit, but only for the implementation of complex operations. Performance benefits may be realized because of the increased execution speed of the complex operations and because of the reduced redundancy of the instructions that implement the complex operations.

Adder design in the GaAs environment. Many different adder designs have been considered for use in silicon processors (Table 4). Four example adder designs, in order of increasing complexity, are ripple-carry, carry-select, conditional-sum, and carry-lookahead. For a silicon implementation, it is generally true that the designs requiring the larger transistor count also provide the faster addition times. This is certainly true for SSI/MSI implementations. For VLSI implementations, although there are indications that this may not be true, carry-lookahead adders are used in such high-performance silicon processors as the HP-FOCUS and BELLMAC-32.

In the GaAs environment, simple adder designs such as ripple-carry and carry-select are better candidates than carry-lookahead. The justification presented earlier for sim-

ple register cell designs is also appropriate here. Again, the reasoning is that the tradeoff of high speed for reduced resource requirements is advantageous for GaAs datapath designs. There is, however, another reason why simple adders are more attractive. The carry-lookahead design is plagued with very large gate fan-ins and fan-outs. As mentioned earlier, GaAs gates are now often characterized with low fan-in and fan-out capabilities. Therefore, additional gates must be used implement a carry-lookahead adder. Because carry-lookahead is an irregular adder design, it has a large area requirement. This combined with the need for additional gates may make carry-lookahead adders inappropriate for a GaAs processor.

The ripple-carry design is the simplest and most regular of the three and so is advantageous from the VLSI point of view. The carry-select approach is the next best. Because the limited fan-in of GaAs gates degrades the performance of the partial carry-lookahead approach so severely, the nonregularity and long wirelengths associated with this technique make it undesirable for a GaAs/VLSI implementation. The ripple-carry approach is nearly as fast as a parallel approach in a silicon VLSI environment for a word length of 32 bits. Because of the limited fan-in of GaAs gates, the ripple-carry approach may be faster for a GaAs VLSI implementation. Even if not the fastest, the ripple-carry approach may still be preferred because of its low layout area requirements.

Multiplier/divider design in the GaAs environment. Multiplication and division operations show a wide variation in frequency of use. For example, scientific applications require these operations much more often than general-purpose applications. Therefore, the application environment has a large influence on the selection of appropriate multiplication and division techniques.

Several multiplier designs have been used in silicon processors. Some processors, such as the UCB-RISC, utilize an adder and an iterative add-and-shift algorithm that requires n steps, where n is the word length. A variation of this method incorporates a recorded number system, such as a modified Booth algorithm used in the Fairchild F9450, which requires only n/2 steps. Alternatively, more hardware can be used, such as in the design used by the TMS320, which

Adder type	Transistor count	Gate delays
Ripple-carry	1.0K	66
Carry-lookahead	2.0K	20
Carry-select	2.2K	19

Table 4. Comparison of three 32-bit adders.

uses a modified Booth algorithm implemented in hardware. Parallel, array multipliers have also been used, such as in the NEC IPP. Also, bit-serial multipliers have been presented. A survey of the topic and some interesting novel solutions for GaAs can be found in reference 13.

Many different divider designs are also evident in silicon processors. Some designs, such as the SU-MIPS, utilize an iterative subtract-and-shift algorithm requiring n steps. Cellular array and bit-serial dividers have been studied. A division-by-repeated-multiplication technique has been used in several processors, including the IBM 360/91.

As is the case for adder design in the GaAs environment, the use of simple hardware is desirable for multiplier/divider design. The "cheapest" techniques in terms of hardware requirements require only one adder and little control logic. These are the add/subtract-and-shift methods mentioned above, and they are good candidates for GaAs implementation. Next in complexity is the add-and-shift multiplication technique with a modified Booth algorithm. This requires very little additional logic and is also a promising technique for GaAs implementation. Bit-serial hardware, parallel to the main datapath, is next in complexity and another promising method. The other techniques mentioned above require too much hardware for implementation into a general processor. However, these designs may be appropriate for implementation into a coprocessor.

The three multiplication techniques and two division techniques appropriate for a GaAs implementation show increasing performance with increasing hardware requirements. As already mentioned, the standard add/subtract-and-shift multiplication/division approaches require only the main datapath adder and require n steps. The modified Booth multiplication scheme requires only a small increase in hardware and reduces the number of steps by half, so this is a cost effective approach.

Both of the above approaches use an iterative algorithm and may be implemented in

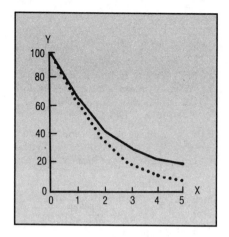

Figure 13. Effects of multiply fill-in. X—Number of NOOPs to eliminate; Y—Percentage of time that NOOPs are sucessfully eliminated.

several ways. For illustration purposes, consider the multiplication of two 32-bit numbers using the standard add-and-shift method.

In one approach, two add-and-shift instructions are used with a loop that must be executed 16 times. Because of the overhead associated with loop execution in a vertical architecture (calculating the branch address, etc.), this method is over twice as slow as some other methods.

In another approach, 32 different instructions are fetched from instruction memory. Each instruction implements a single add-and-shift. However, this method has features that lessen its appeal for a GaAs implementation. Since 32 instructions must be fetched, there is a higher likelihood that a cache miss will occur during the execution of the multiply than if just one instruction is fetched. Also, if 32 instructions must be located in memory for each multiply operation, then other instructions must be relegated to storage in slower memory.

A third approach is to include the 32 instructions in a runtime support routine where it need only be stored once. The disadvantage of this method is that a subroutine call and return must be performed for each multiply.

An alternative approach resembles the execution of silicon microcoded CISCs in that only one instruction (macroinstruction) is fetched from memory. This has the desirable effect of reducing the memory bandwidth and storage requirement, which is a major concern in the GaAs environment. However, it also complicates the control logic. In the GaAs environment this ap-

proach deserves strong consideration for implementation.

A third alternative design for GaAs processor implementation is the bit-serial approach off the main datapath. A multiplier may be implemented that executes in 2n steps. This method exploits a principal GaAs advantage—its high switching speed. Each step of the multiplication process requires only a full addition and flip-flop access, so a very high clock rate can be used. A multiply operation using this approach may be executed in the time needed to execute only five or so standard instructions.

Not only is the raw speed of the hardware multiplier better than the other two methods, but there is also a potential performance enhancement due to "multipler fill-in." Since multiplication occurs off the main datapath, other instructions requiring the datapath may be executed in parallel with multiplication. A sophisticated optimizing compiler like that used for branch fill-ins in the SU-MIPS is required here in order to find the instructions that may be executed in parallel with the multiplication. A preliminary investigation performed at Purdue University[14] indicates that for some applications a substantial performance gain may be realized if such a scheme were implemented. These results are presented in Figure 13.

Shifter design in the GaAs environment. Many modern microprocessors allow variable-length shifts on data from 0 to $n-1$ bits, where n is the word length. One example is the TMS 320. However, the inclusion of such a shifter may violate the RISC philosophy since the frequency of multiple-length shifts may not justify its inclusion, especially if an off-datapath multiplier/divider is incorporated. The designers of UCB-RISC indicate that the incorporation of a (0-31)-bit barrel shifter was a mistake.[8] Because of the large hardware requirements of such a variable-length shifter, a thorough analysis is required to determine if it is appropriate for a GaAs processor.

Some of the applications for a barrel shifter include data alignment for memory loads and stores, data alignment for immediate operands, multiplication/division support, and fast multiplication when either the multiplier or multiplicand is a power of two. Also, some high-level languages, such as C, have a shift statement that must be supported.

Typically, only a small subset of the shift distances are required for data alignments and multiplication/division support. For example, in the SU-MIPS, for data align-

ments for memory accesses the shift distance is a multiple of eight. In order to use the shifter directly for multiplication, the value that is a power of two must be known at compile time so that the appropriate shift operation can be used to replace the multiply operations. The frequency of these occurrences is probably low. The frequency of the shift statements in C programs should be determined in order to discover the shifter's value in this regard. It may be the case that it is used infrequently.

The number of gates needed to implement a barrel shifter is approximately 3n log n, where n is the word length. Therefore, significant hardware savings may be realized if a shifter design is used that provides only the functionality absolutely required, e.g., 1, 2, and 8, or a similar subset.

Instruction set design and optimization. The careful design of the processor instruction set is extremely important in a GaAs environment. There are two desirable and conflicting instruction set characteristics. First, the instruction set should be simple. There should be a small number of instruction formats, and the same instruction fields should be used in each format whenever possible. Also, the number of different operations should be kept small and the operations themselves should be kept primitive. Secondly, an effort should be made to design the instruction set so that program memory requirements are minimized. There exists a rationale for these goals as well as techniques for achieving compact instructions. However, the dual goals of instruction set simplicity and program compactness are conflicting.

Because of the relatively small number of transistors within a GaAs processor, the circuitry devoted to instruction decoding and control must be minimized. This is achieved primarily by keeping the instruction set simple. Such an approach is one of the primary reasons why the RISC design philosophy is appropriate for GaAs implementation study.

The high off-chip propagation delays characteristic of the GaAs environment make compact programs very beneficial. Compact programs are desirable for several reasons.

The difference in access times (in terms of instruction cycles) between the various levels of the instruction memory hierarchy will probably be large for a GaAs processor. Therefore, the ability to maximize the likelihood that a required instruction is in the higher levels of the hierarchy is important. It has been shown that the hit ratio of a cache depends primarily on the cache size. [15] Since a reduction in instruction size has the same effect as an increase in the size of the memory containing it, compact instructions have a very positive effect on hit ratios of the higher levels of the memory hierarchy and, consequently, on performance.

Instruction packing is a technique that was mentioned earlier as a method for increasing the information bandwidth between a GaAs processor and its external environment. However, because of the pin limitations of a single-chip processor, a short instruction format is necessary in order for packing to be possible. It is also necessary to implement the packing in a way that minimizes decoding and control complexity.

A primary disadvantage of using silicon RISC processors for GaAs implementations is the low information content of the instructions. Because of this, single-cycle instruction execution may be a less worthy goal for GaAs RISCs than for silicon RISCs. In order to maintain single-cycle execution, all complex operations must be synthesized from primitive operations. However, in some relatively frequent complex operations, such as multiply and divide, the same primitive operation is repeatedly executed. Therefore, the information content of each primitive instruction is very low, and this results in a potentially large increase in program size. In the GaAs environment, this has a more negative effect on performance than in the silicon environment; therefore, the addition of complex instructions to the instruction set may be justified for GaAs processors. Again, care must be taken to minimize the negative effects this has on control complexity.

Several techniques for reducing the instruction size have been studied; three techniques may be appropriate for a GaAs implementation. The first is based on Huffman-like variable-length encodings. [16] The second involves replacing common instruction sequences with a single instruction. The third approach consists of the selection of the optimal data addressing mechanism.

Huffman coding is a frequency-based technique that yields a minimum-sized encoding. A variation of this technique was utilized for the Intel iAPX 432. The essence of the algorithm is that the opcodes that appear most frequently receive the smallest encoding. In a related technique, referred to as "conditional coding," the encoding is also dependent on a number of prior in-

structions, as well as the current instruction. Although these techniques theoretically lead to the most compact instructions, the compactness is program-dependent since it relies on instruction frequencies. More importantly, complicated decoding logic is required and the decoding must be performed sequentially, which reduces execution speed. Because of these negative characteristics, Huffman-like coding is not desirable for a GaAs processor.

The second technique is to increase the level of opcode encoding by replacing frequently occurring instruction sequences with a single instruction. One example of this is the inclusion of multiply and divide instructions, which was mentioned earlier. This technique also results in increased instruction decoding complexity, but may be justified by the expected performance gains in the GaAs environment.

There has been much debate over the instruction compactness of stack, register, and memory-to-memory architectures. Although it appears that memory-to-memory addressing leads to more compact code than "traditional" register or stack architectures, this kind of addressing is probably not appropriate for a GaAs implementation because of the long off-chip memory access time. As mentioned earlier, it is very desirable to keep frequently accessed data on-chip. If a large, multiwindow register file can be accommodated, then this would result in faster execution than a memory-to-memory architecture. [17] Furthermore, it would probably lead to more compact code as well, since register accesses would be very frequent and only a small number of bits are needed to specify register addresses.

The implementation of microprocessor architectures in the GaAs environment is a very promising and challenging area of research. The characteristics of GaAs demand different architectural solutions than those found in silicon designs. With proper modifications, the reduced instruction set computer design philosophy is a good candidate for GaAs implementations. However, research is needed for the development of special computer architecture strategies optimized for the GaAs environment. □

Acknowledgments

The authors appreciate the assistance they received from W. Heagerty, W. Moyers, and S. Undy.

References

1. R. C. Eden, A. R. Livingston, and B. M. Welch, "Integrated Circuits: the Case for Gallium Arsenide," *IEEE Spectrum,* Vol. 9, No. 12, Dec. 1983, pp. 30-37.

2. R. C. Eden et al., "The Propsects for Ultrahigh-Speed VLSI GaAs Digital Logic," *IEEE J. Solid-State Circuits,* Vol. SC-14, No. 2, April 1979, pp. 221-239.

3. G. Nuzillat et al., "GaAs MESFET IC's for Gigabit Logic Applications," *IEEE J. Solid-State Circuits,* Vol. sc-17, No. 3, June 1982, pp. 569-584.

4. R. Yamamoto et al., "Design and Fabrication of a Depletion GaAs LSI Hi-Speed 32-Bit Adder," *IEEE J. Solid-State Circuits,* Vol. SC-18, No. 5, Oct. 1983, pp. 592-599.

5. G. Leopold, "New Approach Promises GaAs Interconnections," *Electronics Week*, Vol. 58, No. 22, June 3, 1985, p. 27.

6. D. A. Patterson and D. R. Ditzel, "The Case for the Reduced Instruction Set Computer," *ACM SIGARCH Computer Architecture News*, Vol. 8, No. 6, Oct. 1980, pp. 25-32.

7. J. Hennessy et al., "The MIPS Machine," *Digest of Papers*, Spring COMPCON 82, San Francisco, Feb. 1982, pp. 2-7.

8. M. G. H. Katevenis, *Reduced Instruction Set Computer Architectures for VLSI,* PhD thesis, UC, Berkeley, Oct. 1983.

9. D. A. Patterson and R. S. Piepho, "Assessing RISCs in High-Level Language Support," *IEEE Micro,* Vol. 15, No. 11, Nov. 1982, pp. 9-19.

10. D. W. Clark and W. D. Strecker, "Comments on 'The case for the reduced instruction set computer,' by Patterson and Ditzel," *ACM SIGARCH Computer Architecture News,* Vol. 8, No. 6, Oct. 1980, pp. 34-38.

11. D. R. Ditzel and H. R. McLellan, "Register Allocation for Free: The C Machine Stack Cache," *Proc. Symp. Architectural Support for Programming Languages and Operating Systems*, Palo Alto, Calif., March 1982, pp. 48-56.

12. B. W. Lampson, "Fast Procedure Calls," *Proc. Symp. Architectural Support for Programming Languages and Operating Systems*, Palo Alto, Calif., March 1982, pp. 66-76.

13. B. Hoefflinger, *Design of Very-High Throughput Rate GaAs Multipliers,* technical report, Purdue University, March 1984.

14. K. Keirn, *Studies of the RISC Architecture in GaAs,* internal report, Purdue University, 1984.

15. J. E. Smith and J. R. Goodman, "A Study of Instruction Cache Organizations and Replacement Policies," *Proc. Tenth Ann. Symp. Computer Architecture*, Stockholm, Sweden, June 1983, pp. 132-137.

16. D. A. Huffman, "A Method for the Construction of Minimum Redundancy Codes," *Proc. I.R.E.*, Vol. 40, No. 9, Sept. 1952, pp. 1098-1101.

17. G. J. Myers, "The Case Against Stack-Oriented Instruction Sets," *ACM SIGARCH Computer Architecture News*, Vol. 6, No. 3, Aug. 1977, pp. 7-10.

Veljko M. Milutinovic is on the faculty of the School of Electrical Engineering, Purdue University. He received the PhD degree from the University of Belgrade, Belgrade, Yugoslavia. He has published over 60 technical papers, two original books, and five edited books. His research has been published in *IEEE Transactions, IEEE Proceedings, IEEE Computer,* and other refereed journals. His book on microprocessor-based design has been published in several languages. He is the editor of the IEEE PRESS Tutorial on Advanced Microprocessors and High-Level Language Computer Architectures for VLSI. He is the coeditor of the IEEE PRESS Tutorial on Advanced Topics in Computer Architecture. He has been appointed to serve as a chair for panels on GaAs computers at the nation's leading conferences, including ICCD-85 (Port Chester, N.Y., October 1985) and HICSS-19 (Honolulu, Hawaii, January 1986).

He has lectured in Europe and North and Latin America. His current interests include VLSI computer architectures for GaAs, high-level language computer architecture, distributed task allocation, artificial intelligence computer architectures, and multiprocessor systems for signal processing. He has been involved in consulting activities for a number of high-tech companies, including Aerospace Corporation, Intel, Honeywell, NASA, RCA, and others. He is currently involved in the industrial implementation of a 32-bit VLSI microprocessor in GaAs technology, with responsibilities in the microarchitecture domain. He is a member of the IEEE and is on the EUROMICRO board of directors.

David A. Fura is a graduate student in the School of Electrical Engineering, Purdue University. He received dual BSE degrees in Electrical Engineering and Computer Engineering from the University of Michigan. Before entering Purdue, he spent three years as an electrical design engineer with Texas Instruments, Inc. His current research activity is in the area of computer architecture design for high-speed digital circuit technologies. His interests include reduced instruction set computer architectures and dataflow systems. He is currently involved in the industrial implementation of a 32-bit VLSI microprocessor in GaAs technology. He is a member of the IEEE Computer Society, ACM SIGARCH, and Eta Kappa Nu.

Walter A. Helbig is a unit manager at RCA's Advanced Technology Laboratories heading the Advanced Computation Systems unit for the Systems Engineering Laboratory. He joined RCA in 1952 and has been involved in the design and application of computer systems and in the construction of support software programs since. He directed the architecture design of a GaAs 32-bit RISC and is presently a consulting architect for the design of a 32-bit silicon RISC and for the construction of an 8-bit GaAs RISC Technology Demonstration System. His recent background includes work in the area of CAD tool design, construction and evaluation. Previously, he directed the design of two versions of the RCA ATMAC microprocessor, all of their support software, and several single and multiboard systems using the ATMAC.

Helbig has had several years of recent experience in the area of design and construction of computer system hardware and software; communication security equipment design and construction; and system design, construction, and debug for an advanced passive autonomous sonar system, A. He has also developed video display systems and communication systems.

Helbig holds a BSEE degree from the Milwaukee School of Engineering. He has thirteen US patents and has authored and coauthored numerous papers. He was a senior member of the IEEE.

For more information about this article, contact Milutinovic at School of Electrical Engineering, Purdue University, West Lafayette, IN 47907.

COMPUTER

A GaAs E/D MESFET demonstration wafer that has digital logic (1-micron two-level metal). (Photo courtesy of RCA Advanced Technology Laboratories.)

Issues of Importance in Designing GaAs Microcomputer Systems

Reprinted from *Computer*, October 1986, pages 45-57. Copyright © 1986 by The Institute of Electrical and Electronics Engineers, Inc.

Veljko Milutinović, Alex Silbey, David Fura,

Kevin Keirn, and Mark Bettinger

Purdue University

Walt Helbig, William Heagerty, Richard Zieger,

Bob Schellack, and Walt Curtice

RCA Corporation

Many more factors are proving to be drivers of GaAs VLSI architecture than was ever the case with silicon. However, the possibility that GaAs may make possible throughput five times greater than that achievable with silicon continues to encourage research.

In 1984, RCA began projects that would lead to the development of equipment constructed with GaAs digital VLSI technology. Continuing the approach taken in developing VLSI design capability for CMOS and CMOS/SOS, three technique-development projects were undertaken and, in this case, a fourth was added. The three previously followed were standard logic-cell circuit design, CAD program development for automatic chip placement and routing, and one or more chip architecture designs. The new technique-development project concerned chip packaging and interconnect for GaAs VLSI technology that would operate in the 100-MHz to 400-MHz range.

Initially, the four projects were all company-sponsored efforts, and the architecture example chosen was an 8-bit reduced instruction set computer (RISC) designed along the lines of a Stanford University multiprocessor without interlocked stages (MIPS). Subsequently, a contract was obtained from the US Government to direct similar architecture design efforts toward the design of a 32-bit

computer (designed as a RISC) that would have a 200-MIPS throughput.

In pursuing both the 8-bit and 32-bit computer efforts, it was immediately recognized that there were a number of limitations associated with GaAs digital circuits that would affect the design and assembly of such computer systems. These limitations made it necessary (1) to re-evaluate many technique proposals that were made during the early days of silicon VLSI development and (2) to develop new techniques to solve old problems.

For example, some of the ideas that were considered for GaAs architectures were silicon technology designs that had been discarded because they did not provide enough benefit. However, because of the differences in GaAs and silicon technology parameters, some ideas that are unusable or rarely used in silicon designs seemed to make sense for GaAs. One example is migration of hardware functions back into software. [1-2]

The difference between silicon technology parameters and GaAs technology parameters is much greater than the difference between the parameters of two different silicon technologies. Most designers already know that when minor technology changes occur, the basic design strategy remains the same (for example, when the instruction pipeline depth is forced to change from three to four because of a slight increase in the CPU speed). But when one or more parameters change from a half to a full order of magnitude (as is sometimes the case when changing from silicon to GaAs parameters), the strategy must change as well. For example, the cache memory was created to fill a sudden gap between CPU speed and memory speed caused by technology changes in the 1960's.

Technology changes affect both processor and system design. The processor design issues were covered by Milutinović, Fura, and Helbig[3]; here we cover system design issues. Although these two types of issues are essentially different, they are highly interrelated.

Silicon CMOS and E/D MESFET GaAs technologies. Different GaAs design processes are characterized by different computer design parameters, and the same is true of the various silicon technologies. Therefore, it is important to keep in mind that this article deals only with (1) the E/D MESFET process currently being used by RCA[4] and (2) with the CMOS silicon process developed at RCA. ("E/D MESFET" stands for enhancement/depletion-mode metal semiconductor field effect transistor.)

One of the most critical differences between CMOS silicon technology and E/D MESFET GaAs technology is that the GaAs wafers have a higher density of defects. This results in a very low chip yield and indirectly limits individual chip area. Whereas some CMOS silicon designs *reliably* have up to approximately two hundred thousand transistors on a single chip, the highest *reliable* level of integration achieved so far in GaAs technology has been below thirty thousand transistors.[3]

One of the other crucial differences between CMOS silicon technology and E/D MESFET GaAs technology is the ratio of off-chip memory access speed to on-chip memory access speed. Because the penalty for accessing off-chip memory is much higher in GaAs technology than in silicon technology,[3] a restructuring of the silicon CMOS memory hierarchy to minimize the number of off-chip accesses, or, alternatively, to minimize the penalties for going off-chip, is necessary.

Another major difference between CMOS silicon and E/D MESFET GaAs is the more limited fan-in/fan-out capability of GaAs. Whereas an experienced silicon technology designer can choose to specify

a 3-input NAND gate in his designs, the GaAs technology designer simply may not have such an option. Furthermore, each extra output on a GaAs NOR gate results in a relatively large increase in switching time.

To make evaluations of the many proposals, extensive simulations were felt to be necessary. For this purpose, RCA chose to employ the assistance of Purdue University. Both the RCA group and the Purdue group wrote hardware-description models and ran simulations of various design approaches and construction parameters. This article is a summary of what was learned in the specific areas of interconnection technology, as well as in a GaAs computer system's memory, arithmetic coprocessing, and I/O.

Memory design in the GaAs environment

We found that memory-related design issues are affected by GaAs more than other system-design issues (more than, for example, I/O, arithmetic, or coprocessing).

Cache-based memory. The design of cache memories is strongly influenced by the characteristics of the underlying technology.

Technology characteristics relevant for cache design. One extremely important difference between silicon technology and GaAs technology is the much lower transistor-count capability of GaAs memory chips. Because of this, GaAs caches will generally be much smaller than their silicon counterparts.

The dissimilar ratios of off-chip memory access speed to on-chip memory access speed is another important difference between the technologies. The higher penalty for off-chip access in a GaAs environment requires a careful structuring of the memory hierarchy to minimize the penalty.

The lower chip yield of current GaAs technology also necessitates a different approach for GaAs cache design. Techniques that increase chip yield are more appropriate for designing GaAs memory chips than for designing silicon memory chips, which have a relatively high yield.

Finally, the limited fan-in/fan-out capability of GaAs gates can impact cache design, too. Implementing the capability for wide associative searches (for associative cache memories) is expensive in GaAs. Additional chip area is required to implement the fan-in/fan-out trees required by associative logic.

Cache hierarchy in the GaAs environment. Because of the speed at which information is transferred between a

GaAs processor and main memory, examination of a second-level cache deserves consideration.[5]

The composition and physical placement of the second-level cache are extremely important to ensuring the timely transfer of information between the first-level cache and the GaAs processor. To achieve maximum memory density at a suitable speed, the first-level cache should consist of GaAs chips. Also, to minimize the damaging effect of propagation delays, the first-level cache should be placed on the processor package.[3]

More flexibility is possible in both composition and physical placement when a second-level cache is added to a GaAs coprocessor and a first-level cache. GaAs technology may not be appropriate for the second-level cache, unless it is absolutely necessary for reasons like radiation hardness. The relatively large size of this cache will require that the cache use a large number of the relatively sparse GaAs chips, and this use will create a large distance between the GaAs processor and the farthest memory chips. Higher density silicon chips may actually supply faster access times because of their closer proximity to the GaAs processor, even though their raw speed is lower than that of the GaAs memory chips. For this reason, careful study is required to select a configuration involving a second-level cache.

Fetch policies in the GaAs environment. Static prefetching is of considerable interest in helping reduce the miss ratio in a GaAs microprocessor cache. *Static prefetching* is done at compile-time, and it involves predicting the blocks most likely to be needed to be moved into the cache. The compiler is able to do this more intelligently than the hardware because of its knowledge of the semantics of the code. For example, the compiler can recognize an unconditional branch in a high-level language code and prefetch the target of that branch. The small cache size, common in GaAs systems, means that static prefetching should be used sparingly so as to avoid polluting the cache with data that is never referenced. If static prefetching is used only when the prefetched block is certainly (or nearly certainly) going to be referenced, the danger of memory pollution is lessened.

In conclusion, for a GaAs microprocessor system, the static prefetch method has three advantages over the *dynamic prefetch* method, which is carried out at run time.

• First, static prefetching can be "smart." Memory pollution can be avoided or reduced by using knowledge of program semantics to make accurate prefetch decisions.

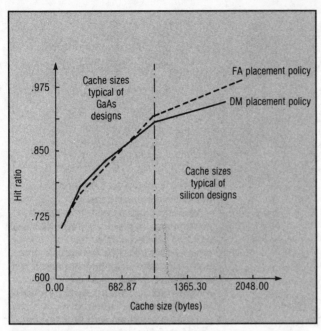

Figure 1. A comparison of the hit ratios achieved by the direct mapped (DM) placement policy and the full associative (FA) placement policy.

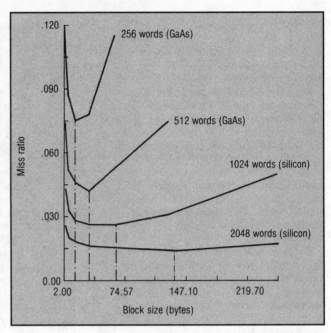

Figure 2. The relationship between miss ratio and block size as plotted for four different cache sizes.

• Second, static prefetching does not increase the hardware complexity of the cache.

• Third, the miss ratio decrease that occurs when static prefetching is used results without a corresponding increase in the traffic ratio (that is, in the total references versus program-generated references).

However, the burden in static prefetching is moved to compile-time; the effect this has on compiler complexity will be described in Milutinović et al.[1]

Placement policies for the GaAs environment. Placement policies regulate the location of blocks after they are transferred from main memory into the cache as a result of the fetch policy. There are three common placement policies: *direct-mapped (DM), set-associative (SA),* and *fully associative (FA)* (in order of increasing hardware complexity). The criteria for selecting a placement policy include the miss ratio, the complexity of the hardware, and the access time of the cache.

• *The effect of placement policy on net cache area.* The FA and SA placement policies allow more flexibility than the DM policy in the placement of individual data blocks. However, along with the increased flexibility of the FA and SA policies goes the need for a *replacement policy* to decide which block to replace in the cache when the cache is full. The FA and SA placement policies require that some overhead bits be used to store usage information on each block. When the commonly used least recently used (LRU) replacement

policy is invoked, the amount of overhead is $\log_2 N$ bits per block, where N is the number of blocks in an FA cache and N is the "set size." These overhead bits can be used for net data storage when a DM placement policy is used, since the DM policy requires no replacement policy. Another advantage of the DM placement policy is that the same cell can be used for memory and tags. Since no special associative search between tags and requests by processor memory for blocks has to be made, there is no reason to have special cells for the tag bits. The net storage area gained by using the DM placement policy could be significant, since the overall number of bits in a GaAs cache is restricted by transistor count limitations.

• *The effect of placement policy on hit ratio.* In general, the overall ranking of these three placement policies in order of increasing hit ratios is DM, SA, then FA. However, for small caches, it is not always true that the FA placement policy results in a higher hit ratio than the DM policy. Results from experiments with general-purpose code traces on a 32-bit minicomputer indicate that the DM policy performs comparably to the FA policy for cache sizes up to 1024 bytes.[6] The results are shown in the Figure 1 graph, in which the solid line indicates the DM policy and the broken line indicates the FA policy. For small caches, the DM placement policy provides equal or superior hit ratios.[6] The hit ratios are equal at cache sizes of about 900 bytes, and remain close

to each other until cache size reaches about 1K byte. Between 1K byte and 8K bytes, the FA placement policy provides a considerably better hit ratio. At sizes larger than 8K bytes, the placement policy has little effect on the hit ratio, since the ratio asymptotically approaches 1.0 as the cache size increases. Figure 1 indicates the cache sizes for which GaAs is practical (those to the left of the dotted-dashed line).

Block size in the GaAs environment. After net cache size, block size probably has the largest effect on the performance of a cache memory. The *block size* is the number of bytes of cache memory associated with each address tag in the cache.

Different block sizes can have dramatically different influences on the miss ratio. As already indicated, the miss ratio is even more important in GaAs than in silicon because of the huge penalty in computing speed caused by a miss in a GaAs cache.[3] Results from experiments show that the optimum block size for smaller caches is smaller than the optimum block size for larger caches.[7] However, even in a large cache, the block size must be restricted because of the danger of memory pollution. Figure 2 shows the experimentally derived relationship between miss ratio and block size for four cache sizes.[7] Note that the minimum block size should be larger than or equal to 1 + the pipeline branch latency.

Storing data. There are two common techniques for storing data: write-through and copy-back. These either (1) immediately transfer modified data words to the main memory (*write-through*) or (2) transmit the entire modified data block to main memory when a miss occurs and the block is selected to be replaced (*copy-back*).

In the write-through implementation, all write instructions result in the immediate transmittal of the datum to main memory. Thus, the processor must wait (if there are no buffering facilities) for the write to complete before it can continue processing. In a GaAs microprocessor system, however, buffering may not be needed, since, as we discuss later, pipelined memory is an efficient solution to the problem of long off-chip latency. With a pipelined memory, there is no way that a read request and write request can get out of sequence. The pipelined memory also eliminates the wait for the completion of the write. Write-through also ensures that an updated copy of the cache contents always exists in main memory.

The copy-back method uses a "dirty bit" to indicate blocks in the cache that have been modified. When the replacement policy decides that a modified block is to be replaced, then that block has to be written back to main memory before a new block can take its place. Another disadvantage of the copy-back scheme for a GaAs microprocessor system is that it requires additional logic to maintain the dirty bits and to initiate the fetch-on-write and copy-back-on-replacement.

Multi-distance memory. When dealing with a new technology, such as GaAs, unconventional memory design techniques deserve greater levels of attention than they would normally receive. One idea that has found little use in the silicon technology environment and that may be appropriate for a GaAs system is a *multi-distance memory* (that is to say, a memory system in which the access time for different portions of the main memory is different). A multi-distance memory is beneficial because it improves the program execution time without run-time decision making (and consequently, without incurring hardware overhead costs). The disadvantages of this approach are the loss of locality exploitation and the loss of flexibility in program and data placement within the memory system.

Storage overhead. An important design consideration for both RISC and GaAs system architects is the movement of run-time complexity to compile time.[1] In the case of multi-distance memory, instead of using chip resources for the implementation of caches, the task of placing frequently used information in the fastest memory can be moved to the compiler.

How much extra area is needed in a cache as compared with an ordinary memory or with a multi-distance memory? A clue to the answer can be obtained by looking at a silicon-based design: that of the Zilog Z80,000 32-bit microprocessor's on-chip cache. The overhead in a cache is on a per-block basis, that is, the extra circuitry needed for a cache is replicated once per block. In the Z80,000, each block holds 16 bytes of data, eight data-validation bits, four bits for least recently used (LRU) data, 28 tag bits, and one tag validation bit, giving a total of 169 bits.[8] A total of 128 of the 169, or about three fourths of the cache bits, are used for net storage. The remaining one fourth cache bits, for overhead, use up approximately one half of the cache area because the overhead bits are relatively irregular in design (in contrast to the highly regular structure of the net storage cells). Further, since GaAs technology has more stringent fan-out limitations than silicon technology has,[3] one can assume that the overhead bits will consume an even larger proportion of the area in the former than they do in the latter. Thus, the net result is that the area available for data storage in a GaAs cache is less than half of that available for storage in a regular (non-cache) GaAs memory. Consequently, if a multi-distance memory is used, and if its "shortest-distance" part is placed on the same package as the CPU chip, the total storage capacity of the on-package memory will be about twice the net storage capacity of an on-package cache.

Cost of compile-time control. The loss of temporal and spatial locality exploitation capability is a major disadvantage of multi-distance memories. However, the additional burden placed on the compiler also deserves attention.

One anomaly in a multi-distance memory is that the various data may not arrive at the processor in the order that would seem indicated by the order of fetch instructions. Consider the effect of two consecutive fetches to memories at different distances:

(inst. *i*):   Load R1,distant_memory*
(inst. *i* + 1): Load R2,close_memory*

Because the close memory takes less time to respond to the fetch request than the distant memory, it is possible that its data will arrive at the processor before the data from the distant memory. This is called the *sequencing problem.*

This problem can be solved in a manner similar to the approach taken by the delayed fetch in the Stanford MIPS architecture.[9] The *delayed fetch* reorganizes the code to ensure that such problems do

* "Inst." stands for "instruction."

not occur. The reorganization happens at compile time, which implies that it will work only if the system for distribution of code to the distant memory elements is a static one. This solution may not work directly in a dynamic allocation system because the location of code is not known at compile time. Using dynamic code allocation in a multi-distance memory requires that there be some hardware mechanism (tags, for example) to aid in ensuring the orderly arrival of data from the memory.

Pipelined memory. Pipelining is a very effective method for achieving dramatic performance increases for relatively small costs. The classic example of silicon pipeline technology consisting of instruction-fetch, decode, and execution stages is a good illustration.

When one observes a relative increase in the instruction-fetch time that results from technological reasons, one can remedy the problem by breaking the instruction-fetch stage into multiple substages.[3] It is very fortunate that the relative memory-access time for GaAs systems—which is longer than that for silicon systems—lends itself well to pipelining. The longer GaAs memory system delay does not result from the lower raw speed of the memory itself, but from longer relative propagation delays between the CPU and the memory. By proper physical positioning of intermediate latches, the propagation delays are easily pipelined.

Figure 3 provides an illustration of a pipelined memory system with three stages. In the first stage the processor transmits the address (and data if write) to a latch physically near the memory. In the second stage the memory is accessed and the data is stored in the latch physically close to the memory (if read). In the third stage (if read), the data is propagated back to the processor.

Pipelining is a technique that can be employed in both cache-based and multi-distance memories, and for both instructions and data. Because pipelined memory systems can completely match the effective processor-memory bandwidth with the processor's requirements, they are extremely promising for GaAs.

The disadvantage of pipelined memory systems is that the increased pipeline depth they cause places severe requirements on the optimizing compiler. The reason for this is that branch delays[9] are longer, and early compiler efforts to replace the no-op instructions in the fill-in slots are most successful for short branch delays.[9] The implications of GaAs technology on these aspects of compiler implementation will be discussed by Milutinović et al.[1]

Virtual memory. The virtual memory (VM) system design is not impacted too severely by the use of GaAs technology. In many cache-design issues, the design of a GaAs microprocessor virtual memory system parallels some silicon-based design. The problems related to GaAs virtual memory management are treated by Silbey.[7]

Arithmetic coprocessors

In designing arithmetic coprocessors for a GaAs environment, as in designing the CPU for such an environment, one should follow the RISC design philosophy.

Because of the different transistor count limitations of GaAs and silicon, certain operations typically included in silicon coprocessors cannot be included directly in GaAs coprocessors, and these operations must be synthesized. This is done by finding a small set of minimally complex operations that are sufficient to synthesize complex operations easily, yet require a transistor count low enough for implementation on a GaAs coprocessor.

The IEEE floating-point standard presents some problems in the GaAs environment. These exist because the standard requires several special cases for representation of numbers. Since GaAs

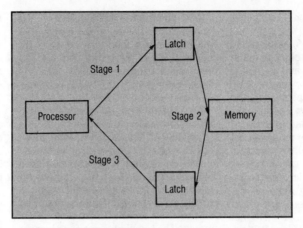

Figure 3. A three-stage pipelined memory.

works best with the RISC philosophy of "provide primitives, not solutions," the special cases should be handled by software rather than hardware. The IEEE standard provides a good general guideline for software implementations. However, the standard was designed with silicon architectures in mind. Since the GaAs coprocessor will be a small-area chip, exact adherence to the IEEE standard will probably not be possible for GaAs coprocessor implementations.

The essence of this discussion is that in a GaAs environment, the transistor count

limitations play a major role. For example, in Figure 4, we present the relationship between number of devices per chip and speed for two IEEE format double-precision floating point coprocessors, one GaAs and one silicon, both designed by RCA and tested with the 1750A mix.[10]

An important consideration for the implementation of an arithmetic coprocessor is the method of communication with the CPU. The following paragraphs examine several possible schemes for implementing coprocessors in a GaAs environment, to determine the advantages and disadvan-

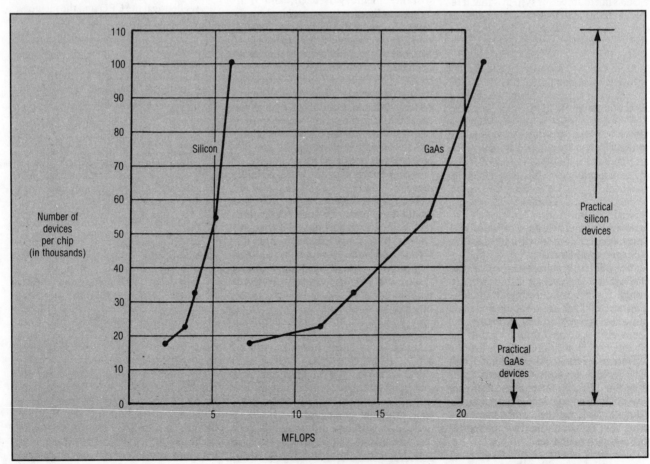

Figure 4. The relationship between coprocessor speed and device count for a silicon coprocessor and a GaAs coprocessor.

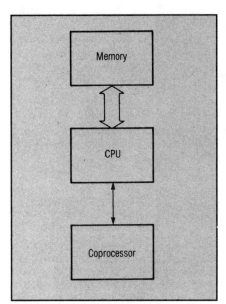

Figure 5. The coprocessor slave configuration.

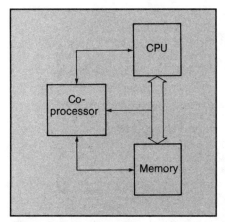

Figure 6. A set of possible coprocessor communication links.

tages of each. The two configurations discussed are a slave configuration and an expanded configuration.

Probably the simplest way of implementing a coprocessor in a system is to include it as a slave to the CPU. A block diagram illustrating this approach is shown in Figure 5. In this approach, the coprocessor is isolated from the rest of the system. All communication with the coprocessor is done through the CPU, and the coprocessor receives all instructions from the CPU. Unfortunately, there are several disadvantages to this approach; for example, because the coprocessor is a slave, the CPU must guide the coprocessor through each operation.

One way of reducing CPU involvement in coprocessor operation is to establish ad-

ditional communication links—from the coprocessor to the rest of the system. The two most likely links are between the coprocessor and the system bus, and between the coprocessor and the memory. Figure 6 shows a set of possible coprocessor communication links.

We compare here the estimated design and performance parameters for RCA's E/D MESFET GaAs and CMOS silicon coprocessors.[10] In the first case, the number of devices is between 20K and 25K, and the number of floating-point registers is four. In the second case, the number of devices is between 60K and 75K, and the number of floating-point registers is 16. The expected performance ratio of the former to the latter is about 2:1 (11.6 MFLOPS versus 5.05 MFLOPS), for the 1750A mix. The expected cost ratio is about 100:1.

Input/output

The design of I/O systems for GaAs technology is not influenced by the change from silicon to GaAs as heavily as memory design. Nevertheless, GaAs technology does have a major impact on I/O design in the areas of I/O coprocessor design, DMA, and interrupt processing. The interested reader is referred to Bettinger.[11]

The concepts behind GaAs I/O coprocessor design are similar to those discussed for arithmetic coprocessors by Helbig and Milutinović,[12] since some of the interprocessor communication issues are similar. One design possibility is to move more "intelligence" into the I/O coprocessors. First and foremost among the benefits of intelligent I/O is the reduced amount of work assigned to the main processor. Giving intelligence to the I/O coprocessors minimizes the amount of interchip communication, which is important for GaAs.

The relative latency changes in the new technology, partly because applications and requirements may not have changed. Because of this, one can assume that it is safe to check for interrupts at the same time intervals as in silicon designs. During those same intervals, more instructions may be executed, which points out the possibility of interrupting the CPU on time boundaries other than instruction boundaries. This principle can be modified slightly to allow interrupts only on some common instructions such as load, store, or move. The compiler can then make sure that no sequence of instructions will leave an excessive gap in which interrupts cannot be recognized.

Because pipelined memories will very likely be used in GaAs systems, there are very few cycles for the DMA to steal. Some of those few might occur during

cache misses, or during the no-op instructions, which are inserted concurrently with off-chip communications. Also, due to increased relative latencies, cycle-stealing DMA may become very difficult to implement.

Packaging technology for GaAs

Packaging considerations take on great importance in the GaAs environment.

Balance between processing, memory, and packaging technologies. Traditionally, in the context of a particular implementation environment, computer designers have striven to achieve a balance between processing capability and memory capability. A system with such a "matched" design provides the maximum performance for a given set of cost constraints. When rapid advances in processing power disrupted the balance between processing and memory in the 1960's, implementation strategies were invented in an attempt to regain this lost balance. As a result, various means, (caches, for example) have become widely utilized to enhance the capabilities of memory systems.

In the present-day implementation environment for silicon technology, on-chip logic and wiring delays significantly exceed off-chip delays. In this environment, packaging considerations are relatively unimportant and, as a result, packaging innovations to reduce off-chip delays have been less stressed than processing and memory improvements. In the GaAs environment, however, packaging design has become a critical bottleneck. Interchip signal delays are significant, and design techniques must be used to compensate for this undesirable characteristic.

Research in packaging materials and manufacturing techniques may once again allow computer designers to treat interchip communication as an ignorable problem.

However, as progress is made in packaging techniques, equally significant progress is being made in IC technology.

GaAs design methodology now consists of balancing the capabilities of three resources. Since advances in both processing and memory power are derived from IC technology advances, one expects only moderate difficulty in maintaining a balance between these two.

However, packaging advances are obtained independently of IC technology advances. Therefore, one can expect more difficulty in maintaining the constant balance of processing and memory with packaging, which is necessary if one is to be able to ignore interchip communication costs. To achieve balance between all three areas, there must be an increased emphasis on packaging technology improvements.

Issues in packaging. In spite of advances in packaging and interconnecting, the high switching speeds in GaAs force designers to view off-chip signal lines as transmission lines. This requires either that all signal lines be impedance matched, or that reflections be tolerated on the signal lines. Such matching of signal line impedances on a line that has multiple sources and sinks is quite difficult. This problem is of considerable importance when one is designing the memory system in GaAs computers.

The maximum speed of signals travelling between two chips is limited to the speed of light, that is, 1.0167 ns per foot. This is the *maximum,* however, and in practice the signals are much slower because of two factors.

• First, the signal flow in a medium other than air is slowed down by the medium's dielectric constant.

• Second, the signal flow is slowed because of capacitance loading on the signal lines and because of the signal-driver internal resistance.

Interchip wiring is generally laid out as screened or etched lines on a non-conducting medium. Common examples are printed wire boards on glass epoxy, and thick or thin film conductors on ceramic boards. The velocity of signal propagation relative to the speed of light is inversely proportional to the square root of the dielectric constant of the board material. Consequently, propagation delays of two inches per nanosecond are not uncommon.

In this interchip wiring environment, which is critical for GaAs, it is convenient to use transmission-line-type signal paths. For this reason, microstrip transmission lines are used, since they work well as surface lines on a medium with a ground plane. The microstrip lines are normally designed to have a constant, characteristic impedance, which is a function of the ratio of line width to dielectric thickness. The delay through these lines varies because of the impedance and, therefore, because of the "effective" dielectric constant variation caused by line width. Figure 7 plots the signal delay (in nanoseconds/ inch versus dielectric constant) for a family of line impedances that start at zero ohms (at which point the line width to thickness ratio—w/h—equals infinity) with no fringing and go to a maximum impedance (w/h going to zero) without a ground plane. Since the zero-ohm case is devoid of any fringing field, the effective dielectric constant is equal to the material dielectric constant. Therefore, the upper curve is also the delay curve for stripline trans-

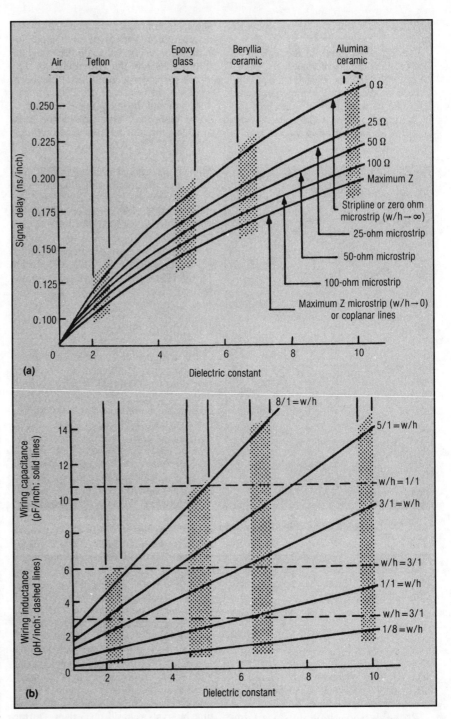

Figure 7. Wiring delay, capacitance, and inductance of various dielectrics. **(a)** Circuit delay versus dielectric constant (E_r) for several microstripline impedances (variable widths), including fringing and stripline (0 Ω microstrip has no fringing). **(b)** Capacitance and inductance versus E_r for several line width/thickness ratios (w/h).

mission lines (line impedance is not a factor), in which the line is completely buried in the media between two ground planes. Conversely, the lower curve, which represents 0 ground, is applicable to coplanar lines. Microstrip lines much over 100 ohms

are not realizable because of the narrow line widths required. Figure 7 also shows the common materials used and the range of their dielectric constants.

Two other factors affect the interconnection problem, and these result from having a data width of a large number of bits.

The first is the length of the lines to be used to make the interconnections. With, for example, 32 lines to go from one chip to another, even if the line impedance and delay can be controlled (or matched) for all lines, the length of the lines must be the same for all lines or bit skew will result.

The solution is to either make all lines the same length (or close to the same length) or to build the electronics to de-skew the bits at the receiving end. (Actually, an approach that incorporates a little bit of both options is the best.)

The second factor is the physical difficulty associated with making the lines equal lengths. This must be done without causing the undesirable effects that result from signal reflection, but it must be done without taking up an excessive amount of board (package) space. (An example of the types of lines needed and the layout techniques required is shown in the picture of the GaAs chip in Figure 8. (Note the curves and the mirrored corners used to prevent reflections. And note the "waves" in the lines that are used to make the lines the same length.) If one uses too much space to make the lines the same length, then the board gets too big to manufacture, or the number of parts per board gets too low to result in an efficient design.

What is likely to happen is that, in the attempt to make large groups of lines equal in length, the package will be made of several layers. This will make the manufacturing easier and the control of characteristic parameters of the interconnects easier. However, multilayer packaging has an added difficulty: Feedthroughs, which are normally a 90 degree turn in the line, have to be made without reflection points (that is, they have to have 90-degree turns without mirror edges).

Another factor to consider is that buses are very difficult to implement. Having a source in the center of a matched impedance line means that both ends of the line must be terminated—making, for example, the effective impedance 25 ohms for a driver driving a line with a characteristic impedance of 50 ohms (and thereby requiring larger drivers). Second, having multiple loads on the line makes it difficult to control the impedance because the locations of the loads influence the ef-

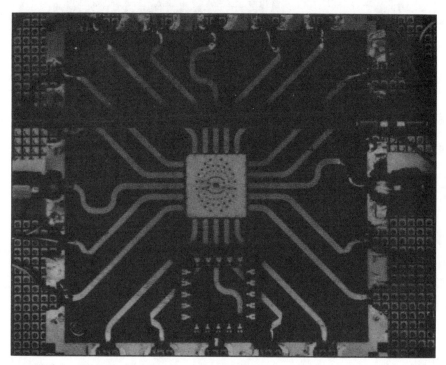

Figure 8. A packaged GaAs chip. (Photo used by permission of TriQuint.)

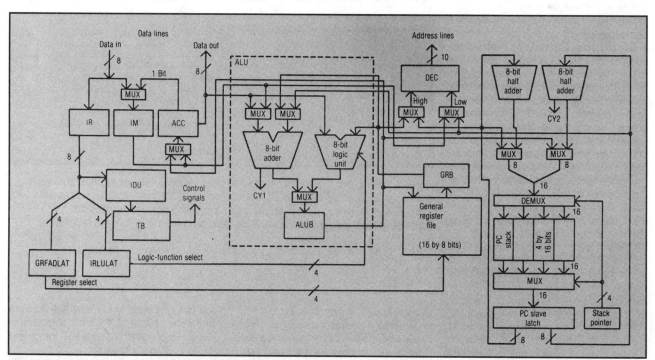

Figure 9. A block diagram of RCA's 8-bit GaAs Technology Demonstration Microprocessor system. ("ALUB," "GRB," "GRFADLAT," "IR," and "IRLULAT" are latches. "ACC" stands for accumulator; "CY1/2" stands for cycle #1/2. The "DEC" is a small combinational decoder and latch. "IDU" stands for instruction decoding unit. "IM" stands for immediate field buffer. The "TB" is the timing block. It includes an output latch.)

fective impedance. Third, the more one tries to simplify the operation by incorporating a bus, the harder it is to make the lines equal in length and not to have reflection points.

Examples of GaAs systems

An 8-bit GaAs demonstration system. The 8-bit GaAs Technology Demonstration Microprocessor (GTDM) is a pipelined, RISC machine.[4] It was originally targeted for 200-MHz operation and 100-MIPS performance. (Subsequently, it was redesigned for 200-MIPS performance.) A pioneering effort in GaAs technology, it has provided a vehicle for the development of a GaAs design methodology. A version of the GTDM consisting of the CPU, 512 words of memory, and some I/O capability is being constructed with leadless ceramic chip carriers. A block diagram of the microprocessor is shown in Figure 9. The VLSI layout, which was generated through extensive use of CAD techniques, is shown in Figure 10. A block diagram of the system is shown in Figure 11. The physical placement of chips on the board is shown in Figure 12.

GaAs fabrication in general is developing rapidly and is currently capable of integration of 1000 to 4000 gates with yields of 10 percent to 20 percent. A 1-micron double-level-metal E/D MESFET process is used in the GTDM. A single power supply is required, and the 0.2- and 0.8-volt levels represent logic zero and logic one, respectively. The design is primarily standard cell, with two handcrafted or custom-designed macrocells. These two macrocells are a 16-bit by 8-bit general register file, and a 4-bit by 16-bit program counter stack. Typical gates in the experimental GaAs E/D standard-cell family have delays between 100 and 500 picoseconds, and a maximum fan-out of four. The processor chip is 185 by 167 mils, and it dissipates about 858 milliwatts. It is packaged in a 48-pin leadless ceramic chip carrier.

The processor's instruction set consists of 23 instructions, 19 of which are 8 bits long and four of which are 16 bits long. The 100-MIPS goal required that an instruction be fetched every 10 nanoseconds. This processing rate is achieved through the use of simple, fast-executing, hardware-frugal instructions, and a pipeline that permits the simultaneous processing of several instructions.

The system includes four 256-by-4-bit Gigabit Logic 3-nanosecond GaAs memories (providing 512 8-bit bytes), 12 ECL input/output chips, and the 8-bit

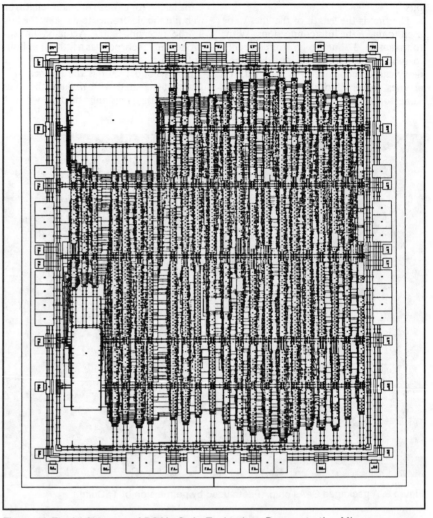

Figure 10. The VLSI layout of RCA's GaAs Technology Demonstration Microprocessor. (Photo courtesy of RCA Advanced Technology Laboratories.)

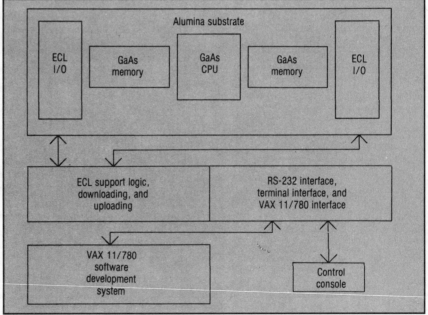

Figure 11. A block diagram of the GaAs Technology Demonstration Microprocessor system.

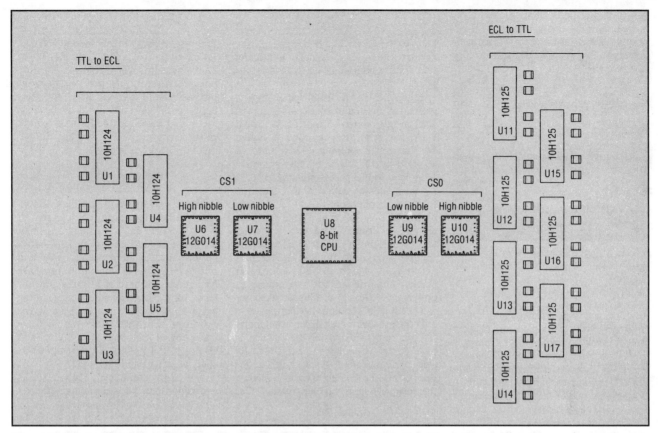

Figure 12. Physical placement of chips on the RCA GaAs Technology Demonstration Microprocessor board.

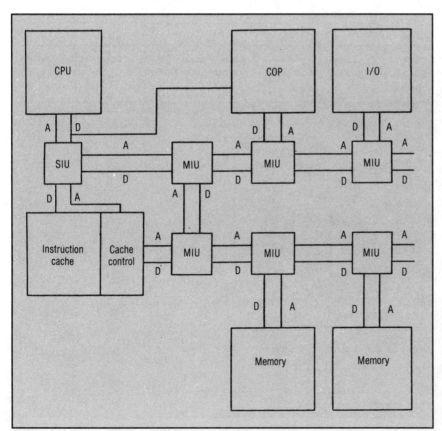

Figure 13. A block diagram of RCA's 32-bit GaAs microprocessor. ("A" stands for address bus; "D," for data bus; "COP," for coprocessor; "CPU," for central processing unit; "I/O," for input/output controller; "MIU," for memory interface unit; and "SIU," for system interface unit.)

processor. A 16-bit address width allows for memory expansion to 64K bytes.

The 512 memory locations are high-order interleaved to provide the option of separate program and data storage in memory. If a program requires less than 256 bytes of memory, then it can be stored in one bank while data is stored in another. This arrangement allows two experiments to be run on the system. For programs requiring less than 256 bytes, no memory part is accessed more often than every 10 nanoseconds. Otherwise, if a program requires more than 256 bytes, it can request data from the same memory chip in the form of current instructions. This causes memory chip accesses to be 5 nanoseconds apart. If the system does not permit access at 5-ns intervals, then the clock frequency is lowered until the system works, thereby testing the cycle time of the memory parts as they function in the system.

System-level packaging of the microprocessor, GaAs memory chips, and ECL/TTL translators is done on an alumina substrate. Typical signal propagation delay time for transmission line interconnects built on alumina substrates is 250 picoseconds/inch. This translates into a delay time per inch that is 5 percent of the microprocessor cycle time.

A 32-bit GaAs system. RCA is also currently developing a 32-bit GaAs computer

Figure 14. A GaAs E/D-MESFET test wafer. (Photo courtesy of RCA Advanced Technology Laboratories.)

system based on a single-chip GaAs processor. A block diagram of the system is shown in Figure 13. As shown in this block diagram, the system interface unit (SIU) multiplexes the two data streams that it receives (from a memory interface unit, or MIU, and the instruction cache) to send them to the CPU. The MIUs provide the necessary drive- and signal-conditioning functions to communicate from board to board.

A GaAs E/D MESFET demonstration wafer that has digital logic (1-micron two-level metal) related to that of the 32-bit GaAs microprocessor is shown in Figure 14. This wafer contains a 32-bit adder, a 16-word by 32-bit register file, a control PLA, and some process-monitor logic.

The processor design is based on the RISC design philosophy. A block diagram of the CPU is given in Figure 15. This allows for simple instruction decoding, which results in low resource requirements for decoding/control logic. The execution units (ALU, register file, and so on) also employ simple designs for low resource requirements. Details of this architecture can be found in Helbig and Milutinović. [12]

In the processor design, much emphasis was placed on maximizing the size of on-chip storage to reduce the need for off-chip communication. As a result, the resources saved elsewhere were allocated to the relatively large on-chip register file.

The system components shown in Figure 13 are all part of a large pipeline. In the 32-bit system, the MIUs are junction points. Therefore, the delay between the processor and the closest MIU, the delay between MIUs, and the delay between MIUs and associated peripherals (coprocessor, memory, and so on) are all multiples of the processor cycle time.

At present, both computer-development projects are in progress under RCA funding. The 8-bit computer logic redesign for 200-MIPS performance has been finished. Standard cells to be used in its implementation have been redesigned several times and are now ready for the implementation stage of the project. Layouts of the chip and the hybrid on which it is to be mounted are underway. Processing of the chip and testing of the system are expected to be completed in early 1987.

The 32-bit computer's register stacks and adder have been laid out on the test

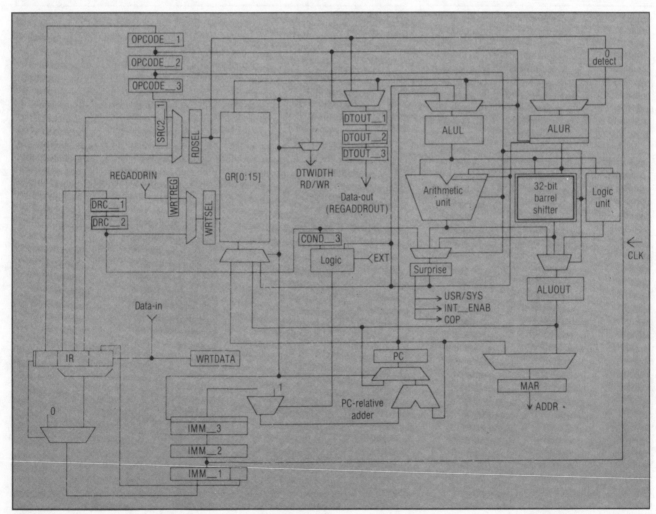

Figure 15. A block diagram of an experimental 32-bit GaAs CPU.

chip shown in Figure 14. Testing of this test chip is underway to verify design correctness and circuit performance.

Because of the high cost and low yield of GaAs wafers produced today, only a limited number of these test chips are available for testing. Even so, the register stack design has been proven correct and 5-ns access times have been measured. (The access time needed for 200 MIPS operation is 2.5 ns. The difference between the design goal and the measured performance is due to the measurement process. When used within the confines of a CPU, the register stack should provide the proper speed because it will not have to drive output lines with measurement equipment hanging on them.)

The development of the hybrid for the 8-bit machine has verified all expectations and fears. A delay to get the set of signals for memory referencing off of the CPU, to the memory, and back without detrimental skew has been accomplished. However, the design process required extra care and the total operation delay was, as expected, greater than one machine cycle time even for this machine's small memory capacity.

While this article discusses only a few of the system-level considerations for GaAs VLSI computer design and assembly, the critical ones have been identified. Unfortunately, most of the items discussed have been verified by the example systems under construction. ("Unfortunately" because they have verified that many more factors must be considered as architecture drivers than it was ever necessary to consider for silicon VLSI systems.)

Designing computers that incorporate GaAs VLSI will require greater effort than the corresponding effort required for silicon VLSI design. GaAs chips will be more expensive than silicon chips, and GaAs computer assembly will be more expensive than silicon computer assembly. The corresponding support software (compilers, assemblers, and code reorganizers) will have a lot more work to perform on the application programs, making code production slower and more expensive. However, reaching the goal of an increase over silicon system throughput of perhaps five times will be worth it.

The next things that must be tackled are the design of the interim system and compatible I/O systems. Interrupt systems are difficult to design in the GaAs environment because such an environment demands that instructions, data, and control-signal flow be of a pipelined nature and because of the severe limitation in the number of logic elements that can be put on any one chip. (One design has been conceived that will work; however, the response time to external interrupts is relatively slow.) GaAs I/O systems are difficult to design because of the increased ratio (over silicon) of CPU throughput to I/O channel throughput and because of difficulty involved with building a bus with GaAs circuits.

Considerably more work is needed to learn how to design and build GaAs VLSI computers. With the high payoff, though, the price will likely be paid.□

Acknowledgments

The authors appreciate the assistance they received from Wayne Moyers of RCA, and Chi-Hung Chi of Purdue University.

This research was sponsored by RCA.

References

1. V. Milutinović et al., "Compiler/Architecture Synergism in GaAs Computer Systems," to be published in 1987.

2. J. Hennessy and T. Gross, "Postpass Code Optimization of Pipeline Constraints," *ACM Trans. Programming Languages and Systems,* Vol. 5, No. 3, July 1983, pp. 422-448.

3. V. Milutinović, D. Fura, and W. Helbig, "An Introduction to GaAs Microprocessor Architecture for VLSI," *Computer,* Vol. 19, No. 3, March 1986, pp. 30-42.

4. W. A. Helbig, R. H. Schellack, and R. M. Zieger, "The Design and Construction of a GaAs Technology Demonstration Microprocessor," *Proc. Midcon 85,* Session 23, Chicago, Ill., Sept. 1985, pp. 1-6.

5. M. Horowitz and P. Chow, "MIPS-X," *Proc. Wescon 1985,* San Francisco, Calif., Nov. 1985, pp. 6/1/1-6/1/6.

6. J. E. Smith and J. R. Goodman, "A Study of Instruction Cache Organizations and Replacement Policies," *Proc. 10th Annual Int'l Symp. Computer Architecture,* Stockholm, Sweden, June 1983.

7. A. Silbey, "A Study of Cache Design and Virtual Memory Management in the GaAs Environment," Purdue/RCA Internal Report No. 14, May 1985.

8. D. Alpert, "Performance Trade-offs for Microprocessor Cache Memories," Stanford University Technical Report 83-239, Dec. 1983.

9. T. Gross, "Code Optimization of Pipeline Constraints," Stanford University Technical Report 83-255, Dec. 1983.

10. W. Helbig, "RISC vs. CISC, GaAs vs. Silicon, and Hardware vs. Software," *IEEE-CS Joint MTT/ED Meeting,* Princeton, N.J., Jan. 23, 1986.

11. M. Bettinger, "A Study of I/O Design Issues in the GaAs Environment," Purdue/RCA Internal Report No. 17, May 1985.

12. W. Helbig and V. Milutinović, "A 32-Bit GaAs Microprocessor," in *High-Level Language Computer Architecture,* V. Milutinović, ed., Computer Science Press, New York, 1986.

V. M. Milutinović's biography and photo appear following the Guest Editor's Introduction.

Alexander Silbey is a member of the technical staff of Gould, Inc.'s Computer Systems Division. He has an MS degree in electrical engineering and two BS degrees in engineering, all from Purdue University. He has published papers on high-level language computer architecture and advanced microprocessors, as well as on computer architecture for GaAs. His research interests include high-level language computer architectures for GaAs and parallel architectures for numeric processing. He developed cache and virtual memory approaches for a GaAs microprocessor as part of his research at Purdue University.

David Fura is a doctoral student in the Dept. of Electrical Engineering and Computer Science at Purdue University. His current research activity is in high-performance and highly reliable computer-system design. He received BSE degrees in electrical engineering and computer engineering from the University of Michigan in 1981, and the MS degree in electrical engineering from Purdue University in 1985. His master's thesis research consisted of processor architecture studies for the industrial implementation of a GaAs computer system. Before entering Purdue, Fura spent three years as a design engineer at Texas Instruments, Inc.

Kevin Keirn received his BS degree in electrical engineering in 1984 and his MS degree in electrical engineering in 1985 from Purdue University. He is currently a member of the technical staff of the Manufacturing Test Division of Hewlett-Packard Co. in Loveland, Colo. Prior to joining Hewlett-Packard, he was employed with Delco Electronics, Kokomo, Ind. His current research interests are programming languages, artificial intelligence, and computer architecture.

Mark Bettinger is a doctoral student in the Dept. of Electrical Engineering of Purdue University. His current research activity is in concurrent simulation of digital networks. He received the BS degree in electrical engineering from Purdue University in 1984 and the MS degree in electrical engineering from Purdue University in 1985. His master's thesis research consisted of system architecture studies for the industrial implementation of a GaAs computer system. While completing his BSEE he worked as a cooperative education student at the Federal Systems Division of IBM.

Walter Helbig is the unit manager for advanced information-processing techniques development in the Advanced Technology Laboratories of RCA Corp. He has been involved in all aspects of computer system development: working with both hardware and software, developing and applying both computers and peripheral equipment, and developing and applying both application and operating-system software for real-time applications. Helbig was one of the principal designers of the RCA 4100 series machine (a RISC type machine). He is presently technical director for both hardware

and software designs for a reduced instruction set computer to be built in GaAs. Helbig received the BS degree in electrical engineering from the Milwaukee School of Engineering in 1952. He has published seven papers and has 13 patents.

William Heagerty is the unit manager of the Technology Development Laboratory in the Advanced Technology Laboratory of RCA Corp. He was program manager on the Purnell-II contract, which involved the manufacture of two VLSI microprocessors, an I/O controller, and program software. He was involved in the design of CMOS/SOS LSI and linear circuitry with emphasis on radiation-hardened applications. Heagerty is presently responsible for the introduction and application of new IC technologies. He has directed RCA's GaAs I R&D program entitled "Gigabit Logic Technology" for the past two years. He received the BS degree from Syracuse University in 1960 and the MS degree from the University of Pennsylvania in 1967, both in electrical engineering. He has published seven papers and has four patents.

Richard Zieger is a member of the technical staff in the Advanced Technology Laboratory of RCA Corp. His past assignments have included system architecture simulation studies and the design of a 3-nanosecond 32-bit GaAs adder. He is currently a principal designer of an 8-bit pipelined GaAs processor. Zieger received the BS degree in computer engineering from Lehigh University in 1984, and is presently a graduate student in the Electrical Engineering Dept. of Villanova University.

Bob Schellack is a senior member of the engineering staff at RCA Advanced Technology Laboratories. He is the project engineer of GaAs technology development for use in digital integrated circuit designs. His recent work has been involved in the design and fabrication of GaAs Manchester Encoder circuits and GaAs microprocessors. In addition, he has been the principal investigator for RCA's internal research and development of GaAs technology for the past three years. Schellack received his BS in electrical engineering from Drexel University in 1980 and his MS from Drexel University in 1983.

Walt Curtice joined RCA Laboratories, Princeton, N.J., in 1973 as a member of the technical staff in the Microwave Technology Center. Initially, he directed the development of second-harmonic-extraction TRAPATT amplifiers for X-band operation. He later developed the two-dimensional electron-temperature model of GaAs field-effect transistors and an improved MESFET model for GaAs integrated-circuit simulation; more recently, he has been directing the nonlinear-device modeling effort. In 1984 he received an RCA Laboratories Outstanding Achievement Award for the development of advanced techniques for the computer simulation of III-V compound FETs. Curtice has published more than 40 technical papers and has eight US patents. He received the BEE, MS, and PhD degrees from Cornell University in 1958, 1960, and 1962, respectively.

Readers may write to Veljko Milutinović at the Purdue University School of Electrical Engineering, West Lafayette, IN 47907.

Architecture/Compiler Synergism in GaAs Computer Systems

Veljko Milutinovic and David Fura
Purdue University

Walter Helbig
RCA Corporation

and

Joseph Linn
Institute for Defense Analyses

Architecture/Compiler Synergism in GaAs Computer Systems

Reprinted from *Computer*, May 1987, pages 72-93. Copyright © 1987 by The Institute of Electrical and Electronics Engineers, Inc.

Veljko Milutinovic, Purdue University

David Fura, Purdue University

Walter Helbig, RCA Corporation

Joseph Linn, Institute for Defense Analyses

One way to overcome the joint effects of low chip density and long off-chip delays in GaAs systems is by migrating some traditional hardware functions into software and by performing appropriate compile-time optimizations.

Gallium arsenide (GaAs) has begun to attract serious attention from computer system designers, in addition to the traditional interest of device physicists. This is due not only to the much heralded switching speed advantages of GaAs, but also to the rapid progress seen in GaAs digital chip densities over the past few years. Lured by potential applications in supercomputer, military, aerospace, telecommunications, and high-speed testing areas, several companies are currently pursuing GaAs technology.

Currently, such companies as Gigabit, Harris, Vitesse, and TriQuint Semiconductor have already been marketing GaAs chips for digital applications.[1] In addition, several laboratory designs exhibiting higher performance have been presented; these include a 2000-gate gate array[2] and a 16K-bit static RAM,[3] with transistor counts of 8.2K bits and 102.3K bits, respectively.

These new GaAs designs are expected to eventually replace silicon emitter-coupled logic (ECL) circuits in current SSI/MSI-based vector supercomputer implementations. However, GaAs technology also offers the potential for dramatic performance improvements for general-purpose

applications not exhibiting the highly regular data required for efficient vector supercomputer execution.

GaAs computer system design has already generated considerable interest. GaAs computer design considerations have been presented earlier by Gilbert of the Mayo Clinic.[4] According to Karp of DARPA, the US government sponsored three teams in relation to a 32-bit GaAs microprocessor effort.[5] The participating companies were McDonnell Douglas, Texas Instruments with Control Data, and RCA. DARPA's creative leadership has advanced the state of GaAs technology and GaAs computing in the United States tremendously. As a result, an 8-bit processor design based on GaAs technology has already been presented by RCA.[6]

In this article we describe an approach to computer system design that we feel is very attractive for GaAs technology. Our strategy involves the use of a single-chip GaAs processor, an increased role for the compiler, and an aggressive migration of functions from hardware to the compiler. In fact, we believe that the advantages of GaAs technology cannot be fully exploited without further developments in compiler technology. This article follows previous papers on GaAs processor design[7] and

GaAs system design,[8] and completes our overview of GaAs technology-based computer system design.

Explanation of our methodology

In this section we describe the strategy that we believe is desirable for GaAs computer system implementations. As will be seen, in addition to drastic improvements in packaging technology, compiler improvements will be necessary to allow GaAs to approach its potential. We believe that packaging and compilation are the major two bottlenecks in the area of GaAs computing.

We begin by describing the characteristics of GaAs that affect our system design strategy. We then describe how sophisticated compiler capabilities have already been introduced by the designers of reduced instruction set computer (RISC) processors. We conclude by demonstrating that the increased reliance on compilers typical for silicon RISCs is very advantageous for GaAs processors, and, in fact, the characteristics of GaAs indicate that an even stronger compiler capability is desirable.

GaAs characteristics relevant for computer system design. Several different device and logic circuit designs have been used in GaAs implementations. However, because of the superior maturity of published GaAs enhancement-mode driver/depletion-mode load, metal-semiconductor field effect transistor (E/D MESFET) designs, we will limit our discussions to the GaAs MESFET family. It is typically used in direct-coupled FET logic (DCFL) circuit configurations.[9]

There are three principal characteristics of E/D-MESFETs that differentiate GaAs computer design techniques from those used for silicon designs.

One, GaAs has an inherent advantage in gate switching speed. This is due to the higher mobility of GaAs electrons—six to eight times that of silicon electrons.[9]

Two, the on-chip speed advantage that GaAs enjoys is not matched by an equal off-chip speedup. Interchip signal propagation delays are determined primarily by packaging considerations rather than integrated circuit technology[8]; therefore, more time is lost in off-chip communication, in terms of instruction cycles, for GaAs processors than for silicon processors. This

is an area that should benefit greatly from improved compiler technology.

Three, the lower maximum transistor count of GaAs chips further limits the capability of GaAs designs. Current problems with yield and the higher power requirements of GaAs limit transistor counts of GaAs chips to roughly one-tenth the corresponding value for silicon MOS chips.[7] Therefore, it is mandatory that some traditional hardware functions be migrated into the compiler to overcome the negative effects of having to build the system with a smaller number of devices.

Compiler advances associated with silicon RISCs. The RISC philosophy has caused a reevaluation of computer architecture design methodology. RISCs have (supposedly) shown better performance than the customary complex instruction set computer (CISC) style by utilizing streamlined instruction sets (see, however, Fleming and Wallace[10]). Example RISCs include the University of California-Berkeley RISC I and II (UCB-RISC),[11] the Stanford University MIPS (SU-MIPS),[12] and the IBM 801.[13] Much of the credit for the RISC performance advantage is given to the fact that RISCs execute frequently occurring instructions very fast. What is frequently overlooked are the requirements that RISC architectures place on compiler technology in order to achieve these results.

First, in order to help minimize the instruction cycle time, a conscious effort to transfer hardware functions into software is performed. Examples of this are the elimination of hardware timing hazard interlocks[14] in the SU-MIPS and the elimination of hardware sequencing hazard interlocks[14] in the UCB-RISC and SU-MIPS. The IBM 801 has hardware interlocks, but the optimizing compiler tries not to use them.

Also, in order to reduce decoding complexity and achieve a shorter cycle time, the instruction set is reduced to a small set of primitives comparable to vertical microinstructions on a microprogrammed machine. This presents new opportunities in that many compiler optimizations not available on CISC macroinstruction sequences are possible for RISC instruction sequences because the compiler has access to the fine-grained RISC primitives. One example of this is the data load fill-in of the IBM 801 compiler.[13] As described later, a RISC compiler is able to reduce the performance degradation due to long-latency data loads by scheduling other use-

ful instructions during the latency period. In a memory-to-memory instruction of a CISC, however, the full data fetch latency must be absorbed because the compiler is not able to (and does not) "get inside" this type of course-grained atomic instruction.

A third reason for increasing compiler capabilities is the fast rate of RISC instruction execution itself. An extremely fast processor such as a RISC will not achieve its potential unless its surrounding environment is able to support this speed. Since off-chip memories have traditionally not been able to do so, except for relatively small memories, compiler algorithms to reduce the penalty induced by the off-chip environment have been developed. The compiler for the IBM 801 uses a very sophisticated register coloring algorithm in order to maximize the register lifetime and minimize the need to fetch off-chip data.[15] The IBM 801 also incorporated special instructions that allow the compiler to override the runtime caching mechanism whenever the compiler determines a better placement policy.[13] The SU-MIPS designers developed a packing scheme to allow their processor to fetch two instructions concurrently,[12] a strategy that is especially effective in environments with slow off-chip memory access and that required the SU-MIPS compiler to perform the instruction packing.

GaAs computer system design. We are interested in computer system designs that utilize VLSI ($>10,000$ transistors) GaAs chips for both the processor and the highest level(s) of the memory hierarchy (cache). VLSI-based designs are desirable because they require less board area and power, and exhibit greater performance and reliability than systems built exclusively from SSI and MSI parts. In a GaAs processor implementation, VLSI designs are especially advantageous because they minimize the need for interchip communication.

Single-chip VLSI GaAs processors must necessarily inherit the general characteristics of RISCs that make the processors so compiler-dependent for optimal performance. In fact, the successful exploitation of GaAs technology in single-chip processor designs requires even stronger compiler capabilities. Obviously, the limited transistor count of the processors dictates that the transfer of functionality from hardware to the compiler is highly desirable for GaAs designs. Also, the extremely fast switching speeds of GaAs increase the need for the compiler to reduce the negative effects of a slow off-chip environment.

As already indicated, the successful exploitation of GaAs in single-chip processor configurations depends considerably on our ability to utilize compiler capabilities to their fullest. In the silicon domain, very high levels of integration are available to better enable the full use of increasingly fast data path transistors in a relatively slow off-chip environment. In the GaAs environment fast gate switching speeds are accompanied by a lower level of integration. Without the assistance from an increasingly sophisticated compiler technology, GaAs processors will struggle to attain a speed advantage over silicon processors near the level marked by their gate speed advantage. We believe this compiler technology-GaAs technology relationship is analogous to the CAD-VLSI relationship of several years ago, in that the full capabilities of VLSI could not be fully utilized without appropriate advances in CAD technology.

Compiler enhancement and compiler migration candidates

Several functions that may be wanted in a GaAs system compiler fall into one of the two following general groups of compiler functions:

(1) functions traditionally implemented in hardware, which could be migrated into the compiler (for better exploitation of the scarce on-chip transistor count), or *migration candidates*; and

(2) functions to add to the compiler (to enhance its capabilities in fighting the increased off-chip communication delays), or *enhancement candidates*.

We briefly describe each compiler function and discuss the rationale behind its selection. Then we present algorithms which may be used to implement each function, and discuss the areas where algorithm advances are necessary. Several of these compiler functions are borrowed from silicon designs, but the characteristics of GaAs technology make them differ considerably in their implementation. For example, the number of branch delay slots to fill in is now about one-half order of magnitude larger; also the number of potential pipeline hazards has increased.

Our presentation is divided along architectural boundaries. We first discuss

two control functions that are typically implemented in hardware. Next, we present several memory system functions for which compiler support may be beneficial. We continue with two compiler functions associated with arithmetic, and two compiler functions associated with various instruction formats. We conclude with external communications.

Control. There are two migration candidates for compiler implementation that have traditionally been performed by hardware in silicon pre-RISC designs. These are examples of a direct migration of hardware responsibilities into the compiler.

Pipeline interlock (timing hazards): compilation candidate. The pipelining of processors introduces the potential for conflicting claims for resources among multiple pipeline stages and/or multiple instructions. These conflicts may be referred to as timing hazards,[14] three classes of which are destination-source conflicts, source-destination conflicts, and destination-destination conflicts. A destination-source conflict occurs when the result of a pipeline stage has not been stored before a succeeding pipeline stage requires it. A source-destination conflict occurs when a pipeline stage of instruction i requires a result produced from an earlier pipeline stage in instruction $i + k$. A destination-destination conflict occurs when a resource is written concurrently by pipeline stages of two different instructions. If not avoided, all three of these conflicts may result in incorrect execution of an otherwise correct program.

The pre-RISC silicon CISC approach to these conflicts has traditionally been a hardware one. For example, the CDC 6600 utilized a "scoreboard" to keep track of its hardware resources at runtime.[16] In addition to approaches such as this, some silicon RISCs also employ hardware solutions. The UCB-RISC utilized an internal forwarding bus in order to eliminate one possible cause of destination-source conflict. This was used for situations when the result of an ALU operation was needed as a source operand for the succeeding operation.

Some silicon RISC designers have gone to extremes in avoiding the use of hardware resources for resolution of these conflicts. The SU-MIPS designers required the compiler to avoid generating instruction sequences with any such conflict. They even declined to provide an internal forwarding bus as was used in the UCB-RISC.

An SU-MIPS designer claimed that, in addition to a reduction in hardware complexity, software pipeline interlocks reduced the instruction cycle time by 10 percent.[17]

The software solution to timing hazard detection and avoidance is advantageous for GaAs processors primarily because of its reduction in hardware resource requirements, and also because of the possible reduction in instruction cycle time it allows. Because GaAs instruction pipelines can be expected to be longer than silicon pipelines,[7] the pipeline interlock hardware for a GaAs processor would probably be even more complex. The hardware resources not required for timing hazard prevention can have a great positive impact on performance in a resource-scarce GaAs processor, if they can be utilized elsewhere within the processor.

The longer instruction pipelines expected for GaAs processors not only increase the benefits of a software approach, but also change the requirements placed on the compiler algorithms that implement the pipeline interlocking function. Compiler algorithms used for relatively shallow silicon pipelines are generally not efficient in the case of relatively deep GaAs pipelines; therefore, as discussed next, advances in compiler technology (with respect to this issue) will greatly increase the performance of GaAs processors.

Pipeline interlock (timing hazards): compiler algorithms. Many of the compiler techniques in migrating function from hardware to software are based on the method of "code reorganization," or "horizontal code compaction," assuming that more than a single machine primitive is executed from a fetched instruction memory unit. The technique is primarily useful in the removal of timing hazards, but it can be used in a number of different ways, as will be discussed later.

The task of reorganization, then, is to accept an input program and to rearrange the instructions so that no timing hazards are present in the output program. Specifically, the instructions are to be arranged taking cognizance of pipeline delays so that data is passed between these instructions correctly. For instance, if there is a two-cycle delay between the initiation of an instruction and the writeback of its calculated result, then the reorganizer must ensure that at least two instructions are placed between the instruction and any other instruction that utilizes the result.

In addition, the reorganizer must also ensure that no machine utilization constraints are violated. Such constraints may be formulated as statements like "loads may occur no more frequently than every six cycles" (typical for some GaAs systems), or "the bits of these instructions must not cross over a quadword boundary." In the following discussion, these constraints are referred to as "resource requirements." For a particular architecture/implementation, the specification of resource requirements may range from the trivial (none is needed) to the simple (each cycle has a small set of "resources" available and a subset of these is "consumed" on each cycle) to the very complex (as for highly horizontal architectures with several levels of decoding). Fortunately, the last case is not of particular interest for GaAs implementations because of the limited number of gates and pins available.

Thus, reorganization may be viewed as a two-pronged problem, that is, a sequencing problem dealing with the input and output registers of the instructions, and a resource utilization problem with the machine resource requirements of the instructions. The overall procedure of reorganization can be specified as follows: first, convert the input program into a directed acyclic graph, called the data precedence graph or DPG, that captures all of the register sequencing constraints, and, second, schedule each instruction for execution according to some topological ordering on the DPG. Of course, the scheduler must keep track of what resources are available on each cycle so that it can determine the feasibility of issuing a particular instruction on a particular cycle. Moreover, depending on the exact form of the initial DPG and on the scheduling algorithm, the DPG may require updating as the scheduling ensues.

In the DPG, there are three types of relationships that must be represented: (1) data dependency, (2) data antidependency, and (3) output dependency. These relationships are straightforward and easy to understand. An instruction I2 is data dependent on instruction I1 by register r if I1 writes a value into register r that is subsequently read by I2. In the DPG, we would have a data dependency arc from I1 to I2 labeled with register r. Second, I2 is data antidependent on I1 by register r if I1 must read a value from register r before I2 overwrites that value. This situation is represented by a data antidependency arc from I1 to I2 labeled with r. Last, I2 is output dependent on I1 by register r if I1 must

write register r before I2 writes register r; here, an output dependency arc is needed. The first two relationships are clearly required to ensure each instruction reads the correct values; the most intuitive use of output dependencies is to ensure the preservation of live registers. As it happens, there are less obvious ones. A thorough treatment of building and maintaining the DPG is found in Linn.[18]

The arcs of the DPG represent not only data sequencing constraints but timing constraints as well. For example, suppose that we have a data dependency arc labeled with register r3 from I1 to I2, that I1 writes register r3 in the sixth cycle after issue, and that I2 reads r3 in the third cycle after issue. Then, clearly, we may deduce that I2 may not be issued fewer than three cycles after I1. The best situation is obtained if there are other instructions from the program that are available for execution in these three cycles. Otherwise, "No-Operation" instructions (No-Ops) must be used. Obviously, the true instruction execution rate is reduced whenever these extra No-Ops are required.

The scheduling algorithm operates by considering at each time t all of the instructions that are "available" at time t, that is, each instruction with both the property of having all of its ancestors in the DPG having already been scheduled sufficiently far in advance to satisfy write/read delays and the property that all of the resources required for execution are available. Of these, the "best" one (according to some heuristic) is chosen to be issued at time t. If more than one instruction may be issued from the same instruction register load, the process is repeated until no more instructions can be issued in the current cycle. Then the algorithm applies the considerations at time $t + 1$; this is continued until no more instructions remain to be scheduled.

Let us consider a simple example to get a flavor of this process. In Figure 1 (a-b), a fragment of an HLL program and its realization in a MIPS-style assembly language are depicted. Here, we assume the rK, rL, and rM are registers that contain the values of K, L, and M from the program fragment, respectively; this convention continues throughout our discussion. Figure 1c shows the DPG. Let us further assume that the architecture has the following properties:

- A three-address instruction, op r1,r2,r3, executes in a three-stage pipeline, where r1 is read in the zeroth cycle

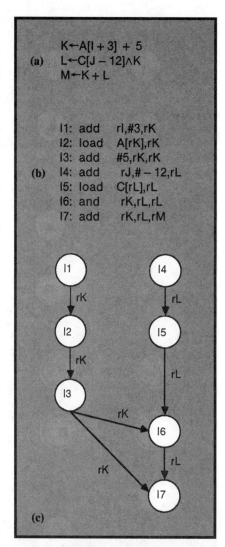

Figure 1. (a) Fragment of program in HLL. (Note the $\wedge$ is the logical "and" operator.) (b) Fragment of program in the MIPS-style assembly language. (c) DPG of the program fragment.

after issue, r2 in the first cycle after issue, and r3 is written in the second cycle after issue. The reads on a cycle occur before the writes; the result of this is that if r3 is utilized by a subsequent instruction, then two cycles must intervene if r3 is the first read register, but only one if r3 is the second.

- For a load A[r1],r2, r1 is read on the first (origin zero) cycle, and r2 is written in the fourth cycle. Again, an instruction may not read a value from a register in the same cycle that it is written into the register.

133

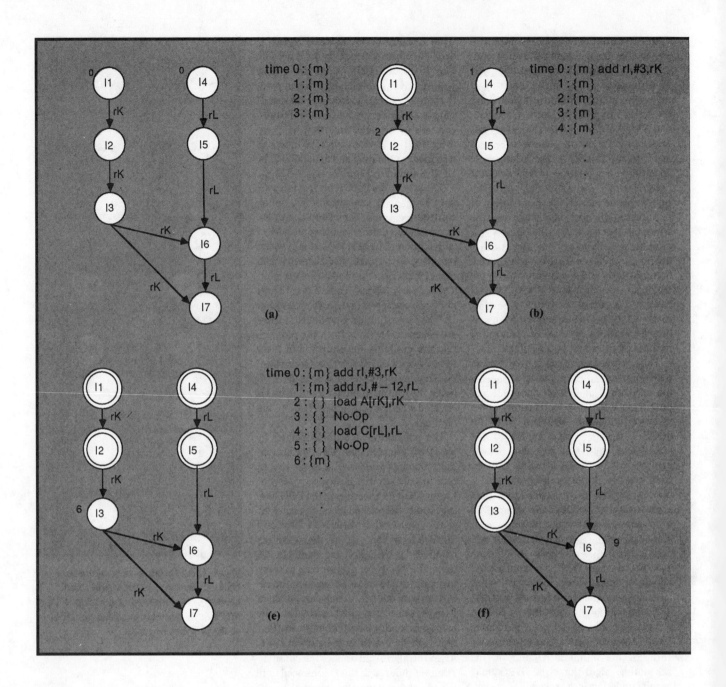

time 0 : {m}
1 : {m}
2 : {m}
3 : {m}

(a)

time 0 : {m} add rl,#3,rK
1 : {m}
2 : {m}
3 : {m}
4 : {m}

(b)

time 0 : {m} add rl,#3,rK
1 : {m} add rJ,# − 12,rL
2 : { } load A[rK],rK
3 : { } No-Op
4 : { } load C[rL],rL
5 : { } No-Op
6 : {m}

(e)

(f)

- Because of a lack of external memory address buffers, a load instruction may not be issued in the cycle immediately following another load instruction.
- Only one instruction may be issued from a single instruction register load.

Now, let us trace the execution of the reorganizer in Figure 2.

Figure 2a illustrates the initial setup. Note that instructions I1 and I4 each has all of its ancestors already scheduled. Thus, both are available at time = 0. For this architecture, we define a pseudoresource m

to keep track of whether a load instruction may be issued in any particular cycle. Initially, load instructions are enabled for all cycles. On the basis of the fact that I1 has one more descendent than I4, we choose to schedule I1. The updated situation is shown in Figure 2b. Note that I1 has been marked as scheduled, the available time for I4 has been updated, and I2 has become available, though not until time = 2. Also, note that if rK were read on the zeroth cycle in I2, instead of the first, then I2 would not have become available until time = 3. At time = 1, I4 is the only instruction availa-

ble. Figure 2c shows the updated state at time = 1.

At time = 2, I2 is the only available instruction. After verifying that its required resources are available at time = 2, I2 is scheduled there (as depicted in Figure 2d). Note that the scheduling of I2 also causes the removal of m at time [5] 3. This prevents the "two-reads-in-a-row" problem. At time [5] 3, I5 is data available, but cannot be scheduled because the m is not available. Since no instruction is both data and resource available, a No-Op is generated, and I5 is then scheduled at time = 4.

COMPUTER

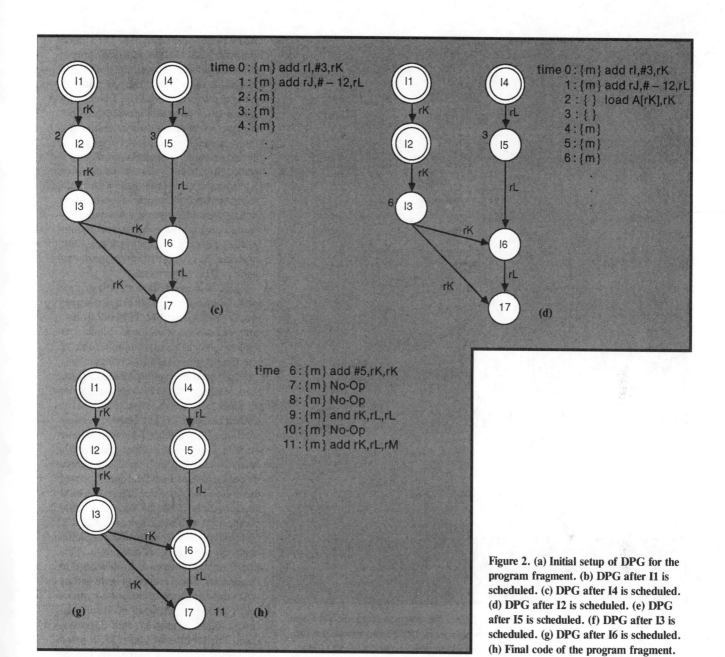

Figure 2. (a) Initial setup of DPG for the program fragment. (b) DPG after I1 is scheduled. (c) DPG after I4 is scheduled. (d) DPG after I2 is scheduled. (e) DPG after I5 is scheduled. (f) DPG after I3 is scheduled. (g) DPG after I6 is scheduled. (h) Final code of the program fragment.

Since I3 is not available until time = 6, another No-Op is generated at time = 5. The state after time = 5 is shown in Figure 2e.

Figure 2f shows the situation after I3 is scheduled at time = 6. I6 becomes available at time = 9 since it may not read rK until three cycles after I3 is issued. Since "and" is commutative, it might sometimes make sense to have the reorganizer automatically recode I6 as "and rL,rK,rL"; not in this case, however, since I6 must wait five cycles after the issuing of I5 to read rL. Figure 2g shows the situation after I6 is sched-

uled at time = 9 and Figure 2h shows the final code.

It is important to keep in mind that the code generated by this scheduling process does not generally execute "stand alone"; rather, the code is probably a fragment of a larger program. Thus, measures must be introduced to ensure that hazards are not produced as program fragments are pieced together. Figure 3 (a-b) shows a program fragment and flow graph, respectively, to illustrate the problem. A common approach to reorganization (called local reorganization) is to reorganize each of the

basic blocks of a program (that is, maximal single-entry, single-exit fragments) and to glue the resulting pieces together. Figure 3c shows possible reorganizations of each of the basic blocks of the fragment considered independently. Although each reorganized fragment executes correctly if independent, the sequential execution of the code will not produce the desired result.

To see this, consider the code sequence executed when Block2 and Block3 are concatenated, as shown in Figure 3d. Note that I7 (at the top of Block3) will read the wrong value, that is, not the one produced

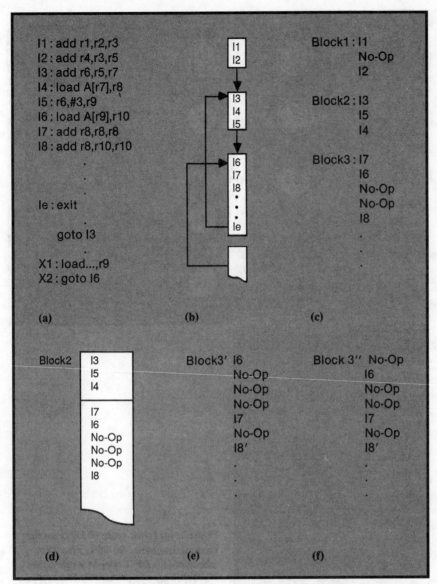

```
I1 : add r1,r2,r3        I1          Block1 : I1
I2 : add r4,r3,r5        I2                    No-Op
I3 : add r6,r5,r7                              I2
I4 : load A[r7],r8       I3
I5 : r6,#3,r9            I4          Block2 : I3
I6 : load A[r9],r10      I5                    I5
I7 : add r8,r8,r8                              I4
I8 : add r8,r10,r10      I6
       .                 I7          Block3 : I7
       .                 I8                    I6
Ie : exit               • • •                  No-Op
       .                 Ie                    No-Op
    goto I3                                     I8
                                                .
X1 : load...,r9                                 .
X2 : goto I6                                     .

(a)                      (b)                   (c)


Block2   I3        Block3'  I6       Block 3''  No-Op
         I5                 No-Op               I6
         I4                 No-Op               No-Op
                            No-Op               No-Op
         I7                 I7                  I7
         I6                 No-Op               No-Op
         No-Op              I8'                 I8'
         No-Op              .                    .
         No-Op              .                    .
         I8                  .                    .

(d)                      (e)                   (f)
```

Figure 3. (a) A program fragment. (b) Flow graph of the program fragment. (c) Basic blocks of the program fragment. (d) Code sequence when Block2 and Block3 are concatenated. (e) Code sequence of Block3 after repacking with respect to I4. (f) Code sequence of Block3 after repacking with respect to Block2-Block3 boundary.

by I4. A few moments of reflection will reveal that this problem may be solved by repacking the blocks, as shown in Figure 3e. (I8' is "add r10,r8,r10.") Again, incorrect execution results since now we have a load (I6) immediately following another load (I4). Figure 3f gives a packing that is legal with respect to the Block2-Block3 boundary; whether it is completely legal depends on how the block-containing instruction X1 is packed.

Again, two problems arise when "piecing" the blocks together—a data sequencing problem and a resource problem. Only

trivial solutions have been obtained for the resource problem. The most common solution is not to allow resource utilization to propagate beyond block boundaries. In this case, such a strategy requires that a No-Op be appended to the code for Block2. This results in a wasted cycle if the instruction at the top of the next block is not a load. This problem can be especially thorny if long resource utilizations are needed, such as for a nonpipelined floating-point coprocessor. This is discussed in greater detail in a later section.

Two solutions are possible when consid-

ering interblock data delays. The simple approach is not to allow data delay propagation as above. However, the data delay problem is significantly simpler than the resource utilization problem. This occurs because in the data delay problem it is only necessary to determine the maximum delay that is carried into the block by any write; in the resource utilization problem we would have to find all possible resource "starting states" for the block. This could be very difficult if resources are consumed for long periods. However, it is straightforward to determine the maximum amount of delay propagated into any block. But, applying this information naively can result in a very poor code.

Figure 4a shows the flow graph for a program fragment in which the two upper blocks (Block1 and Block2) both propagate delay into the lower block. As depicted, Block1 brings four units of delay into Block3, whereas Block2 brings in only one unit. Assume that Block2 is the textual predecessor of Block3 in the program; that is, Block3 is entered from Block2 if the branch in Block2 is not taken. A simple solution to this problem is shown in Figure 4b. The problem here is that, if Block3 is entered mostly from Block2, then three wasted cycles have been introduced most of the time. The solution of Figure 4c would be a good one if Block1 were the textual predecessor of Block3 instead of Block2. Figure 4d potentially introduces additional delay on the Block1-Block4 path. This might be costly depending on execution frequencies. The solution in Figure 4e may not even be implementable for an architecture with a branch delay of more than three, which is typical in some GaAs systems. The solution of Figure 4f, copying the destination block, is the most general. However, it increases the size of the program. Indeed, in order to save the most cycles, many of Block3's descendants must be copied as well. If the fragment shown is part of a loop and if an instruction cache is employed, then the effectiveness of the cache may be reduced by the larger code size. Thus, no completely effective solution for this problem has been formulated. More work is needed in several areas.

When write delays become several cycles in length, which is the case in GaAs microprocessors, it is frequently the case that typical blocks do not contain a sufficient number of unrelated instructions to cover over the timing delays. Consequently, too many No-Ops are required to be inserted, and efficiency decreases dramatically. In such cases, the efficiency of the

COMPUTER

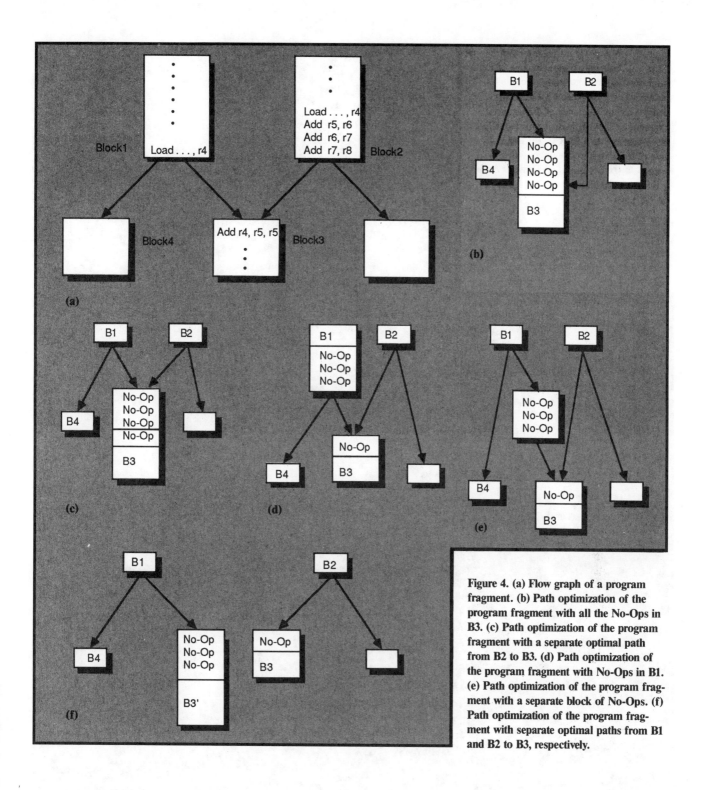

Figure 4. (a) Flow graph of a program fragment. (b) Path optimization of the program fragment with all the No-Ops in B3. (c) Path optimization of the program fragment with a separate optimal path from B2 to B3. (d) Path optimization of the program fragment with No-Ops in B1. (e) Path optimization of the program fragment with a separate block of No-Ops. (f) Path optimization of the program fragment with separate optimal paths from B1 and B2 to B3, respectively.

reorganization process can frequently be increased by finding instructions from other blocks to fill in the "holes." Consider the fragment shown in Figure 5a. An extraordinarily good code generator might provide the code shown in Figure 5b. Here, we have assumed that a marginal index vector M is available and, further, that the row stride of the array is available in register

rSTRIDE. The column stride size is equal to one.

Focusing on the T-block and the Y-block, Figure 5c shows how the blocks might be compacted individually; the code quality is not very impressive. Figure 5d shows how the code can be improved by pushing instructions from the X- and Y-blocks into the T-block. The code improves by 17 per-

cent. It is somewhat biased in favor of executing along the T-X path instead of the T-Y path. If we bias completely in favor of the T-X path, that is, if we assume that its probability of being executed is far greater than for the T-Y path, then we obtain the code of Figure 5e. This code is optimal with respect to execution of the T-X path. However, Figure 5f gives code that executes the

Figure 5. (a) A program fragment in HLL. (b) Assembly code sequence of the program fragment generated. (c) Code sequences of T-block and X-block. (d) Improved code sequence of the program fragment by moving instructions from X- and Y-blocks into T-blocks. (e) Optimal code of the program fragment with respect to the T-X path. (f) Optimal code of the program fragment with respect to the T-Y path.

(a)

```
if A[I,I] > 0 then
    B←(A[I,J + 1] − A[I,J − 1])
else
    B←(A[I + 1,J] − A[I − 1,J]);
```

(b)

```
T1: load M[rI],r1
T2: add rI,r1,r2
T3: load A[r2],r2
T4: bge #0,r2,Y1

X1: add #1,rJ,r3
X2: add r1,r3,r3
X3: load A[r3],r3
X4: add # − 1,rJ,r4
X5: add r1,r4,r4
X6: load A[r4],r4
X7: sub r3,r4,rB
    goto JOIN

Y1: add rSTRIDE,rJ,r5
Y2: add r1,r5,r5
Y3: load A[r5],r5
Y4: sub rJ,rSTRIDE,r6
Y5: add r1,r6,r6
Y6: load A[r6],r6
Y7: sub r5,r6,rB
    goto JOIN
```

(c)

```
T1: load M[rI],r1
No-Op
No-Op
No-Op
T2: add rI,r1,r2
No-Op
T3: Load A[r2],r2
No-Op
No-Op
No-Op
T4: bge #0,r2,Y1

X1: add #1,rJ,r3
X4: add # − 1,rJ,r4
X2: add r1,r3,r3
X5: add r1,r4,r4
X3: load A[r3],r3
No-Op
X6: Load A[r4],r4
No-Op
No-Op
No-Op
X7: sub r3,r4,rB
```

(d)

```
T1: load M[rI],r1
X1: add #1,rJ,r3
X4: add # − 1,rJ,r4
Y1: add rJ,rSTRIDE,r5
T2: add rI,r1,r2
Y4: sub rJ,rSTRIDE,r6
T3: load A[r2],r2
X2: add r1,r3,r3
X5: add r1,r4,r4
Y2: add r1,r5,r5
T4: bge #0,r2, Y2; label not very meaningful

X3: load A[r3],r3
No-Op
X6: load A[r4],r4
No-Op
No-Op
No-Op
X7: Sub r3,r4,rB
```

(e)

```
T1: load M[rI],r1
X1: load M[rI],r1
X4: add # − 1,rJ,r4
Y1: add rJ,rSTRIDE,r5
T2: add rI,r1,r2
X2: add r1,r3,r3
T3: load A[r2],r2
X5: add r1,r4,r4
X3: load A[r3],r3
Y4: sub rJ,rSTRIDE,r6
X6: load A[r4],r4
T4: bge #0,r2,...

No-Op
No-Op
X7: sub r3,r4,rB
```

(f)

```
T1: load M[rI],r1
X1: add #1,rJ,r3
X4: add # − 1,rJ,r4
Y1: add rJ,rSTRIDE,r5
T2: add rI,r1,r2
X2: add r1,r3,r3
T3: load A[r2],r2
X5: add r1,r4,r4
X3: load A[r3],r3
Y4: sub rJ,rSTRIDE,r6
X6: load A[r4],r4
Y2: add r1,r5,r5

Y5: add r1,r6,r6
T4: bge #0,r2,...

X7: sub r3,r4,rB
```

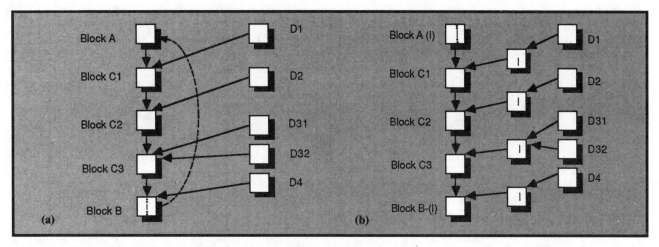

Figure 6. (a) A program fragment where instruction I in block B will be moved to block A. (b) Necessary modification of the program fragment for moving instruction I. (Note that the "block B-{I}" means the block B without instruction I.)

T-X path just as fast, and executes the T-Y path two cycles faster. Interestingly, even code so biased in favor of one execution path is actually optimal, as long as the probability of the T-X path is at least as large as the probability of the T-Y path.

Although this example shows only movement of instructions between adjacent blocks, it is possible to look arbitrarily far ahead in the program to find "free" instructions. Details of this procedure may be found in Linn.[19] It should be noted, however, that moving instructions around can lead to decreased execution times, and also to potentially large increases in program size. Figure 6a shows a program fragment where it is determined that instruction I in block B will be moved to block A. While faster execution may result along the A-C1-C2-C3-B path, the program must be modified as shown in Figure 6b, in order that the semantics of the program be preserved.

As a final note, the reorganization procedure outlined here is frequently utilized as a post-pass activity that is initiated only after code generation and register allocation are completed. In fact, we may expect that very good code may be obtained only when the register assignment phase has the knowledge of what shape the reorganized code is likely to have. The PL.8 compiler for the IBM 801 actually performs reorganization both before and after the register assignment phase. In this way, it tries to avail itself of final code shape information during register assignment, and to use reorganization to cover any remaining No-Ops as well.

Branch delay fill-in (sequencing hazards): compilation candidate. The negative effect of branch instructions on the performance of pipelined processors has long been recognized. In a typical pipelined processor, the condition evaluation portion of a conditional branch is not complete before the next sequential instruction is fetched. Therefore, if the condition evaluates to true, the branch is taken and the instruction that was just fetched must be discarded.

Silicon CISC approaches to the solution of the branch delay problem generally rely on a hardware mechanism to inhibit the execution of the sequential instruction. More ambitious techniques involve predicting the outcome of the condition evaluation and fetching the appropriate instruction. A wrong choice here again requires the inhibition of the execution of an already fetched instruction.

The silicon RISC design approach relies on the concept of delayed branching,[17] a technique used widely in microprogramming. In this approach, a fixed number of instructions after the branch instruction are always executed. In order to preserve the correct program execution, only a subset of instructions are legal candidates for insertion after branch instructions. For example, instructions influencing the outcome of the condition evaluation cannot be moved to a location following the branch instruction. Silicon RISC architectures rely on the compiler to move as many instructions as possible to positions following branches in order to increase performance, while also preserving the correctness of program execution.

The delayed branching approach is appealing for GaAs processor implementations. First, it reduces hardware complexity because there is no need to inhibit instruction execution, undo partial executions, etc. The advantages of this approach for a resource-scarce GaAs processor are clear. In addition, the delayed branching technique leads to faster execution because the reduced hardware complexity reduces the basic instruction cycle time, and because successfully filled branch delay slots cause no performance degradation, in contrast to most hardware approaches.

However, the increased instruction pipeline length expected for GaAs processors requires increased compiler algorithm capabilities. This is because an increased pipeline length also increases the branch delay, that is, the number of instructions always executed after branch instructions. The compiler for the SU-MIPS was very successful at finding one instruction to move behind branches, but performed relatively poorly when attempting to find two or more[20]; therefore, new branch fill-in algorithms are very desirable in the GaAs environment.

Branch delay fill-in (sequencing hazards): compiler algorithms. As already indicated, there are essentially three ways to handle sequencing hazards. The first, hardware interlocks, is not felt to be reasonable for GaAs systems, both because of the additional hardware required and because the inclusion of interlocks has a lengthening effect on the basic machine cycle time. The second way is an architectural solution that

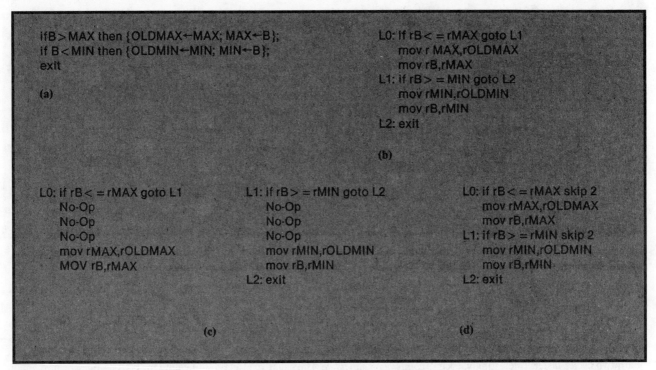

```
ifB > MAX then {OLDMAX←MAX; MAX←B};          L0: If rB < = rMAX goto L1
if B < MIN then {OLDMIN←MIN; MIN←B};             mov r MAX,rOLDMAX
exit                                             mov rB,rMAX
                                             L1: if rB > = MIN goto L2
(a)                                              mov rMIN,rOLDMIN
                                                 mov rB,rMIN
                                             L2: exit

                                             (b)


L0: if rB < = rMAX goto L1    L1: if rB > = rMIN goto L2    L0: if rB < = rMAX skip 2
    No-Op                         No-Op                         mov rMAX,rOLDMAX
    No-Op                         No-Op                         mov rB,rMAX
    No-Op                         No-Op                     L1: if rB > = rMIN skip 2
    mov rMAX,rOLDMAX              mov rMIN,rOLDMIN              mov rMIN,rOLDMIN
    MOV rB,rMAX                   mov rB,rMIN                   mov rB,rMIN
                              L2: exit                      L2: exit


            (c)                                                         (d)
```

Figure 7. (a) A program fragment in HLL. (b) A possible realization for the program fragment. (c) Code sequence of the program fragment with branch delays of three cycles. (d) Code sequence of the program fragment with "conditional skip of n cycles" primitive.

attempts to avoid conditional branches by providing other forms of conditional execution. The third solution is completely compiler based, and consists of having the compiler attempt to move instructions into the branch fill slots (that would otherwise have been occupied by No-Ops). This last option is the main thrust of this section.

First, however, let us briefly consider the second solution. Figure 7 (a-b) shows a code fragment and a possible machine realization. Figure 7c shows the code that must be used if we assume a branch delay of three cycles, which is typical for some GaAs systems. Note that even for the case where neither of the consequents is executed, nine cycles are required for execution. Figure 7d shows a realization that is possible if we assume that a different conditional execution primitive—the conditional skip of *n* cycles—is available. Such a primitive is readily implemented. Many pipelined computers already contain the appropriate mechanisms to support precise interrupts.

Now, we consider the software solution. The solution may be further decomposed into: (1) the case where moving instructions into the branch fill occurs after individual blocks of the program are already reor-

ganized and (2) the case where the filling occurs during reorganization. Clearly, the former solution is utilized in conjunction with local reorganization and the latter in conjunction with global reorganization. Only the local reorganization method is discussed here. The global method requires wholesale changes in the flow graph of the program that are even more sweeping in scope than the ones indicated previously for global reorganization. The interested reader should refer to Linn.[19]

Figure 8 depicts in a general way all the different places that the compiler can look to find instructions to plug into the branch fill. Here, we are assuming that block B is the textual successor of block A, so that execution proceeds from A to B, if the conditional branch is not taken. Otherwise, execution proceeds with block C. All three blocks shown can provide instructions to be moved into the branch fill following the conditional branch. The first place to look for such instructions is in block A. It may be that instruction A*n* writes neither of R3 and R5. If so, the order of A*n* and the branch can be reversed; in this way, one slot of the branch fill is used up. As usual, this move can also be a drawback as in the case where C1, say, is data dependent on A*n*. By

interchanging A*n* with the branch, A*n* takes up a unit of the branch delay, but the branch does not take up a unit of A*n*'s write delay. Such problems can be resolved only optimally by considering all possible cases; clearly, this is infeasible.

If the branch delay is more than one, we could continue by considering instruction A[*n*−1], A[*n*−2], etc., in turn until we have completely utilized the branch fill. If we do not allow ourselves to repack block A, then the procedure may terminate without utilizing all of the slots, either if block A is shorter than the branch delay or if any of the instructions write registers utilized by the branch. As a last note, we must ensure that the branch instruction is not scheduled so early that it attempts to read register values that have not yet been set. This method of obtaining instructions to use in the branch fill is called type-1 branch optimization in Gross.[14]

Figure 9a shows a block as it might exist after reorganization, and Figure 9b shows the effects of type-1 optimization. Note that the No-Ops shown will not be covered using any of the methods based on local reorganization. This is one of the advantages of proper global reorganization. For type-1 to be truly effective, the local reor-

COMPUTER

ganizer should do all that it can to give priority to instructions that write into registers used by the branch instruction (if any) that terminates the block the branch instruction is part of. In the current example, an additional No-Op would have been required if the reorganizer had chosen to schedule the "add r3,..." instruction first in the block, since the branch instruction cannot be scheduled sooner than three cycles after the "ldA[r2]...." Actually, the code generator can do a great deal to facilitate the efficient removal of sequencing hazards as well. Figure 10 (a-b) shows a for-loop construct and a possible realization. However, the realization of Figure 10c is superior (note that the increment is in the branch fill) since the branch condition does not depend on the new value of I, and since the increment is done in the branch fill. This realization cannot actually be specified in most assembly languages since the concept of a delayed branch is not supported.

Referring again to Figure 8, a second place to find instructions is from block C. This method is called type-2 optimization.[14] The conditions under which the top instruction under consideration in block C can be moved into the branch fill are these:

- The instruction from C must not be moved so high in the branch fill that a timing hazard would be created.
- The instruction from C must not violate the resource state.
- The instruction from C must "fit" into the branch fill. This is important if multiple instruction lengths are utilized. For example, a two-word instruction cannot be moved into the last word of the branch fill since this will result in incorrect execution if the branch is not taken.
- The instruction must not write any register that is live at the top of block B.

Assuming that all of these conditions are met, the instruction can be moved into the branch fill at the appropriate slot. What this means is that the text of the instruction is moved into the appropriate slot, and the branch target address is increased by one. Consider Figure 11a, where a short fragment is depicted; temporarily we assume a branch delay of four cycles. Figure 11b shows that situation after type-2 optimization is performed. In essence, instructions C1 and C2 have been moved into the branch fill. Several items are noteworthy. First, C1 has been moved to slot A7 instead of A6 so that a timing hazard is not created. Second, when a No-Op is needed

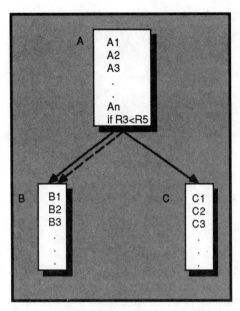

Figure 8. Locations where instructions can be found to plug into the branch fill.

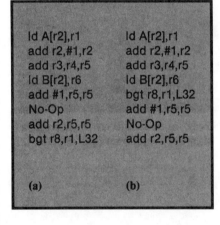

```
ld A[r2],r1        ld A[r2],r1
add r2,#1,r2       add r2,#1,r2
add r3,r4,r5       add r3,r4,r5
ld B[r2],r6        ld B[r2],r6
add #1,r5,r5       bgt r8,r1,L32
No-Op              add #1,r5,r5
add r2,r5,r5       No-Op
bgt r8,r1,L32      add r2,r5,r5

  (a)                 (b)
```

Figure 9. (a) A block of code that may exist after reorganization. (b) Effects of type-1 optimization on the block of code in a.

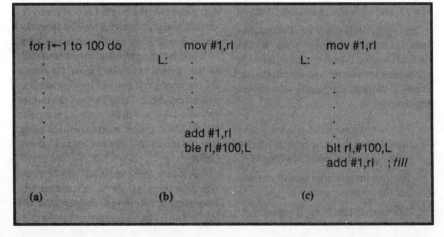

Figure 10. (a) A typical for-loop construct. (b) A possible machine realization for the for-loop construct. (c) A modified machine realization for the for-loop construct.

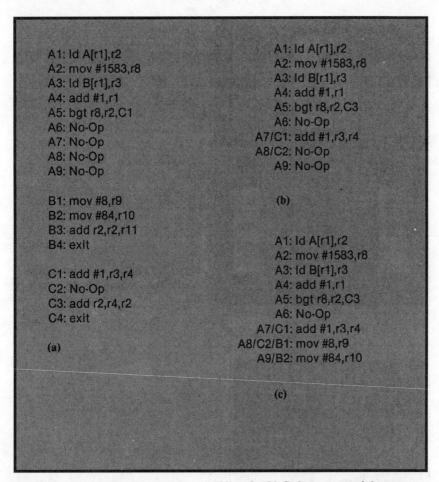

```
A1: ld A[r1],r2
A2: mov #1583,r8
A3: ld B[r1],r3
A4: add #1,r1
A5: bgt r8,r2,C1
A6: No-Op
A7: No-Op
A8: No-Op
A9: No-Op

B1: mov #8,r9
B2: mov #84,r10
B3: add r2,r2,r11
B4: exit

C1: add #1,r3,r4
C2: No-Op
C3: add r2,r4,r2
C4: exit

(a)
```

```
A1: ld A[r1],r2
A2: mov #1583,r8
A3: ld B[r1],r3
A4: add #1,r1
A5: bgt r8,r2,C3
A6: No-Op
A7/C1: add #1,r3,r4
A8/C2: No-Op
A9: No-Op

(b)
```

```
A1: ld A[r1],r2
A2: mov #1583,r8
A3: ld B[r1],r3
A4: add #1,r1
A5: bgt r8,r2,C3
A6: No-Op
A7/C1: add #1,r3,r4
A8/C2/B1: mov #8,r9
A9/B2: mov #84,r10

(c)
```

Figure 11. (a) A program fragment in assembly code. (b) Code sequence of the program fragment after type-2 optimization. (c) Code sequence of the program fragment after type-2 and then type-3 optimization.

in block C for timing reasons, it must be treated as a normal instruction to be moved. Last, we could not move instruction C3 into slot A9, because C3 writes register r2, and r2 is live at the top of B.

Obviously, the last place to find instructions to move will be in block B. The method is called type-3 optimization. The conditions to be met are essentially the reverse of the ones for type-2 optimization; they are

- The instruction from B must not be moved so high in the branch fill that a timing hazard would be created.
- The instruction from B must not violate the resource state.
- The instruction from B must "fit" into the branch fill.
- The instruction must not write any register that is live at the top of block C.

Assuming that all of these conditions are met, the instruction can be moved into the branch fill at the appropriate slot. However, the actual movement is a little different. Since B is the textual successor to A, we may simply remove a No-Op from the end of block A for each instruction word of B that is to be moved into the branch fill. In the current example, Figure 11c shows the result of performing type-3 optimization after type-2. Table 1 shows the results produced by a working reorganizer for RCA's 32-bit GaAs microprocessor using the "standard" benchmarks from Gross.[14]

Obviously, these methods can be combined in various ways. A particularly interesting combination was implemented by Gross.[14] The reorganizer for the SU-MIPS machine was implemented in such a way that only a very small amount of the program was resident in memory at any particular time. A small symbol table was

maintained that contained the first few instructions of each block that had been reorganized. If a backward branch was encountered, the branch fill routines could utilize the table information to perform type-2 optimization. So, type-1, type-2, and type-3 reorganization was attempted. In the case of a forward branch, the fill routines had no knowledge of the code at the branch target. Thus, only type-1 and type-3 was attempted. In this way, only the symbol table and approximately one block worth of code remained memory-resident simultaneously.

Memory. There are several memory-related areas where a compiler can provide enormous performance benefits for a GaAs processor. As already pointed out, GaAs chips will be limited to a relatively low transistor count; therefore, on-chip processor memory will be small. Because of the large signal propagation delays between chips, the cost of accessing even the fastest off-chip memory will be high. Meanwhile, accessing memory at the lower levels of the memory hierarchy will introduce extremely large amounts of dead time in which the processor will be idled.

The compiler is able to ameliorate the off-chip memory access problem in two ways. First, the compiler is able to increase the reusability of information at the higher levels of the memory hierarchy. Second, the compiler is able to overlap program execution and the fetching of information into the higher levels of the memory hierarchy (through various prefetching techniques). In other words, the compiler should first try to minimize the need for off-chip communications, and then should try to overlap any remaining communication with useful on-chip processing. We next discuss how information reuse and overlap may be employed at three levels of the memory hierarchy: register file, cache, and main memory.

Register file lifetime maximization: compilation candidate. In a GaAs processor incorporating a register-to-register execution model, data loads and data stores are extremely costly. Large performance degradation may result for two reasons. First, a large delay may be directly introduced because of the long-latency off-chip environment, especially for data loads. Second, the presence of load and store instructions increases the program size, and this can be expected to result in decreased hit ratios at the higher levels of the instruction memory hierarchy.

COMPUTER

Unfortunately, data loads and stores are used frequently in silicon processors. For typical silicon RISCs, approximately 10 and 20 percent of all executed instructions are data stores and loads, respectively.[17] Obviously, once data is loaded into the register file, it is very desirable to keep it there until it is no longer needed. One method of increasing the reusability of register data is to incorporate a larger register file—a method that is feasible in a silicon processor but one that faces a severe implementation problem in GaAs because of transistor limitations. An alternative approach that is more applicable to GaAs is to increase the register data reusability through compilation techniques.

Register file lifetime maximization: compiler algorithms. In order to maximize utilization of the register file on a machine, two separate problems must be solved. The first of these is the elimination of common subexpressions. Clearly, the number of data items that must be retained can have a large effect on the percentage of such items that are found in a register file at any given time. Thus, common subexpression elimination not only decreases the number of instructions executed but also may greatly decrease the number of data items. Local and global common subexpression elimination are now the standard fare of optimizing compilers; Aho and Ullman[21] provide a very good overview of such techniques.

The second consideration for maximizing register lifetimes is to determine globally a truly good set of items to keep in registers at any particular time. This is a very difficult problem. The graph coloring algorithm of Chaitin[22] provides an excellent framework for considering the problem and (as mentioned previously) has been utilized for the PL.8 compiler on the IBM 801 machine. The technique used is to convert a program flow graph, decorated with ''live variable'' information and ''reaching definition'' information, into a graph coloring problem. The nodes of the graph are the instructions of the program. The edges of the graph represent ''interferences'' between instructions. Here, two instructions are said to interfere if the register definitions of the two instructions must be live simultaneously. Clearly, if the definitions must be live simultaneously, then the values computed by the instructions must not reside in the same register.

Reorganization is performed before register allocation so that the scheduler of the reorganizer need not be constrained by a

Table 1. Percentage of branch fills accomplished by the current reorganizer (static count)

Benchmark	Static count					Total
	Total branches	3-fills (%)	2-fills (%)	1-fills (%)	0-fills (%)	fills (%)
Realmm (8 × 8)	29	31.0	20.7	13.8	34.5	49.4
Bubble (20 items)	23	26.1	17.4	13.4	43.5	42.0
Cal	89	34.8	13.5	26.7	24.7	52.8
FFT	124	24.2	17.1	45.2	13.7	50.5
Weight	131	37.4	17.6	25.2	19.1	57.5
Puzzle	84	8.3	9.5	8.3	73.8	17.5
Parse	81	23.5	19.8	8.6	48.2	39.5
Average	80 +	26.5	16.5	20.2	36.8	44.2

physical register assignment. Then, the resulting program is converted into its interference graph. A polynomial time approximation for graph coloring is utilized to color the graph since graph coloring in general is NP-complete. Essentially, the algorithm tries to 32-color the graph since the 801 has 32 registers. The method used is to reduce the graph by one node at a time (utilizing appropriate heuristics for picking good nodes) until the graph is empty. If the algorithm never encounters a node of degree 32 or higher, then the procedure is quite simple and a reasonable coloring assured. Otherwise, it must find some way (normally by spilling to memory or recomputing the stored value) of reducing the maximum degree of the graph. Note, by the way, that the existence of high-degree nodes doesn't necessarily mean that the algorithm will have to spill if some color (register) is duplicated.

Thus, the method provides a very convenient framework for considering the problem. Note that since the program is considered globally, interferences caused by live registers at block boundaries that are considered in sequencing hazard elimination can easily be modeled in the graph. Essentially the algorithm provides hooks for two sets of heuristics: (1) the choosing of a node to color and the color to use and (2) the choosing of a node to spill/recompute when coloring has failed. The algorithms utilizing the heuristics outlined in Chaitin[22] are reported to provide excellent results for the 801 (32 registers), as well as for the IBM S/370 architecture with only 16 registers. Register files of size 16 seem to be well within the capabilities of today's GaAs; thus, work in this area

should concentrate on utilizing this evolving framework for register allocation.

Register file prefetching: compilation candidate. As discussed in the previous section, data loads and stores are both costly and relatively frequent. In the previous section, techniques were described that reduce the need to access information not contained in the register file. A second approach for reducing the negative effects of data loads is to overlap data loads with the execution of other useful operations.

As already indicated, RISC processors allow a compiler optimization to be utilized that is not available to compilers for CISC processors. As discussed earlier in this article, RISC compilers can overlap the latency associated with data loads with the execution of useful instructions through a technique known as load fill-in. Note that the load fill-in optimization may be viewed as a technique for moving useful instructions into the fill-in slots after the data load instruction. Our viewpoint of this optimization as a prefetching technique is based on the observation that the data load instruction is advanced, so that the initiation of the load request is performed before the data is actually required by a succeeding instruction; that is, it is prefetched. Because the load fill-in delay will likely be longer for a GaAs processor, the effectiveness of the fill-in implementation will have a more pronounced effect on performance.

Just as the increased branch delays for GaAs processors introduce the need for fundamental compiler algorithm improvements, so too do the longer load delays.

Register file prefetching: compiler algorithms. From the point of view of the compiler, the load delay is treated identically as other write delays. In the previous example of Figures 1 and 2, the load instructions were assumed to have a write delay of four cycles. In this example, the reorganizer is only partially successful in filling instructions into the load fill-in slots. The essential reason here is the relatively small number of instructions under consideration and therefore the small number of free instructions at any particular instant. The example of Figure 5 shows that significantly better performance should be obtained when global reorganization is utilized. However, we do not have sufficient experience yet with global reorganization versus local reorganization for architectures with long delays as in GaAs.

An important point should be made here about the usefulness of this technique. If no interlocks are provided (as is proposed), the write delay utilized will have to be the maximum possible delay. For example, if a load resulting in a cache hit has a write delay of three, whereas a miss causes a write delay of 12, then either the reorganizer must always assume a delay of 12 or the machine must take an interrupt (its only form of interlock) on a cache miss. If misses are frequent and the interrupt handling sequence is longer than 12 cycles, considerable performance will be lost. The 801 machine, conversely, supports interlocks. The 801 compiler in the above situation would attempt to pack between three and 12 instructions into the load fill depending on what instructions might be free. Considerable experimentation needs to be initiated to determine whether the performance loss of supporting interlocks is greater than the performance gained by assuming (and frequently hitting) minimum write delays.

Cache lifetime maximization: compilation candidate. Cache memories are used in virtually all high-performance silicon computer systems. Caches have proved to be successful at providing nearly cache-level access speeds while introducing little to the overall system cost. The reason for the success of cache memories is that they successfully exploit the locality of memory references.[23] Memory reference address patterns are not completely random. Once a memory location is accessed, there is a high likelihood that the same address will be reaccessed a short time later (temporal locality). Also, when a memory location is accessed, there is a high probability that the nearby addresses will be accessed soon

(spatial locality). However, note that the level of locality will decrease after the code motion related to the global code optimization, which has been advocated here in several places.

The performance level of a cache memory depends considerably on the cache hit ratio, that is, the fraction of memory references accessing a value actually in the cache. The penalty for cache misses, in terms of instruction cycles, will be higher for a GaAs processor than for a silicon processor. This is due to the relatively long access times of main memory because of extremely long propagation delays, if GaAs memory chips are used, or because of slower raw memory access speed, if silicon memory chips are used. Because of the lower density of GaAs chips, GaAs caches will likely be smaller than caches for silicon processors. Since cache memory capacity is the single most important parameter to influence the hit ratio,[24] GaAs processor systems may experience significant performance degradation from cache misses.

One way to reduce cache miss ratios is to ensure that, once a block of data is loaded into the cache from main memory, the maximum usage of the block is achieved before it is restored to main memory. That is, we would like to maximize the reusability of the cache block information. There are two ways in which a compiler can be helpful.

In the first approach, the compiler works with the runtime block replacement policy by appropriately grouping together instructions and data. The goal here is to increase the correlation between the temporal and spatial localities of reference of particular information. In other words, the compiler increases the degree of spatial locality in programs. Consequently, all the information used within a short time span should also be contained within the minimum number of cache blocks. Note, that one of the parts of the Parafrase* system actually revises the locations of data in memory, to increase the locality.

A second approach is to allow the compiler to override the runtime block replacement policy whenever it detects a more optimal replacement sequence. Because a runtime replacement policy must operate with little overhead, it must necessarily be somewhat primitive. A common runtime approach is the least recently used (LRU)

*Kuck & Associates, Inc.

method or an approximation. As its name indicates, the LRU approach replaces the block having the earliest time of last use. Since a compiler has a view of the entire program, and presumably more time to implement its replacement algorithm, it should also select better blocks for replacement.

Because of the relatively small penalty for cache misses in a silicon processor implementation, the motivation for compiler algorithm advances to improve cache performance (of the type discussed above) is also relatively small. However, one of the first-generation silicon RISCs, the IBM 801, incorporated special instructions to allow its compiler to override the runtime cache placement policy whenever it detected a better policy.[13] Still, in general, current compiler algorithms for improving cache performance are at a primitive state and need improvement for a better utilization of GaAs technology.

Cache lifetime maximization: compiler algorithms. For any but the most trivial programs, it is very difficult for a compiler to determine the set of blocks in memory at any given time; thus, it is difficult for the compiler to give much assistance to the replacement policy. There are a few cases, however, where the compiler can assist in identifying good candidate blocks to be replaced. Consider a flow graph of the type shown in Figure 12a. Here, we see a loop and an if-test inside. If the compiler knows (from traces, for example) that the consequent of the if statement is *not* executed a very large percent of the time, then the compiler might consider instructing the cache that Block B is an excellent candidate for the next replacement in its cache set. Figure 12b shows a program with two loops. The compiler here would instruct the cache to mark for replacement appropriate cache frames from the first loop. In this way, runtime routines shared between the two loops may be spared an inopportune replacement. Marking data (as opposed to instructions) for replacement is a much more difficult task.

The effects of packing the program in such a way, as to minimize the number of cache frames active at any particular time, could be a very effective way to obtain an apparent increase in cache size. For instruction blocks, this essentially amounts to ensuring that labels in the program fall on appropriate addresses relative to the start of memory frames. Consider the program of Figure 13. Here, we have a program with

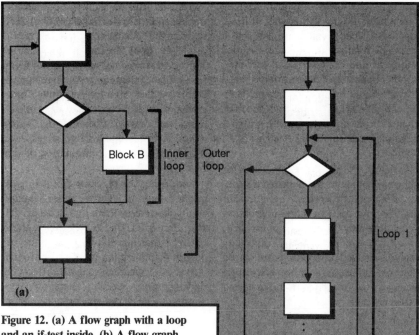

Figure 12. (a) A flow graph with a loop and an if-test inside. (b) A flow graph with two loops. (Note that the diamond box represents a test block.)

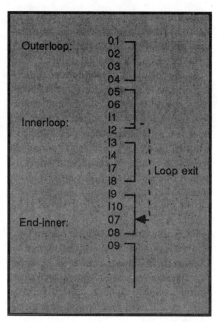

Figure 13. Code sequence for the loops from Figure 12.

an outer loop and an inner loop. The brackets indicate cache/memory frames. Note that because of the alignment of the program, the inner loop actually requires three cache frames instead of two. Thus, the probability that one of the frames will be displaced is 50 percent higher than if I1 were aligned on a cache frame boundary; for inner loops with complicated flow graphs the percentages can increase dramatically.

Similar considerations could be given to data frames. For example, one could determine the influence of the affinity of access that various data objects display. The various components of a stack frame, or the fields in a frequently accessed record type, could be subjected to such analysis. In the case of record fields, the fields would be rearranged so that items that are accessed similarly (in time) would be packed together into the fewest possible frames.

Their history has been that cache memories have enjoyed high hit rates and/or low penalties for misses. Such assumptions are not necessarily valid for GaAs architectures; nevertheless, little work has been reported in attempting to apply such software-controlled cache techniques. Our opinion is that these techniques are unlikely to produce large improvements in the efficiency of GaAs systems; however,

there have been no experimental validations of these "engineering intuitions."

Cache prefetching: compilation candidate. As discussed in the previous section, memory accesses resulting in cache misses can reduce the performance of GaAs proces-

sor systems significantly. In the previous section, we described compilation techniques for reducing the number of replacements (of cache blocks) containing data that will soon be needed by the processor. There are compilation techniques for reducing the cache miss rate by loading information into the cache just before it is required by the processor, in parallel with on-going on-chip processing (another approach is to try to reduce the negative effects of cache miss).

Runtime techniques for prefetching cache blocks must be simple to minimize overhead delays. One example approach is the "one block lookahead" method.[25] In one variation of this approach, the hardware ensures that block $i + 1$ is in the cache when block i is accessed. If block $i + 1$ is not resident in the cache, it is then fetched. As with most runtime memory management techniques, this approach yields benefits because it successfully exploits the locality of references, in this case spatial locality. A compiler-based approach is advantageous because it is not forced to rely exclusively on locality exploitation. The compiler has a much broader view of program behavior than the runtime mechanism just mentioned. For example, the compiler can detect occurrences of branch instructions well before a runtime mechanism can. With the ability to correctly predict the cache blocks to prefetch, compiler algorithms offer a potentially large performance enhancement capability.

Again, the smaller reward for compiler-based cache block prefetching in the silicon environment has limited the motivation for developing sophisticated compiler algorithms. In GaAs processor implementations, however, increased potential benefits encourage algorithm advances to exploit this compiler optimization opportunity.

Cache prefetching: compiler algorithms. While it is possible to allow the software to completely manage the cache in the same way that it manages its registers, such a situation is unlikely to be completely acceptable since a well-understood source of parallelism may be forfeited in the process. Further, the amount of process state that must be saved and restored at a context switch would be greatly increased. Thus, caches will probably continue to support primitive demand policies such as LRU. However, a compiler armed with trace probabilities could likely do a superior job to such crude policies as "fetch $i + 1$". At the entry to any basic block of code, the compiler would insert cache management instructions to ensure that successive cache frames are available as needed. Additionally, the compiler could ensure that the cache frames, where likely successor blocks are situated, fall in different cache frames, compared to the last few frames of the current block, in order to be able to prefetch these as well. Thus, program addresses could be assigned by picking likely traces through the program and ensuring that addresses likely to be executed in the same time frame are allocated in different cache sets. As a special case, prefetching across subroutine boundaries should be relatively straightforward, particularly if cache set sizes greater than one are supported. As on the 801, special instructions should be provided for prefetching; the ability to prefetch several consecutive blocks simultaneously could be useful. However, high interrupt densities might reduce the positive effects of this process.

Similar methods could be applied to data frames. A very important consequence of moving the prefetching to software instead of hardware is that the number of incorrect prefetches should be greatly decreased. For example, several authors have noted that branches occur very often in compiled code. Thus, the "fetch $i + 1$" strategy will end up fetching a great many frames that are not utilized. For GaAs caches, this will mean that a reasonable number of frames are discarded before the end of their useful lifetimes. Another important consideration is that a software-based solution for data prefetching can take array strides into account, whereas this is not possible with any simple implementation of the "fetch $i + 1$" method.

As before, the historic assumptions for cache environments have created a situation in which little work has been done in this area. Our opinion is that instruction prefetching may likely result in excellent performance improvements, especially when the prefetch instructions are placed where No-Ops would have been. No experimental validation of these opinions has yet surfaced.

Main memory lifetime maximization and prefetching: compilation candidate. The size of the main memory of computer systems has increased enormously in the last several years as silicon technology has continued to develop. The main memory for a GaAs processor will very likely consist of silicon memory parts for at least two reasons. First, because of the much lower density of GaAs parts, an enormous number would be required in order to implement a large memory. The propagation delay between the processor and furthest memory chips would be very large, especially if they are on separate boards. Therefore, the access delay for a GaAs main memory would probably not be significantly better than for a silicon main memory. Second, the large cost of such a great number of relatively expensive GaAs chips would be prohibitive for all but the most demanding applications.

In some applications requiring the capabilities of a GaAs processor, there may be no need for a backing store memory such as a magnetic disk. However, in those applications that do use a backing store, the cost of accessing it is very high. Magnetic disk access typically requires several milliseconds; therefore, a GaAs processor would waste a significant amount of time waiting for disk accesses to complete, or perhaps lose performance because of frequent context switching overhead. Minimizing the number of disk accesses is certainly important for a silicon processor system, but is more important for a system that hopes to exploit the speed advantages of a GaAs processor.

Systems utilizing backing store memories generally transfer large blocks of data between the backing store and main memory. These blocks are usually referred to as either pages or segments. Pages are of fixed size, while segments correspond to logical entities within high-level language programs, such as procedures or data structures, and are of variable size. Main memory then is divided into pages, segments, or perhaps a combination of the two.

Paralleling the previous discussion of cache memories, what we desire here are compilation techniques that decrease the frequency of backing store access or, alternatively, that increase the reusability of data in main memory (another approach is to try to decrease the negative effects of backing store access). There are two approaches, which are similar in their basic goal, but different in the algorithms to be employed.

In the first approach, the compiler restructures instructions and data to increase the effectiveness of the runtime page/segment replacement policy. The compiler attempts to place into the same page, or set of pages, all the information that will be used within nearby intervals of time.

In the second approach, the compiler selectively overrides the runtime page/segment replacement policy when it discovers more effective replacement strategies. For reasons noted in the previous section, the compiler can be expected to implement a better replacement policy than a runtime mechanism can.

Note that the above two approaches can be combined, which has been done in some systems.

Memory requests requiring backing store access, for example, magnetic disk, can penalize a GaAs processor severely. Instead of using methods for keeping useful data in main memory, there are compiler-based techniques for loading information into main memory before the processor requires it.

Main memory runtime prefetch strategies must be very simple for the same reason discussed for cache runtime prefetch techniques. However, because the compiler can sometimes predict the usage of instructions and data, it seems to offer the potential for a highly successful prefetch mechanism. A compiler-based algorithm may be used for either a paged or segmented memory. For example, if a procedure is to be eventually called from within the currently executing procedure, the instructions for the new procedure may be prefetched. The effectiveness of this approach is severely limited by the extremely long seek times and access latencies of backing stores. Because context switches are normally performed when a page/segment fault is encountered, a prefetch algorithm is less profitable here than in the case of cache misses. Nevertheless, the fast instruction cycle times of GaAs processors create a higher potential performance enhancement if adequate compile-time algorithms could be found.

Main memory lifetime maximization and prefetching: compiler algorithms. This potentially significant research area has been essentially abandoned in recent years. As memory sizes have increased, the notion that virtual memory systems utilizing demand paging and simple runtime replacement policies has become firmly rooted. Just as main memory caches have decreased the apparent access time of main memory, so too has disk caching been employed to reduce the effective access time of disk memories. Thus, the environment has been that there was no payoff for techniques involving program restructuring.

Thus, the problems and solution possibilities offered here have been essentially ignored for a decade. But, the new programs in GaAs may provide an impetus for renewed research, and Hatfield and Gerald,[26] Hatfield,[27] Smith,[28] Ferrari,[29] and Trivedi[30] are elements of a good starter set of references in this area.

Multilevel cacheless memory systems: compilation candidate. As discussed earlier, cache memories of small capacity greatly improve computer system performance because they successfully exploit temporal and spatial localities of reference. The standard caching mechanism is implemented in hardware within the memory system. However, a hardware caching mechanism has two characteristics that reduce its desirability for implementation in a GaAs processor system. First, cache memories require a significant amount of hardware overhead for their implementation. This extra hardware may introduce signal propagation delay problems because it causes other hardware elements to be located farther from the processor, perhaps even to another board. Second, caches generally add a delay to the memory access time to determine whether the desired block is present in the cache, even when a

translation lookaside buffer is used. This delay may be effectively eliminated if it is implemented as a stage in a memory pipeline. Yet this adds another instruction to the branch and load fill-in delays and is, therefore, not desirable either.

Registers are advantageous in that they require no caching overhead. Extending the register file concept to main memory may prove to be advantageous in a GaAs processor system, and we will now describe some of the advantages of this technique.

First of all, just as registers are accessed directly through their physical address, so too are the main memory locations in a cacheless system; therefore, a logical-to-physical address translation is not required for main memory accesses.

Extending the register file concept to main memory may prove to be advantageous in a GaAs processor system.

The cacheless memory system exploits the spatial and temporal localities of reference in the same manner as a cache-based system. The major difference is that the cacheless memory system with the same hardware complexity as a cache-based system will have more of its hardware devoted to instruction and data storage.

Finally, the cacheless memory system requires the compiler to explicitly load instructions and data into main memory in the same manner that a conventional compiler must load data into the register file of a conventional processor. A cacheless memory system allows the compiler to perform load fill-in on these loads. This is in contrast to a hardware-imposed pipeline suspension when a cache miss occurs in a cache-based system.

The cacheless memory system concept requires a sophisticated compiler in order to take advantage of the additional opportunities for optimization, as well as to implement the replacement policy.

Multilevel cacheless memory systems: compiler algorithms. While we are not aware of any ongoing research in this area, there are essentially two methods that could be employed here, utilizing existing algorithms and knowledge. Both of these techniques attempt to map the problem onto the register allocation problem statically. The first approach would operate in

the manner of naive but not trivial register allocators that assign the most frequently used items in a program fragment (say, a procedure) to permanent locations in the fast memory and use the rest of the faster memory as a buffer for the rest of the memory locations. If the faster memory were large, the overhead of the spilling and reloading operations could be managed. Such an algorithm would be simple to implement and would be very effective if the code being executed changed very slowly. Data access within a program beyond what could be held in a reasonable register file does not seem to be accessed along nearly so regular patterns. For many situations, the program would be better off just accessing the data from the slower memory without the overhead of first fetching it into the fast memory.

A second alternative (and others are possible) is to use a more sophisticated algorithm such as the graph coloring algorithm mentioned earlier to find a reasonable mapping. The code would be divided into frames. Frames would be said to interfere if they need to be in fast memory at the same time for fast execution. Again, graph coloring could be used to find an appropriate static mapping between the program frames and physical frames in the fast memory. The compiler then adds code to ensure that frames are in memory before they are executed. This technique could also be applied to moderate-size data sets, that is, the size of an activation record. However, for large data sets (i.e., the atoms in a Lisp program) the computation would not be feasible.

Finally, dynamic techniques could also be employed. However, we are not aware of any ongoing research in this area.

Memory-initiated instruction prefetching: compilation candidate. Instruction fetching and instruction execution are fairly independent operations. Instruction fetching is mainly a memory system function, with some processor participation, while instruction execution is a processor responsibility. Because it makes sense in a GaAs-type environment, where communication costs are large, to perform locally as much work as possible, it may be useful to move the instruction fetching mechanism local to the main memory, when possible. A similar approach was studied in Patterson et al.[31]

An instruction memory system has all the information necessary to calculate the address of the next instruction (program counter) to be executed, independently of the processor in most cases. In sequential execution, the PC is simply the current PC incremented by one. On unconditional branches, the memory system can perform the destination address calculation, if a PC-plus-displacement operation is used. On conditional branches, however, the memory system must rely on help from the compiler to better decide which instruction to fetch. The compiler can indicate its choice by setting a bit in the instruction. However, it is not until the processor has completed the condition evaluation that the memory system knows whether it has fetched correctly.

The advantage of such an approach, beyond the benefits of parallel address calculations, is that it eliminates the delay for propagation of the address from the processor to memory. This delay may represent one entire pipeline stage in a GaAs processor.

Memory-initiated instruction prefetching: compiler algorithms. We have assumed throughout that the compiler is capable of determining appropriate branch probabilities for a program (even though this may be quite difficult). Thus, having the compiler set a bit in the instruction to predict the branch direction is well within current technology. Besides this, and filling with instructions during the branch fill for conditional branches, the compiler can be of little additional benefit here.

Arithmetic. The use of low-transistor-count processors requires the implementation of hardware-intensive arithmetic units external to the processor chip. One such candidate for implementation into an arithmetic coprocessor is the multiplication function. Other candidates that may be considered include floating-point hardware, etc.

Complex arithmetic delay fill-in: compilation candidate. The use of low-transistor-count processors requires the implementation of hardware-intensive arithmetic units external to the processor chip. One such candidate for implementation into an arithmetic coprocessor is the multiplication function. Other candidates that may be considered include floating-point hardware, etc. The following discussion applies to all these cases.

One problem with coprocessors is the long latency involved in providing the processor with the result after the proces-

sor requests it. Compilation techniques may be used to reduce the negative consequences of such long latencies.

The compiler-derived benefits here are much the same as for the load delay fill-in solution. In both cases the compiler attempts to keep the processor data path busy at the same time that a parallel resource is active. However, restrictions related to the fill-in contents (instructions available for fill in) are different. In a GaAs processor implementation, the benefits derived are very substantial. First of all, as indicated earlier, the limited transistor count of GaAs almost certainly dictates that some type of coprocessor will be implemented. Secondly, the high penalty of off-chip communication means that a large potential performance gain will be achieved through a sophisticated compiler implementation.

As in the case for both the branch fill-in and data load fill-in optimizations described earlier, current compiler algorithms for performing arithmetic delay fill-in are ineffective for the longer latencies presented by a GaAs processor. Compiler algorithm advances are necessary for a greatly improved fill-in capability. Note that similar algorithms can be applied to I/O.

Note also that multiple coprocessors associated with a single CPU and running multiple job streams could result in a good utilization of the CPU's computational capability.

Complex arithmetic delay fill-in: compiler algorithms. There are actually two problems here. In one, the delays involved are on the same order as that for a memory load, or even a little longer. In the other, delays an order of magnitude worse than a memory load are encountered. In the first case, the methods presented in discussing how to deal with timing hazards are quite adequate. For example, an on-chip, off-data-path serial multiplier might have a delay of five cycles. It is straightforward to deal with such delays.

Conversely, a floating-point coprocessor chip might have a delay of 140 cycles for an operation such as floating-point divide. In such cases, one would like to attempt to overlap the computation with as much of another part of the program as possible. As was pointed out earlier, this type of arrangement is beyond the scope of the current global reorganization algorithms, both because of the long resource utilization requirements and because of the fact

that the current techniques cannot account for the delay time utilized by loops. Much more work in this area is needed.

As a last resort, the floating-point coprocessor in the above example could be treated exactly like an I/O device, and the processor's attention could be switched to another process when such operations are initiated.

Strength reduction: compilation candidate. GaAs processor systems lose much of their performance advantage over silicon systems when performing arithmetic operations outside of the central processor. In fact, using early GaAs technology, a GaAs processor may achieve a 5:1 speedup over a silicon processor, yet a GaAs arithmetic coprocessor only experiences a 2:1 speedup.[32]

There are two reasons for the relatively poor performance of a GaAs arithmetic coprocessor. First, the communication necessary to perform a coprocessor function requires more time, in terms of instruction cycles, for a GaAs processor. Second, the severe transistor and area limitations typical for GaAs restrict arithmetic function designs to those utilizing iterative approaches rather than parallel approaches.

In order to achieve maximal speedup through the use of GaAs technology, the frequency of complex operation execution should be minimized. There are techniques for reducing the frequency of complex arithmetic operations.

Strength reduction: compiler algorithms. Reduction in strength is achieved by compilers in essentially three ways.

The first way is to do a special case analysis on the operands of any particular operation to determine if a cheaper implementation is available. Typical examples of this include adding instead of multiplying by two (or three), right-shifting instead of dividing, etc.

The second method is the substitution of addition for multiplications when the multiplications are found in a loop and one of the operands is proportional to the loop index. These are standard compiler fare and the appropriate algorithms are found in Aho and Ullman.[21]

The third technique for achieving a reduction in strength is by caching. Examples of this include the use of displays for stack frame offsets, and the use of marginal index vectors. In each case, a relatively lengthy computation is replaced by a memory reference. For example, a marginal index converts multiplications into memory references. In the case of a GaAs processor, neither memory nor multiplications are cheap; thus, this type of optimization must be used with great care.

Instruction format. An appropriate choice of instruction format will enable the employment of different instruction packing schemes. Instruction packing effectively increases the memory bandwidth, which is so desirable in GaAs systems. On the other side, it imposes new challenges for compiler writers.

Among a variety of different approaches to instruction packing, we have chosen two to discuss here. We refer to them as MIPS-style packing,[12,14] and transputer-style packing.[33] In the first case, two instructions with short or no immediate fields are packed together under the condition that no pipeline conflicts will be created. In the second case, all instructions are of the same 8-bit length, and four of them can be packed together. In both cases, 32-bit units are fetched from the main memory at one time.

MIPS-style packing: compilation candidate. This type of packing is more efficient; that is, more instructions could be packed if the instruction format has shorter immediate fields. However, shorter immediate fields pose certain constraints to be overcome by the compiler. Constraints are even more severe if we insist on single-word instructions, which is especially important in GaAs systems.

MIPS-style packing: compiler algorithms. The ability to pack multiple instructions into a single word complicates the model of instructions significantly, but has surprisingly little effect on the required reorganization algorithm (in silicon systems). What actually happens is that an instruction is considered to have several "versions," each with its own resource utilization and read/write delays.

With these simple additions, it is clear how the reorganization algorithms must be modified. First, when we are trying to arrive at a set of available candidates, we must check to see if any version of an instruction fulfills the current resource utilization constraints. Next, we must use the write delay of the version actually scheduled to determine when data dependency successors become data available. Last, we must check to ensure that the read delay of a version under consideration is

truly sufficient to allow the data to be passed. These additional constraints are easily supported within the general context of the reorganization algorithm presented earlier. A formal presentation of all the details is found in Linn.[18]

Transputer-style packing: compilation candidate. This type of packing may be very appealing for GaAs systems. The instructions tend to be more primitive compared to "traditional" RISC instructions. Consequently, we expect that optimization opportunities will increase.

Transputer-style packing: compiler algorithms. Code optimization for transputer-style packing should be based on the same approaches as discussed above. Note that more primitive machine instructions potentially offer better code optimization capabilities.

Multiprocessing: compilation candidate. Communication mechanisms in multiprocessor systems deserve very special attention. Intersystem (interprocessor)

Instruction packing effectively increases the memory bandwidth, which is so desirable in GaAs systems.

---

communication delays have to be minimized and equalized through both hardware design and compiler efforts. Compile-time partitioning of complex programs, into the tasks to be associated with different processors, has different requirements in GaAs systems. Note that a combined dataflow/reduction approach may be better suited for GaAs systems than conventional control-flow approaches. This is because data are forwarded to appropriate destinations when available and not when requested. The first method is less sensitive to the relatively large intersystem delays typical of GaAs.

Multiprocessing: compiler algorithms. In systems such as these, the compiler and operating system work together to simplify the execution problems, to make execution more efficient. Graph simplification by the compiler is required to eliminate as much interprocess communications as possible. Then the task assignment and scheduling must be done with communication costs in mind, as well as the usual time and memory costs.

Compiler optimizations for a real GaAs processor

As part of RCA Corporation's deep involvement in GaAs computer system design, an optimizing compiler development effort is currently underway. As will be seen in this section, many of the optimizations presented earlier are integral components of this GaAs processor compiler.

The original development plan for the optimizing compiler was to utilize the Stanford U-CODE compiler to produce MIPS-style code and to use post-pass reorganization to eliminate the sequencing and timing hazards. The U-CODE compiler actually performs a great number of the traditional compiler optimizations mentioned here, including common subexpression elimination, code motion for loop invariant code, tree height reduction for expressions, and induction variable elimination. The decision to use this decomposition was made for commercial rather than technical reasons—the customer mandated that post-pass reorganization would be used. Thus, the benefits of pre- and post-reorganization for register allocation were lost. Also, the decision was made to utilize the same strategy as the Stanford project that had been very successful—that is, local reorganization and type-1, -2, and -3 branch optimization. Because of the longer delays involved, an extra pass was required in the reorganizer to deal with interblock write delays; interblock resource utilization was not permitted.

It is interesting to consider some of the characteristics of the prototype architecture to get a feeling for the utility of the issues discussed here. The write delay for a typical ALU instruction was three cycles for a single-length instruction, and four cycles for a double-length instruction. (Note that two different instruction lengths were needed; this is easily handled with the resource utilization mechanisms.) The branch delay is six cycles; the load delay is seven cycles.

The reorganizer has been implemented in LISP and is approximately 2500 lines in length. It was implemented in 3.5 months. After only limited testing, with hand-generated input programs, several issues have become quite clear. First, local reorganization is not sufficient to find enough independent instructions to fill over load and branch delays. Interestingly, load delays are rarely a problem, because most

Table 2. Performance statistics for RCA's 32-bit GaAs microprocessor. Pre-Op: before code optimization; Post-Op: after code optimization.

Benchmark	No-Ops (%)				Extrapolated real execution time* (Peak speed 40 MIPS)	
	Static		Dynamic			
	Pre-Op	Post-Op	Pre-Op	Post-Op	Pre-Op	Post-Op
Realmm (8 × 8)	34.8	17.7	19.1	10.2	30.93	34.16
Bubblesort (20 items)	47.1	25.1	45.1	19.9	21.09	30.35
Weight	—	14.9	—	10.1	—	34.72
Puzzle	51.4	31.1	32.5	16.3	24.21	29.29

*Assumes an infinitely large cache.

scalar references can be held in registers. For example, in the Bubblesort program, there were usually enough instructions available to fill in the load delays. In the case of branch delays, the story is quite different.

Even after keeping the whole program graph resident simultaneously (in virtual memory, naturally) so that all of type-1, -2, and -3 branch optimizations could be attempted, the program was able to fill fewer than half of the branch fill slots. A brief analysis of the program revealed that global reorganization would have filled approximately 30 percent of the ones remaining. By knowing the first six instructions of various runtime library routines and their register usage, another 30 percent could have been saved. Approximately, 15 percent of the slots could not have been filled by any of the current techniques. Last, approximately 25 percent of the slots were due to complicated branching among short blocks. The architectural solution to sequencing hazards described earlier could have been used to cover these.

Table 2 presents statistical performance data for RCA's 32-bit GaAs microprocessor, using the above described synergism methodology and the "standard" benchmarks from Gross.[14] Data from Table 2 show a relatively good performance. Still, strong research efforts are needed in the area of code optimization, in the conditions typical of GaAs technology. When analyzing data from Table 2, keep in mind that the peak speed of this microprocessor is 200 MIPS. For the GaAs machine the branch latency would be six and the load latency would be seven (with the store latency equal to zero). The peak speed of the silicon counterpart microprocessor is 40 MIPS. For comparison purposes, in the

RCA's 32-bit silicon machine,[5] the branch latency is three and the load and store latencies are also three. Both machines have an ALU latency of one.

Gallium arsenide technology is rapidly approaching VLSI levels of integration. In order to better exploit the strength of this new technology, its weaknesses must be avoided as well. Presently, we have identified the low transistor count of GaAs chips and the relatively slow off-chip environment as the principle limitations to achieving the improvement factor indicated by gate speed alone. Because GaAs does not have the transistor count capability to offset the slow off-chip environment, it must rely on the compiler writer to enable a system to present an optimum execution environment, and to make up for what the architect cannot achieve with his hardware design. Of course, the architect must provide a hardware design that lets the compiler designer make optimal use of existing hardware resources.

The optimal solution is in achieving a synergism between the hardware and the compiler ("synergism methodology"). In that case, together they achieve performance that neither of the two can achieve alone. In this article we have shown several examples of this cooperation, which we perceive as vital for the best exploitation of this new technology. We are currently working on algorithmic details necessary to improve the above strategy.

Acknowledgments

The authors are thankful to Hank Dietz, David Meyer, and Chi-Hung Chi of Purdue University and to Nancy Chen, Tom Geigel, and Robert R. McMahon of RCA for their help.

This research has been sponsored by RCA Advanced Technology Laboratories. David Fura was sponsored by NCR World's Headquarters.

References

1. H. Bierman, "Move Over, Silicon! Here Comes GaAs," *Electronics*, Vol. 58, No. 48, Dec. 2, 1985, pp. 39-44.

2. N. Toyoda et al., "A 42-ps, 2K-Gate GaAs Gate Array," *Proc. 1985 IEEE Int'l Solid-State Circuits Conf.*, Feb. 1985, pp. 206-207.

3. Y. Ishii et al., "Processing Technologies for GaAs Memory LSIs," *Proc. IEEE GaAs IC Symp.*, Boston, Oct. 1984, pp. 121-124.

4. B. K. Gilbert, "Design and Performance Trade Offs in the Use of Si VLSI and Gallium Arsenide in High Clockrate Signal Processing," *Proc. IEEE 1984 Int'l Conf. Computer Design*, Port Chester, NY, Oct. 1984, pp. 260-266.

5. C. Barney, "DARPA Eyes 100-MIPS GaAs Chip for Star Wars," *Electronics Week*, Vol. 58, No. 20, May 20, 1985, pp. 22-23.

6. W. A. Helbig, R. H. Schellack, and R. M. Zieger, "The Design and Construction of a GaAs Technology Demonstration Microprocessor," *Proc. Midcon/85*, Chicago, Sept. 1985, pp. 23/1.1-23/1.6.

7. M. Milutinovic, D. Fura, and W. Helbig, "An Introduction to GaAs Microprocessor Architecture for VLSI," *IEEE Computer*, Vol. 19, No. 3, March 1986, pp. 30-42.

8. M. Milutinovic et al., "Issues of Importance in Designing GaAs Computer Systems," *IEEE Computer*, Vol. 19, No. 10, Oct. 1986, pp. 45-57.

9. G. Nuzillat et al., "GaAs MESFET IC's for Gigabit Logic Applications," *IEEE J. Solid-State Circuits*, Vol. sc-17, No. 3, June 1982, pp. 569-584.

10. P. J. Fleming and J. J. Wallace, "How Not to Lie with Statistics: The Correct Way to Summarize Benchmark Results," *CACM*, Vol. 29, No. 3, March 1986, pp. 218-221.

11. M. G. H. Katevenis, *Reduced Instruction Set Computer Architectures for VLSI*, Report No. UCB/CSD 83/141, University of California at Berkeley, Oct. 1983.

12. J. Hennessy, "The MIPS Machine," *Digest of Papers, Spring COMPCON 82*, San Francisco, Feb. 1982, pp. 2-7.

13. G. Radin, "The 801 Minicomputer," *IBM J. R&D*, Vol. 27, No. 3, May 1983, pp. 237-245.

14. T. Gross, *Code Optimization of Pipeline Constraints*, Tech. Report No. 83-255, Stanford University, Dec. 1983.

15. M. Auslander and M. Hopkins, "An Overview of the PL.8 Compiler," *Proc. ACM SIGPLAN Symp. Compiler Construction*, Boston, June 1982, pp. 22-31.

16. J. E. Thorton, "Parallel Operation in the Control Data 6600," reprinted in Siewiorek, Bell, and Newell (eds.), *Computer Structures: Principles and Examples*, McGraw-Hill Book Company, New York, 1982.

17. D. A. Patterson, "Reduced Instruction Set Computers," *CACM*, Vol. 28, No. 1, Jan. 1985, pp. 8-21.

18. J. L. Linn, "Improved Models and Algorithms for Local Horizontal Microcode Compaction," submitted to *IEEE Trans. Computers*, 1986.

19. J. L. Linn, "Horizontal Microcode Compaction," to appear in S. Habib and S. Dasgupta (eds.), *Handbook of Microprogramming*, Van Nostrand, New York, 1986.

20. J. Hennessy, *Design of a High Performance VLSI Processor*, Tech. Report No. 236, Stanford University, Feb. 1983.

21. A. V. Aho and J. D. Ullman, *Principles of Compiler Design*, Addison-Wesley, Reading, Mass., 1977.

22. G. J. Chaitin, "Register Allocation and Spilling via Graph Coloring," *Proc. SIGPLAN '82 Symp. Compiler Construction*, Boston, June 1982, pp. 98-105.

23. P. J. Denning, "On Modeling Program Behavior," *Proc. Spring Joint Computer Conf.*, 1972, pp. 937-944.

24. J. E. Smith and J. Goodman, "A Study of Instruction Cache Organizations and Replacement Policies," *Proc. Tenth Ann. Symp. Computer Architecture*, Stockholm, June 1983, pp. 132-137.

25. K. Hwang and F. A. Briggs, *Computer Architecture and Parallel Processing*, McGraw-Hill Book Company, New York, 1984.

26. D. Hatfield and J. Gerald, "Program Restructuring for Virtual Memory," *IBM Systems J.*, Vol. 10, 1971, pp. 168-192.

27. D. Hatfield, "Experiments on Page Size, Program Access Patterns, and Virtual Memory Performance," *IBM J. R&D*, Vol. 16, No. 1, 1972, pp. 58-62.

28. A. J. Smith, "Sequential Program Prefetching in Memory Hierarchies," *IEEE Computer*, Vol. 11, No. 12, 1978, pp. 7-12.

29. D. Ferrari, "The Improvement of Program Behavior," *IEEE Computer*, Vol. 9, No. 11, 1976, pp. 39-47.

30. K. Trivedi, "Prepaging and Applications to Array Algorithms," *IEEE Trans. Computers*, C-25, Sept. 1976, pp. 915-921.

31. D. Patterson et al., "Architecture of a VLSI Instruction Cache for a RISC," *Proc. Tenth Ann. Symp. Computer Architecture*, Stockholm, June 1983, pp. 108-116.

32. W. Helbig, *Architectural Tradeoff for Hardware and Software for a RISC Type Machine*, Presentation at the Joint Chapter Meeting: IEEE MTT/ED Societies and the Computer Society, Princeton, Jan. 1986.

33. *A High-Level Language View of the T424 Instruction Set*, Inmos Technical Note #8, Inmos, Inc., 1983.

Veljko M. Milutinović is on the faculty of the School of Electrical Engineering, Purdue University. He has published over 60 technical papers, two original books, and four edited books.

Milutinović's current interests include VLSI computer architecture for GaAs, high-level language computer architecture, and artificial intelligence computer architecture. He has consulted for a number of high-tech companies and is currently involved in the industrial implementation of a 32-bit VLSI microprocessor for the GaAs technology, with responsibilities in the microarchitecture domain. Milutinović received his PhD from the University of Belgrade in 1982. He is a senior member of the IEEE and is on the EUROMICRO board of directors.

David A. Fura is a doctoral student in the School of Electrical Engineering at Purdue University. His current research activity is in the area of computer architectures for very high speed integrated circuits. His master's thesis research consisted of processsor architecture studies in support of the industrial implementation of a 32-bit GaAs microprocessor.

Fura received BSE degrees in electrical engineering and computer engineering from the University of Michigan in 1981 and the MSEE in computer engineering from Purdue in 1985. Before entering Purdue, he worked for three years as a design engineer with Texas Instruments. He is a member of IEEE and ACM.

Walter A. Helbig is a unit manager at RCA's Advanced Technology Laboratories, heading the Advanced Computation Systems unit for the System Engineering Laboratory. He joined RCA in 1952 and has been involved in the design and application of computer systems and in the construction of software support programs since. He directed the architecture design of a GaAs 32-bit RISC and is presently a consulting architect for the design of a 32-bit silicon RISC and for the construction of an 8-bit GaAs RISC technology demonstration system.

Helbig has had several years of recent experience in the area and construction of computer system hardware and software; communication security equipment design and construction; and system design, construction, and debug for an advanced passive autonomous sonar system. He has also developed video display systems and communication systems. Helbig holds a BSEE degree from the Milwaukee School of Engineering. He has 13 US patents and has authored and coauthored numerous papers. He is a senior member of the IEEE.

Joseph L. Linn has been a member of the research staff in the computer and software engineering division of the Institute for Defense Analyses since early 1986. He is currently the chair of the Technical Committee on Microprogramming of the Computer Society of the IRRR and the vice chair of SIGMICRO of the ACM.

Linn received his BS and PhD from Vanderbilt University in 1974 and 1980, respectively. Current research interests include computer architecture, compiling, programming languages, microprogramming, and, particularly, compilers for high-level microprogramming languages for interesting microarchitectures. He is a member of the IEEE, the CS/IEEE, and the ACM.

Readers may write to Milutinović at the School of Electrical Engineering, Purdue University, West Lafayette, IN 47907.

High-speed GaAs logic systems require special packaging

When designing logic systems that operate in the gigahertz range, packaging considerations are critical to proper system performance. Even your choice of pc-board material affects signal-propagation delays.

Tushar Gheewala *and* **David MacMillan**,
GigaBit Logic Inc

The first article in this series (EDN, March 22, pg 239) reviewed the increased circuit performance provided by high-speed gallium-arsenide ICs. These circuits, now becoming commercially available, promise unprecedented 100-psec gate delays and 1-nsec access times in static RAMs. Their corresponding fast rise and fall times of roughly 150 psec demand special considerations in their packaging and use. This article reviews the packaging and interconnect approaches for GaAs logic ICs, emphasizing gigabit-per-second applications.

GaAs applications fall into two major groups. The first includes communications and instrumentation, where you find clock rates of 1 to 4 GHz and relatively short logic paths. The second group of applications includes digital signal processing and very fast computing systems, which are characterized by somewhat slower clock rates (100 to 500 MHz) but longer logic paths, as in multipliers, adders or cache-memory access.

Systems in the first class generally require small- to medium-scale circuit integration, fit on small pc boards and often employ direct chip-on-board or hybrid techniques. Systems in the second class typically use more gates and thus demand large-scale integration with more I/O paths, fan-outs and large multilayer pc boards. Despite these differences, the general packaging design rules for both types are similar.

Specifically, your choice of packaging and pc-board material for high-speed GaAs systems should adhere to the following requirements:

- Reduce signal-propagation delays in proportion to the reduction in circuit delays (this is the most important requirement). To shorten these delays, reduce interconnect lengths with high wiring

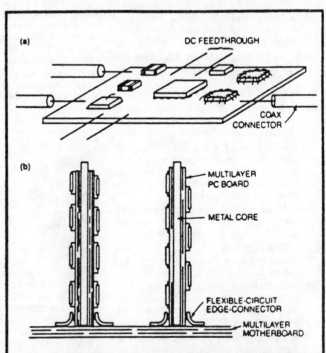

Fig 1—These two packaging schemes *for high-speed GaAs-based systems suit different classes of applications. Using RF/microwave techniques, the scheme in (a) serves communication and instrumentation systems with clock rates of 1 to 4 GHz; the scheme in (b) suits large systems with many ICs such as signal processors or computers systems.*

densities and multilayer pc-board materials. To increase signal velocity, use low-dielectric-constant materials.

- Reduce the ringing caused by transmission-line impedance mismatches and discontinuities due to pins, vias and pads. To minimize ringing, use constant-impedance signal lines to compensate for rise times. Also reduce the lengths of unterminated transmission-line sections known as stubs.
- Minimize crosstalk between signal lines. Crosstalk arises from mutual coupling. Careful signal layout and the use of multiple ground planes can solve the problem.
- Minimize power-supply disturbances through low-impedance power-supply distribution and decoupling capacitors.
- Minimize signal-rise-time degradation and attenuation. These phenomena are caused by line resistance, skin effects and dielectric losses at very high frequencies.

GaAs packages contain decoupling caps

Fig 1 shows two possible packaging schemes for high-speed systems. The scheme in (a), derived from RF/microwave methods for packaging discrete devices, uses ICs in packaged and dice forms, along with coaxial connectors, for system signal I/O. This method is limited to the first class of applications, such as fiber-optic data multiplexer/serializers or frequency synthesizers. The second method (b) suits larger systems, such as signal processors and general-purpose and scientific computers. It relies on multilayer pc-

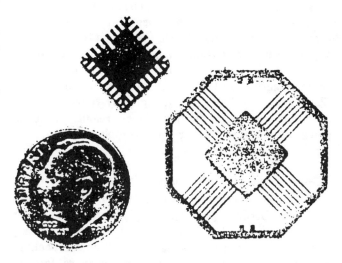

Fig 2—GaAs logic comes in leaded and leadless chip carriers. *These packages are small to minimize lead lengths, and they often contain decoupling capacitors to attenuate power disturbances.*

board materials for high-speed modules as well as mother boards. It also includes low-inductance, flexible-circuit-based edge connectors to carry signals to and from pc boards.

Both approaches use surface-mounted GaAs ICs to improve packaging density and to minimize lead inductances. These packages, illustrated in **Fig 2**, include leaded and leadless chip carriers for surface mounting. You would use the dice form for applications requiring the highest performance. When packaged,

TABLE 1—PC-BOARD MATERIAL CHARACTERISTICS (GIGABIT APPLICATIONS)

PC-BOARD MATERIAL	DIELECTRIC CONSTANT (ϵ_R)	PROPAGATION SPEED (C, IN CM/ NSEC)	LOSS FACTOR (ψ)	CONDUCTOR LAYERS (MAXIMUM)	MINIMUM WIRE PITCH (IN./MM)	VIA COVER-DOT DIAMETER (IN./MM)
THIN-FILM CERAMIC	10	9.5	0.002	2	0.002/0.05	0.010/0.25
COFIRED CERAMIC	10	9.5	0.002	30	0.015/0.38	0.015/0.38
POLYIMIDE	4	15	0.01	20	0.010/0.25	0.025/0.64
TEFLON	2.2	20	0.002	10	0.010/0.25	0.050/1.27

many GaAs ICs contain decoupling capacitors to bypass power-supply transients caused by high-speed driver switching. Furthermore, these packages are very small and contain low-dielectric-constant materials to minimize the ringing caused by package loading.

High-speed GaAs ICs also encourage the use of surface-mounted, low-inductance chip capacitors and terminating resistors. With few exceptions, system signals travel over constant-impedance lines terminated in matching load resistors. In instrumentation and communication systems, transmission-line impedance (Z_o) is generally 50Ω. In large digital systems, however, a higher characteristic impedance results in lower power dissipation, smaller power-supply transients and higher wiring densities.

PC-board materials key in gigahertz range

The time spent transmitting signals from one chip to another is becoming an increasingly significant portion of total system delay, especially in systems with many ICs. It's therefore important to minimize package delays, and to do so you must optimize several factors. You must carefully partition and place system components, minimize chip count with large-scale integration (LSI/VLSI), achieve high-density packaging with finer line widths and vias on multilayer pc boards, minimize wire lengths with improved automatic placement and wiring tools, and use low-dielectric-constant pc-board materials. The pc board's dielectric constant (ϵ_R) directly affects propagation speed, with a lower ϵ_R yielding higher speeds.

A pc-board material's wiring density isn't a simple function of its wiring pitch, via density and dielectric constant. Rather, it requires a careful analysis of crosstalk, losses and stub lengths at the desired characteristic impedance. Another important consideration in selecting pc-board materials is their skin and dielectric losses at gigahertz frequencies. These losses degrade rise and fall times of high-speed signals, especially when signals such as system clocks travel over long lines.

Table 1 summarizes the characteristics of some leading pc-board materials used in gigabit-rate GaAs-based systems. They include thin-film ceramic—which serves small systems only—and multilayer ceramic, polyimide and Teflon, all well suited to use in large systems. Glass-epoxy, although commonly used, isn't included, because it's not generally suitable at gigahertz frequencies due to its high dielectric losses. It does find use, however, in special cases where high-speed interconnects are short (ie, a few centimeters).

Teflon-based materials have the lowest dielectric constant and hence provide the fastest propagation speeds. However, the via density in Teflon isn't as good as that in polyimides or cofired ceramics, being limited by its thermoplastic nature. Even so, the dielectric loss properties of Teflon and ceramics are excellent even at frequencies to 10 GHz, which corresponds to rise and fall times of roughly 40 psec—much faster than the 150-psec times encountered in current GaAs off-chip drivers. Also note that the dielectric losses of quartz or Kevlar-reinforced polyimides are generally acceptable for GaAs systems, except at clock frequencies higher than 2 to 3 GHz. However, take care when using certain polyimides: Their dielectric losses degrade rapidly when they absorb moisture.

Another important consideration in estimating a pc-board material's wiring density is the line width necessary to obtain a specific transmission-line characteristic impedance. **Table 2** lists typical dimensions for 50, 60 and 70Ω transmission strip lines. Note that because of Teflon's low dielectric constant, you must use line widths that are wider than the available minimum to obtain the correct impedances.

With cofired ceramics, on the other hand, you must use thicker dielectric layers to avoid violating minimum-line-width rules. You should typically keep the spacing between signal lines equal to, and for ceramics even greater than, the line width needed to minimize crosstalk between adjacent lines. (There's no entry for ceramic at 70Ω because it's impractical to make strip lines that small using today's ceramic technology. In fact, using ceramic at 60Ω pushes the limits of the technology.)

Given these facts, you can now estimate a material's wiring density. To compare materials, evaluate the total length of 50Ω transmission line in centimeters that

TABLE 2— TYPICAL STRIP-LINE DIMENSIONS

CHARACTERISTIC IMPEDANCE (Z_O IN Ω)	TEFLON $\epsilon_R = 2.2$		POLYIMIDE $\epsilon_R = 4$		CERAMIC $\epsilon_R = 10$	
	W	t	W	t	W	t
50	0.016 (0.4)	0.010 (0.25)	0.0095 (0.24)	0.010 (0.25)	0.005 (0.13)	0.015 (0.38)
60	0.012 (0.31)	0.010 (0.25)	0.0065 (0.17)	0.010 (0.25)	0.003 (0.08)	0.020 (0.51)
70	0.009 (0.23)	0.010 (0.25)	0.0065 (0.17)	0.015 (0.38)	—	—

DIMENSION (IN. (MM))

Ringing arises from transmission-line mismatches, discontinuities

fits in a unit area of the material, allowing one via and cover dot for every three signal lines. Then define unit area as the square of the distance a signal travels in 1 nsec to factor in the dielectric properties of different materials. Thus, as shown in **Fig 3**,

$$\text{PACKAGE WIRING DENSITY} = \frac{N}{2} \times \frac{3c^2}{(3W + 4S + D)}, \quad (1)$$

where the final value is in centimeters per nanoseconds squared and

- N=the number of conductive layers (N is divided by 2 to allow for alternating ground and voltage planes)
- c=the velocity of signal propagation in the dielectric (in centimeters per nanosecond)
- W=the width of 50Ω strip lines (in centimeters)
- S=strip-line spacing (in centimeters)
- D=via cover-dot diameter (in centimeters).

Table 3 lists the equivalent wiring densities of 50Ω transmission lines using various packaging approaches.

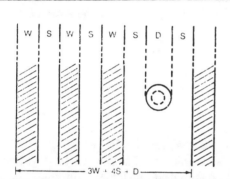

Fig 3—Use this configuration to evaluate a package's wiring density. *It corresponds to Eq 1 and represents the length of a 50Ω transmission line in centimeters per unit area, allowing one via with a cover dot for every three signal lines.*

TABLE 3— EQUIVALENT WIRING DENSITIES (CM/NSEC²)

	MULTILAYER PC-BOARD MATERIALS		
	CERAMIC	POLYIMIDE	TEFLON
50Ω WIRE LENGTH PER UNIT NORMALIZED AREA WHERE WIDTH = SPACING (S/W = 1)	31.5k	29k	14.7k
SPACING/WIDTH RATIO ADJUSTED TO MAKE COUPLING COEFFICIENT K_L, $K_C \leqslant 0.1$	19.6k (S/W = 2.5)	29k (S/W = 1)	18.3k (S/W = 0.5)
WIDTH ADJUSTED TO MAKE LOSS FACTOR $\alpha_{SK} + \alpha_D \leqslant 0.01$ AT f = 3 GHz	10.8k	29k	18.3k

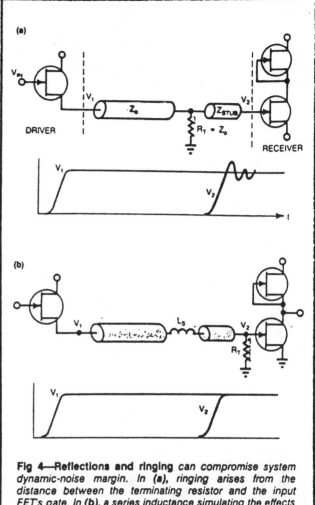

Fig 4—Reflections and ringing *can compromise system dynamic-noise margin. In (a), ringing arises from the distance between the terminating resistor and the input FET's gate. In (b), a series inductance simulating the effects of a via, pin or wire bond causes rise time to slow down.*

The first row illustrates the simple case where S=W, and it uses data from **Tables 1 and 2**. Here, multilayer cofired ceramics provide the highest wiring density for 50Ω systems. This advantage vanishes, however, when you consider crosstalk and high-frequency losses, as indicated in the table.

Watch for reflections and ringing

Ideally, all off-chip signals travel over constant-impedance transmission lines that terminate in matching resistors. In reality, however, this case rarely occurs, so you must deal with signal-line reflections and ringing that can compromise system dynamic-noise margin and cause inadvertent switching. These irregularities arise from many factors, including terminating resistors' inequality with transmission-line impedance, nonuniform transmission-line impedances, inductive vias and capacitive pads, unterminated line sections (stubs), and nonideal resistors.

Fig 4 illustrates two possible causes of signal reflec-

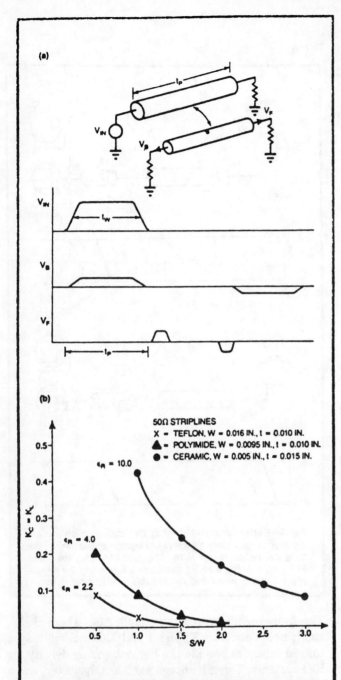

(a)

(b)

50Ω STRIPLINES
X — TEFLON, W = 0.016 IN., t = 0.010 IN.
▲ — POLYIMIDE, W = 0.0095 IN., t = 0.010 IN.
● — CERAMIC, W = 0.005 IN., t = 0.015 IN.

$\epsilon_R = 10.0$

$\epsilon_R = 4.0$

$\epsilon_R = 2.2$

Fig 5—Forward and backward crosstalk (a) *is a function of the capacitive and inductive coupling coefficients K_C and K_L, which vary with the pc-board material's dielectric constant and transmission-line configuration (b).*

down in rise time for the shunt capacitance of load devices or soldering pads.

You can determine the maximum series inductance, shunt capacitances and stub lengths that yield acceptable discontinuities from the following equations:

$$L_S \leq \frac{t_R Z_0}{3}$$

$$C_P \leq \frac{t_R}{3 Z_0}$$

$$t_{STUB} \leq \frac{t_R}{3}.$$

To minimize stub length, choose low-dielectric-constant pc-board materials. **Table 4** lists the maximum allowable stub lengths for various dielectric materials and rise times. The previous discussion also makes it clear that you should keep overall chip-carrier size less than $2t_R/3$, unless the carriers provide terminating resistors. For this reason, GaAs ICs come in small packages.

Minimizing crosstalk decreases density

Crosstalk also has considerable effect on wiring density, and you can determine the crosstalk between two long transmission lines with the equations

$$\frac{V_B}{V_S} = \frac{K_C \pm K_L}{4}$$

$$\frac{V_F}{V_S} = \frac{K_C - K_L}{2}\left(\frac{t_P}{t_R}\right),$$

where

- V_S=signal amplitude
- V_B=amplitude of backward-propagating crosstalk
- V_F=amplitude of forward-propagating crosstalk
- K_C=capacitive coupling coefficient
- K_L=inductive coupling coefficient
- t_P=propagation delay of the lines
- t_R=signal rise time.

tions and ringing. It shows waveforms at the output of an ECL-compatible GaAs source-follower driver and at the load device's input. In (a), ringing arises from the distance between the terminating resistor and the chip (limited by the chip carrier's size), resistor size and via density; (b) illustrates the rise-time degradation due to a series inductance in the transmission lines that simulates a via, pin or wire bond. You'll see similar slow-

TABLE 4—
MAXIMUM ALLOWED STUB LENGTHS

RISE TIME t_R (pSEC)	STUB LENGTH (MM)		
	CERAMIC (ϵ_R = 10)	POLYIMIDE (ϵ_R = 4)	TEFLON (ϵ_R = 2.2)
100	3	5	6.7
150	4.5	7.5	10
200	6	10	13.3

Surface-mounted GaAs devices increase density, reduce lead inductance

Fig 5a illustrates typical signal and crosstalk waveforms. You can reduce the coupling coefficients between the lines by increasing their separation or by bringing the ground plane closer to them. For a uniform dielectric medium, capacitive and inductive coupling coefficients are equal, making forward crosstalk equal to zero. However, this statement is not true when many vias are present, when the X and Y signal planes are sandwiched between a set of ground planes, or when you use composite dielectrics.

To see exactly how the capacitive and inductive coefficients, and thus crosstalk, vary with the ratio of line width and spacing, look at **Fig 5b**. It plots K_L and K_C for 50Ω strip lines (see **Table 2**) as a function of spacing/width ratio. You can keep backward crosstalk between strip lines at acceptable levels by using a spacing/width ratio greater than unity; minimize forward crosstalk by using only one wiring plane (X or Y) between a pair of ground planes, shortening line lengths and using a lower dielectric constant. **Fig 5b** also shows that you must use relatively larger spacing between signal lines for high-dielectric multilayer ceramics to keep crosstalk at an acceptable level ($K_C = K_L \le 0.1$). This results in a lower wiring density for the multilayer ceramics (see **Table 3**).

Some GaAs logic includes decoupling caps

High-speed GaAs logic circuits are very sensitive to power-supply disturbances. This fact proves especially true for supplies feeding output drivers that can switch as much as 40 mA (a 2V signal into a 50Ω load) in as little as 150 psec.

You can estimate power-supply disturbances with this formula, which uses nomenclature from **Fig 6**:

$$\Delta V = Z_{OP} \cdot I_S \cdot \frac{t_P}{t_R} = \frac{(L_P)(I_S)}{t_R}, \quad (2)$$

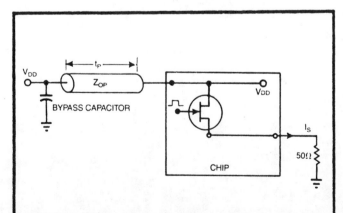

Fig 6—Use this model along with Eq 2 to estimate power-supply disturbances that occur when output drivers switch at high rates.

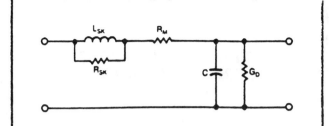

Fig 7—This transmission-line model helps you calculate the loss mechanisms that lead to signal degradation in high-speed circuits.

where Z_{OP} is the power bus's characteristic impedance, I_S is the signal amplitude, t_P is the propagation delay to the nearest power reservoir (capacitor) and t_R is the signal rise time. The $Z_{OP} \times t_P$ product also equals L_P, the power-bus inductance connecting the driver circuit to the capacitor. For ultra-high-speed GaAs circuits, limiting this product to less than a few nanohenries keeps power-supply disturbances to less than a few hundred millivolts. This fact also explains why some companies provide power-supply bypass capacitors inside GaAs packages. The output source-follower FET is designed to stay in saturation mode throughout the full range of the voltage disturbances. Thus, little of the power-supply disturbance feeds into the output signals.

Dielectrics minimize signal degradation

In any circuit, you will want to minimize signal degradation, but this problem can become acute with GaAs logic. You can avoid serious degradation for signals as high as a few gigahertz by using pc-board materials with low dielectric-loss properties, such as ceramics, Teflon or certain polyimides (**Table 1**).

Signal degradation arises primarily from three loss mechanisms: conductor series resistance (R_M), skin resistance (R_{SK}), and dielectric conductance (G_D). The model in **Fig 7** illustrates these factors.

You can examine losses in signal amplitude with the expression

$$V_{OUT} = e^{-\alpha L} \cdot V_{IN},$$

where α is the loss factor and L is the transmission-line length. Now you can get a value of α for each of the three loss mechanisms to use in that equation.

The loss factor due to series resistance is given by

$$\alpha_R = R_m / 2 \, Z_o,$$

where R_M=series resistance/centimeter and Z_o=transmission-line characteristic impedance.

The losses due to series resistance in conductor materials are generally negligible when compared with the skin and dielectric losses. You can calculate losses

PC-board wiring density requires careful evaluation of many factors

TABLE 5— TYPICAL LOSS FACTORS IN 50Ω STRIP LINES

	PC-BOARD MATERIALS		
	TUNGSTEN ON CERAMIC	COPPER ON POLYMIDE	COPPER ON TEFLON
SKIN-LOSS FACTOR α_S AT f = 3 GHz	0.02	0.006	0.003
DIELECTRIC LOSS FACTOR α_d AT f = 3 GHz	0.003	0.005–0.01	0.001

for short stub lengths will drive chip carriers toward smaller sizes and the use of low dielectric materials and tighter I/O pitch. Building on this knowldege, the final article of this series will consider some practical design cases and address the ways of interfacing these new devices to other logic families. **EDN**

due to skin resistance with the equation

$$\alpha_S = \frac{\pi}{W \, Z_0} \sqrt{\frac{f}{\sigma'}}$$

where σ=conductivity (per ohm-centimeter), f=signal frequency (in gigahertz) and W=conductor width (in centimeters).

Finally, you calculate the dielectric loss factor with the equation

$$\alpha_D = \frac{\pi\psi}{C} \cdot f,$$

where ψ=dielectric loss factor, f=frequency (in gigahertz) and c=velocity of light in the medium (in centimeters per nanosecond).

Table 5 shows typical values of skin and dielectric losses at f=3 GHz for the three pc-board materials under consideration, using the 50Ω strip-line dimensions listed in **Table 2**. With the exception of skin losses in tungsten conductors, these losses aren't very significant for lines less than 10 cm. Furthermore, to reduce skin losses when using tungsten lines on multilayer ceramics, you should keep line widths greater than the minimum allowed value. Doing so, however, adversely affects this material's wiring density, as indicated in **Table 3**.

Radical packaging changes are not needed

You see now that you can take advantage of high-speed GaAs ICs without deviating radically from existing trends in pc-board technologies, especially through the use of surface-mounted leaded and leadless chip carriers on 2-sided, multilayer boards. Also, the need

Optical Interconnections for VLSI Systems

JOSEPH W. GOODMAN, FELLOW, IEEE, FREDERICK J. LEONBERGER, SENIOR MEMBER, IEEE,
SUN-YUAN KUNG, SENIOR MEMBER, IEEE, AND RAVINDRA A. ATHALE

Invited Paper

Reprinted from *Proceedings of the IEEE*, Volume 72, Number 7, July 1984, pages 850-866. Copyright © 1984 by The Institute of Electrical and Electronics Engineers, Inc.

The combination of decreasing feature sizes and increasing chip sizes is leading to a communication crisis in the area of VLSI circuits and systems. It is anticipated that the speeds of MOS circuits will soon be limited by interconnection delays, rather than gate delays. This paper investigates the possibility of applying optical and electrooptical technologies to such interconnection problems. The origins of the communication crisis are discussed. Those aspects of electrooptic technology that are applicable to the generation, routing, and detection of light at the level of chips and boards are reviewed. Algorithmic implications of interconnections are discussed, with emphasis on the definition of a hierarchy of interconnection problems from the signal-processing area having an increasing level of complexity. One potential application of optical interconnections is to the problem of clock distribution, for which a single signal must be routed to many parts of a chip or board. More complex is the problem of supplying data interconnections via optical technology. Areas in need of future research are identified.

I. INTRODUCTION

There are several roles that optics can play in the field of computation. Best known are the well-demonstrated applications of optics to analog computation. Examples include acousto-optic spectrum analyzers, convolvers, and correlators [1], [2], as well as systems for forming images from synthetic-aperture radar data [3], [4]. Such analog approaches offer very high processing speeds, but low accuracy and limited flexibility in terms of the types of operations that can be performed. These shortcomings have led to a search for applications of optics to digital [5], [6] or other types of numerical computation [7], [8].

A digital computer or computational unit consists primarily of nonlinear devices (logic gates) in which input signals interact to produce output signals, and interconnections between such devices or groups of devices of various sizes and complexity. The nonlinear interactions required of individual computational elements are realized in optics

Manuscript received February 3, 1984.
J. W. Goodman is with the Department of Electrical Engineering, Stanford University, Stanford, CA 94305, USA.
F. J. Loenberger is with Lincoln Laboratory, Massachusetts Institute of Technology, Lexington, MA 02173, USA.
S-Y. Kung is with the Department of Electrical Engineering-Systems, University of Southern California, University Park, Los Angeles, CA 90080, USA.
R. A. Athale is with the Naval Research Laboratory, Code 6530, Washington, DC 20375, USA.

only with considerable difficulty. Various kinds of optical light valves have been utilized to realize a multitude of parallel nonlinear elements [9], [10], but the speeds at which such devices can operate are exceedingly slow by comparison with equivalent electronic elements. Recent discoveries in the area of optical bistability have generated renewed interest in the possibility of constructing optical logic gates that are even faster than their electronic counterparts, but currently the efficiency of such devices is low and the device concepts are too little explored to allow a full assessment of their potential. It seems safe to say that the construction of optical logic gates with speeds, densities, and efficiencies equaling or exceeding those of electronic gates remains problematical, although future progress is certainly possible.

While optics lags behind electronics in the realization of the needed nonlinear elements, nonetheless the horizon for electronics is not without clouds. It is generally realized that the exponential growth of semiconductor chip capabilities cannot continue indefinitely, and that indeed important limits are beginning to be felt already. These limits arise not from difficulties associated with the further reduction of gate areas and delays, but rather from the difficulties associated with interconnections as dimensions are further scaled downward and chip area continues to increase [11]–[13].

Given the above facts, it is natural to inquire as to whether optics might offer important capabilities in overcoming the interconnect problems associated with microelectronic circuits or systems. Encouragement is offered by the observation that the very property of optics that causes difficulty in realizing nonlinear elements (it is difficult to make two streams of photons interact) is precisely the property desired of an interconnect technology. Further encouragement is offered by the noted successes of fiber optics in satisfying modern communication needs on a more macroscopic scale.

The purpose of this paper is to explore the possible means by which optics might contribute to the solution of interconnect and communication problems in integrated circuits (ICs) and systems. Attention is by no means limited to fiber optics, but rather places emphasis on integrated optics and free-space interconnection techniques as well. The ideas are admittedly speculative to some degree, but an attempt is made to introduce realistic numbers wherever possible. To our knowledge there has been no previous attempt to systematically explore the area of optical interconnections in a comprehensive way.

Section II provides an overview of the current state of IC technology, with emphasis on the limitations posed by interconnect requirements. Section III provides further motivation by considering the implications of signal/image processing algorithms with respect to interconnections. Some algorithms require only local interconnects, while others fundamentally benefit from global or more flexible interconnect capabilities. Section IV reviews the current state of the art of optical technology relevant to the interconnect problem. Section V introduces a number of specific optical approaches to interconnections, at various levels, including intrachip, interchip, and interboard (machine-to-machine communication is excluded from consideration, due to the large attention it has already received by others). Finally, Section VI identifies the outstanding problems that must be solved for optical interconnections to find real application in the microelectronics field, and suggests future directions for research.

II. Overview of Integrated Circuit Technology and Interconnect Limitations

The purpose of this section is to give a brief overview of the current state of metal–oxide–semiconductor (MOS) IC devices and systems, to outline the limitations posed by the interconnect problem, and to very briefly discuss some VLSI architecture issues. The treatment is far from exhaustive, but rather focuses on aspects that are relevant to the central question addressed in this paper; namely, what role might optics play in helping to solve the interconnect problem. Emphasis here is on silicon (Si) MOS circuits, since they are the base for the vast majority of VLSI-based computational power. Comments on the use of optical interconnections in hybrid GaAs–Si circuits as well as high-speed Si bipolar and GaAs ICs are found in Sections V and VI.

A. MOS Circuits [14]

MOS circuits are typically constructed from n-channel enhancement and depletion transistors (NMOS), or n-channel and p-channel enhancement transistors (CMOS). An n-channel transistor is made in a p-type substrate, whereas a p-channel transistor is made in an n-type substrate. In an n-channel transistor, the drain and source regions are created by n-type diffusions. The gate is made of a conductor (polysilicon) over a thin oxide covering the region between the drain and source diffusions. When the voltage of the gate is raised with respect to the drain, source, and substrate voltages, electrons are attracted to the surface of the substrate. Above a certain threshold, the number of electrons is so large that they form a conducting channel between the source and the drain.

The basic MOS module is the inverter circuit. Fig. 1 shows basic NMOS and CMOS inverter circuits. Usually, the transistor connected to ground is called the pulldown transistor, while the transistor connected to V_{dd} is called the pullup transistor. The pullup transistor of the NMOS inverter is a depletion-mode transistor, i.e., it is always on. The pullup transistor of the CMOS inverter is a p-channel enhancement-type; it will be on only when the voltage at

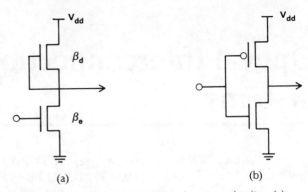

Fig. 1. Basic NMOS and CMOS inverter circuits. (a) NMOS-depletion load static inverter. (b) CMOS static inverter.

the gate is low with respect to the voltages at the drain and source. When the inverters are properly designed, their outputs can be used to drive the input of the next inverter stage.

A major difference between NMOS and CMOS is the power dissipated. A CMOS inverter draws power only in a transient condition, due to the fact that normally only one of the transistors is on. An NMOS inverter, on the other hand, draws power whenever the pulldown transistor is conducting. One way of alleviating this problem is to use dynamic logic, which is however more difficult to design and requires more area. Consequently, CMOS is in general preferable to NMOS.

B. Integrating Circuits on a Chip

A strong point of VLSI is the availability in the near future of a *hierarchical* and *multilevel* design method and the associated software packages. Such approaches are imperative due to the extremely large (> 100 000) numbers of MOS gates per chip in current technology. Usually four description levels are considered: 1) architectural, 2) register transfer, 3) logic/circuit, and 4) layout. An upper level description should be an elegant and powerful abstraction of the more detailed implementation at the lower level. For instance a control unit can be simply a box at the architectural level, one or more finite-state machines (FSM) at the register transfer level, an MOS programmable logic array (PLA) circuit description at the circuit level, and a collection of rectangles at the layout level. At each of the description levels the cells are hierarchically specified to decrease the complexity of the description. In order to reduce the design costs, a modular design approach is used; it is often less expensive to implement a general module that can be used in a number of different places than to implement a specific module that can be used only once.

The actual process of designing the layout of a VLSI chip is fairly well supported at the moment. Existing interactive layout editors and design rule checkers relieve the designer from most of the tedious work of specifying and checking the layout. An important aid in specifying the layout of a VLSI circuit is the so-called "stick diagram" [14]. A stick diagram specifies the topology of the circuit, i.e., the relative positions of the transistors and their interconnections. In a stick diagram the transistors are symbolically depicted as the crossing of polysilicon and diffusion lines. A stick diagram adequately models the functional behavior (i.e., the logic gates and their interconnections) of the circuit. However, it does not allow the specification of certain capacitive effects, such as bootstrapping.

At the circuit level, we decompose the circuit into three major types of building blocks. The basic *memory* module is the one bit register cell; the basic *logic* module is the AND-OR-INVERT gate, and the basic *arithmetic* module is the full adder. Fundamentally, a VLSI circuit consists of these three types of modules. A somewhat special (but widely used) logic module is the PLA. A PLA can be used to implement any set of Boolean equations, and if combined with a state register, can even implement a complete FSM. A PLA can be generated directly from a register transfer level specification. In general, with the increasing use of high-level design aids, we see more and more programs that are able to synthesize large portions of a VLSI circuit from a high-level (register transfer) specification.

The building block approach, described above, when combined with high-level tools such as silicon compilers/assemblers, gives the VLSI designer the flexibility and modularity needed to cope with the ever increasing complexity of VLSI design.

C. Effects of Scaling on Device and Interconnection Delays

The exponential growth of IC complexity and capabilities experienced since the birth of the industry has been caused by a combination of scaling down of the minimum feature size achievable, and a scaling up of the maximum chip size, both subject to the constraint of reasonable yield. The scaling process has many beneficial effects, but also eventually causes difficulties if combined with "stuffing," i.e., the addition of circuitry in order to realize more complex circuits in the same area of silicon that was used before scaling [15]. Here we wish to briefly discuss the good and bad effects of scaling.

We will assume that all the dimensions, as well as the voltages and currents on the chip, are scaled down by a factor α (an α greater than one implies that sizes or levels are shrinking). Consider first the effects of device scaling. Obviously, when scaling down the linear dimensions of a transistor by α, the number of transistors that can be placed on a chip of given size scales up by α^2. In addition, the power dissipation per transistor decreases by a factor α [16], due to the fact that both the threshold voltage and the supply voltage are scaled down by α. Finally, we note that the switching delay of a transistor is scaled down by α, due to the fact that the channel length is decreased by a factor α.

Scaling also affects the interconnections between devices. Fig. 2 depicts the effect of scaling down a conductor

by a factor α. Since the cross-sectional area of the conductor is decreased by a factor α^2, the resistance per unit length will increase by a similar factor. If the length of the conductor is scaled by α (as simple scaling implies), then the net increase of resistance is in proportion to α. At the same time, scaling implies changes of the capacitance of the interconnection. Regarding the conductor as one plate of a parallel-plate capacitor, scaling down of both linear dimensions of the plate by α implies a decrease of the capacitance by α^2. However, scaling down also implies a decrease by α of the thickness of the oxide insulating layer separating the plates of the capacitor. Hence the capacitance of a fixed interconnection scales down by α. We see the scaling up of resistance and down of capacitance exactly cancel, leaving the RC time constant and the interconnect delay unchanged.

It is well-recognized in the IC literature that the scaling laws outlined above will eventually pose serious problems for the VLSI industry [11]-[13], [17]-[19]. First, it is clear that since gate delays decrease with scaling while interconnect delays remain constant with scaling, eventually the speed at which a circuit can operate is dominated by interconnect delays rather than device delays. However, the situation is actually somewhat worse than the above considerations imply, due to the fact that as scaling and stuffing occur, the lengths of the interconnects required do not scale down with the inverse of α, as was assumed. Rather, as the complexity of the circuit being realized increases, the distances over which interconnections must be maintained on a chip of fixed area may stay roughly constant. It has been argued from statistical considerations [20] that a good approximation to the maximum length L_{max} of interconnection required is given by

$$L_{max} = \frac{A^{1/2}}{2} \tag{1}$$

where A represents the area of the chip. Note that if in addition to scaling, chip size is increased, the interconnect problem becomes further exacerbated. As a consequence of these considerations, it has been estimated that by the late 1980s, chip speeds will be limited primarily by interconnect delays [11]. The tantalizing possibilities for bringing optics to bear on this interconnection bottleneck are prime motivating factors for the considerations of this paper.

D. Effects of Scaling on Numbers of Interconnections Required

In accord with the hierarchical nature of design, a complicated VLSI chip can be regarded as consisting of a multitude of subunits of circuitry, called "blocks," connected to form larger circuit units, called "super-blocks" [11]. As scaling proceeds, the complexity of the blocks can be made greater, and the number of blocks that can be realized in a single super-block also grows. As the number of elements in a block increases, the number of interconnections required from that block to other blocks also increases. If the assumption is made that interconnections to or from a given block must be supplied around the perimeter of that block, then the limitation imposed by the amount of available perimeter implies that the number of interconnections that can be supplied grows as the square root of the area of the block, or equivalently as the square root of the number of devices contained within the block. However, there is a

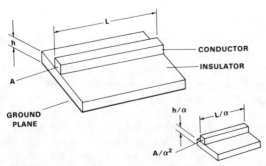

Fig. 2. Scaling of a conductor (scaling factor α).

well-known empirical relation, known as *Rent's rule*, which specifies that the number of interconnections M required for a block consisting of N devices grows as approximately the 2/3 power of N, i.e.,

$$M \approx N^{2/3}. \tag{2}$$

At the chip level, the disparity between the number of interconnections that can be realized and the number required becomes more and more severe as the number of devices within the chip grows larger through scaling and stuffing. For example, a circuit consisting of 100 000 gates requires about 2000 interconnections. For a 10 mm × 10 mm chip works out to a connection pad every 20 μm. It should be noted that Rent's rule applies only to circuits consisting of logic elements. Memory cells require fewer interconnections. In addition, it is required that each circuit be a small "random" subset of the entire logic system [13].

At the chip level, some of the limitations implied by Rent's rule can be overcome by use of metal bump technology for making interconnections possible from the interior of a chip, rather than just from the edges. Optical techniques may ultimately provide an alternate and more flexible means for providing interconnections directly to the interior of a chip.

As the number of devices realizable on a single chip grows, the assumptions underlying Rent's rule may become invalid, and the exponent associated with that rule may fall to less than 0.5. Nonetheless, from a practical point of view, connections to and from a chip are likely to remain a problem area, due to the bandwidths and driving powers required, as well as the continuing need to distribute signals to and from the interior of the chip.

E. Effects of Scaling on Electromigration

There is one further negative effect of feature size scaling that should be mentioned, namely *electromigration*. While current is scaled down inversely as α, the cross-sectional area through which that current must flow is scaled down inversely with α^2. The net result is that current density increases in proportion to α. Such an increase leads to greater electromigration effects, by which is meant the movement of conductor atoms under the influence of electron bombardments, resulting ultimately in the breaking of conductor lines. The potential of optical interconnections as a means for reducing the electromigration problem is of considerable interest here.

F. System Considerations

Arrays of identical VLSI processing elements can be organized to perform a variety of signal processing functions, as will be reviewed in the next section. Interconnections in such VLSI systems are customarily implemented in a two-dimensional circuit layout with a few crossover layers. With such technology, communication is ideally restricted to localized interconnections, since communication is very expensive in terms of area, power, and speed [14]. Dynamic interconnections are desirable for general-purpose computing and in certain signal processing applications.

The timing framework is a very critical issue in system design. There exist two different timing schemes, *globally synchronous* and *locally synchronous* approaches. In the globally synchronous scheme, a global clock network must distribute the clocking signals throughout the entire system. Clock skew associated with global clock distribution

has become an increasingly important factor in limiting achievable clock speeds. Under such circumstances the locally synchronous approach has some advantages, in that there need be no global clock, and information transfer is by mutual convenience and agreement between each processing element and its immediate neighbors. The performance of such a scheme is less affected by the scaling of technology than is the globally synchronous scheme, and it can be implemented with a simple handshaking protocol [21]. Optics may provide an alternative method for solving these synchronization problems, as discussed in greater detail in Section V.

III. ALGORITHMIC IMPLICATIONS OF INTERCONNECTS

Further motivation for considering optical interconnections is provided by algorithmic considerations. The capabilities and limitations of the interconnect technology utilized in realizing a computational or signal processing unit play a substantial role in determining the speed and flexibility of the operations that can be achieved by that unit. Different algorithms require different degrees of interconnect globality, and it is the implications of such considerations, particularly as they pertain to electronic and optical interconnections, that are the subject of this section.

To effectively exploit the special features of optical and electronic technologies, the mathematical operations needed in signal processing and computational operations must be cast in suitable algorithms. Optical signals can flow through three-dimensional space to achieve the required interconnect pattern between elements of a two-dimensional data array before executing the desired operation between them. Current VLSI-based electronic systems, on the other hand, are inherently two-dimensional in nature. While work on three-dimensional VLSI is in progress, success in this endeavor will primarily increase the density of computational elements, rather than alleviating the constraints imposed by interconnect limitations. For current VLSI technology, the interconnect paths as well as the processing elements have to share what is essentially a common plane. These topological considerations, as well as cross-talk and interconnect delay limitations, impose a restriction to nearest neighbor interconnections as being highly desirable in VLSI parallel-processing systems. The algorithmic mapping of the same mathematical operation with optical interconnects and electronic interconnects may be quite different in order to conform to the different constraints of the interconnect patterns. In subsequent discussion, we will consider four different classes of signal processing operations that are defined by the type of interconnect patterns that are needed to implement those operations on a parallel array of processors.

A. Point Operations

In this category of operations, each point in the one- or two-dimensional data array is processed completely independently. If the one-dimensional input is a time sequence, then these operations are referred to as "memoryless" operations. All the points in the input array may be processed in the same way or each could have its own independent instruction set. In either case, it is clear that once the input data array is loaded into the array of processing elements, then each element can carry out its own predetermined processing task completely independently of the rest of the elements in the array. The interconnectivity required by these operations is therefore minimum and will be apparent only while loading the data into or unloading the data from the processor array. These operations can therefore be carried out in parallel, whether interconnections are provided by optical or electronic means.

Optical interconnections have the advantage of being able to input the entire two-dimensional data array in parallel using the third dimension for data propagation. On the other hand, in an electronic parallel processor, such as the Goodyear Massively Parallel Processor (MPP) [22], the data can be input and output only along the edges of the two-dimensional array, one row/column at a time.

In those cases where the operations needed are complex, the overhead associated with the data input and output may be small compared to the computational load of the main operation, thus minimizing the need for a completely parallel input/output link between the processing element and the outside world. Examples of such operations can be found especially in the field of image processing. The value of a picture element can be transformed according to a prescribed nonlinear function in order to modify its contrast. Another example would involve correcting for spatially varying sensitivity of a two-dimensional sensor array by suitable post-processing. Addition/subtraction of matrices is yet another example of this type of operation.

B. Matrix Operations

A large number of signal and image processing algorithms can be expressed in terms of matrix operations. The multiplication of two matrices is one of the most basic operations in matrix algebra (a vector–matrix multiplication can be considered as a special case of this more general operation). Such a multiplication is described mathematically as follows:

$$C_{ij} = \sum_{k=1}^{N} A_{ik} B_{kj}, \qquad i, j = 1, \cdots, N \tag{3}$$

where A, B, and C are assumed to be $N \times N$ square matrices, for the sake of convenience. Alternatively, the output matrix C can be defined as a sum of N outer product matrices formed by multiplying column vectors of A by corresponding row vectors of B

$$C = \sum_{k=0}^{N} C^{(k)}$$

$$C_{ij}^{(k)} = A_{ik} B_{kj}, \qquad i, j = 1, \cdots, N \tag{4}$$

where the second line defines the outer product between the kth column of A and the kth row of B. It is evident from the above equations that this operation involves a high degree of interconnectivity between the elements of the input matrices and the output matrix. Thus all the elements in a given row of A and a given column of B will contribute to one element of the output matrix C. Conversely, one element of matrix A (or B) contributes to all elements of the corresponding row (or column) of matrix C.

Taking advantage of these properties, the global interconnect capabilities of optics can be exploited to build high-speed, high-throughput parallel optical processors to perform matrix multiplication [23]. On the other hand, the regular nature of the interconnectivity suggested in (3) and (4) implies that these operations can also be carried out via recursive and locally interconnected algorithms implemented with systolic architectures in VLSI [21], [24]. In such algorithms, all processors perform nearly identical tasks and each processor repeats a fixed set of tasks on sequentially available data. A recursive algorithm is said to be locally interconnected if the space indices of the data elements input to the same processor in successive recursions are separated by no more than a given limit [21]. In matrix operations, these indices are found to differ by 1, thus indicating nearest neighbor type of interconnectivity.

It can be seen from (3) and (4) that the computation involved in matrix multiplication grows as $O(N^3)$, where N is the dimension of the matrices. The use of a two-dimensional array of processing elements that perform multiplication and addition of two numbers along with a suitable nearest neighbor interconnection network can be shown to carry out the matrix multiplication in $O(N)$ time. Thus the global interconnection capability offered by optics does not provide any significant computational advantage over systems using only nearest neighbor interconnections when dealing with simple matrix multiplications.

It is worth noting that some algorithms for matrix operations, more complicated than the simple product discussed above, have been proposed that require nearest neighbor connectivity on a three-dimensional surface (e.g., a torus) [25]. Clearly, the communication problem posed by cutting such a surface for compatibility with a planar processor geometry offers opportunities for contributions by optical interconnections. Another potential role for optical interconnections is in the problem of clock distribution in a globally synchronous systolic processor (see Section VI for more detailed consideration of the clock distribution problem).

C. Fourier Transforms and Sorting

Fourier transformation and sorting are two important signal processing operations that entail global interconnections between all the elements of the input array. In other words, every element of the output array is affected by all elements of the input array, and conversely, each element of the input array affects all elements of the output array. The computations involved in the Fourier transform are complex multiplication and addition, whereas in sorting it is the comparison operation.

The discrete Fourier transform (DFT) of a one-dimensional sequence is defined by

$$X(k) = \sum_{i=0}^{N-1} x(i) W_N^{ik}, \qquad k = 0, \cdots, (N-1) \tag{5}$$

where

$$W_N^{ik} = \exp \left[-j 2\pi (ik)/N \right].$$

It can be seen that if implemented in a straightforward fashion, this operation involves computation that grows as $O(N^2)$. But the regular structure of the problem as well as the periodic nature of the W_N^{ik} suggest a more efficient algorithm, in which the computation grows as $O(N \log N)$ [26]. However, this computational savings comes at the expense of a global and more complicated interconnection pattern between the input elements than that implied by

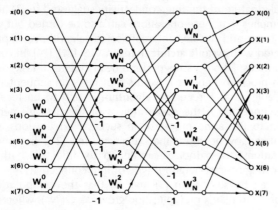

Fig. 3. Flowgraph for the FFT.

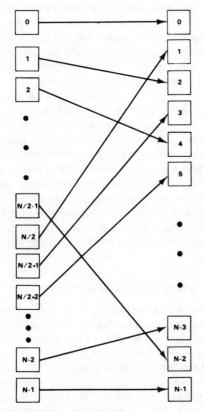

Fig. 4. Perfect shuffle interconnections.

(6). Fig. 3 shows the familiar butterfly diagram of a fast Fourier transform (FFT), which indicates that the interconnections change at different stages of the computation. This requirement for dynamic interconnections can be avoided by resorting to a fixed but global interconnect pattern known as the "perfect shuffle" and shown in Fig. 4. The perfect shuffle can be applied repeatedly at each stage of the FFT to produce the interconnect pattern required for that stage [27], presumably at a cost of extra time required to complete the interconnections.

The operation of sorting a sequence of numbers involves elementary operations of comparing two numbers and arranging them in descending order at the output. One algorithm for efficient sorting is Batcher's bitonic sort algorithm [28]. The basic principle behind this algorithm is the "divide-and-conquer" method of breaking a large problem

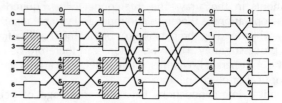

Fig. 5. Sorting network for eight items based on Batcher's bitonic sort algorithm.

into several smaller problems, and then combining their solutions at the output to generate a solution to the more general problem. The network for implementing Batcher's sort algorithm is shown in Fig. 5. Again it is seen that the interconnections between elements are global and dynamic. Since the FFT algorithm is also based on the divide-and-conquer principle, it should come as no surprise that the interconnections required for both operations are identical and hence can be generated by repeated application of the perfect shuffle [27].

Thus both of the operations discussed above belong to the class of operations requiring global and dynamic interconnection between the different elements of the input array. The regularity and structure of the different interconnect patterns leads to a simpler realization of the dynamic interconnects via repeated use of a global but fixed interconnect network (the perfect shuffle network in the case discussed). If either the fixed or the dynamic interconnect networks can be implemented easily and efficiently using optics, then a speedup of the throughput without a corresponding increase in the hardware can be achieved.

D. Space and Time Variant Operations

In image restoration and pattern recognition, one is interested in studying structures of various sizes in images, from a single point and its nearest neighbors to an image covering the entire available field. The interconnectivity between each input point and all object points is determined by the degree of globality of the operation under consideration. When the size and nature of the interconnectivity of the operation to be performed is invariant over the image space, as well as in time, then the problem is considerably simpler, and fixed optical or electronic (depending on the degree of globality required) interconnection networks can be used.

For problems encountered in restoration of images degraded by atmospheric turbulence and in processing signals obtained from a dynamic sensor array, the interconnectivity varies in space and time. Furthermore, the interconnect patterns could be data-dependent (as often is assumed in modeling the human visual system), making it impossible to foresee the interconnect requirements at different stages of processing without having foreknowledge of the input.

The computational throughput of a parallel processor implementing these types of operations will be critically affected by the availability of a dynamic and global interconnect network. Without such a capability, the processors could be idle for a significant number of cycles while the data are routed to the correct processors. A much higher degree of supervision on the part of the controller would be required, and there would be many more input/output operations to and from memory. All these considerations decrease the computational efficiency of the parallel processors and point to the importance of flexible interconnects.

E. Overview

The four classes of signal/image processing operations discussed above require varying amount of complexity on the part of the interconnect network that routes signals to processors. As the complexity increases, so does the impact of a flexible interconnect technology on the throughput of a parallel processor, whether optical or electronic. In the case of point operations, the motivation for a flexible and global interconnect capability is weak; interconnects are most important in this case when many input/output operations to the processor array are required in practice. In the second category, namely, operations involving matrix algebra, the global but fixed interconnects inherent in the operations can be converted to nearest neighbor interconnects via the recursive formulation. The computational throughput can be high when pipelining is used. Therefore, in this type of application, global interconnections will be beneficial only when the nature of the application produces frequent breaks in the pipelining of the processor. The third category of operations involves global and dynamic interconnects, which can be reduced to repeated application of a global but fixed interconnect network. If these fixed interconnects are implemented in a fast and efficient way, perhaps with the help of optics, then a high computational throughput can be achieved without excessive hardware and without a dynamic interconnect structure. The last category considered contains operations with a minimum amount of regularity and structure, along with possible data and time dependency in the interconnect requirements. A global and programmable interconnect network will be vital to achieving high throughput and high efficiency with parallel processors implementing these operations.

IV. Overview of Electrooptic Technology as it Pertains to the Interconnect Problem

The rapid growth of the fiber telecommunications industry has been in part due to the development of near-infrared optical sources, modulators, and detectors. These components are particularly attractive for solving the interconnect problem. In this section the state of the art of these components, as well as of the transmission media for directing light to specific locations, will be reviewed.

A. Light Sources, Modulators, and Detectors

The alternatives for optical sources are diode lasers and light-emitting diodes (LEDs) [29]. While much of the telecommunications effort is now directed at InP-based devices whose emission wavelengths match the 1.3–1.5-μm optimum fiber band, the 0.85-μm range of GaAs/GaAlAs emitters is of most interest here because of the wavelength sensitivity compatibility with on-chip Si detectors. Typical efficient low-threshold GaAs lasers are of the index-guided type and emit 3–15 mW with threshold currents of approximately 30 mA and differential efficiencies in the 20–30-percent range. The spectral bandwidth is of the order of 20 Å (about 0.2 percent). Typical active laser area is

500×2 μm, but packaged chips are generally wider for bonding. Such lasers are edge emitters with cleaved mirrors and emission patterns typically 10×35 degrees in width. They have projected lifetimes in the $\geq 10^5$-h range. In the laboratory, a number of techniques have been proposed for noncleaved mirrors for more compact devices. Although surface-emitting GaAs lasers have seen limited development, both distributed feedback [30] and heterointerface-mirror [31] types have been reported. These devices are to date relatively inefficient and in the latter case require cryogenic cooling.

LEDs are well developed and can be designed for edge or surface emission. In contrast to diode lasers, they are inefficient (100-mA drive) with a low power output (of the order of 1 mW) that has a broad emission pattern (Lambertian for a surface emitter) and a wide spectral range (≈ 450 Å). However, they are more stable and, in particular, less temperature sensitive than diode lasers.

To modulate these sources, either direct current modulation or external modulation can be used. Diode lasers can be large-signal modulated to rates of approximately 2 GHz with minimal pattern effects, and LEDs are generally limited to < 100-MHz modulation but have recently been reported to operate at rates up to 500 MHz [32]. These sources present dynamic resistive loads of approximately 10 Ω. For situations where driving a capacitive load is preferred, one may use external modulators. Here full on–off modulation requires approximately 4 V in a waveguide modulator for a bandwidth to about 3 GHz with a capacitance of approximately 3 pF. [33] The use of LiNbO$_3$ waveguide modulators to monitor interchip signals in VHSIC circuits has recently been reported [34].

For modulating an optical wavefront propagating through free space, a large variety of electrically addressed light modulators can be used. Recently, several devices have been proposed with drive requirements compatible with Si integrated circuitry, and hence are particularly relevant to this study. These include a LiNbO$_3$ phase modulator [35], a cantilevered beam-deflector made in Si [36], and a deformable mirror device [37]. The last two approaches, being mechanical in nature, are somewhat limited in their speeds (≈ 10 kHz) while the phase modulator needs a complicated optical system for conversion of phase modulation to intensity modulation. A recent proposal for using the electroabsorption effect in GaAs with guided or unguided optical waves has the advantage of potentially high-speed operation (≈ 1 GHz) and of direct intensity modulation [38].

In the detector area, avalanche photodiodes, p-i-n photodiodes, and photoconductors are candidate devices [29]. Avalanche devices require large biases (≈ 50 V) and are relatively temperature sensitive, and photoconductors have a relatively low impedance. Thus p-i-n photodiodes are the most attractive for interconnects. These diodes require only a few volts bias and have quantum efficiencies of approximately 70 percent. High-performance devices have been made in GaAs as well as Si. Self-scanned Si detector arrays are also well developed with scanning rates up to 40 MHz available commercially.

B. Circuits

For circuit interconnects, it is quite relevant to ask what overall transduction efficiency is obtainable using optoelectronics. Laser efficiencies for devices with uncoated mirrors can approach approximately 30 percent, but minimum power dissipation will remain in the 1-mW range, due to the 1-V diode turn-on and 1-mA current fundamentally needed for lasing [39]. Optical signals in the 0.5-mW range could produce signals from a photodiode–transimpedance preamplifier of approximately 100 mV. To achieve this signal level (at frequencies typically $\leqslant$ 100 MHz) requires at least two transistors; subsequent amplification to volt level logic states will require a few additional transistors. Thus it is not unreasonable to consider integrating these detection circuits on silicon ICs if the photodiode fabrication process can be made compatible with logic circuit fabrication. This could be more of a difficulty with MOS than with bipolar technology.

An alternative method for changing logic states is by direct optical injection into a gate. Initial results utilizing this technique have been reported for both Si [40] and GaAs [41] circuits. At present the peak optical power levels required exceed those available from the low-threshold diode lasers discussed here, but more progress in this area is anticipated.

C. Interconnect Elements

Optics is attractive for interconnects because of the inherent noninteraction of multiple photon beams passing through or near one another. Here, media to be considered include free space, optical fibers, and integrated optical waveguides. An attractive means for exploiting optical beam noninteraction is to use free-space propagation with either focused (e.g., holographic) or unfocused techniques. Holographic optical elements are fairly well developed. They may be written with visible light in dichromated gelatin or silver halide emulsions. Reflective elements with efficiencies limited only by surface reflections (i.e., with efficiencies in the high 90 percentiles) can be realized in dichromated gelatin when imaging with visible light [42]. In bleached silver halide materials, high diffraction efficiencies are hard to achieve in reflective elements due to the limited spatial frequency response of even high-resolution materials, but efficiencies of the order of 70 percent are readily achieved on transmission [43]. Comparable performance should be possible in imaging diode laser or LED emission in the near infrared. Computer-generated holograms can also be constructed, in some cases with the help of electron-beam lithography for writing the hologram. In any of these cases, the equivalent of $F/1$ optical systems can be achieved.

Due to fiber-optic systems, multimode fibers and associated components such as microoptic lenses, star couplers, and wavelength multiplexing modules are under development with some commercial availability. These components could lend themselves to signal distribution. For example, an N-port fiber star coupler can distribute a signal at one of N input ports equally to N output channels. Recently, a coupler with $N = 100$ was reported with total channel loss of 5 ± 0.05 dB over that expected for equal power division [44].

Another candidate for signal distribution is integrated optics. While most work has been reported for guides in electrooptic materials such as LiNbO$_3$ and GaAs [45], numerous workers have fabricated guides in glass or in oxide films on Si substrates. These latter guides can have quite low propagation loss ($<$ 0.1 dB/cm) [46] and passive components such as couplers and splitters can be formed. Here the work on multimode as well as single-mode devices is relevant.

The interconnection can be made changeable by inclusion of an active element in these schemes. With holographic optical elements, a tantalizing (though long-range) possibility is the incorporation of dynamic holographic materials, such as those now being studied for four-wave mixing applications. A shorter term solution might entail a bank of holographic mapping elements in conjunction with a real-time mask which selects the appropriate interconnection pattern. Some candidates for such a real-time mask are matrix-addressed liquid-crystal devices, and the matrix-addressed magnetooptic spatial light modulator [47]. Another approach for a dynamic interconnect could be the implementation of an optical crossbar switch as a special case of an optical matrix–vector multiplier [48]. Dynamic interconnects can also be obtained in the domain of guided-wave optics using integrated directional couplers in LiNbO$_3$ [49]. Cascading several such two-port switches can yield an arbitrary interconnection with high speed capabilities.

D. Hybrid and Monolithic Approaches

To discuss the use of optics in electronic interconnections raises immediately questions of materials technology, since optical sources cannot be formed from silicon. Hybrid and monolithic approaches are conceivable. In the former area, hybrid laser–amplifier circuits are available from a number of suppliers. For detection, hybrids containing a Si diode and preamplifiers are available. These hybridization techniques have to date followed conventional technological approaches to achieve several hundred-megahertz bandwidth. Although monolithic approaches can minimize parasitic capacitance for increased performance, there has been only limited work on monolithic Si photoreceivers, due to process compatibility issues and limited needs for bandwidth.

In the monolithic area, there have been limited reports of GaAs edge-emitting lasers monolithically integrated with electronics. In particular, FET drivers with lasers have been reported, including modulation up to 1 GHz [50]. Recently, a 4 : 1 multiplexer and laser were reported with speeds to 150 MHz [51]. Monolithic GaAs p-i-n diode–FET amplifiers have also been reported by several groups, and response times compatible with 500 Mbits/s have been achieved [52]. In each case, difficulties associated with process incompatibility between optoelectronic and electronic device requirements had to be overcome.

Similar efforts on both monolithic and hybrid InP-based circuits are being pursued because of the important telecommunications applications. However, these sources typically emit at 1.3 μm, a wavelength not readily detected by Si diodes. Thus this work will have most relevance to wideband fiber interconnects between machines which may be remotely located, a topic which, as previously mentioned, will not be discussed here.

An exciting topic in monolithic integration is the emerging area of heteroepitaxy. Here one attempts to grow crystalline films of one semiconductor on a dissimilar (and thus not lattice matched) crystalline substrate. The most recent relevant example for the interconnect application is the growth of GaAs on Si and the subsequent fabrication of devices in both materials on the same wafer. Initial reported growth results utilized an intervening layer of Ge to relieve part of the lattice mismatch [53], but dislocation densities were too high (10^7 cm^{-2}) to fabricate practical devices. Recently an overgrowth technique has been reported which has reduced the dislocation density to 10^3–10^4 cm^{-2} [54], so that optoelectronic device fabrication in the GaAs layers looks promising.

V. Possible Applications of Optical Interconnects

A. Introduction

Some of the difficulties expected in the further extension of integrated electronic technology to circuits and systems with ever greater complexity have been mentioned in Section II. In what respects does optics offer a potential solution to some of these problems?

Propagation of signals on metallic interconnections is governed by the basic laws of circuits containing distributed elements. The exact character of the distributed elements depends on whether interconnections are considered at the chip level or the board level. At the chip level, interconnections can be viewed as distributed and unterminated RC transmission lines [11], [18]. At the board level, the transmission lines may contain significant distributed inductance and may be terminated or unterminated. The velocity of signal propagation on such transmission lines depends on the capacitance per unit length. Thus as more and more devices having capacitive components of admittance are attached to an interconnection, the velocity of propagation decreases, and the time required for charging the line to a predetermined voltage level increases.

By way of contrast, propagation of optical signals, whether confined to waveguides or through free space, takes place at a speed that is independent of the number of components that receive those signals, namely, at the speed of light in the medium of concern. Thus we identify the first of several advantages of optical interconnects, namely the *freedom from capacitive loading effects*. Such freedom is responsible for the greater flexibility of optical interconnections with respect to fan-in and fan-out, vis-a-vis electrical interconnections.

A second advantage of optical interconnections over their electronic counterparts is their superior *immunity to mutual interference effects*. The stray capacitances that exist between proximate electrical paths introduce cross-coupling of information to a degree that increases with the bandwidth of the signals of interest. In contrast, optical interconnects suffer no such effects, although care must be exercised to assure that light scattering does not introduce a similar result (of different origin). In any case, there is no electrical coupling between the high-frequency modulations of two proximate beams of light.

A third potential advantage of optical interconnect technology lies in *freedom from planar or quasi-planar constraints*. Waveguides can pass through waveguides without significant cross-coupling (provided the angle of intersection exceeds about 10°), and free-space light beams can pass through free-space light beams without significant interaction. Such flexibility can simplify the problems associated with routing signals on a complex chip or board.

A fourth advantage to be considered lies in the potential for certain types of optical interconnections (namely, free-space focused interconnects, to be discussed in more detail shortly) to achieve *reprogramming by means of a dynamic optical interconnect component*. In principle, the interconnection pattern associated with a chip can be changed at will, by writing appropriate information to the interconnect element. Such a capability would be rather difficult to realize using conventional electronic interconnect technology.

Finally, a fifth reason for considering optical interconnections lies in the possibility (discussed in Section IV-B) of *direct injection of optical signals into electronic logic devices*. Such intimate coupling of optical signals into electronic devices, with the bypassing of separate detectors for optical-to-electronic conversion, could greatly simplify the interface between the optical interconnect and electronic device technologies, as well as offer significant speed advantages vis-a-vis purely electronic connections to the logic, provided suitable low-power approaches can be found.

For optoelectronics to be useful for VLSI interconnections, the size, efficiency, and power requirements must be compatible with IC environments. This is in fact the case, based on the previously given review of component capabilities. For example, detector areas of about 100-μm diameter with about 1 mW of incident optical power should have acceptable power dissipation and signal levels. The overall efficiency of laser drive current to detector output current can approach 20 percent and only a modest number of transistors should be needed after the detector to produce logic-level signals.

B. Classification of Optical Interconnect Problems

In order to discuss the optical interconnect issue, it is useful to describe a hierarchy of connections with some perspective on size considerations. The fundamental chip we take for example is a 10×10-mm MOS chip, having $\geqslant 300\,000$ transistors. This level of complexity is less than that of recently reported NMOS circuits, but in general, at this level of complexity the chip can be wiring dominated and the "pin-out" problem can be severe. Such chips have typically 100-μm center-to-center spacing for bond pads at the periphery and are mounted on a chip carrier with about 50-mil spacing between contacts at its outer edge.

Levels of interconnects to be considered include within a single chip, at the wafer level between undiced chips, between packaged chips on a common board, and between boards. Here it is assumed that a board will be about 1×1 ft and will contain about 100 chips. As previously mentioned, the highest level interconnect, between machines, will not be considered here.

Within this hierarchy of interconnections it is appropriate to consider several types of signal distribution. The most straightforward case is clock distribution. Here an identical signal is distributed to a large number of nodes. Since only one-way fixed communication channels are involved, the source can be a separate discrete circuit. The more general case is the distribution of data and control signals. Here more specialized and two-way links would be desirable. In addition, since various degrees of flexibility in the interconnects are desirable, both static and dynamic interconnects need to be explored. In the following sections, both clock and data distribution will be considered. For each case, the hierarchy of interconnections will be matched to the available optical technologies summarized previously.

C. The Problem of Clock Distribution

A problem that appears amenable to immediate attack using optical technology is that of clock distribution at the chip, wafer, or board level. Most (but not all) computing architectures require synchronous operation of a multitude of devices, circuits, and subsystems. Synchronism is maintained by distributing to all parts of the system a timing signal, called the clock. One of the chief difficulties encountered in designing circuits and systems for high-speed operation is the phenomenon known as "clock skew," a term which refers to the fact that different parts of the circuit or system receive the same state of the clock signal at different times. In this section we consider several possible approaches to using optics for distribution of the clock, with the aim of minimizing or eliminating clock skew. Attention is first focused on the problem of distributing the clock within a single chip. Consideration is then given to the problem at the wafer and board levels.

1. Intra-Chip Clock Distribution: The interconnections responsible for clock distribution are characterized by the facts that they must convey signals to all parts of the chip and to many different devices. These requirements imply long interconnect paths and high capacitive loading. Hence the propagation delays are large and depend on the particular configuration of devices on the chip. Here we consider methods for using optics to send the clock to various parts of the chip. It is assumed that optics is used in conjunction with electronic interconnects, in the sense that optical signals might be used to carry the clock to various major sites on the chip, from which the signals would be further distributed, on a local basis, by a conventional electronic interconnection system.

The clocks used in MOS technology are generally two-phase [14]. Presumably only one of these phases will be distributed optically, the other being generated on the chip after the detection of the optical timing signal.

A variety of optical techniques can be envisioned for accomplishing the task at hand, and therefore we devote some time to delineating these various approaches and specifying their strengths and weaknesses. The main distinction between these approaches occurs in the method used to convey light to the desired locations on the chip.

Index-guided optical interconnections: The first major category of optical interconnect techniques we refer to as "index guided." Light is assumed to be carried from some single source generating an optical signal modulated by the clock to many other sites by means of waveguides. The waveguides could be of either of two types. One type could use optical fibers for carrying the optical signals. The second type could use optical waveguides integrated on a suitable substrate.

If fibers are chosen as the interconnect technology, then the following approach, illustrated in Fig. 6, might be used. A bundle of fibers is fused together at one end, yielding a core into which light from the modulated optical source (probably a lasing diode) must be coupled. Light coupled in

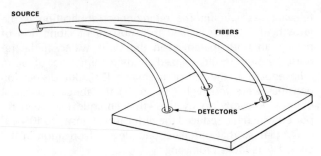

Fig. 6. Distribution of the clock by means of fibers.

at the fused end is split as the cores separate, and transmitted to the ends of each of the fibers in the bundle. Each fiber end must now be carefully located over an optical detector that will convert the optical clock to an electrical one. Alignment of the fiber and the detector might be accomplished with the help of micropositioners (analogous to a wire bonding machine), and UV-hardened epoxy could be used to hold the fiber in its proper place permanently. The difficulties associated with the fiber-optic approach stem from the alignment requirements for the fibers and detectors, and from the uniformity requirements for the fused-fiber splitter. It should also be noted that the fibers cannot be allowed to bend too much, for bends will cause radiation losses that may become severe. Lastly, we should mention that the use of fibers, and the requirements regarding allowable degrees of bending, imply that this interconnect technology will occupy a three-dimensional volume, rather than being purely planar, and this property could be a disadvantage in some applications.

If integrated optical waveguides are chosen as the interconnect technology, then the geometry might be that shown in Fig. 7. The waveguides might be formed by sputtering of

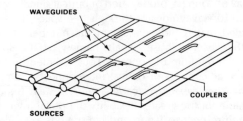

Fig. 7. Distribution of the clock by means of integrated optical waveguides.

glass onto a silicon dioxide film on the Si substrate. These guides are shown as straight in the figure, a configuration chosen again because of the large losses anticipated if this type of light guide is bent at a large angle. Optical signals must be coupled into each of the separate guides. Such signals might be generated by a single laser diode and carried to the waveguides by fibers, or separate sources might drive each of the guides, with the clock distributed to the different sources electrically. Presumably light must be coupled out of each of the straight waveguides at several sites along its length, with a detector converting the optical signal to electronic form at each such site. The difficulties associated with the waveguide approach to the problem, neglecting the bending problem which has been intentionally avoided, stem primarily from the requirement to efficiently couple into and out of the guides. Careful alignment of the sources or fibers with the integrated waveguides is required, and couplers with short lengths are desired to remove the light from the guides and place it onto the appropriate detectors. Present waveguide technology requires distributed couplers with rather large dimensions (5 μm $\times$ 1 mm) compared with the feature sizes normally thought of in electronic IC technology. A major advantage of the integrated optics distribution system lies in its planar character and the small excess volume it requires. A disadvantage is the comparatively inflexible geometry dictated by the necessity to avoid large bends of the waveguides.

Free-space optical interconnections: A second major category of optical interconnects can be referred to as "free-space" techniques. For such interconnects, the light is not guided to its destination by refractive index discontinuities, but rather by the laws that govern the propagation of light in free space. It is helpful to distinguish between two types of free-space interconnect techniques, "unfocused" and "focused."

Unfocused interconnections are established simply by broadcasting the optical signals carrying the clock to the entire electronic chip. One such approach is shown in Fig. 8. A modulated optical source is situated at a focal point of

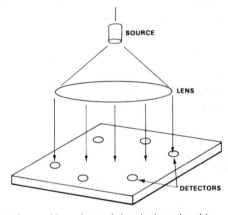

Fig. 8. Unfocused broadcast of the clock to the chip.

a lens that resides above the chip. The signal transmitted by that source is collimated by the lens, and illuminates the entire chip at normal incidence. Detectors integrated in the chip receive the optical signals with identical delays, due to the particular location of the source at the focal point of the lens. Hence in principle there is no clock skew whatever associated with such a broadcast system. However, the system is very inefficient, for only a small fraction of the optical energy falls on the photosensitive areas of the detectors, and the rest is wasted. Inefficient use of optical energy may result in requirements for the provision of extra amplification of the detected clock signals on the chip, and a concomitant loss of area for realizing the other electronic circuitry required for the functioning of the chip. Moreover, the optical energy falling on areas of the chip where it is not wanted may induce stray electronic signals that interfere with the proper operation of the chip. Therefore, it is likely that an opaque dielectric blocking layer would be needed on the chip to prevent coupling of optical signals at

places where they are not wanted. Openings in this blocking layer would be provided to allow the optical signals to reach the detectors. Alternate unfocused interconnection techniques could be imagined that use diffusers rather than a lens. Note that all such techniques require a three-dimensional volume in order to transport the signals to the desired locations.

The last category of optical interconnections is free-space "focused" interconnections, which can also be called "imaging" interconnections. For such interconnections, the optical source is actually imaged by an optical element onto a multitude of detection sites simultaneously. As indicated in Fig. 9, the required optical element can be realized by

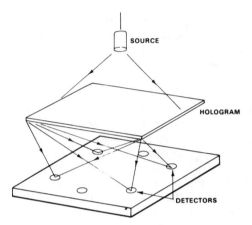

Fig. 9. Focused optical distribution of the clock using a holographic optical element.

means of a hologram, which acts as a complex grating and lens to generate focused grating components at the desired locations. The efficiency of such a scheme can obviously exceed that of the unfocused case, provided the holographic optical elements have suitable efficiency. Using dichromated gelatin as a recording material, efficiencies in excess of 99 percent can be achieved for a simple sine wave grating. When a multitude of focused spots are to be produced, the efficiency will presumably be lower, but should be well in excess of 50 percent. The flexibility of the method is great, for nearly any desired configuration of connections can be realized.

The chief disadvantage of the focused interconnect technique is the very high degree of alignment precision that must be established and maintained to assure that the focused spots are striking the appropriate places on the chip. Of course, the spots might be intentionally defocused, decreasing the efficiency of the system, but easing the alignment requirements. Thus there exists a continuum of compromises between efficiency and alignment difficulty. Fig. 10 illustrates a possible configuration that retains high efficiency but minimizes alignment problems. The imaging operation is provided by two two-element lenses, in the form of a block with a gap between the elements. A Fourier hologram can be inserted between the lenses, and it establishes the desired set of focused spots. The hologram itself consists of a series of simple sinusoidal gratings, and as such the position of the diffracted spots is invariant under simple translations of the hologram. The source is permanently fixed on the top of the upper lens block after it has been aligned with a detector at the edge of the chip,

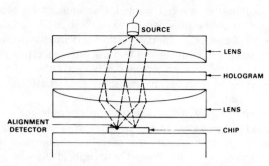

Fig. 10. Configuration for focused clock distribution that minimizes alignment problems.

thereby establishing a fixed optical axis. The only alignment required for the hologram is rotation. The position of the image spots is determined by the spatial frequencies of the gratings in the hologram, which could be established very precisely if the hologram were written, for example, by electron-beam lithography.

Focused interconnect systems, like the unfocused ones, require a three-dimensional volume above the chip. If holographic elements are used, thought must be given to the effects of using a comparatively nonmonochromatic source such as an LED. A spread of the spectrum of the source results in a spread of the focused energy, so the primary effect is to reduce the efficiency with which light can be delivered to the desired detector locations.

2. Clock Distribution at the Wafer and Board Levels: Clock distribution at the wafer and board levels is also a strong candidate as an application for optical interconnections. The primary differences in the optical requirements in the two cases derive from the different physical sizes of chips, wafers, and boards, as discussed above. At the chip and wafer levels, the discussion of the previous sections carries over essentially without change. At the board level, the physical areas are sufficiently large that the free-space and integrated optics approaches could at best be used for coverage of only a portion of an entire board. The preferred approach seems to lie with the use of optical fibers for conducting signals to remote parts of a single board, between which the greatest clock skews would otherwise be anticipated. Hierarchical schemes can also be envisioned, in which a network of fibers distributes the clock to a series of widely separated sites, from which either integrated optical waveguides or free-space connects are used to distribute these signals more locally to detectors, where the optical signals are converted to electronic form and distributed on an even more local scale to the various devices that require the clock signal.

D. Data Interconnects

The clock distribution problem discussed above is a particular case where long propagation distances are encountered. The more general case is data exchange between different components of a system. It was seen earlier that, if the process of scaling down feature size and increasing chip size is continued, then at a certain point the speed of the chip will be limited by the delay time associated with the interconnections between different components of the circuit, rather than the switching times of the components themselves. Therefore implementing the longer intercon-

nections optically could potentially enhance the performance of the chip. Communications between different chips are often limited by the number of pins available on the chips for communication with other chips. In addition, as interconnection lengths increase, the size and power requirements of the drivers on the chip also increase. Thus it becomes difficult to communicate with chips that are widely separated, and to have a large fan-out.

In addition to these hardware considerations, several important applications in signal and image processing demand much more flexible interconnections between processing elements of a VLSI-based parallel processor than electronic interconnect technology can provide. It was seen in Section III that some important classes of algorithms require global and dynamic interconnections between the elements of the processor array. Optical interconnections could make valuable contributions to these problems for all levels of integration, from one processor per chip to an entire array of processors on a single wafer.

The optical data interconnects utilize some components (the detectors and the interconnect elements) that are common with the problem of optical clock distribution. However, the conversion of signals from electronic to optical form poses much greater demands in the case of data interconnects. The different technologies available for direct modulation of sources, as well as external modulators (as reviewed in Section IV) will be particularly relevant here. As with the case of clock distribution, we discuss the problem of data interconnects at the two levels of intrachip and interchip communication.

1. Intrachip Data Communication: As a first scheme to be considered, a GaAs chip with optical sources is connected in a hybrid fashion (with conventional wire bond techniques) to a Si chip such that light is generated only along the edges of the Si chip (see Fig. 11). The sources

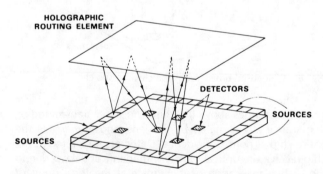

Fig. 11. Hybrid GaAs/Si approach to data communication.

could be of the edge-emitting or surface-emitting type. The optical signals are routed to the appropriate locations on the Si chip using conventional and/or holographic optical elements. The Si chip will contain detectors to receive the optical data streams generated by the sources. Since the detector–amplifier combinations can be fabricated in Si, every computational component on the Si chip could be capable of receiving data. Free-space propagation of optical signals allows a large fan-out as well as the possibility of changing the routing via a programmable two-dimensional mask, such as a reflective spatial light modulator.

In the second scheme to be considered, index-guided

structures are used for routing signals instead of free-space propagation. This scheme can be well illustrated by a specific example involving a one-dimensional parallel processor array which is interconnected by a perfect shuffle network (see Section III). The schematic diagram of the system for the case of 4 processing elements is shown in Fig. 12. The Si chip contains 4 processing elements which

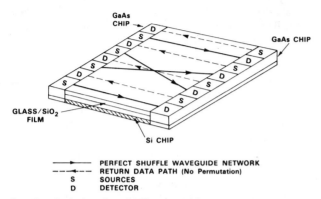

Fig. 12. Optical perfect shuffle network.

output data to the left and accept data from the right. Each processing element is associated with source–detector pairs in the GaAs chips that are mounted on both sides of the chip. Thus there exists a bidirectional optical data path for each processing element. The routing of optical data is performed by a crossing network of channel waveguides that can be formed in glass/SiO$_2$ layers grown on top of the Si chip. The waveguide network connecting the sources on the output side of the processor array (i.e., the left side) with the detectors on the input (right) side perform a perfect shuffle while the reverse optical paths correspond to a processing element connected to itself (no permutation). Using this scheme it is possible to shuffle data as many times as necessary to obtain the desired interconnect pattern before processing by the electronic part of the system. Since the sources and detectors can operate at several hundred megahertz rates (or more), and the optical interconnection delays are negligible, the permutation operation could be performed extremely rapidly. Such a processor design would be very efficient in implementing the FFT or Batcher's sorting algorithm.

An alternative approach to the same problem would use waveguides formed in a LiNbO$_3$ substrate, with active switches incorporated in the permutation network. Such a network would be programmable. A further modification might allow detection to be distributed throughout the Si chip, coupling light from LiNbO$_3$ waveguides to detectors via tapping mechanisms, such as grating couplers, evanescent wave coupling, etc.

In the third scheme to be discussed, electrical-to-optical conversion is carried out via external modulation of a uniform optical wavefront. In this scheme, the routing of optical signals is carried out via conventional and holographic optical elements and free-space propagation. The different modulation mechanisms were mentioned earlier along with their speed limitations. Fig. 13 shows the schematic diagram of this approach to optical interconnects, where the modulators are operated in a reflection mode.

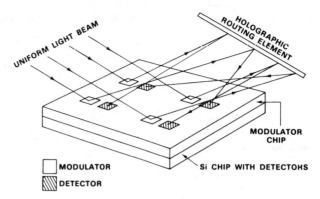

Fig. 13. Optical interconnections using external modulators operating in reflection mode.

The optical elements that perform the routing after the uniform light signals have been modulated could include a dynamic mask, thus introducing programmability in the interconnect patterns. The main advantage of using external modulators is their low power consumption and the relative ease with which components in the interior of the chip can be accessed. It should be noted that the problems encountered here in realizing the electrical-to-optical converters are somewhat similar to those encountered in the development of spatial light modulators. There are significant differences, however, in that the modulation mechanisms required for interconnect schemes need much faster response times (several megahertz versus tens of kilohertz), but need only binary (rather than analog) output (1 bit versus 10 bits).

An alternative approach to the same concept can achieve high-speed operation with low voltage levels via integrated optical modulators. As previously described, such modulators are highly asymmetric, being typically a few millimeters long and only tens of micrometers in width. Due to this shape, such an approach would make most sense when the communication distances involved are more than a few millimeters. The small widths can be exploited to fabricate a number of such modulators on a chip in order to provide one modulator for each source of data on the chip. Thus the two-dimensional arrangement of the processing elements in an array will be converted into a linear light distribution. This linear distribution can then be mapped into another linear distribution in an arbitrary fashion (including one-to-many mappings, if needed) via an optical crossbar switch, which can be realized using an optical matrix–vector multiplier, such as has been reported in the literature [48]. When the matrix mask that encodes the interconnect pattern is changeable in real time, a programmable interconnect network of the processing elements in an array is obtained. Fig. 14 shows the schematic diagram of such a system. The main limitation of this scheme will be the total number of components that can be connected this way within a chip. The theoretical maximum will be given by the number of integrated optical modulators that can be accommodated within the linear dimension of the chip. Since the routing is still performed by free-space propagation and focusing/imaging optics, the entire system will be three-dimensional, requiring large volume and a highly stable optical system. A hybrid version can also be envisioned, where the final delivery of the permuted optical data streams

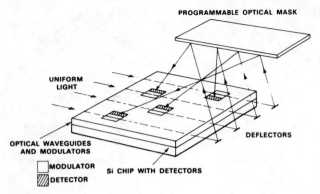

Fig. 14. Optical interconnections using integrated optical modulators.

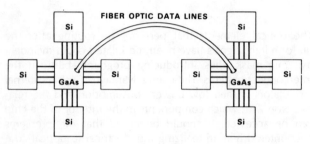

Fig. 15. Configuration with clusters of Si chips around GaAs chips, and with communication between GaAs chips via optical fibers.

to the detectors at appropriate locations on the chip can be performed with permanently bonded optical fibers.

A fourth and final approach to the data-routing problem is a monolithic one that presupposes the successful development of heteroepitaxial growth of GaAs on Si and subsequent construction of devices in both materials. The sources in the GaAs might be of the surface-emitting type. The optical routing could then be performed via free-space propagation and imaging components. The main advantage to such an approach is the optical access it provides to data sources that may be interior to the Si chip, rather than requiring that data be routed electrically to the edge of the chip before being converted into optical form.

2. Interchip Data Communication: Unlike the case of electrical interconnections, an increase in the length of optical data paths does not reduce the bandwidth of the link (all the paths of concern here are so short that optical attenuation is assumed to be insignificant). Therefore, the schemes discussed previously for intrachip communication using free-space propagation or fibers are equally applicable to interchip communication. The arguments are somewhat similar to those made for wafer- and board-level clock distribution with optics. Some advantages of this type of interchip data communication (above and beyond the potential for higher bandwidth and lower mutual interference afforded by optics) are the ability to access interior components of a chip directly and the potential for realizing programmable interconnects using real-time masks. On the other hand, optical data routing using imaging optics and free-space propagation requires careful alignment and uses the third spatial dimension, requiring a larger volume than would otherwise be the case. Therefore, optical fibers may be preferred as the communication medium at the board level.

A novel way of exploiting the large information carrying capacity of fiber optic systems would entail the use of time multiplexing. Thus several electrical connections could be replaced by a single high-speed fiber-optic line. Additional multiplexing and demultiplexing circuitry would be required on a GaAs chip. Conceptually, one can imagine a cluster of Si chips connected to a GaAs chip with short electrical connections. The GaAs chip performs the multiplexing and electrical-to-optical conversion before sending the data over a fiber-optic line to another cluster. The GaAs chip will also have detectors and demultiplexing circuits. The idea is described pictorially in Fig. 15.

VI. FUTURE DIRECTIONS

In this section our goal is to identify the most likely and profitable directions in which research on optical interconnections might move in the next few years. The view is based on the considerations discussed in previous sections, but inevitably has an element of subjectivity. These opinions should not be construed as ruling out the possibility of a "breakthrough," conceptual or practical, not foreseen in the previous discussions.

A. Clock Distribution

In many respects the problem of optical clock distribution seems to be the easiest to attack with current technology. The problem is a real and serious one. A single off-chip source is needed, and the distribution system can be as simple as global broadcast, with no focusing of light. However, presumably the extra efficiency of a focused distribution system will result in higher detected current and voltage levels, thus minimizing the need for extra amplification on the chip. The tradeoffs between optical efficiency and amplification needed on chip are interesting ones and worthy of future study.

Some experience with optically supplied clocks is needed before the benefits and drawbacks of the idea can be fully understood. Probably a combination of a macroscopic optical clock distribution feeding a collection of more local electrical distribution systems on the chip will be optimal. If unfocused broadcast is to be used, opaque overcoating layers will be needed to prevent introduction of unwanted signals at locations other than detectors. Experimentation with these ideas is badly needed.

If focused distribution systems are to be used, methods for relieving alignment problems, such as that illustrated in Fig. 10, must be developed. Further optical studies of the efficiencies of holographic optical elements in the infrared would be helpful.

B. Hybridization

Many of the proposed interconnect techniques rely on the mating of Si and GaAs chips. In some cases the GaAs provides only the optical source, but in others a more complex optoelectronic chip is needed. Initial efforts could focus on previously developed techniques for chip placement and bonding of the two dissimilar types of chip. However, to maximize the efficiency of relieving the interconnect and pin-out problems in large-scale Si circuits, the development of techniques that minimize the length of interchip interconnect lines, and in effect eliminate the bonding pads, are needed. The pads are considerably larger than the device lines, and pins on the conventional ceramic package are even larger, as described previously. Two examples of approaches that could be pursued are a metal-bump technique and a close-packed planar hybrid. In the former technique, the electrical and optoelectronic chips would be vertically mated by a series of metal posts formed on one of the circuits. This technique has been used, for example, to connect infrared detector arrays to Si chips [55]. In the latter approach, the chips could be butted up to one another and interchip metallization formed on an intervening planarizing dielectric [56]. Manufacturable versions of these technologies could allow both more interconnects to the Si and the efficient utilization of GaAs chips.

C. Monolithic Approaches

The integrating on GaAs of both optical and electrical devices is an exciting area currently in early development, and progress was summarized in Section IV-B. Progress in integrated optoelectronics will be paced by the development of GaAs ICs. If ICs with medium-scale integration or higher complexity can be fabricated with high yield, there may be strong motivation to use optics for interconnects in all-GaAs high-speed or radiation-tolerant processors.

A long-term and conceptually appealing technique for realizing optical interconnects is to grow single-crystal GaAs on Si and then form the appropriate devices in each material, thereby eliminating the need for hybridization. In addition to optoelectronic devices, GaAs electronic devices could also be formed (e.g., high-speed digital circuits for multiplexing signals to Si circuits). This technology could lend itself to many circuit configurations, including the formation of strategically located GaAs islands on a large Si wafer. To date, initial efforts have focused on materials issues, as discussed in Section IV-D. The demonstration of heteroepitaxial circuits, of course, requires the careful determination of process-compatible approaches to Si circuit formation, GaAs layer growth, and GaAs fabrication. For example, at present the GaAs growth occurs at temperatures of $\approx 680°C$, suggesting that higher temperature Si processing steps may have to occur prior to GaAs growth. This technique could, in the long run, realize in single-chip form many of the GaAs/Si hybrid approaches described earlier.

D. Perfect-Shuffle Exchange Network

The realization of a global but fixed interconnect network like the perfect shuffle with optoelectronic techniques could have a large impact on special-purpose, high-performance signal processing systems. The scheme discussed in Section V is just one possible approach. If the processing elements on the VLSI chip are not arranged in a simple linear form, as assumed in that scheme, then the use of LiNbO3 guided-wave modulators to perform the electrical-to-optical signal transduction, as shown in Fig. 14, could be used. The optical permutation network chip consisting of linear arrays of sources and detectors, as well as the passive network of optical waveguides, can then be physically dissociated from the Si chip. In this way the processing

elements could all be on one chip, or could be distributed among different chips. In any case, the components that need most development are the individual addressable arrays of laser diodes and LiNbO3 guided-wave modulators that can be directly addressed by a Si chip at high speed.

E. Electrically Addressed Optical Modulators

One of the most important elements of an optical data interconnect system is the external modulator that can operate on guided or free-space optical wavefronts and can be directly addressable by a Si IC. Although several schemes have been proposed and demonstrated, as reviewed in Section IV, special attention is needed to make these modulators compatible with VLSI circuits with respect to size, power consumption, and speed. A matrix-addressed light modulator can also find application in dynamic interconnect schemes involving real-time masks. Depending on the applications, the update rate of these masks could be significantly lower than the clock rates of the VLSI circuits. On the other hand, these masks will be required to have a rather large space–bandwidth product in order to provide high interconnect flexibility. Thus in general future work will be required in developing high-speed, low-power, and small-size modulators.

F. High-Speed ICs

The focus of this paper has been on alleviating the interconnect problem for VLSI MOS circuits which at present operate at clock rates no greater than 30 MHz. A potentially equally important area for optical interconnects may be for smaller scale circuits that operate at very high speeds (100 to 2000 MHz). Si ECL circuits are commercially available with clock rates greater than 100 MHz, and gigahertz circuits in short-gate Si MOS and GaAs MESFET technology have been demonstrated. While the gate counts of such circuits are at least 1 to 2 orders of magnitude smaller than for VLSI chips, their higher speed places severe stress on the isolation and capacitance of the interconnects. In such cases, the inherent high speed and low crosstalk of optical approaches is very appealing. While there are cases where incorporating an optimum number of gates on a chip can minimize the number of high-speed interconnects [57], optics could still play a significant role. Many of the hybridization techniques described earlier could be applied to these high-speed situations. Hybridization of optical chips with fast complex Si circuits is especially attractive due to the recent report of integration of fast CMOS circuits with bipolar circuitry [58]. This achievement could eliminate the need for scaling up the MOS devices (and thus using wafer area and potentially slowing down the devices) in order to drive the optical sources. The most appealing long-term solution for high-speed applications may be the development of all-GaAs systems, since obviously the optical devices could then be integrated, as described above.

ACKNOWLEDGMENT

This paper was the result of an Army Research Office Palantir study. These studies address the physical foundations of approaches to solutions of important technological problems with the aim of stimulating new avenues for progress toward their solution. The participants in the study consisted of the authors of this paper. S. Y. Kung served as chairman. The authors thank Dr. B. Guenther of ARO for his sponsorship and assistance. One of the authors (F. J. L.) wishes to acknowledge partial support by the Department of the Air Force.

REFERENCES

[1] *Proc. IEEE* (Special Section on Acoustooptic Signal Processing), vol. 69, no. 1, pp. 3–5, 48–118, Jan. 1981.
[2] N. J. Berg and J. N. Lee, *Acousto-Optic Signal Processing*. New York, NY: Marcel Dekker, 1983.
[3] L. J. Cutrona, E. N. Leith, L. J. Porcello, and W. E. Vivian, "On the application of coherent optical processing techniques to synthetic aperture radar," *Proc. IEEE*, vol. 54, no. 8, pp. 1026–1032, 1966.
[4] A. Kozma, E. N. Leith, and N. G. Massey, "Tilted plane optical processor," *Appl. Opt.*, vol. 11, no. 8, pp. 1766–1777, 1972.
[5] For a review of this area, see H. J. Caulfield, J. A. Neff, and W. T. Rhodes, "Optical computing: The coming revolution in optical processing," *Laser Focus*, vol. 19, no. 11, pp. 100–110, 1983.
[6] D. Psaltis, D. Casasent, D. Neft, and M. Carlotto, "Accurate numerical computation by optical convolution," *Proc. SPIE*, vol. 232, pp. 160–167, 1980.
[7] A. Huang, Y. Tsunoda, J. W. Goodman, and S. Ishihara, "Some new methods for performing residue arithmetic operations," *Appl. Opt.*, vol. 18, no. 2, pp. 160–167, 1980.
[8] C. Y. Yen and S. A. Collins, Jr., "Operation of a numerical optical processor," *Proc. SPIE*, vol. 232, pp. 160–167, 1980.
[9] A. A. Sawchuk and T. C. Strand, "Fourier optics in nonlinear signal processing," in *Applications of Optical Fourier Transforms*, H. Stark, Ed. New York, NY: Academic Press, 1982, ch. 9.
[10] C. Warde, A. M. Weiss, and A. D. Fisher, "Optical information processing characteristics of the microchannel spatial light modulator," *Appl. Opt.*, vol. 20, no. 12, pp. 2066–2074, 1981.
[11] K. C. Saraswat and F. Mohammadi, "Effect of scaling of interconnections on the time delay of VLSI circuits," *IEEE Trans. Electron Devices*, vol. ED-29, no. 4, pp. 645–650, 1982.
[12] R. W. Keyes, "Communication in computing," *Int. J. Theor. Phys.*, vol. 21, nos. 3/4, pp. 263–273, 1982.
[13] A. J. Blodgett, Jr., "Microelectronic packaging," *Sci. Amer.*, vol. 249, no. 7, pp. 86–96, 1983.
[14] C. Mead and L. Conway, *Introduction to VLSI Systems*. Reading, MA: Addison-Wesley, 1980.
[15] D. J. Kinniment, "VLSI and machine architecture," in *VLSI Architecture*, B. Randell and P. C. Treleaven, Eds. Englewood Cliffs, NJ: Prentice-Hall, 1983, pp. 24–33.
[16] F. Anceau and R. Ries, "Design strategy for VLSI," in *VLSI Architecture*, B. Randell and P. C. Treleaven, Eds. Englewood Cliffs, NJ: Prentice-Hall, 1983, pp. 128–137.
[17] R. W. Keyes, "Fundamental limits in digital information processing," *Proc. IEEE*, vol. 69, no. 2, pp. 267–278, 1981.
[18] P. M. Solomon, "A comparison of semiconductor devices for high-speed logic," *Proc. IEEE*, vol. 70, no. 5, pp. 489–509, 1982.
[19] G. W. Preston, "The very large scale integrated circuit," *Amer. Scientist*, vol. 71, no. 5, pp. 466–472, 1983.
[20] R. W. Keyes, "The evolution of digital electronics towards VLSI," *IEEE Trans. Electron Devices*, vol. ED-26, no. 4, pp. 271–278, 1979.
[21] S. Y. Kung, K. S. Arun, R. J. Gal-Ezer, and D. V. Bhaskar Rao, "Wavefront array processor; language, architecture, and applications," *IEEE Trans. Comput.* (Special Issue on Parallel and Distributed Computers), vol. C-31, no. 11, pp. 1054–1066, 1982.
[22] P. A. Gilmore, "The massively parallel processor (MPP): A

large scale SIMD processor," *Proc. SPIE*, vol. 431, pp. 166–174, 1983.
[23] R. A. Athale, "Optical matrix algebraic processors," in *Proc. 10th Int. Optical Computing Conf.*, IEEE Cat. No. 83CH1880-4, Apr. 1983, pp. 24–31.
[24] H. T. Kung, "Why systolic architectures?" *IEEE Computer*, vol. 15, no. 1, pp. 37–46, 1982.
[25] R. S. Schreiber, "On the systolic arrays of Brent, Luk, and van Loan," *Proc. SPIE*, vol. 431, pp. 72–76, 1983.
[26] A. V. Oppenheim and R. W. Schafer, *Digital Signal Processing*. Englewood Cliffs, NJ: Prentice-Hall, 1975, pp. 284–337.
[27] H. S. Stone, "Parallel processing with the perfect shuffle," *IEEE Trans. Comput.*, vol. C-20, no. 2, pp. 153–161, 1971.
[28] K. E. Batcher, "Sorting networks and their applications," in *1968 Spring Joint Comp. Conf.*, AFIPS Proc., vol. 32 (Washington, DC, 1968).
[29] See, for example, H. Kressel, *Semiconductor Devices for Optical Communications*. Berlin, Germany: Springer-Verlag, 1982.
[30] D. R. Scifres, R. D. Burnham, and W. Streifer, "Output coupling and distributed feedback utilizing substrate corrugations in double heterostructure GaAs lasers," *Appl. Phys. Lett.*, vol. 27, no. 5, 1975.
[31] K. Iga, H. Soda, T. Terakado, and S. Shimizu, "Lasing characteristics of improved GaInAsP/InP surface emitting injection lasers," in *Proc. 4th Int. Conf. on Integrated Optics and Optical Fiber Communications* (Tokyo, Japan, June 27–30, 1983), pp. 198–199.
[32] H. Grothe, G. Muller, and W. Harth, "560 Mb/s transmission experiments using 1.3 μm InGaAsp/InP LED," *Electron. Lett.*, vol. 19, no. 22, pp. 909–911, 1983.
[33] R. A. Becker, "Broad-band guided-wave electrooptic modulators," to be published in *IEEE J. Quantum Electron.*, vol. QE-20, pp. 723–727, July 1984.
[34] R. A. Boenning, V. B. Morris, and E. G. Vaerewyck, "PC board test signal extraction," presented at the 29th Int. Instrumentation Symp., Instrument Society of America, Albuquerque, NM, May 1983.
[35] R. V. Johnson, D. L. Hecht, R. A. Sprague, L. N. Flores, D. L. Steinmetz, and W. D. Turner, "Characteristics of the linear array total internal reflection (TIR) electrooptic spatial light modulator for optical information processing," *Opt. Eng.*, vol. 22, no. 6, pp. 665–674, 1983.
[36] K. E. Petersen, "Micromechanical light modulator array fabricated on silicon," *Appl. Phys. Lett.*, vol. 31, p. 521, 1977.
[37] D. R. Pape and L. J. Hornbeck, "Characteristics of the deformable mirror device for optical information processing," *Opt. Eng.*, vol. 22, no. 6, pp. 675–681, 1983.
[38] R. A. Kingston, B. E. Burke, K. B. Nichols, and F. J. Leonberger, "Spatial light modulation using electroabsorption in a GaAs charge-coupled device," *Appl. Phys. Lett.*, vol. 41, no. 5, pp. 413–415, 1982.
[39] J. N. Walpole, MIT Lincoln Laboratory.
[40] M. L. Levy, "An investigation of flaws in complex CMOS devices by a scanning photoexcitation technique," in *Proc. 15th Annu. IEEE Reliability Symp.*, pp. 44–53, 1977.
[41] R. K. Jain and D. E. Snyder, "Switching characteristics of logic gates addressed by picosecond light pulses," *IEEE J. Quantum Electron.*, vol. QE-19, no. 4, pp. 658–663, 1983.
[42] B. J. Chang, "Dichromated gelatin as a hologram storage medium," *Proc. SPIE*, vol. 177, pp. 71–81, 1979.
[43] K. Biedermann, "Silver halide photographic materials," in *Holographic Recording Materials*, H. M. Smith, Ed. Berlin, Germany: Springer-Verlag, 1977, p. 69.
[44] Y. Fujii, M. Suzuki, and J. Minowa, "A 100 input/output star coupler composed of low-loss slab waveguide," in *Proc. 4th Int. Conf. on Integrated Optics and Optical Fiber Communication*, (Tokyo, Japan, June 27–30, 1983), paper 29C2-4, pp. 342–343.
[45] See, for example, *Tech. Digest of the Topical Meeting on Guided Wave Optics* (Asilomar, CA), IEEE Cat. No. 82CH 1719-4, 1982.
[46] S. Dutta, H. E. Jackson, and J. T. Boyd, "Scattering loss reduction in ZnO optical waveguides by laser annealing," *Appl. Phys. Lett.*, vol. 39, no. 3, pp. 206–208, 1981.

[47] W. E. Ross, D. Psaltis, and R. H. Anderson, "Two-dimensional Magneto-optic spatial light modulator for signal processing," *Proc. SPIE*, vol. 341, p. 191, 1982.

[48] J. W. Goodman, A.R. Dias, and L. M. Woody, "Fully parallel, high speed incoherent optical method for performing the discrete Fourier transform," *Opt. Lett.*, vol. 2, no. 1, pp. 1–3, 1978.

[49] M. Kondo, Y. Ohta, M. Fujiwara, and M. Sakaguchi, "Integrated optical switch matrix for single-mode fiber networks," *IEEE J. Quantum Electron.*, vol. QE-18, no. 10, pp. 1759–1765, 1982.

[50] M. Kim, C. Hong, D. Kasemet, and R. Milano, "GaAlAs/GaAs integrated optoelectronic transmitter using selective MOCVD epitaxy and planar ion implantation," in *Proc. GaAs IC Symp.*, pp. 44–47, Oct. 1983.

[51] J. Carney, M. Helixal, and R. Kolby, "Gigabit optoelectronic transmitter," in *Proc. GaAs IC Symp.*, pp. 48–51, Oct. 1983.

[52] For a review, see N. Bar-Chaim, S. Margalit, A. Yariv, and I. Ury, "GaAs integrated optoelectronics," *IEEE Trans. Electron Devices*, vol. ED-29, no. 9, pp. 1372–1381, 1982.

[53] B. Y. Tsaur, M. W. Geis, J. C. C. Fan, and R. P. Gale, "Heteroepitaxy of vacuum-evaporated Ge films on single-crystal Si," *Appl. Phys. Lett.*, vol. 38, no. 10, pp. 779–781, 1981.

[54] B. Y. Tsaur, R. W. McClelland, J. C. C. Fan, R. P. Gale, J. P. Salerno, B. A. Vojak, and C. O. Bozler, "Low dislocation density GaAs epilayers grown on Ge-coated Si substrates by means of lateral epitaxial overgrowth," *Appl. Phys. Lett.*, vol. 41, no. 4, pp. 347–349, 1982.

[55] D. H. Pommerrenig, D. D. Enders, and T. E. Meinhardt, "Hybrid silicon focal plane development: an update," *Proc. SPIE*, vol. 267, pp. 23–30, 1981.

[56] A. Chu, MIT Lincoln Lab., private communication.

[57] B. Gilbert, T. Kinter, S. Hartley, and A. Firstenberg, "Exploitation of GaAs digital integrated circuits in wideband signal processing environments," in *Proc. GaAs IC Symp.*, pp. 58–61, Oct. 1983.

[58] J. Miyamoto, S. Saitoh, H. Momose, H. Shibata, K. Kanazaki, and S. Kohyama, "A 1.0 μm N-well CMOS/bipolar technology for VLSI circuits," in *Tech. Dig. Int. Electron Device Meet.*, pp. 63–66, Dec. 1983.

Analysis of Crosstalk in Very High-Speed LSI/VLSI's Using a Coupled Multiconductor MIS Microstrip Line Model

SHOUHEI SEKI AND HIDEKI HASEGAWA, MEMBER, IEEE

Abstract —Crosstalk in very high-speed LSI/VLSI's is analyzed using a coupled multiconductor metal–insulator–semiconductor (MIS) microstrip line model. Loss in the substrate is ignored for simplicity. A periodic boundary condition is used, and the mode analysis is done using the Green's function method. Effects of line length, spacing, substrate thickness, and output impedance of gates are investigated. The "lumped capacitance" approximation for interconnections is shown to be inadequate for crosstalk evaluation when the circuit speed is less than 200–300 ps in LSI circuits. The result indicates that crosstalk considerations based on a transmission-line model is very important in the design of very high-speed LSI/VLSI circuits. Provisions of adjacent shield lines are shown to be significantly effective in reducing crosstalk, but at the risk of dynamic ringing and at the sacrifice of wiring capacity. A shielded multilevel interconnect scheme is proposed for reduction of crosstalk without reduction of wiring capacity.

I. INTRODUCTION

IN ORDER TO meet the increasing demands for higher speeds in areas of high-speed computation, signal processing, data links, and related instrumentation, very high-speed integrated circuits with a propagation delay time per gate t_{pd} of below 100 ps have to be developed. In SSI/MSI integration levels, t_{pd} reaching 10-ps range has already been realized with various technologies [1]–[3]. However, as one tries to achieve high speeds in LSI/VLSI levels, difficulties are anticipated to arise from increased lengths of interconnections. The purpose of this paper is to analyze the crosstalk in the interconnection system of high-speed LSI/VLSI circuits. Delay due to interconnection is analyzed in our separate paper in this issue [4].

Previous analyses on crosstalk were based either on the "lumped capacitance" approximation [5] or on the distributed-parameter models with a limited number of conductors [6]–[9]. In this paper, interconnections are modeled as a coupled multiconductor metal–insulator–semiconductor (MIS) microstrip line system having many conductors. The present model is particularly applicable to semicustom gate arrays where many closely spaced interconnections run parallel for a long distance. Loss in the semiconductor substrate is ignored for simplicity, making the model applicable to IC's formed on semi-insulating GaAs or InP substrates or silicon-on-sapphire (SOS) substrates. A periodic boundary condition is used and this greatly simplifies

the analysis without too much loss generality. Mode capacitances evaluated using a Green's function method. Section II explains the model and mathematical formulation, and the result concerning crosstalk amplitude and its reduction is presented and discussed in Section III. Section IV gives the conclusion.

II. MODEL AND FORMULATION

A. Model and Boundary Condition

The MIS microstrip line model with n strip conductors is shown in Fig. 1(a). Interconnections are formed on a surface passivated semiconductor substrate with a metallized back. This model provides a good first-order approximation for closely spaced interconnection tracks in high-speed semicustom gate arrays, as shown in Fig. 2. For such a case, n corresponds to the track number or wiring capacity of the channel. Loss in the substrate is ignored, since a complicated situation due to the slow-wave mode propagation and mode transition takes place in the conducting substrate, as discussed in our separate paper [4].

As the boundary condition exists on both sides of the stripline system, a periodic boundary condition is adopted where it is assumed that the same n-conductor stripline system is repeated infinitely, as shown in Fig. 1(b). This is a convenient boundary condition for simplifying the problem, as often employed in solid-state physics. In the crosstalk problem, we are more interested in the interrelationship of strip conductors inside the wiring channel rather than effects of the channel boundaries which depend on the device and layout design. Thus, the periodic boundary condition is useful to provide a first-order estimate of crosstalk without going into the specific design details.

B. Normal Modes

Obviously, there exists n quasi-TEM normal modes on this stripline system. Let us consider an excitation in which the phase angle difference of voltage and current between two adjacent strip conductors is constant and equal to θ, and call such an elementary excitation the "θ-mode." Possible values of θ that satisfy the cyclic boundary condition are then given by

$$\theta = 0, \frac{2\pi}{n}, \cdots, \frac{2k\pi}{n}, \cdots, \frac{2(n-1)\pi}{n}. \tag{1}$$

Manuscript received May 22, 1984.

The authors are with the Department of Electrical Engineering, Faculty of Engineering, Hokkaido University, Sapporo, 060 Japan.

Reprinted from *IEEE Transactions on Microwave Theory and Techniques*, Volume MTT-32, Number 12, December 1984, pages 1715-1720. Copyright

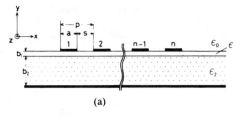

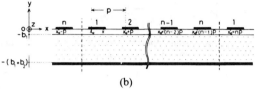

Fig. 1. (a) A coupled multiconductor MIS microstrip line model having n conductors and (b) a periodic boundary condition applied to the model.

The characteristic impedance $Z_{0\theta}$ and the phase velocity v_θ of the θ mode are given in terms of the static capaci-

$$G_\theta(x, x_0) = \sum_{m=-\infty}^{\infty} \frac{1}{p} \cdot e^{-j\beta_m(x-x_0)} \cdot \frac{1}{|\beta_m|} \frac{\epsilon_1 \coth|\beta_m|b_1 + \epsilon_2 \coth|\beta_m|b_2}{(\epsilon_2 \coth|\beta_m|b_2)(\epsilon_0 + \epsilon_1 \coth|\beta_m|b_1) + \epsilon_1(\epsilon_1 + \epsilon_0 \coth|\beta_m|b_1)} \quad (4)$$

tance per conductor per unit length corresponding to the θ-mode excitation

$$Z_{0\theta} = \frac{1}{v_\theta C_\theta} \qquad v_\theta = c_0 \sqrt{\frac{C_{\theta 0}}{C_\theta}} \quad (2)$$

where $C_{\theta 0}$ is the static capacitance of the θ mode without dielectric loading, and C_θ is that with dielectric loading. c_0 is the light velocity in vacuum.

C. Line Voltage and Current

In terms of the above normal modes, the voltage and current on the kth conductor can be expressed by the following equations:

$$V_k(z) = \sum_\theta \Big(A_{\theta f} e^{-j(k-1)\theta} \cdot e^{j\omega(t-(z/v_\theta))}$$

$$+ A_{\theta r} e^{-j(k-1)\theta} e^{j(t+(z/v_\theta))} \Big) \quad (3a)$$

$$I_k(z) = \sum_\theta \Big(\frac{A_{\theta f}}{Z_{0\theta}} e^{-j(k-1)\theta} e^{j\omega(t-(z/v_\theta))}$$

$$- \frac{A_{\theta r}}{Z_{0\theta}} e^{-j(k-1)\theta} \cdot e^{j\omega(t+(z/v_\theta))} \Big) \quad (3b)$$

where $A_{\theta f}$ is the amplitude of the θ-mode forward voltage wave and $A_{\theta r}$ is that of the backward voltage wave, z is the position on the conductor, and ω is the angular frequency. By providing terminal conditions at both ends of each conductor, mode wave amplitudes are determined. The pulse response can be obtained by a numerical inverse Laplace transform of the above equations.

D. Determination of Mode Capacitances by Green's Function Method

Values of static mode capacitances are calculated here by the Green's function method. Referring to Fig. 1(b), let $G_\theta(x, x_0)$ denote the Green's function on the strip plane

Fig. 2. A schematic diagram of a semicustom gate array.

$(y = 0)$ for the θ-mode. It is defined as the potential at a point x on the strip plane when a unit charge with a phase factor of $\exp(-jm\theta)$ is placed at points $x_0 + mp$ with p being the pitch in Fig. 1(b) and $m = 0, \pm 1, \pm 2, \cdots, \pm \infty$. $G_\theta(x, x_0)$ can be determined by making a Fourier transformation of the two-dimensional Laplace's equation and solving the resultant equation with respect to y, as was done by Yamashita *et al.* [10]. The result is

where

$$\beta_m \equiv \frac{2m\pi + \theta}{p}.$$

Then, the following Fredholm integral equation of the first kind can be set up for the charge density function $\rho_\theta(x)$ for the θ-mode at point x on the strip conductor:

$$V_0 = \int_{-a/2}^{a/2} G_\theta(x, x_\theta) \rho_\theta(x_0) \, dx_0 \quad (5)$$

where V_0 is the potential on the strip under consideration. This equation can be easily solved numerically by the standard procedure [11]. Then, the static capacitance per conductor of the θ-mode can be calculated as

$$C_\theta = \frac{1}{V_0} \int_{-a/2}^{a/2} \rho_\theta(x) \, dx. \quad (6)$$

III. RESULTS AND DISCUSSION

A. Frequency-Domain Analysis

Before going into the pulse analysis, it is desirable to check the validity of the mode analysis. To our knowledge, an analytic expression based on the conformal mapping is available for the characteristic impedance of the π-mode [12]. This analytic formula is applicable for the case of $b_1 = 0$ and $b_2 = \infty$. The values of the mode characteristic impedance calculated by the present method are compared for various a/p (a: strip width, p: pitch) ratios in Table I with those by the analytic formula. The numerical computation is done by dividing the strip into 100 segments and taking 1000 Fourier terms. As seen in Table I, the agreement between two methods is excellent with the difference being less than 0.3 percent. The calculated characteristic impedance $Z_{0\theta}$ is plotted versus a/p for various modes in

TABLE I
COMPARISON OF CALCULATED π-MODE CHARACTERISTIC IMPEDANCE

a/p	Green's Function Method	Conformal Mapping
0.1	194.20 ohms	193.87 ohms
0.2	152.06	151.95
0.3	126.75	127.00
0.4	108.61	108.81
0.5	94.15	94.12
0.6	81.48	81.42
0.7	69.67	69.76
0.8	58.16	58.31
0.9	45.72	45.70

The values by conformal mapping are obtained by using an analytic expression in [12].

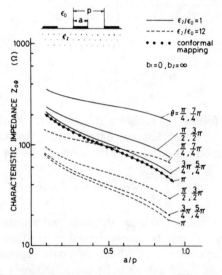

Fig. 3. Calculated characteristic impedance Z_0 of the various modes.

Fig. 3. The high-impedance nature of the modes is noted; this is because of the lack of a common ground plane in this case. However, the high-impedance nature of the interconnection system remains true in the practical situation of, for instance, $a = 2$ μm, $p = 4$ μm, and $b_2 = 200$ μm, because of the small value of a/b_2.

B. Long Interconnections

The pulse response of the stripline system is calculated by the inverse Laplace transform of (3a) and (3b) under various excitation and loading conditions. Unless otherwise stated, the 2-μm rule ($a = 2$ μm) is used for the interconnection width, and the substrate thickness and relative permittivity of $b_2 = 200$ μm and $\epsilon_2 = 12$, and those of the insulator of $b_1 = 1$ μm and $\epsilon_1 = 4$ are assumed, respectively, throughout this paper.

The calculated crosstalk amplitudes in semi-infinite interconnections are shown in Fig. 4. The number of the

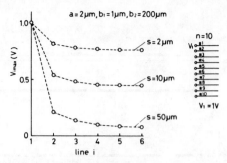

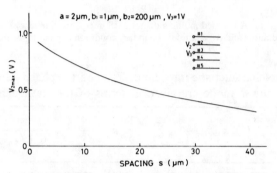

Fig. 4. Calculated crosstalk amplitude at the ith interconnection for a semi-infinite coupling length.

Fig. 5. Crosstalk amplitude at the adjacent interconnection for a semi-infinite coupling length plotted versus spacing s.

strips n is chosen to be ten and the input end of each strip is open circuited. A step voltage is applied to strip 1 and the induced voltage V_i at strip i is plotted versus i. This is essentially equal to the crosstalk constant as calculated from the static capacitance. It should be noted that $V_i = V_{12-i}$ because of the periodic boundary condition. Since a/b_2 is small, the shielding effect by the metallized back is small, and a voltage on one strip tends to have its effect over a long range. Fig. 5 shows the variation of induced voltage at an adjacent strip versus the spacing s ($= p - a$) calculated for $n = 5$. The long-range nature is again seen here.

C. Dynamic Excitations

In the computation of pulse waveforms on the finite-length interconnections, the input and output impedances of a logic gate are represented by a capacitor C_L and a resistor R_S. A standard 1-μm-gate GaAs MESFET with a gate width of 20 μm has approximately an input capacitance of 20 fF. The output signal impedance of a gate consisting of FET-type devices is approximately equal to the inverse of the transconductance g_m of the switching or load device which is taking part in the transient.

An example of calculated crosstalk pulse waveforms is shown in Fig. 6. The excitation and loading conditions are shown in the inset. The voltage waveform at the input of the gate terminating interconnection 4 is shown. The dashed curve shows the response calculated by the "lumped capacitance" approximation of the interconnection (explained in the Appendix) where interconnections are represented by a capacitance network shown in the inset. Clearly the "lumped capacitance" approximation becomes inadequate

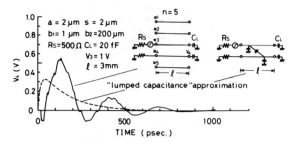

Fig. 6. Calculated step-response waveforms. The dashed curve is the waveform by the "lumped capacitance" approximation.

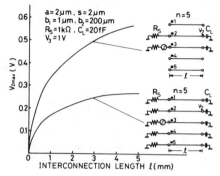

Fig. 7. Crosstalk amplitude plotted versus the interconnection length.

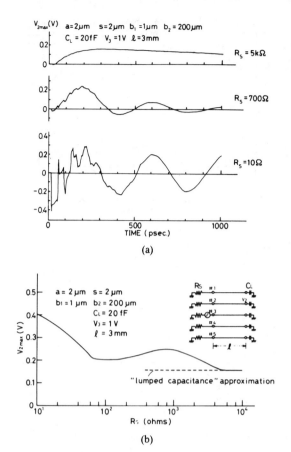

Fig. 8. (a) Crosstalk waveforms for different signal source resistances R_s of the gate and (b) the crosstalk amplitude plotted versus R_S.

in high-speed circuits. The results of the calculation showed that this approximation is applicable to interconnections of a few millimeters long, only when the circuit rise time is above 200–300 ps. The response waveform in Fig. 6 shows an initial time delay and a ringing-type decaying oscillation with ripple-like smaller oscillations being superposed. The initial delay is due to the propagation of wavefront, and small oscillations are due to the velocity difference of the various modes involved. On the other hand, the large amplitude oscillation with a much slower period than the round-trip times of the normal modes is due to an LC-type oscillation where the zero-mode ($\theta = 0$) with a high characteristic impedance (several kilohms) provides an effectively large lumped inductance and becomes resonant with the load capacitance.

The crosstalk amplitude is plotted versus the interconnection length in Fig. 7 for the terminal conditions shown in the inset. As seen in Fig. 7, the presence of floating interconnections has a large effect on the crosstalk amplitude because it effectively increases mutual coupling by reducing the line capacitances.

The dependences of the crosstalk waveform and amplitude on the signal source resistance R_S are shown in Fig. 8(a) and (b), respectively. The lumped capacitance approximation holds when R_s is above 2–3 kΩ and the response is slow. As the signal source resistance is reduced, the above-mentioned lumped LC oscillation becomes dominant and determines the crosstalk amplitude. With further reduction of R_s down to several tens of ohms, multiple reflection of the wavefronts of the low-impedance modes appears at the initial stage and the first negative

peak of this transient determines the crosstalk amplitude. Thus, the dependence of the crosstalk amplitude on the R_s becomes complicated, as shown in Fig. 8(b), showing in the medium resistance range of 10^2–10^3 Ω a significant deviation from the general trend of increased crosstalk amplitude with the decrease of R_s.

D. Reduction of Crosstalk

From the above results, reduction of crosstalk seems imperative for successful realization of very high-speed LSI/VLSI's with sufficient noise margins to ensure reliable operation. The reason for large crosstalk is that the conventional interconnection system does not have a solid shielding ground plane in its vicinity. Therefore, one obvious way to reduce crosstalk is to reduce the substrate thickness. The effect of substrate thickness on the coupling in semi-infinite interconnections is shown in Fig. 9. It is clear that this approach is not too effective unless the substrate thickness is reduced to 10 μm, which is practically impossible unless a new technology such as SOI is employed.

Another way of reducing crosstalk is to provide adjacent shielding ground lines. A result of dynamic response calculation to investigate its effect is shown in Fig. 10 for the terminal conditions shown in the inset. Thus, it is significantly effective in reducing crosstalk. However, the computed pulse waveforms at the centers of the active line, shield line, and adjacent line, as shown in Fig. 11, exhibit dynamic ringing due to the aforementioned LC-type oscil-

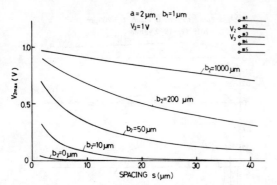

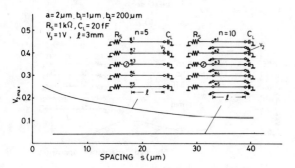

Fig. 9. Crosstalk coupling coefficient versus spacing for various substrate thickness.

Fig. 10. The effect of shield lines on crosstalk.

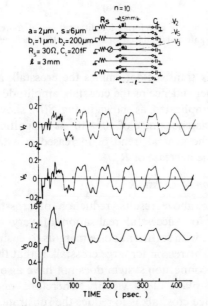

Fig. 11. Waveforms at the centers of the adjacent line (V_2), the shield line (V_S), and the active line (V_3).

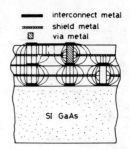

Fig. 12. A proposed shielded multilevel planar-interconnect scheme.

lation. The potential on a narrow shield line cannot be made null all the way along the line, even if the line is grounded at both ends. Additionally, shield lines reduce the wiring channel capacity a great deal in spite of the fact that availability of interconnection capacity itself is a big problem in LSI/VLSI design.

An alternative shielded multilevel planar interconnect scheme is schematically shown in Fig. 12. The coupling in this scheme is roughly equal to the case of $b_2 = 0$ in Fig. 9 and is very small. This allows reduction of crosstalk without reducing the wiring channel capacity. The risk of dynamic ringing is reduced for a fixed value of R_s because reduction of inductance shifts the ringing frequency towards higher frequencies. Additionally, each interconnection can be regarded as a separate transmission line in this scheme, thereby facilitating the timing and layout design a great deal. On the other hand, such a scheme, of course, lowers impedance and increases capacitance. To achieve high speed and a high integration level by this scheme, devices should therefore possess high transconductance and low power consumption. Such a requirement is an essential one in any well-shielded interconnect structure, including the present one, unless the chip size is greatly reduced or the basic architecture of the integrated circuits is modified in such a way that only short interconnections are required.

IV. CONCLUSION

The main conclusions of the present study are as follows.

1) Crosstalk consideration is supremely important in very high-speed LSI/VLSI design with t_{pd} below a few 100 ps.

2) When the circuit speed is less than 200–300 ps in the LSI level, the "lumped capacitance" approximation for interconnection is inadequate in calculating the crosstalk waveform and amplitude, and a proper microwave consideration becomes a necessity.

3) The length, spacing, and termination conditions of interconnection, substrate thickness, and output impedance of gates have large and complicated effects on crosstalk.

4) Shield lines reduce crosstalk, but there is a risk of dynamic ringing. They also limit the wiring capacity. A shielded multilevel interconnect scheme is proposed which reduces crosstalk with reduced risk of ringing and without reduction of wiring capacity. It also facilitates timing and layout design.

APPENDIX
CROSSTALK IN THE "LUMPED CAPACITANCE" APPROXIMATION

Using the circuit model shown in the inset of Fig. 13, the crosstalk amplitude $V_2(t)$ at time t is given by

$$V_2(t) = \tfrac{1}{2}\left(e^{-t/\tau_1} - e^{-t/\tau_2}\right) \qquad (A1)$$

where

$$\tau_1 = R(C + C_L) \qquad \tau_2 = R(2C_m + C + C_L). \qquad (A2)$$

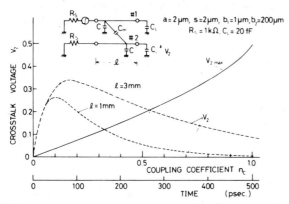

Fig. 13. Crosstalk waveform and amplitude based on the "lumped capacitance" approximation.

The maximum crosstalk amplitude is given by

$$V_{2\,max} = \frac{1}{2}\Big(e^{-(1-n_c)/(2n_c)\ln(1+n_c)/(1-n_c)}$$
$$- e^{-(1+n_c)/(2n_c)\ln(1+n_c)/(1-n_c)} \Big) \quad (A3)$$

where n_c is the capacitance coupling coefficient, and is given by

$$n_c = \frac{c_m}{c_m + C + C_L}. \quad (A4)$$

The crosstalk waveform and the maximum crosstalk amplitude is plotted versus time and n_c, respectively, in Fig. 13.

ACKNOWLEDGMENT

The authors would like to express their sincere thanks to Dr. H. Ohno, Hokkaido University, and Dr. A. Masaki, Hitachi Central Research Laboratory, for their useful discussions and comments.

REFERENCES

[1] K. Yamasaki, Y. Yamane, and K. Kurumada, "Below 20ps/gate operation with GaAs SAINT FET's at room temperature," *Electron. Lett.*, vol. 18, no. 14, pp. 592–593, 1982.

[2] M. Abe, T. Mimura, N. Yokoyama, and H. Ishikawa, "New technology toward GaAs LSI/VLSI for computer applications," *IEEE Trans. Electron Devices*, vol. ED-29, pp. 1088–1094, July 1982.

[3] C. P. Lee, D. L. Miller, D. Hou, and R. J. Anderson, "Ultra high speed integrated circuits using GaAs/GaAlAs high electron mobility transistors," in *Proc. Device Research Conf. IIA-7*, June 1983.

[4] H. Hasegawa and S. Seki, "Analysis of interconnection delay on very high-speed LSI/VLSI chips using MIS microstrip line models," *IEEE Trans. Microwave Theory Tech.*, vol. MTT-32, no. 12, pp. 1721–1727, Dec. 1984.

[5] H-T. Yuan, Y-T. Lin, and S-Y. Chiang, "Properties of interconnection on silicon, sapphire, and semi-insulating gallium arsenide substrates," *IEEE Trans. Electron Devices*, vol. ED-29, pp. 639–644, Apr. 1982.

[7] J. A. DeFalco, "Reflection and crosstalk in logic circuit interconnections," *IEEE Spectrum*, pp. 44–50, July 1970.

[8] F-Y. Chang, "Transient analysis of lossless coupled transmission lines in a nonhomogeneous dielectric medium," *IEEE Trans. Microwave Theory Tech.*, vol. MTT-19, pp. 616–626, Sept. 1970.

[9] J. Chilo and T. Arnaud, "Coupling effects in the time domain for an interconnecting bus in high-speed GaAs logic circuits," *IEEE Trans. Electron Devices*, vol. ED-31, pp. 347–352, Mar. 1984.

[10] E. Yamashita, "Variational method for the analysis of microstrip-like transmission lines," *IEEE Trans. Microwave Theory Tech.*, vol. MTT-16, pp. 529–535, Aug. 1968.

[11] P. Silvester, "TEM wave properties of microstrip transmission lines," *Proc. Inst. Elec. Eng.*, vol. 115, pp. 43–48, Jan. 1968.

[12] Y. C. Lim and R. A. Moore, "Properties of alternately charged coplanar parallel strips by conformal mappings," *IEEE Trans. Electron Devices*, vol. ED-15, pp. 173–180, Mar. 1968.

✦

Shouhei Seki was born in Hokkaido, Japan, on November 16, 1956. He received the B.S. and M.S. degrees in electrical engineering from Hokkaido University, Sapporo, Japan, in 1980, and 1982, respectively. He is working towards the Ph.D. degree at the same department.

His research interests include design and analysis of very high-speed integrated circuits and microwave IC's.

Mr. Seki is a member of the Institute of Electronics and Communication Engineers of Japan, and the Japan Society of Applied Physics.

✦

Hideki Hasegawa (M'70) was born in Tokyo, Japan, on June 22, 1941. He received the B.S., M.S., and Ph.D. degrees in electronic engineering from the University of Tokyo, Tokyo, Japan, in 1964, 1966, and 1970, respectively.

In 1970, he joined the faculty of the Department of Electrical Engineering, Hokkaido University, Sapporo, Japan, as a Lecturer. In 1971, he became an Associate Professor and, in 1980, a Professor, both at the same department. From 1973 to 1974, he was on sabbatical leave at the Department of Electrical and Electronic Engineering, the University of Newcastle-upon-Tyne, England, as a Visiting Research Fellow. His current research interests include MBE and OM VPE growth, characterization and processing of III–V compound semiconductors, surface and interface properties of compound semiconductors, high-speed logic, microwave and O/E IC's using GaAs, InP, and related compounds. He is also interested in growth, characterization, and device applications of a-Si films.

Dr. Hasegawa is a member of the Institute of Electronics and Communication Engineers of Japan, the Japan Society of Applied Physics, the Institute of Electrical Engineers of Japan, and Japan Association of Crystal Growth.

Reprinted from *Proceedings of the GaAs IC Symposium*, 1985, pages 143-146.
Copyright © 1985 by The Institute of Electrical and Electronics Engineers, Inc.

REQUIREMENTS AND INTERIM SOLUTIONS FOR HIGH-SPEED TESTING OF GaAs ICs

Tushar R. Gheewala*

Gigabit Logic, Newbury Park, CA   91320

ABSTRACT

The test system requirements for GaAs digital ICs are identified. The main limitations of the presently available automated testers are the generation and acquisition of gigabit rate test patterns with high accuracy, and the test-fixtures required to probe wafers and packaged components. Solutions to the above limitations are now becoming available in the form of GaAs ICs such as high-speed Static RAMs and 2 - 3 GHz rate MUX/DEMUX ICs and novel test-fixture techniques based on polyimide flexible circuits, elastomers and gold-dot connectors. Several interim test techniques must be employed until these techniques become commercially available at reasonable costs. One of the most cost-effective test technique is to use D.C. testing prior to H.S. test to screen out the three most common failure modes i.e. defects, inadequate noise margins, and poor transconductance of MESFETs. Correlation between high-speed performance and such parameters as ring-oscillator speeds, MESFET transconductance, power supply current levels can also be used to minimize the dependence on the high-speed testers and thus cut the cost of testing the GaAs ICs. Finally some novel on-chip test techniques are discussed.

INTRODUCTION

Over the past three years significant progress has been made towards the solutions to many of the practical problems facing the commercialization of high speed Gallium Arsenide Integrated Circuits. The quality of the starting material has improved dramatically with the wide availability of good quality 3" diameter LEC wafers. The reproducibility and yield of the IC processes have been improved to a point where MSI level circuits have now become manufacturable. Significant progress has also been made in the area of high speed packaging whereby several approaches are now available to meet the requirements of up to 5 GHz components. However, in the area of testing these high-speed ICs, very little progress has been made to date. As a result, no general purpose GaAs IC tester is available today, forcing the GaAs IC manufactures to employ slow and expensive, 'rack-and-stack' instrumentation that is capable of testing SSI/MSI level circuits. These test systems are generally dedicated to specific applications and cannot readily be employed to test a wide range

* Present Address: Sperry Corporation, Semiconductor Operations, 1500 Towerview Drive, Eagan, MN   55122.

of components, adding significantly to the cost of testing. In this review paper we will examine the requirements for general purpose high speed automated test equipments, and some interim strategies that can be employed until such equipment becomes available. The discussion will focus mainly on the digital ICs since they represent the more difficult and complex testing problem. Although this paper addresses the question of testing GaAs ICs, the test issues are applicable to other high-speed technologies such as Silicon ECL.

The problem associated with the testing of a new, highest performance technology is a perennial one. Generally, the circuit technology is ready before the compatible test equipment can be manufactured, often based on the same new high speed technology. What makes the problem much more acute for the Gallium Arsenide technology are two factors:

1) The switching speeds and the rise and fall times have become comparable to the signal propagation delays over very short distances. In order to test these ultra-high-speed properties, the test equipment must also have very short delays and extremely short interconnect discontinuities of the order of one milimeter;

2) The magnified importance of propagation delays relative to the circuit performance also demands that the new technology must be packaged very densely, or in other words, LSI to VLSI levels of integration must be attempted in the infancy of the emerging technology.

Thus, the testing of the digital GaAs ICs requires the development of a tester technology capable of testing LSI/VLSI ICs, at Gigahertz rates, with roughly 100ps rise and fall times, and extremely short packaging delays and discontinuities. Clearly, the development of such a tester is going to require an extensive use of high-speed GaAs components, very aggressive packaging techniques and a highly pipelined tester architecture. The prospects for a near term availability of such testers are not very bright, specially in the light of the relatively small demand for such systems. In the meanwhile, we must look at alternatives such as on-chip tests, correlation between D.C. parametric tests and high-speed performance, and test strategies and product selection aimed at lowering the cost of testing. We will discuss the requirements of an ideal high-speed tester and some interim solutions in the following sections.

GaAs IC Symposium

TEST SYSTEM REQUIREMENTS

The electrical requirements for a GaAs digital IC systems can be separated into two different categories, the first ones being related to electrical signals and the second ones being related to the test fixturing. The electrical signals requirements are listed in Table 1 and are contrasted with the capabilities of the best available testers today. It is seen that a ten fold improvement in the performance of the state-of-the-art testers is necessary to meet the general requirements for the testing of GaAs ICs.

The two most critical components of the high-speed tester are the pattern generator and the data acquisition units. Both these units can achieve significant performance enhancements from the use of GaAs technology. For example, the use of high-speed SRAMs in conjunction with gigahertz rate GaAs MUX/DEMUX ICs can meet the objectives of gigahertz rate pattern generation and acquisition. Similarly, the use of GaAs comparators and digital-to-analog convertors can solve the problem of accurately sensing voltage amplitudes at gigahertz rates. Thus one can conclude that although no tester is available today that can meet the requirements for testing GaAs ICs, the technology to generate and capture high-speed signals accurately will be available in the near future. Meanwhile, specific test techniques must be developed to test the early SSI/MSI level components. Some examples of such specific test techniques would be the use of high-speed synchrnous counters to test the cycle time of SRAMs or the use of a gigahertz rate bit error rate generator system to test the MUX/DEMUX ICs.

Features	GaAs Tester Requirements	State-of-art Testers
Data Rate	$0.5GH_Z$ - 2GH$_Z$	50MH$_Z$ - 100 MH$_Z$
Signal Rise & Fall Times	100ps - 150ps	700ps - 1,500ps
Timing Accuracy	10ps - 20ps	300ps - 700ps
Voltage Measurement Accuracy	10mV	1mV - 10mV
No. of high-speed pins	64 - 128	128 - 256

Table 1. Electrical Requirements

High Speed Test Fixtures

The other set of requirements on a high-speed tester for the Gallium Arsenide technology rise from the need for extremely short discontinuities in the propagation of high-speed signals over transmission lines. Test fixtures such as wafer probe-cards, quick disconnect sockets and load-boards on which switches and resistors are mounted, must all exhibit constant impedance at frequencies up to about 5 GHz.

In other words, the discontinuities posed by such structures as connectors, pins, probes, etc. should have an inductance of no more than about 2 to 3 nH, which would correspond to about 2 to 3 mm in physical length. There is one major exception to this requirement in the case of the power supply and ground distribution. The total series inductance in such a case should be significantly lower because of the large rate of change of currents in these lines. This requirement can be met by the use of multiple connectors in parllel to minimize the inductance and by the incorporation of microwave quality capacitors to reduce the rate change of current.

In addition, a 1 GHz tester must also exhibit time-of-flight delays between the tester I/Os and the device under test which are significantly less than a nanosecond. For a dielectric constant of 2, this requirement would constrain the maximum diameter of the load-board to about 5 cms. We can work around this requirement by calibrating each I/O lead length by the means of jumper devices that bypass the device under test. However, under such conditions, certain features such as tri-state drivers may not be tested at full cycle speeds.

WAFER PROBES SCHEMATIC DIAGRAM	MATERIALS	STUB LENGTH (MM)	TYPICAL INDUCTANCE (nH)	F$_{MAX}$ (GHz)
1) MODIFIED GLASS-EPOXY RING PROBE	TEFLON CABLES WITH PALINEY NEEDLES	5-7	8-10	1
2) CERAMIC BLADE PROBE	POLYMIDE BOARD CERAMIC BLADES PALINEY PROBE NEEDLES	3-4	4-5	2
3) COPLANAR CERAMIC PROBES	CERAMIC WITH GOLD PLATED BUMPS	0.5	0.5	18
4) POLYMIDE FLEXIBLE PROBES	CERAMIC POLYMIDE GOLD PLATED TI/W BUMPS	2	2	5

Figure 1
High-Speed Wafer Probe Techniques

Some of the test fixture technologies available to meet these requirements are illustrated in Fig. 1 and 2. The wafer probe techniques shown in Fig. 1 range from the extension of the established epoxy-ring probes to the recent coplanar ceramic probes and a proposed multilayer polyimide probe technology. The coplanar ceramic probes have demonstrated the highest performance exceeding 18 GHz [1]. However, they also have the limitations of very high cost, fragile construction and very few I/Os. The proposed polyimide technique is similar to the Tape Automated Bonding (TAB) concept used for packaging ICs. Copper leads are patterned on a flexible film of polyimide and plated with Titanium, Tungsten and Gold bumps where they would contact the pads on the ICs. The polyimide probes can be manufactured using photolithographic processes and can provide a large number of I/Os at acceptable cost and performance.

GaAs IC Symposium

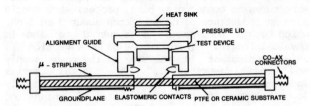

Figure 2
High-Speed Package Test Fixture

The package test fixtures such as the one shown in Figure 2 are relatively easy to make. They generally comprise of micro-striplines on a high-performance dielectric substrate such as either ceramic of Teflon and are connected to the test equipment by SMA or similar high frequency connectors. The quick-release connection between the test board and the device under test is usually a low-inductance pressure contact made of a gold-plated elastomer such as silicone rubber.

AVAILABLE TEST SYSTEMS

It may take more than a few years before automated, reconfigurable, gigahertz rate testers become available. Until such systems become available, the only available solutions are a combination of the following test strategies:

1. 'Rack-and-Stack' test systems made of various instruments such as signal generators and digital sampling oscilloscopes running on the IEEE488 bus. These systems are slow, expensive, provide very limited capabilities and are not easily reconfigured to test different devices.

2. A hybrid test strategy based on a combination of D.C. and high-speed testers. The D.C. testers are used to test functionality and features that the high-speed testers can not test due to their limited I/O capabilities. The D.C. testers can also screen out a large percentage of failures and thus reduce the load on the high-speed test systems.

3. On-chip test structures ranging from simple ring oscillators to psuedo-random test-pattern generators can be included on the ICs to measure circuit delays and clock-speeds.

These three techniques are examined in more detail in the following sections.

A typical IEEE488 bus based test system is shown schematically in Figure 3. The cost of such a test system, including the cost of the test fixtures and the R.F. switch network used to relay the I/O signals to the signal generators or the sampling oscilloscopes, would be about $250,000. The capabilities of such a system would include sinewave generators to 10 GHz, pulse generators up to 1 GHz, word generators up to 200 MHz, psuedo-

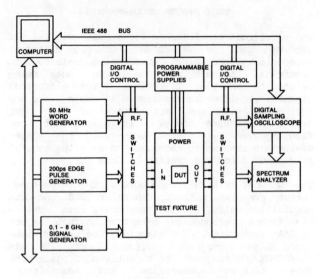

Figure 3
IEEE488 Based Test Instrumentation

random bit pattern generator up to about 2 GHz, spectrum analyzers over 10 GHz and sampling oscilloscopes with +20ps accuracy. The limitations of such systems are many; such as slow throughput time of the order of minutes to test SSI components, limited number of I/Os, can not be re-configured under computer controlled to test different products, etc.

The IEEE488 based systems are, however, capable of testing many of the popular test instrumentation components such as Quad-NOR, Clock-drivers, Comparators, Multi-plexers, Demultiplexers, and Static RAMs. Thus the components needed to build the automated test equipments can be manufactured, breaking the chicken-and-egg cycle.

The Importance of D.C. Testing

The D.C. testing includes parametric and functional testing of the components at low speeds. It can be easily accomplished using readily available, low-cost test systems and it can have significant positive impact on the quality and the cost of testing GaAs ICs. Thus D.C. testing should be an important component of the GaAs test strategy during the interim period before the high-speed full testers become available. The three most common failure modes that can be detected using the D.C. testers are:

1. Defects such as opens and short,
2. Poor noise margins, and,
3. Poor transconductance resulting in inadequate switching currents.

The D.C. testing can be used as a screen to reduce the throughput requirements on the more expensive and slow high-speed testers. In Figure 4, the cost of three different test strategies are compared ranging from A) full test on high-speed tester only; B) high-speed test following D.C. test at

GaAs IC Symposium

every stage; and C) high-speed test only as a final test, all other tests being only D.C. The parts are assumed to be tested three times: at wafer level, after packaging and after burn-in. There are several assumptions made in this analysis, some of which are: the cost of packaging a part is roughly $10.00; MSI levels of integration; package assembly and burn-in yield is 95% and D.C. wafer yield is the average of H.S. wafer yield and 100. Further, the test equipments are assumed to be used over two shift operations. The last assumption may be too optimistic for dedicated high-speed test equipments which can only be used to test a specific product. In that case, the cost of high-speed testing may increase by a large factor. It should also be pointed out that availability of a general purpose high-speed tester in future would bring the cost of testing MSI level components down to 2-3$ dollars range. However, because of the design constraints it would be nearly impossible to combine high-speed and D.C. parametric test capabilities on a single tester. Therefore, D.C. testing and screening of GaAs ICs would continue to be used.

No general theories exist to predict the correlation between D.C. testing of device parameters and the high-speed performance. At simple circuit level the correlation between gain-bandwidth and such D.C. parameters as transconductance and capacitance is obvious. For more complex circuits and in fine-tuned designs where the signal levels do not saturate but operate in the class A amplifier mode, the correlation must be experimentally established.

On-Chip Test Techniques

On-chip test techniques are being employed to solve the problems of testing complex VLSI ICs. Similarly, on-chip test methods must be employed to test the high-speed characteristics of the GaAs circuits. The range of options vary from the inclusion of simple ring-oscillators to incorporation of linear feedback shift-register chains to generate psuedo-random test patterns, as well as to hold the results. One of the other techniques available to the circuit designers is the use of multiplexers on the output pins to output either the signal or a reference timing edge. The delay between the two output signals can then be used to infer the critical path delay to that output.

SUMMARY

In summary, although no adequate general purpose tester exists to test the high-speed GaAs ICs, the necessary electronic components and test fixture technologies are becoming available. Meanwhile, a combination of different techniques can be employed to test many of the specific devices. These techniques are based on the use of test instrumentation controlled by a computer over a networking bus such as the IEEE488 bus. D.C. testing prior to the high-speed testing can be used to improve the quality of test and to reduce the load on the more expensive high-speed tester. On-chip high-speed test structures such as ring

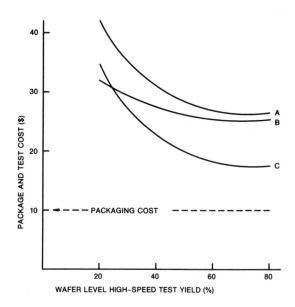

Figure 4
Cost of testing and packaging GaAs ICs as a function of high-speed wafer-probe yield. A) high-speed test only, B) high-speed test following D.C. screening, and C) high-speed test only during final test following burn-in.

oscillators and linear feedback word generators and acquisition registers will become increasingly necessary as the complexity of GaAs circuits grow to LSI and VLSI levels.

ACKNOWLEDGEMENTS

The author would like to thank Thomas Bunch, Tanwei Chung, Elwood Clarke, Richard Eden, Michael Mocanin, Robert Mouro and Dao Ngo for their help in the development of the test methods discussed in this paper.

REFERENCES

[1] K. R. Gleason, T. M. Reeder, and E. W. Strid, MSN, p. 55, May 1983.

Chapter 4: Advanced GaAs System Examples

This chapter surveys several major gallium arsenide (GaAs) design efforts that are currently underway.

In the first paper entitled "GaAs Microprocessors and Memories for High Speed System Design," Becker describes a family of GaAs bit-slice components that are currently being marketed by Vitesse Electronics Corporation. The author discusses his company's strategy for introducing GaAs parts into the silicon-dominated marketplace; he describes the parts, some design considerations, and the intended application environment.

Helbig et al. describe an 8-bit GaAs microprocessor developed by RCA Corporation in their paper entitled "The Design and Construction of a GaAs Technology Demonstration Microprocessor." They discuss the GaAs technology used, packaging issues, the microprocessor architecture, and the design tools used. This paper is the first published description of a microprocessor designed for GaAs technology.

In "A 32-Bit RISC Implemented in Enhancement-Mode JFET GaAs," Rasset et al. describe a 32-bit GaAs microprocessor-based system developed by McDonnell Douglas Corporation. They describe in considerable detail the architecture of their microprocessor, including the instruction pipeline and the ALU. They also discuss a GaAs floating-point coprocessor and the memory interface.

Fox et al., in their paper entitled "Reduced Instruction Set Architecture for a GaAs Microprocessor System," describe the architecture of another 32-bit GaAs microprocessor-based system, this one developed by Control Data Corporation and Texas Instruments, Inc. They describe in great detail their microprocessor architecture, including the instruction set, the instruction pipeline, and the datapath. They also describe their GaAs floating-point coprocessor and their memory system.

Hein et al. describe the design of a systolic array for GaAs technology in "Design of a GaAs Systolic Array for an Adaptive Null Steering Beamforming Controller." They discuss the applications and algorithms for which the array is intended, the system architecture, and the processing element design.

In "Toward a GaAs Realization of a Production-System Machine," Lehr and Wedig discuss the realization of a production system machine in GaAs technology. They describe the modularization of their machine, which they call "RISCF." For each module, they estimate the propagation delay to arrive at an approximate system performance figure.

McDonald et al., in "Wafer Scale Interconnections for GaAs Packaging," describe the wafer scale implementation of a RISC processor using GaAs integrated circuits of different gate densities. They discuss the motivation for their approach, describe the RISC architecture under consideration, and present the performance figures for systems using 200-gate chips and 1000-gate chips.

Fouts et al. describe the architecture of a GaAs digital integrated circuit tester in "System Architecture of a Gallium Arsenide One-Gigahertz Digital IC Tester." They discuss the system architecture, the design of the modules comprising the system, and some of the difficulties they faced.

Morgan, in the final paper of this chapter entitled "The Role of Gallium Arsenide in Highly Parallel Symbolic Multiprocessors," describes the architecture of a GaAs processor designed for symbolic processing applications. He discusses some of the characteristics of LISP programs, for which the processor, named GAELIC, is intended. He describes the architecture of GAELIC and presents its estimated performance.

EH0266-7/88/0000/0187$01.00 © 1988 IEEE

GaAs MICROPROCESSORS AND MEMORIES FOR HIGH SPEED SYSTEM DESIGN

Thomas F. Becker
Applications Engineering Manager
Vitesse Electronics Corporation
741 Calle Plano
Camarillo, Ca. 93010

Introduction

Since the introduction of silicon based TTL logic in 1964, system designers have had an insatiable desire for circuits with higher performance. Many power sensitive designs have been satisfied with TTL and CMOS families. Other designs that required higher speeds turned to Emitter Coupled Logic (ECL). TTL and ECL device families have been made exclusively from silicon technology.

While 10K and 100K ECL are the fastest logic families available, their high power dissipation has limited chip size and functionality. For example, production ECL devices are limited by power to small scale adders and multipliers that make large system designs impractical. Improvements in ECL processes continue to be made, but ECL is a mature technology and is fast approaching it's performance limit. Future enhancements will be difficult and costly compared to advances in Gallium Arsenide integrated circuits.

It is difficult to implement high levels of integration with a logic family that dissipates more than 1 milliwatt of power per gate. Figure 1 is a diagram of the most popular logic families, with a "gate integration" scale at the bottom that assumes 5 watts of device power dissipation.

GaAs Status

Gallium Arsenide (GaAs), a compound made of gallium and arsenic, has been demonstrated as a circuit technology in research laboratories throughout the world since the 1960's. It's higher inherent speed compared to silicon has always excited system designers, but various material and process problems

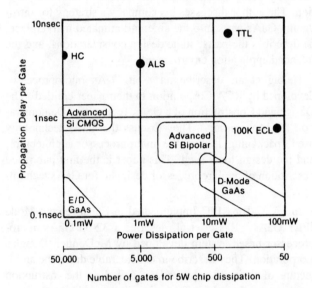

Figure 1. Speed/Power diagram of various logic families.

have prevented it's widespread use. Now, most material and processing problems have been solved, and digital LSI building blocks using GaAs technology are a reality.

GaAs has several significant advantages over silicon as a material for making integrated circuits. The electron mobility of GaAs is five to six times that of silicon, which makes GaAs transistors inherently faster than their silicon counterparts. This basic speed advantage is dramatically demonstrated in products produced by "first generation" manufacturing processes. Faster performance will be realized in the future, as GaAs manufacturers go down the steep part of the learning curve.

Reprinted from *Proceedings of MIDCON '86 Conference*, 1986, pages 1-9.
Copyright © 1986 by The Institute of Electrical and Electronics Engineers, Inc.

Another advantage of GaAs is a higher energy bandgap than silicon, which permits it to operate over a wider temperature range. The lack of an insulating oxide in GaAs insures a much lower sensitivity to radiation than silicon. Gallium Arsenide is a semi-insulating substrate which simplifies circuit design, because GaAs transistors are naturally isolated from one another and do not require extra processing steps for isolation. This results in fewer processing steps for GaAs vs. silicon, which should result in better yields in the future.

Until now, circuit design in GaAs has been accomplished using depletion mode MESFETS (Metal Semiconductor FETS). These are similar to depletion mode MOSFETS from the silicon world. Using all depletion mode FETs requires more active elements for a typical gate (see Figure 2) which results in a high power dissipation (1 - 10 mw/gate) making higher circuit densities impractical.

The solution to this problem is combining both enhancement and depletion mode FETS in the same circuit. This is commonly referred to as the enhancement/depletion (E/D) mode. The E/D mode results in fewer elements (see Figure 3), lower power dissipation, and a need for only one power supply. Vitesse is among the first U.S. based companies to devote production resources solely to the E/D process, which has been embraced by Japanese semiconductor makers as the "standard" GaAs approach.

Lower power dissipation (0.1 - 0.25 mw/gate) of the E/D mode is achieved with nearly the same gate speed as the depletion mode (125 - 400 picoseconds/gate). Building LSI devices with the E/D mode has been difficult until recently due to poor substrate material and sensitive processing steps. With better wafer quality and some process technology improvements transferred from the silicon world, Vitesse has perfected it's E/D process and is now manufacturing digital LSI building blocks.

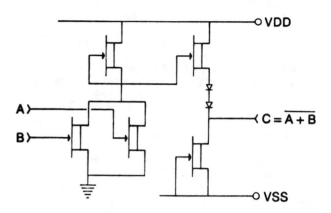

- 1-10mW/gate
- 2 power supplies
- 7 elements

Figure 2. Two input NOR gate using depletion mode FETs.

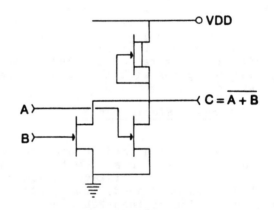

- 0.1-0.25mW/gate
- 1 power supply
- 3 elements

Figure 3. Two input NOR gate using enhancement/depletion FETs.

While the major incentive for higher levels of integration has been economic in the past, for circuits using the E/D process the motivation is largely performance and cost. GaAs propagation delays are so small that a significant amount of speed is lost in input and output buffers (see Figure 4). For example, in Vitesse's Gallium Arsenide microprocessor (the VE29G01), 31% of the total delay from input to output pins is consumed in the input receiver and the output drivers.

The input and output buffers are designed to interface directly with ECL devices, and a significant amount of power is consumed in the I/O circuitry. Only 29% of the total chip power is consumed in internal logic, and the remaining 71% is consumed in the I/O buffers.

At the system level, when board propagation delays of up to 2 nanoseconds/foot are included, a design made up of SSI level GaAs devices will lose 30% - 40% of it's AC performance due to I/O buffers and chip-to-chip delays. The only solution is to integrate more functionality onto each chip, and as devices get larger power dissipation goes up. The E/D mode, with it's low internal power dissipation (0.1 - 0.25 milliwatts per gate), is the only viable process in Gallium Arsenide that will allow chip densities in the range of 5000 - 10000 equivalent gates within the next few years.

Product Significance

Choosing standard products to design and market in a new technology is a classic risk-versus-reward problem. On one hand, new functions running at faster-than-ECL speeds with unusual power and signal levels would attract a lot of attention, but designers are frequently wary of new functions, new signal levels, and new technology all at once. A more sensible approach is to use industry standard benchmarks, such as bit-slice devices and static RAMS, which are familiar to most high-speed circuit designers. Devices such as these, with standard I/O levels and power supplies, would be viewed as logical performance upgrades to existing systems.

VE29G01 DELAY BUDGET

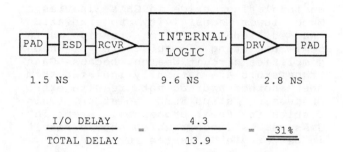

$$\frac{I/O\ DELAY}{TOTAL\ DELAY} = \frac{4.3}{13.9} = \underline{31\%}$$

FIG. 4: VE29G01 DELAY BUDGET

The latter approach is the one that Vitesse has taken. Through an agreement with Advanced Micro Devices (AMD), the most popular bit slice components in use (the 2900 family) have been implemented in GaAs using industry standard signal levels and power supplies. Also, a 4K static RAM with registers onboard was designed to complement the bit slice components. The goal of the entire family of products is to target those speed-critical system paths with the fastest devices commercially available, and to coexist with silicon technology which will continue to fill all other non speed-critical paths.

Product Descriptions

The most important devices in a bit slice design are the microprocessor and the microsequencer. The VE29G01 is a 4 bit processor compatible with microcode written for AMD's 2901. It contains a 16 word by 4 bit dual port RAM, a high speed arithmetic logic unit, and all the necessary shifting, multiplexing, and decoding circuitry needed to decode it's 9-bit microinstruction field. The microinstruction field selects the ALU's function, source operands, and the destination of the ALU's result. The initial version of the VE29G01 is capable of executing an instruction every 14 nanoseconds, and higher speed versions are planned.

The control loop of a typical bit slice design requires a sequencer to control the sequence of execution of microinstructions that are stored in memory. The VE29G10A can generate a new 12 bit address every 10 ns, originating from one of four possible sources: a microprogram address register which is usually incremented on every cycle, an external 12 bit address, a stack that is nine addresses deep, or a register which retains an address loaded on a previous cycle. Most of the 16 sequence control instructions are conditional so an external condition input to the chip can exert program control.

Since the performance of a bit-slice system depends on it's computational speed, a lookahead carry generator is useful in processing ALU carry status outputs. The VE29G02 provides this carry lookahead capability across four ALUs and can be cascaded for larger word lengths.

The memory devices used for microcode storage are often the time bottleneck since access time saved translates into system performance increase. Designers can use pipelining to avoid this dependence on memory access timing. When pipelining is used, memory access time is hidden by the other delays in the control and data loops. Vitesse has designed a 1K X 4 static RAM, the VE12G474, with a 5 ns access time making it ideal for microcode storage. The VE12G474 has onboard registers that allow designers to implement pipelining without resorting to external registers. In the synchronous mode, the VE12G474 can provide data every 3.5 nanoseconds. Figure 5 is a block diagram of the VE12G474.

Signal Interface Levels

A current trend in device design is using smaller logic swings to achieve smaller propagation delays. This benefit is due to the decreased time required to charge up parasitic capacitances. Several logic families are used at Vitesse depending on the design situation, but the most flexible family taking advantage of this lower swing is Direct Coupled FET Logic (DCFL).

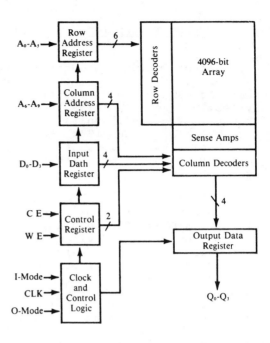

Figure 5.   VE12G474 1024 word by 4 bit Registered Static RAM.

DCFL offers a simple configuration, high speed, and low power due to it's low internal logic swing (530 mv). It is particularly useful for constructing wide fan-in NOR gates. DCFL's logic levels (-100mv HIGH, -630mv LOW) have to be translated to 100K ECL levels (-900 mv HIGH,- 1750 mv LOW) which consumes a considerable portion of the total propagation time through the device. These low logical swings are possible in ECL and GaAs because there is minimal transient noise. This contrasts with TTL, where large noise spikes occur as transistors change state.

The benefit to the user of an ECL interface outweighs the slight loss in speed, because the device looks just like a 100K ECL device with significantly lower internal propagation delays. Now system designers can use existing ECL devices freely to support a GaAs design, as well as relying on their own ECL design experience and methods. Output stages have been designed to support a 25-ohm load, allowing designers to use these devices with a doubly-terminated 50 ohm transmission line directly.

Power Supplies

Another design consideration for a new technology is the selection of power forms necessary to utilize the devices. Vitesse's chips require Vcc (ground), Vee (-4.5 volts), and Vtt (-2.0 volts). Since 100K ECL designs use a Vee of -4.5 volts, this supply is necessary to interface with other 100K logic.

To achieve the low logic swings inherent in GaAs DCFL design, the -4.5 source could be divided on chip (increasing the device power dissipation), or a separate supply could be furnished. Since most system designers would rather keep chip power dissipation as low as possible, Vitesse chose to use the commonly available termination supply -2.0 volts (Vtt), to power the on chip internal logic. This decrease in chip power dissipation will increase device life and reduce the requirement for system airflow.

Packaging

One of the most critical demands in designing a sub-nanosecond device is the type of package to hold the finished product. The package must have small inherent delays to maintain the highest system level performance and to minimize ringing caused by loading effects. Cross-talk and power supply interference must be minimized, and the package must meet mechanical, thermal, and cost tests.

For these reasons a custom ceramic leadless chip carrier was designed. A square cavity slightly larger than the die results in minimum bond wire length, which decreases the inductance on signal lines. A surface mount package is preferable to a dual in line (DIP) package, because the DIP has to interface with a socket and finally with the circuit board. Other advantages of the LCC approach are the lower impedance ground path that it offers and the smaller board space it occupies.

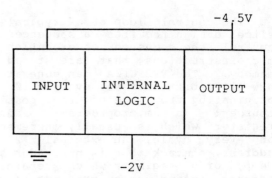

FIG.6: POWER SUPPLIES

Design Considerations

Several books and guides exist to help system designers in design and layout of high-frequency circuit boards, and Vitesse will publish applications notes to assist designers with particular products and techniques. Below is a summary of considerations and general rules that high-speed system designers typically follow:

● A low impedance ground system is an absolute must. Any noise on the ground line can be coupled onto signal lines, and point-to-point voltage differential on the ground bus subtracts from noise margin.

● Bypass capacitors between Vcc and Vee should be used on all ECL and GaAs circuits. A 0.1uF RF quality bypass capacitor should be connected once for every three or four packages. A 1.0 uF capacitor should be connected on the circuit board as close as possible to the power supply inputs.

● Unterminated lines (stubs) can be used but controlled impedance lines are preferred. Undershoot must be controlled as it can cause a signal excursion into the threshold area of common loads, which can cause false triggering. Ringing generally will be controlled if the two-way delay on the line is less than the amount of time the signal takes to rise from 20% to 80% of it's full value. Stub length should be kept to a minimum if stubs are used.

192

• Either series or parallel terminations can be used, depending on the design situation, and each has it's own advantages. Factors which affect this decision are interconnect distances, capacitive loading, resistive loading, and allowable overshoot and undershoot design goals.

• Crosstalk between signal lines must be prevented. Mutual coupling from close proximity lines causes coupling, so careful signal layout must be followed. Multiple ground planes help decrease crosstalk and keep ground plane impedance low.

Applications

Bit slice microprocessors and sequencers have been applied to a variety of design problems and the most prevalent use has been in the design of microprogrammed hardware systems using MSI and LSI components.

Microprogramming is a method of control design in which hardware control signal selection and sequencing information are stored in a memory, called a microinstruction memory. Each microinstruction specifies which control signals should be activated at a certain time, and the location of the microinstruction which should be executed next in the sequence.

A group of microinstructions that is related is called a microprogram, and since the program exists in software rather than hardware, system designers can implement microprogrammed control units that are far more flexible than their hardwired counterparts. Microprogramming is used in systems wherever typical microprocessors have been unable to meet the speed requirement. It is a popular technique in the design of computers, where a control unit selects a sequence of microinstructions to execute a single machine language instruction.

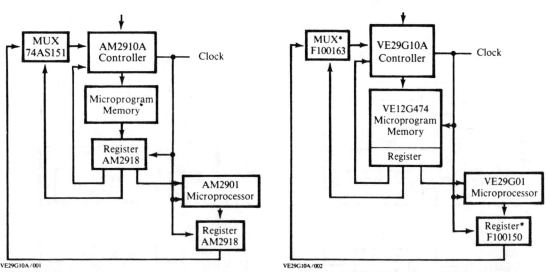

Device	Path	Delay
Pipeline Register (AM2918)	Clock ►Output	13ns
MUX (AS151)	Select ►Output	15ns
AM2910A	$\overline{CC}$►Y	30ns
PROM (AM27535)	ADDR ►Output	35ns
Register (AM2918)	set-up	5ns
	minimum cycle time	98ns

Device	Path	Delay
Pipeline Register (VE12G474)	Clock ►Output	3ns
MUX (100163)	Select ►Output	4ns
VE29G10A	$\overline{CC}$►Y	10ns
Registered Static RAM (VE12G474)	ADDR ►Output	5ns
	minimum cycle time	22ns

* MUX and Register are 100K ECL devices.

Figure 7. Comparison of minimum control loop cycle time. 16 bit system, single level pipeline.

193

To demonstrate the minimum cycle time that can be achieved using Vitesse's family of bit slice components and static RAMS, a comparison was done between a typical bipolar 16 bit design and a design using GaAs devices. The control loop is usually analyzed for the worst case path delay, then the data path is analyzed for it's worst case delay. The longest delay of either control or data paths is a useful indication of the cycle time limit of the system.

Figure 7 is a diagram of the control loop and figure 8 is the data loop. No attempt was made to optimize the bipolar case, since it is a "generic" case that is commonly used to compare bit-slice designs. Significant delays could be eliminated by using faster RAM (writeable control store) instead of PROMS, and a faster register could be used as the pipeline register for better results. The use of GaAs bit slice devices and memories can conservatively cut the minimum cycle time from 98ns down to 30 ns, a speed increase of 3X.

A more specific application of high-speed bit slice processors to high speed design is in the area of computer graphics. The sharply lower price of memory has made building bit-mapped graphics systems more economical, with a consequence of much higher computational demands. As bit mapped displays get larger, several system needs emerge that will benefit from the speed of GaAs and the functionality of LSI.

Implementation of high level graphics commands causes the need for emulation capability that bit slice processors can provide. Program control applications require both the utility of a wide microinstruction word and the ability to change the word width in the future. The need for sophisticated algorithms such as line drawing, fast fills, and raster operations on primitives requires both the speed and programmability of bit slice ALUs and sequencers.

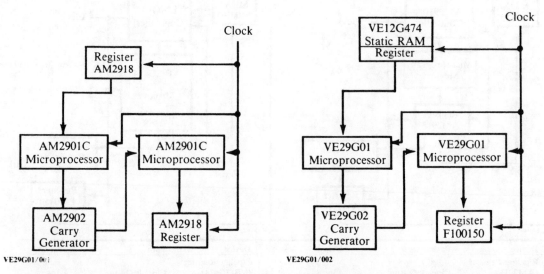

Device	Path	Delay	Device	Path	Delay
Pipeline Register			Pipeline Register		
(AM2918)	Clock ►Output	13ns	(VE12G474)	Clock ►Output	3ns
AM2901C	A,B ►$\overline{G},\overline{P}$	37ns	VE29G01	A,B ►$\overline{G},\overline{P}$	14ns
AM2902A	$\overline{G}_0, \overline{P}_0 ►C_{n+z}$	7ns	VE29G02	$\overline{G}_0, \overline{P}_0 ►C_{n+z}$	5ns
AM2901C	$C_n ►C_{n+4}$, OVR, . F3, F=0, Y	25ns	VE29G01	$C_n ►C_{n+4}$, OVR, F3, F=0, Y	6ns
Status Register (AM2918)	set-up	5ns	Status Register (ECL 100150)	set-up	1ns
	minimum cycle time	87ns		minimum cycle time	29ns

Figure 8. Comparison of minimum data loop cycle time.
16 bit system, single level pipeline

194

A commercial product that uses a 16 bit 2901 architecture to implement high level graphics is the T4 color graphics controller from Microfield Graphics. The T4 controller is a 1024 by 800 pixel 4-plane graphics processor based on bit slice technology. It emulates the IBM Color Graphics Adapter (CGA) and is programmable so that the user can change the microcode to create specialized graphics commands. Sixteen colors are available from a palette of 4096, and the T4 is built on a single PC/AT compatible card.

Figure 9 is a block diagram of the T4. The 16 bit 4X2901 processor controls the PC/AT bus interface and translates higher level commands into low level commands like read/write memory and exclusive-OR functions. The processor uses a 64-bit control word which is stored in a portion of the frame buffer memory. The T4 is capable of filling a structure at 30 nanoseconds/pixel, and drawing a structure at 240 nanoseconds/pixel.

The 4X2901 used by the T4 is manufactured by IMI (International Microcircuits) and is capable of operating at a cycle time of 140 nanoseconds. The implementation of the 4X2901 is flexible enough to allow for variable cycle times, matching the complexity of the instruction. Actual cycle time for the bit slice loop on the T4 varies from 180 to 500 nanoseconds, depending on the instruction being emulated.

The T4 uses the 2901 architecture to implement a variety of functions including program control, comparing operands, instruction emulation and actual vector calculation. A design implemented with GaAs devices would allow the system speed to increase by a factor of four. Even though board performance would probably not increase by a full factor of four, using GaAs bit slice devices and RAMS would provide significant performance improvement and preserve exisiting microcode - and rewriting microcode is a big expense in designing bit slice systems.

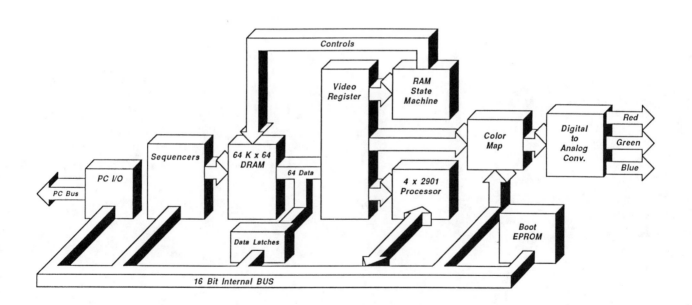

Figure 9. Microfield Graphics T4 Color Graphics Controller

Conclusions

Gallium Arsenide has already proved itself as a usable technology in the microwave world where it has been used successfully for years in making depletion-mode transistors. Rapid advancements in substrate quality and processing have made the low-power enhancement/depletion mode a viable method of making LSI devices in GaAs, with 4K RAMS and bit-slice microprocessors now available. In the future, the E/D mode will dominate GaAs development in both LSI and VLSI areas, with very complex devices (5000 - 10000 gates) available in the next few years. The qualities of GaAs should make it appealing in many speed-critical application areas, including Digital Signal Processing, Computer Graphics, and general control system design.

GaAs devices will fit well into high-speed systems that require high radiation hardness. Any designs that can be partitioned into speed-critical paths will find GaAs components the ideal solution to complement slower silicon circuitry. Finally, designs that need both computation power and memory with access times under 5 nanoseconds will find GaAs components a good alternative.

References

1) Samuel W. Mallicoat, "A Building Block Approach to Computer Graphics". Society for Information Display Proceedings, May 1986.

2) John Hayes, "Computer Architecture and Organization". McGraw-Hill 1978.

W.A. Helbig | R.H. Schellack | R.M. Zieger

The design and construction of a GaAs technology demonstration microprocessor

Is gallium-arsenide technology catching up to silicon for integrated circuits?

The technology maturity of gallium arsenide (GaAs) in processing digital integrated circuits is equivalent to that of silicon in the early 1970s. Today we can integrate between 1000 and 4000 GaAs gates on a single circuit. Yields for these medium-scale integration circuits are generally between 10 and 60 percent.

The major factor that currently constrains larger integration levels with better yields is the variation in pinch-off voltage of the GaAs transistors. Improvements with GaAs processing technology are occurring at a rate that is three times what occurred in silicon processing during the 1970s and early 1980s. Many silicon processing tech-

Abstract: *Because technology has reached the point where we may integrate a few thousand gates on a single chip, RCA's Advanced Technology Laboratories (ATL) is designing and constructing an 8-bit, reduced instruction set microprocessor as a test case for technology development and demonstration. We expect to produce the first operational system by January 1986. This article discusses the technology status, design choices, and project progress and schedule.*

© 1986 RCA Corporation.
Final Manuscript received November 20, 1985
Reprint RE-31-1-12

niques that have been refined over the years apply directly to the processing of GaAs. As a result, integration levels approaching 10,000 gates are now being seen.[1]

With the low gate delays that the technology provides, a GaAs 100-million instructions-per-second central processing unit (CPU) was easy to design. However, construction of a complete system to operate at this speed presents some unique challenges in the designs of the system architecture, demonstration board, and support software. For example, chip-to-chip communication along conduction paths on the board (an insignificant problem in the silicon environment) is greatly complicated because propagation delays are about 5 percent of the CPU cycle per inch of conductor length, which makes control of data skew and delay a significant factor in board layout.

We are using the double-level-metal enhancement/depletion (E/D) process provided by TriQuint Corporation to construct the CPU. The chip is partially handcrafted and partially designed using standard cells, and was laid out using RCA CADDAS tools. A system that consists of the CPU, 512 words of memory, and a minimum I/O capability is being constructed using leadless ceramic chip carriers (LCCCs) and emitter-coupled logic (ECL) glue chips. It will be mounted on a single board made of alumina.

TriQuint's E/D foundry services

RCA is currently using the GaAs enhancement/depletion E/D process provided by TriQuint Semiconductor of Beaverton, Oregon. TriQuint is a newly formed subsidiary of Tektronix, also in Beaverton, Oregon. Research in GaAs technology began at Tektronix in 1978. Two processes are available from Tri-Quint: depletion-mode and enhancement/depletion-mode (E/D) processing. RCA is using the low-power, high-speed E/D process to build an 8-bit, reduced-instruction set CPU (RISC) microprocessor on a single chip.

The E/D process requires a single, 2-volt power supply. The E/D logic family is designed to have a 0.6-volt logic swing. Logic 0 and 1 levels are represented by 0.2 and 0.8 volts, respectively. The E/D logic family has a typical delay time of 200 ps that is varied based on the gate's output loading. Figure 1 illustrates output delay times with respect to loading for the E/D gate family.[2]

The E/D logic family generated for the 8-bit microprocessor design was created for use in a standard cell layout implementation. In this approach, the layouts for all gates in the family have the same cell height, and the length varies as a function of the gate fan-in. This permits automatic placement and routing of all standard cells.

The E/D logic family consists of 28 gate types for logic design, ranging from an inverter to a 10-input AND/OR logic

Reprinted with permission from *RCA Engineer*, Volume 31, Number 1, January/February 1986, pages 76-80. Copyright © 1986 by RCA Corporation.

gate. Because we used standard cells to implement the logic, the 8-bit microprocessor—except for its general register file and four program counters—requires 1150 gates. We estimate that this level of standard-cell integration, combined with the register file and program counters, should dissipate 427 mW of power for the entire microprocessor circuit.

Alumina substrate packaging

We will use an 84-pin leadless-ceramic chip carrier (LCCC) to package the 8-bit microprocessor circuit. System-level packaging of the microprocessor with GaAs memory chips (in 40-pin LCCC packages) and emitter-coupled logic/transistor-to-transistor logic (ECL/TTL) translators will be done on an alumina substrate. The alumina substrate provides the support platform for the system and interconnection (on multiple levels) of signals between CPU, memory, and ECL input/output (I/O). Typical signal propagation delay time for transmission line interconnects built on alumina substrates is 250 ps/inch. This translates into a delay time per inch that is 5 percent of the microprocessor cycle time.

We considered alternative materials for packaging the system—beryllia, epoxy glass board, and Teflon—but problems with them dictated the use of alumina.

All the interconnects among the microprocessor, memory, and ECL interface parts are uniform transmission lines that have characteristic impedances of 50 to 100 ohms with adequate load terminations. This ensures that the rising- and falling-edge times of 1 ns do not produce unacceptable noise levels that would be caused by mismatched transmission lines.

Architecture

The GaAs technology demonstration CPU's low level of integration limits it to an 8-bit machine. A 16-bit address allows for memory growth to 64k bytes. The instruction set contains 23 instructions; 19 are 8 bits long and 4 are 16 bits long. Our goal of 100 million instructions per second (MIPS) requires that an instruction be fetched every 10 ns. To reach the 100-MIPS goal, we used a 400-MHz clock, a RISC philosophy[3] of sim-

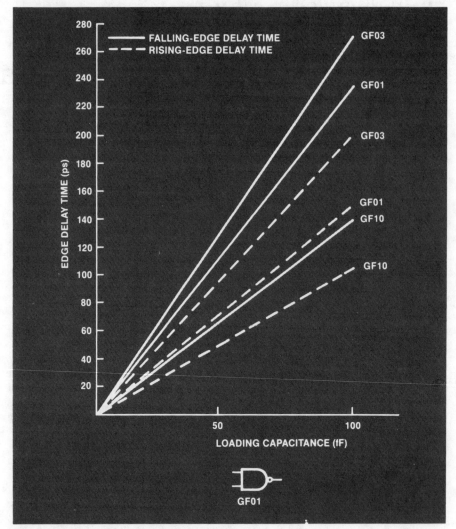

Fig. 1. *Delay versus loading for GaAs E/D standard cell family.*

ple, fast-executing, hardware-frugal instructions, and a pipeline[4] that permits the concurrent processing of several instructions. Table I lists the CPU processes.

A single chip-select bit divides the 512 available 8-bit memory locations into two sets of 256 by 4-bit memories. We did this so the lower 256 addresses fall into two of the four memory chips and the upper half of the addresses fall into the other two. The reason for this stems from the nature of instruction and data fetches from memory.

At 100 MIPS, an instruction fetch occurs every 10 ns. The data fetches occur between the instruction fetches. While future memory parts will be able to handle requests every 5 ns, we were uncertain that the available memory parts could do so. With this memory-chip-selection method, we can run two experiments on the system.

A program shorter than 256 (8 bits)

instructions can reside in the lower half and access data in the upper half of memory. In this experiment, no memory part is accessed more often than every 10 ns. This experiment uses a form of interleaved memories.

A program that is longer than 256 instructions can request data from the same memory chip as current instructions. This will cause memory chip accesses 5 ns apart. If the system does not permit access at 5-ns intervals, then

Table I. *CPU processes*

CPU Pipestage	Duration (ns)	Phase
Request Instruction	2.5	3
Wait	15.0	4, 1
Receive Instruction	2.5	2
Decode Instruction	5.0	3, 4
Execute Instruction	2.5	1
Write-back Result	5.0	2, 3

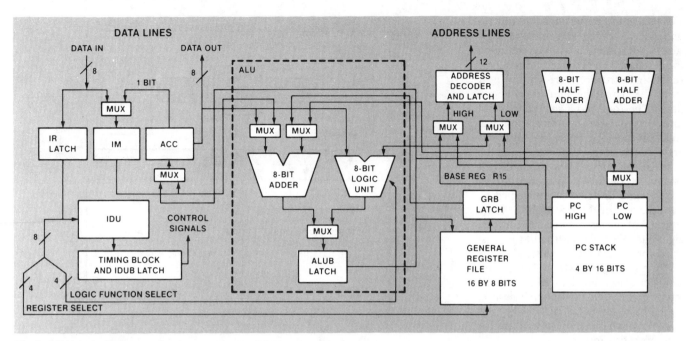

Fig. 2. *CPU block diagram.*

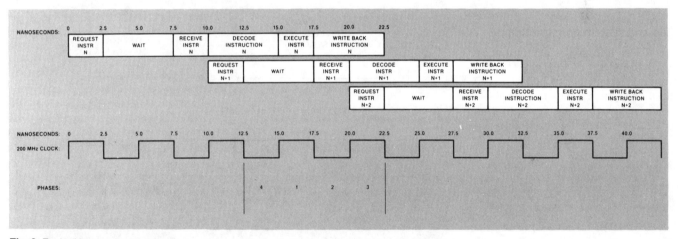

Fig. 3. *Typical instruction sequence.*

we can lower the clock frequency until the system works, and thus test the cycle time of the memory parts as they function in the system.

Figure 2 is a block diagram of the CPU developed from these goals and limitations. The general register stack consists of sixteen 8-bit registers, and the program counter (PC) stack consists of four 16-bit registers. The arithmetic logic unit (ALU) consists of an 8-bit ripplecarry adder, an 8-bit logic unit, and an 8-bit output latch (ALUB). All two-operand arithmetic and logic function instructions take one operand from the accumulator and the other operand from a register in the general register stack. All branching is relative to the value in the PC; the 8-bit offset is found in the 16-bit instruction.

All loops are implemented with a conditional branch. All subroutines require a push, a branch, and a pop. (The current address in the PC is saved, which is the push; the subroutine is executed, the branch; and the original address is retrieved, the pop, and loaded into the PC.) The PC stack exists only to save the return addresses that make subroutines possible. With four PC registers in the PC stack, subroutine nesting is limited to a depth of three.

The load and store instructions use addresses that reside in the general register stack. The most-significant 8 bits of the address are taken from register 15, and the least-significant 8 bits are taken from a general register that is specified in the instruction.

The typical instruction sequence given in Fig. 3 shows that an instruction request occurs every 10 ns and a pipeline depth of two to three instructions is processed at once. The instructions depicted in Fig. 3 represent 8-bit instructions, or the first half of a 16-bit instruction.

The instruction register sends the lower four bits of every instruction to the general register stack as a register address. It sends the upper four bits of every instruction to the logic unit to choose one of the 16 possible logic functions of two operands. The logic unit's result is disregarded for all instructions that are not among the chosen six logic function instructions. The general register stack's output will be disregarded for instructions that do not require an operand from the general register file.

This method assigns opcodes (operation codes) to the two-operand logic function instructions without choice by the designer. The two-operand nonlogic function instructions are chosen next from the remaining unused combinations. The four 16-bit instructions fall into the non-two-operand, nonlogic function category. Their first eight bits are decoded in the same manner as the 8-bit instructions. Their second eight bits are a constant or a branch offset; the constant or offset is anticipated by the decoding of the first eight bits (the opcode) of the instructions. The second eight bits of a 16-bit instruction are destined for the IM register instead of the instruction-register (IR). These constants or offsets are allowed into the IR latch register, but prevented from executing by resetting the IR latch register to zero, which is one of the opcodes for a no-operation instruction.

Chip and system construction

The GaAs technology demonstration system includes the CPU chip, four 256 by 4-bit GaAs memories, and ECL I/O parts. The system is shown in Fig. 4.

The GaAs technology demonstration CPU chip includes custom-designed macrocells for the general register file and the program counter stack. The rest of the chip is implemented with 1150 standard cells. If we had designed the entire chip with standard cells, there would have been about 2000 gates.

RCA's MP2D layout tool allows the engineer to specify the corners in which the macrocells are to be placed. Then, MP2D will fit the standard cells into the remaining chip space as efficiently as it can. Figure 5 shows a floor plan of the CPU chip.

The CPU will be packaged on an 84-pin leadless ceramic chip carrier (LCCC). There will be ten address lines, eight data-in lines, eight data-out lines, one 400-MHz clock input, one reset input, and one read/not-write output. This totals 29 signals. There will be 16 power and ground pins and 39 unused pins.

We have simplified the I/O of the technology demonstration CPU chip. The CPU is kept in a dormant state by the reset pin until the memories have been loaded. Then, the CPU goes into a no-operation instruction loop when the program is finished. The system's I/O

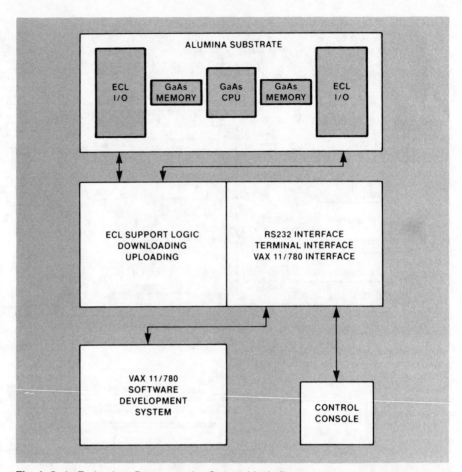

Fig. 4. *GaAs Technology Demonstration System block diagram.*

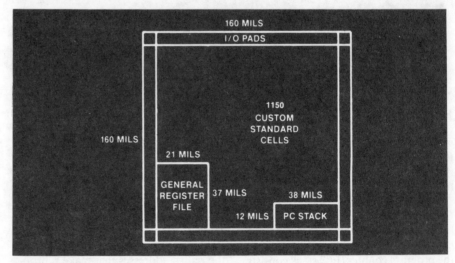

Fig. 5. *CPU chip floor plan.*

involves loading the GaAs memories through the ECL interface parts from a Digital Equipment Corporation VAX 11/780 computer.

Support software/documentation

In the CPU development, we have used several approaches that are consistent with RCA's commitment to use formal hardware-descriptive languages. First, we wrote a behavioral model using ISP'. With this model, the assembler and linker in the ISP' tool set are being used for software production. Initially, we used the N.mPc simulator to test the instruction set and the functional interrelationships of the system components.

Later on, we will use it to debug software.

Next, as the structural design progressed, we expressed the design in RCA's hardware descriptive language, CADL, and simulated the design using RCA's gate-level simulator, MIMIC. Subsequently, we transferred the design to a hierarchical description using Texas Instrument's hardware description language (HDL), and resimulated the design using Texas Instruments' simulator INTSIM. A translator has been written that fetches the connection list from the HDL database and converts it into the proper format for the RCA MP2D layout program. This provides a direct link from a high-level description of the design—in RCA's standard cells—to a complete artwork file (mask-making drive tapes.) Of course, other programs handle macrocells.

Currently, three other related software development projects are in various stages of completion. First, an assembler/reorganizer program is being written to translate the DARPA core set assembly language into inputs for the ISP' linker, reorganizing (optimizing) it along the way to obtain maximum performance from a pipeline machine.[5,6,7,8,9] Second, a set of diagnostic/demonstration routines is being produced to exercise all aspects of the system finally produced. This will help us debug the system and study construction aspects, with an eye toward expansion. And, third, a loader routine is being produced that, after hand-loading into the system, will enable us to load programs and data directly from the support software host, a VAX 11/780 computer.

Status and plans

On December 31, 1985, we were ready to begin layout of the 8-bit GaAs technology demonstration microprocessor.

Both the 16 by 8-bit general register stack and the 4 by 16-bit program counter stack have been hand-crafted and are complete. Work on the standard cell layouts for all 20 cell types is completed.

Final layout of the complete microprocessor circuit was done after we completed some final circuit simulations. These simulations address the timing and control of all major elements of the microprocessor.

We delivered a complete design tape

Authors, left to right: Helbig, Schellack, and Zieger.

Walter Helbig is Unit Manager of the Advanced Computation Systems Group in ATL's Systems Engineering Laboratory. He is responsible for the design and implementation of advanced computer system architectures. He directed the design of the GaAs 32-bit RISC architecture, and is participating in the construction of the 8-bit GaAs RISC Technology Demonstration System. Previously, he directed the design of two versions of the RCA ATMAC microprocessor, including all of the supporting software, as well as systems utilizing an ATMAC. Walt has a BSEE degree from the Milwaukee School of Engineering. Contact him at:
Advanced Technology Laboratories
Moorestown, N.J.
Tacnet: 253-6530

Robert Schellack is a Senior Member of the Engineering Staff in ATL's Microelectronics Laboratory. His work involves GaAs device modeling and circuit analysis for high-speed digital applications. He is incorporating automated design capability for high-speed digital GaAs ICs into RCA's CADDA system. He is also Principal Investigator for a study of advanced GaAs IC technology. Bob has BSEE

and MSEE degrees from Drexel University. Contact him at:
Advanced Technology Laboratories
Moorestown, N.J.
Tacnet: 253-6519

Richard M. Zieger is a member of the engineering staff of ATL's Systems Engineering Laboratory, where he is involved in designing and developing computer architecture. He has worked with a System Architecture Simulator (SARSIM), modeling and simulating a high-speed signal processing system. Recently, he completed the architecture and logic design of an 8-bit gallium arsenide (GaAs) microprocessor, a pipelined, RISC architecture to be implemented in 1-micron double-level-metal enhancement/depletion MESFET technology. The microprocessor is designed to operate at a 200-MHz rate and perform 100 MIPS. Mr. Zieger holds a BS in Computer Engineering from Lehigh University, and has recently begun work on an MSEE at Villanova University. Contact him at:
Advanced Technology Laboratories
Moorestown, N.J.
Tacnet: 253-6518

to TriQuint Semiconductor for generation of masks and fabrication.

Work on the development of the demonstration system and its support software is scheduled to continue into the beginning of 1986.

References

1. Roosild, Sven A., "Survey of Manufacturing Capabilities for GaAs Digital Integrated Circuits," *1984 IC Symposium Technical Digest*.
2. Flegal, T., LaRue, G., Rode, A., "A High-Yield GaAs Gate Array Technology and Applications," *1983 GaAs IC Symposium Technical Digest*.
3. Hennessy, J.L., Jouppi, N., Baskett, F., Gross, T.R., Gill, J., and Przybylski, S., "Hardware/Software Tradeoffs for Increased Performance," *Proc.*, SIGARCH/SIGPLAN Symposium on Architectural Support for Programming Languages and Operating Systems, ACM, Palo Alto, Cal., pp 2-11, (March 1982).
4. Hennessy, J.L., Jouppi, N., Przybylski, S., Rowen, C., Gross, T.R., Baskett, F., and Gill, J., "MIPS: A Microprocessor Architecture," *Proceedings*, Micro-15, IEEE, pp. 17-22, (October 1982).
5. Gross, T.R., "Code Optimization of Pipeline Constraints," PhD thesis, Stanford University (August 1983).
6. Gross, T.R., and Hennessy, J.L., "Optimizing Delayed Branches." *Proceedings*, Micro-15, IEEE, pp. 114-120, (October 1982.)
7. Gross, T.R., "Code Optimization Techniques for Pipelined Architectures," *Proc. Compcon Spring '83*, IEEE Computer Society, San Francisco, Cal., pp. 278-285 (March 1983).
8. Hennessy, J.L. and Gross, T.R., "Code Generation and Reorganization in the Presence of Pipeline Constraints," *Proc. Ninth POPL Conference*, ACM, pp. 120-127 (January 1982).
9. Hennessy, J.L. and Gross, T.R., "Postpass Code Optimization of Pipeline Constraints," *ACM Trans. on Programming Languages and Systems*, Vol. 5, No. 3, (July 1983).

Reprinted from *Computer*, October 1986, pages 60-68. Copyright © 1986 by The Institute of Electrical and Electronics Engineers, Inc.

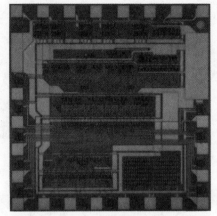

The MDC2901, a 4-bit GaAs microprocessor circuit that contains 1860 transistors. (Photo courtesy of McDonnell Douglas Microelectronics Center.)

A 32-bit RISC Implemented in Enhancement-Mode JFET GaAs

Terrence L. Rasset, Roger A. Niederland, John H. Lane,

and William A. Geideman

McDonnell Douglas Astronautics Company

This CPU architecture exemplifies the special design approaches being developed to take advantage of GaAs technology for high-speed processing.

Recently, considerable attention has been focused on gallium arsenide (GaAs) semiconductor process technologies for very high speed digital integrated circuits. This attention is motivated primarily by the ability of GaAs transistors to switch much faster with lower power consumption than transistors in silicon technologies. [1,2] Soon to be available with higher switching speed and more transistors than the fastest silicon technology (emitter-coupled logic), GaAs digital ICs will be a boon to developers of supercomputers and specialized high-speed microprocessors, such as digital signal processors. GaAs transistors are also much more resistant to temperature extremes and to ionizing radiation than silicon, important features for applications requiring operation in harsh environments.

This does not mean that GaAs will replace silicon; rather, where the higher cost of GaAs is warranted by application requirements that only GaAs can satisfy, it will augment silicon. The high cost of GaAs chips is due mainly to the scarcity of gallium and the inferior quality and difficulty in manufacturing the gallium arsenide compound. Unlike silicon, which is very uniform and pure, GaAs has many defects and its characteristics may vary considerably from ingot to ingot, affecting yield. Also, the wafers have a tendency to break during processing.

GaAs material defects and problems controlling noise margins across the chip affect processing yields and limit chip die sizes, thus limiting the number of possible transistors on a chip. Power consumption also limits the chip size. Although GaAs consumes much less power than silicon ECL, it usually consumes more than silicon MOS processes. As in silicon, power consumption is related to the switching speed of the transistors; generally, the faster the gates, the more power they consume.

As the quality of the GaAs material has improved and the processing technologies have matured, greater circuit densities have been achieved. During the last few years, a great deal of development work has centered on gate arrays and memory chips, resulting in significant advances. By 1983 experimental 1K static RAMs had been announced, and in 1985 4K and 16K static RAMs and 2000-gate arrays were announced. [3] Recent announcements have included experimental 5K-gate arrays.

To fully exploit GaAs in digital logic circuits requires special design approaches. Because gates switch so fast, the ratio of on-chip propagation delays to off-chip communication delays is greater than in silicon. Even in today's supercomputers, which use very high speed ECL logic, chip-to-chip communication is a more important factor in the computer's cycle time than on-chip gate delays. This suggests that higher levels of integration and novel computer architectures are necessary before GaAs technology will pay real dividends in high-performance computers.

A number of efforts to develop GaAs computers are currently in progress. One of these projects is at McDonnell Douglas Astronautics Company, where a single-chip GaAs microprocessor and a single-chip floating-point coprocessor in a proprietary GaAs junction field effect transistor process are under development. The goal of this project is twofold: first, to develop and demonstrate GaAs JFET technology, and, second, to produce a microprocessor for very high data rate real-time processing.

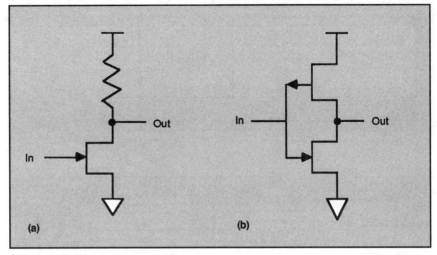

Figure 1. GaAs inverter circuits: resistive load inverter (a), and complementary inverter (b).

GaAs E-JFET process

The N-channel enhancement mode junction field effect transistor (E-JFET) is fabricated by ion implantation in a semi-insulating GaAs wafer.[4,5] The process steps are similar to silicon wafer processing except that no furnace diffusion steps are used and all etching is dry, using plasma and reactive ions. The JFET P-N junction is formed by implanting silicon ions to form the N-region and then implanting magnesium over the silicon-implanted region to form the P-region.

An added advantage of the JFET process is that the implantation steps can be reversed to produce a P-channel device. Thus, P-channel and N-channel transistors can be combined on the same wafer to produce complementary logic in GaAs.

The schematic for both the complementary and resistive load inverters is shown in Figure 1. Both of these circuits can be manufactured on the same wafer, giving the circuit designer the ability to save power where speed is not critical. These are simple, low-transistor-count devices with no level-translation required between any of the different circuit combinations, as is required with many other GaAs processes. Thus, they allow the use of direct coupled FET logic (DCFL), with a voltage swing of about 0.8 volts and a noise margin of 200 millivolts.[4]

The low power dissipation, simple transistor configurations, low transistor count per logic gate, and ease of processing make the GaAs E-JFET technology a good candidate for large-scale integrated circuits. This has been demonstrated with the successful design and fabrication of a 1K static RAM with a wafer yield of 47 percent, and a fully functional emulation of the Advanced Micro Devices AM2901 four-bit microprocessor slice. A 4K static RAM containing over 25,000 transistors on a 4.6 mm × 4.1 mm die is currently in processing, with functional parts expected by the end of 1986.

Even though the GaAs JFET technology is still maturing, it has proven viable for high-speed and low-power digital integrated circuit applications. The JFET process has performed well in adverse environmental conditions, not only outperforming all silicon technologies but also all other GaAs processes in resistance to radiation effects.[6]

Currently, E-JFET logic gates are sensitive to circuit loading, which limits gate fan-outs, and to other types of gate loading. The loading on a particular net is composed mainly of interconnect resistance, capacitance between interconnects, interconnect crossovers, and gate capacitance of the transistors connected to the net. This sensitivity has a significant effect on the circuit designs developed and puts an extra burden on the architecture, logic, circuit, and layout designers, who must work as a close-knit team to produce desirable results. The loading effects will be reduced in the near future with self-aligned gate structures, which will reduce the sidewall capacitance of the gate. The effects of interconnect are being reduced by lowering the sheet resistance of the interconnect and by decreasing the dielectric constant of the insulating material between the interconnect layers to lower the interconnect capacitance.

The GaAs JFET sensitivity to loading also has a considerable effect on off-chip communication, in which it can adversely affect system performance. In GaAs, the ratio of on-chip delay to off-chip delay is much greater than in silicon technologies, thus making the system partitioning problem even more critical than in silicon,[3] where the slower gates and larger scale of integration lessen chip-to-chip communication effects. Therefore, the search for a suitable GaAs computer architecture is strongly influenced by the need to lessen

interchip communication. This implies that large-scale integration capable of producing single-chip microprocessors and compact systems is even more important in GaAs than in silicon.

Architectural overview

In developing the GaAs microprocessor, we wanted an architecture that could be initially implemented in less than 25,000 transistors, yet would support the Ada programming language and be viable well into the next decade. Because the GaAs process is maturing and higher levels of integration will be available by the end of the decade, the architecture should be able to grow, to take advantage of these increased levels of integration. For efficient support of Ada, the architecture has to be a good compiler target and should provide a large address space. To provide sufficient precision for the planned applications and a large linear address space, we preferred a 32-bit architecture.

To achieve our rather ambitious architectural goals within such a small transistor budget, we followed the reduced instruction set computer philosophy in developing our architecture.[7,8] The RISC approach favors simplified instruction sets with few format options or addressing modes. It requires that the implementation cost of every instruction and hardware feature be justified in terms of frequency of use in the execution of programs, resulting in a streamlined, efficient instruction set architecture.[9] With a simple instruction set, the hardware can be optimized to execute the instructions that are used most frequently in the application programs. Other, more complex instructions are synthesized, as needed, out of the simpler instructions. In this way, for complex operations, such as a procedure call, we can generate the code

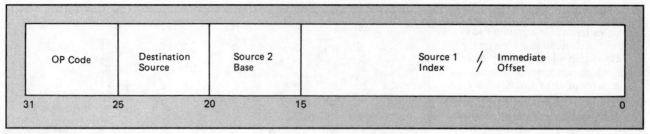

Figure 2. Instruction word format.

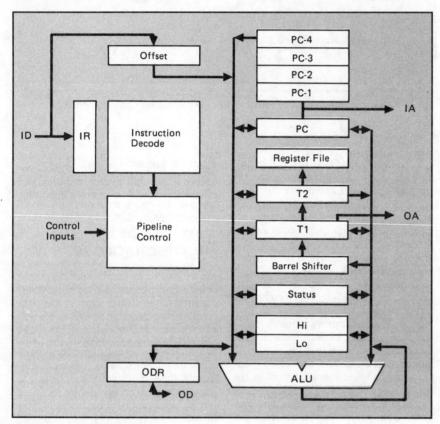

Figure 3. CPU block diagram.

at the machine instruction set level.

A unique feature of the MIPS microprocessor that was incorporated into our GaAs microprocessor is the use of pipelined instruction execution without hardware interlocks to detect resource conflicts. Instead, the code emitted by the compiler is rearranged to eliminate conflicts by a tool called a reorganizer. There are two main advantages to reorganizing at compile time rather than detecting at run time: first, the hardware necessary to control resource allocation and detect conflicts is eliminated, and, second, execution is faster because no instructions are suspended while waiting for an earlier instruction to finish using a resource (e.g., waiting for an instruction to write to a register).

In addition to rearranging code to eliminate pipeline conflicts, the reorganizer also attempts to replace NOPs (null operations) that result from branch delays and data load latencies with useful instructions. Delayed branches [13] are another feature of the RISC philosophy. Rather than fetch and discard the instructions immediately following a branch that is taken (as most CISCs do), most RISCs execute these instructions. At the worst, NOPs are inserted into these instruction slots, but with a one-instruction branch delay the MIPS reorganizer was able to move a useful instruction into the branch delay slots 90 percent of the time. Another way to look at this is that data taken from the MIPS shows that an average of 21 percent of the executed instructions were performed in the delay cycle following a taken branch. [8] If these instructions were fetched and not executed, 21 percent of the cycles would be wasted. Similar data was gathered for programs executing on a VAX 11/780. [14]

The architecture we developed is very simple and regular, yet has hardware resources in the data path that are not found on more complex microprocessors. All instructions are one word long, are available in either an immediate or register-to-register format as shown in Figure 2, have fixed fields, and execute in one cycle. Unlike most complex instruction set microprocessors, the critical delay path in this microprocessor is in the data

optimally for each instance, rather than creating a large, complex instruction that attempts to deal with all cases (and probably satisfies few). The RISC approach results in a greatly simplified control structure (usually hardwired), which, in addition to being very fast, leaves more chip area available for performance enhancements to the data path.

At the time we started developing the architecture, the leading RISC projects were the University of California at Berkeley RISCs I and II, [10] the Stanford University MIPS, [8] and the IBM 801. [11] Of these, the Stanford MIPS project influenced our architecture the most. The MIPS microprocessor was implemented in an NMOS silicon semiconductor process using approximately 25K transistors. The architecture of the MIPS was compiler driven; that

is, the instruction set was determined on the basis of its utility as the target for an optimizing compiler. The MIPS group felt that compiler optimization techniques have reached such a level of sophistication that computer architecture assumptions with regard to the execution of compiled code must be reexamined. They concluded that a simplified load-store architecture (i.e., only load and store instructions reference data memory; all others are register to register) with no hidden microarchitecture could deliver better performance in the execution of compiled code than could a complex instruction set computer (CISC). [12] The MIPS approach requires sophisticated register allocation and other optimization techniques in the compiler to achieve full performance. MIPS was not intended to be hand programmed path, not the control path. That is, the execution cycle time is completely determined by the time it takes to access the operands, perform an ALU operation, and save the result.

The microprocessor. The microprocessor architecture and implementation were driven by the constraints of the GaAs process. So that the microprocessor would be buildable in the near term, a strict transistor budget was established at less than 25,000 transistors.

The fixed format of the instruction leads to a very simplified instruction decode, reducing both the number of transistors needed for its implementation and increasing the speed of the decode. The instruction decode accounts for less than two percent of the total transistor budget and controls the functional blocks of the microprocessor with only 31 control lines. The only other significant control circuitry on the microprocessor is the pipestage control, leaving 95 percent of the transistor budget for implementing the data path.

The microprocessor's data path is partitioned into functional units as shown in Figure 3. These functional units are used to implement the instructions in a manner which gives the most performance for the transistors. The PC contains the current program counter plus the three most recent values for exception recovery. The register file contains 17 general-purpose registers and a constant zero generator. A 32-bit word can be shifted in either direction any number of bits in either a logical or arithmetic manner in the barrel shifter. The two registers in Hi and Lo can be used as general-purpose registers but they also contain multiply and divide support circuitry. The ALU performs all logical and arithmetic calculations. Offset provides alignment for immediate data. The operand data register (ODR) communicates with operand data memory. The temporary registers, T1 and T2, are used for pipestage alignment and are transparent to the user. A status register is contained in Status. All of these registers are mapped into the register file address field (except the temporary registers), as in Figure 4.

All instructions contain either three register operand addresses or two operand addresses and 16 bits of data. All register address fields are five bits long, allowing up to 32 registers in the architecture, of which 22 are implemented. Program-accessible registers are addressed by these five-bit fields in the instruction, providing a simple, uniform view of the register set.

Since the transistor budget would not allow the implementation of a full multiplier, a two-bit-per-cycle iterative Booth's algorithm was implemented. The

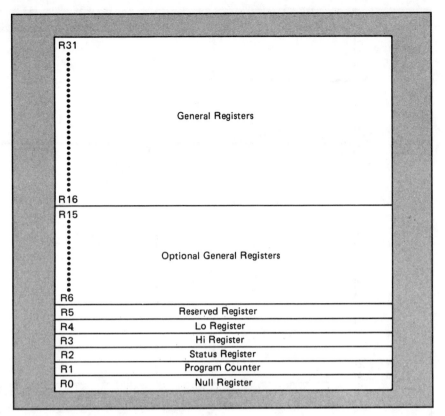

Figure 4. CPU register set.

multiplication control circuitry is incorporated in the Hi and Lo register pair and the ALU. This added a minimum of transistors and provided a means to accomplish a 32-by-32-bit multiply in 16 cycles. The Hi and Lo registers are also used to implement an iterative, nonrestoring divide algorithm. A 64-bit dividend can be divided by a 32-bit divisor, yielding a 32-bit quotient and a 32-bit remainder in 32 cycles.

All of the functional units are utilized during different instruction pipe stages. The pipe stages provide the flow necessary for overlapping instruction execution to increase resource utilization, resulting in superior performance.

Determining the number of pipeline stages. A difficult (and contentious) decision, intimately involved with the memory system design, was the choice of the number and type of execution pipeline stages. The decision centered on the problem of extending the execution pipeline into the memory and pipelining memory references. We quickly concluded that the four-stage pipeline discussed below was the ideal minimum. But increasing the number of stages to five or six, with the extra stages added to the memory access stages, would allow more time for memory accesses and therefore would make the memory system easier to build (or, some would argue, buildable at all). The six-stage pipeline would provide two stages for instruction fetch and two for operand read/write. This would require that the memory system be pipelined, the address being sent to the memory in the first stage and the data accessed and delivered to the microprocessor in the second. A new memory access would be achieved on every cycle by overlapping the address decoding with memory chip accessing and data delivery. This means that the memory word received by the microprocessor during cycle j would be the word read using the address sent out on cycle $j - 1$. For the five-stage case, only the data memory accesses would be extended to two cycles. This is based on the fact that most instruction references are sequential and very localized, which means that an effective instruction cache memory is more realizable than an effective data cache.

At first the six-stage pipeline seemed to offer considerable relief from a very difficult problem. Unfortunately, nothing is given for free: The six-stage pipe increases branch delays from one cycle to two and load latencies to two cycles. Data gathered from benchmark programs taken from real-time system applications and applied to four-, five-, and six-stage pipelines showed that the reorganizer was not able to effectively move useful instructions into the extra delay slots. The performance loss

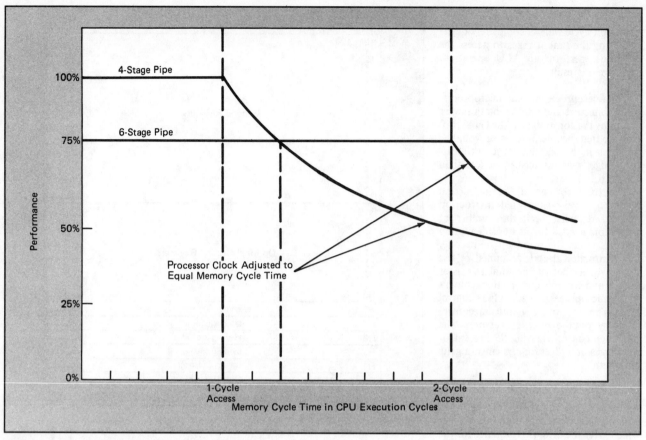

Figure 5. Performance model: 4-stage pipe vs. 6-stage pipe.

due to NOP insertion was from 20 to 30 percent for the six-stage pipeline and approximately half of that for the five-stage pipe relative to the four-stage pipe. The effect on microprocessor performance is illustrated by the graph in Figure 5, which shows microprocessor performance degradation for the four- and the six-stage pipelines as the memory cycle slows relative to the microprocessor cycle speed. The vertical axis is the net microprocessor throughput normalized to the four-stage implementation and the horizontal axis is the effective memory system access time. In reality, due to extra logic delays and problems inherent in clocking the memory pipe stages synchronously with the microprocessor clock, performance with six stages actually falls off before the memory access time reaches twice the microprocessor cycle time. Another problem with the six-stage pipeline is that it would require a more complex master pipeline control due to the extra states, more transistors for saving an additional copy of the PC, and another temporary register in the data path. The extra registers also add extra loads that must be driven by the data buses, which would have some effect, albeit small, on the execution cycle. With a four-stage pipeline, we can run the microprocessor's clock at least 25 percent slower

than with a six-stage pipeline and still achieve the same net throughput.

The pipeline. The instructions can be divided into two general categories: computational and memory reference. The instructions finish their execution in four pipe stages though some instructions do not use all four. These stages are shown in Figure 6.

The instruction addressed by the program counter is accessed during the first pipe stage, called instruction fetch. The lower half of the fetched instruction may contain a data value; therefore it is loaded into the offset register concurrently with the instruction register loading.

The instruction register contents are used in the ALU pipe stage. The operand address fields of the instruction register require no decoding and are sent directly to the registers so the operands can be accessed immediately. The simple instruction decode allows the control lines to become valid before the access of the operand is complete; therefore an instruction decode pipe stage is not necessary. The operands are latched at the arithmetic unit and the barrel shifter, allowing both buses to be used during the second half of the pipe stage. The result is computed and transferred to T1, where it is loaded at the

end of the ALU pipe stage. The results may also be loaded into the program counter, the Hi or Lo register, or the status register. If a store operation is in progress, the data is transferred to the operand data register (ODR) during the second half of the ALU pipe stage.

At the beginning of the third pipe stage, operand fetch, the contents of T1 will either contain the result of a computation or an operand address. In either case the contents are available on the operand address bus (OA). This provides not only the address for the operand memory, but a window into the microprocessor for testing purposes. The operand memory can be read or written to during this stage. If it is a read operation, the operand memory outputs the contents of the addressed location on the operand data bus, which is enabled onto the internal bus, making the data available to T2 during the second half of the pipe stage. T2 will be loaded with the operand memory contents during a load operation, displacing the address in T1. Otherwise, T1 is simply transferred to T2.

During the last instruction pipe stage, write back, T2 is transferred into the register file, if that was the destination.

The minimum microprocessor cycle time is the time it takes for the critical path

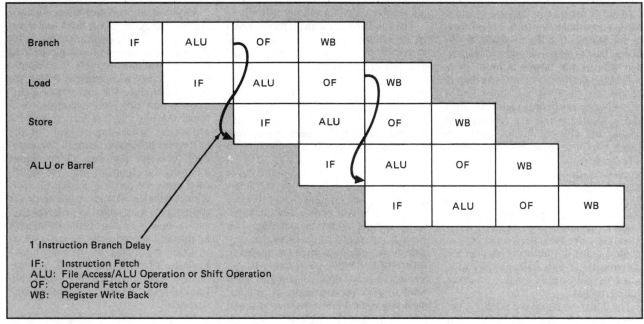

Figure 6. CPU pipeline flow.

in the ALU pipe stage, which starts with the instruction register outputting the operand addresses and ends with T1 being loaded with the results. Between these operations, the register file must be accessed, the operands transferred to the ALU, the add performed, and the results loaded into T1. Forty percent of the cycle is allocated for transferring data over the internal buses between the functional units; the rest of the cycle is split between the adder and the register file access.

Traditional microprocessor design uses buses for communication between different functional blocks, but, in order to get the most performance out of the GaAs circuits, interconnects must be kept short, with as few crossovers as possible.

Just as in silicon, precharging techniques are used to reduce the bus transfer time. The time available for precharging the buses is equal to the slowest functional unit. The functional units operate at much higher speeds than their equivalents in silicon, making the time available for precharging in GaAs significantly less than in silicon. Unfortunately, the bus loading is not significantly different. Also, clock skew must be controlled very closely to regulate this short precharge time. The bus design is a major factor in the critical path of the microprocessor and therefore received considerable attention.

A two-phase nonoverlapping clock scheme is used. This scheme maps well with the bus, giving two active pulses per pipe stage when the buses can be used for transferring data. The clocks have to be controlled so that the clock skew is kept

below half a nanosecond between the registers. The loading and interconnect lengths must be tuned for each branch of the clock distribution tree. To reduce the effects of clock skew across a 32-bit data path, all registers are clocked from the least significant bit, giving the adder more time since its most significant bits are a function of the least significant bits.

Exceptions, memory wait states, and hold states are handled by the microprocessor's pipe stage controller, a simple state machine with eight states, the majority used for startup and wait states. When an exception is taken, the state machine is forced to the IF state. All of the information necessary for a complete recovery from any exception is obtainable from the program counter's history file and the status register. The history file contains the three previous values of the program counter. A startup sequence is necessary to start the pipe stages after an exception; this is provided by the states IF, ALU, OF, and Exe. Exe is the normal operating state.

When the memory needs added time for access, the machine goes from Exe to the wait state. It will remain there inhibiting all pipe stages until the memory is ready; then on the next clock edge it returns to its normal state. Each of the states in the startup sequence has a wait state associated with it.

ALU implementation. A good example of the circuit design decisions that must be made in GaAs is the implementation of the microprocessor's arithmetic logic unit. Because the ALU is in the microprocessor's critical timing path, a good, high-speed design is essential. The ALU is decomposable into separate adder and logic sections, with the adder being by far the more complex. A high-speed adder design in GaAs should keep gate loading to a minimum, simultaneously keeping the number of gates in the longest path to a minimum. The adder must be 34 bits wide to implement the multiply algorithm. The four candidates considered for the adder design are listed in Table 1.

Table 1. Adder types.

	Transistors in Critical Path	Average Load	Maximum Load
Ripple-carry	82	1	2
Carry-select	37	1.9	18
Carry-lookahead	11	3.4	8
Modified* Brent & Kung	23	1.5	3

*Includes logical unit; all others exclude logical functions.

Many of the criteria followed in selecting an adder design for GaAs are the same as for silicon, but the emphasis is different. Due to crossover and communication effects, the layout is much more critical for performance in GaAs than in silicon. As in other integrated circuit technologies, an efficient use of transistors and a regular layout are preferred. In silicon, the efficient use of transistors makes economic sense; in GaAs it is absolutely essential. In silicon, gate delays are so dominant that other factors can be ignored and extra complexity can be introduced if it reduces the number of gate delays in the critical path. For implementation in the GaAs JFET process, we rejected the carry-lookahead adder because of the number of transistors required and the irregular layout. Delays attributed to crossovers were nearly equal to the delays due to fan-out.

The adder we chose is a modified version of an adder described by Brent and Kung.[15] This adder is characterized by simple cells with low gate fan-out and a very regular layout. The critical path contains 23 gates (compared with 11 in the carry-lookahead adder) with an average load of 1.5 gates. The maximum loading on any one gate is three gates. In addition, the loading from interconnects and crossovers is minimal since most of the connections are local.

Another advantage of the modified Brent-Kung adder is that its layout and control signals made it possible to superimpose the logical unit over the adder. This added only seven transistors and one resistor per bit and one gate delay to the critical path.

The ripple-carry adder has a very regular structure with exceptionally low fan-out, but with a 34-bit adder the number of gates in the critical path (82 gates) is unacceptable for a high-speed circuit. The carry-select adder, with 37 gate delays in the critical path, has a gate driving 18 loads, slowing the adder to an unacceptable speed.

The floating-point coprocessor

For efficient execution of floating-point arithmetic, an optional floating-point coprocessor chip is also being developed. The coprocessor is optimized to perform floating-point arithmetic on either single precision (32-bit) or double-precision (64-bit) data in the IEEE format. Due to the complexity of floating-point operations, the coprocessor does not follow the single-cycle instruction execution scheme of the microprocessor. Rather, each floating-point instruction is a complete floating-point operation, including programmable rounding and normalization.

The full IEEE standard is too complex to be implemented fully in hardware; therefore only the essential computational elements were included. To implement the full standard, software must be used to augment the core hardware resources. For example, arithmetic exception detection is fully implemented in hardware but exception handling is not. Whenever an exception, such as overflow or underflow, is detected by the coprocessor, a signal is sent to the microprocessor. A software handler executed by the microprocessor determines the cause by reading the coprocessor status register and performing the application-specific exception handling. This strategy results in a control area that consists of two relatively small (compared to other IEEE floating-point units) PLAs. The coprocessor does contain full hardware support for arithmetic operations, including eight double-precision operand registers and double-precision significand- and exponent-processing units.

The coprocessor depends on the microprocessor to perform all memory accesses. The coprocessor monitors the instruction stream, picking off the floating-point instructions as they are fetched by the microprocessor. During the execution of floating-point arithmetic operations, the coprocessor functions independently of the microprocessor. For floating-point load or store instructions, the microprocessor computes the memory address and initiates the memory accesses; then it allows the coprocessor to load data from or enable data onto the operand bus. For conditional branches on floating-point conditions, the coprocessor provides a True/False-valued signal to the microprocessor. The microprocessor computes the branch target address and loads this into the PC if the signal from the coprocessor is True.

To reduce the demands placed on the microprocessor for instruction fetching and to allow greater concurrency between the microprocessor and the coprocessor, two coprocessor arithmetic instructions are packed into a 32-bit instruction word. To further support parallel, concurrent operations, two floating-point coprocessors (plus two other coprocessors) may be used with a single microprocessor. This feature was added to the interface design primarily to support multiply-intensive applications. Because a full multiplier would not fit on the coprocessor chip, the multiply instruction uses an iterative, two-bit per cycle algorithm. The result is multiply execution times three to four times slower than add instruction execution times. The reorganizer assists the compiler in packing floating-point instructions and in scheduling two floating-point and one fixed-point computational streams.

Coprocessor implementation. Figure 7 is a block diagram of the main functional units in the floating-point coprocessor. Independent, dedicated processing elements are used wherever possible to maximize the parallelism of operations within the coprocessor chip. The coprocessor is partitioned into two semi-independent sections: the bus interface section and the arithmetic processing section. In the arithmetic processing section, the exponent processor performs all operations involving the exponents while the significand processor performs arithmetic operations on the significands. Some hardware components were added to make the execution time of all instructions fixed, with no operand dependencies, to facilitate instruction scheduling by the reorganizer. Exclusive of peripheral circuits, approximately 80 percent of the coprocessor chip transistors are dedicated to computational elements.

The same implementation considerations hold for the coprocessor as were discussed for the microprocessor. However, due to the nature of the operations performed by the coprocessor, data busing and control signal distribution are much simpler in the coprocessor. Each floating-point arithmetic operation follows a fixed sequence of operations that requires multiple processing cycles per instruction, unlike the microprocessor, which must execute a new instruction on every cycle with a new set of operands. The coprocessor reads a set of operands from the register file at the start of an instruction execution, and then, at the end of several execution steps, the result is written into the destination register. This reduces the requirements on the internal operand data buses and allows the control signals to be decoded in advance and routed to the data path components without strict time requirements. Thus, there is no need to allow any control decode time in the length of a processing cycle, and the cycle time is based entirely on the data path delays.

The floating-point coprocessor contains in a status register condition codes that are set as a result of arithmetic operations. The bus interface section uses these flags to execute conditional branch instructions concurrent with arithmetic instruction execution in the arithmetic processing section. This allows the microprocessor to branch on coprocessor busy or on the results of the first of the two arithmetic instructions while the second is being executed. In this way, instruction fetch delays that would otherwise result from a branch to a new block of code can be avoided.

The coprocessor uses the same clock as the microprocessor. This is necessitated by the close cooperation with which the two processors must operate. In particular, the bus interface design requires the coprocessor to load instructions and operands, and to output results, at the correct point in the microprocessor's execution cycle. During conditional jump instructions, the coprocessor presents to the microprocessor the valid conditional test line at the correct time during the appropriate microprocessor pipeline stage. To facilitate this, the microprocessor's internal state information is available to the coprocessor on microprocessor output pins. The coprocessor uses this state information to detect bus wait states and exceptions by tracking the pipeline stage sequencing in the microprocessor. If the microprocessor causes a bus fault during a memory fetch, the coprocessor bus interface must be aware of it and may have to abort a bus operation.

A common clock is essential for synchronization between the microprocessor and coprocessor during bus operations and conditional branching on floating-point conditions. The coprocessor bus interface latches the bus input data or enables output data on the same clock edge that the processor uses. This is the most critical timing and is controlled by very simple gating to minimize potential problems. Hold times provided by the memory system and the data bus assist in providing safe margins.

To ensure that the two chips, the microprocessor and coprocessor, are able to operate together, the clock signals will be generated from a common external source and carefully routed to each chip. Within each chip, critical synchronization functions will be controlled by a minimum of logic gates. The chip IO pads and buffers will be identical on both chips to ensure compatible input and output delay times. The microprocessor's short execution cycle does not leave a very large margin for error or clock skew, so this area must be designed very carefully.

The memory interface

The high memory bandwidth required by the microprocessor led to separate instruction and operand buses. Consequently, the chip die size is determined by the input-output pad spacing, not by the number of transistors. The empty die area between the active die area and the input-output pads will be filled in a future version with on-chip instruction cache. Since all instructions are 32-bits long, the instruction memory is word addressable. But to support 8-, 16-, and 32-bit data types, the operand memory is byte addressable.

As with any high-cycle-speed microprocessor, the memory interface and the memory system are integral, and vitally important, parts of the design. Com-

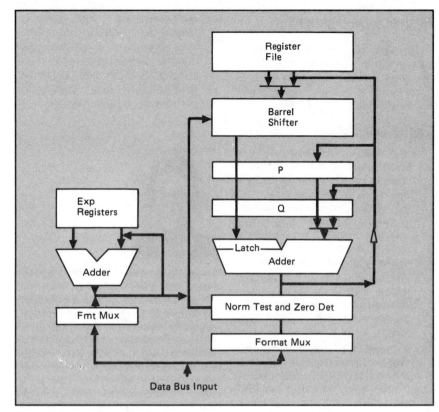

Figure 7. Coprocessor data path.

munication delays play a much more prominent role in GaAs than in silicon, compounding the problem of memory chip access delays. With an ultimate goal of a five-nanosecond execution cycle, the time it takes for a signal to travel down a wire to the memory and back becomes significant. One soon comes up against physical limits that no clever design will solve.

To retain performance, the memory system's access time must match the microprocessor's execution cycle time on the majority of memory accesses. A hierarchical memory system will be necessary for all but the smallest implementation. This approach will place a small, very fast cache near the microprocessor. For many systems, an intermediate buffer between main memory and the cache may be used to temporarily store data deleted from the cache in case it is soon needed again. Not only do physical delays affect data signals but they also exaggerate clock skew between the microprocessor and the cache. Current estimates predict that clock skew will account for 5 to 10 percent of the total cache access time.

The dual instruction and operand buses, with demultiplexed address and data lines, will greatly simplify the cache system design. Not only can separate caches be designed to suit the unique characteristics of the individual memories, but

each cache can be made smaller than a single cache without decreasing the hit rate. The instruction cache will be much simpler than the operand cache due to greater locality and absence of writes. Developing an operand cache that will provide acceptable hit rates will be one of the greatest challenges of this project.

We have described the design and implementation of a 32-bit microprocessor and floating-point coprocessor in gallium arsenide using N-channel enhancement mode junction field effect transistors. We have identified areas of the architecture and design that were critical to the GaAs implementation and explained our reasons for making the decisions that we made. Both chips have been simulated using the Endot N.2 behavioral simulator (Endot, Inc.) to verify and evaluate the architecture. During 1986 a cache memory design will be evaluated with this simulator to obtain design parameters and hit rates for a cache memory system on a dual bus microprocessor. The chip level design and chip layouts will be completed by the end of this year, and processing will begin early next year. We expect to have functional chips in 1987. With improvements in the GaAs JFET currently in development, our goal is an execution cycle of 5 nanoseconds. □

Acknowledgments

The authors appreciate the assistance they received from W. Loutensock and R. Roberts, both of the McDonnell Douglas Astronautics Company, and R. Zuleeg of the McDonnell Douglas Microelectronics Center.

References

1. R. C. Eden, A. R. Livingston, and B. M. Welch, "Integrated Circuits: the Case for Gallium Arsenide," *IEEE Spectrum,* Vol. 20, No. 12, Dec. 1983, pp. 30-37.

2. B. K. Gilbert, "Design and Performance Tradeoffs in the Use of VLSI and Gallium Arsenide in High Clockrate Signal Processors," *Proc. IEEE ICCD 84,* Port Chester, N.Y., Oct. 1984, pp. 260-266.

3. V. M. Milutinović, D. A. Fura, and W. A. Helbig, "An Introduction to GaAs Microprocessor Architecture for VLSI," *Computer,* Vol. 19, No. 3, Mar. 1986, pp. 30-42.

4. R. Zuleeg, J. K. Notthoff, and G. L. Troeger, "Double-Implanted GaAs Complementary JFETS," *IEEE Electron Devices Letters,* Vol. EDL-5, Jan. 1984, pp. 21-23.

5. R. Zuleeg et al., "Femto-Joule High-Speed Planar GaAs E-JFET Logic," *IEEE Trans. on Electron Devices,* Vol. ED-25, June 1978, pp. 628-639.

6. R. Zuleeg, "Radiation Effects in GaAs Integrated Circuits," Chapter 11 in Vol. 11, *VLSI Electronics, Microelectronic Science,* Academic Press, New York, 1985.

7. D. A. Patterson and D. L. Ditzel, "The Case for the Reduced Instruction Set Computer," *ACM Sigarch Computer Architecture News,* Vol. 8, No. 6, Oct. 1980, pp. 25-32.

8. J. L. Hennessy, "VLSI Processor Architecture," *IEEE Trans. Computers,* Vol. C-33, No. 12, Dec. 1984, pp. 1221-1246.

9. J. L. Hennessy, N. Jouppi, F. Daskett, T. R. Gross, and J. Gill, "Hardware/Software Tradeoffs for Increased Performance," *Proc. Sigarch/Sigplan Symp. Architectural Support for Programming Languages and Operation Systems,* ACM, Palo Alto, Calif., March 1982, pp. 2-11.

10. M. Katevenis, "Reduced Instruction Set Computer Architectures for VLSI," PhD dissertation, University of California, Berkeley, Oct. 1983.

11. G. Radin, "The 801 Minicomputer," *Proc. Sigarch/Sigplan Symp. Architectural Support for Programming Languages and Operation Systems,* ACM, Palo Alto, Calif., March 1982, pp. 39-47.

12. F. Chow, "A Portable, Machine-independent Global Optimizer—Design and Measurements," PhD dissertation, Stanford Univ., Stanford, Calif., 1984.

13. T. R. Gross and J. L. Hennessy, "Optimizing Delayed Branches," *Proc. Micro-15,* IEEE, Oct. 1982, pp. 114-120.

14. D. Clark and H. Levy, "Measurement and Analysis of Instruction Use in the VAX 11/780," *Proc. Ninth Annual Symp. Computer Architecture,* ACM/IEEE, Austin, Tex., April 1982.

15. R. P. Brent and H. T. Kung, "A Regular Layout for Parallel Adders," *IEEE Trans. Computers,* Vol. C-31, No. 3, March 1982, pp. 260-264.

Terrence Rasset received his BS degree in mathematics from Western Washington University in 1978 and his MS in information and computer science from the University of California, Irvine, in 1985. Since 1978 he has worked for the McDonnell Douglas Astronautics Company in Huntington Beach, California. He is currently manager of the processor advanced technology group and is responsible for the development of custom real-time processor systems and support software. His interests include advanced computer architectures for VLSI, real-time software, and application support tools. He is currently developing the architecture for an all-GaAs digital signal processor.

John H. Lane received his BS degree in physics from the New Mexico Institute of Technology in Socorro in 1955 and his MS in electrical engineering from the University of New Mexico in Albuquerque in 1961. Since 1971 he has worked for McDonnell Douglas Astronautics Company. He currently is a staff manager responsible for computer architecture and system design. Previously he was responsible for the architecture of the MDC281 MIL-STD-1750A processor chip set as well as other general-purpose and special-purpose computer architectures.

Roger Niederland received his BS in electrical engineering from Rutgers University in 1980. Currently employed by McDonnell Douglas Corporation in Huntington Beach, he is working in the processor development group and is group leader for integrated circuit design. Previously he was involved with the design of the MDC281, a 1750A-MIL-STD microprocessor chip set.

William A. Geideman received his BS in physics from Iona College, New Rochelle, New York, in 1957 and his MS in physics from Stevens Institute of Technology, Hoboken, New Jersey, in 1960. He joined McDonnell Douglas in 1973 and is currently a staff senior manager for microelectronics applications in the Astronautics Division in Huntington Beach. Prior to this he was the chief engineer for GaAs digital circuit design and fabrication in the microelectronics center. He is responsible for the application of GaAs digital circuits to internal system programs as well as for prime government contracts.

Readers may contact the authors at the McDonnell Douglas Astronautics Company, Huntington Beach, CA 92647.

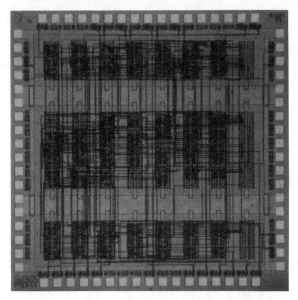

An 820-gate, programmable function interval timer (PROFIT) circuit implemented on a TI 1K GaAs gate array. (Photo courtesy of Texas Instruments.)

Reduced Instruction Set Architecture for a GaAs Microprocessor System

Eric R. Fox, Kenneth J. Kiefer, Robert F. Vangen, and Shaun P. Whalen

Control Data Corporation

Reprinted from *Computer*, October 1986, pages 71-81. Copyright © 1986 by The Institute of Electrical and Electronics Engineers, Inc.

RISC architecture characteristics of low hardware requirements, large register files, and pipelining accommodate the gate count constraints and preserve the inherent speed of GaAs technology.

Gate densities that permit the integration of an entire microprocessor on a single chip have been reached in GaAs technology. A reduced instruction set computer, or RISC, architecture is well suited to implementation in GaAs because of its low hardware requirements. The large register file and pipelined architecture typical of RISCs [1-2] complement the high on-chip gate speeds of GaAs by reducing off-chip communication. In late 1984 Texas Instruments and we at Control Data, under DARPA sponsorship, began a one-year project to develop a GaAs microprocessor system with a RISC architecture. The system we developed consists of a CPU, a floating-point coprocessor, or FCOP, a memory management unit, or MMU, and a cache. The streamlined architecture minimizes latencies between instructions while allowing for parallel operation between the CPU and the FCOP. The MMU manages the cache to provide a high hit rate. The tight coupling between CPU, FCOP, and MMU achieves a peak throughput of 200 MIPS.

Technology

In order to make it possible to successfully build a fully functional chip, we had established that a maximum gate count of 10,000 was necessary. Also in order to obtain the fastest possible machine cycle time interaction between GaAs chips had to be kept to a minimum to preserve the inherent speed of the GaAs gates. This required that we put entire logical functions on one chip. To place the CPU on one chip we had to eliminate control gates as much as possible while implementing as many on-chip registers as possible to minimize off-chip activity. The RISC architecture was a natural choice to satisfy these requirements.

When ready for large-scale production the CPU, COP, and MMU circuits are to be fabricated using GaAs heterojunction integrated injection logic, or HI^{2}L, technology. Analysis shows this is a good choice for the implementation of the GaAs microprocessor system. The HI^{2}L nand gates require only one transistor, which permits high gate density and smaller chip size. With a substrate ground and only one voltage bus needed, power distribution is greatly simplified. With HI^{2}L good control of logic thresholds over temperature and voltage ranges is obtainable since doping levels have little effect on thresholds. Control over gate speeds may be individually programmed by selecting the value of the base resistor with a single mask step. This flexibility permits designing very fast gates as needed in critical paths while using slower and lower power gates where they can be tolerated. This is important to allow reaching the 10,000 gate limit without using excessive power.

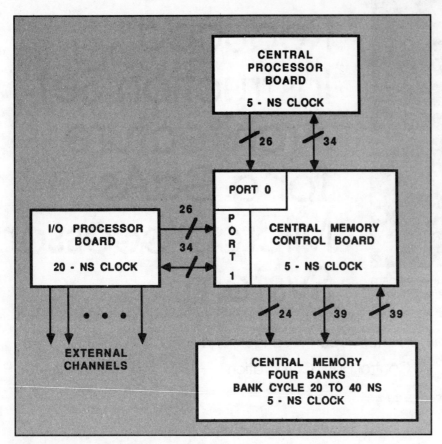

Figure 1. GaAs microprocessor system logical configuration.

System overview

Figure 1 is a logic diagram of the GaAs microprocessor system. The system has full 32-bit data paths throughout and supports a 64M-byte virtual and real address space. The objective of the system is to operate using a 5-ns clock cycle, thereby attaining a 200-MIPS peak execution rate. All elements in the system operate from the same clock system. The CPU chip is the heart of the system and generates all memory addresses for both instructions and operands. The CPU, FCOP, and MMU chips each are capable of executing their own specific instructions using a common instruction bus. Each chip controls a six-stage pipeline so an orderly exit and return can be taken to an interrupt routine. The MMU supports a fully segmented and paged virtual memory system. It also controls independent instruction and data caches, which allow parallel access. The I/O processor and CPU have separate ports on the central memory control, or CMC, board to a multibank central memory to minimize contention and conflict delays.

The GaAs microprocessor system central processor board consists of a CPU chip, a FCOP chip, two MMU chips, two processor board interface chips, along with several RAMs and support chips utilized as cache memories. The CPU, FCOP, and MMU chips are GaAs custom circuits using approximately 10,000 gates and 136 I/O pins. The processor board interface chips are GaAs gate arrays. The cache memories are built using 256- × 4-bit and 1K- × 4-bit GaAs RAMs.

Error detection logic is not included in the chips. Parity protection is included on both the cache tag and cache data memories. The central memory is protected by a single-bit error correction double bit error detection, or SECDED, code that is generated and checked by the CMC board. When a parity error is detected, an error interrupt is sent to the CPU, FCOP, and MMU chips.

Instruction set architecture, or ISA

An initial instruction set was developed based on simulation statistics in the literature,[1,3] and from our own studies. The GaAs microprocessor system instruction set design was modified by the introduction of a core instruction set require-

ment. A core instruction set was defined at an intermediate level between the hardware-dependent GaAs microprocessor system instruction set and a high-level language. Once a program is compiled to the core instruction set, a hardware-dependent translator transforms the code to the machine instruction set and performs any machine-dependent optimizations. The focus of the GaAs microprocessor system instruction set was changed from emulating macro functions in high-level language statements to supporting macro functions in the instructions of the core instruction set.

The instruction set is divided into three parts corresponding to the three elements of the GaAs microprocessor system: the CPU, the FCOP and the MMU (Figures 2a, 2b, and 2c).

Floating-point operations cannot be executed in a single cycle even with fast GaAs logic. Floating-point operations may be partitioned for single machine cycle execution. The FCOP instruction set consists of instructions that perform parts of a given floating-point operation. For example, single-precision floating-point add is performed by executing the following:

DADDS   Denormalize operand with smaller exponent. Add the mantissas of the two operands. Compare exponents of the two operands to give result exponent. Convert mantissa sum/difference from two's complement to sign magnitude format.

NRMRNS   Normalize and round result mantissa to single precision.

The three instruction sets provide an integrated system that includes floating-point and memory management capability. The CPU performs instruction and operand addressing for the system. Instructions fetched by the CPU may be executed by the CPU, FCOP, or the MMU. The CPU controls the system interrupt behavior. Upon receiving an interrupt, the FCOP and MMU suspend their pipelines while the CPU performs a context switch. The MMU and FCOP are informed of changes in the address privilege, address mapping, and cache usage by the monitor, map, and cache bypass signals. The CPU, FCOP, and MMU may communicate by passing data directly from one to the other. Conditions evaluated on the FCOP are available to the CPU via the coprocessor condition signal.

The architecture allows for a maximum of four coprocessors in the system. Other coprocessor instruction sets must support memory access and data movement between processors in the same way that these operations are supported in the CPU, FCOP, and MMU.

Single-precision integer add	ADD,SRC1,SOURCE2*,DEST	Load word indexed	LDW,SOURCE2[SRC1],DEST
Single-precision integer add with carry	ADDC,SRC1,SOURCE2,DEST	Load halfword indexed	LDH,SOURCE2[SRC1],DEST
Single-precision integer subtract	SUB,SRC1,SOURCE2,DEST	Load byte indexed	LDB,SOURCE2[SRC1],DEST
Single-precision integer subtract with carry	SUBC,SRC1,SOURCE2,DEST	Store word indexed	STW,SRC2,SYMBOL[SRC1]
Single-precision integer subtract reverse	SUBR,SRC1,SOURCE2,DEST	Store halfword indexed	STH,SRC2,SYMBOL[SRC1]
Single-precision integer multiply step	MSTEP,SRC1,SRC2,DEST	Store byte indexed	STB,SRC2,SYMBOL[SRC1]
Logical AND	AND,SRC1,SOURCE2,DEST	Store word direct	STW,SRC2,LITERAL
Logical inclusive OR	OR,SRC1,SOURCE2,DEST	Store halfword direct	STH,SRC2,LITERAL
Logical exclusive OR	XOR,SRC1,SOURCE2,DEST	Store byte direct	STB,SRC2,LITERAL
Shift right arithmetic by one	SRA,SOURCE2,DEST	Trap conditional	TRAPCND,COND,TRAP_CODE
Shift right logical by one	SRL,SOURCE2,DEST	Jump indexed	JMP,SOURCE2[SRC1]
Move register or immediate	MOV,SOURCE2,DEST	Call indexed	CAL,SOURCE2[SRC1]
Implicit source move	MOV,IMPL_SRC,DEST	Return from trap	RETT,LITERAL,DST
Implicit destination move	MOV,SOURCE2,IMPL_DEST	Branch conditional	BRC,COND,SOURCE2
Load high immediate	LDHI,HO_BITS,DEST		

(a)   *SOURCE2 is either a sign extended literal or the register indicated by src2.

Figure 2. (a) CPU instruction set; **(b)** MMU instruction set; **(c)** FCOP instruction set.

	Purge page map	PMAP
	Purge cache	PCACH
	Load inst mmu page map	LDW,SOURCE2[SRC1],MDEST
	Load oper mmu page map	LDW,SOURCE2[SRC1],MDEST
	Implicit Source move reg from mmu to cpu	MOV,MIMPL_SRC,DEST
(b)	Implicit Destination move reg from cpu to mmu	MOV,SRC2,MIMPL_DEST

	No operation	NOP
	Single-prec denormalize, add, convert to sign magnitude	DADDS,CSRC1,CSRC2
	Single-prec denormalize, sub, convert to sign magnitude	DSUBS,CSRC1,CSRC2
	Double-prec denormalize, add	DADDD,CSRC1,CSRC2
	Double-prec denormalize, sub	DSUBD,CSRC1,CSRC2
	Convert to sign magnitude, lower half of double prec	CSML
	Convert to sign magnitude, upper half of double prec	CSMH
	Single-prec convert integer to floating point	FLOATS,CSRC1
	Double-prec convert integer to floating point	FLOATD,CSRC1
	Single-prec normalize and round to nearest	NRMRNS
	Double-prec normalize and round lower half to nearest	NRMRNDL
	Round double-precision upper half	RNDH
	Single-prec multiply floating start	MFSTS,CSRC1,CSRC2
	Single-prec multiply integer start	MISTS,CSRC1,CSRC2
	Single-prec multiply step	MSTEP
	Single-prec multiply floating finish	MFINFS
	Single-prec divide floating start	DFSTS,CSRC1,CSRC2
	Single-prec divide integer start	DISTS,CSRC1,CSRC2
	Single-precision divide step	DSTEP
	Single-precision divide floating finish	DFINFS
	Implicit Source move reg from fcop to cpu	MOV,CIMPL_SRC,DEST
	Implicit Destination move reg from cpu to fcop	MOV,SRC2,CIMPL_DEST
	Load register file high	LDHI,SOURCE2[SRC1],CDEST
	Load register file low	LDLO,SOURCE2[SRC1],CDEST
	Load register file, convert to single prec	LDCV,SOURCE2[SRC1],CDEST
	Store register file high	STHI,CSRC1,SYMBOL[SRC1]
	Store register file low	STLO,CSRC1,SYMBOL[SRC1]
	Store register file, convert from single prec	STCV,CSRC1,SYMBOL[SRC1]
	P1 register high to register H	MOV,P1,H
	P1 register low to register L	MOV,P1,L
(c)	Source 1 to P1, Source 2 to P2	MOV,CSRC1/CSRC2,P1/P2

Pipeline

Pipelining is an effective method for reducing interchip communication while increasing performance. The GaAs microprocessor system was initially designed with a four-stage pipeline. Fetching one instruction every cycle gives a high instruction bandwidth while permitting the instruction format to be simply encoded.

The cache memory access could not support the 5-ns memory cycle required by the four-stage pipeline. A pipelined memory preserved the 5-ns cycle time by permitting the memory to be accessed over two cycles. The resulting six-stage pipe consists of instruction fetch cycle 1 (I1), instruction fetch cycle 2 (I2), ALU execute (EX), memory access cycle 1 (M1), memory access cycle 2 (M2), and write register file (WR). (See Figure 3.)

The nonmemory access pipestages EX and WR execute the instruction and write the register file. The memory access pipestages I1, I2, M1, and M2 put the memory address out during the I1 or M1 cycle and latch the returning instruction or operand data during I2 and M2. The memory chips have pipeline registers integrated on-chip with the memory array to support pipelined access. The pipelined memory access increased the complexity of the design but decreased the cycle time by 39 percent.

The GaAs microprocessor system has some hardware pipeline interlocks. Data dependencies between register-to-register instructions are resolved in hardware. (See Figure 4.)

Scheduling of operations in the instruction slots after a branch is not provided by the hardware. On a branch, the software must ensure that instructions in the pipe after the branch do not depend upon the destination of the branch. If no benign instruction can be found to fit into the delay

```
I1  I2  EX  M1  M2  WR
    I1  I2  EX  M1  M2  WR
        I1  I2  EX  M1  M2  WR
            I1  I2  EX  M1  M2  WR
                I1  I2  EX  M1  M2  WR
                    I1  I2  EX  M1  M2  WR
```

Figure 3. Final GaAs microprocessor pipeline.

```
ADD, R0, R1, R2   R2=R1+R0   I1  I2  EX  M1  M2  WR
SUB, R2, R3, R4   R4=R2−R3       I1  I2  EX  M1  M2  WR
```

Figure 4. Data dependencies. Although the ADD does not write R2 until the WR pipestage, the hardware shortstopping logic provides the sum of R1 and R0 to the SUB instruction in its EX pipestage.

```
0000    BRC, GT, $F000    I1   I2   EX   M1   M2   WR
0001    NOP                    I1   I2   EX   M1   M2   WR
0002    NOP                         I1   I2   EX   M1   M2   WR
F000    ADD,...                          I1   I2   EX   M1   M2   WR
```

Figure 5. Branch delays. The branch delay for a six-stage pipeline is two. The two instructions after a branch are always executed since these instructions are already in the pipeline when the branch is evaluated during EX.

slot, then it must be filled with a no operation instruction (nop). (See Figure 5.)

The pipeline organization has a direct impact on performance by determining the number of delay slots after a branch. The number of branch delays in the four-stage pipeline is one. The number of branch delays for the six-stage pipeline is two. Although it is more difficult to fill two branch delays than one with useful instructions, simulations show that the six-stage pipeline net MIP rate is 39 percent better than the four-stage pipeline.

The interrupt convention followed in the GaAs microprocessor system architecture stops interrupted instructions from completing, shuts down the pipeline, fixes the cause of the interrupt, and restarts the interrupted instruction stream. Shutting down the pipeline involves two tasks: saving the addresses of the interrupted instruction stream and saving the state of the system. The addresses of the instructions in the M2, M1, and EX pipestages are saved to allow the instruction stream to be restarted upon return from the interrupt. The state of the system is preserved by preventing the interrupted instructions from altering permanent registers, the register files, or memory.

Returning from an interrupt is performed by jumping to the addresses of the three instructions saved when the interrupt occurred. The return from interrupt routine also restores the system to its original status.

Software

All software is written in a high-level language such as Pascal or Ada. This software then passes through a compiler, translator, reorganizer, assembler, and linker/loader before execution, as shown in Figure 6. The process begins with the compiler, which translates programs written in Pascal or Ada into the MIPS Core ISA assembly language.

The translator searches the core ISA code and by using a combination of macros, procedures, and machine code sequences translates the core ISA to machine ISA. For most instructions, the mapping from the core instruction to low-level instruction is a direct translation into the machine instruction.

The reorganizer takes the translated machine ISA and repositions instructions. The reorganization of instructions results in more efficient program code. Code reorganization packs the branch delay slots with useful instructions when possible. Also, memory reference instructions cannot be immediately followed by instructions that use the memory reference; they must be delayed two instructions. In such cases, the translator will

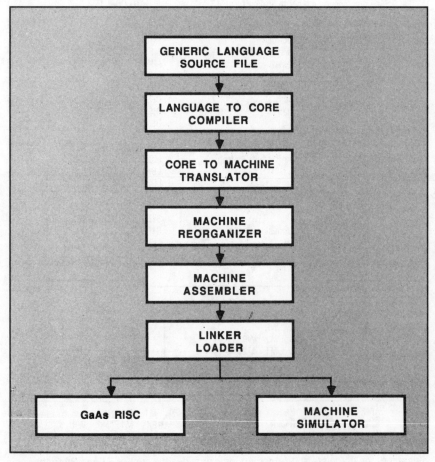

Figure 6. Support software overview.

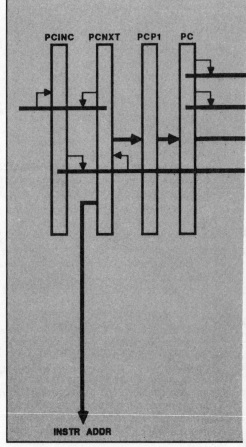

Figure 7. CPU data path.

load the pipeline with nops, relying on the reorganizer to eliminate as many as possible by replacing them with position-independent instructions.

The assembler and linker and loader complete the translation process, either producing a loadable simulator file or a binary file executable by the GaAs microprocessor system.

Central processor unit, or CPU

The CPU incorporates interfaces, data paths, and control to execute efficiently the CPU instruction set. The CPU has dedicated buses for operand and instruction memory access. The memory interface consists of a 24-bit wide instruction address bus, a 32-bit wide instruction data bus, a 26-bit wide operand address bus, and a 32-bit wide operand data bus. Instructions are word addressed. Operands are byte addressed. Operand data may be in byte, halfword, or word format. The control interface provides status, memory read/write control, and interrupt information to the system or the CPU.

The CPU execution model (read two operands, perform an ALU operation, write the result) is supported by a 32-bit wide data path. The major data path elements are the register file, the temporary registers, the ALU, the PSW, and the program counters. (See Figure 7.)

Data flows through the data path from the register file through the ALU and back to the register file. An instruction is fetched using the address in PCNXT during I1 and I2. During EX, the register file is read onto the a and b buses. Alternatively, the contents of result1, result2, or result3 may be "shortstopped" to one or both buses. The ALU performs the arithmetic, logical, or shift operation. The ALU result is latched by the result1 register on ALU and memory instructions, sent to the PCNXT on control transfer instructions, or latched by the PSW on an implicit move to the PSW instruction. During M1, the result1 contents are sent to the result2 register. The result1 contents may be used as an address for an operand cache access. The condition codes, if set by the instruction, are evaluated during M1 and latched in the PSW. During M2, the result3 register latches the ALU output, the result2 contents, or the memory interface.

During WR, the register file is written by the result3 register. During each pipestage, the instruction address is passed from one program counter to the next. Therefore, PCNXT, PCP1, PC, PCM1, and PCLST hold the addresses of the instructions in the I1, I2, EX, M1, and M2 pipestages, respectively.

The streamlined instruction set and pipeline structure result in a simple state machine. The state machine has six states. The initial state after an interrupt is the TR1 state. This state enables only the I1 pipestage. All interrupts except reset are disabled upon entering TR1 state. The successive states enable the next pipestages in the pipeline until the state machine returns to the NORM state, where all six pipestages are executing. The simple state transitions permit a small state machine. (See Figure 8.) Memory waits suspend the state machine until the memory is ready.

Context switches for interrupts complicate a load/store architecture. The register file is the destination or source of loads and stores. The program counters must be accessed directly on an interrupt to avoid corrupting the register file. To avoid the increased complexity and gate count of store and load program counter instructions, the state machine and the primitive instructions synthesize these functions. On an interrupt, the program

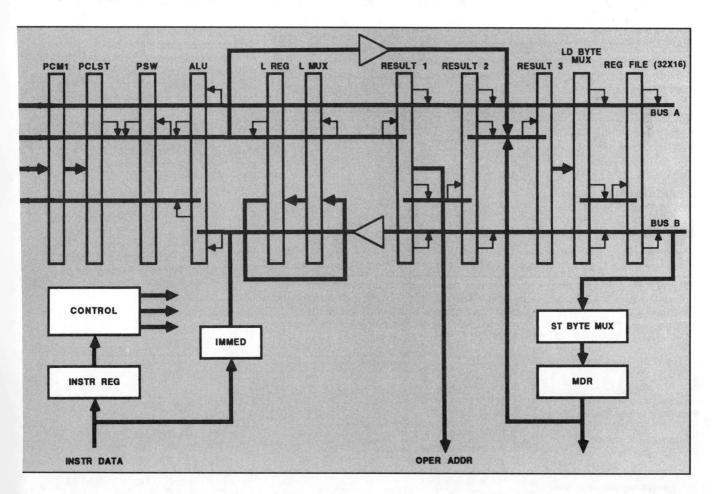

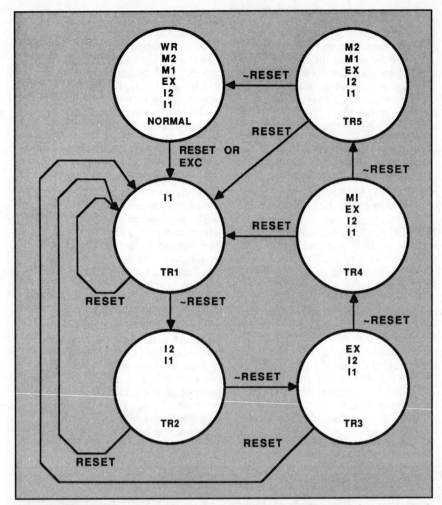

Figure 8. State machine. State transitions are determined by the reset, interrupts, and interrupt enables. EXC is the sum of product terms involving the interrupts and their respective enables.

```
I1   I2   EX   M1   M2   WR
     I1   I2   EX   M1   M2
          I1   I2   EX   M1
               I1   I2   EX
                    I1   I2
                         I1
STWD,R0,$0000              I1   I2   EX   M1   M2   WR
STWD,R1,$0004                   I1   I2   EX   M1   M2   WR
STWD,R2,$0008                        I1   I2   EX   M1   M2   WR
MOV,PCLST,R0                              I1   I2   EX   M1   M2   WR
MOV,PCLST,R1                                   I1   I2   EX   M1   M2   WR
MOV,PCLST,R2                                        I1   I2   EX   M1   M2   WR
 t   t+1 t+2 t+3 t+4 t+5 t+6 t+7 t+8 t+9
```

Figure 9. Pipestage activity during an interrupt. An interrupt occurs during the pipestage at t+ 5. All pipestages are disabled except for I1, which begins fetching the interrupt service routine at location zero. The first six instructions of the interrupt routine move registers R0, R1, and R2 to memory and move the program counters into the register file.

Figure 10. Pipestage activity on a return from trap. The RETT instruction fetches the first return address and intends to write it to register R0. The JMP instruction notes that the destination of the RETT is the same as its source and short-stops the contents of the temporary register to be used as the target address of the jump.

```
RETT,$0000,R0           I1   I2   EX   M1   M2   WR
RETT,$0004,R1                I1   I2   EX   M1   M2   WR
RETT,$0008,R2                     I1   I2   EX   M1   M2   WR
JMP,R0,$0000                           I1   I2   EX   M1   M2   WR
JMP,R1,$0000                                I1   I2   EX   M1   M2   WR
JMP,R2,$0000                                     I1   I2   EX   M1   M2   WR
first return instruction                              I1   I2   EX   M1   M2   WR
second return instruction                                  I1   I2   EX   M1   M2   WR
third return instruction                                        I1   I2   EX   M1   M2   WR
```

counters are inhibited from changing until three registers in the register file have been saved. After three locations have been freed in the register file, the program counters may be moved there and then to memory. (See Figure 9.)

A return from interrupt requires that the return instruction addresses be fetched from memory without going through the register file. The return from trap instruction loads the return address from memory into a temporary register, where it may be used by a jump instruction to transfer control. The temporary register is not written to the register file. (See Figure 10.)

The return from trap returns the system to its original context without corrupting the register file.

FCOP

The FCOP, or floating-point coprocessor, contains the hardware to execute the floating-point portion of the instruction set. The FCOP also contains hardware support for fast integer multiply and divide. The FCOP conforms to IEEE standard floating-point format for single-and double-precision operands.

The FCOP interface reflects its role as a coprocessor in the system and receives instructions and operands over two dedicated 32-bit buses. The FCOP control interface contains the status inputs, interrupt signals, memory wait conditions, the coprocessor condition, and two signals to indicate the binary code of a particular FCOP if more than one coprocessor is in the system.

The data path of the FCOP consists of the following major elements: 4- × 64-bit register file, exponent control, 64-bit shift unit, 34-bit arithmetic unit, and FCOP PSW. (See Figure 11.)

Floating-point operations require a more complex execution model than integer operations. The FCOP hardware is used iteratively to perform the various parts of a floating-point operation. For example, a double-precision floating-point addition begins by reading the two

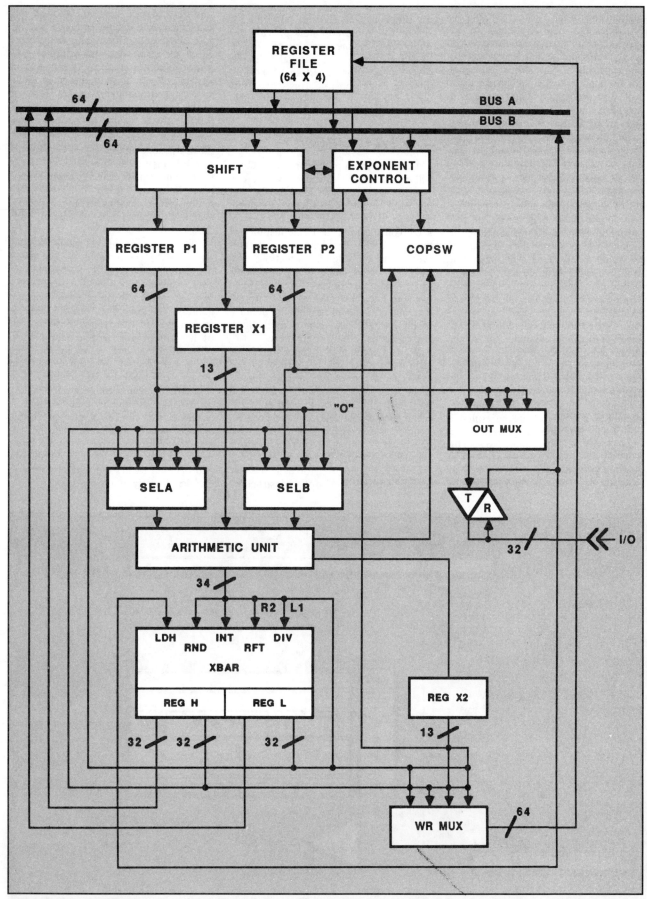

Figure 11. FCOP data path.

October 1986

operands out of the register file during the EX pipestage. The exponents of the operands are compared and the appropriate shift amount sent to the shifter for denormalization. The shifter denormalizes the mantissa with the smaller exponent. The preliminary result exponent is latched in the X1 register and the mantissas in the P1 and P2 registers. During the M1 pipestage, the arithmetic unit adds the low parts of the two mantissas. The carry out is saved and used during M2 to add the upper parts of the two mantissas. The next instruction converts the lower part of the arithmetic unit two's complement output to sign magnitude. The next instruction uses the arithmetic unit in the M2 pipestage to convert the upper part of the result mantissa to sign magnitude form. The sign magnitude mantissa is normalized in the next instruction during the M1 pipestage. During M2, the low part of the mantissa is rounded. The final instruction uses the arithmetic unit during the M2 pipestage to round the upper part of the normalized mantissa, reformat the result into double-precision format with the exponent, and write it to the register file. The floating-point condition codes in the PSW are updated in different pipestages depending on whether they are the result of a shift or add operation.

The FCOP typically cannot issue an instruction every cycle because of resource conflicts between instructions. These instruction cycles must be filled with nops if no other useful instructions can be scheduled. These nop slots provide the opportunity for the execution of CPU or MMU instructions in parallel with the FCOP's operation. The translator/reorganizer is responsible for scheduling CPU and FCOP instructions for maximum parallelism.

Cache memory

The GaAs microprocessor system CPU will require a 32-bit instruction word every 5 ns. Program statistics have shown that up to one-third of all instructions executed are load or store instructions. In order to avoid contention at the cache memory, a two-port cache would be required. But even if this were done, instructions and operands could contend for the same cache locations, reducing the cache effectiveness. For these reasons, separate instruction and operand caches are defined to allow parallel accessing of instructions and operands without contention.

When a cache miss is encountered, an eight-word block will be fetched by the MMU and processor interface. During the cache fetch process, the CPU will be in a wait state and will not proceed until the cache fetch is complete. When a store instruction is executed, the data will always be written to central memory. If the store instruction encounters a hit in the cache, the word will also be stored in the appropriate cache cell. Use of the instruction and performance simulator showed this implementation would improve the hit rate of the operand cache by 45 percent. Since the cache does not monitor I/O writes to central memory, the operating system software ensures that stale cache data is not created by I/O writes. To assist in this operation, the cache can be cleared with a purge cache instruction, and bypassed at the direction of the CPU. The cache memory addressing mechanism is shown in Figure 12. The cache size of 1K words and single element organization were chosen as a trade-off between optimum system clock cycle time, expected available circuits, and satisfactory hit ratios.

The cache contains 128 single element sets of eight words each. In the direct mapped technique, bits 5-11 of the virtual address are used to index the tag memory sets that contain the top 14 bits of a virtual address. The tag entry from the selected set is compared with the high-order 14 bits of the virtual address to determine a hit or miss condition. The same address bits along with bits 2-4 are used to read the proper word from the data memory. If a hit condition occurs, the data word read is passed on the data bus to its destination. If a miss occurs, the GaAs microprocessor system is put into a wait state while the real memory address is used to fetch the missing word into the cache. The instruction and operand caches are separate but are identical in design.

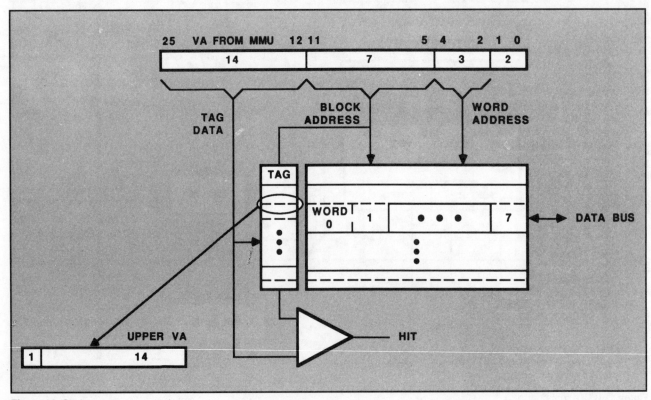

Figure 12. Cache memory operation.

Each cache is controlled by a separate MMU and each has its own address and data path so parallel referencing of instructions and data can be accomplished. The cache memories are designed to be accessed in two pipelined clock cycles. Each cache contains 1K 34-bit entries organized as 128 one element sets with eight words per set.

Process to virtual address mapping

The virtual address mapping is taken from that utilized in the MIPS processor built at Stanford.[4] When the system is in mapped mode, the MMU translates the process address received from the CPU to a virtual address using the process identifier, or PID, and mask, or MA, register contents. The translation logic substitutes the PID register contents into the high-order bits of the process address for as many bits as are set in the MA register. Since the PID register is limited to 12 bits,

the smallest segment permitted by a process is then 4096 words. In the process address translation to a virtual address, the top n bits of the address are removed and replaced by an n bit PID. During the field length check the top $(n + 1)$ bits of the process address are checked to be all zeros or all ones. The value n is given by the number of bits set in the MA register. Since the process address is 26 bits, the accessible portion of the process address space is split into the low $2^{25 - n}$ bytes and the high $2^{25 - n}$ bytes. An attempt to access bytes outside of this range results in a field length error. The field length error causes an MMU interrupt and a field length error bit is set in the MMU PSW register along with the virtual address reference attempted.

Page map operation

The page map provides for virtual address to physical memory address translation. This translation is done through a set associative page map that contains en-

tries for the most recently used pages. The MMU will interrupt the CPU when a page map miss is encountered. The CPU will search central memory and load the page map with the appropriate entry. During this search, the CPU may encounter a page fault that will require the page to be loaded from virtual address space to a physical memory address. The page map may be preloaded using CPU instructions.

The page map address mapping mechanism is shown in Figure 13. The page size is 2K bytes and is fixed. The map contains 8 two-element sets that provide the real memory address. In the set associative technique, the low order three bits of the page number are used to index a pair of tag elements. The tag entry from each element is compared with the high-order 15 bits of the virtual address. The two comparisons are made in parallel.

If a match is found, the real memory address is formed from the page offset and the 15 bit address from the matching real memory address element. If a match on the tag memory contents is not made, a

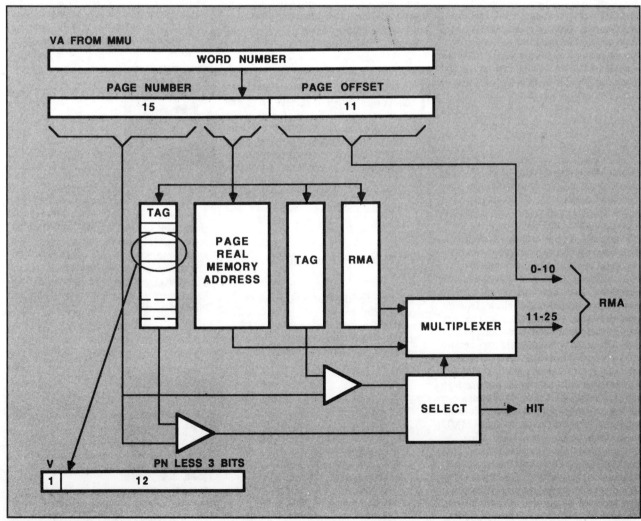

Figure 13. Page map operation.

Table 1. GaAs microprocessor simulation results.

Benchmark	Gibson mix number	Sieve prime search	String	Linked list
e = Executed instructions	716	7474	892	277
n = Number of nops	215	2290	256	114
L = Number of loads	65	258	66	32
i = Instruction cache hit rate	93%	99%	99%	96%
o = Op-cache hit rate	91%	96%	95%	94%
R = Rate (1) with simulated cache hit rate average = 91.0 MIPS	65.2 MIPS	117.4	117.0	67.2
R = Rate (2) with 100% cache hit rate average = 134.7 MIPS	139.9 MIPS	138.7	142.6	117.7

$$(1) \quad R = \frac{e-n}{[e+(1-i)\,ce+(1-o)\,cL]\,t} \qquad (2) \quad R = \frac{e-n}{et}$$

c = Cache service delay = 16 cycles
t = cycle time = 5 ns

page map miss fault results that results in a MMU interrupt signal being sent to the CPU, COP, and paired MMU. The MMU interrupt signal is used by the MMU to trap the page number of the virtual address, or VA, that was missed or had an access violation in the MMU PSW register. The page map can be bypassed at the direction of the CPU and can be purged using the purge page map instructions.

Performance summary

The GaAs microprocessor system can operate with a 200-MHz clock rate because of the efficiency of its highly pipelined architecture, but the average system net throughput, as shown in Table 1, is less than 200 MIPS because of the CPU pipelining that requires nops and because of limited operand and instruction MMU cache hit rates. During each machine cycle, stages of six different instructions are executing, thus allowing up to one instruction completion per clock. One instruction must be fetched from memory every clock cycle, with simultaneous access to required operands via the operand data bus for maximum net throughput. To minimize this memory bottleneck, the two GaAs MMUs are each used to manage a cache. The limits on memory bandwidth show up in the instruction and operand cache hit rates, and the MMU time required to service a cache miss. The average GaAs microprocessor system net throughput then is 200 MIPS, reduced by 32 percent because of required nops, and then reduced by another 32 percent because of the memory bandwidth limits. This results in an average net throughput

of 91 MIPS, as shown in the benchmark simulation results of Table 1. Design enhancements are being made to the system to improve the average net throughput by reducing the number of nops in the reorganized code and improving the memory bandwidth.

In summary, the RISC system architecture exploits the high speed aspects of GaAs technology to achieve up to one instruction completion every five ns, while demanding a minimal number of gates per chip. The increased demands on memory bandwidth caused by the RISC approach are answered by including two GaAs caches. Through a balanced system design philosophy, a complete system architecture was fitted to the constraints of GaAs technology. □

Acknowledgments

Funding for the GaAs Microcomputer was provided by the Defense Advanced Research Projects Agency, or DARPA, under contract 84-F-167880; Texas Instruments; and Control Data Corporation.

References

1. D. Patterson and C. Sequin. "RISC I: A Reduced Instruction Set VLSI Computer," *Proc. 8th Ann. Symp. Computer Architecture,* May 1981, pp. 443-457.
2. J. Hennessy et al. "The MIPS Machine," *Proc. Compcon,* Feb. 1982, p. 107.
3. J. Hennessy et al., "Hardware/Software Tradeoffs for Increased Performance," *Proc. Symp. Architectural Support for Programming Languages and Operating Systems,* March 1-3, 1983, pp. 2-12.
4. S. A. Przybylski et al., *Organization and VLSI Implementation of MIPS,* Stanford Computer Systems Laboratory tech report no. 84-259, April 1984, pp. 8-10.

Eric R. Fox is currently working on the GaAs microprocessor system demonstration and test hardware and software. Prior experience includes design of a VLSI chip, a CPU context cache, a CPU arithmetic unit, and a portion of a floating-point firmware package.

Fox is a member of Tau Beta Pi and Eta Kappa Nu, has received a Control Data Employee Excellence Award, and holds a BSEE from Purdue University.

Kenneth J. Kiefer is a technical consultant at Control Data Corporation. He is currently involved in developing architectures for Avionics

Computers and in applying GaAs technologies to these architectures. Prior to taking this position, he worked in the development of high-performance mainframes at Control Data.

Kiefer holds a BA from Loras College, Dubuque, Iowa, and a BSEE from the University of Iowa, Iowa City.

Robert F. Vangen is the GaAs Microprocessor Project Manager, and is also on the design team to develop a vector coprocessor for the GaAs microprocessor system. Present interests include high-performance computer architecture and signal processing. Prior professional experience includes development of a CAD system for design of integrated circuits. He has also designed computer peripherals, digital communication systems, and airborne computers.

Vangen has been granted one patent, is a member of Eta Kappa Nu, and has a BSEE with distinction and an MBA, both from the University of Minnesota.

Shaun P. Whalen is currently an electrical engineer with the Avionics Computer Architecture department of Control Data Corporation. His technical interests include streamlined computer architectures for high-level languages.

Whalen is a member of IEEE, Eta Kappa Nu, and Tau Beta Pi. He received his BS degree from the University of Notre Dame in 1983 and his MS degree from the University of California, Berkeley, in 1984.

Readers may write to the authors at Control Data Corporation, 8800 Queen Ave., South, Minneapolis, MN 55440.

Design of a GaAs Systolic Array for an Adaptive Null Steering Beamforming Controller

Carl E. Hein, Richard M. Zieger, and Joseph A. Urbano

Advanced Technology Laboratories
Moorestown Corporate Center, Route 38
Moorestown, New Jersey 08057

Introduction

The Gallium Arsenide (GaAs) systolic array beamforming controller described in this paper demonstrates the feasibility of using a top-down approach for designing an adaptive radar system. Because of its speed and its unique characteristics, the GaAs technology chosen to implement the systolic array significantly influenced the design of the internal processor architecture. The array will be configured as a single instruction, multiple data (SIMD) machine, in which each processing site communicates only to its nearest neighbors. The array will be used in digital radar beamforming with automatic null steering, which is just one of many uses for systolic arrays.

Background

A typical far-field radar antenna array pattern consists of a main beam, and multiple sidelobes and nulls as shown in Figure 1. This particular one dimensional pattern results from the finite size of the unweighted aperture (windowing effect) and the 12 elements of the antenna. The structure is analogous to one derived from the discrete Fourier transform of a time domain signal sampled at a finite number of points for a finite duration in a conventional digital signal processing system (DSPS). The analogy can be understood best if a linear array of antenna elements in a phased array antenna system (PAAS) is compared to a set of time samples in a DSPS. The spacing of the antenna elements in the PAAS is equivalent to the sampling period of the DSPS system; the frequency response of the DSPS is analogous to the antenna pattern of the PAAS.

The magnitude of the sidelobes in a PAAS is particularly important and can be reduced by amplitude weighting. In either the PAAS or DSPS case, amplitude weighting softens the edges of the sample window by multiplying the samples by real weights that progressively attenuate the samples at the edges of the window. A typical weighting curve is shown in Figure 2. The application of the weights reduces the height of the sidelobes but increases the width of the main beam slightly. This tradeoff is usually acceptable. Various weighting curves are popular, particularly Taylor weighting; which approximates the optimality of the Dolph-Chebyshev approach [1].

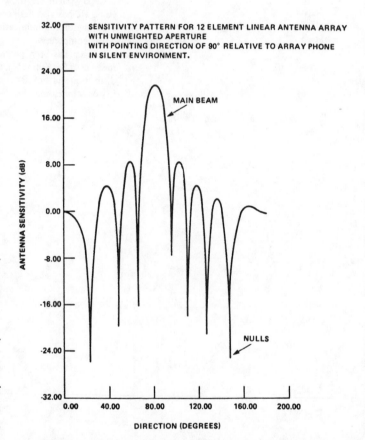

Figure 1: A typical radar antenna array pattern.

In addition to amplitude weighting, both the DSPS and PAAS perform a transform on the sampled values. An implementation of the transform T is shown in Figure 3.

The transform T is expressed as:

$$T = \sum_{i=1}^{N} x(i) \cdot w(i)$$

where:

N = the number of antenna elements or samples
w(i) = the ith transform coefficient.

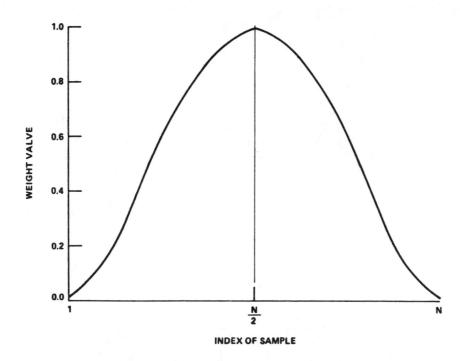

Figure 2: A typical (cosine squared) weighting curve.

The antenna pattern of Figure 1 was plotted by performing the transformation above for each value along the θ (horizontal) axis. The values of the θ axis correspond to the orientation of a signal source at angle θ with respect to the antenna. The incoming signals are assumed to be in the narrow band around the central frequency. For each incident angle θ, the phase of the received x(i) values is unique. The relative phase difference ϕ, between two adjacent elements spaced a distance d, with a path difference d sin (Figure 4) is:

$$\phi = \frac{\Delta\lambda}{\text{wavelength}}$$

$$\phi = \frac{d * \sin(\theta)}{\text{wavelength}}$$

The transform coefficients used to produce the plot in Figure 1 were calculated to maximize the output energy from

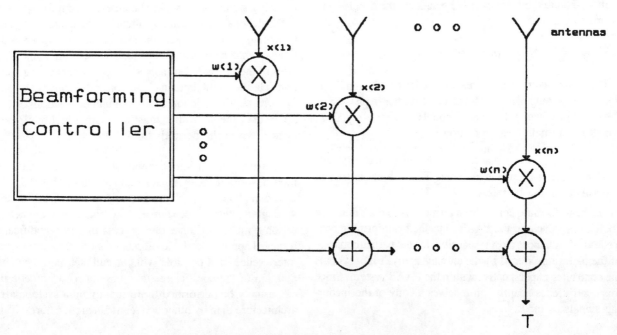

Figure 3: Diagram of the beamforming system.

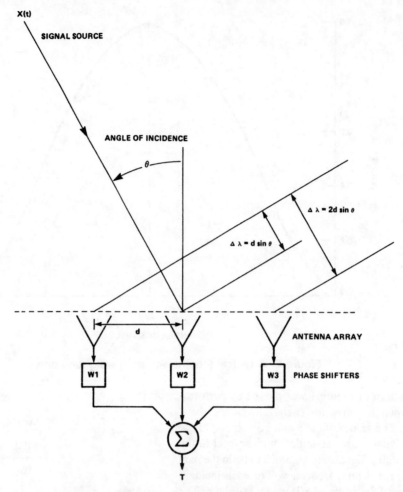

X(t)

SIGNAL SOURCE

ANGLE OF INCIDENCE

θ

$\Delta \lambda = 2d \sin \theta$

$\Delta \lambda = d \sin \theta$

d

ANTENNA ARRAY

W1   W2   W3   PHASE SHIFTERS

Σ

T

Figure 4: Relative phase difference Φ.

signals incident from the desired "look" direction Ω. Although there are many possible solutions, the simplest one seems to be:

$$w(i) = d*i*\sin(\Omega)$$

This solution ensures that each product of the signal and the corresponding coefficient will sum together in phase with the other products only when Ω equals or nearly equals θ, which is the main beam direction.

The many algorithms that exist for deriving the coefficients produce differing antenna patterns. This subject is treated extensively in the literature [5,6,7,8].

The beamforming controller's purpose is to determine the coefficient values for the PAAS, thus the beamforming controller is the element most responsible for the particular shape of the pattern produced by the antenna array. Figure 3 puts the controller in perspective within the PAAS system. Since this controller is adaptive, it receives a copy of the incoming signals as input.

This system is intended for use in radar applications where jamming signals may strike the antenna from many different directions. To maximally attenuate the jamming signals, the beam controller generates a set of coefficients that produce an antenna pattern in which the nulls are in the directions of the unwanted signals. As the jammers change position relative to the antenna, the controller moves the nulls to correspond continuously to the jammer positions. At the same time, the controller must maintain a highly directive main beam in the desired "look" direction.

Figure 5 shows an example of the beam controller's modification of the original beam pattern of Figure 1. This is accomplished by placing a null in the direction of a 40-degree interference source. A comparison of the modification with the original plot reveals that the modification achieved approximately 30 dB more cancellation of unwanted interference than possible without null steering. The computation of the coefficients involves matrix arithmetic that can usually be performed more rapidly by a systolic array architecture than by other conventional architectures. Table

Table 1. Digital Beamformer Target Specifications

Number of complex input channels	12 (12 real, 12 imaginary)
Number of beams	1
Null depth	50 dB (relative to main beam)
Iterations to converge	24
Input signal resolution	9 bits
Update time per coefficient vector	5 μsec

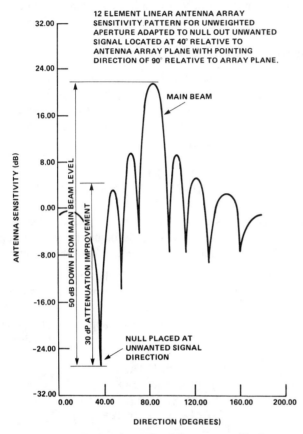

Figure 5: Example of the beam controller's modification of the original beam pattern.

1 lists the specifications to be met by the radar system in which the beamformer controller will be installed.

Survey of Current Systolic Arrays

Currently, both universities and industry are considering the uses of several systolic arrays. The WARP machine is one of the few systems constructed that is ready for use in research. Carnegie Mellon University designed and constructed the WARP machine in cooperation with General Electric and Honeywell [2]. This system consists of a one-dimensional array of identical processing units. Each processing unit of the WARP offers 10 MFLOPS with 32-64K words of memory on a 15″×17″ wire-wrap board. WARP is currently being applied to image processing research under DARPA's autonomous land vehicle program.

The Naval Ocean Systems Center (NOSC) designed another array that is scheduled for construction by June 1987. This 16-node, 4×4 two dimensional prototype systolic array is fully programmable and optimized for real-time signal processing applications. The NOSC system derives its computational power from an 8 MHz Weitek floating-point chip set and uses the AM2910A microcode sequencer. Each processing node occupies a 16×18 inch wirewrap board. An IBM PC serves as host for the system [3].

RCA has also investigated a Gram-Schmidt preprocessor in the form of a one-dimensional systolic array of specialized processors. It performs the Gram-Schmidt orthoganization procedure for adaptive sidelobe canceling in radar antennas.

Most systolic array systems which are intended for beamforming are composed of programmable computing elements. This has caused these arrays to have limited speed and to be of large size. The size penalty limits the number of processing elements that may be combined to form the array and restricts the use of such systems in portable applications. The GaAs systolic array design was driven by the need for a system composed of thousands of high performance processors. Since the application for the system is fixed, the GaAs systolic array system and processors were custom designed to perform only one algorithm. In comparison to the other systolic arrays, the GaAs systolic array is not programmable. The algorithm was hardwired into the control structure to minimize and simplify hardware and improve processing speed.

Algorithm Selection

Selecting an algorithm that adaptively generates the complex coefficient vector was the first step in the design process. Many such algorithms have since been studied. Most are similar in some respects; some can be ideally implemented on a systolic array. In general, the main beam direction is supplied to the beamformer as a steering vector, and the environment is supplied as a digitized signal from each antenna element of the array. The classical approach to computing the coefficients from the steering vector and antenna signals was described by Howells [4] and developed and applied by Applebaum [5] and others. Most of the algorithms usually attempt to minimize the error in an approximation of the inverse of the signal autocovariance matrix. They are based on approximations to the optimal Weiner-Hopf solution:

$$W = R^{-1} S$$

where:

W = vector of adapted coefficients
R = received signal autocovariance matrix
S = steering vector

The algorithm search identified three algorithms that offer the best combination of performance, stability, and ease of systolic implementation. These are MSR3 [6], Gram-Schmidt [7], and Givens [8]. Performance was judged by the algorithm's speed of convergence, the depth of nulls, and the shape of the antenna pattern produced. Each of these algorithms was simulated at the highest level (the algorithmic level) for further analysis. Figure 6 shows the comparative convergence curves obtained from the simulations and how quickly the maximum null depth is reached in terms of iterations.

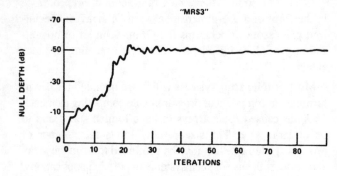

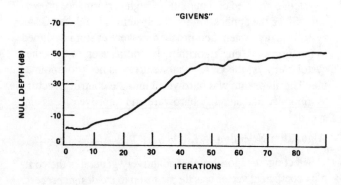

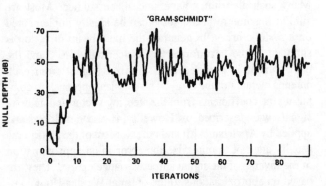

Figure 6: Comparison of convergence speed and null depth for three beamforming algorithms.

The authors have proved that these algorithms are similar and that they can be expressed so that they differ by only a few lines of code. Once identified, the effect of these lines explained the difference in characteristic performance of the algorithms. For the most part, the differences formed filters that affected the shape of the convergence curves. The MSR3 algorithm, which was a compromise between the other two, was selected to guide the design of the systolic array. The MSR3 algorithm forms an estimation of the square root of the covariance matrix R, which is then inverted and multiplied by the steering vector to produce the coefficients.

System Architecture

The computational core of the algorithm consists of a pair of double nested DO loops with several arithmetic operations inside. Such a sequential code structure implies a two-dimensional systolic array of processors [9,10]. In general, for a computation loop such as:

FOR i := 1 to N DO
    X(i+1) := X(i) * Y(i)

an N-node linear systolic array can be configured so that each node i, performs one operation on X(i), then passes the result X(i+1), to its neighboring node i+1, as shown in Figure 7.

For a doubly nested loop, a two dimensional array of processing nodes can be used, where each node corresponds to an iteration of the outer loop, and each column corresponds to an iteration of the inner loop. In this application, the inner array index limit is dependent on the outer array index:

FOR i := 1 to N DO
    FOR j := 1 to i DO
        X(i+1, j) := X(i,j) * Y(i,j);
        Y(i, j+1) := X(i,j) * Y(i,j);

This eliminates half of the node positions and results in a triangular array (Figure 8), where data flow through each processing node (i,j) is:

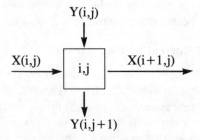

A doubly nested loop can be implemented as a linear array, where each node performs every iteration of the inner loop for each iteration of the outer loop. However, executing the inner loop sequentially in each processor results in an unbalanced processing load because the i=1 processing node has only one iteration to perform, while the i=N processing node has N iterations.

226

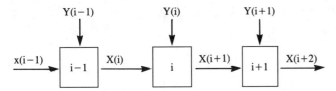

Figure 7: Example data flow for a linear systolic array.

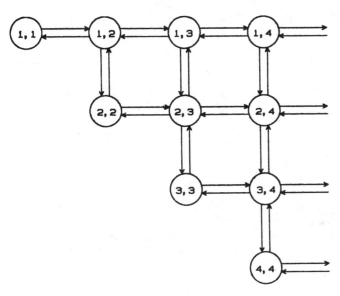

Figure 8: GaAs systolic array system nodal processor and FIFO interconnection, Version 1.

The arithmetic in the computational core of the algorithm consists of multiply and add operations with one real divide in the outer loop. The original algorithmic simulations were written in FORTRAN at a level that does not contain information about the physical structure of the computing elements. As a result, the simulation computed the algorithm by performing each operation in sequence. To assist in determining the order of data transfers and operations in the full array of processors running in the steady state, the original algorithmic simulation was modified from a sequential format into one that recognizes the parallel execution of the array with distribution of variables in space and time.

From this version of the simulation, the sequence and location of the data transfers between nodes were easily traceable. Of the algorithm's two pairs of DO loops, the second pair has a deleterious effect on the performance of the array because it is indexed in reverse order from the first. In the systolic array, data flow in the first DO loop pair flows from left to right and from top to bottom, while in the second DO loop pair, data flows from right to left and bottom to top. The implication is that, instead of the algorithm propagating in continuous waves across the array, one wave must

propagate across the array in one direction, then another wave must propagate across the array in the opposite direction. This destroys the ability to efficiently pipeline the operation and results in the majority of nodes being idle most of the time.

Several remedies are possible. A second triangular array of nodes can be constructed on top of the first, and the two arrays can be interconnected at each node through FIFO registers (see Figure 9). In this scheme, the first array performs the operations in the first pair of DO loops, and the second array performs the operations in the backward DO loops. The FIFO registers pass data between corresponding elements of the two arrays. This allows pipelining and full use of all nodes. Unfortunately, more connections per node and twice the number of processing nodes are required; moreover, the FIFO length varies with its position in the array.

Another solution is to roughly approximate the algorithm data flow and let both waves run simultaneously in opposite directions on the original single array (Figure 8). This minimizes hardware and fully uses all nodes. However, experimentation with the simulation revealed that this expedient significantly degrades the accuracy of the computation under transient conditions.

The chosen system architecture achieves the proper algorithmic data flow, WITHOUT approximation, by providing storage locations at each node that allow both waves to run simultaneously in opposite directions on one triangular array of processors. It does this by creating a pipeline of operations with a depth equal to twice the number of processors along the diagonal of the array. The storage registers accommodate the numerous stages of the pipeline by saving the critical values from each stage. In this way, the data flow of the algorithm is preserved in space by skewing operations in time.

As in the original determination of data transfers and operations in the full array, spatial simulation aided in the determination of this system architecture. The addition of these storage registers (labelled "R" in the planar array shown in Figure 10) to the planar array makes it execute the algorithm without approximation. Therefore, the process is algorithmically equivalent to the double array shown in Figure 9.

To aid in developing continually lower level details of the design, a simulation using the S simulator was written. The S simulator is a medium level system design simulator developed by RCA. The S simulation contains more detail than either of the previous algorithmic simulations. Useful in determining bottlenecks and critical paths at the system level, it employs information about length of time and about data produced and consumed by each operation.

Although theoretical methods have been postulated [11], the intricate data and time dependency within the systolic

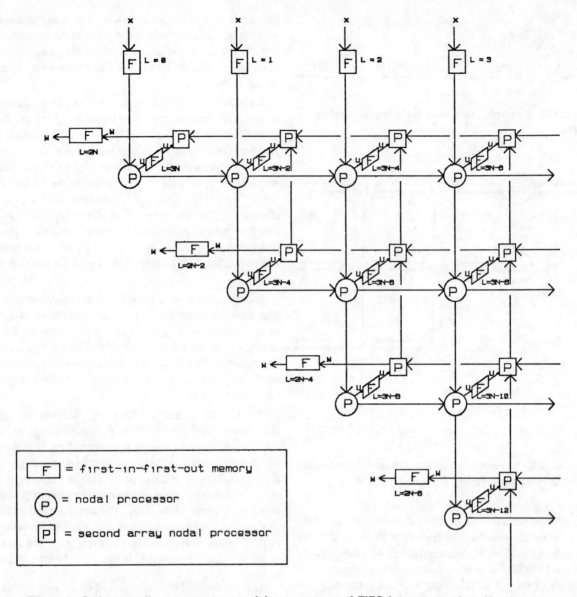

Figure 9: GaAs systolic array system nodal processor and FIFO interconnection, Version 2.

array is so complicated that it is virtually impossible to continue the design correctly without simulation at the system level. Initially, the length of time required to perform each operation was estimated. These estimates revealed that the proposed architecture was feasible for executing the algorithm. As the design progressed and more information became available, the simulation determined more precisely the time constraints of each operation and data transfer.

The medium level S simulation demonstrated that under steady state processing, the processors in the array can be made to run the single sequence of operations in three phases with 100% utilization of interior processors: every third processor can execute the same instruction. For example, consider an operation sequence consisting of instructions 1, 2, and 3 to be executed in sequence (see Figure 11). Since

the machine is SIMD, each processor executes the same instruction stream as its neighbors. However, to accommodate smooth operand flow, each processor executes the instructions in the stream out of phase relative to each other. In this example, instruction 3 can correspond an operation inside the backward indexed DO loops of the MSR3 algorithm. Results indicate that the most reliable way to achieve the steady state condition is to initialize the state of the array to the steady state condition on startup.

The system of processors can be controlled by three instruction sequencers, where each of the three sequencers control one phase of the instruction stream. Each sequencer would drive one-third of the processors in the array. All array processors that are members of one phase would be hard-wired to the sequencer which controls that phase. The three

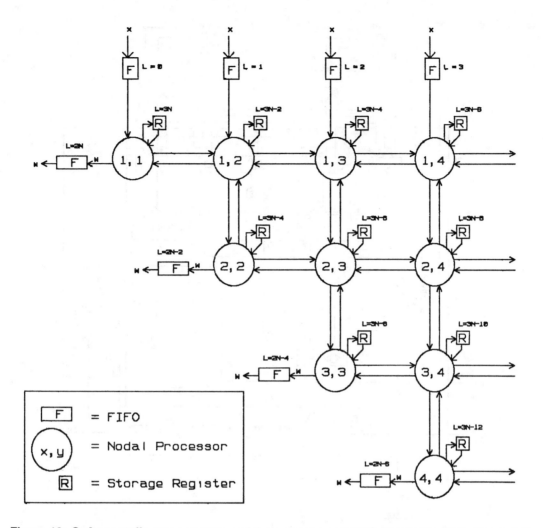

Figure 10: GaAs systolic array system nodal processor and FIFO interconnection, Version 3.

```
2 3 1 2 3 1 2 3
  3 1 2 3 1 2 3
    2 3 1 2 3 1
      1 2 3 1 2      T = 0
        3 1 2 3
          2 3 1
            1 2
              3

1 2 3 1 2 3 1 2
  2 3 1 2 3 1 2
    1 2 3 1 2 3
      3 1 2 3 1      T = 1
        2 3 1 2
          1 2 3
            3 1
              2
```

Figure 11: Snapshot of array executing 1-2-3 instruction sequence in three phases.

sequencers must be synchronized to maintain the proper phase relationship between them.

The system architecture of a systolic array can be made fault tolerant if a nodal interconnection scheme is provided so that a failed processing node can be bypassed to use processing nodes in spare rows and columns. Investigations using the S simulation showed that the addition of three spare rows and columns avoided catastrophic failure from up to an average of eight separate faults.

The system architecture set certain constraints on the internal architecture of the nodal processor and dictated its functionality. Communication ports going in and out are required on each of the four sides of the nodal processor. The simplicity of the operations and the construction advantages suggest that all circuitry for a processing node be partitioned on one chip. The data ports were serialized by nibbles to lessen the number of I/O pins. The algorithm in combination with the system architecture dictated the nodal processor's register set, which consists of four general registers

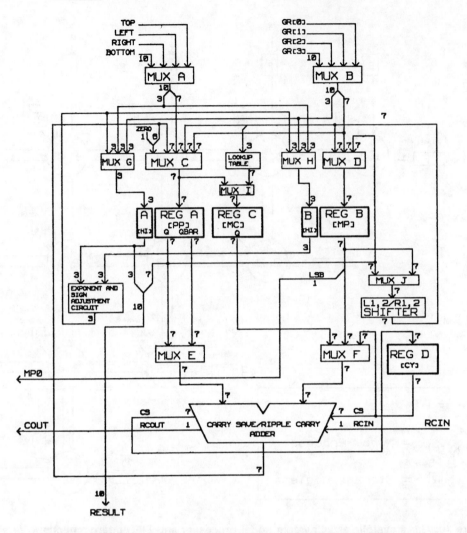

Figure 12: Systolic array nodal processor chip's ALU block diagram.

used for holding critical values of the algorithm between operations.

The current throughput requirement on the order of five microseconds per coefficient update indicates the need for clock rates in the 100 MHz range. Future throughput requirements will far exceed these rates. Such clock rates are currently reachable with GaAs parts. Unfortunately, GaAs fabrication capabilities are not as advanced as those of silicon. Consequently, the internal architecture of the nodal processor reflects many tradeoffs in circuit complexity. Since the processor is being custom built to perform this algorithm, only the minimum set of data paths are provided, and control is effected through logic driven by a state counter.

The design of the ALU capitalizes on GaAs speed, while optimizing and minimizing the logic to perform multiplies, adds, and divides. A special adder-multiplier was designed with ripple-carry and carry-save adders (see Figure 12). A fast approximation divide algorithm was chosen that uses the adder-multiplier.

Circuit complexity was further reduced 25 percent by selecting a special pseudo floating-point number format that offers the equivalent range of 14-bit fixed point representation using only 10 bits. This format was developed to meet range and accuracy requirements of the beamforming application. This format reduces the interchip communication burden by 29 percent.

The special format uses a 2-bit exponent field, a 7-bit unnormalized mantissa, and a sign bit. The exponent can put the value of the mantissa into four ranges. The value of each range is four times greater than the previous range. This is accomplished with a 0, 2, 4, 6 shifter that is merely a four input multiplexer. An unnormalized mantissa is used so that interface to the outside world can be accomplished easily in fixed point. Table 2 shows how the four ranges of numbers are represented for the mantissa length chosen above.

Gallium Arsenide Technology

Gallium Arsenide (GaAs) technology offers important advantages for real-time signal processing applications. High

Table 2. Pseudo-Floating-Point Ranges

Numeric Range		Mantissa Range		Exponent
lower	upper	lower	upper	
0	(+/−)255	0000000	1111111	00
(+/−)256	(+/−)1023	0100000	1111111	01
(+/−)1024	(+/−)4095	0100000	1111111	10
(+/−)4096	(+/−)8192	0100000	1111111	11

speed is GaAs's primary advantage. That GaAs is more radiation hard for the total dose and more temperature tolerant than silicon are other advantages. However, GaAs's radiation hardness is limited because single-event upset probabilities increase with decreasing device size and because GaAs devices in current designs are often in the micron or submicron range. Moreover, GaAs digital technology is also limited by low integration, high wafer density dislocations (low yield), and high cost. GaAs also has a smaller noise margin, and rapid enough testing equipment is lacking. Fortunately, most GaAs problems are expected to be temporary [12].

The GaAs technology being developed at RCA's Advanced Technology Laboratories (ATL) has progressed enough to make it possible to design and fabricate a 32-bit ALU test chip, and a Manchester Encoder, and to design an 8-bit microprocessor and a Manchester Decoder [13,14]. The fabricated Manchester Encoder chips deliver 500 Mbit/s performance. The 8-bit microprocessor, using instruction-stream pipelining and RISC design philosophies, promises to deliver 200 MIPS performance. Triquint Corp. of Beaverton, Oregon, fabricates ATL's GaAS chips. The Triquint process chosen involves low power dissipation (a typical gate dissipates about 780 microwatts) and 1-m enhancement/depletion MESFET technology in both gate array and standard cell options.

GaAs technology was chosen to meet future processing requirements without the need for redesigning the processing elements. If MOS technology were used, processing speed would be obtained by introducing parallelism by increasing hardware size.

Logic Design

The standard cells used in the systolic array are limited to 1-, 2-, 3-, 4-, and 5-input NOR gates. The standard cell family also includes AND-NOR gates, in which the AND component is accomplished through a dual-gate MESFET. However, this dual gate MESFET is the source of recent yield problems. Because of these yield problems, only the five NOR gates listed above will be employed in the design of this systolic array.

The systolic array includes single-chip standard cell GaAs processing nodes. Each processing node chip has approximately 2100 gates of the relatively small NOR gates. MIMIC, RCA's logic simulator, was used in the gate-level design process. Before final logic design, the register-transfer-level (RTL) will be simulated, using the N.2 simulator from Endot, Inc.

Features of the NODAL Processor Chip

Working from specifications of data transfer rate, coefficient update rate, and GaAs technology limitations (gates, pins), the authors determined the minimum clock rate, the number and type of chips, and the number of handshaking lines required.

In the array, only one processor design was used. In this design, fault tolerance is included on the system level; the clock rate is 80 MHz; the data transfer rate between processors is 12 MHz; the number of I/O pins is 42. The system updates the coefficients for the multiple beams every five microseconds.

Data is transmitted serially over eight lines (two unidirectional lines on each of four sides of a processing node in the array). Of the sixteen handshaking lines, there are two for each data line ("data valid" and "acknowledge"). The operation of the 2-line handshaking system used is demonstrated in Figure 13.

The processor contains an ALU optimized to perform only the functions needed by the algorithm. The partitioning of the algorithm was influenced by choosing the functions implemented with the most efficient (lowest gate count) hardware circuits designed in the hardware-frugal GaAs technology. (A RISC-like philosophy of hardware-toward-software trading-off was used to meet the low gate count restriction.) The basic architecture of the nodal processing chips is shown in Figure 14.

The number of registers in the processor and their interconnection, minimized to meet the stringent gate limitation, were carefully tailored to the algorithm. All data flowing between processors and into the ALU is assumed to be normalized. The ALU renormalizes its outputs to assure that the next process receives normalized data. (Normalized means that the leading one is in the first or the second most significant bit position of the 7-bit mantissa.) The only seemingly unnormalized numbers allowed are very small, occurring only when the exponent is zero.

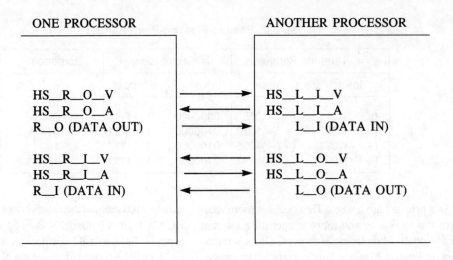

ONE PROCESSOR   ANOTHER PROCESSOR

HS_R_O_V → HS_L_I_V
HS_R_O_A ← HS_L_I_A
R_O (DATA OUT) → L_I (DATA IN)

HS_R_I_V ← HS_L_O_V
HS_R_I_A → HS_L_O_A
R_I (DATA IN) ← L_O (DATA OUT)

where:
    HS = handshaking
     R = right
     L = left
     O = out
     I = in
     V = valid
     A = acknowledge

Figure 13: Standard interface for all sides of the nodal processor.

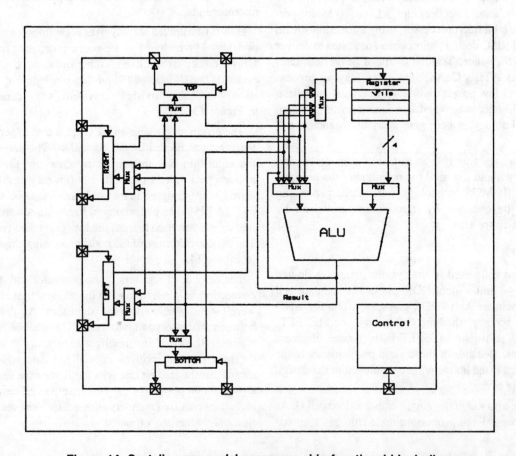

Figure 14: Systolic array nodal processor chip functional block diagram.

Features of the ALU

The ALU has two 10-bit inputs and one 10-bit output. It assumes that the 10-bit package includes a 2-bit exponent, a sign bit, and a 7-bit mantissa. The number representation system and the normalization scheme were described earlier. Upon receiving the normalized data, the ALU assumes that the binary point is between the most significant bit and the next most significant bit, so that each mantissa assumes a value between one-half and two.

The ALU is composed of two 10-bit and two 7-bit registers. One 7-bit register is a simple latch; the other three are masterripple-slave flipflops. The ALU also has a 7-bit combination carry/carry-save adder, a 7-bit shifter, exponent and sign handling circuits, and the necessary multiplexers. Table 3 shows the ALU gate count estimate of approximately 2100 gates.

Table 3. Systolic Array Nodal Processor ALU Gate Count Estimate

Logic Block		Gate Count
CS/RC Adder		132
Muxes:	A (4:1 10 bits)	136
	B (4:1 10 bits)	136
	C (5:1 7 bits)	204
	D (4:1 7 bits)	106
	E (2:1 7 bits)	36
	F (3:1 7 bits)	68
	G (3:1 3 bits)	30
	H (3:1 3 bits)	30
	I (2:1 7 bits)	36
	J (2:1 7 bits)	36
Registers:	A (10 bits)	146
(master-slave)	B (10 bits)	146
	D (7 bits)	112
Latches:	C (7 bits)	54
Shifter:		44
Reciprocal lookup table:		19
Exponent and sign adjustment circuits:		201
Control:		425
Total gates:		2097

The processes of normalization, denormalization, complementation, and various shifting functions are required to manipulate the mantissa during addition, subtraction, multiplication, and reciprocation. The ALU functions shown in Table 4 assume that normalization has already been performed.

The shifter is needed as a left 1/2 shifter for reciprocation's normalization and as a right 2/4/6 shifter in preparation for add/subtract. The algorithm also requires an instruction for shifting the contents of the B register to the right 1 place. The familiar tradeoff between speed and gate count must be considered in choosing a shifter. A minimal-hardware shifter requires extra steps to perform longer shifts; whereas, a hardware-liberal shifter requires many more gates. In the interest of conserving gates, a small shifter (L-1, 2/R-1,2) was chosen. Although the smaller shifter requires two or three steps to perform the four and six right shifts, these longer shifts occur infrequently.

Table 4. ALU Functions

Function Set	Suboperations	Number of steps
1 A + B	shift, add, shift	3
2 B − A	shift, add, shift	3
3 A*B	7 csadd, 1 rcadd	8
4 A shr 1	shift	1
5 -A (two's comp)	add	1
6 1/B (reciprocal)	shift, mult, complement, move, mult, shift	22

The above functions do not include the load-and-store operations because these functions are required in the instruction sequences.

The architecture of the ALU design focused on a special 7-bit adder circuit, minimal registers, and minimal additional hardware. The adder circuit is special because it can operate in either carry-save or ripple carry mode. The carry-save mode provides fast multiply operation. Ripple-carry is needed to propagate the carries from the final stage of multiplication, and also for normal ADD and SUBTRACT capability.

The adder uses operands A and B. Operand A is always supplied by operand register A. Operand B is selected from either the operand B register or is the result of the adder operation (known as the accumulator or partial product). Operand A requires shift-leftby-1 capability. The partial product source operand requires shift-right-by-1 capability. This shifting capability is necessary only during multiplication. Multiplication of two n-bit numbers produces a 2n-bit result. During the first n/2 iterations of a multiplication, only one operands shifts. The other operand shifts during the remaining n/2 iterations to perform the most efficient multiplication possible since it reduces the storage of bits that must be stripped away to fit in the register length.

To produce a set of coefficients every five microseconds, a real multiply must be performed on the order of every 150 nanoseconds. Logic simulations indicated that the ALU can perform a real multiply in less than 45 nanoseconds. Therefore, the current design incorporates a healthy threefold safety margin.

Reciprocation

Because of stringent constraints on the number of allowable gates per processing element, the reciprocator hardware was kept to a minimum. The added hardware consists of a lookup table implemented in combinational logic and an additional multiplexer in the ALU. Because of its minimum hardware implementation, the reciprocation process chosen takes slightly more time than some other methods. However, this does not present a problem because reciprocation only occurs in the main diagonal nodes, which have less computational load than the other nodes in the array. The medium level S simulations revealed that the reciprocation process can take up to eight times longer than a multiplication without causing a bottleneck. Since the reciprocator requires two multiplications for each iteration, up to four iterations are possible.

Since a multiplier and two's complementer were already needed in the ALU, a convergence algorithm using only multiplication and two's complementing was chosen to approximate reciprocation. The reciprocation process is performed by hardware implementation of the following algorithm [15]:

$$Dn = \text{normalized denominator } (0.5 < Dn < 1.0)$$
$$P(0) = \text{initial guess (from lookup table)}$$
$$A(0) = P(0) * Dn$$
$$A(i) = A(i-1) * [2 - A(i-1)], \ i=1,2,3,\ldots,N$$
$$P(i) = P(i-1) * [2 - A(i-1)]$$
$$P(N) \sim 1/Dn$$

$A(i)$ and $P(i)$ are intermediate values, with $P(i)$ being the stepwise approximation to the reciprocal of Dn. The number N is the number of iterations required to converge on the solution. As $A(i)$ approaches 1, $P(i)$ approaches $1/Dn$. Greater precision requires a larger number of iterations. Using simulations of the algorithm having numbers with fixed point notation and fixed word length means that a 7-bit word length requires only one iteration to converge on the solution (using an 8-value lookup table for the initial guess). Therefore, only two multiplications (for A0 and P1) are performed for each reciprocation. The 8-value lookup table, implemented using combinational logic, requires minimal hardware (about 19 gates).

The hardware required for normalization and denormalization consists of a shifter and some control logic. A general purpose shifter was designed to perform normalization and denormalization for the reciprocator along with mantissa adjustment needed to maintain our pseudo-floating-point notation (described previously). The shifter can shift right once or twice, or left once or twice. The ALU registers are used to latch and temporarily store all intermediate values.

Conclusion

The increasing processing power requirement of many signal processing applications is rapidly exceeding the capacity of conventional uniprocessor systems. Multiprocessor systems, like the systolic array, offer a cost effective advantage in processing power. GaAs ICs are well suited for this application because of their high speed and because the processing nodes do not require a high level of integration. The efficient design procedure reported here has resulted in the design of a realizable, special purpose, hardware-efficient systolic array with realtime performance unmatchable by any realizable uniprocessor system.

Acknowledgements

The authors would like to thank Walter Helbig, B.A.Deresh, Doris Mozer of RCA, and Pin-Yee Chen for their valuable comments.

References

[1] W.D. Stanley, G.R. Dougherty, and R. Dougherty, *"Digital Signal Processing,"* Reston Publishing Co., Reston, VA, 1984, p. 232. and M. Skolnik, *"Introduction to Radar Systems,"* McGraw-Hill Book Company, New York, 1980, pp. 257 and 426.

[2] H.T. Kung, "A Programmable Systolic Array Machine and Its Applications," *IEEE Parallel Architectures for Signal Processing Presentation*, Philadelphia, Penn., April 1986.

[3] J. Loughlin, Naval Ocean Systems Center, San Diego California, Conversation held January 13, 1987.

[4] P.V. Howells, "MOSAR-Array Multiplex Beamforming Technique," *Symposium Record, 9th Annual Radar Symposium*. Ann Arbor, Mich., June 1963.

[5] S.P. Applebaum, "Electronic Scanning of Circular Arrays," *U.S. patent 3,076,193*, January 29, 1963.

[6] N.A. Carlson "Efficient Digital Algorithm for Adaptive Arrays," *Final Technical Report*, Rome Air Development Center, New York, 1981, p. 38.

[7] S.M. Yuen, "Algorithm and Systolic Architecture for Solving Gram-Schmidt Orthogonalization Systems," *RCA/GSD and MSR*, Moorestown, N.J.

[8] W. Givens, "Computation of Plane Unitary Rotations Transforming a General Matrix to Triangular Form," *Journal of the Society for Industrial Applied Mathematics*, Volume 6, Number 1, March 1958.

[9] D.I. Moldovan, "Mapping an Arbitrarily Large QR Algorithm into a Fixed Size VLSI Array," *Proceedings of the 1984 International Conference on Parallel Processing*, Bellaire, Mich., August 1984.

[10] P. Quinton, "Automatic Synthesis of Systolic Arrays from Uniform Recurrent Equations," *11th Annual Symposium on Computer Architecture, Conference Proceedings*, Ann Arbor, Mich., June 1984.

[11] D.I. Moldovan, "Tradeoffs Between Time and Space Characteristics in the Design of Systolic Arrays," *1985 Inter-*

national Symposium on Circuits and Systems, Kyoto, Japan, June 1985.

[12] Velijko Milutinović, "GaAs Microprocessor Technology," Computer, Volume 19, Number 10, October 1986.

[13] Veljko Milutinović, Alex Silbey, David Fura, Kevin Keirn, Mark Bettinger, Walter Helbig, William Heagerty, Richard Zieger, Robert Schellack, and Walter Curtice, "Issues of Importance in Designing GaAs Microcomputer Systems," Computer, Volume 19, Number 10, October 1986.

[14] Walter A. Helbig, Robert H. Schellack, and Richard M. Zieger, "The Design and Construction of a GaAs Technology Demonstration Microprocessor," Proceedings of Midcon 85, Session 23, Chicago, Ill., September 1985, pp. 1-6.

[15] K. Hwang, Computer Arithmetic: Principles, Architecture, and Design, John Wiley and Sons, Inc., New York, 1979.

Toward a GaAs Realization of a Production-System Machine

Theodore F. Lehr and Robert G. Wedig

Carnegie Mellon University

Reprinted from *Computer*, April 1987, pages 36-48. Copyright © 1987 by
The Institute of Electrical and Electronics Engineers, Inc.

The computation and memory demands of OPS5 production systems suggest that the underlying production-system machine architecture can take advantage of a high-speed realization technology.

Production systems are a special class of expert systems. *Expert systems* are tailored programs or system environments that are designed to handle problems whose solution normally requires human expertise in a particular area. In this article, we attempt to demonstrate the issues involved in realizing a GaAs processor designed for efficient execution of the OPS5 production-system language. [1-3] We review the state of GaAs D-MESFET technology, which is a mature technology, and discuss how its capacities can be exploited by a reduced instruction set computer (RISC) called RISCF.* RISCF was designed at Carnegie Mellon University.

A *production-system machine* is a machine whose architecture and implementation are optimized for the execution of production-system languages. The OPS5 production-system language is currently being researched and used at Carnegie Mellon University, as well as at a number of industrial sites.

OPS5 has several advantages over other production-system languages. It is generally easier to encode rules in OPS5 than in other types of expert-system languages. Unfortunately, OPS5 suffers from the same problem that plagues all production-system languages—insufficient execution performance.

Research on improving the execution speed of production systems has been conducted at Carnegie Mellon on three basic fronts:

- investigation of the maximum amount of parallelism that can be built into a production system,
- the evaluation and development of special-purpose architectures for production-system execution, and
- investigation of alternative implementation technologies for production-system machines.

Only through the combination of parallelism, architecture, and technology can the highest system performance be achieved.

Investigation of parallelism in production systems was performed by Anoop Gupta and Lanny Forgy, both of Carnegie Mellon. Their work has been reported by Gupta [3,5] and will not be discussed here except to note that they determined that a small number of processors connected by means of a tightly coupled network can at-

---

An earlier version of this article appeared on pp. 246-252 of the *Proceedings of the 19th Hawaii International Conference on System Sciences* under the title "The GaAs Realization of a Production-System Machine." © 1986 IEEE.

*RISCF conforms to the definition of a RISC given by Cowell et al. [4]

tain a significant amount of the parallelism available in OPS5 production-system programs.

Jim Quinlan of Carnegie Mellon performed a study[6] of the suitability of different architectures for production-system machines. In this study, he compared a number of commercial computers that run production-system programs with each other and with two proposed special-purpose machines. The results of the architectural analysis indicate that when a custom RISC processor is given the same cycle time as a complex microcoded architecture designed solely for the execution of production-system programs, it can perform as well as the microcoded architecture, or better.

Our work is to investigate the issues involved in realizing a RISC processor in gallium arsenide to obtain estimates of parameters like the cycle time and the basic system requirements of such a processor. The work reported in this article is a feasibility study of a GaAs implementation of RISCF. This study, which was performed with the cooperation of the Honeywell Corporate Systems Development Division near Minneapolis, Minnesota, focuses on the feasibility, design, and layout of, and performance estimates for, a D-MESFET implementation of a customized processor for the execution of production-system languages. It was carried out by the authors from the fall of 1983 until December of 1985. The work was performed solely by the authors, although Honeywell provided the packaging, density, and technology specifications and the CAD facilities for verifying the accuracy of the design. Ours was a feasibility study, and the design has not been implemented; however, through this work, we have been better able to determine the feasibility of GaAs as a system-realization technology, and we have helped to push back the limits of the execution speed of production-system programs.

Quinlan's study of five architectures[6] suggests that two proposed architectures—a microcoded machine with long, semantically complex instructions and a specially designed RISC processor (RISCF)—are best suited for executing production systems. Since these architectures are markedly dissimilar, it may seem odd that microcoded and RISC processors have comparable performance for OPS5 applications. Quinlan points out, however, that computer-system issues, such as available processor-memory bandwidth, are critical factors affecting the relative

performance of both these machines.

In this article, we assume that each serves a host machine as either a dedicated accelerator or a coprocessor. The systems issues that arise when they are dedicated processors or coprocessors that execute only OPS5 are different from those that arise when they are machines of more general utility. In the case of RISCF, we also assume that we have access to high memory bandwidth. By "realization," we mean roughly the semiconductor technologies on which a machine is built. "Implementation" refers to the machine's register-transfer-level description, and "architecture" usually refers to its instruction-set design, although the boundary between "implementation" and "architecture" is not constant across all machines. We are indebted for our use of the terms to an unpublished manuscript by Blaauw and Brooks.[7]

For purposes of illuminating the issues that arise when one attempts to realize a processor in GaAs, we have made the GaAs realization of the RISCF production-system machine our principal thrust in this article. Given the complexity of the microcoded architecture, any reasonable implementation would be quite large, and hence we do not consider that a feasible realization in GaAs is possible with today's technology. RISCF, however, has single-cycle instruction execution, is predominantly load/store in design, and is composed of relatively few instructions. It also has a regular instruction format and a fixed 32-bit instruction width. In Lehr,[8] the implementation of this architecture is discussed, and a number of its interesting features are presented.

Every semiconductor technology—whether it be NMOS, ECL, or MESFET—has fabrication and design rules that uniquely affect the implementation of a system. In our researches, we used GaAs D-MESFET logic because it is one of the most established GaAs technologies. (Companies like Honeywell and Rockwell offer product lines based on D-MESFET technology.)

OPS5 and the Rete algorithm

OPS5 is an efficient production-system language in which rules are codified in the form of a search tree called the *Rete tree*.[1,2]

The less efficient production systems typically store a list of rules in one memory space and a formal description of the problem in another. Searching for a match between the LHS of the rules and the elements of the problem is performed in these systems by indexing through the two memories in such a way that each entry in one is compared with every entry in the other. Although the inefficiency of this method can be mitigated with techniques like hashing the lists by means of certain keys, these are frequently just *ad hoc* improvements because they seldom take advantage of behavior indigenous to production systems.

In contrast, the OPS5 search tree is constructed to take advantage of the propensity in production systems for parts of conditionals to exist in the LHS of more than one rule. For example, in Figure 1, R1, R2, and R3 represent three rules in a hypothetical production system for auto-engine diagnostics. (Of course, in actual OPS5 code, these rules would be formally specified.) Since R1 and R2 share the condition "low compression" in their LHSs, the tree guarantees that when this condition is found in the problem space, each rule will simultaneously instantiate the "low compression" part of its LHS. That is, both rules concurrently get their LHSs partially satisfied. Despite the prevalence of such shared conditions, previous production-system languages did not exploit them.

The Rete tree is part of the more general *Rete matching algorithm*. As we just noted, the tree takes advantage of structural similarities between the LHSs of rules in OPS5 production systems. In addition to exploiting this property, Rete also capitalizes on temporal similarities between the elements in the problem. As we noted earlier, production systems make

R1: IF light blue exhaust smoke AND
low compression THEN check piston rings

R2: IF unburned gas in exhaust AND
low compression THEN check valves and valve seats

R3: IF compression ratio < 6.5:1 THEN low compression

Figure 1. Some rules from a hypothetical production system.

several passes through a problem, updating it each time rules are satisfied. The Rete algorithm recognizes that it does not need to look for a match in the entire updated problem, only in the part of the problem that has just changed. Consequently, Rete records those aspects of the problem that have been altered and applies the rules to only those altered parts. For example, should a 5:1 compression ratio be one of the problem elements in the hypothetical engine-diagnostic system mentioned earlier, rule R3 would add the element "low compression" to the problem description. Then, in the next pass through the problem, the Rete algorithm would attempt to match only "low compression" to the LHSs of the rules, since any partial matches from the first pass would still exist. In this case, rules R1 and R2 would be partially instantiated. If the element "light blue exhaust smoke" had been found in the first pass, R1 would be fully instantiated in the second pass, which would indicate that the rings should be examined.

A study of the Rete algorithm's implementation demands shows that where conventional processors are involved, the kinds of computations it performs after a memory access are usually simple. Once data is resident in a conventional processor, only simple arithmetic instructions are needed to perform the matching tests. Heavy memory traffic and a preponderance of simple instructions are two key run-time characteristics of the Rete algorithm. They are also characteristic of matching algorithms for less efficient production systems, since the computation most often done in production systems is the comparison of two operands.

A third characteristic of the Rete algorithm is the prevalence of branch instructions over other types. One of the reasons for this is that part of the Rete algorithm consists of the Rete tree, which is built upon the antecedent parts of all the rules in the production system. The Rete tree is a complex structure that implements not only the sharing of parts of antecedents, but also implements a number of other features of the Rete algorithm. It must be traversed while the algorithm tests for matches. The tree, however, is mapped onto the sequential code of a uniprocessor. Consequently, when moving among the branches of the Rete tree, the processor is frequently forced to jump to noncontiguous localities in the instruction stream. The jump frequency is heightened further because the processor is usually executing iterative loops when it is at branch nodes in the tree.

These three characteristics—high memory traffic, the simplicity of instructions in OPS5, and frequent branching—drive designs for the architecture and implementation of the processor for executing OPS5. We do not know if a preponderance of branching instructions is a property of other production systems, although the simple, repetitive nature of searching for matches makes this likely.

The architecture and implementation of RISCF

When compiled into assembly-language instructions, the Rete algorithm consists of many Load-Jump and Compare-Jump sequences. It does not need complex instructions, but requires only a few simple Load, Compare, and Jump types. A sequential processor dedicated exclusively to executing OPS5 can be based on a small core of simple instructions that have the potential for being executed in a single cycle. Other Rete characteristics favor a processor that can efficiently support both (a) heavy data traffic in and out of memory and (b) frequent branching.

An OPS5-executing processor that is built on a set of simple instructions and optimized to support all these Rete characteristics can achieve a speedup over an uncustomized OPS5-executing processor that supports numerous complex instructions. This is so because the overhead of supporting instructions superfluous to OPS5 execution is eliminated. Such a processor architecture—one built primarily of simple Load-Store instructions, each of which executes in one machine cycle—suggests a RISC-like architecture. John Cock of IBM initiated the seminal work on RISC architectures with the 801 minicomputer.[9] This machine inspired work done at Berkeley[10] and Stanford[11] and has affected the design of some recently introduced commercial machines.

The instruction set of RISCF, the RISC we developed for executing OPS5, is streamlined to accommodate the properties of the Rete algorithm. (The "F" in "RISCF" refers to Charles L. Forgy of Carnegie Mellon, the developer of the Rete algorithm.) Compare-and-branch and Load-and-branch instruction sequences are implemented under a static branch-prediction strategy. Memory-reference instructions use simple addressing techniques, and Arithmetic-logic instructions are decoded and executed in a single machine cycle. All of RISCF's instructions are 32 bits long. The main data type is the 32-bit integer, and the only arithmetic operations are Add and Subtract. RISCF has four addressing modes: absolute, immediate, base register plus displacement, and register. The functional integrity of all RISCF subsystems except the caches has been verified in a simulation done on the MIMOLA Software System.[12,13]

The RISCF branch-prediction strategy is integrated into a three-stage data pipeline. Ordinarily, a heavily pipelined machine suffers performance degradation when it runs programs with incessant branching. The degradation occurs because a branch to a different program location usually requires that the pipe be flushed, which reduces the concurrency available on the machine. The degradation is most serious when it frequently happens that the data in the pipeline is dependent on previous or subsequent data, or when there are frequent cache misses. Both the simplicity of RISCF's single-cycle instructions and its branch-addressing mode, however, curtail such data dependencies. We applied statistics on the runtimes of typical OPS5 programs[14] to RISCF instruction sequences that were generated by James Quinlan.[6] The results show that a static branch-prediction scheme speeds up RISCF's execution of the Rete algorithm by 15 percent over RISCF execution of the algorithm without branch prediction.

In developing a processor's pipeline, the types of instructions, the instruction sequences, and the frequency of cache misses are important design parameters. The simplicity of the RISCF instruction set and the regularity of RISCF operations allow for uncomplicated pipelining. The only data dependencies that exist between instructions and can cause pipe breaks are those between Branch-prediction instructions and Branch instructions. An internal forwarding mechanism handles any dependencies that arise between instructions requiring common registers. Despite the value of the pipeline, the high number of branch instructions used in the Rete algorithm might indicate incessant pipe breaks and recurrent cache misses. However, the RISCF pipeline is structured to permit the decoder to decode all instruction sequences without pipe breaks except when those sequences harbor incorrectly predicted branches. These isolated sequences are slower than straight line code by one machine cycle.

The efficiency of the pipeline is also enhanced by the structure of RISCF's register file. The register file is a large, 128-bit × 32-bit structure consisting of two read ports and a single write port. It is meant to hold critical elements from the problem space and pointers to various matching tests in the Rete tree. The register file's ports are essential components in establishing RISCF's three-stage pipeline. If the processor-control state asks for parallel reading and writing of the same register, the write data is forwarded internally, which guarantees that the most up-to-date data is sent to the ALU. RISCF does not require an ALU with complex functionality because the predominant operation performed by the processor is the comparing of an operand from data memory with a register operand. Consequently, the ALU is a simple structure with only 10 functions.

RISCF derives some of its performance from logically separate instruction and data caches. For a RISC processor, especially one realized in GaAs, memory bandwidth is a critical performance factor. Executing an instruction every machine cycle requires memory fast enough to supply the instructions. The dual RISC caches permit simultaneous fetching of one instruction while the operand of another is retrieved. Without the additional cache, the processor would need to delay the instruction fetch each time data was fetched from memory. Lehr[8] suggests that a large data cache (32K bytes × 32 bytes or larger) can hold over 90 percent of all data references. It is not likely, however, that such a large cache would operate fast enough for a GaAs RISC. Fortunately, data references in OPS5 frequently exhibit a high degree of locality, so a smaller cache is probably sufficient. The architecture of the memory interface is an important area for further research.

RISCF is a superior uniprocessor architecture for production systems—and for OPS5 production systems in particular—because its instruction set is tailored to executing the Rete algorithm and because the size and simplicity of its instruction set permit the machine to fetch an instruction every machine cycle. The RISCF instructions are basically a modified subset of the instruction sets found on larger, more complex machines (there are Compare-and-predict-to-branch instructions, for example). RISCF instructions are basically those that are usually used to

implement the Rete algorithm on these larger machines. The computational requirements of the Rete algorithm, including those for making control-flow decisions, are simple enough that an instruction set designed to support the algorithm can be implemented on a machine that offers single-cycle execution. Such a machine—RISCF is an example—takes maximum advantage of the available memory bandwidth, since *with respect to the Rete algorithm*, RISCF has a very high ratio of useful computations per memory reference. This high ratio is usually not a characteristic of RISC machines designed

---

RISCF is a superior uniprocessor architecture for production systems.

---

for a broader range of applications, but RISCF is intended for a single application.

The notion of useful computations per memory reference is a complex and subtle one. The ratio depends on the meaning assigned to "useful," and therefore on the application being executed. The microcoded machine proposed by Quinlan[6] tries to maximize the ratio of useful computations per memory reference, but does so by raising the architectural level of the machine above typical assembly-language instructions to that of an instruction set that more directly executes the primitive operations of the Rete algorithm. Quinlan carefully discusses the assumptions behind RISCF and the microcoded machine, and he analyzes the performance that results when OPS5 is executed on architectures like the VAX/780. With its shorter cycle times, RISCF is superior to the microcoded machine when the problem of increased processor-memory bandwidth (a problem inherent in RISC machines) is mitigated.

It is difficult to compare machines as dissimilar as a VAX/780 and RISCF, for the VAX is a computer *system* designed for a multiprogramming environment, while RISCF is a dedicated *processor* designed for executing OPS5. How well the processor architectures of the 780 and RISCF execute production systems depends on their implementations and on the systems in which they are placed. In addition, while the 780 is a successful commercial product on which physical experiments can be made directly, RISCF is

a set of architecture and implementation specifications whose performance has been verified through computer simulations. In his study, Quinlan[6] derives performance estimates for the architectures by means of such metrics as instruction/data traffic and the number of machine cycles required to execute OPS5 programs. One of the metrics attempts to base the estimate of the execution times on more of a *processor-to-processor* analysis by decoupling the VAX architecture from its memory-management system. This decoupling is done by packing the Rete code in tight loops, which enables the 780 to obtain nearly a 100 percent hit ratio in cache memory. In such a case, the match time of OPS5 running on a VAX/780 that accesses cache every 200 ns is approximately two to four times longer than the match time of RISCF that is realized in NMOS VLSI and has a 300-ns cycle time.

As a RISC machine, however, RISCF can take greater advantage than a VAX can of the higher speeds that come from reduced chip counts. Consequently, a high-speed realization of RISCF in GaAs is likely to widen the performance gap. Because of RISCF's architectural simplicity, a silicon realization would require a relatively small amount of real estate. This simplicity means that it is worth considering whether a GaAs realization is viable. In considering this, one must first analyze those characteristics of GaAs devices that affect system-design issues.

Factors affecting the performance of GaAs ICs

Questions of the viability of realizing RISCF in GaAs and of the advantages RISCF might obtain from such a realization suggest that one should examine how GaAs differs from silicon with respect to the logic structures, scale of integration, and signal-propagation behavior.

Available logic structures. Designing digital circuits in GaAs D-MESFET technology is attended by two major constraints not encountered when one designs with silicon technology in mind.

The first constraint arises because only depletion-mode transistors are used. This constraint means that at least two voltage sources must be used. If a depletion-mode transistor has its source tied to ground and its drain connected to some positive potential, it can only turn off if a potential less than or equal to its pinch-off voltage is applied to its gate. Consequently, unless two or more sources are available, or unless elaborate charge-pump circuits are used, D-MESFETs will always be on.

The second constraint is a consequence of the small pinch-off voltage usually found in depletion mode MESFETs (the usual pinch-off voltage is $V_p \approx -1$ volt) and of the range of the output-voltage swings ($\Delta V_{out} \approx 1.0$ volt).[15] At a fixed gate potential, small V_p (that is, when V_p is close to zero) do not permit channels to conduct as strongly as they conduct for larger V_p. Since the channels are less conductive, there is a comparatively large drop in the drain-source voltage (V_{ds}) across the transistor. This relationship between V_p and V_{ds} removes basic NAND gates and most pass transistors from the set of viable design alternatives.[16] The large voltage drop across each of the NAND pull-down transistors when they are off raises the low-voltage logic levels of GaAs chips dangerously high. This prevents the gate from driving load transistors. Although NAND gates and pass transistors can be fabricated, the designer must either accept reduced switching speeds or have access to very fine process control to produce circuits of the quality necessary to prescribe the device parameters accurately. Typically, however, the low logic levels and diminished noise margins obtained by placing two MESFETs in the usual pull-down configuration of an NMOS NAND gate are unacceptable. Pass transistors suffer the same effects from that configuration: large drain-source voltage drops and diminished noise margins.

To the integrated circuit designer accustomed to the variety offered by silicon MOSFETs, the absence of NAND gates and pass transistors imposes onerous constraints on the complexity and functionality that can be packed into a given chip area. The designer can no longer implement a simple multiplexer that incorporates an array of pass transistors selected by inverted and noninverted control signals, but must instead derive the canonical expressions for the multiplexer and coax them into a form generally consisting of NOR gates. Consequently, a GaAs multiplexer and some other integrated structures require more transistors than their silicon MOSFET alternatives. If the GaAs version of a structure uses more gate stages than a functionally identical silicon circuit, the effect of the structure on the speed advantage enjoyed by in-

dividual GaAs devices is diminished. The inability to map silicon gate structures directly onto functionally similar structures in GaAs also affects comparisons of the achievable scales of integration in the two technologies.

The scale of integration in GaAs. In order for large digital systems to benefit from the intrachip speeds of GaAs, the scale of integration must increase so that greater functionality can be placed on a single chip. The number of transistors that can be placed on a single GaAs chip with acceptable yield has recently tipped 25,000 in the implementation of highly regular structures like static RAMs. Less densely packed systems include gate arrays and parallel multipliers that contain between 1000 and 10,000 transistors.[17-19] Each of the integrated circuits exhibits the high-speed, low-power characteristics usually associated with GaAs, but usually also endures weak fan-out performance. For example, the Honeywell HGAS-500 gate array is a fast (~ 0.25 ns per logic gate) aggregate of NOR/OR-NAND gates, but it has maximum dc fan-outs of only two for unbuffered NOR and OR-NAND gates and of five for buffered NOR gates.[20] The low fan-out of GaAs buffers is a stumbling block to designers: It will force them to confront dismal interchip propagation delays for large systems until GaAs advances from LSI to VLSI.

The move to VLSI and the advantages that may be derived from it hinge on process-control improvements and the kinds of gates that may be fabricated. As was noted in the section on "Available logic structures," the circuit geometries of transistors in silicon MOSFET structures and those in functionally equivalent GaAs MESFET structures are not mirror images of one another. Since D-MESFET circuits cannot use NAND gates and pass transistors, they typically require more transistors for implementation of a digital system than a MOSFET circuit would. This discrepancy may disappear, however, as decreases in feature sizes, in voltage swings, and in tolerances for threshold-voltage variations cause difficulties in implementing NAND gates and pass transistors in future silicon VLSI technology. In addition, the advent of reliable heterojunction bipolar transistors (HJBTs) will eventually introduce NAND gates and pass transistors to GaAs, but this technology is still years away from being a viable VLSI alternative. Although larger chip areas are required for circuits limited

to NOR and compound-logic gates, this is not the principal obstacle impeding successful VLSI fabrication in GaAs.

The major impediment to reducing both the sizes of features and the voltage swings of GaAs integrated circuits is that chip yield is very poor.[16,21] As integration scales increase, the swing of gate voltages must decrease so that manageable power-dissipation levels can be maintained. Decreasing gate-voltage swings necessitates the reduction of threshold-voltage deviations across a wafer. Threshold voltages are not constant over a wafer, but deviate from an ideal threshold voltage according to some statistical distribution. In order to ensure that many of the chips on the wafer function correctly, the range of gate-voltage swings must be adjusted to accommodate the worst-case threshold values. This is required so that one can be certain that the transistors having those values will be forced to turn on and off. In light of this, it can be seen that the poor control over threshold voltages in GaAs technology forces voltage swings in the logic to widen. As was just noted, the larger voltage swings cause the typical transistor to dissipate more power, and if the power dissipation is too large, it must be countered by increasing device sizes—which means lower circuit-integration scales. Once GaAs performance parameters achieve the sensitivity necessary for VLSI circuits, the advantages of the faster device speeds will be realized more easily. Off-chip delays will then be less critical, since the logic that used to be distributed over several chips will be present on one. Long intrachip paths, however, might occur more frequently. Since only SSI, MSI, and LSI circuits are currently available in GaAs, any timing studies of systems as large as RISCF must look at both on- and off-chip signal propagations.

Propagation delays. Interchip signal propagation comprises a significant part of the circuit delays in both GaAs and silicon systems. Although intrachip signals propagate faster than interchip broadcasts, the geometry of an integrated circuit can pose difficult problems in timing subcircuits for harmonious operation. Long intrachip buses occasionally confiscate substantial chip area for routing, and they usually diminish the effects of fast device speeds by loading driver transistors. Though delays resulting from the length of intrachip buses are not endemic to gallium arsenide, integrated circuits in GaAs are more vulnerable to them than their silicon cousins in that as bus lengths increase, the speed advantage that GaAs has over silicon begins to decrease.[18] However, since GaAs integrated circuits have not yet reached the VLSI level, the predominant propagation delays continue to be at interchip interfaces.

The advantage RISCF would obtain from a GaAs technology that has not matured to the VLSI level would depend on how well RISCF could be modularized to reduce the effects of interchip delays. The decomposition of RISCF into modules depends on transistor counts, communication paths, and the number of I/O pins permitted on each chip module.

Modularizing RISCF for gallium arsenide

The modularization of RISCF that we discuss below is based on conservative estimates of the numbers of gates for different structures and on an upper pin-out bound of around 80.

Since D-MESFET systems can be scaled no further than the LSI level, RISCF must be decomposed into modularized chips if it is to be realized in this GaAs technology. Dissecting RISCF requires determining the approximate number of gates needed for each substructure, the shared communication paths, and the maximum pin-out allowed for a GaAs chip. An estimate of the speed of the modularized processor requires that one know approximate intrachip delays and the nature of interchip loading. Our modularization of RISCF is contrived in part from the performance-affecting factors (available logic structures, integration scale, and propagation delays) that were discussed in the section on "Factors affecting GaAs performance," and in part from information acquired from the Honeywell, Inc., Physical Sciences Center located outside of Minneapolis, Minnesota.[20] (We used the Honeywell data in our analysis of the main substructures of the processor—the analysis is given below—and we used the analysis, in turn, to arrive at an estimate of the machine-cycle time.)

We have selected the logic of each of the substructures primarily for its simplicity, not for gate conservation or for attractive performance characteristics. By limiting each substructure of the processor to configurations of NOR and NOT gates and by using rudimentary logic implementations, we have established a conservative upper

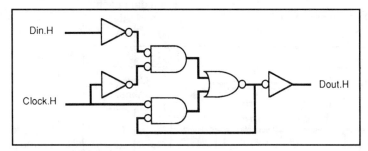

Figure 2. A single static-latch bit.

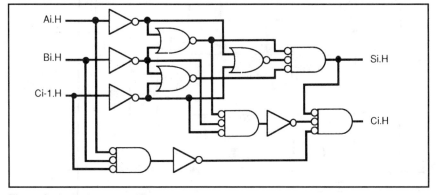

Figure 3. A ripple-carry adder.

bound on the number of gates needed by each major substructure. For example, though a parallel adder will most likely outperform a simple ripple-carry type, the implementation considerations for a parallel adder are more complex and its logic structure is more elaborate. Since the modularization of RISCF makes intermodule communication the major source of performance degradation, it would be premature to select elaborate logic implementations for their potential performance gains before the modularity is established. More significantly, the purpose of selecting gate configurations is not to ascertain the optimal modularity of RISCF, but to help realize a modularization that has the advantage of simplicity.

Gate geometries of RISCF substructures. The substructures of RISCF include register-transfer-level (RTL) units like registers, incrementers, the ALU, multiplexers, and other structures of similar complexity. In assigning the gate geometry to these structures, we have used only NOR and NOT gates and we have paid no attention to the different transistor configurations used in GaAs to implement these gates.

We assume that the inputs and outputs of the structures described below are asserted high.

Register. Since reliable pass transistors cannot be implemented in GaAs MESFET

technology, a GaAs static register cell consists only of standard NOR and NOT gates. Figure 2 depicts a single static-latch bit. A latch contains six gates per bit.

Multiplexer. The absence of pass transistors most strongly affects the implementation of multiplexers. Instead of being implemented as an array of pass transistors that are all controlled by a single input-select unit, a GaAs multiplexer is implemented with an armada of combinational logic. A GaAs multiplexer requires $2n + 1$ gates per bit, where n is the number of inputs.

Adder. The number of gates in the single adder cell shown in Figure 3 also reflects the absence of pass transistors. The central goal in synthesizing a modularization scheme is to arrive at a rough estimate of processor-cycle time. Consequently, we have made no special efforts to implement a fast adder, since it would not contribute to the accuracy of the estimates. The adder is a simple ripple-carry type. It contains 10 gates per bit.

Incrementer. In GaAs, an incrementer is a simplified adder in which one of the summands is a single bit equal to one. Consequently, we have constructed the incrementer out of half-adders that add the carry of the previous bit to the current bit. An incrementer has seven gates.

Decrementer. The logic construction of a GaAs decrementer is similar to that of the incrementer. Like the incrementer, it

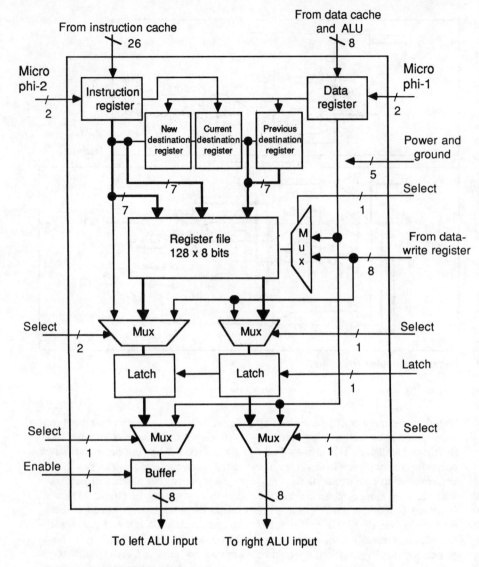

Figure 4. A register-file module.

has seven gates per bit.

ALU. The arithmetic-logic unit of RISCF can perform one of six operations each machine cycle. The operations are

• *Addition.* The geometry of the logic of the ALU's addition function can be much like that of the adder structure shown in Figure 3, but the geometry is somewhat constrained because of the other ALU operations.

• *Subtraction.* This operation is implemented in the form of the gate geometry of the addition function; however, it includes the simple two-complement converter on one of the inputs.

• *Signextend.* The first 19 bits of input *a* are passed directly to the output. The nineteenth bit's value is passed to each of the succeeding bits and is transferred to their output. Passing the bit value on to the succeeding bits is easily achieved if a two-gate drive is placed every three bits or so.

• *Hiload.* The values of the lower 16 bits of input *a* are passed to the upper 16 bits of input *b* and are concatenated with the lower 16 bits of input *b*. The modified *b* value is sent to the output. The bit values to be passed can simply be gated into their proper locations.

• *Passleft* and *Passright.* In Passleft, the left input is selected to be passed to the ALU output. (In Passright, it's the right input.) The gating is relatively trivial.

• *Or, And, Xor,* and *Not.* These logic instructions can be implemented simply, and their gating is trivial.

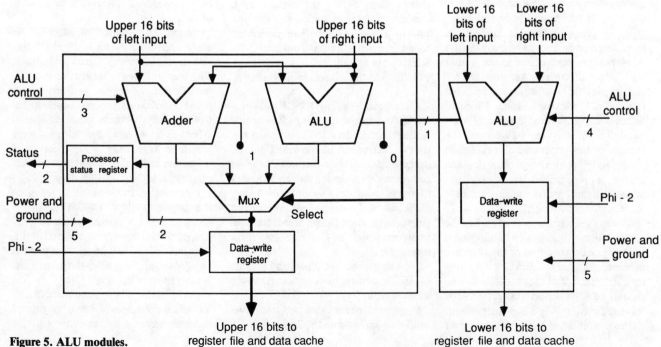

Figure 5. ALU modules.

We do not discuss in this article the gate geometries of the *Select* logic for the ALU and multiplexer, since these geometries are not complex. They have physically large realizations, however, so that they can drive control signals across the structures, but these large realizations are only significant if the gate counts per module approach LSI limitations.

In addition, there are several logic structures in the control section of RISCF that check for equality, inequality, and other relationships, but these are typically not very wide and occur infrequently.

A possible modularization scheme. The gate geometries just discussed permit approximations of the number of gates belonging to the individual modules of a given modularization scheme. A good modularization scheme attempts to decompose RISCF in such a way that critical paths and closely related substructures are kept within individual modules. Figures 4, 5, 6, and 7 depict our RISCF decomposition scheme, which attempts to satisfy the demands of pin-out, of requirements concerning numbers of gates, and of communication paths. The pin-out and communication-path requirements relegate the problem of gates per module to insignificance, since even in the case of large, highly regular structures like the register file modules, the number of gates is below 10,000. Figure 4 shows one of four register files, together with the multiplexers and the supporting latches. The four-module

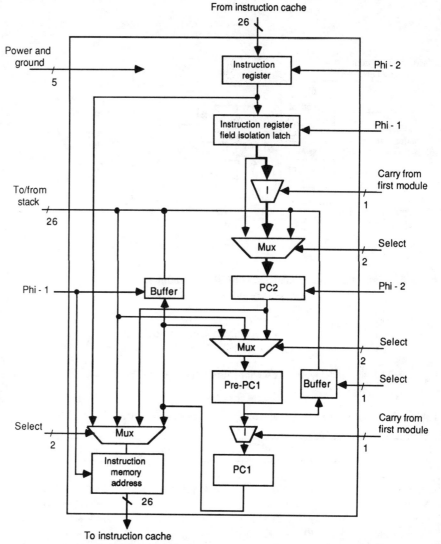

Figure 6. The instruction-fetch module.

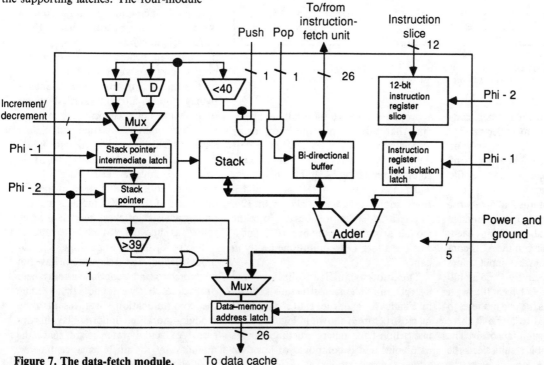

Figure 7. The data-fetch module.

243

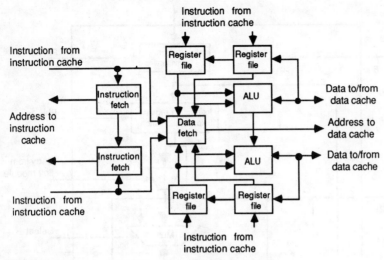

Figure 8. A layout showing juxtaposition of RISCF modules.

Total delay = 15 (gate delay)   + 65 x (unit fan-outs)
                + 0.16/micron x (unit fan-outs) (first metal)
                + 0.14/micron x (unit fan-outs) (second metal)

Figure 9. The typical delay, in picoseconds, for a 10μ-wide MESFET.

Table 1. Propagation delays, in picoseconds, for various structures.

Structure	Data Paths	Select Logic	Worst Case
Register (write)	320	—	320
Multiplexer (2:1)	320	110/bit	3500 (32 bits)
Adder[1]	600/bit	—	8960 (16 bits)
Incrementer	390 + 290/bit	—	7540 + drivers
Decrementer	390 + 290/bit	—	7540 + drivers
Register file (write)	3000	4500	4500
Register file (read)	2800	4500	4500
ALU (32 bit)[2]	12,500	400	12,500
Driver	250/stage	—	1500 (6 stage)

1. Delay for the ripple-carry adder shown in Figure 3.
2. Delay for dual, carry-selected adders in the highest 16 bits.

macrostructure of which it is a part contains more gates than any other macrostructure and has the widest data path of them all (approximately 37,000 gates, of which those in the multiport register file make up over 95 percent).

The ALU and the status and data-write registers, shown in Figure 5, are combined into two modules of about 60 pins each. The most significant slice of the ALU contains two adders—with carry-input values of zero and one, respectively—and a multiplexer for selecting between them. A design like this permits the two modules to work concurrently and to arrive at three separate 16-bit results simultaneously. The carry of the lower 16-bit result selects the appropriate upper 16-bit result, an operation that incurs only the extra delay associated with the multiplexer instead of the delay that would result from another 16-bit computation. A 16-bit ripple-carry adder needs less than 180 gates, and a 16-bit multiplexer uses only about 120. This split-adder feature does not force the module's total gate count over 1000, and it cuts the adder's execution time nearly in half.

The more significant half of the instruction-fetch macrostructure is shown in Figure 6, and the entire data-fetch macrostructure is shown in Figure 7. The instruction-fetch macrostructure consists of 62 pins and is composed of less than

2500 gates. The instruction-address stack and the stack pointer reside in the data-fetch macrostructure, a module with 74 pins and about 2000 gates.

The PLA controller, which is not shown in any of the figures in this article, comprises comparatively few gates, and can be subsumed into either the instruction-fetch module or the data-fetch module. The approximate module-gate totals are computed by identifying the principal substructures, which include the input/output buffers in the applicable module, and summing their respective subtotals.

Juxtaposition and timing. There is some overlap of functionality among the nine modules (chips). For example, slices of the instruction latch are contained in both of the instruction-fetch modules and in each of the four register-file modules. The replication of shared structures in the different modules reduces the penalties of interchip delays. As we have discussed, interchip signal propagation among both GaAs and silicon circuits is a principal source of performance degradation. Since GaAs circuits are low in power, the problems associated with driving off-chip signals are relatively greater than they are for silicon technologies like NMOS or bipolar logic, and the degradation suffered is more profound because of the high intrachip speeds of GaAs circuits. Consequently, until VLSI GaAs circuits appear, the problems of interchip signal propagation will continue to haunt the designer who wishes to build in gallium arsenide. Honeywell, Inc., is investigating a form of wafer scale integration called hybrid wafer-scale integration (HWSI), in which previously fabricated chips are deposited onto a substrate wafer and the interconnect is laid down subsequently. Such a scheme, though difficult, takes advantage of both the lower capacitances resulting from the common substrate and the absence of highly capacitive DIP pins. It also has potential for higher yields than would be obtained through general wafer-scale integration. Both our discussion of the juxtaposition of the RISCF modules and our timing analysis of these modules, which follow, assume a HWSI implementation.

Figure 8 shows a possible RISCF-module layout. In this layout, we have not attempted to find an optimal arrangement of modules, but we did note that keeping the communication distances between modules short is an important layout concern. An actual wafer might space the modules by as much as a centimeter.

Honeywell is researching special, low-dielectric chip interconnects that reduce interchip delays if sufficiently powerful off-chip drivers that are compatible with the interconnect medium are used. The typical on-chip delay for a 10μ-wide MESFET is shown in Figure 9.

As can be seen from Figure 9, unless a gate is driving a long bus ($> 500~\mu m$), the most significant loads on the gate come from the devices connected to the gate's output. Since we have not established the circuit layout of each module, our timing estimates use only the intrinsic gate delay and the delay arising from load devices that is explained by the expression in Figure 9. Although delays owing to bus length are excluded from these estimates, the fact that the implementations of the structures that we discussed earlier are not optimal helps to compensate for the absence of bus-length-related delays in the estimates. The values in Table 1 and other calculations described below assume that unit-sized gates (10-μm-wide FETs) are used for all on-chip functions except those performed by the off-chip drivers, and the off-chip drivers are scaled appropriately. We use the approximate delay in picoseconds for each of the major intrachip structures discussed above to analyze the critical paths through each of the modules and to ascertain an approximate machine-cycle time.

We have obtained a measure of the delay for each of the Table 1 structures except the register file by applying the expression for gate delay (the expression does not include the delays resulting from bus length) to a logic representation like that shown in Figure 2. The estimates of the read/write and access times of the register file were drawn from comparisons of available GaAs SRAM circuits.[22] We assume that the register file consists of parallel 128-bit $\times$ 32-bit SRAMs and that each SRAM pair supports parallel read/write operations. The delay time for the multiplexer is based on an analysis of the logic multiplexer described previously. The driver delay takes on a successor stage, or a load three times larger than the load it presents to the preceding driver.

The critical paths in each of the four macromodules—the register-file, ALU, instruction-fetch, and data-fetch modules—are shown by the dark, heavy lines in Figures 4, 5, 6, and 7. The choice of path is based on the propagation delays of the structures the paths contain. These delays determine the maximum time to be allotted to the machine for intrachip opera-

tions. Every RISCF module latches a state during at least one of the two phases of the machine cycle. That is, each module contains a minimum of one latch between its inputs and outputs, and therefore requires that the processor bridge the interchip media only once during a clock phase. Consequently, an estimate of the period of the machine cycle is derived by summing the longest intrachip delay incurred during the first phase with the longest such delay incurred during the second, then adding the result to the approximate interchip delay.

Estimated machine-cycle time. The longest intramodule delay for Φ_1 operations is about 11 nanoseconds, and the longest for Φ_2 is about 15 nanoseconds. We have not yet ascertained the effect of the drivers except in the special case of ALU operations. If, as Table 1 indicates, the delay from a six-stage driver is 1.5 nanoseconds, then a more accurate estimate of the phase periods is 13 nanoseconds for Φ_1 and about 17 nanoseconds for Φ_2, which makes for a total machine-cycle time of roughly 30 nanoseconds.

The GaAs alternative

Although the previous calculations are approximate (they leave out delays that result from bus length), they give a ballpark estimate of the RISCF machine-cycle time. More precise estimates would require both detailed layouts for each of the modules and more information on the advantages of HWSI. The six-stage drivers used in our analysis may be larger than we need for GaAs implementation of RISCF, since, according to one text[23] on MOS VLSI design, a six-stage driver in which each successive stage is three times larger than its predecessor should efficiently drive loads more than 700 times larger than that of a minimum-sized driver. Of course, the drive capability of the six-stage driver is actually less, since larger drivers require longer buses, which places a greater load on the drivers. Investigations of a more detailed kind that are conducted about possible layouts and gate organizations will yield more precise estimates, but given the conservatism of the estimates discussed here, any estimates relying on more intricate evaluations of a RISCF realization in GaAs will probably come up with an even faster machine cycle.

The appeal of such a fast processor should not overshadow the difficulties

impeding its realization. A 30-ns cycle time is of little value unless caches with compatible access times are available. In fact, with the recent success of alternative device and packaging technologies for GaAs, RISCF's cycle time could be even shorter. The question still remains, however, of how a machine of single-cycle instructions with, say, a 10-ns cycle time will maintain an unbroken supply of instructions. It is feasible that small (4K-byte $\times$ 32-byte) memories could be used to achieve a 30-ns memory-access time. A

Recent successes in alternative device and packaging technologies for GaAs may mean that RISCF's cycle time will be shorter than 30 ns.

---

small cache, however, might not provide sufficient support for the memory demands of Rete. Consequently, designing for GaAs-related speedups brings tradeoffs into the design of an integrated-processor system for executing OPS5; indeed, it brings tradeoffs into all processor-architecture design.

According to simulations and physical experiments, if RISCF is designed with a 300-ns cycle time, it executes OPS5 code two to four times faster than a VAX/780 that accesses memory exclusively from the cache. If a RISCF with a 30-ns cycle time had access to memory that supplied an instruction every 30 nanoseconds, it would increase this performance by almost a factor of 10. Of course, if the performance of the 780 processor is improved by implementation and realization enhancements, RISCF's performance advantage decreases.

Although gallium arsenide devices promise high speed, they have substantial fabrication and implementation problems. Currently, the GaAs systems that have been realized consist of SRAMs, gate arrays, and multipliers. Recently, some experimental GaAs RISC-like machines have been developed that are addressing the system issues we have alluded to in this article.[24,25]

We have illustrated some of the problems that arise when one attempts to realize a RISC machine in GaAs D-MESFET technology, which is a mature gallium arsenide technology. Owing to the comparatively low levels of integration and the poor fan-out characteristics of D-MESFET logic, systems as complex as a RISC machine cannot yet enjoy the full advantages of the speed of gallium arsenide. To compound the difficulties, there is the question of whether caches and other supporting subsystems can accommodate the speed of a GaAs processor at reasonable costs. However, given the progress that researchers have made in improving the GaAs integrated circuit, the future holds some promise for RISC processors and other systems that display a similar type of complexity. Improving alternative GaAs technologies, such as HEMT, HBJT, and enhancement/depletion logic, may eliminate some of the logic-design constraints and fan-out problems endemic to D-MESFETs.

At Carnegie Mellon, current research into improving the speed of production systems concentrates on algorithm design and investigations of appropriate parallel-processor architectures. Although the speedup of a processor such as RISCF over machines that are more general-purpose in nature is not insignificant, the importance of actually realizing a physical GaAs RISCF is mitigated by the as yet unanswered higher level issues currently under investigation. For example, the prevalence of new multiprocessors on the market has created an environment in which very fruitful investigations can be performed on how to exploit parallelism in production systems.

Our investigation of a customized GaAs processor design provides a means to approximate an upper bound for the execution speed that can be expected from a single processor for OPS5 or other production-system languages. Our research goals, however, do not make the actual building of a GaAs RISCF a high priority because experimental GaAs RISC machines are being investigated by others and because Quinlan's comparison[6] has suggested to us that though RISCF has a performance advantage over a particular uncustomized RISC architecture when it is built with similar technologies, this small advantage is not significant enough to outweigh the costs we would incur in building a RISCF machine.

As a result of efforts by researchers to produce GaAs systems, the viability of realizing a GaAs production-system machine will likely improve.

We anticipate that subsequent investigations of GaAs RISC processors are likely to yield promising results if alternative technologies are pursued. □

Acknowledgments

We would like to thank Jim Quinlan, Charles Forgy, Alan Newell, and Anoop Gupta for the helpful discussions we had with them and for their comments on this work.

References

1. C.L. Forgy, "On the Efficient Implementation of Production Systems," PhD thesis, tech. report CMU-CS-79-107, Jan. 1979, Carnegie Mellon University, Computer Science Dept., Pittsburgh.

2. C.L. Forgy, "Rete: A Fast Algorithm For the Many Pattern/Many Object Pattern Match Problem," Artificial Intelligence, Vol. 19, No. 1, Sept. 1982, pp. 17-37.

3. C.L. Forgy, "OPS5 Users Manual," tech. report CMU-CS-81-135, 1981, Computer Science Dept., Carnegie Mellon University, Pittsburgh.

4. A. Gupta, "Parallelism in Production Systems," PhD thesis, tech. report CMU-CS-86-122, Mar. 1986, Computer Science Dept., Carnegie Mellon University, Pittsburgh.

5. J. Quinlan, "A Comparative Analysis of Architectures for Production System Machines," master's thesis, tech. report CMU-CS-85-178, May 1985, Carnegie Mellon University, Computer Science Dept., Pittsburgh.

6. R. Cowell et al., "Computers, Complexity and Controversy," Computer, Vol. 18, No. 9, Sept. 1985, pp. 8-19.

7. G.A. Blaauw and F.P. Brooks, "Computer Architecture," unpublished manuscript.

8. T.F. Lehr, "The Implementation of a Production-System Machine," Proc. 19th Annual Hawaii Int'l Conf. System Sciences, Jan. 1986, Computer Society Press, Los Alamitos, Calif., pp. 177-186.

9. G. Radin, "The 801 Minicomputer," Proc. Symp. on Architectural Support for Programming Languages and Operating Systems, Mar. 1982, ACM, New York, pp. 39-47.

10. D.A. Patterson and Carlo H. Sequin, "A VLSI RISC," Computer, Vol. 15, No. 9, Sept. 1982, pp. 8-21.

11. J. Hennessy et al., "Hardware/Software Tradeoffs for Increased Performance," Proc. Symp. on Architectural Support for Programming Languages and Operating Systems, Mar. 1982, ACM, New York, pp. 39-47.

12. G. Zimmerman and P. Marwedel, "MIMOLA Report Rev. 1 and the MIMOLA Software System User's Manual," tech. report Bericht Nr. 2/79, May 1979, Christian-Albrechts-Universitat, Kiel, West Germany.

13. G. Zimmerman et al., "MIMOLA Primer," tech. report CTC-83-7: 8214 ed., 1982, Honeywell Corporate Systems Development Division, 1000 Boone Ave., North Golden Valley, Minn.

14. A. Gupta and C.L. Forgy, "Measurements on Production Systems," tech. report CMU-CS-83-167, Dec. 1983, Dept. of Computer Science, Carnegie Mellon University, Pittsburgh.

15. C. Mead and L. Conway, Introduction to VLSI Systems, Addison-Wesley, Reading, Mass., 1980.

16. A.F. Podell, "GaAs Logic Circuits," VLSI Design, Vol. 4, No. 4, July/Aug. 1983, pp. 68-69.

17. S. Evanczuk, "Designers Test Limits of Process Technology," Electronics, Vol. 57, No. 4, Feb. 23, 1984, pp. 131-132.

18. S. Taylor, "Gearing Up for GaAs," VLSI Design, Vol. 5, No. 4, Apr. 1984, pp. 59-62.

19. R.C. Eden et al., "Integrated circuits: the case for gallium arsenide," IEEE Spectrum, Vol. 20, No. 12, Dec. 1983, pp. 30-37.

20. Honeywell Optoelectronics Division, "Gallium Arsenide HGAS-500 Gate Array," product description, 1984, Honeywell Physical Sciences Center, 10700 Lyndale Ave., South Bloomington, Minn.

21. R.C. Eden, "Comparison of GaAs Device Approaches for Ultrahigh-Speed VLSI," Proc. IEEE, Vol. 70, No. 1, Jan. 1982, pp. 5-12.

22. N. Yokoyama et al., "A 3-ns GaAs 4K x 1b SRAM," Solid-State Circuits Conf. Digest of Technical Papers, Feb. 1984, IEEE, New Jersey, pp. 44-45.

23. S.I. Long et al., "High-Speed GaAs Integrated Circuits," Proc. IEEE, Vol. 70, No. 1, Jan. 1982, pp. 35-45.

24. T.L. Rasset et al., "A 32-Bit RISC Implemented in Enhancement-Mode JFET GaAs," Computer, Vol. 19, No. 10, Oct. 1986, pp. 60-68.

25. E.R. Fox et al., "Reduced Instruction Set Architecture for a GaAs Microprocessor System," Computer, Vol. 19, No. 10, Oct. 1986, pp. 71-81.

Theodore F. Lehr is a PhD candidate in the Electrical and Computer Engineering Dept. at Carnegie Mellon University. He has won a General Electric Foundation Graduate Fellowship and a Burroughs Graduate Fellowship. His current research is bogged down in architectural considerations for parallel-programming environments.

Lehr is a member of IEEE, Tau Beta Pi, and Phi Beta Kappa.

He received his master's degree in 1985 from Carnegie Mellon. In 1983, he received bachelor's degrees in electrical engineering and in philosophy from Bucknell University.

Robert G. Wedig is an independent consultant doing business as Wedig Consulting Services. He currently consults in the area of the design and analysis of parallel and pipelined processors, VLSI systems, and memory hierarchies.

He was an assistant professor of electrical and computer engineering at Carnegie Mellon University from 1979 to 1985.

He has been active in the design of machine architectures for running production-system languages and in the implementation of architectures for GaAs.

Wedig received his PhD in electrical engineering from Stanford University 1979, and he holds a BS from the University of Dayton and an MS from the University of Southern California—both in electrical engineering.

Readers may write to Theodore F. Lehr at Carnegie Mellon University, Dept. of Electrical and Computer Engineering, Pittsburgh, PA 15213.

Wafer Scale Interconnections for GaAs Packaging—Applications to RISC Architecture

Reprinted from *Computer*, April 1987, pages 21-35. Copyright © 1987 by
The Institute of Electrical and Electronics Engineers, Inc.

Jack F. McDonald, Hans J. Greub, Randy H. Steinvorth, Brian J. Donlan, and

Albert S. Bergendahl

Rensselaer Polytechnic Institute

This article describes a high-speed, high-density, wafer scale packaging technology for the implementation of GaAs systems.

After years of research, gallium arsenide (GaAs) digital circuits have begun to emerge as commercial products. Harris and Tektronix/ TriQuint appear to be at the forefront of commercialization, offering SSI and MSI as well as gate array products. New start-up companies such as Vitesse and Gigabit Logic have specialized in GaAs. Traditional military electronics suppliers such as Rockwell and Honeywell offer GaAs foundry services, while Raytheon, Texas Instruments, and GE/RCA support internal GaAs services. Analog GaAs monolithic microwave integrated circuits (MMICs) have also begun to show increasing levels of system integration. The immediate advantage of GaAs is the high-speed or wide-bandwidth performance achievable relative to silicon. This is due to gallium arsenide's higher electron mobility and drift velocity available at low electric field strengths. Gate propagation delays below 200 ps are readily obtainable. In one stunning example, Hughes has announced 0.2-μm channel-length GaAs MESFET BFL/CEL flip-flops that toggle at rates of 14-18 GHz. Additionally, the large energy band gap of GaAs provides a high-resistivity, semi-insulating bulk substrate that reduces wiring capacitance and device isolation parasitics. Finally, an increase in total-dose radiation hardness is observed with GaAs MESFETS compared to silicon technology.

On the negative side, GaAs is currently much more expensive than silicon. The GaAs material cost is itself about $80-$200 for a three-inch wafer. Furthermore, these substrates are extremely fragile, necessitating highly automated wafer handling. Relevant automated silicon-based equipment must be modified to take into account the higher wafer mass and different position sensor properties of GaAs relative to silicon. Fabrication and low throughput currently account for the bulk of the finished cost per wafer, which can be as high as $13,000. Dramatic cost reductions are possible as demand increases (perhaps by an order of magnitude or more). Nevertheless, unless extraordinary improvements in yield occur, the primary impediment for exploitation of this exciting technology is likely to be packaging. More importantly, even when these yield increases are realized, there will be a continuing need for alternatives for

Parts of this paper were presented at the 1985 IEEE International Conference on Computer Design.

high-frequency packaging in many large digital systems.

Low yield has always been a problem for GaAs, unlike silicon. The GaAs material itself contains a significant number of defects. The boule-growing technology for GaAs has recently undergone some dramatic improvements with the introduction of indium doping and improved thermal control. The tendency for the GaAs to disassociate during growth has been reduced somewhat by a kind of electromagnetic stirring operation. Sumitomo now offers wafers with two orders of magnitude lower defect density than only a few years ago. Unfortunately, the defect density is still higher than for silicon. Large 1-cm dies have been made, but with terrible yield and consequently at high cost.

Yield is currently so low that dies containing 70 to 500 gates are currently the norm. Larger circuits containing as many as 6000 gates have been made, but with slower gates. Digital systems involving 250,000- to 500,000-gate equivalents, which are typical of some computer architectures would require thousands of expensive, bulky, high-frequency packages. Except in special digital architectures, the resulting signal propagation delays would largely negate the potential for high-speed performance promised by the underlying device technology.

Greiling et al.[1] have presented arguments that are even more unsettling regarding the impact of interconnections on the performance of LSI GaAs circuits. They modeled the interconnections internal to GaAs random logic circuits using Rent's rule.[2,3] They assumed a specific form for the wiring channels to predict average gate delay due to the loading effect of this wiring. Utilizing only two layers of thin interconnections and fixing the total circuit power dissipation at 2 W, they showed that the loaded gate delay increased substantially once the size of the circuit exceeded a critical number of gates (roughly 1000). The wiring demands in such systems force the active devices apart, resulting in a low surface density requiring longer wires, larger device sizes and drive capabilities, and greater power dissipation. More structured circuits such as memories, programmed logic arrays, and functionally partitioned logic blocks can have shorter average wire lengths than random logic.[4] However, yield considerations currently limit the ability to exploit such dense building blocks. The solutions for this problem include the incorporation

of multiple layers of interconnections into the circuit to permit shorter, denser wiring; the improvement of the electromagnetic characteristics of this wiring; the development of superior devices for driving the lines fast; and improved heat removal methods.

Wafer scale integration

The current yield problems for GaAs technology are similar in some respects to those that existed in the early days of silicon processing.[5] In 1966, Texas Instruments produced the first LSI circuits (of 1000-gate complexity) by testing much smaller sized dies on an intact substrate and then wiring the components found to be functional directly on the same wafer. This approach was termed wafer scale integration (WSI), and the specially designed wiring (which had to be different on each wafer) was termed discretionary wiring.

All the efforts to implement WSI to date have demanded more processing or repair steps for fabrication than conventional processing. In 1966, the most pressing market demands for silicon integration were eventually met by the LSI produced by conventional methods using improved clean room procedures, new lithography tools, and purer chemicals. The resulting yield advances for conventional silicon processing proved more cost-effective than WSI. The demand for larger scales of silicon integration did not substantially outstrip the yield "learning curve" until 1980, at which point WSI began to be "rediscovered."

By comparison, the yield for GaAs is limited by a variety of defects. The number and types of defects are much greater than found in silicon. The most significant defects, however, have to do with a lack of uniformity across the wafer of various device thresholds. While great strides have been made to improve the yield of GaAs, some of the problems seem so profound that a quick advance to overtake silicon densities appears to be only a remote possibility. Wafer scale integration could provide a technology that would permit GaAs to advance in one bold step from SSI to much larger gate counts.

Traditionally, full WSI can be regarded as a special form of packaging in which extra wiring, normally used to interconnect packages containing working dies, is fabricated on the surface of a wafer substrate containing dies and mounted

inside a *single* package. The electromagnetic characteristics of this internal wiring can be designed to control or eliminate many of the problems encountered in printed circuit boards or ceramic carriers. Interconnection densities are enhanced by the small dimensions of the wire and the closeness of the dies in WSI. The footprint of the multiple packages conventionally used on boards can take up an order of magnitude more space than the dies themselves. Wiring over the dies (where possible) eliminates the space in between the dies, which is usually consumed by interconnections. Reduced wiring length, in turn, increases the system speed and decreases power requirements for I/O drivers. In general, one can realize a large net decrease in overall system wiring capacitance that is a result of the reduction in wiring area achievable with WSI. Thus, the total amount of charge that has to be moved onto a wire to change its logic state from low to high voltage is reduced, and the power supply current and I/O driver size requirements are reduced.

One drawback of traditional WSI is the statistical uncertainty in the wiring delays resulting from the wiring of the random collection of working dies. That is, since the locations of the working cells are not fixed, the wiring delay of a given path may vary from wafer to wafer. However, since these delays can be much shorter than those found in most other packaging arrangements, this could be less of a problem than might be expected. Moreover, one of the tasks of the CAD placement and routing software tools is to manage these timing uncertainties and assure that the critical path constraints are met.

Nevertheless, if the die size can be made large enough (e.g., 4 mm × 4 mm) with acceptable yield, then the aforementioned timing uncertainty can be eliminated by scribing the wafer, separating the dies, and remounting them on a substrate (similar to the IBM ceramic substrate used in its Thermal Conduction Module, or TCM) in assigned positions and interconnected by fixed wiring.[6] The propagation delay inside the TCM is adversely affected by the high dielectric constant of the ceramic used for the substrate. Although the top layers of TCM wiring can involve gold lines embedded in a low dielectric constant polyimide, the wiring pitch has been on the order of several mils. Recently, research efforts have been directed toward developing inexpensive, multilayer metal-polyimide structures at a wiring pitch of only a few microns.[7-11] An advantage of this approach, which is variously termed the wafer scale hybrid (WSH) or wafer transmission module (WTM), is that all the wiring capacitance can be made small as a result of the low dielectric constant of polyimide. Figure 1 shows a prototype WTM. With a fully developed WTM bonding technology, the die spacing could be made extremely tight, resulting in an effective gate density approximating an ultralarge scale integrated (ULSI) circuit.

The resulting multilayer structure resembles a miniaturized printed circuit board with dies and other components directly bonded to the surface. Such a hybrid package can also be regarded as supplying additional layers of interconnections needed to improve the active device density to better exploit the speed of GaAs. Unfortunately, the yield of GaAs is currently so low that dies with a 16 mm^2 area and utilizing the maximum achievable device density are extraordinarily expensive. The alternative would be to artificially restrain the device density to improve the yield while maintaining a manipulatable die size. This underutilizes the technology, with resulting performance or cost degradation. Hence, when the dies cannot be made sufficiently large with good yield to successfully and cost effectively mount them in fixed positions on a substrate, then the WSH approach will not work, and the on-the-wafer or in-situ wiring scheme of traditional full wafer scale integration is an attractive alternative worth considering. The fact that an aggressive high-speed technology such as GaAs usually implies the use of small dies suggests that full WSI should be seriously examined. For example, if the dies cannot be fabricated with reasonable yield at dimensions greater than 2 mm × 2 mm, then roughly 1000 of these dies would be needed to achieve a density comparable to in-situ WSI wiring. The mechanical difficulties of mounting so many dies on a common substrate and guaranteeing wire bond or solder integrity for all of them is severe. Unfortunately, the GaAs wafer is extremely fragile. The tendency for the substrate in full WSI to crack is an additional problem. Recent efforts to fabricate E/D MESFET circuits in GaAs grown on silicon (with a stress-relief buffer layer of Ge) indicate one approach to strengthening the substrate.[12] Residual stress in this structure degrades MESFET performance somewhat, but this may be overcome by further development. The silicon substrate described here would also have superior heat removal capability.

Figure 1. A prototype wafer transmission module (WTM). (*Source:* J. F. McDonald and A. J. Steckl, "Multilevel Interconnections for Wafer Scale Integration," *J. Vacuum Science & Technology A*, Vol. 4, No. 6, Nov./Dec. 1986, p. 3135.)

Figure 2 shows a 3-inch-diameter circle representing a GaAs wafer with space for more than 4000 1-mm square dies. Yield would be high enough even with current design and fabrication strategies for these small dies that most of them would work, and the device density could approach the limit achievable with the underlying GaAs technology. An appropriate multilayer interconnection structure and fast line drivers and receivers would be needed to form a complete system from these dies. In addition, a special problem exists for solder bonding of GaAs to a thermally dissimilar substrate. The GaAs material is piezoelectric and thermal stress can induce unwanted threshold shifts. In this regard, GaAs WSI is definitely not a simple extrapolation of Si WSI technology.

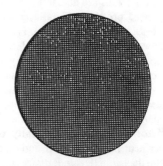

Figure 2. Three-inch wafer with 1-mm dies (actual scale). (*Source:* J. F. McDonald et al., "Fabrication and Performance Considerations for Gallium Arsenide Wafer Scale Integration," *IEEE Proc. Int'l Conf. Computer Design: VLSI in Computer*, Oct. 1985, p. 404. Source of Figure 3 also.)

April 1987

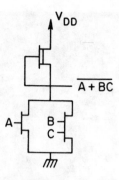

Figure 3. Typical GaAs E/D DCFL MESFET logic gate.

The Tektronix-TriQuint E/D foundry

In order to understand the potential for GaAs WSI, we will specifically examine the Tektronix-TriQuint 1.0-μm enhancement/depletion (E/D) MESFET foundry[13] as a source for cells to be used as the building blocks of the wafer scale integrated system. Honeywell, Rockwell, and AT&T have also demonstrated E/D processes, and AT&T has even demonstrated an E/D high electron mobility transistor (HEMT) circuit. However, a great deal of information (especially concerning yield) is available for the Tektronix-TriQuint foundry.

The absence of a stable native oxide in GaAs FET processing prevents fabrication of the metal-oxide-semiconductor sandwich used in silicon MOSFET gate structures. Instead, a Ti-Pd-Au metal-semiconductor (MESFET) Schottky interface is used to obtain a recessed gate definition over the channel implantation regions (Si$^+$ ions are implanted through an annealed protective SiO$_2$ layer using photo resist as the implant mask). The current between the separately defined source and drain regions is controlled by the voltage on the metal gate. The semi-insulating nature of the GaAs substrate provides the device isolation. By employing separate dose levels for two kinds of transistor channels, a normally off enhancement (E) mode device and a normally on depletion (D) mode device can be fabricated.

The result can be exploited to produce an "NMOS"-like circuit style termed E/D direct coupled FET logic (DCFL), where E-mode active pull-down devices are combined with the D-mode pull-up devices. The gate fan-in is typically limited to three for DCFL because of the turn-on charac-

teristics of the E-mode switch. Figure 3 shows a typical E/D DCFL circuit diagram. One attractive feature of this circuit class is the immediate adaptability of a broad collection of CAD tools for design layout and simulation, because of its similarity to NMOS circuits. Many circuit designers can readily be retrained for the minimal design rule changes that apply. However, the consideration of bypass capacitances and parasitic inductances in the power distribution system becomes very important in the layout of DCFL circuits.

A more significant advantage of the E/D DCFL circuit is the power dissipation reduction per logic gate, which is obtained by the use of the depletion mode load transistor in combination with the E-mode devices. This produces a 1/4-mW dissipation for a gate typically exhibiting a 200-ps propagation delay. Hence an aggregate of 250,000 gates (if these are integrated on a single wafer) would dissipate 62.5 W. While this may seem high, one must observe that this level of integration discussed here is nearly an order of magnitude larger than those recently discussed in connection with the silicon bipolar technology by Trilogy (30,000 gates per wafer at around 1200 W dissipation).[14] The feasibility of realizing this level of integration can be estimated by noting that a three-inch wafer provides a total 4560 mm^2 of surface area. Each one mm square could easily contain 70 logic gates, using 1.0-μm design rules, along with a set of reduced area bond pads and fast output drivers appropriate in number for such a small cluster of logic. The small size of these bond pads must, of course, be consistent with test fixture considerations. Tektronix has earlier reported an 83 percent yield for 70-gate systems in the literature, which were fabricated in a class 10,000 clean room facility.[13] At such yields, most of the area of the wafer could be productively utilized in WSI, leading to circuit densities greater than achievable with board or ceramic multipackage carriers such as the IBM TCM.

One drawback of the E/D MESFET process is the necessity to obtain good threshold voltage tracking for the two different types of transistors, which are implanted separately. Therefore, the E/D yield is necessarily less than D-mode-only circuit designs. On balance, however, the lower power dissipation afforded by the E/D DCFL circuit is a property singularly attractive for integrating a large number of gates (200,000-500,000) on a single wafer. In contrast, the power dissipation for

D-mode-only logic circuits varies from 2.5 mW per gate (1.9 GHz) to 40 mW per gate (5.0 GHz),[15] exceeding even the power dissipation of ECL silicon bipolar circuits. In other words, the use of the E-mode in conjunction with the D-mode device results in reduction of power dissipation per gate of between 10 and 160, respectively! Clearly, integration of a system of 200,000 gates in D-mode only at 5.0 GHz would dissipate on the order of eight kW, which would preclude implementation on a single wafer. On the other hand, the E/D DCFL GaAs MESFET logic circuits deliver a 200-ps typical gate delay at much lower power than bipolar ECL at comparable speeds. Therefore, it would seem that, for the moment at least, GaAs technology can deliver digital performance in a unique and desirable range. By changing the gate width and loading, the gate propagation delays can be made as low as 66 ps with only 1/2-mW dissipation. This speed can be realized on certain critical signal paths by employing the faster gates there and using lower power gates on noncritical paths.

The processing sequence for fabricating the Tektronix E/D DCFL MESFET is summarized in Figure 4. One of the points worth mentioning about this sequence is the special alloy (Au-Ge-Ni) required to obtain an ohmic contact to the sources and drains. Schottky junctions are readily formed on GaAs, but ohmic contacts are more difficult to produce. The fact that Schottky junctions are so readily made can be exploited in fabricating fast Schottky barrier diode (SBD) clamps.

Another important feature of the process shown in Figure 4 is the use of air bridge metal interconnections for the final metallization. A temporary dielectric is used to fabricate these metal lines. After these wires are completely formed, the temporary dielectric is etched away from under the metal, leaving air as the dielectric. Metal posts are located every 60 μm to support this metal. Air has a dielectric constant essentially equal to unity, which makes these lines very fast and of low capacitance. Subsequent filling of this air bridge by wafer scale dielectrics can lead to a performance reduction. In some cases, this will be severe enough to lead one to consider etching away a portion or all of the WSI dielectric to produce WSI air bridges.

One important fabrication consideration for in-situ GaAs WSI wiring is the tendency of the underlying substrate and device structures to decompose or degrade at the elevated temperatures encountered in many common processing steps. For example, the Au-Ge-Ni alloyed ohmic contacts are formed at 45° C. Temperatures over 300°C will begin to alter the ohmic properties of these contacts. Furthermore, at 600° C the GaAs itself begins to disassociate with the release of arsenic vapor. Consequently, all in-situ WSI wiring processing steps must be limited to low temperatures (preferably no higher than 300° C). Therefore, use of plasma enhanced processing is preferred. Plasma enhanced chemical vapor deposition (PECVD) of insulator or encapsulant material commonly requires a temperature of only 200° C. Reactive ion etching (RIE) and metal deposition can also be carried out at low temperatures. For this reason these are the most desirable fabrication tools for introducing wafer scale interconnections on the substrate. Great care is required so that these processing steps do not damage dies that have been tested and found functional prior to creation of the wafer scale interconnections.

Propagation delay of WSI interconnections

In the TTL IBM 308X series of machines, roughly 50 percent of the CPU cycle time can be traced to wiring delays in both the TCMs and the mounting panels supporting them. Gate density in the TCM is low (approximately 50,000 gates per TCM in the ECL 309X series). The increased gate speed of GaAs would lead to only modest improvements in system performance in such an environment. Only by packing a larger numbers of gates (perhaps an entire system) onto a wafer could wiring delays be substantially affected and system speed improved.

The reduced wiring length achievable in WSI would not necessarily translate into reduced propagation delay unless the other wire dimensions (specifically thickness dimensions) are scaled properly. This fact appears to have been overlooked in many recent efforts to implement WSI commercially, although designers of microwave circuits are familiar with the problem.

For example, suppose a metal wire of rectangular cross section with length l, width w, and thickness t is located a distance d from a ground plane of the same metal (Figure 5). Then the RC charging delay of the distributed system is approximately given by[16]

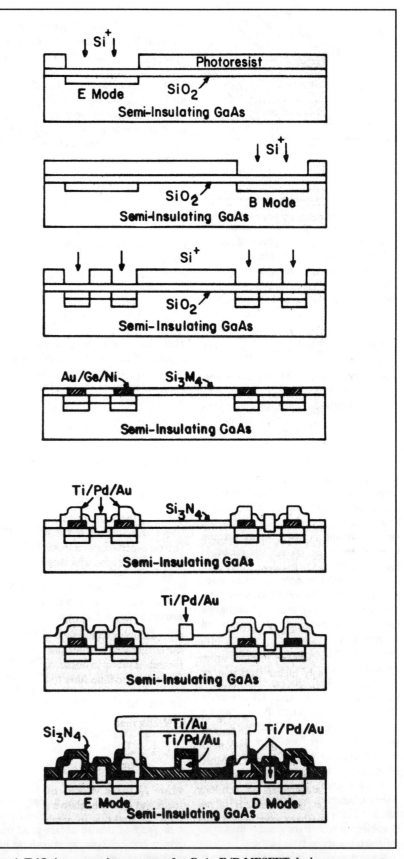

Figure 4. TriQuint processing sequence for GaAs E/D MESFET devices. (*Source:* **J. F. McDonald et al., "Fabrication and Performance Considerations for Gallium Arsenide Wafer Scale Integration,"** *Proc. Int'l Conf. Computer Design: VLSI in Computer,* Oct. 1985, p. 404.)

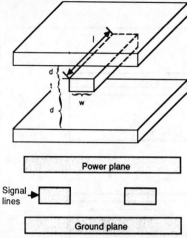

Figure 5. Wire geometry for analysis of a conductor over a ground plane. (*Source: J. F. McDonald et al., "Gallium Arsenide Wafer Scale Integration," AGARD Conf. Proc. No. 380, May 1985, p. 12-11. Source of Figure 8 also.*)

$$T_{RC} = \frac{1}{2} \frac{2\rho l}{tw} \frac{\epsilon l w}{d} = \frac{\rho \epsilon l^2}{td} \quad (1)$$

A line of length $l = 20$ cm made of aluminum ($\rho = 2.63 \times 10^{-6}$ Ω cm) on SiO_2 ($\epsilon_r = 3.9$) with the following dimensions (which are typical of integrated circuit lines):

$$l = 20 \text{ cm}, \ t = d = 0.5 \ \mu m$$

would have a charging time of 160 ns, or roughly 1/6 μs! On the other hand, an electromagnetic wave traveling through a homogeneous SiO_2 dielectric with the same length and dielectric constant would have a delay of only 1.3 ns. If the dielectric constant could be reduced to unity, then the delay would be only 600 ps or three E/D DCFL gate delays at 200 ps per gate. This is more than two orders of magnitude faster than the metal line of conventional IC processing thickness.[17] Furthermore, the bandwidth of a wave propagating through a unity dielectric medium would be correspondingly higher than that exhibited by the thin wire. Of course, a 20-cm run of wire probably represents a worst case length for WSI wiring on wafers of diameter from three to four inches, especially with consideration for noise margins at the end of the run. Moreover, it is possible to improve the speed by inserting repeater amplifiers on such long wires.[18] However, in this case it is still not possible to approach the speed of light in an infinite homogeneous dielectric.

Nevertheless, it is possible to obtain such high propagation speeds using simple extensions of existing technology. This can be achieved by fabricating thick film *LC* transmission lines rather than thin film

lines with *RC* charging behavior. The criterion for just how thick to make the lines can be deduced from the following simple argument.

The characteristic impedance Z_0 for a lossless TEM transmission line having the given cross-sectional geometry is related to the capacitance per unit length C/l, and the velocity of propagation ν by the formula

$$Z_0 = \frac{1}{\nu \left(\dfrac{C}{l} \right)} \quad (2)$$

If we now consider the introduction of a small amount of loss, then the line would exhibit an attenuation α given by

$$\alpha = \frac{(R/l)}{2Z_0} = \frac{(RC/l^2)\nu}{2} \quad (3)$$

where Z_0 is still the characteristic impedance of the lossless line. For a line of length l to exhibit a low value of α and hence be useful as a transmission line one would require

$$\alpha l = \frac{RC\nu}{2l} << 1 \quad (4)$$

This would be fairly well satisfied if

$$R/2Z_0 = \frac{\rho \epsilon \nu l}{td} << 1 \quad (5)$$

That is, if the total end-to-end resistance R of the wire is much less than the characteristic impedance of a lossless wire of the same cross section and length l using the given dielectric thickness d and dielectric constant ϵ_r, then LC transmission line performance will be discerned.

We note that the width w is absent in Eq. (5). This holds true only if the width w is still larger than the wire thickness t, but the formula is useful in obtaining estimates of how thick the films have to be in order to achieve the desired transmission line behavior.

Noting that for a TEM wave

$$\nu = \frac{1}{\sqrt{\epsilon \mu_0}} = \frac{\nu_0}{\sqrt{\epsilon_r}} \quad (6)$$

where ν_0 is the velocity of light in free space and ϵ_r is the relative dielectric constant, we find that to obtain good transmission line behavior we must have films sufficiently thick that

$$\rho \sqrt{\epsilon_r} \ \epsilon_0 \nu_0 l << td \quad (7)$$

is satisfied. For a polyimide dielectric ϵ_r can be as low as 2.8 (in one sample we ob-

tained from General Electric). Hence for lines as long as 20 cm, if we make $t = d = 4.5$ μm, we can satisfy the requirement in Eq. (7). In practice, somewhat larger thicknesses ($t = d = 8$ μm) are used because the resistivity of Al lines rarely equals that of bulk Al. A high temperature (450° C) anneal of Al would be undesirable for GaAs WSI. Lines made of Cu or Au could approach the condition of Eq. (7) more readily.

Requirements for the resistivity in Ω/□ can be derived from Eq. (7) by dividing by t:

$$\rho_\square = \frac{\rho}{t} < \frac{1}{\sqrt{\epsilon_r} \ \epsilon_0 \ \nu_0 \ (l/d)} \quad (8)$$

in which it can be seen that the resistivity expressed in this manner depends only on the line length measured in multiples of dielectric thickness. For polyimide with $l = 20$ cm and $d = 5$ μm we have $\rho_\square = 10^{-4}$ Ω/□.

Coupling between the WSI interconnection lines is reduced by introducing both power and ground planes above and below the signal lines, as shown in Figure 5. The presence of these planes provides conductor surfaces to attract electric field lines that would normally terminate on another signal line. The magnetic field lines are similarly confined by the reduced space around the signal conductor. Furthermore, the rise time-dependent coupling is suppressed in this configuration, which satisfies the so-called homogenous dielectric condition.

The high propagation velocity achievable with the thick (>4 μm) film transmission lines is realizable only if line reflections from impedance discontinuities do not cause "ringing." The lossy behavior of these lines damps these reflections in a manner similar to series damping resistors used in ECL. Termination in Z_0 is unattractive because it establishes a DC current path that dissipates a great deal of power and causes signal level droop. The use of Schottky barrier diode (SBD) clamps at the ends of the slightly lossy WSI lines can prevent overshoot or undershoot while providing a current path only during conduction.[7] The diodes can readily be fabricated on highly doped regions in the semi-insulating substrate in any available space (such as found in the scribe space; normally left between the dies). These diodes must also be fabricated in such a way that they do not generate low-amplitude, high-frequency shot noise.

The bandwidth of WSI interconnections

Although the thick (5-10 μm) film transmission lines we have been discussing can exhibit quasi-TEM behavior, they are lossy and this factor alone can introduce dispersion. Even without the skin effect (which becomes important at high frequencies) the nonzero resistivity we have assumed causes a rise time degradation (as well as bandwidth reduction) in pulses traveling along these lines.

If one forms the Laplace transform of a forward traveling wave on a semi-infinite line, one obtains

$$V_+ \ (z,s) = V_p(s)e^{-\gamma(s)z} \tag{9}$$

where z is the distance along the transmission line, $V_p(s)$ is the pulse launched at $z = 0$, $V_+(0,s)$, and

$$\gamma(s) = \sqrt{(R+Ls) \ (G+Cs)} \tag{10}$$

One can plot the magnitude of this transform as a function of frequency ($s = j\omega$). This shows a decreasing bandwidth as a function of increasing loss, as shown in Figure 6. By inverting the transform it is possible to compute the rise time at a point z along the line in response to a step input. This is shown in Figure 7 for a sequence of different line thicknesses. The waveform for sufficiently low resistance has an abrupt rise followed by a slow charging behavior. The step response for more lossy lines shows shorter segments of abrupt rise, and a slow charging segment that approaches the usual RC exponential at higher resistance, eventually completely dominating the abrupt rise. In all cases the onset of the rise is preceded by a time of transmission delay determined by the velocity of propagation along the line.

The model shown in Eqs. (9) and (10) does not include skin effect resistance, but Figures 6 and 7 do. At 10 GHz Au has a skin depth of 0.8 μm. Therefore, pulse frequency components around this frequency degrade the abrupt rising edge, as shown in Figure 7.

The skin effect introduces an additive series impedance per unit length, which is given by

$$Z_s = k(1+j) \tag{11}$$

The factor k depends on the skin depth, which is proportional to the square root of the radian frequency ω. If r is the radius of a circular section wire and the ratio r/δ is

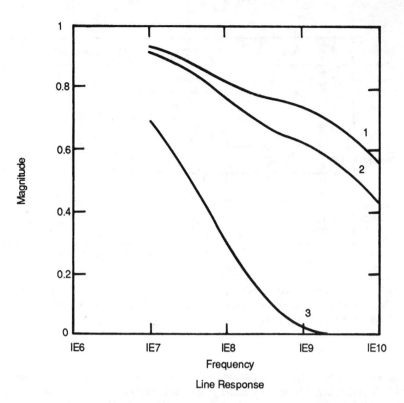

Figure 6. The line frequency response for 10μm × 7μm metal wire on 7 μm of polyimide (top curve, labeled 1), a 10 μm × 5 μm metal wire on 5 μm of polyimide (middle curve, labeled 2), 5 μm × 0.75 μm metal wire on 1 μm of SiO$_2$ (lower curve, labeled 3). Total line length is 5 cm.

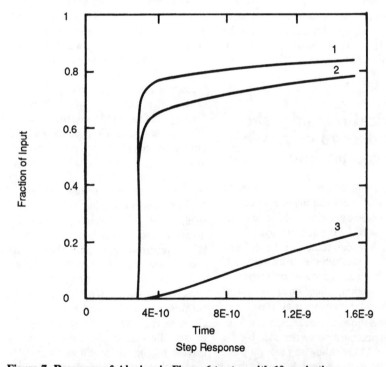

Figure 7. Response of Al wires in Figure 6 to step with 10-ps risetime.

greater than 1.5, k may be approximated by

$$k = \frac{1}{2 \pi \sigma \delta (r - \delta/2)} \tag{12}$$

where the skin depth is

$$\delta = \sqrt{\frac{2}{\omega \mu \sigma}} \tag{13}$$

Both the magnitude and phase of the frequency transfer function of the line

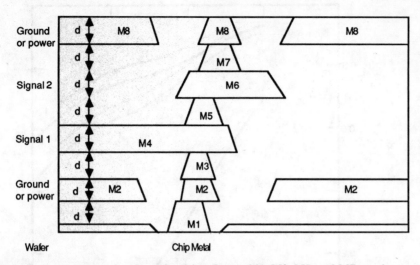

Figure 8. Cross section of wafer scale wiring. Layers M1, M3, M5, and M7 are via studs; M2 and M8 are ground and power planes; and M4 and M6 are signal wiring layers. The thickness d is 5-10 μm.

change when the skin effect is considered.

The discussion here has been for wafer length wires. Needless to say, some WSI wires are much shorter than 20 cm and their bandwidth and delay are correspondingly improved. In fact, by locating these shorter lines on other, thinner layers, the bandwidth can be further improved, as it is only the longer lines that demand the thicker films for achieving transmission line performance.

Fabrication and yield considerations for WSI interconnections

The thick films that favorably effect the propagation times can also help improve the discretionary wiring yield, depending on the type of fabrication employed.[19]

One fabrication technique that is being examined at Rensselaer is a thick film liftoff process,[20] which is a scaled-up version of more conventional thin-film methods used successfully for many years at IBM.[21]

Figure 8 shows a cross section of a four-layer interconnection system suitable for WSI or WSI consisting of a ground plane (at the bottom), X and Y signal planes containing discretionary wiring, and a top power distribution plane. The thick power and ground planes handle the supply currents required for the large numbers of circuits on the wafer and prevent electro-migration. These planes also help reduce interline coupling in the signal layers,

guarantee a low resistance in the signal ground return paths, decouple these paths from the underlying signal layers, and shield against "slow" waves in the substrate.[17,22] The vias between layers are solid pillars or studs rather than eyelets. This strategy helps keep the via resistance low. It also reduces yield problems associated with the poor step coverage that arises when one uses steep sloped via walls for the purpose of minimizing the total via area.

Each of the eight processing layers (including the stud via layers) shown in Figure 8 are fabricated using the thick film liftoff process shown in Figure 9. First a 10 μm planarizing dielectric layer is spun on and cured in several layers to avoid or reduce pinhole effects. After this, the wafer is coated with a release layer (R) of Mo or soluble organic film and then a thin shield layer of Al. Finally, the pattern definition resist layer is spun on. After lithographic resist patterning the thin Mo and Al layers in the exposed regions are etched. An anisotropic dry etch opens a deep vertical walled trench or well with a slight metal shield overhang. Next the thick metal layer is directionally deposited. Because of the shield overhang and the directional deposition, the metal in the trench or well is not connected to the top layer metal. A final lateral etch of the release layer releases the top metal, permitting it to be "lifted off" under mild agitation.

The yield of this thick film liftoff process is extremely high, although there are many processing steps involved in its im-

plementation. First, the planarization of the top surface of each dielectric layer greatly reduces the defects due to topological features.[23] Second, the use of solid stud vias reduces the step coverage problem, which the thick layers would aggravate. Third, the vertical walled trenches or wells help reduce interwire shorts on a given layer by embedding each wire deeply in the dielectric. Fourth, pinholes in all layers are of reduced significance because of the extreme thickness of these layers. Small pinholes in the patterned Al shield layer will form small "wormholes" in the anisotropically etched polyimide. Since the thick Al is directionally deposited, small pinholes in the etch shield will tend to seal themselves before forming a complete stud in the polyimide wormhole below. This effect is illustrated in Figure 10. Finally, the use of only moderate processing temperatures reduces thermal stress on the wiring.

The use of liftoff is not without its disadvantages. Pinholes in the release layer can result in unwanted adhesion of the liftoff metal, causing shorts. Very large pinholes in the resist or metal shield result in metal studs of partial or full height, which may cause shorts. Failure in planarization thickness control results in lap-over bridging shorts, poor endpoint verification, and poor cleaning of via interface surfaces. These defects most often result in surface bridging faults and open or highly resistive vias. Highly resistive vias could prevent the onset of *LC* transmission line behavior. One approach to the repair of these defects is discussed in conjunction with the focused ion beam (FIB). To enhance long-term reliability an encapsulation layer can be used to passivate the metal or dielectric layers.

One of the principal advantages of the fabrication of thick film micro transmission lines by liftoff is its generic applicability to a broad class of underlying wafer technologies. The method is equally applicable to submicron CMOS or GaAs processing. Any foundry can be used to fabricate the wafers.

E-beam lithography

The patterning of the resist is readily accomplished with direct-write electron beam lithography. E-beam use eliminates the need for creation of expensive mask plate sets for the different wiring and via configuration on each wafer. Rensselaer is fortunate to have received a grant from

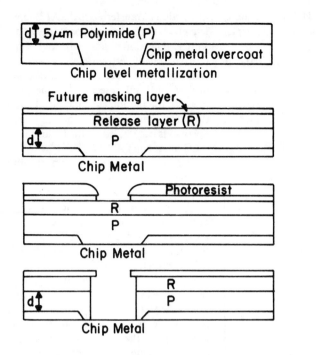

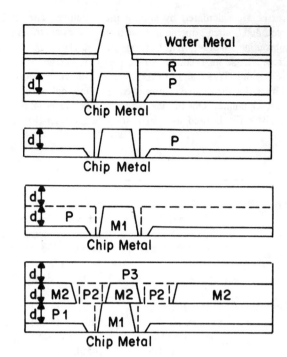

Figure 9. Fabrication sequence for thick film liftoff process. Steps are repeated identically for all layers of the multilayer interconnect structure including the pillar vias. (*Source:* J. F. McDonald et al., "Gallium Arsenide Wafer Scale Integration," *AGARD Conf. Proc. No. 380,* May 1985, p. 12-12.)

IBM of an EL-2 direct-write electron beam lithography machine. Using the recently available Perkin-Elmer AEBLE system, a wafer throughput of 30 wafers per hour is possible. Hence, commercial WSI fabrication can enjoy competitive wafer throughput. The use of optical masks for fixed vias or feedthrough layers can keep the number of more expensive E-beam operations to a minimum.

Focused ion beam repair

The focused ion beam (FIB) is a relatively new processing tool. One of the process capabilities of this tool is focused ion milling of fine features, which can be done in registration on the wafer. Using an integral scanning electron microscope (SEM) attachment on the FIB, it is possible to scan metal layers to look for large pinholes, and to compare fully patterned lines against the pattern database to find bridging faults. Using the milling action of the ion beam, it becomes possible to cut short circuit metal spurs or redundant connections. The FIB can also be used to clean or verify vias. Using an integral secondary

ion mass spectrometer (SIMS), a precise endpoint verification can be made for each via, thus ensuring clean, low-resistance metal interfaces. Although the FIB is a relatively slow tool for some operations, these discrete repair, cleaning, and verification operations can be performed quite quickly since the number and size of these regions requiring repair are small.

A 32-bit GaAs RISC in wafer scale technology

The application of wafer scale technology to the implementation of a 32-bit RISC[24] in GaAs using an E/D gate array will be examined now. The point of view taken will be that of traditional WSI rather than WSH or WTM packaging, although clearly these may be used. The instruction set of the register file based processor is shown in Figure 11.

The Source 2 operand can be replaced with a 12-bit immediate constant and it can further be shifted one or two bits left or one bit right. The immediate constant used in the BRANCH and LOAD# instructions is 20 bits wide and can be complemented. I/O

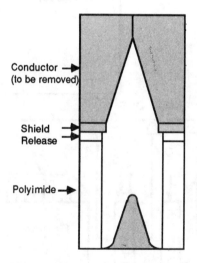

Figure 10. Since the thick metal film is directionally deposited, the interlayer "wormholes" resulting from small pinholes in the shield layer tend to seal themselves before forming a complete stud, thus improving the WSI wiring yield. (*Source:* J. F. McDonald and A. J. Steckl, "Multilevel Interconnections for Wafer Scale Integration," *J. Vacuum Science and Technology A,* Vol. 4, No. 6, Nov./Dec. 1986, p. 3135.)

addresses are calculated by adding the Source 1 and Source 2 operands. Note that no subroutine call or return instructions are available. These instructions can be performed by the STORE and LOAD instructions by setting the Source 1 operand equal to the stack pointer. One of the registers in the register file is used as system stack pointer. The GETLASTPC instruction is necessary to save the return address after an I/O trap or interrupt occurs.

The architecture of the GaAs RISC is shown in Figure 12. The data path has two internal buses: the L-Bus and S-Bus; its two external buses are the Instruction-Bus and Data-Bus. The Source 2 operand of an instruction is transferred to the ALU input latch B on the S-Bus and goes through the shifter. The shifter has only four functions: pass, shift left, shift left by two, and shift right, since the lack of pass transistors in GaAs MESFET technology increases the cost for the implementation of multiplexers considerably. The Source 1 operand is transferred on the L-Bus to the ALU input latch A.

The dual-port read, single-port write register file with 16 registers allows the CPU to access two ALU operands concurrently and to perform a read and write operation in a single system cycle. An ALU result is transferred on the L-Bus to the feed forward register, from where it will be written into the register file during the next cycle. This delayed write scheme reduces the system cycle time or instruction time by eliminating the relatively long register file write delay from the cycle time. If one of the source operands is equal to the destination register of the previous instruction, the operand will automatically be read from the feed forward register, and not from the register file that has not yet been updated. This eliminates data dependencies that would occur because of the delayed write scheme.

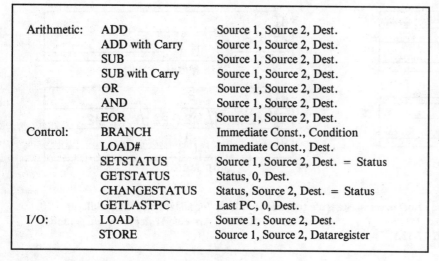

Arithmetic:	ADD	Source 1, Source 2, Dest.
	ADD with Carry	Source 1, Source 2, Dest.
	SUB	Source 1, Source 2, Dest.
	SUB with Carry	Source 1, Source 2, Dest.
	OR	Source 1, Source 2, Dest.
	AND	Source 1, Source 2, Dest.
	EOR	Source 1, Source 2, Dest.
Control:	BRANCH	Immediate Const., Condition
	LOAD#	Immediate Const., Dest.
	SETSTATUS	Source 1, Source 2, Dest. = Status
	GETSTATUS	Status, 0, Dest.
	CHANGESTATUS	Status, Source 2, Dest. = Status
	GETLASTPC	Last PC, 0, Dest.
I/O:	LOAD	Source 1, Source 2, Dest.
	STORE	Source 1, Source 2, Dataregister

Figure 11. Instruction set of register file based processor.

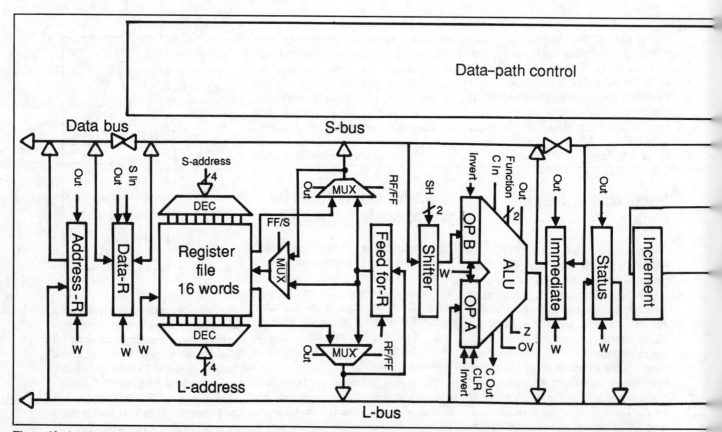

Figure 12. Architecture of GaAs RISC. (*Source*: H. Greub, J. F. McDonald, and H. Merchant, ''The Effect of Die Yield Evolution on a Wafer Scale Implementation of the GaAs RISC,'' *Hawaii Int'l Conf. System Sciences*, Jan. 1987, p. 57. Source of Figure 13 also.)

The ALU has only four functions: ADD, AND, OR, and EOR. The subtraction is implemented by inverting one of the operands and inverting the carry in. The carry select scheme over four bits is used to speed up the adder. The carry out for four bits is calculated for a carry in of zero and a carry in of one. The actual carry in selects only the output carry from one of the two carry chains. The carry propagation delay over four bits is therefore reduced to the carry output multiplexer delay, once the four-bit carry chains have settled. This adder speed-up scheme was chosen because it offers a good speed versus gate count trade-off. [25]

The program counter logic includes four registers, an incrementer, and an input and output multiplexer. The NEXT PC is normally loaded from the incrementer, but in case of a BRANCH instruction it can be loaded with the jump address from the ALU, or in case of a exception due to a reset, interrupt, or I/O trap, it will be loaded with the corresponding exception vector. The value of the current PC is transferred on the L-Bus to the ALU for jump address calculations. The output multiplexer actually puts the value of the NEXT PC on the bus because the NEXT PC is equal to the current PC at the time of the transfer. The LAST PC can also be transferred to the L-Bus to save the return address after an interrupt or trap. The previous and last PC values are necessary because of the pipelining of the data path. Output multiplexers have been included in the register file and PC logic to reduce the bus-loading and the I/O pins on the bit slices used to implement the corresponding sections.

The separate instruction and data buses and the pipelining allow the RISC to execute an instruction fetch, a data I/O, and an ALU operation concurrently. One instruction leaves the three-stage pipeline per system cycle. The instruction length is fixed to 32 bits since all instructions must be executed in three cycles (instruction fetch, execute cycle, data I/O). The cycle time is given by the delays on the critical path: instruction decoder = > address decoder = > register file (read) = > shifter = > ALU latch = > ALU (add) = > register (write).

The system cycle time was estimated using proprietary information on a new gate array with a high fan-out from Tri-Quint. A gate delay model was used with a basic delay for each gate type plus an incremental delay for the number of fan-outs. Further, it was assumed that fast, high-power I/O cells with E/D logic threshold are used. The resulting system cycle time is 15.8 ns. Twenty-three percent of the cycle time is due to driver and receiver, while only 22 percent is due to transmission line delays. With a cycle time of 15.8 ns the GaAs RISC will execute 63 million instructions per second. However, data dependencies after load instructions and the delayed branch scheme will reduce this figure, depending upon the application. To achieve near-maximum throughput, the memory must be able to transfer one instruction and one data word per system cycle to the CPU. This would require a memory bandwidth of 506 megabytes per second. Fast data and instruction caches are therefore necessary to reduce the main memory bandwidth. The system architecture with the two cache memories is shown in Figure 13'.

For the implementation with the E/D-mode MESFET gate array from TriQuint, [13] the ALU, the PC logic, and the registers are divided into four-bit slices. Only the register file with the feed forward logic has to be divided into one-bit slices. Figure 14 shows the building blocks for the GaAs

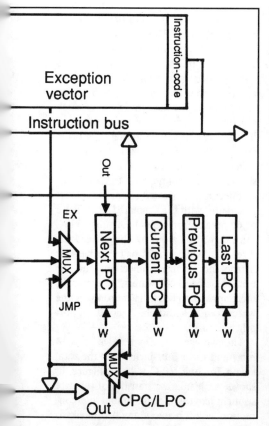

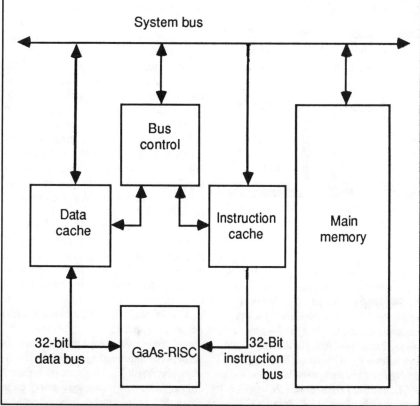

Figure 13. System architecture. Two independent cache memories are used to reduce the main memory bandwidth.

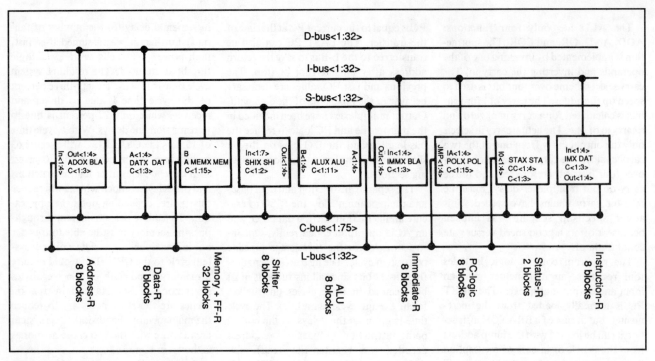

Figure 14. Block structure of data path.

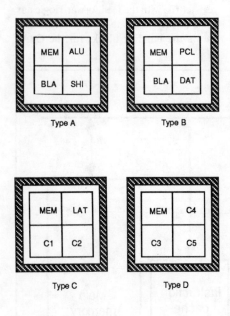

Figure 15. Division of the four gate array types into four independent blocks. MEM: Register file and feed forward register—1 bit slice; ALU: carry select adder and [AND, OR, EOR]—4 bit slices; BLA: bus-latch for address-R and immediate-R—4 bit slices; SHI: 4-to-1 multiplexer for shifter—4 bit slices; PCL: program counter and PC-registers—4 bit slices; DAT: data I/O register—4 bit slices; LAT: data latch for instruction-R—4 bit slices; and C1-C5: control logic.

RISC data path. A slice or building block should have less than 180 gates since the yield drops exponentially with the number of gates in a block. The yield of a block with 180 gates is currently above 60 percent.[13] All gate array sites are therefore divided into four small and independent blocks that have a high yield. The number of gate array types is currently restricted to four because of the use of step and repeat lithography by the foundry. This restriction severely affects the design since it limits the number of block types to 16, and some of the block types have even to be repeated several times because they are used more often. This limitation can be avoided using WSH or WTM die mounting systems with some loss in surface density. Figure 15 shows the four gate array types required for the implementation of the RISC architecture. Four blocks have to share the 64 I/O pins of the gate array. If the restriction of only four different gate array types on a wafer is lifted by the foundry, the support of byte and half-word (16-bit) instructions becomes feasible. Further hardware support for a second-order Booth multiply algorithm could be implemented to give the GaAs RISC signal processing capability. Various amounts of improved multiplication hardware are possible. The area of memory cells in gate array technology is very large compared to custom-designed memory cells. This RISC design has therefore no multiple-window register file in contrast to the Berkeley RISC, and the cache mem-

ories have to be implemented on a structure similar to the wafer transmission module[11] with custom-designed GaAs memories.

After processing at the foundry the wafer is tested and the location of the fully functional blocks is fed to the placer and router software. The testing must also verify if the threshold levels on the wafer are compatible and span the so-called burn-in period for reliability. The placer and router has to give special attention to critical paths like the carry chain or clock distribution tree. The seven segments of the carry chain must be shorter than 10 cm (560-ps transmission delay) to achieve a system cycle time of 15.8 ns. Figure 16 shows the interconnections for *two* RISC architectures fabricated on the same four-inch wafer with the simulated yield figure of 60 percent for a block. A single RISC can easily fit on a three-inch wafer. Using three-inch wafers might be better because of the shorter interconnections and the brittleness of GaAs wafers. In any case, there appears to be sufficient room on the wafer to add additional logic to support other features.

The average wire segment length is 14 mm, and on a four-inch wafer the total length for one RISC is 18 m. Figure 17 shows the histogram statistics of the wire segment lengths. The maximum interconnection length between any two blocks is less than 10 cm. The total wire capacity of two layers at 20-micron pitch for the four-inch wafer is roughly 500 m.

The GaAs RISC architecture requires 12,000 gates for its implementation, which is well below the wafer capacity. The static power consumption of the gates and drivers is estimated to be 36 W if the blocks can be powered up independently. The dynamic power consumption is estimated to be quite low because of the low input capacitance of the gates and the transmission line interconnections. The full RISC package is therefore expected to dissipate only about 40 W per RISC architecture. If the power distribution plane is split in two halves, the two CPUs could be powered up independently. Special considerations not described here must apply for implementing quiet power distribution throughout the wafer. Precise clock wiring is especially critical for the four-phase clock required to drive this pipelined architecture. The CAD software must ensure this during placement and routing.

When the GaAs process technology reaches the point where 1000 gates per die can be fabricated with high yield, the speed of the RISC can be improved significantly by partitioning the architecture into larger blocks or cells, resulting in fewer wafer interconnect delays. The wafer interconnect delays are, despite the transmission line behavior, much greater than the interconnect delays on a die because of the driver and receiver delays and the much higher length of wafer interconnections. To reduce the cycle time, the ALU and the shifter would be incorporated in one eight-bit slice, thereby saving the wafer interconnect delay between the ALU and the shifter. By using the carry select scheme over eight bits instead of four bits, the carry propagation over the full 32 bits becomes faster and the wafer interconnect delays in the carry chain are reduced from seven to three. These changes would decrease the adder delay from 11.34 to 6.45 ns. Further, the control logic could be built with fewer blocks, saving again a wafer interconnect delay of 0.90 ns. All these improvements would result in a system cycle time of only 10 ns. This shows that a wafer scale integrated RISC will gain speed as the yield of the circuit technology improves.[26] The 15.8-ns RISC assumes 100 cells of 12 different cell types containing no more than 180 gates (which happen to be implemented here on a quarter of a gate array reticle, as shown in Figure 14). The 10-ns RISC assumes 23 cells of seven different die types containing no more than 1000 gates per die. The wiring layout for the rectangular WTM

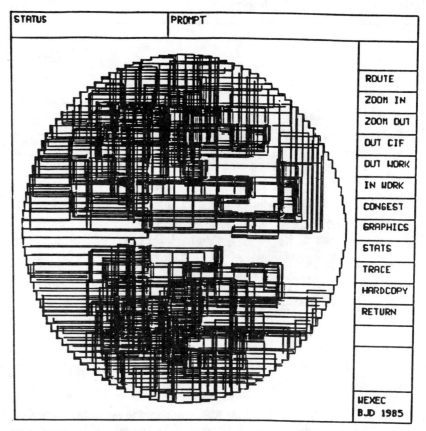

Figure 16. Interconnections on a four-inch wafer for two RISC architectures.

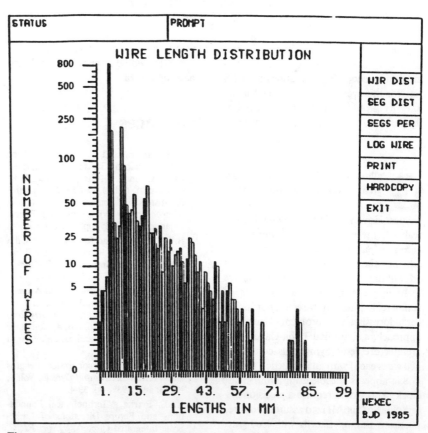

Figure 17. Distribution of wire length for interconnect of two RISC architectures on a four-inch wafer.

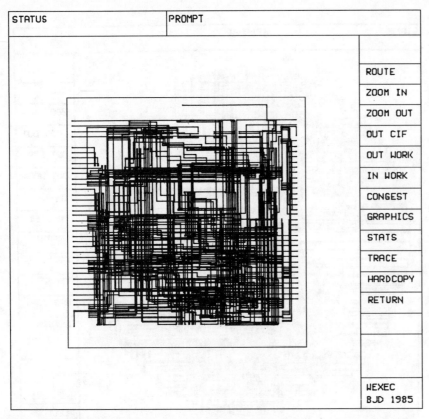

STATUS	PROMPT

ROUTE

ZOOM IN

ZOOM OUT

OUT CIF

OUT WORK

IN WORK

CONGEST

GRAPHICS

STATS

TRACE

HARDCOPY

RETURN

WEXEC
BJD 1985

Figure 18. Routed WTM layout for GaAs RISC partitioned to use 23 dies containing less than 1000 gates per die. (*Source*: H. Greub, J. F. McDonald, and H. Merchant, "The Effect of Die Yield Evolution on a Wafer Scale Implementation of the GaAs RISC," *Hawaii Int'l Conf. System Sciences,* Jan. 1987, p. 61.)

supporting these 23 dies is shown in Figure 18. This layout was used to obtain the wiring delays needed for estimating the MIPS rate for this architecture.[27] Special signal integrity problems must be considered in the design to achieve this performance.[28-29]

G allium arsenide logic circuits hold great promise for use in high-frequency digital microelectronics. However, if this potential is to be realized, the system designer must have access to packaging and interconnection schemes that will not negate the speed advantages of the underlying device technology. Many of the concepts of wafer scale integration seem appropriate for addressing this problem. Using this approach, a simplified 32-bit GaAs RISC architecture (employing cells containing 180 gates each) with an instruction time of l5.8 ns appears feasible using a four-phase clock. This would require a precision system clock of 506 MHz to assure the desired precision timing. If cells with l000 gates each can be fabricated with reasonable yield, the repartitioned architecture could be designed to have an instruction time of

l0 ns; however, a four-phase system clock of 800 MHz would have to be distributed to accomplish this.□

References

1. P. T. Greiling and C. F. Krumm, "The Future Impact of GaAs Digital Integrated Circuits," in N. G. Einspurch and W. R. Wisseman (eds.), *VLSI Electronics Microstructure Science,* Vol. 11 (*GaAs Microelectronics*), Academic Press, Orlando, Fla., l985, pp. 138-171.

2. B. S. Landman and R. L. Russo, "On a Pin-Versus-Block Relationship for Partition of Logic Graphs," *IEEE Trans. Computers,* Vol. C-20, No. 12, Dec. 1971.

3. W. E. Donath, "Placement and Average Interconnection Lengths of Computer Logic," *IEEE Trans. Circuits and Systems,* Vol. CAS-26, No. 4, Computer Society Press, Los Alamitos, Calif., April 1979, pp. 272-277.

4. D. K. Ferry, "Interconnection Lengths and VLSI," *Circuits and Devices,* Vol. 1, No. 4, July 1985, pp. 39-42.

5. R. L. Petritz, "Technological Foundations and Future Directions of Large-Scale Integrated Circuits," *Proc. FJCC,* 1966, pp. 65-67.

6. A. J. Blodgett and D. R. Barbour, "Thermal Conduction Module: A High Performance Multilayer Ceramic Package," *IBM J. R&D,* Jan. 1982.

7. A. Deutsch and C. W. Ho, "Thin Film Interconnection Lines for VLSI Packaging," *Proc. IEEE International Conf. Computer Design,* Rye, N. Y., Oct. 1983, pp. 222-226.

8. C. Huang et al., "Silicon Packaging—A New Packaging Technique," *Proc. IEEE Custom Integrated Circuits Conf.,* Rochester, N. Y., May 1983, pp. 142-146.

9. R. R. Johnson, "The Significance of Wafer Scale Integration in Computer Design," *Proc. IEEE Int'l Conf. Computer Design,* Oct. 1984, pp. 101-105.

10. J. F. McDonald et al., "The Trials of Wafer Scale Integration," *IEEE Spectrum,* Oct. 1984, pp. 32-39.

11. B. J. Donlan et al., "The Wafer Transmission Module," *VLSI Systems Design,* Jan. 1986, pp. 54-90.

12. T. Ishida et al., "GaAs MESFET Ring Oscillator on a Si Substrate," *IEEE Trans. Elec. Dev.,* Vol. ED-32, No. 6, June 1985, pp. 1037-1041.

13. A. Rode, T. Flegal, and G. LaRue, "A High Yield GaAs Gate Array Technology and Applications," *Proc. IEEE GaAs IC Symp.,* Oct. 1983, pp. 171-181.

14. D. L. Peltzer, "Wafer Scale Integration—The Limits of VLSI?," *VLSI Design,* Sept. 1983, pp. 43-47.

15. F. S. Lee, "VLSI GaAs Technology," in G. Rabbat (ed.), *Hardware and Software Concepts in VLSI,* Chap. 11, Van Nostrand-Reinhold Press, 1983, pp. 257-295.

16. A. S. Bergendahl, "Thick Film Stripline Micro Transmission Line Interconnections for Wafer Scale Integration," *Proc. ECS Meeting on VLSI,* Vol. 85-5, May 1985, pp. 175-184.

17. B. J. Donlan et al., "Computer Aided Design and Fabrication for Wafer Scale Integration," *VLSI Design,* March 1985.

18. B. H. Bakoglu and J. D. Meindl, "Optimal Interconnect Circuits for VLSI," *Proc. 1984 IEEE ISSCC,* Feb. 22-24, 1984, pp. 164-165.

19. T. E. Mangir, "Sources of Failure and Yield Improvement for Restructurable Interconnections for RVLSI and WSI. Part I—Sources of Failures and Yield Improvement for VLSI," *Proc. IEEE,* Vol. 72, No. 6, June 1984, pp. 690-708.

20. A. Bergendahl et al., "A Thick Film Lift-Off Process for Wafer Scale Integration," *Proc. IEEE 1985 VLSI Multilayer Interconnection Conf.,* (V-MIC), Santa Clara, Calif., June 1985, pp. 54-62.

21. R. Larsen, "A Silicon and Aluminum Dynamic Memory Technology," *IBM J. R&D,* May 1980, pp. 268-282.

22. H. Hasegawa and S. Seki, "Analysis of Interconnection Delay on Very High Speed LSI/VLSI Chips Using an MIS Microstrip Line Model," *IEEE Trans. Electron Devices,* Vol. ED-31, No. 12, Dec. 1984.

23. M. R. Gulett, "Dual-Metal CMOS for Semicustom or Custom Designs," *VLSI Design,* Jan. 1985, pp. 84-90.

24. Manolis G. H. Katevenis, *Reduced Instruction Set Computer for VLSI,* MIT Press, Cambridge, Mass., 1984.

25. R. W. Sherburne, *Processor Design Tradeoffs in VLSI,* doctoral thesis, University of Calif., Berkeley, 1984.

26. H. Greub, J. F. McDonald, and H. Merchant, "The Effect of Die Yield Evolution on a Wafer Scale Implementation of the GaAs RISC Architecture," *Proc. Twentieth Ann. Hawaii Int'l Conf. System Sciences,* HICSS-20, Vol. 1, Jan. 6-11, 1987, pp. 53-61.

27. J. Donlan and J. F. McDonald, "A Placement and Routing System for Wafer Scale," *Proc. IEEE Int'l Conf. CAD,* ICCAD 86, Nov. 11-13, 1986, pp. 462-465.

28. H. Greub, J. S. Kim, and J. F. McDonald, "On the Possibility of Standing Wave Resonance in the Bypass Capacitor Structure for WSI," *Proc. 1986 VLSI Multilayer Interconnect Conf.,* Santa Clara, Calif., June 9-10, 1986, pp. 250-258. (IEEE Cat. No. 86CH2337-4.)

29. J. S. Kim, H. J. Greub, and J. F. McDonald, "High Frequency Electromagnetic Characterization of Lossy Transmission Lines for WSI," *Proc. IEEE Region 1 Tech. Workshop on Electromagnetic Field Computation,* Schenectady Section, N.Y., Oct. 20-21, 1986, Paper 4, Solid State Devices Session.

Randolph H. Steinvorth is a professor at the University of Costa Rica. His main research interests are in computer architectures and wafer scale integration.

He received the BSEE and a licensiature in electrical engineering from the University of Costa Rica. He also holds MS and PhD degrees in computer and systems engineering from Rensselaer Polytechnic Institute.

Brian J. Donlan is a captain in the US Air Force. He is stationed at Wright-Patterson Air Force Base in Ohio, and he is an assistant professor at the Air Force Institute of Technology.

Donlan received the BS degree from the State University of New York and the MSEE degree from Rensselaer Polytechnic Institute. He just earned a PhD at Rensselaer Polytechnic Institute.

Albert S. Bergendahl is at IBM Corp. in Essex Junction, Vt. He is also an adjunct professor at Rensselaer Polytechnic Institute.

Bergendahl received the BEE, the MS in geology, and the PhD in chemistry at Rensselaer. His main research interest is in IC fabrication.

Readers may write to Jack F. McDonald at the Center for Integrated Electronics, Rensselaer Polytechnic Institute, Troy, NY 12189.

John F. McDonald joined Rensselaer Polytechnic Institute as an associate professor, and he is currently a full professor at the Rensselaer Center for Integrated Electronics. He has served as an assistant professor at Yale University.

McDonald received the BSEE degree from the Massachusetts Institute of Technology, and the M.Eng. and PhD degrees from Yale University.

Hans J. Greub is pursuing a PhD at Rensselaer Polytechnic Institute under a Tektronix fellowship.

His main research interests are in computer architectures and wafer scale integration.

He holds the BSEE and MSEE degrees from the Swiss Federal Institute of Technology. With the aid of a Fulbright fellowship, he earned an MS degree in computer and systems engineering from Rensselaer Polytechnic Institute.

April 1987

System Architecture of a Gallium Arsenide One-Gigahertz Digital IC Tester

Douglas J. Fouts, John M. Johnson, Steven E. Butner, and Stephen I. Long
University of California, Santa Barbara

Reprinted from *Computer*, May 1987, pages 58-70. Copyright © 1987 by
The Institute of Electrical and Electronics Engineers, Inc.

A team from UCSB has an approach for testing full-custom GaAs ICs. The tester they've developed is a hybrid of GaAs digital ICs, high-speed silicon logic, and a standard microprocessor.

The technology to support full-custom GaAs integrated circuits is now emerging. It is still an evolving technology with few standards, relatively low density, and poor yield. The promise of GaAs is its speed; the challenge is in harnessing that speed.

Why a tester?

This article describes the architecture of an early GaAs system, a 1-GHz digital integrated circuit tester. The motivation for this project was the development of a graduate-level course in GaAs integrated circuit design at the University of California, Santa Barbara (refer to the sidebar description of the course on page 60). UCSB's course produces a multiproject GaAs chip every year (Figure 1), and the tester is a tool for evaluation of the projects after dicing and packaging. The multiproject chips are also the source of custom GaAs ICs that will be used to build the high-speed portions of the IC tester.

The tester serves a twofold purpose. First, very high speed test equipment is needed for exercising and evaluating custom GaAs chips and subsystems. Since the speed of these chips and subsystems far exceeds the capabilities of existing digital test equipment, there is little choice but to make the required tool. Secondly, the tester serves as a focus for the first round of designs. It is during this round that standards are set: pads and pad drivers are created, voltage swings are established, interconnect impedances and packaging standards are set, and clocking techniques formulated. The first project undertaken—in this case a "bootstrap" project—sets the design style for more complex systems yet to come. Because of the complexity of designing GaAs systems, the design team chose not to build a computer as the first project. Rather, the high-speed functional tester project was selected. Once the tester project is accomplished, the team has plans to apply what has been learned toward the design of a very high speed GaAs computer system.

The goals of the UCSB tester project are as follows:

(1) The tester should be able to test chips with a clock rate of up to 1 GHz.

(2) It should be versatile enough to test GaAs unbuffered FET logic, buffered FET logic, Schottky diode FET logic, direct-coupled FET logic, as well as silicon emitter-coupled logic.

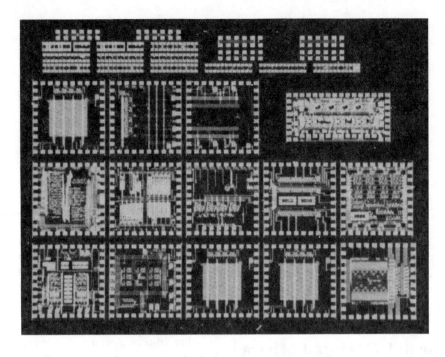

Figure 1. GaAs multiproject chip.

(3) The system should be easy to reconfigure in order to test a chip with a different pin-out, or to run a different test on the same chip.

(4) It must be possible to specify an arbitrary set of test vectors (subject to a reasonable size limitation) for use as a set of stimuli to the unit under test. The system must be able to apply digital signals from that set in either a single-shot or continuous (looping) mode at full test speed.

(5) The tester should be able to capture and store the response of the unit under test on a per-pin basis at full test speed.

(6) The speed of application of the test should be adjustable with high resolution over a wide range, with particular emphasis on the region near the highest speed.

Some test methods. There are several methods that can be used for testing digital integrated circuits. As the density available in conventional MOS integrated systems has risen, so has the trend toward using built-in circuitry to perform self-test. This approach minimizes the need for special test gear—the chip or subsystem simply tests itself. Such an approach generally incurs a reasonably high overhead that, given the present density and yield of custom GaAs chips, is not justified. In special cases, however, where the amount of additional circuitry is small, the built-in test approach is the best approach.

Falling short of complete built-in self-test, but still better than zero designed-in testability, is the technique of using generic structures (usually programmable logic arrays, or PLAs) that can be tested without regard for the function they realize. Gallium arsenide densities and yields are not yet ready to support large PLAs, and thus such an approach cannot currently be used.

Since built-in test circuits often are not practical, special-purpose external test equipment is required. Parametric testing—the measurement of ac and dc parameters of the circuits within the chip—can be done for the most part at low speeds and with existing general-purpose laboratory equipment. Digital testing at device speeds (which are running well into the gigahertz range), however, is impossible with any known test equipment. Thus the choice of a functional high-speed, general-purpose digital test stand as a project not only serves to focus our initial design effort, but also fills a void in the spectrum of test equipment available for general use.

A number of lower-speed functional testers are currently available.[1-4] High-speed testers, such as the one described in this article, are very similar to their lower-speed counterparts mentioned above. High-speed testers, however, are exposed to unique problems that must be solved at the system or architectural level. Among these problems are

- interconnection of signals with short rise and fall times,
- skew and distribution of high-speed control signals and clocks,
- design of custom high-speed components,
- selection and screening of high-speed components,
- physical placement of high-speed parts,
- distribution and bypassing of power,
- ground distribution, and
- dissipation of heat.

Test assumptions and conditions. The tester we have designed is intended to fill a need at the extreme speed range of the testing spectrum. Not all chip technologies will be testable. The types of chips targeted for support in our prototype test stand are those that are likely to operate at or above 200 MHz, and those having ECL-compatible external logic levels and noise margins. These assumptions allow most GaAs logic families as well as silicon ECL to be tested. It will be necessary to package all chips before testing them at high speed. Probe-type testing can be accomplished before dicing. We use microwave probe cards[5] to weed out nonfunctional chips and to get partial performance evaluation data before packaging.

Standardization of logic levels for GaAs logic families has not yet occurred. To maintain compatibility with existing high-speed silicon logic, F100K series ECL logic levels and noise margins have been chosen as standard.[6]

- Voh(min)   = −1.025 volts
- Voh(max)   = −0.88 volts
- Vol(min)   = −1.810 volts

  Vol(max)   = −1.620 volts
- Vih(min)   = −1.165 volts

  Vih(max)   = −0.88 volts
- Vil(min)   = −1.810 volts

  Vil(max)   = −1.475 volts

All our custom GaAs unbuffered FET logic, buffered FET logic, and Schottky diode FET logic circuits are equipped with pad drivers and pad receivers that convert to these external specifications. Even if a chip does not have compatible external logic levels, it can still be tested by the tester if its external logic swing is between 0.2 and 1.0 V. This is possible because the power for the chip under test comes from different supplies than does the power for the tester. Testing a chip with incompatible logic levels is accomplished by skewing the power supply voltages to the chip under test such that the logic swing of the chip under test crosses the logic threshold of the tester.

Because there is little or no theoretical work available on fault models for GaAs subsystems, we have chosen to support functional testing. This decision is based on maximizing flexibility and test speed so that virtually any fault model and associated testing philosophy can be supported once theoretical results for GaAs do become available. Functional testing, simply speaking, is exercising the circuit under test in a manner similar to its normal intended operation. Functional testing stands apart from other approaches, which generally exercise the circuit under test only so as to cause detection of possible faults from a known class, for example, the single or multiple line stuck-at faults.[7] This type of testing—which we shall call fault-model-based testing—is usually not performed at high speeds, except to minimize overall test fixture occupancy. It is also the case that the test vectors often do not represent a "real" environment such as would be seen by the chip under test when it is placed in the application system.

The hardware required to support functional testing is sufficient to support fault-model-based testing as well. The capability to stimulate any pin of the circuit under test with an arbitrary predefined pattern at full speed must exist. All such input pins (from the point of view of the circuit under test) must be synchronized at the test fixture. In addition, the test stand must have the capability to sample and store the output of any pin of the circuit under test. Not all pins in today's digital systems are purely input or output. Bidirectional, tristate pins are typical. Because of the extreme speed capabilities and corresponding environmental requirements of GaAs chips and the significant performance penalty and packaging complexity incurred by using buses and tristate devices, the use of such devices in GaAs subsystems is not thought to be advantageous. The prototype test stand will not provide support for bidirectional pins of the circuit under test.

Architectural problems unique to GaAs digital systems

The architectures of most contemporary computers and digital systems are influenced more by function and applica-

---

The GaAs IC design course at UC-Santa Barbara

Over the past five years, silicon VLSI design courses have become quite prevalent at many universities. These courses present a structured design approach that when used together with CAD layout and simulation tools result in project circuits that are in many cases fabricated by the DARPA-funded silicon VLSI project ("MOSIS"), and later returned to the university to be tested by the students.

A GaAs IC design course is being taught at UCSB that builds on this, by now, established format. The objective of this course is to present an introduction to GaAs devices and their application in digital ICs sufficient for the student to complete a design project of SSI/MSI complexity (up to about 200 gates). Because of the emphasis on high-speed circuits, the UCSB course tends to stress understanding of the GaAs devices and their interactions with interconnections, load capacitance, transmission lines, and packages to a greater degree than is usual for a VLSI structured design course. Also, because of the logic voltage swing limitations, more emphasis is placed on gate level analysis of noise margins and speed. A modified version of Spice2 equipped with a GaAs MESFET model is used in homework assignments and for the design project. Recently, Spice3 has been used to support this modeling work. Other CAD tools that have been adapted for GaAs include Caesar (a tool for creat-ing and editing IC mask structures), Lyra (a design rule checking program compatible with Caesar), and, more recently, Magic (a technology-independent VLSI CAD system). Magic supports both node extraction and design rule checking. All the CAD programs (originally from UC-Berkeley) were modified to be compatible with the GaAs design rules and device characteristics.

Fabrication of the class projects is being made possible by DARPA contracts that have been awarded to establish GaAs foundries at Rockwell and Honeywell. Funding was provided to UCSB by DARPA through NASA and JPL to support fabrication of the circuits in the foundry, to develop documentation for GaAs IC design and fabrication through foundries, and to support the tester project described here. The composition of the multiproject chips has been more constrained than is typical for silicon VLSI multiproject chips because of the direct-step-on-wafer projection lithography required for the 1-micron GaAs process. Rather than populating the entire wafer with different projects, an 8-mm field must contain all chips, which then are repeated 44 times on the 3-inch GaAs wafer. Therefore, a total of 12 projects were included on the first mask set. In addition to the UCSB circuits on the first set of project chips, circuits designed by JPL and Kent Smith of the University of Utah have also been included.

---

tion than by implementation. If this approach is taken with a GaAs system, the result will quite probably be a less-than-optimal design because GaAs digital systems can suffer from several technology-related problems. These problems are only partially solvable during the implementation phase of a project. Therefore, if a design is to be efficiently implemented in GaAs, these technology-related problems must be taken into consideration during the architectural design phase of the system.

One of the biggest technology-related problems that affects the architectural design of a GaAs computer or digital system is caused by fast signal transitions propagating from chip to chip. Spice simulations[8-9] of the GaAs digital ICs designed for this tester indicate that the chips will generate output signals with rise and fall times in the vicinity of 75 to 150 ps. These subnanosecond square waves will have components that are many multiples of the fundamental frequency. With such high-speed signals, interconnections as short as a few millimeters will behave like transmission lines.[10] It is therefore necessary to use impedance-controlled transmission line structures for all high-speed interconnect lines.

The two most practical types of transmission line structures for interconnecting devices on the same printed circuit board (PCB) are microstrip (Figure 2) and stripline (Figure 3). The impedance (Z_0) of these types of transmission lines is determined by the width (W) and thickness (T) of the traces, and by the thickness (H or B) and dielectric constant (ε_r) of the board material. Equations for calculating Z_0 are readily available.[11]

The dielectric constant of a board is, of course, dependent upon the type of board material. The thickness of the conductors and the distance between the conducting planes of the board are usually determined by the number of planes, the overall thickness of the board, and processing tolerances. Thus the parameters of conductor thickness and ground plane to signal trace distance are usually determined by practical and processing considerations. Conductor line width is therefore the only parameter that can be varied at will to control the characteristic impedance of an interconnection.

For TTL or MOS circuits the interconnection traces can be made as narrow as processing limitations allow, thus providing more room for interconnect. However, the width of traces that need to be impedance controlled cannot be made arbitrarily small just for the sake of increased interconnection density. For high-speed interconnect, traces must usually be widened to lower their characteristic impedance to the normally used 50-ohm standard. The wider the traces for a given size board, the fewer traces the board can hold. Thus the interconnection density of a PCB designed for high-speed logic may be significantly less than the interconnection density of a similar board designed for lower-speed logic. The stripline used on the PCBs for the described tester is twice as wide as it would be if it were designed to interconnect TTL or MOS chips. Because of these wide traces, the tester PCBs can support only about 50 percent of the interconnect density that would be possible using minimum line widths.

The interconnection problem is even worse when high-speed signals need to be sent from one PCB to another. This must be done with high-frequency coaxial cables and connectors. The described tester uses low-loss coaxial cables and SMA connectors rated at 12 GHz for circuits that are clocked at slightly above 1 GHz. For higher frequency circuits, correspondingly higher frequency cables and connectors must be used. The problem with these high-frequency components is that they utilize additional space and are difficult to work with when compared to printed circuit backplanes, wire wrap, or ribbon cable.

The best solution to the low-density problem of high-speed interconnect is to design an architecture that minimizes the amount of high-speed interconnect. It may not be possible to eliminate all the high-speed clocks and control signals, but structures such as high-speed buses should be avoided. The described tester's architecture is such that most of the PCBs require only two high-speed signal interfaces from/to each board.

Another technology-related problem awaiting the GaAs computer is the low density (compared to MOS, TTL, and ECL) of GaAs ICs. Current technology is such that GaAs LSI logic is just now becoming practical. VLSI is still years off. This problem works against a GaAs digital system because more chips are required to implement a specified function, and more chips means more interconnect, which is undesirable.

One obvious possibility is to design large circuit boards that can hold many ICs and still have room for a sufficient amount of microstrip or stripline interconnect. Expe-

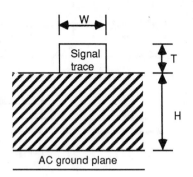

Figure 2. Microstrip transmission line.

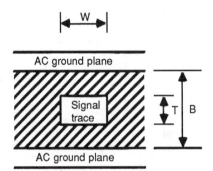

Figure 3. Stripline transmission line.

rience has shown that large PCBs with many chips and interconnects usually have at least some long interconnect lines, extending perhaps as long as 12 inches. This approach introduces three new problems.

Problem one is that of signal attenuation. Most PCBs are made from substances such as glass-epoxy or polyimide. These materials have a fairly high attenuation (loss) factor when compared to air. The attenuation is usually negligible at low (TTL and MOS) speeds or over short distances of a few inches. However, when distances are increased to as much as 12 inches, signal attenuation at high frequencies causes pulse dispersion and begins to degrade noise margins. Equations for calculating signal loss in microstrip and stripline as a function of frequency of operation (due to skin effect and dielectric losses) can be found in Gupta et al.[11]

Another problem introduced by long PCB interconnect is related to signal propagation delay. Typical propagation delay through PCB transmission line structures is usually greater than 1 ns per foot. For a system running with a 1-GHz clock, such a signal would take more than one clock period just to travel across a 12-inch board. Similar problems occur for signals

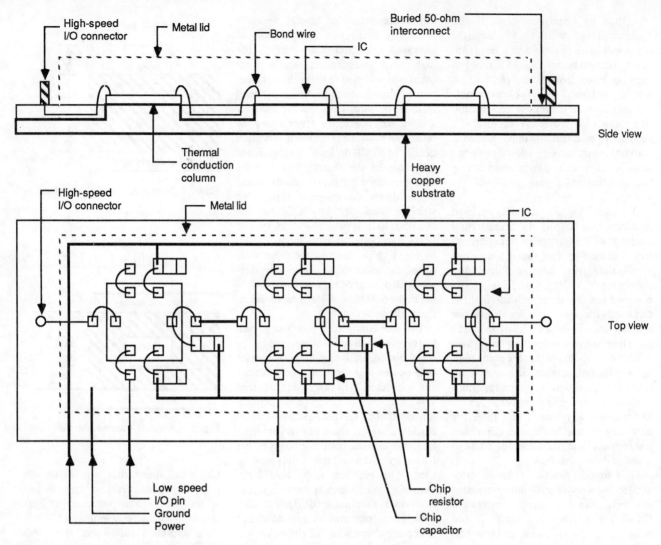

Figure 4. Hybrid semiconductor module.

that travel between boards over coaxial cables.

The third problem introduced by long PCB interconnect is crosstalk. When signal lines must be routed in parallel for several inches, crosstalk (undesired coupling between lines) must be considered. Crosstalk is proportional to the length of interconnection lines and signal speed, as well as other parameters. It is therefore desirable to minimize the length of interconnections for high-speed logic. Crosstalk is inversely proportional to the distance between two traces. In some cases it may be necessary to space signal traces farther apart than the minimum distance allowed by processing tolerances. This will further reduce interconnection density. However, in the described tester, signal traces are allowed to be as close to each other as processing limitations will allow (0.008 inch). It should be noted that the tester

uses stripline-type transmission line because microstrip-type transmission line structures have more crosstalk than stripline-type structures. This is because the wave propagation in microstrip is not purely transverse electromagnetic (TEM). Therefore, different propagation velocities are obtained for each transmission mode. Stripline, because of its symmetry, is TEM and forward crosstalk components are precisely canceled.

Another factor that affects crosstalk is signal reflections from impedance discontinuities. The load and source of a transmission line structure must be impedance matched to the line. Research at UCSB has shown that reflections can also be caused by receiving chips, right angle corners in traces, and vias (plated-through holes that are used to change layers). Receiver circuits should have high impedance inputs. The custom GaAs ICs for the tester use source

follower input pad receivers with an extremely high input impedance.

Printed circuit board vias that are used to interconnect different board layers are not impedance-controlled structures and can cause severe reflections. The use of vias should be kept to a minimum. It should be noted that thinner PCBs have shorter vias and thus less severe reflections. Right angle corners in signal traces are not as bad as vias, but they can still cause problems. Trace corners should be rounded if CAD tools and processing allow it. If not, use of corners in traces should be minimized.

The subject of crosstalk in digital systems and coupling in transmission line structures is too vast for further treatment here. Readers interested in more information on this subject should consult references 10-12, or other texts on pulse and digital techniques and transmission line theory.

One comprehensive solution to all the above-mentioned problems is to design an architecture that is modular. Modules should be designed such that all the high-speed components that need to communicate with each other are in the same module. The use of this technique will minimize the high-speed interconnect between modules. When the design is implemented, each module can be packaged as a hybrid semiconductor module similar to that shown in Figure 4. Using hybrids will minimize the length and maximize the density of the high-speed interconnect between the components. The hybrid semiconductor modules contain all the chips, the high-speed interconnect, and termination for the interconnect. The hybrids also contain provisions for distributing power and ground, bypassing the power supplies, and dissipating heat. The described tester contains 25 hybrid semiconductor modules, all identical.

Even with a carefully designed architecture and hybrid semiconductor modules, it may still be necessary to have some high-speed signals travel distances of 12 inches or more. Such is the case for the clock and control signals of the tester. This problem can be overcome by using asynchronous communication techniques between high-speed modules. The choice of using carefully engineered synchronous communications was made for the tester project, however.

If synchronous communication techniques are used, then special steps are required to maintain synchronization. In the described tester, all synchronized signals originate from the same board, which is centrally located. The cables from the sending board to the receiving boards are all the same length, the length of the longest required cable. Loading of the high-speed signals is exactly the same for every cable.

In addition to these techniques, a fan-out and phasing chip has been developed. When a synchronous signal is received on a board or hybrid module, it is routed through the fan-out and phasing chip shown in Figure 5. The chip can be programmed by the tester's controlling microprocessor to select an experimentally determined amount of delay such that the received signal is kept in phase with the rest of the signals in the system.

The last problem discussed here that affects GaAs system architecture is the problem of cost and availability of GaAs digital ICs. It would be nice to think that this problem does not exist, and perhaps it

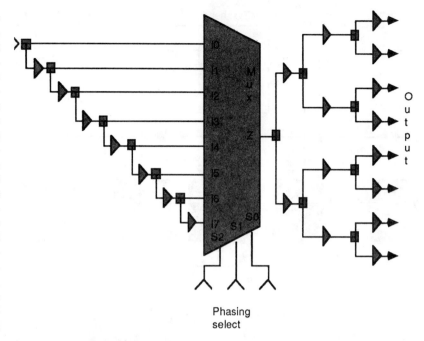

Figure 5. Phasing and fan-out chip.

does not if one is only interested in an academic exercise. However, the construction of a system such as the described tester would not be possible unless the architecture was designed around parts that can be obtained, and obtained within the appropriate budgetary constraints. There are very few "standard" GaAs parts available, and most of these are of very small scale integration. For this reason, the tester architecture is a hybrid design that uses the minimum possible number of high-speed GaAs parts. In order to minimize the number of GaAs chips, custom chips were designed specifically for the tester. These parts are utilized in the part of the architecture that is the limiting factor for the tester's speed. The rest of the system is designed from off-the-shelf high-speed silicon ECL, TTL, and MOS logic.

Tester system architecture

The tester is designed around a conventional microprocessor system. The overall system architecture of the tester can be seen in the block diagram of Figure 6. The microprocessor acts as an intelligent controller for the tester. The main memory is used to store programs for the microprocessor, test vectors for the chip under test, and result vectors for analysis.

The purpose of the high-speed interface modules is to provide a link between the

low-speed (8 MHz) microprocessor and the chip under test, where signals are clocked at 1 GHz. When connected to input pins of a chip under test, the high-speed interface modules store up test vectors at low speed and then apply them to the chip under test at high speed. When connected to output pins, the high-speed interface modules store up result vectors at high-speed and then send these vectors on to the microprocessor at low speed.

The clock and control module has two jobs. Job one is to distribute the high-speed clock, which is generated by an external programmable frequency generator. Although it is not shown in the block diagram, the frequency generator is attached to the microprocessor through an I/O port so that the microprocessor can control the clock frequency. Job two of the clock and control board is to synchronize, generate, and distribute all the required high-speed control signals.

The main purpose of the test head is to provide a method for connecting the chip under test to the high-speed interface modules without having to solder the chip down. The test head provides impedance-matched 50-ohm connections to all 24 I/O pins, and also provides the chip under test with power, ground, terminating voltage, and a method for dissipating heat.

Not shown on the block diagram of Figure 6 are the power supplies. The power supplies for the chip under test are completely separate from the supplies that

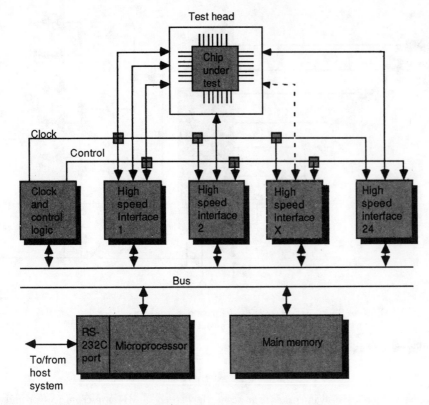

Figure 6. Overall system architecture of the tester.

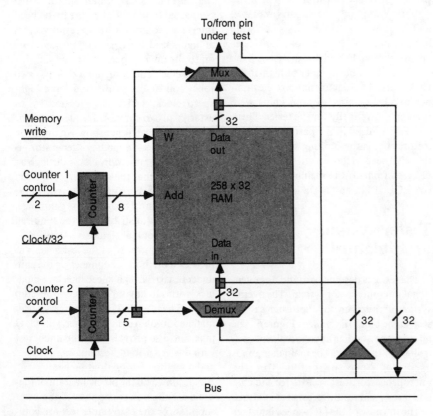

Figure 7. Memory-multiplexer architecture.

power the tester, and are connected to the microprocessor through an I/O port. This allows the microprocessor to control the power supply voltages to the chip under test. This makes the tester more versatile because it can test any chip, regardless of the chips power requirements, so long as the chip has appropriate external logic levels and noise margins.

The overall system design of Figure 6 has many advantages and few disadvantages. Some of the more important advantages of this system design are the following:

(1) All the high-speed parts of the tester can be controlled by the microprocessor, and because the microprocessor can be controlled by the host system, the tester is versatile, easy to use, and easy to reprogram.

(2) There is a minimum number of modules running at 1 GHz and, with the exception of the clock and control board, these modules are all the same.

(3) The tester can store a large amount of test vectors, result vectors, microprocessor software, and other information in its main memory.

(4) The tester can be easily expanded to test chips that have more than 24 I/O pins by adding more high-speed interface boards.

(5) Expansion to a stand-alone test system is straightforward, by adding a hard disk and an operating system.

The most crucial part of the tester, and the most difficult to design, is the high-speed interface module. Three competing architectures were evaluated before proceeding with the design of these modules. Selection of an architecture was based entirely on its ability to perform the necessary tasks at the required speed (1 GHz). The primary issues concern (1) the local storage of test and result vectors during the performance of a test, (2) the parallel-to-serial conversion of test vectors (in the input mode), and (3) the serial-to-parallel conversion of test results (in the output mode). Two of the architectures (memory-multiplexer and memory-shift register) provide for the storage of test vectors and result in a high-speed (ECL) RAM. The third architecture utilizes a long chain of GaAs shift registers for local data storage.

Memory-multiplexer architecture. The memory-multiplexer architecture (Figure 7) provides, for each pin of the chip under test, local storage capabilities for a 4096-bit

COMPUTER

test vector (or test result). Data is stored as 32-bit words in an ECL RAM. The custom GaAs components required in this architecture are a multiplexer, a demultiplexer, and some latches (not shown in Figure 7). Parallel-to-serial conversion of input test data is accomplished via a 32:1 multiplexer, controlled internally by a 5-bit counter. Conversely, serial-to-parallel conversion of test results is provided by a 1:32 demultiplexer.

The operation of the tester proceeds as follows. When configured for input (i.e., the pin under test is an input pin), data is loaded into the RAM in parallel from the microprocessor bus. RAM addresses are generated by the 8-bit counter, under control of the microprocessor. Loading of test data necessarily occurs at the speed of the MOS components and testing begins only after the entire test vector has been loaded into the RAM.

On initiation of the test, RAM addressing is again accomplished via the 8-bit counter, now running at the full clock speed of the test divided by 32. Thirty-two-bit words are applied to the multiplexer for parallel-to-serial conversion while, simultaneously, the next 32-bit word is accessed from the RAM. In the output mode, the demultiplexer/counter provides for the serial-to-parallel conversion of test results in an analogous manner to that described above.

A detailed analysis of the timing and synchronization requirements of this architecture brought to light a number of difficulties in implementation (see Figure 7). The most serious of these is the need for two high-speed clocks ("clock" and "clock/32" in the figure) operating in phase. At the full speed of the tester, correct operation requires tight synchronization between the ECL components operating at 31.25 MHz (in the figure, the 8-bit counter and RAM), and the custom GaAs components at 1 GHz (the 5-bit counter, multiplexer, demultiplexer, and latches in the figure).

Memory-shift register architecture. The memory shift-register architecture (Figure 8) for the high-speed interface modules is very similar to the memory-mux architecture in that local data storage is provided via an ECL RAM. The principal difference is that the parallel-to-serial/serial-to-parallel conversions are carried out by a GaAs shift register (with parallel I/O capabilities) rather than the multiplexer/demultiplexer combination. Operation is,

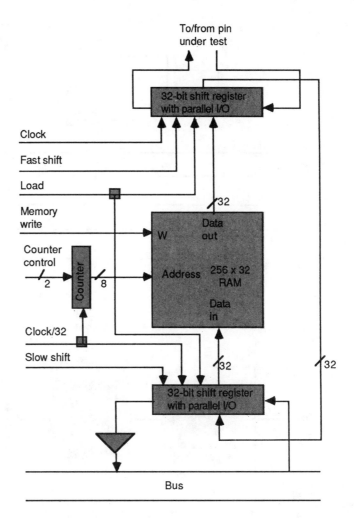

Figure 8. Memory-shift register architecture.

of course, similar to that of the memory-mux architecture.

The advantage of this architecture over the memory-multiplexer architecture is the use of a single (and possibly simpler) custom GaAs chip; all other components are off-the-shelf parts. However, the disadvantages associated with the complexity of control and synchronization at high speeds remain.

The shift register architecture. The third potential architecture for the high-speed interface module utilizes a chain of GaAs shift registers for local data storage, removing the control complexity imposed by the memory-based architectures. Figure 9 illustrates this architecture.

This approach maintains a number of advantages over the memory-based architectures and, as such, was chosen for implementation. Here, the speed of the

tester is limited by the speed of the shift register chain, rather than by the control circuitry. Additionally, only a single high-speed clock is required during test performance.

Two custom GaAs chips are required in this implementation: a 32-bit serial I/O shift register and a 4-bit parallel/serial I/O shift register. The size of the serial I/O shift register is constrained by die acreage and the parallel I/O component by packaging limitations (a 36-pad frame was provided for all the multiproject GaAs chips).

Operation of this tester is considerably simpler than the memory-based architectures discussed previously. In the input mode test vectors are loaded into the shift register chain, in parallel 4-bit words, from the microprocessor bus. The register is then shifted left 4 bits and another word is loaded. This cycle continues until the entire test vector is loaded into the shift chain. On

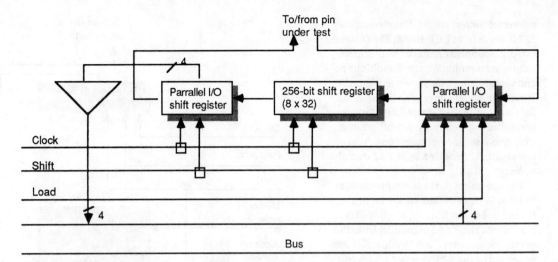

Figure 9. Shift register architecture.

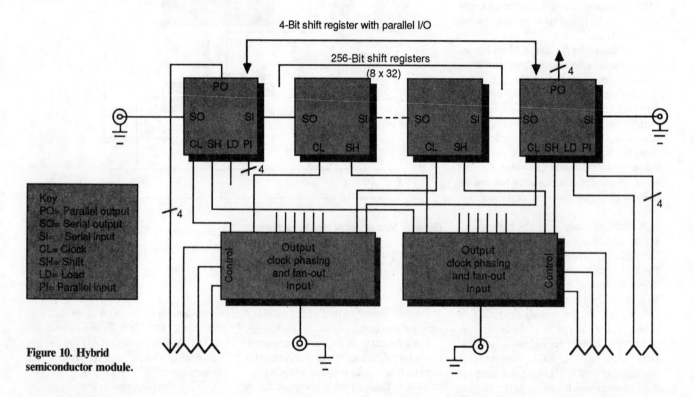

Figure 10. Hybrid semiconductor module.

Key
PO= Parallel output
SO= Serial output
SI= Serial input
CL= Clock
SH= Shift
LD= Load
PI= Parallel input

initiation of the test, the data are then applied to the pin under test at the speed of the programmable clock. Output pins are tested in a complementary fashion, with test results provided to the output shift register chains.

The current design allows for a test vector length of 264 bits. Expansion of test vector length can be accomplished by adding more shift registers to the chain.

Tester implementation

The tester is constructed around a VME system card cage and backplane. This allows the use of off-the-shelf microprocessor components for controlling the tester. The VME bus was chosen over other high-performance microprocessor buses because it has a large amount (64) of uncommitted backplane pins. These are used for distribution of power to the boards containing GaAs and ECL components, and as auxiliary grounds. The CPU board has a Motorola MC68000 microprocessor running at 8 MHz and a built-in PROM monitor. The CPU board also has three RS-232 serial ports for external communication and control. The RAM board contains 512K bytes of memory plus refresh circuitry. Future plans include the addition of a hard disk so that the tester can maintain its own library of diagnostics, automatic test generation software, and a small specialized operating system.

The tester's architecture follows all the guidelines that were set forth previously. The architecture is such that there are no high-speed buses, and thus very little high-speed interconnect exists between boards. The small amount of high-speed interconnect that does run between boards is done with coaxial cables and SMA connectors. The architecture is modular in design with most of the GaAs logic being contained in hybrid semiconductor modules of the type previously described. The modules are built on a 10-layer polyimide structure laminated to a copper substrate. Five of the polyimide layers are conducting layers and are used to create a 50-ohm stripline-type transmission line for use as a high-speed interconnect. Each module contains 12 custom GaAs digital ICs, 36 microwave "chip"-type capacitors for power supply bypassing, and several microwave "chip"-type resistors for terminating a high-speed interconnect. To aid in the dissipation of heat, all the ICs are mounted on thermal conduction columns connected through the polyimide layers to the heavy copper substrate. There are 15 low-speed I/O pins on each module, and four SMA connectors for high-speed I/O. A block diagram of the hybrid modules is shown in Figure 10.

A few of the chips used in the tester will not be placed in hybrid modules. These chips are to be packaged in leadless ceramic chip carriers that have been specially designed for packaging high-speed digital logic.[13] These are the same carriers used to package the chips to be tested by the tester. Because of certain restrictions, details on the carriers cannot be given in this article. Readers that are interested in the leadless ceramic chip carriers should obtain a copy of reference 13.

A block diagram of the high-speed interface boards is shown in Figure 11. There is one of these boards for every pin of the chip under test. Each board consists of one hybrid semiconductor module, and some associated logic for addressing, control, and logic level translation. Each board is configured as either an input or an output. If a board is configured as an output, then the serial output of the board's hybrid module is connected to the test head. If the board is configured as an input, then the serial input of the board's hybrid module is connected to the test head. Connections are made with coaxial cables and 12-GHz SMA connectors.

A block diagram of the clock and control board is shown in Figure 12. The main parts of this board are a pulse generator and some fan-out logic. The pulse generator is capable of generating a shift register control pulse that is from 1 to 264 clocks in length, and is synchronized with the high-speed clock. This is accomplished by loading a string of 1's of appropriate length into a high-speed shift register chain identical to those used for interfacing

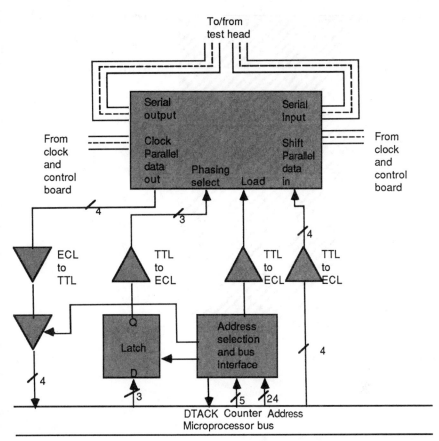

Figure 11. High-speed interface boards.

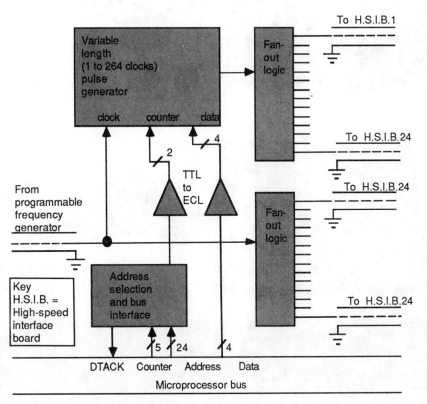

Figure 12. Clock and control board.

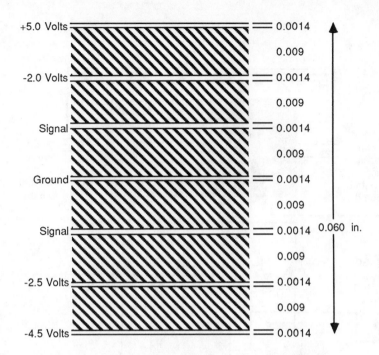

Figure 13. Tester PC boards.

to/from pins of the unit under test. As this register chain is clocked at full test speed, the result is the desired programmable pulse. After it has been generated, the shift control signal and the clock are distributed to the 24 high-speed interface modules. There is also some logic on the clock and control board for bus interface, address selection, and control.

The hybrid semiconductor modules and other components are mounted on fairly standard but carefully designed PCBs. The PCBs are 0.060-inch-thick multilayer glass-epoxy boards, as shown in Figure 13. There are seven conducting layers, five of them buried. The signal layers are sandwiched between two ac ground planes. This creates a 50-ohm stripline transmission line, which is used for all on-board high-speed interconnects. The high-speed interconnect is terminated with 50-ohm chip-type resistors, and all power planes are bypassed at all chip locations with chip-type capacitors. Off-board high-speed interconnect is done with coaxial cables and SMA connectors.

The purpose of the test head was mentioned in the previous section. Figure 14 shows the test head, along with two leadless ceramic chip carriers that fit into the test head. The test head fixture is constructed of a polyimide structure that is laminated to a copper substrate. The polyimide structure provides 50-ohm impedance-matched connections between the socket for the chip and the SMA connectors on the back of the substrate.

Tester operation

The tester is not a stand-alone unit, but operates as a slave to a personal computer, workstation, or mainframe computer. In Figure 6, a test is started by the host system loading input test vectors and other information into the tester's main memory through the RS-232C port. The microprocessor then takes over control of the tester and transfers the input test vectors and clock phasing commands, via the microprocessor bus, to the appropriate high-speed interface modules. Next, the frequency generator and power supplies are programmed to the values specified by the test. The clock and control board is then programmed with the length of the test vectors; this is done via the microprocessor bus.

At this point, everything is ready and the clock and control board is given a signal to

Figure 14. (a) Test head, top view; (b) test head, bottom view.

start the test. The clock and control board sends out a shift command to all the high-speed interface boards. The high-speed interface boards connected to input pins of the chip under test shift their data out to the test head. The high-speed interface boards connected to output pins of the chip under test shift in data from the test head. After the appropriate number of clocks (as specified by the length of the test vectors) the clock and control board stop the shifting, and control is returned to the microprocessor.

When a high-speed test has thus been completed, the result vectors are unloaded from the high-speed interface boards at low-speed, and stored in the main memory. The result vectors can either be sent back to the host or can be analyzed by the microprocessor. The tester can also be put into a loop mode, where the same test or a series of tests can be run over and over again. This mode of operation is useful for oscilloscope viewing and for testing certain state-intensive chips, for example, counters.

The tester also has the ability to perform functional tests on itself. This is useful for the following three reasons:

(1) It provides a means for initial debugging of the tester after construction.

(2) It provides a means for debugging the tester should the system fail.

(3) It serves as a confidence test to ensure that the tester is functioning properly.

The tester's self-test operates under the assumption that the power supplies are working correctly, that the RS-232C interface to the host system is working correctly, and that there is no failure in the system jamming the microprocessor bus. The test has three parts: a CPU board confidence test, a main memory confidence test, and a high-speed interface module functional test.

The CPU board confidence test is stored in EPROM on the CPU board and is run whenever the system is powered up, or whenever the reset switch on the front panel is pushed. The test exercises the microprocessor, the EPROM, and the memory mapping and protection circuitry to determine if they are functioning properly. If errors are detected, then appropriate messages are sent to the host system.

The main memory confidence test is also stored in EPROM on the CPU board. It is automatically run after the CPU board confidence test is run. It tests all locations

in memory for stuck bits, shorted bits, and address independence. Errors are reported to the host system.

The high-speed interface module functional test is performed under the control of the host system, and can be run whenever the user feels the need. The test requires that the user connect the input of every high-speed interface module to its own output. The host system then downloads specific test vectors to the tester. The tester is programmed to load the test vectors into the high-speed interface modules, and to program the clock and control board with the appropriate test vector length. The test vectors are then shifted out of each high-speed interface module and back around to each module's input. The vectors are then read out of the high-speed modules and checked for data corruption. Any errors are reported to the host system. This process is repeated several times with test vectors of various sizes, including the smallest and largest possible test vectors.

Future plans for the tester include the addition of a hard disk and a specialized operating system. With these additions it will be possible for the tester to operate as a stand-alone system, not requiring a host computer or workstation. Future plans also include the porting to the tester of automatic test generation software that is

currently under development at UCSB. This software will allow the tester to automatically generate input and result test vectors for a chip, given a description of the chip's logical functions.

We have designed and are building a very high speed digital system using GaAs custom integrated circuits. Because of the extremely fast signals, packaging and clocking considerations have dominated the architecture, leading to a modular design with local high-speed interconnects. The speed of the resulting system will be limited only by the speed of the GaAs custom parts and not by other portions of the architecture. □

Acknowledgments

The authors wish to thank Martin Buehler (Jet Propulsion Laboratory) both for his support and for his technical leadership on this project. We also thank Brent Blaes (also of JPL) and Joy Shetler (UCSB) for their chip designs and other technical contributions. The work described herein has been funded by DARPA under contract #NAS7-918.

References

1. W. Ponik, "Teradyne's J967 VLSI Test System," *IEEE Design & Test*, Dec. 1985, pp. 57-62.

2. T. Moore and S. Garner, "Autoprobing on the L200 Functional Tester," *IEEE Design & Test*, Dec. 1985, pp. 44-49.

3. R. Powell, "IBM's VLSI Logic Test System," *Proc. IEEE Int'l Test Conf.*, Phila., Pa., Nov. 1981, pp. 388-392.

4. S. E. Butner, "Testing and Characterizing Prototype VLSI Chips in a University Environment," *IEEE Phoenix Conf. Computers and Communications*, March 1985.

5. D. Carlton, K. Gleason, and E. Strid, "Microwave Wafer Probing Achieves On-Wafer Measurements Through 18 GHz," *MSN and Communications Tech.*, May 1985.

6. *F100K ECL User's Handbook*, Fairchild Camera and Instrument Corp., Mountain View, Calif., 1982.

7. D. Siewiorek and R. Swarz, *Theory and Practice of Reliable System Design*, Digital Press, Bedford, Mass., 1982.

8. E. Lekakis and S. Long, "Dynamic Performance Studies of GaAs IC's," *IEEE*

Trans. Elect. Dev., ED-30, Nov. 1983, pp. 1585-1586.

9. T. Takada, "A MESFET Variable Capacitance Model for GaAs IC Simulation," *IEEE Microwave Theory and Tech.*, MTT-30, May 1982, pp. 719-723.

10. A. Barna, *High-speed Pulse and Digital Techniques*, John Wiley & Sons, New York, 1980.

11. K. C. Gupta, R. Garg, and R. Chadha, *Computer-Aided Design of Microwave Circuits*, Artech House, Dedham, Mass., 1981, pp. 57-72.

12. A. Feller, H.R. Kaupp, and J.J. Diagiacomo, "Crosstalk and Reflections in High-Speed Digital Systems," *Proc. Fall Joint Computer Conf.*, 1965, pp. 511-525.

13. B.K. Gilbert, *Leadless Chip Carrier Packaging and CAD/CAM-Supported Wire Wrap Interconnect Technology for Subnanosecond ECL*, Mayo Clinic/Mayo Foundation, Special-Purpose Processor Development Group, Dept. of Physiology/Biophysics; Avionics Laboratory, Air Force Wright Aeronautical Laboratories, Air Force Systems Command, Wright-Patterson Air Force Base, Ohio 45433, pp. 4-22.

Douglas J. Fouts is a teaching associate, research assistant, and PhD student in the Department of Electrical and Computer Engineering at the University of California at Santa Barbara. His current research interests include computer architecture and the design of high-clock-rate digital systems, GaAs IC design, VLSI design, and system software.

Fouts received his bachelor's degree in computer science from the University of California at Berkeley in l980, and his MS degree in electrical and computer engineering from UCSB in 1984. From 1980 to 1983 he worked as a design engineer for Burroughs Corporation (now Unisys). A member of the Computer Society of the IEEE and of the ACM's SIGArch, Fouts is also the first trombone player of the Algorhythms, the UCSB CS/ECE Department jazz band.

John M. Johnson is a research assistant and teaching associate in the Department of Electrical and Computer Engineering at the University of California, Santa Barbara. His research interests include asynchronous GaAs architectures, digital integrated circuits, multiple-valued logic, and VLSI design.

Johnson received the BS degree in electrical engineering from Worcester Polytechnic Institute in 1978 and the MS degree in electrical and computer engineering from UCSB in 1984. He is currently working toward the PhD degree in electrical and computer engineering at USCB. From 1978 to 1983 he was a design engineer with Raytheon Company, working primarily in the area of digital subsystem design for radar and electronic countermeasures systems. Johnson is a Hughes Aircraft, Santa Barbara Research Center fellow and a member of the IEEE and the Computer Society of the IEEE.

Steven Butner is an assistant professor of electrical and computer engineering at the Santa Barbara campus of the University of California. His research interests include design for testability, test generation, and computer architecture for high-performance and/or high-reliability applications.

Butner received the BS-EE degree from the University of Kansas (1969), the MS-EE from the University of Pennsylvania (1971), and the PhD (EE) from Stanford University (1982). He has industrial experience with General Electric, Honeywell, GTE, and Bell Northern Research. He is a member of IEEE, ACM, and Tau Beta Pi.

Stephen I. Long joined the Electrical and Computer Engineering Department of the University of California, Santa Barbara in 1981, and is currently a professor. His research interests are in the design and fabrication of high-speed III-V compound semiconductor devices and GaAs digital and analog integrated circuits.

Long received a BS degree in engineering physics from the University of California, Berkeley in 1967, and an MS and PhD degree in electrical engineering from Cornell University in 1969 and 1974, respectively. A senior member of IEEE and a member of Tau Beta Pi, he received the IEEE Microwave Applications Award for development of InP mm-wave devices in 1978.

Readers may write to Butner at the Department of Electrical and Computer Engineering, University of California, Santa Barbara, CA 93106.

The Role of Gallium Arsenide in Highly Parallel Symbolic Multiprocessors

Michael L. Morgan
Magnavox Electronic Systems Company
Fort Wayne, Indiana

Abstract

Highly parallel processors have been shown to have enormous potential in symbolic computing over the past few years. Likewise, gallium arsenide (GaAs) technology has recently demonstrated VLSI capability; GaAs processing elements for multiprocessors should soon be feasible. Because of the limitations of off-chip memory access speed in GaAs, and the expected limit of about 30,000 transistors, GaAs processors cannot simply be copies of existing silicon designs. This paper explores the issues of processing element complexity, or granularity, and interprocessor communications, for highly parallel computers. A design for a medium-grained GaAs processing element optimized for LISP, with general communications, is described.

1. INTRODUCTION

One ingredient for powerful, cost-effective knowledge-based systems is faster processors. This goal is being pursued by a variety of means, including multiprocessors, innovative architectures, and materials with higher electron mobility. In this paper we explore the effects of combining these means, and describe the design of a gallium-arsenide-based processing element for a highly parallel symbolic multiprocessor.

1.1 HIGHLY PARALLEL MULTIPROCESSORS

The recent demand for higher speed knowledge-based systems has made it clear that highly parallel processors will play an important role in the future of computer design. These machines may be characterized as having either a large number of simple processors, called fine-grained machines, or a smaller number of more complex processors, called coarse-grained machines. There are, of course, tradeoffs between these two extremes, called medium-grained multiprocessors.

One advantage claimed for fine-grained architectures is that, since the processing elements (PEs) are simpler, they are less expensive, allowing more of them. This advantage is offset to some extent by the fact most algorithms in use today were written for uniprocessors. Even proponents of fine-grained machines acknowledge that it will be difficult to take advantage of the tens of thousands or even millions of processors which these machines will contain. In those algorithms which can take advantage of massive parallelism, the limiting factor on speed becomes the communications bandwidth between processors.

At the other end of the granularity spectrum is the coarse-grained machine. The ultimate coarse-grained machine is the uniprocessor. The speed of these machines is limited by the raw ability of the PEs to execute instructions. Not all computations can be speeded up by parallelism; coarse-grained machines offer a high-speed alternative for these largely serial algorithms.

Much of the research in the fine-grained architectures has been concentrated on finding new ways to partition computations across vast numbers of processors, and in improving communications between processors. In the uniprocessor community, much of the work is concerned with making individual processors fast. Coarse-grained architectures are often based on networks of fast, off-the-shelf uniprocessors, such as the Motorola 68000 or 68020. Since they use off-the-shelf technology and require relatively few changes to existing algorithms, these machines offer the best short-term solution to the need for increased speed.

In the long run, however, there is a mounting body of evidence that a fine-grained machine with a general interprocessor communications system offers significant advantages over the coarse-grained approach. Hillis (1) has suggested that an architecture may be measured using five parameters:

(1) Size of Memory, in bits

(2) Memory Bandwidth, in bits per second

(3) Processor Bandwidth, in bits per second, without regard for instruction complexity

(4) Communications Bandwidth: total memory size divided by the time required to perform an arbitrary permutation of all the bits in memory

(5) Input/Output Bandwidth in bits per second

Uniprocessors and coarse-grained multiprocessors have a much lower ratio of processing power to memory and thus, by these measures, are less powerful than fine-grained architectures. It is still not clear what advances in software will have to occur to take advantage of this power.

Arvind and Iannucci (2) have suggested two issues which test a processor's power:

(1) ability to tolerate memory latency

(2) ability to share data without constraining parallelism

Although the correlation of these issues with granularity is far from clear, it appears that in fine-grain implementations which associate memory with each PE, such as the Connection Machine, these issues are less of a concern than they are in coarse-grain machines.

A compromise position, often viewed as an extension of coarse-grained systems, is medium granularity. Medium-grained systems typically have several hundred to several thousand processors. The definitions and boundaries between the categories of granularity are necessarily fuzzy.

1.2 GALLIUM ARSENIDE

One approach to increasing the speed of PEs is to change the material on which the processor is built. Digital gallium arsenide (GaAs) circuits are now available in VLSI. Gate arrays containing eight-thousand gates were announced in 1986; even higher densities are expected. It is now possible to consider GaAs in the implementation of high performance processors.

GaAs offers about half an order of magnitude or more speed increase compared with silicon TTL. However, capacitive loading and speed-of-light limitations affect GaAs and silicon equally; the result is that the ratio of GaAs off-chip to on-chip memory access is about half of the corresponding value for silicon (3). In addition, the cost of GaAs is about two orders of magnitude higher than silicon, although this is expected to drop to about one order of magnitude by the end of the decade.

An additional limitation of GaAs is the number of devices. In order to increase yield and to to keep power dissipation below two watts, it is necessary to limit the chip to about 30,000 transistors. Compared with the transistor demands of most coarse-grain processors, this is a very small number. The Motorola 68020, for example, has nearly 200,000 transistors. It is possible, however, to build much smaller processors without sacrificing generality or speed. This is shown by the existence of the Reduced Instruction Set Computers (RISCs) such as RISC and SU-MIPS. Table 1 shows the transistor counts of some of these machines, and some Complex Instruction Set Computers (CISCs) for comparison:

Processor	Transistors (K)	Produced by
RISC I	44	Univ. of California at Berkeley
RISC II	41	Univ. of California at Berkeley
SOAR	35	Univ. of California at Berkeley
MIPS	25	Stanford
Z8000	18	Zilog
M68000	68	Motorola
M68020	190	Motorola
iAPX-432	110	Intel
Focus	450	Hewlett-Packard

TABLE 1. TRANSISTOR COUNTS

2. TRADEOFFS

The use of GaAs offers another alternative in the fine-grain/coarse-grain spectrum described above. It is possible to build a multiprocessor with a small number (on the order of a hundred) medium-grain GaAs processors, each of which is about ten times faster than its silicon counterpart. The weakness of such a design is that, unless care is used in programming and in processor allocation, communications time will dominate the computation and act as the limiting factor. The strength is that programming is less of a concern than it is on processors with hundreds of thousands of PEs; in many algorithms there is enough natural parallelism to support several tens of processors. This is especially true in many artificial intelligence applications, in which much of the work is in searching a large graph.

2.1 ISSUES IN MULTIPROCESSING

2.1.1 Granularity

As processors become less complex in fine-grained architectures, it becomes necessary to limit the width of data paths. This makes it necessary to perform serially many instructions which might otherwise be performed in parallel. On a machine which is used heavily for floating-point operations this can present a serious problem. In most symbolic applications, however, the data type for most operations is a pointer which can be passed down an address bus. Arithmetic and Logic Unit (ALU) operations are primariliy simple comparisons and arithmetic on small integers. In these applications a narrow data path in the ALU which can perform the most common operations in a single cycle can outweigh the problems of having to process wider operands serially.

One way to address the granularity issue is to define *virtual processors*. Virtual processors may be larger or smaller than the physical PE. If larger, the physical PEs must communicate in order to complete the work of the virtual PE. If smaller, one physical PE may emulate several virtual PEs. As long as the virtual PE is smaller than the physical PE, no adverse effect on the loading of the communications network is seen. Having a virtual PE which is smaller than a physical PE does, however, force the physical PE to execute serially what might otherwise be executed in parallel. Defining virtual PEs in software allows the system designer and user to trade overall network speed for cost. Furthermore, the tradeoff between communications network loading and PE loading can be balanced by adjusting the size of the virtual PEs on an algorithm-by-algorithm basis.

2.1.2 Communications

It has already been pointed out that, as the number of processors increase, the percentage of total time consumed by interprocessor communications increases. This means that the overall bandwidth of the communications network must be as high as possible. The relationships between network topology, bandwidth, and scalability and extensibility, are well described in Hillis (4), Hwang and Briggs (5), and in Seitz (6). In general, topologies such as hypercubes, which add bandwidth as the number of processors increases, offer the greatest bandwidth and scalability.

2.1.3 Control

Another issue which must be addressed in designing a multiprocessor is whether instructions should operate on all PEs or only on a single PE. In the first alternative, there is a single instruction stream, often stored on a host computer, and multiple data streams, one on each PE. This style of control is characterized as SIMD (for Single Instruction stream, Multiple Data stream). An alternative is to allow each processor to control its own execution. This is known as MIMD, for Muliple Instruction stream, Multiple Data stream. At issue is the tradeoff between speed and network loading. In a SIMD each instruction must be broadcast over the network. In a MIMD each processor loads the next instruction out of its own local memory.

2.1.4 Fault Tolerance

Even with the high reliability of VLSI, a machine consisting of many hundreds or thousands of components will have an unacceptable rate of failure unless some provision is made for components to fail. In a multiprocessor network it is often possible to choose a communications topology which has redundant paths. This ensures that a PE will not become isolated if one or two of its neighbors should fail.

2.1.5 Scalability and Extendability

As costs for VLSI continue to decrease, and as demand for processing power climbs, it will be necessary to build larger and more powerful networks of processors. A *scalable* architecture is one in which larger versions of the machine can be built for a linear cost increase. An *extensible* architecture is one which is incrementally scalable. In an extensible machine all that is required to add processing power is to add another rack or board of PEs.

2.2 THE ROLE OF GALLIUM ARSENIDE

As part of the "Advanced Microprocessors and High-Level Language Computer Architectures" course offered at Purdue University during the fall of 1985, one component of a GaAs multiprocessor, the high speed processing element, was designed. This project, the Gallium Arsenide Experimental Lisp Integrated Circuit (Gaelic) was based on a combination of three technologies: symbolic computing, gallium arsenide, and the RISC approach to architecture design.

Gaelic assumes that issues such as network topology and control are best decided indepenent of the underlying technology. This is done by defining virtual PEs which are independent of GaAs or silicon tradeoffs, and then adjusting the number of virtual PEs which execute on a physical PE. Thus, a single very fast GaAs processor might carry the same number of virtual PEs as several silicon processors.

An overview of the Gaelic design objectives, architecture, and performance is given below.

3. THE HIGH SPEED PROCESSING ELEMENT

The principal design objectives of Gaelic were to maximize the speed of execution for symbolic programs, and to minimize the

transistor count so that the design would fit into GaAs. RISC architecture was fundamental in achieving both objectives.

3.1 RISC

The RISC design philosophy is as follows:

For the instruction set design,
  (1) First, identify the machine instructions most
      frequently used by the target applications.

  (2) Second, optimize the datapath and timing for these
      instructions.

  (3) Finally, add other instructions to the instruction set
      only if they can be supported by the already-defined
      data path.

For the incorporation of resources, add a new resource only if it is justified by the frequency of use, and if its incorporation will not slow down other resources which are frequently used.

Because the resulting instruction set will not contain many of the complex instructions found in more traditional processors, it is necessary to synthesize such instructions with the compiler. One of the fundamental arguments in favor of RISC is that the resulting object code, which may require more memory than the code on conventional machines, will execute more quickly, since the data path of the RISC is faster than the data path of an equivalent CISC.

The instruction set of Gaelic provides direct support for many LISP primitives. This is because these are the instructions which occur most frequently in LISP programs. This approach differs from the approach used for the Language-Directed Architectures (LDA) which have been widely described. In an LDA the instruction set is intended to closely resemble the statements of the target language. LDA machines have a large, rich instruction set which makes the work of the compiler almost trivial. LISP programmers usually program in complex functions which are, themselves, based on user- or system-defined functions. The complier must decompose these functions into the underlying LISP primitives for execution on Gaelic.

3.2 LISP

Although few large knowledge-based systems are implemented directly in LISP, LISP is usually present at a lower level of the implementation. That is, most knowledge engineers construct their programs in a shell or tool which is, itself, LISP-based. The resulting code is either compiled into LISP or is interpreted by an interpreter which is written in LISP. Furthermore, in those cases where the tool is written in another language, such as C, it has often evolved from a Lisp-based tool, and can benefit from a Lisp-like instruction set. For these reasons LISP was chosen as the target language of Gaelic.

In order to determine which instructions were called most frequently, three sources were examined:

(1) first, the literature on LISP and other symbolic languages

(2) second, the literature on symbolic programs in general purpose languages

(3) third, a small LISP interpreter was built and instrumented to report both static and dynamic usage.

In addition to instruction frequency, several other language parameters were identified which influence architectural decisions. These include the type and source of operands, locality of nesting depth, and variable scoping in procedure calls, instruction and data locality (both spatial and temporal), and the automatic management of storage for dynamic data.

Many LISP programs spend substantial time in garbage collection. Beyond that, LISP code is characterized by high percentages of the following instructions:

(1) call/return

(2) very simple ALU operations such as EQ

(3) CAR (returns the first element of a list)

(4) CDR (returns all but the first element of a list)

(5) CONS (used to build new lists)

(6) COND (LISP's IF statement)

LISP, like many languages, requires fast access to operands. This can be a serious problem in a GaAs design, since the number of cycles required to access off-chip data is much longer than in a silicon design. Yet in GaAs, there is little room for on-chip caches or large register files.

The number of procedure calls in LISP can become quite large. Most programs, however, are dominated by a call pattern of the form "call to depth k, make a significant number of calls from

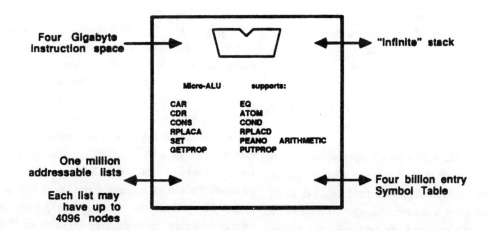

FIGURE 1. COMPILER'S VIEW OF GAELIC PE

level *k* and higher but mostly within a few levels of *k*, before backing out."

3.3 GAELIC ARCHITECTURE

Figure 1 shows the compiler-view of the Gaelic chip itself. Note that there are four address spaces associated with Gaelic: instruction space, list space, the stack, and the symbol table.

To manage these four address spaces, six supporting units are required:

(1) Instruction Manager — keeps track of program progress (the program counters (PCs) are maintained here). Maintains an instruction prefetch buffer and a history stack of old PCs. Executes directives from the compiler, termed *pseudoinstructions*.

(2) Instruction Cache — a backing cache for the instruction manager

(3) Garbage collector — a separate processor which collects garbage and compacts list space in parallel with Gaelic processing (7)

(4) List space — memory for lists. A portion of this address space extends onto the Gaelic chip.

(5) Auxiliary Memory — provides storage for the stack. The top of the stack extends onto the Gaelic chip.

(6) Symbol Space — provides storage for atoms and their attributes. A portion of the symbol table may reside on the Gaelic chip in part of the region normally used for list space.

The Gaelic supporting units are shown in figure 2. Support for coprocessors or memory-mapped I/O may be provided by additional off-chip units.

To the user Gaelic appears as a pure Lisp machine which supports a wide variety of Lisp constructs. Lisp makes no distinction between hardware-supported functions and those defined by the user or in a run-time library. Therefore the "large" LISPs such as Common Lisp, ZetaLisp and Interlisp can run efficiently on Gaelic. Note, however, that many programs in these languages also make extensive use of integer and floating-point arithmetic and array data structures. While

instructions to support these features can be synthesized on Gaelic, it will often be more suitable to run such programs on a multiprocessor which includes both symbolic and numeric processors, so that numeric-intensive code is not run on Gaelic.

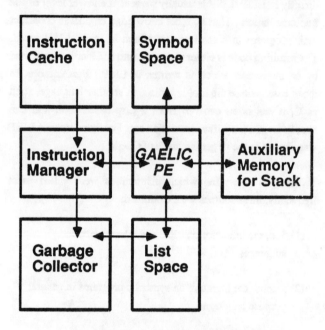

FIGURE 2. SUPPORTING UNITS

Since Gaelic's machine language is so close to the Lisp primitives themselves, the compiler takes the form of a simple code generator and a more complex optimizer. The output of the code generator is executable, but will not be efficient. A series of post-generation optimizing steps rearrange the code to take advantage of the microarchitecture, filling wait states and increasing locality.

The micro-ALU is best defined in terms of what it does *not* support. Gaelic does not support any form of byte or bit manipulation, nor is there any user-accessible form of shift. It is impossible for the user to gain access to the internal representation of lists or atoms. There is no hardware support for floating point numbers, arrays, strings, or records. There is no multiplication in any form; there is no addition or subtraction except for Peano arithmetic (add 1, subtract 1). There is no logical or bitwise AND, OR, XOR, or NOT. There is no provision for testing arithmetic conditions such as less-than, greater-than, or equal-to. There is an EQ predicate, which is primarily intended for comparing atoms to see if they are the same. It is not guaranteed to work on numbers outside the range (−128…127). Because of these extreme limitations in what can at best be called a micro-ALU, most of the instruction

Instruction	Function	
ADD1	Increment element on top of stack	
SUB1	Decrement element on top of stack	
CAR	Returns pointer to first element of list pointed to by top-of-stack	
CDR	Returns pointer to the list which begins with the element following the CAR	
CONS	Builds and returns pointer to the list whose CAR is top-of-stack and whose CDR is the second element on the stack	
BOT	Branch on true to operand	
RPLACA	Equivalent to CAR, but replaces rather than constructs	
RPLACD	Equivalent to CDR, but replaces rather than constructs	
SET	Assigns a value in the symbol table	
PUTPROP	Place a value on a property list	
GETPROP	Return a value on a property list	
EQ	Return T if top two elements of stack are equal	
ATOM	Return T if Top-of-stack points to an atom	
NUMBERP	Return T if Top-of-stack points to a numeric atom	
BIND	Make top-of-stack the value of the atomic operand	
UNBIND	Pop the value stack of the atomic operand	
CALL	Enter function	(Pseudoinstruction)
RETURN	Exit from function	(Pseudoinstruction)
QUOTE	Treats operand like a literal	(Pseudoinstruction)
PROG/RETURN	Set up interative control	(Pseudoinstruction)

TABLE 2. GAELIC INSTRUCTION SET

set typically seen in a microprocessor must be synthesized.

Note also that, because there is no program counter on Gaelic, there are no branch instructions in the traditional sense. There are limited branches, but they are used only as part of the synthesis for COND, CALL, DO, RETURN, and similar instructions.

All ALU instructions are performed relative to the stack. There are no data or address registers. Items are pushed onto the stack using the PUSH instruction from either the symbol table (atoms) or list space. Items are popped from the stack as instructions use them up.

The symbol table may be thought of as a specialized list, in which each element is as shown in figure 3. It will be seen that atoms are more complex than the variables of conventional programming languages. When the value of the atom is one of the self-evaluating atoms such as NIL or a small number, that value is stored explicitly in the atom. When the value is more complex, such as a list, a pointer is stored into list or symbol space as necessary.

The print names may be stored in a reserved region of list space as desired by the compiler designer. Many running programs will have no need to retain print names for most atoms.

At compile time, DEFUN (DEfine FUNction) associates a function definition with an atom. Thus, the function definition pointer will normally point to an address in instruction space. Run-time evaluation and definition of functions is handled as an exception.

The property list is a list of associative pairs stored with each atom. It is accessed by the instructions GETPROP and PUTPROP.

The Lisp equivalent of variable assignment is *binding*. A BIND causes the current value of an atom to be pushed onto a stack which is "hidden" behind the value field. The top of the stack is popped into the value field. No other field in the symbol table is affected. UNBIND reverses the procedure, destroying the old value.

Gaelic uses a compact list representation developed at the University of Illinois at Urbana by Sohi *et al* (8). This representation is based on the fact that Lisp lists are, with few exceptions, simple binary trees. These exceptions are stored in an *exception table* (ET). Exceptions may occur in Gaelic for only five reasons:

(1) nonnumeric atom

(2) numeric atom

(3) end-of-list found

(4) reference counter greater than one

(5) forwarding pointer, pointing to another exception table.

Nodes on the binary tree are numbered by three rules:

(1) The base node of an ET is numbered 1.

(2) The CAR of node n is at node 2n unless node 2n has an exception.

(3) The CDR of node n is at node 2n + 1 unless node 2n + 1 has an exception.

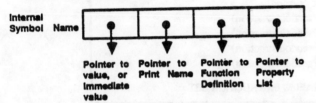

FIGURE 3. INTERNAL REPRESENTATION OF SYMBOL

On Gaelic, the on-chip exception tables are stored in an associative memory. Thus, to find the CAR of node n, the following algorithm is used:

1. Present (CAR n) = 2n to the list file.

2a. If no exception is found, the CAR is at node 2n. Push 2n onto the stack.

2b. If "multiple reference count" exception is found, ignore it. CAR is at 2n.

If either of the "atom" exceptions is found, look up the name of the atom in the ET, and return it on the stack.

If "end-of-list" has been found, return NIL on the stack.

If a forwarding pointer is found, present the forwarding pointer to the list file and go to step 2.

3.4 GAELIC MICROARCHITECTURE

Gaelic uses a hardwired instruction decoder rather than a microprogram. This uses far less space on the chip, and is made feasible by the streamlined instruction set. A block diagram of the Gaelic microarchitecture is shown in figure 4.

Gaelic is a pipelined architecture. The four stages are Instruction Fetch, Instruction Decode, Execute, and Operand Write.

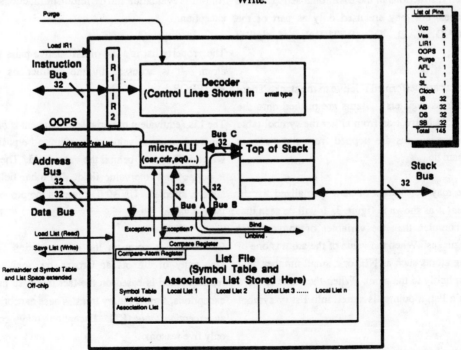

FIGURE 4. GAELIC MICROARCHITECTURE

Four stages were chosen as a compromise between the extra transistors needed to manage additional stages and the speedup available from increased pipelining. In GaAs the greatest delays are anticipated in any off-chip memory access; the chip has therefore been designed to minimize off-chip traffic. A new instruction fetch is normally initiated every fourth machine cycle.

Opcodes for Gaelic fit within a single byte. Since nearly all instructions are stack-oriented, few instructions require more than a single byte for complete encoding. This allows up to four instructions to be packed into one 32-bit word, quadrupling effective instruction bus bandwidth.

Note that two instruction registers (IR1 and IR2) are supported on-chip, for a total of eight instructions available at any given time. These registers appear on the instruction bus, but are also multiplexed onto the stack bus. This allows instructions to be placed in the inactive IR prior to many conditional branches, minimizing wait states due to off-chip memory access. The control signal LOAD IR1 is used to control which register is being loaded from the Instruction Manager.

Consider a function FOO, which processes the elements of a list by processing the first element, and then recursively processing the rest of the list. The function is finished when the end of the list is reached (that is, when the CDR is nil). This is a common construct in Lisp functions.

Since a typical list will have only one nil CDR, FOO will execute many times without taking the branch. When the branch *is* taken, the hardware asserts the OOPS signal to alert the Instruction Manager that it is branching. The processor then checks to see if IR2 is valid. If so, it takes the next fetch from IR2. If not, it waits while the target instruction is pushed onto the chip from the Instruction Manager.

When the instruction stream switches to IR2, the Instruction Manager looks for the next PRELOAD instruction and pushes the next branch target into IR1 on the next free bus cycle. Thus the number of times that the processor must wait for an off-chip fetch is very small, and is confined to those sequences which issue a series of rapid branches interspersed with heavy stack activity.

Since Gaelic fetches on every fourth machine cycle, when a branch is taken there are at most five instructions on-chip (four

in the IR, one being decoded). The processor continues to execute these until the Instruction Manager asserts the control signal PURGE. This allows the optimizer to attempt to fill the slots following a branch with an instruction which does not depend on the stack. For example, the compiler may be able to unbind those atoms which are no longer needed.

During the Instruction Decode stage the instruction is identified by the hardware. The hardware checks for the presence of any required operands. If they are not yet present they are brought on-chip, into the on-chip associative memory. This stage is also used for the management of the stack, symbol table, property lists, and exception tables.

The Execute stage is the most complex stage in the pipeline, since instructions may iterate before completing. An example of this is the recursive definition of CAR, given earlier. Most other instructions are performed along the same lines as CAR.

During the Operand Write stage the instruction manager and the processor take care of any stack, symbol, or list space evacuations. Preloads initiated now will usually be ready by the next Execute stage. The compiler tries to use the slack time during this stage to get the processor ready for the next instruction. This readying process is invisible to the Lisp programmer, but serves to minimize wait states by having operands on-chip when they are required.

4. PERFORMANCE

When clocked at 1 GHz, and with all wait states optimized out, the Gaelic simulators suggest that Gaelic will execute at speeds approaching 1000 MIPS. Including wait states decreases the effective speed by a factor of two to five, depending upon the efficiency of the optimizer. Thus, Gaelic executes its near-LISP machine code at about 300 MIPS. If the program is a typical AI program, such as a backward-chaining inference engine, this is equivalent to between 300,000 and 3 million logical inferences per second (LIPS). When used as part of a 128 PE MIMD hypercube, network speeds on the order of 15 billion LIPS are possible.

5. CONCLUSIONS

The use of RISC architecture, including a compact list representation and parallel garbage collector, results in a processing element capable of performing between ten and 100 times as fast as many commercially available symbolic processors. When used as part of a multiprocessor, speeds are well in excess of the fastest uniprocessors.

While GaAs makes significant speed increases possible, it does so at the cost of relatively long off-chip accesses, and a small transistor budget. Gaelic solves the first problem by using an on-chip associative list file and several on-chip top-of-stack registers. It gets this additional space by dispensing with many features normally found in a processor, such as a microcode ROM and a large ALU.

Additional research is required in this area. VLSI is only now becoming available on GaAs. High speed, high density chip packaging must be perfected. More exploration into the impacts of architecture on performance are required, both within the processing element and in a multiprocessor. As these questions are addressed, the goal of high speed symbolic computing will become economically viable and technologically feasible.

REFERENCES

(1) Hillis, W. Daniel. *The Connection Machine*, The MIT Press, 1985, pages 55 to 59.

(2) Arvind, and Robert A. Iannucci. "A Critique of Multiprocessing von Neumann Style", *Proc. 10th Int. Symp. on Computer Architecture*, June 13 – 17, 1983, pages 426 to 436.

(3) Milutinovic, Veljko, David Fura, and Walter Helbig. "An Introduction to GaAs Microprocessor Architecture for VLSI", *Computer*, March, 1986, page 32.

(4) Hillis, W. Daniel, *op cit.*, pages 67 to 69.

(5) Hwang, Kai, and Fayé A. Briggs. *Computer Architecture and Parallel Processing*, McGraw Hill, 1984, pages 325 to 355 and 481 to 508.

(6) Seitz, Charles L.. "Concurrent VLSI Architectures", *IEEE Transactions on Computers*, Vol. C-33, No. 12, December 1984, pages 1247 to 1265.

(7) Ram, Ashwin, and Janak H. Patel (1985). "Parallel Garbage Collection without Synchronization Overhead", *Proc. 12th Int. Symp. on Computer Architecture*, June, 1985, pp. 84-90.

(8) Sohi, Gurindar S., Edward S. Davidson, and Janak H. Patel. "An Efficient LISP-Execution Architecture with a New Representation for List Structures", *Proc. 12th Int. Symp. on Computer Architecture*, June 1985, pp. 91-98.

(9) Hennessy, John L. "VLSI Processor Architecture", *IEEE Transactions on Computers*, Vol. C-33, No. 12, December 1984.

(10) Beyers, Joseph W., Louis J. Dohse, Joseph P. Fucetola, Richard L. Kochis, Clifford G. Lob, Gary L. Taylor, and Eugene R. Zeller. "A 32-Bit VLSI CPU Chip", *IEEE J. Solid-State Circuits*, vol SC-16, October 1981, pp. 537-541.

(11) Pei, S. S., N. J. Shah, R. H. Hendel, C. W. Tu, and R. Dingle (1984). "Ultra High Speed Integrated Circuits with Selectively Doped Heterostructure Transistors", *1984 GaAs IC Symposium Technical Digest*.

(12) Sussman, Gerald Jay, Jack Holloway, Guy Lewis Steel, Jr., and Alan Bell. "Scheme-79 — Lisp on a Chip", *Computer*, Vol. 14, No. 7, July 1981.

(13) Ungar, David, Ricki Blau, Peter Foley, Dain Samples, and David Patterson. "Architecture of SOAR: Smalltalk on a RISC", *Proceedings of the 10th Annual International Symposium on Computer Architecture*, June 13 – 17, 1983.

(14) Veghdahl, Steven R. "A Survey of Proposed Architectures for the Execution of Functional Languages", *IEEE Transactions of Computers*, Vol C-33, No. 12, December 1984, page 1054.

Michael Morgan is a computer scientist on the staff of the Modernization Program Office of Magnavox. He is responsible for the design of a number of knowledge-based systems, including MEND, a self-improving diagnostic with deep knowledge, and GRILL, a natural language interface to VLSI design databases. His interests include machine learning, natural language processing, and architectures for symbolic processing.

Mr. Morgan holds a Master of Science in Systems Management from Florida Institute of Technology, and a Bachelor of Science in Mathematics from Wheaton College. He is presently completing a Master of Science in Computer Science from the National Technological University.

Chapter 5: Case Study: The Design of a GaAs Microprocessor

This chapter describes the activity behind the design of a 32-bit gallium arsenide (GaAs) microprocessor, along with a description of that processor.

The first paper, entitled "A Study of Pipeline Design for Gallium Arsenide Processors" by Milutinović, Fura, and Helbig, presents experimental results from a processor pipeline study. The authors discuss the motivation for performing the experiment, describe their evaluation methodology, and present their results, which indicate that instruction pipelines with additional stages are most effective in combating long instruction fetch latencies.

The second paper, entitled "Instruction Format Study for a 32-Bit GaAs Microprocessor" by Milutinović, Fura, and Helbig, presents experimental results from an instruction format study. The authors discuss their motivation for performing the experiment and describe their evaluation methodology. They present their results, which indicate that instruction formats with shorter immediate fields or fewer address fields can save code space at the cost of a slight performance penalty. On the other hand, this code size reduction increases the efficiency of cache memory.

"Multiplier/Shifter Design Tradeoffs in a 32-Bit GaAs Microprocessor" by Milutinović, Bettinger, and Helbig presents experimental results from a multiplier/shifter study. The authors discuss the motivation for performing the experiment, describe their evaluation methodology, and present the results together with the related tradeoffs.

"Adder Design Tradeoffs in a 32-Bit GaAs Microprocessor" by Milutinović, Bettinger, and Helbig presents experimental results from a study that compared different adder designs. The authors discuss their motivation for performing the experiment and they describe their evaluation methodology. They present the results, which indicate that serial adder designs have some important advantages (in the GaAs environment) over parallel adder designs.

Helbig and Milutinović describe a 32-bit GaAs microprocessor developed by RCA Corporation in their paper entitled "A DCFL E/D-MESFET GaAs Experimental RISC Machine." They describe the characteristics of the used GaAs technology, introduce the methodology that was used to guide many of their design choices, and briefly summarize the design and the architecture of this experimental microprocessor.

EH0266-7/88/0000/0287$01.00 © 1988 IEEE

A Study of Pipeline Design for Gallium Arsenide Processors*

Veljko Milutinović and David Fura
School of Electrical Engineering
Purdue University
West Lafayette, Indiana 47907
(317) 494-3530

Walter Helbig
Advanced Technology Laboratories
RCA
Moorestown, New Jersey 08057
(609) 866-6530

Abstract

We present here the results of a study related to the design of the instruction pipeline for a 32-bit single-chip gallium arsenide (GaAs) microprocessor. We introduce nine candidate solutions for the instruction pipeline, define a set of technology-dependent and application-related parameters, and present the results of our comparative performance evaluation. We point to important differences between GaAs and silicon, which are relevant for the design of an instruction pipeline, and we determine the quantitative differences between various candidate solutions, which is the major contribution of this research.

1: Introduction

Continued advances in the capability of Gallium Arsenide (GaAs) integrated circuits have begun to attract serious attention from computer system designers. The faster switching speeds of GaAs transistors, and the recently published laboratory designs exhibiting very large scale integration (VLSI) capability, promise a significant role for GaAs in high-performance computer design. Recently announced designs, which use enhancement-mode and depletion-mode MESFETs in direct coupled FET logic circuit configurations (DCFL E/D-MESFETs), include a 2K-gate gate array [ToUcK85] and a 16K-bit static RAM [IsInI84], with transistor counts of 8.2K and 102.3K, respectively.

GaAs computer architecture/design issues have now begun to be addressed. Led by an aggressive U.S. government initiative, several U.S. companies are actively engaged in GaAs-based computer efforts [Barne85]. GaAs computer design strategies have been presented in [Gheew84], [Gilbe86], [FurMi86], [MiFuH86], [MiSiF86], and [MiFuH87], while the first published GaAs microprocessor description was presented in [HeScZ85].

Because GaAs is expected to soon begin making significant contributions to computer system performance, it is important that computer designers appreciate both the strengths and the weaknesses of this new technology. The lack of design experience with GaAs is an obstacle to the full exploitation of the faster switching capability of GaAs transistors. An experimentation-based evaluation methodology is very desirable in order to select the advantageous architectural constructs for the first generation of GaAs processors.

An early participant in the design of GaAs processors, RCA Corporation, teamed with Purdue University to study GaAs computer system design issues. In this paper, we present the results of an experiment undertaken to evaluate several candidate instruction pipeline designs for a single-chip 32-bit GaAs microprocessor.

We begin in Section 2 by discussing motivations for conducting this experiment and in Section 3 by describing general pipeline candidates of interest for the GaAs environment. We continue in Section 4 with the pipeline performance model. Results of the analysis are presented and discussed in Sections 5 and 6.

2: Problem Statement

The advantage that GaAs technology enjoys over silicon technology in faster switching speed is countered by a lower transistor count capability for GaAs integrated circuits as well as a larger penalty for inter-chip communication in GaAs-based systems [MiFuH86]. The characteristics of both GaAs technology (the DCFL E/D MESFET that we were exposed to) and current packaging technology are such that, if a typical silicon datapath (i.e., arithmetic unit, register file, etc.) and an off-chip/on-package instruction

*This research was supported by RCA Advanced Microprocessor Laboratories, in the years 1984 and 1985, and is related to RCA's design of a single-chip 32-bit GaAs microprocessor.

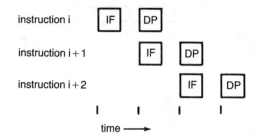

Figure 1: Example Silicon Pipeline.

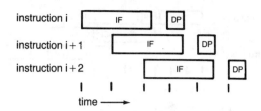

Figure 3: Example GaAs Instruction Pipeline with a Pipelime Memory [FurMi85].

cache are used, then a ratio of instruction fetch delay to datapath delay will be as high as three [Heage85, MiFuH86]. For an off-package instruction cache, this ratio may reach six [Heage85, MiFuH86].

Instruction pipelines for silicon processors typically resemble the one shown in Figure 1. In a GaAs processor environment, with a ratio of instruction fetch delay to datapath delay equal to three, this silicon-type pipeline shows a very poor datapath utilization, as seen in Figure 2. Approaches to alleviate this problem were discussed in [FurMi86], and two of these are represented by Figures 3 and 4. Figure 3 shows an instruction pipeline that results from the use of a pipelined instruction memory, while Figure 4 shows an instruction pipeline that incorporates instruction packing. In our experiments, we determine the effectiveness of these two candidate instruction pipelines in the long-latency off-chip GaAs environment, and we compare them with a conventional pipeline applied to the same type of design environment.

The basic intention of our research was to provide a generic study that would encompass basic approaches to pipeline design that are relevant for the GaAs microprocessor design environment.

3: Instruction Pipeline Candidates

The pipelines we examine in this study are represented by Figures 2, 3, and 4. Figure 2 provides us with a baseline silicon-like pipeline upon which the performances of the other two may be compared. This pipeline will henceforth be called the "normal silicon" pipeline. Pipelines represented by the one in Figure 3 will be referred to as "pipelined

memory" pipelines, while those resembling the pipelines in Figure 4 will be called "packed" pipelines.

Each of the above three pipeline classes will be studied in three different memory configurations. The first configuration consists of an off-chip on-package instruction cache and an off-chip on-package data cache. In this configuration, the ratio of memory access delay to datapath delay equals three for both instruction and data access; hence, this configuration will be referred to as the "(3,3)" configuration. The second configuration, which we call the "(3,6)" configuration, consists of an off-chip on-package instruction cache with an off-package data cache. The ratio of data access delay to datapath delay equals six in this configuration. The final configuration is called the "(6,3)" configuration, because it contains an off-package instruction cache and an off-chip on-package data cache. The ratio of instruction fetch delay to datapath delay equals six in this configuration.

Figures 5 through 13 show the nine pipelines that result from the three generic pipeline types, in the (3,3), (3,6), and (6,3) memory configurations. Figures 5 through 7 show the "normal silicon" pipeline in the three memory configurations. Figures 8 through 10 show the "packed" pipeline in the three memory configurations. Figures 11 through 13 show the "pipelined memory" pipeline in the three memory configurations. Our study's goal was to determine the relative performances of these nine general instruction pipeline types.

4: Pipeline Performance Model

For this study, we choose as our evaluation criterion the number of useful (i.e., non-NOOP) operations executed per

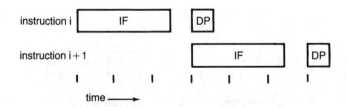

Figure 2: Example Silicon Pipeline Implemented in GaAs [FurMi85].

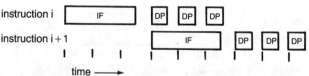

Figure 4: Example GaAs Instruction Pipelined with Instruction Packing [FurMi85].

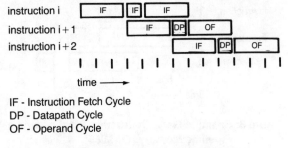

IF - Instruction Fetch Cycle
DP - Datapath Cycle
OF - Operand Cycle

Figure 5: Normal Silicon (3,3) Pipeline.

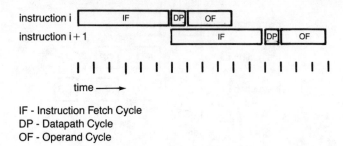

IF - Instruction Fetch Cycle
DP - Datapath Cycle
OF - Operand Cycle

Figure 7: Normal Silicon (6,3) Pipeline.

datapath cycle. The important constraint, which we will obey, is the ratio of instruction fetch delay to datapath delay that is built into the structure of the pipelines themselves.

4.1: Important Notes

In this section, we present some facts that would help to understand better the essence of our contribution. These facts also are intended to underline the generic aspects of our analysis.

First, although our work was related to the design of one particular GaAs microprocessor [MiSiF86], the results of our study are more general. They also can be applied to other technologies characterized with a relatively small on-chip transistor count and a relatively large ratio of the off-chip memory access and the on-chip datapath delay.

Second, one of the major intentions of our research was to determine the numerical differences between the nine candidate pipelines. Actually, some of the candidate pipelines are obviously better than the others [MiFuH86]. However, an important question for a designer is how much better they are and if the performance is improved significantly enough to justify the increased implementational costs.

Third, the study has been conducted [Fura85] for various hypothetical values of the branch delay fill-in probability (owing to space constraints, the results have been presented only for one particular value, 0.6). More details could be found in [Fura85]. The main reason to vary the branch delay

fill-in probability was to determine the impact (on execution time) of the strength of the code optimization mechanism. Actually, if very high values of the branch delay fill-in probability result in a considerably higher execution speed, then it will pay to invest more into a relatively sophisticated code optimization technology. Also, the approach that examines the tradeoffs for various values of the branch delay fill-in probability provides a more general view of the problem.

Fourth, designing a pipeline for a processor also involves issues such as interrupt handling latency and design complexity. However, in our study our only concern was execution speed for the compiled HLL code. This is justified by the following facts: (1) All nine candidate solutions will satisfy the interrupt handling requirements of the targeted applications [HelMi87] and (2) design complexity of all candidate pipelines can be handled by the existing GaAs VLSI design capabilities [Gilbe86].

Fifth, and the most important, in this paper we present one particular methodology that was used to answer the major questions of our research. By choosing the selected methodology, we were able to compare different approaches by using the same compiler. Therefore, the selected evaluation methodology actually avoids the flaw of comparing different architectures by using different compilers, which was done in many other analyses. Recently, an ENDOT-based simulator of all nine candidate architectures was completed, together with a compiler that follows the basic design strategy of the SU-MIPS compiler (again, for com-

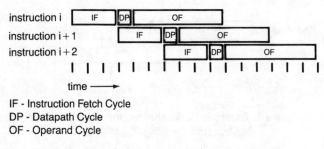

IF - Instruction Fetch Cycle
DP - Datapath Cycle
OF - Operand Cycle

Figure 6: Normal Silicon (3,6) Pipeline.

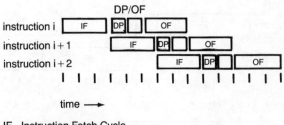

IF - Instruction Fetch Cycle
DP - Datapath Cycle
OF - Operand Cycle

Figure 8: Packed (3,3) Pipeline.

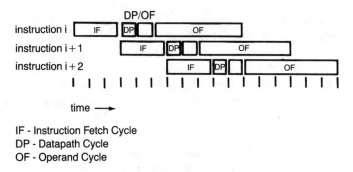

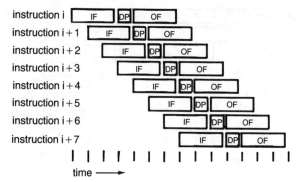

IF - Instruction Fetch Cycle
DP - Datapath Cycle
OF - Operand Cycle

Figure 9: Packed (3,6) Pipeline.

IF - Instruction Fetch Cycle
DP - Datapath Cycle
OF - Operand Cycle

Figure 11: Pipelined Memory (3,3) Pipeline.

parison purposes). Data from the ENDOT-based simulator had shown a fairly good match with the data presented in this paper [HelMi87]. In conclusion, we intentionally used the selected methodology (to be presented later) as the primary evaluation methodology, and the ENDOT-based simulation only as the verification methodology, because the former provides conditions for a more precise comparison.

4.2: Evaluation Tools

We use simulation as our primary evaluation technique. As was already indicated, primary evaluation criterion is the time required to execute compiled high-level language (HLL) programs. To obtain HLL program execution times, a simulation system requires three principal components.

First, an application environment in the form of HLL programs is necessary (benchmarks). Second, a simulation program that implements the architecture description is needed (simulator of the architecture). Finally, a method of translating the HLL programs to the architecture description is required, and this translation should be optimized to exploit any execution speedup opportunities, presented by the architecture (optimizing compiler).

Evaluation tools used in this research have been developed under DARPA sponsorship and were selected by DARPA to support the efforts towards the design of 32-bit GaAs microprocessors [KarRo86].

4.2.1: Workload Model

Because computer system performance depends heavily on the characteristics of the programs it executes, the selection of an appropriate application environment is of considerable importance.

Our application environment consists of a broad mixture of programs written in the high-level language PASCAL. These programs vary considerably in their use of iteration, recursion, and arithmetic. Considered collectively, they represent a fairly general programming environment, while the characteristics of selected individual programs may be used to enhance the responsiveness of execution time to particular architectural variations.

The 10 PASCAL programs that represent our workload model were obtained by us from Stanford University through RCA Corporation [GiGrH83]. They were developed especially for the purpose of testing and comparing the VLSI microprocessors [GiGrH83]. Many of these programs are widely used for benchmarking purposes and appear frequently in the literature:

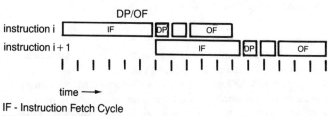

IF - Instruction Fetch Cycle
DP - Datapath Cycle
OF - Operand Cycle

Figure 10: Packed (6,3) Pipeline.

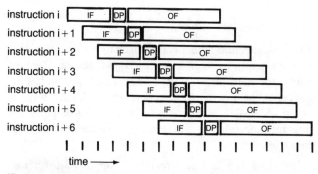

IF - Instruction Fetch Cycle
DP - Datapath Cycle
OF - Operand Cycle

Figure 12: Pipelined Memory (3,6) Pipeline.

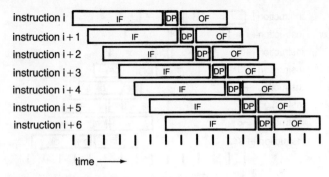

instruction i
instruction i + 1
instruction i + 2
instruction i + 3
instruction i + 4
instruction i + 5
instruction i + 6

time ⟶

IF - Instruction Fetch Cycle
DP - Datapath Cycle
OF - Operand Cycle

Figure 13: Pipelined Memory (6,3) Pipeline.

- Ack—a highly recursive program to compute Ackerman's function.

- Bubble—a program to perform a bubble sort of 5000 integers.

- Fib—a highly recursive program to compute a Fibonacci number.

- Intmm—a computation-heavy program to multiply two 40x40-element integer arrays.

- Perm—a highly recursive program to calculate all permutations of the numbers one through seven.

- Puzzle—an iteration-heavy, computation-heavy program to solve a three-dimensional cube packing problem.

- Queen—a program to solve the Eight Queens problem.

- Quick—a program to perform a quick sort of 5000 integers.

- Sieve—a program that calculates the number of primes between 0 and 8190.

- Towers—a highly recursive program to solve the Towers of Hanoi problem with 18 discs.

4.2.2: Architecture Model

Our architecture model corresponds to a simulation program written in the high-level language C for the Stanford MIPS processor, or SU-MIPS [GiGrH83]. It performs simulation at the machine instruction set level; therefore, it requires SU-MIPS instructions for its input. Its output is the program execution time, in terms of the number of instructions executed.

The SU-MIPS architecture is very appropriate for this study because its transistor count is compatible with current GaAs E/D-MESFET capabilities [KarRo86]. Here we explain several SU-MIPS characteristics to provide a better understanding of the experiments.

First, in our interpretation, SU-MIPS employs delayed branching with a branch delay of one.* This means that the first instruction after every branch operation is always executed, and the compiler is responsible for finding instructions for the fill-in slots such that correct program execution is maintained. If the compiler cannot find a useful instruction for a fill-in slot, it must then insert a NOOP into the slot.

Second, the SU-MIPS compiler must perform a similar function as above for the first instruction after data load operations.

Finally, the SU-MIPS processor employs instruction packing. An SU-MIPS instruction may contain two operations executed sequentially in the time necessary to perform one instruction fetch. Not all operation combinations may be packed, however, and instructions may therefore contain either one or two operations.

In addition to the Stanford University software, we use a cache simulator that was designed and implemented at Purdue University [Betti85]. The cache simulator is implemented as a procedure that is callable from within the SU-MIPS simulator. It receives addresses and possibly data and returns the number of instruction cycles required for access while updating the data and tag information. Modifications to the cache size, prefetch strategy, cache hit delay, and cache miss delay allow for a flexible cache implementation.

In the later stages of the research, the architecture simulator was implemented in the language ISP' (using the ENDOT software package) to prove the same point successfully, using a different experimentation methodology [HelMi87].

4.2.3: Translation Model

There must be some way to translate the PASCAL benchmark programs into a form acceptable to the architecture simulator. The software package that we use for this translation was written by Stanford and again provided to us by RCA. The package consists of a PASCAL compiler, optimizer, code generator, assembler and reorganizer, linker, and loader [GiGrH83].

---

*The SU-MIPS literature states that "indirect branch instruction" (see [GiGrH83]) has a branch delay of two. However, we consider this instruction to be a pair of *operations*—a data load followed by a branch. We are carefully using the term *instruction* to refer to those atomic entities that are fetched into the *processor*, and we use the term *operation* whenever an instruction contains multiple executable pieces. This distinction is important when discussing packed instructions containing multiple operations, in addition to the issue of indirect branch instructions.

The compiler transforms PASCAL programs into an intermediate language, which then receives hardware-independent optimizations before being converted into SU-MIPS-like instructions. The assembler and reorganizer perform the branch delay fill-in, load delay fill-in, instruction packing, etc., and convert the SU-MIPS assembler instructions into machine code. The linker combines this code with the run-time library containing multiplication routines, input-output routines, etc., and the loader logically stores the linked program into memory locations between 0 and 31,999. This loaded program is then written to a file where it is kept until required by the architecture simulation program.

4.3: Modeling Memory, Compiler, and Workload Effects

Here, we describe the details of our experiments by defining appropriate parameters related to memory, compiler, and workload.

4.3.1: Memory Parameters

As was mentioned earlier, one frequently quoted ratio of instruction fetch delay to datapath delay is three when an off-chip/on-package instruction memory is used [MiFuH86]. We, therefore, used this ratio for all on-package accesses throughout the rest of this experiment. For off-chip/off-package accesses, we used six as the ratio of memory access delay to datapath delay since this number corresponds to typical GaAs requirements [Heage85, MiFuH86]. Also, we will assume that the capacity of this off-package memory is infinite, therefore limiting this analysis to a two-level memory hierarchy.

We require six memory parameters, four of which are directly derivable from the pipeline and memory configuration. However, since we require all six parameters in our analytical performance model, we define all six here:

1. nih: Number of effective datapath cycles when a fetch from instruction cache results in a hit. This parameter is equal to one or three if an on-package instruction cache is used; it is one or six otherwise. The value of this parameter differs for *branch taken* and *branch not taken*. The same applies for some other parameters later. Note that the "effective" access delay of a pipelined memory is one.

2. nim: Number of effective datapath cycles for an instruction cache miss. This parameter is four or six if an on-package instruction cache is used; it is six otherwise. Note that an instruction cache miss always results in a delay of three cycles, unless a single-level instruction memory is used.

3. pih: Probability of instruction cache hit. This parameter is not directly derivable from the pipeline and

memory configuration. We will instead use a range of values for this parameter. For the default value, we observe the empirical cache hit ratios presented in [Smith85] for small cache sizes. On the basis of these results, we select a value of 0.8 as our default value.

4. ndh: Number of datapath cycles for a data cache read hit. This parameter is three if an on-package data cache is used; it is six otherwise.

5. ndm: Number of datapath cycles for a data cache read miss. This parameter is always six.

6. pdh: Probability of data cache read hit. As with pih, this parameter is not derivable from our pipeline and memory configurations, so we will use a range of values. From the results in [Smith85], we select a default value of 0.8 for this parameter as well.

There is an assumption implied here for data memory accesses. The parameters ndh, ndm, and pdh are valid for data memory *reads* only. We assume that the data memory is pipelined such that data memory writes cost the processor only one datapath cycle. A similar assumption for data memory reads would add considerable complexity into this analysis.

4.3.2: Compiler Parameters

There are two compiler related parameters required for our analysis. We define them next:

1. pbf: Probability of branch fill. This is the probability that the branch fill-in slots immediately following branch operation contain useful instructions. As in the case of both pih and pdh above, we will use a range of values for this paramenter, because there is no empirical data, to our knowledge, available for a compiler targeted to an architecture with large branch delays, as is the case with our GaAs architecture. We will use 0.6 as our default value because this is the value obtained by the SU-MIPS compiler group for a branch delay of three [HeJoP83]. However, because the SU-MIPS compiler was actually targeted to a machine with a branch delay of one, we do not believe their motivation for successfully filing three slots was especially strong; thus, perhaps our default value is low for a branch delay of three and represents the worst case analysis. However, since we also use branch delays of six in this experiment, we consider our default to be a suitable compromise. Note that the value for pbf is the probability that *all* of the possible slots are filled. Thus, for a branch delay of three and for a pbf of 0.6, there are an average of 1.8 useful instructions and 1.2 NOOPs following each branch operation.

2. plf: Probability of load fill. This is the probability that the load fill-in slots immediately following load oper-

ation contain useful instructions. We will use a range of values for this parameter and, since even less empirical data is available for this parameter than for pbf, we will use the same default value, 0.6. The same note applies here as above.

4.3.3: Modeling the Workload Effects

We now discuss the characteristics of our benchmarks, only those characteristics that we require for our analytical performance model. We first define the workload parameters, and then we present them in Table 1.

Workload Parameter Definitions: There are three causes of non-ideal performance for our three instruction pipelines. These are derived from branches, instruction fetches, and data loads. To determine their total negative effect on program execution time, we must know the number of branches, instruction fetches, and data loads present in our benchmark programs. We will use three abbreviations for these three parameters:

1. ni: Number of instructions in the benchmark program under study, or the average number of instructions if the workload contains multiple benchmark programs.

2. nl: Number of load operations in the benchmark program under study, or the average number of load operations if the workload contains multiple benchmark programs.

3. nb: Number of branch operations in the benchmark program under study, or the average number of branch operations if the workload contains multiple benchmark programs.

In addition to these three parameters, we require three additional parameters that describe the effect of the SU-MIPS compiler on the benchmark programs. Because two of our candidate instruction pipelines do not use packed instructions, and because our analysis is based upon the SU-MIPS instruction format, which does use packed instructions, we must know the number of packed instructions in the benchmark programs. Again, we shall abbreviate this parameter:

4. np: Number of packed instructions in the benchmark program under study, or the average number of packed instructions if the workload contains multiple benchmark programs. Reference [GiGrH83] describes the SU-MIPS instruction set, and the instructions eligible to be packed are evident there. However, just because an SU-MIPS instruction contains space for two operations, does not imply that every instance of this instrucion is packed. The ALU operation piece may contain a NOOP, which is actually a "MOV Rx, Rx" operation. Also, we consider both the conditional branch instruction and the conditional trap instruction

to be packed, since two SU-MIPS operations are clearly required for both of these instructions.

To model the effect of a compiler for a GaAs processor, the analytical model of the next section must include some additional effects of the SU-MIPS compiler on the benchmark programs:

5. pbf0: Probability of branch fill that the SU-MIPS compiler achieved on the given benchmark programs. Determining this value is complicated by the instruction packing of the SU-MIPS instruction set. The approach we have taken is to ignore packing in determining pbf0. If a branch instruction is not packed and could be, this does not affect pbf0. Also, if a fill-in slot after a branch contains at least one operation, then that slot is considered to be filled, otherwise it is unfilled.

6. plf0: Probability of load fill that the Stanford SU-MIPS compiler achieved on the given benchmark programs. The above statements concerning packing apply here as well.

In general, symbol "0" was used to refer to the values typical for the SU-MIPS compiler.

Workload Parameter Values; Through modifications to the SU-MIPS simulation program we obtained the values for the above six workload parameters. The simulator modifications involved, among others, the insertion of appropriate counters into the simulation program. Table 1 contains the results obtained for the 10 benchmark programs. The benchmark average, at the bottom of the table, weights the contribution of each benchmark program equally.

4.4. The Performance Model

We use our pipeline performance model to evaluate each of our candidate pipelines. The ideal pipeline execution rate is one useful operation per datapath cycle or, equivalently, one datapath cycle per useful operation.

Our performance equations represent the total number of datapath cycles required to execute the benchmark programs. These values will then be used to help create the plots shown in the next section.

The performance of the normal silicon pipelines, which are shown in Figures 5 through 7, are given in Equations 1 through 3. The performance of the packed pipelines, which are shown in Figures 8 through 10, are given in Equations 4 through 6. Finally, the performance of the pipelined memory pipelines, which are shown in Figures 11 through 13, are given in Equations 7 through 9.

Performance equations for all general pipeline types of this analysis are given below. Their derivations are straightforward, and they are not included here; however, they may be found in [Fura85].

Table 1: Workload Characteristics Relevant for Pipeline Study [GiGrH83].

Benchmark	ni*	nb*	nl*	np*	pbf0	plf0
ack	1000	216	270	189	0.62	0.90
bubble	1000	217	211	350	0.51	1.00
fib	1000	212	303	212	0.71	1.00
intmm	1000	63	134	637	1.00	1.00
perm	1000	143	304	230	0.75	0.88
puzzle	1000	316	263	489	0.95	0.92
queen	1000	151	299	252	0.63	0.65
quick	1000	208	156	633	0.56	0.97
sieve	1000	249	50	449	1.00	1.00
towers	1000	129	362	203	0.44	0.74
average	1000	190	235	364	0.72	0.91

*Measured per 1000 SU-MIPS instructions.

4.4.1: Normal Silicon (3,3)

$$
\begin{aligned}
\text{Execution time} = \ & ni* (6 - 3 * pih) \\
& + nl* (6 - 3 * pih) * (plf0 - plf) \\
& + nb* (6 - 3 * pih) * (pbf0 - pbf) \\
& + np* (6 - 3 * pih)
\end{aligned} \tag{1}
$$

4.4.2: Normal Silicon (3,6)

$$
\begin{aligned}
\text{Execution time} = \ & ni* (6 - 3 * pih) \\
& + nl* (6 - 3 * pih) * (plf0 - plf) \\
& + nb* (6 - 3 * pih) * (pbf0 - pbf) \\
& + np* (6 - 3 * pih)
\end{aligned} \tag{2}
$$

4.4.3: Normal Silicon (6,3)

$$
\begin{aligned}
\text{Execution time} = \ & ni* 6 \\
& + nl* 6* (plf0 - 1) \\
& + nb* 6* (pbf0 - pbf) \\
& + np* 6
\end{aligned} \tag{3}
$$

4.4.4: Packed (3,3)

$$
\begin{aligned}
\text{Execution time} = \ & ni* (6 - 3 * pih) \\
& + nl* (6 - 3 * pih) * (plf0 - plf) \\
& + nb* (6 - 3 * pih) * (pbf0 - pbf)
\end{aligned} \tag{4}
$$

4.4.5: Packed (3,6)

$$
\begin{aligned}
\text{Execution time} = \ & ni* (6 - 3 * pih) \\
& + nl* (6 - 3 * pih) * (plf0 - plf) \\
& + nb* (6 - 3 * pih) * (pbf0 - pbf)
\end{aligned} \tag{5}
$$

4.4.6: Packed (6,3)

$$
\begin{aligned}
\text{Execution time} = \ & ni* 6 \\
& + nl* 6* (plf0 - 1) \\
& + nb* 6* (pbf0 - pbf)
\end{aligned} \tag{6}
$$

4.4.7: Pipelined Memory (3,3)

$$
\begin{aligned}
\text{Execution time} = \ & ni* (4 - 3 * pih) \\
& + nl* [3 * (1 - pdh) \\
& + (4 - 3 * pih) * (2 + plf0 - 3 * plf)] \\
& + nb * (4 - 3 * pih) * (2 + pbf0 - 3 * pbf) \\
& + np * (4 - 3 * pih)
\end{aligned} \tag{7}
$$

4.4.8: Pipelined Memory (3,6)

$$
\begin{aligned}
\text{Execution time} = \ & ni * (4 - 3 * pih) \\
& + nl * (4 - 3 * pih) * (5 + plf0 - 6 * plf) \\
& + nb * (4 - 3 * pih) * (2 + pbf0 - 3 * pbf) \\
& + np * (4 - 3 * pih)
\end{aligned} \tag{8}
$$

4.4.9: Pipelined Memory (6,3)

Execution time = ni * 1
$$+ nl * (5 + plf0 - 3 * plf - 3 * pdh)$$
$$+ nb * (5 + pbf0 - 6 * pbf)$$
$$+ np * 1 \tag{9}$$

5: Results and Discussion

It is advantageous to study the candidate pipelines in four workload environments. First, we evaluated each pipeline in the workload environment represented by the entire set of benchmark programs. Then, we evaluated each pipeline in arithmetic-heavy, branch-heavy, and load-heavy environments represented by the benchmark programs intmm, puzzle, and towers, respectively. We present here the most essential functional dependencies in Figures 14 through 20. We were aware of the fact that none of the 10 benchmarks alone could be used as a meaningful workload model. Therefore, when using single benchmarks, our goal was to determine the effects of specific machine instructions.

As was indicated in the last section, the ideal pipeline performance standard is one datapath cycle per useful instruction. We instead plot on the vertical axis the number of datapath cycles per 1000 *packed SU-MIPS instructions*. Although not every SU-MIPS instruction contains exactly one useful operation, we do have an easily obtainable basis for pipeline comparison. On the horizontal axis, we have a range of values for either a compiler parameter—pbf or plf, or a memory parameter—pih or pdh. Thus, we are in a position to determine the effects of both compiler and memory system capabilities on the performance of our candidate pipelines.

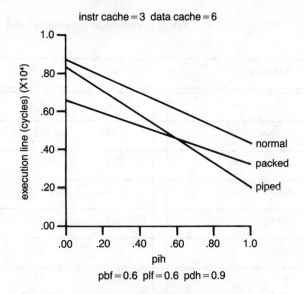

pbf=0.6 plf=0.6 pdh=0.9

Figure 15: Pipeline Performance vs. "pih" in (3,6) Configuration for All Benchmarks.

5.1: Memory Configuration Comparison

Figures 14 through 16 show the performance of the candidate pipelines as a function of pih in the workload environment consisting of all 10 benchmarks. Figure 14 shows the results for the (3,3) configuration, Figure 15 shows the results for the (3,6) configuration, while Figure 16 shows the results for the (6,3) configuration.

The (3,3) memory configuration generally provides the highest performances, followed by the (3,6) configuration, and, finally by the (6,3) configuration. The (3,6) configura-

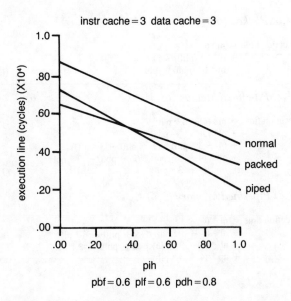

pbf=0.6 plf=0.6 pdh=0.8

Figure 14: Pipeline Performance vs. "pih" in (3,3) Configuration for All Benchmarks.

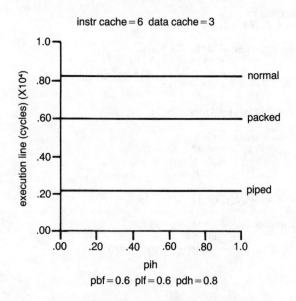

pbf=0.6 plf=0.6 pdh=0.8

Figure 16: Pipeline Performance vs. "pih" in (6,3) Configuration for All Benchmarks.

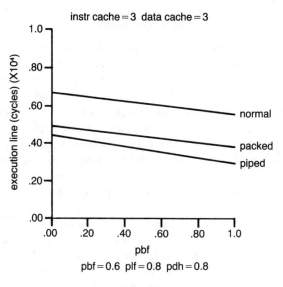

instr cache = 3 data cache = 3

pbf = 0.6 plf = 0.8 pdh = 0.8

Figure 17.

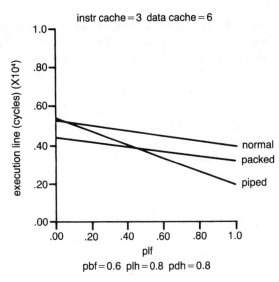

instr cache = 3 data cache = 6

pbf = 0.6 plh = 0.8 pdh = 0.8

Figure 19.

tion generally outperforms the (6,3) configuration because, as is seen in Table 1, instructions are fetched approximately four times as often as data. Note that *the basic intention of our experiments was both to derive answers on qualitative aspects of different pipeline types and to obtain quantitative answers that would help to design a single-chip 32-bit GaAs microprocessor,* as efficiently as possible.

A significant deviation from the general discussion just concluded is the much superior performance of the (6,3) memory configuration, when the pipelined memory pipeline is used. In fact, this combination provides the best performance to be observed in this experiment. The reasons for this are the memory pipelining, which reduces the "effective" instruction delay to one datapath cycle, and the (6,3) configuration, which eliminates the penalty of instruction cache

misses (the off-package memory is assumed to have an infinite capacity).

5.2: Compiler Related Comparison

Figures 17 and 18 show the performance of candidate pipelines for the (3,3) memory configuration and the impact of pbf (probability of the branch-delay fill-in), in the workload environment consisting of one specific benchmark. Figure 17 shows the performance for a branch-heavy benchmark (Ack), and Figure 18 shows the performance for an arithmetic-heavy benchmark (Intmm).

Of all the parameters (pih, pdh, pbf, and plf), the one that most heavily influences pipeline performance is pih. This

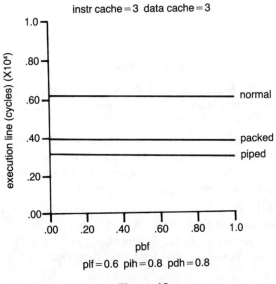

instr cache = 3 data cache = 3

plf = 0.6 pih = 0.8 pdh = 0.8

Figure 18.

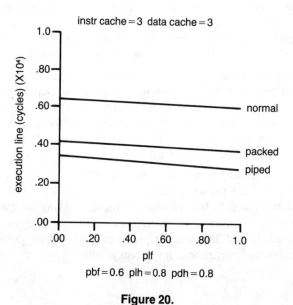

instr cache = 3 data cache = 3

pbf = 0.6 plh = 0.8 pdh = 0.8

Figure 20.

was expected because instruction fetches are more frequent than either data loads or branches. Note that values of all above specified parameters could be influenced by a proper compiler design. Therefore, we believe that this aspect of compiler design is especially important for GaAs.

Figures 19 and 20 show the impact of plf (probability of the load-delay fillin), for the three candidate pipelines, in the (3,3) configuration. Figure 19 shows the effect of a load-heavy environment on performance, while Figure 20 shows the effect of an arithmetic-heavy environment on performance.

For the branch-heavy workload environment we do observe a higher performance dependency on pbf, as we expected. This is because of the high frequency of branches (32 percent) in this benchmark.

For the load-heavy workload environment, we see an increased performance dependency on plf, as also expected. This is again because of the high percentage of loads (36 percent) in this benchmark.

In the arithmetic-heavy workload environment, we observe almost no performance dependency on either pbf or plf. This is because of the extremely low number of branches (6 percent) and loads (13 percent) in this benchmark.

5.3: Comparison of Candidate Pipelines

Clearly, the pipelined memory pipeline is generally superior to both the normal silicon and the packed pipelines. This is not surprising, because the pipelined memory pipeline is the only pipeline of the three potentially able to execute one useful operation per datapath cycle. The packed pipeline can sometimes execute two useful operations per three datapath cycles, while the normal silicon pipeline is limited to one useful operation per three datapath cycles. In only a very few special cases is the silicon pipeline performance equal to the performance of either of the other two pipelines. Clearly, a silicon-like pipeline performs very poorly in our model of a GaAs processor environment.

It is apparent that the pipelined memory pipeline is the most sensitive to variations in all four parameters. This results from the "leanness" of the pipelined memory pipeline. Although it has the highest potential performance, it also experiences the most degradation from unfilled branch fill-in slots, unfilled load fill-in slots, and cache misses.

An interesting result is the lower sensitivity to pih demonstrated by the packed pipeline. This is because fewer instructions must be fetched when instruction packing is used; therefore, the number of instruction cache misses decreases as well. In fact, the packed pipeline out performs the pipelined memory pipeline at low values of pih.

6: Conclusion

There were two basic rationales behind this study. First, the fact that GaAs, compared to silicon, has a radically different impact on computer design, was clearly recognized by early GaAs researchers such as Gilbert and Naused [Gilbe86], and Karp and Roosild [KarRo86]. Moving along these lines, our main goal was to provide a general analysis of pipeline types of interest for the GaAs microprocessor design environment. Our second goal was to show quantitatively what would be performance degradations if a GaAs microprocessor is designed without giving appropriate consideration to technology differences. Third, the immediate goal was the design of a single-chip 32-bit GaAs microprocessor, and it was necessary to examine nine candidate solutions for the instruction pipeline as well as their efficiency in the case of one specific set of benchmarks. Our general conclusions are fairly independent of the choice of benchmarks, but the structure of the "optimal" instruction pipeline could be different for different benchmark sets.

The most significant result of this experiment is demonstration of the superb performance of the pipelined memory pipeline in all environments, even though its performance was hurt in experiments with the branch-heavy and load-heavy benchmarks. In the branch-heavy environment, even at a pbf of zero, the pipelined memory pipeline still performs best. The load-heavy benchmark is more punishing when the (3,6) memory configuration is used, but the pipelined memory pipeline is still best at values of plf above 0.4. In the arithmetic-heavy benchmark, the low frequency of branches and data loads allows the pipelined memory pipeline to excel even at very low values of pbf and plf.

7: Acknowledgments

The authors thank W. Heagerty and W. Moyers of RCA for comments and suggestions related to this work.

8: References

[Barne85] Barney, C., "DARPA Eyes 100-mips GaAs Chip for Star Wars," *Electronics Week*, Vol. 58, No. 20, May 20, 1985, pp. 22-23.

[Betti85] Bettinger, M., "Comparison of CMOS Silicon and E/D-MESFET GaAs for VLSI Processor Design," *Master's Thesis, Technical Report TR-EE 85-18*, Purdue University, West Lafayette, Ind., Dec. 1985.

[Fura85] Fura, D.A., "Architectural Approaches for Gallium Arsenide Exploitation in High-Speed Computer Design," *Master's Thesis, Technical Report TR-EE 85-17*, Purdue University, West Lafayette, Ind., Dec. 1985.

[FurMi86] Fura, D.A. and Milutinović, V.M., "Computer Design for Gallium Arsenide," in *Advanced Topics in Computer Architecture,* ed. by V.M. Milutinović, Elsevier, New York, 1986.

[Gheew84] Gheewala, T.R., "System Level Comparison of High Speed Technologies," *Proceedings of the IEEE 1984 International Conference on Computer Design,* IEEE Computer Society, Washington, D.C. 1984, pp. 245-250.

[GiGrH83] Gill, J., Gross, T., Hennessy, J., Jouppi, N., Przybylski, S., and Rowen, C., "Summary of SU-MIPS Instructions," *Technical Note 83-237,* Stanford University, Stanford, Calif., Nov. 1983.

[Gilbe86] Gilbert, B.K., Naused, B.A., Schwab, D.J., and Thompson, R.L., "Signal Processors based upon GaAs ICs: The Need for a Wholistic Design Approach," *IEEE Computer,* Vol. 19, No. 7, Oct. 1986, pp. 29-43.

[Heage85] Heagerty, W., Advanced Technology Laboratories, RCA Corporation, private communication, 1985.

[HeJoP83] Hennessy, J., Jouppi, N., Przybylski, S., Rowen, C., and Gross, T., "Design of a High Performance VLSI Processor," *Technical Report No. 236,* Stanford University, Stanford, Calif., Feb. 1983.

[HelMi87] Helbig, W. and Milutinović, V., "A DCFL E/D-MESFET GaAs Experimental RISC Machine," *IEEE Transactions on Computers,* 1988.

[HeScZ85] Helbig, W.A., Schellack, R.H., and Zieger, R.M., "The Design and Construction of a GaAs Technology Demonstration Microprocessor," *Proceedings of Midcon/85,* IEEE, New York, Sept. 1985, pp. 23/1.1-23/1.6.

[IsInI84] Ishii, Y., Ino, M., Idda, M., Hirayama, M., and Ohmori, M., "Processing Technologies for GaAs Memory LSIs," *Proceedings of the GaAs IC Symposium,* IEEE, New York, Oct. 1984, pp. 121-124.

[KarRo86] Karp, S.V. and Roosild, S., "DARPA, SDI, and GaAs," *IEEE Computer,* Vol. 19, No. 10, Oct. 1986, pp. 17-19.

[MiFuH86] Milutinović, V., Fura, D., and Helbig, W., "An Introduction to GaAs Microprocessor Architecture for VLSI," *IEEE Computer,* Vol. 19, No. 3, March 1986, pp. 30-42.

[MiFuH87] Milutinović, V., Fura, D., Helbig, W., and Linn, J., "Architecture/Compiler Synergism in GaAs Computer Systems," *IEEE Computer,* Vol. 20, No. 3, pp. 72-93.

[MiSiF86] Milutinović, V., Silbey, A., Fura, D., Bettinger, M., Keirn, K., Helbig, W., Heagerty, W., Zieger, R., Schellack, B., and Curtice, W., "Design Issues in GaAs Computer Systems," *IEEE Computer,* Vol. 19, No. 10, Oct. 1986, pp. 45-57.

[Smith85] Smith, A.J., "Cache Evaluation and the Impact of Workload Choice," *Proceedings of the 12th Annual Symposium on Computer Architecture,* IEEE Computer Society Press, Washington, D.C., 1985, pp. 64-73.

[ToUcK85] Toyoda, N., Uchitomi, N., Kitaura, Y., Mochizuki, M., Kanazawa, K., Terada, T., Ikawa, Y., and Hojo, A., "A 42ps 2K-Gate GaAs Gate Array," *Proceedings of the 1985 IEEE International Solid-State Circuits Conference,* IEEE, New York, N.Y., 1985, pp. 206-207.

Instruction Format Study for a 32-Bit GaAs Microprocessor[*]

V. Milutinović and D. Fura
School of Electrical Engineering
Purdue University
West Lafayette, IN 47907
(317) 494-3530

W. Helbig
RCA Corporation
Advanced Technology Laboratories
Moorestown, NJ 08057
(608) 866-6530

Abstract

This report presents the major results of an instruction format analysis, undertaken to support the design of RCA's single-chip 32-bit DCFL E/D-MESFET GaAs microprocessor. We evaluate ten different instruction formats of interest for GaAs processors of the RISC type. GaAs processor/cache pairs have fewer transistors (less hardware and smaller memories) and faster cycle times (external delays form a larger portion of execution time) than similar Si pairs. One way to compensate for the smaller caches and relatively expensive external delays is to reduce code sizes by denser formats. Thus, this study begins with a MIPS-like RISC processor architecture and explores the potential code space and performance effects resulting from 28, 24, 20, and 16 bit instruction formats. We found that about 10 percent code space can be saved at a slight performance penalty for the set of benchmarks: ackerman, bubblesort, fibonacci, matrix multiply, permutations, puzzle, eight queens, quicksort, sieve, and towers of Hanoi. However, this performance penalty may be recovered through the fact that smaller code size will result in a smaller cache miss ratio, and realistic delays on cache misses may be much longer than those considered in this study.

1: Introduction

Computer design approaches and techniques suitable for GaAs technology have been treated in numerous references [Barne85, EdWeL83, Fura85, HeScZ85, MiFuH86, MiSiF86]. Microprocessor design for GaAs technology has a number of specific problems: faster cycle times make external delays a larger fraction of execution time, less dense circuits lead to less local memory and simpler datapaths, and lower yield leads to small dies and fewer pins.

Here, we discuss only one aspect of the problems, instruction format. In the silicon environment, the RISC philosophy has demonstrated the greater importance of good pipeline design over instruction compactness. However, instruction formats that result in small program sizes can be very advantageous in GaAs implementations. (This factor is explained in detail in Section 1.1). The reasons include the smaller capacity of GaAs memory chips and the higher ratio of off-chip to on-chip delays for GaAs. (For more details on the GaAs/silicon differences of relevance for microprocessor architecture, see [MiFuH86], [MiSiF86], and [MiFuH87].) Therefore, we believe that it is important to determine what effect instruction format compactness can have in a GaAs processor environment.

The use of the RISC design philosophy in GaAs processor design might appear to reduce instruction format design to a trivial problem. Of course this is not so. A particularly strong concern for GaAs processor design is the effect of the instruction format on the timely transfer of instructions to the processor. The instruction bandwidth requirement of a processor is strongly dependent on the instruction format. Although making design decisions on instruction bandwidth alone is not to be encouraged, this architectural metric acquires added significance but should be used within the context of the system design.

For at least two reasons, compact programs require a lower memory-processor bandwidth and are more beneficial in GaAs processor systems than in silicon processor systems.

First, for GaAs processors, the technology used to implement the memory at the highest levels of the memory hierarchy will likely be GaAs. Since GaAs memory chips will likely remain less dense than silicon memory chips, GaAs caches will be relatively small. Memory size has been shown to be the single most important factor to impact the cache hit ratio [SmiGo83]. Moreover, that hit ratio is highly dependent on cache size at small cache sizes while much less so at high cache capacities [Smith85]. Since a decrease

*This research was supported by a RCA Corporation grant to Purdue University.

in program size is equivalent to an increase in the program cache size, compact programs are indeed very desirable in a GaAs processor system.

Second, because of the extremely fast instruction cycle times possible in a GaAs processor, a cache memory access miss in a GaAs processor system will likely entail a longer delay in terms of the number of instruction cycles than a cache memory access miss in a silicon processor system. It is, therefore, more important to minimize these misses in a GaAs processor system. In other words, in GaAs microprocessor systems, cache memory typically resides off the CPU chip but on the same hybrid package. The number of chips that can be placed on a single hybrid package is limited. Therefore, on-package cache memories in GaAs systems are of a relatively small size. The smaller the size of a cache, the higher the miss ratio. However, cache miss is (relatively speaking) much more expensive in GaAs than in silicon. Actually, cache misses in GaAs represent a larger proportion of the smaller execution time achieved by a faster GaAs cycle time. This is predominantly because the number of wait states to insert (on cache miss) into the instruction/data stream may be several times higher, due to the much higher ratio of memory access time and datapath time.

The major disadvantage of the RISC design philosophy in a GaAs implementation is the generally low information content of RISC instructions. Of course, it is the very simplicity of RISC instructions that leads to their low decoding logic requirements. Therefore, any attempt to reduce program size through increased encoding of instructions must be done so as to minimize its impact on decoding complexity.

Here, we will discuss two methods for increasing program compactness in a way that has little impact on a GaAs processor's decoding complexity. The first approach relies on the high dynamic frequency of short immediate fields and few operand addresses; the second approach makes use of the repetitive nature of some complex operations such as multiply and divide.

Some important references (indirectly impacting our work) in the field of instruction formats and code density include [FlyHe63], [FlyHo83], [Patte83], and [Wilne72].

1.1. Frequency-Based Instructions

Techniques based on Huffman codes [Huffm52] are frequently considered in instruction set designs. Huffman coding is a technique for assigning the most frequent instructions to the shorter encoding patterns. A pure Huffman implementation would require sequential decoding and much hardware and, thus, is not a serious candidate for a GaAs processor. However, the concept of providing shorter encoding patterns to frequent occurrences is very applicable for GaAs processor instruction sets.

Compact instruction formats may be designed through the use of small immediate fields and few address fields. The resulting reduction in program size is not due to an explicit encoding function operating on these fields, but results from the high dynamic frequency of small immediate data values and the high dynamic frequency of both one-address and two-address instructions in real programs. In one study of XPL programs [AleWo75], 61 percent of the branch distances required eight bits or less, while 81 percent could be represented with 12 bits. The study also found that 47 percent of the numeric constants could be represented by only four bits and that 87 percent of the numeric constants required eight bits or less. It is also estimated that 87 percent of all assignment statements require only two operand addresses [Myers82].

Compact instruction formats that result from using short immediate fields and fewer operand addresses have three potential benefits for a GaAs implementation.

First, as just mentioned, the proper design of immediate and operand fields can be expected to reduce total program size and provide the benefits for a GaAs implementation.

Second, this approach takes advantage of the dynamic characteristics of program behavior. Small immediate values and fewer operand addresses are not the output of an encoding algorithm but occur naturally and frequently in real programs; therefore, there is no need for a significant decoding function within the processor to "undo" any additional encoding.

Third, compact operations may be packed into a single instruction. Because pin limitations of a GaAs processor will limit the size of instruction fetch transfers, multiple operation fetching (as shown in the instruction pipeline of Figure 1a) is only possible for short operations. A well-designed packed instruction format can improve the performance of a processor in a long-latency off-chip environment.

This form of redundancy removal is not new to instruction set designers. Many silicon instruction sets display varying levels of program compactness, and some even support operation packing, i.e., incorporation of more than one operation into a single instruction [e.g., Gross83]. The longest immediate data values supported by many silicon

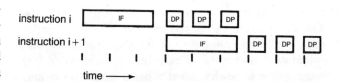

Figure 1(a): Example GaAs Instruction Pipeline with an Instruction Packing [MiFuH86].

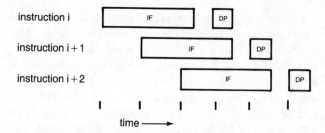

Figure 1(b): Example GaAs Instruction Pipeline with a Pipelined Memory [MiFuH86].

processors require 32 bits of information.* In order to include immediate fields in single-word instructions to represent 32-bit values, extremely long instructions would be required.

Even relatively sparse instruction formats, such as the Berkeley RISC-II [PatPi82], take advantage of the low frequency of use of such long immediate values by only supporting short immediate values within a single instruction. The use of very large immediate values requires two RISC-II instructions [Katev83].

The Stanford MIPS [HeJoG82] limits its maximum immediate field size to 24 bits to allow all immediate values to be used within a single instructions [GiGrH83]. However, the MIPS instruction set takes advantage of small immediate data values by packing a second operation into instructions that require short immediate fields [Gross83]. This operation packing also makes use of the high frequency of one- and two-address operations because the instruction fields for the packed operations are only large enough for two-address operations. The ability of the Stanford MIPS to execute two operations per instruction fetch is limited by the occurrence of long immediate values and by the ability of its compiler to find suitable useful (non-NOOP) packing candidates [Gross83]. A more complex instruction format also results form the MIPS style of packing. This more complex instruction format generates a 10 percent increase in the MIPS instruction cycle time [Patte85], in addition to increased decoding hardware requirements.

The Transputer [Whitb85] relies very heavily on the high frequency of small immediate values, as it only provides four bits of immediate field in every 8-bit instruction. Larger immediate values must be built from multiple instructions, four bits at a time. The small size of its instruction format allows the Transputer to pack four such instructions (from now on we call these *operations*) into a single packed instruction. The Transputer is better able to meet its maximum rate of four operation executions per instruction fetch because of a somewhat different definition of "operation."

---

*The length of immediate data values is a property of programs, not processors.

The Transputer uses even more primitive operations than the MIPS or RISC-II. The use of a large immediate data value is implemented by a sequence of "build immediate field" operations. However, these operations have a 50 percent overhead, as only four of the eight bits contain actual data. However, the rigid field boundaries of the Transputer's instruction format can be expected to result in a simpler decoding function than required by the MIPS instruction format.

Compact instruction formats must be designed with a good understanding of the instruction requirements of the intended application environment. However, the exploitation of the high frequency of usage of small immediate values and fewer operand addresses may provide significant benefits for a GaAs processor implementation.

1.2: Context-Based Instructions

Huffman codes [Huffm52] are based on the frequency of usage of data items without considering the environment surrounding the data items. Because instruction executions are not independent of each other, additional compaction opportunities are available.

A compaction technique that uses context information, in addition to the instruction frequency information used by Huffman-based techniques, is conditional coding [Hehne76]. In this technique, the encoding of the next instruction to be executed is dependent upon the probability of its occurrence in the context of the execution of the current instruction. Therefore, if there are n instructions in the instruction set, then each instruction has n different encodings—one associated with each of the n possible preceding instructions. A strict implementation of this scheme is not practical for a GaAs processor; however, the concept of using context information to reduce program size is applicable.

A less rigorous, but simpler, technique related to the one in [Hehne76] is to replace frequent instruction sequences with a single instruction. In fact, this technique is typically used on microcoded CISCs. A program consisting of CISC macroinstructions is generally more compact than a program containing RISC instructions; this is because each macroinstruction corresponds to a sequence of microinstructions, while each RISC instruction corresponds to a single microinstruction-like instruction. It is possible that this CISC mechanism can be used to good advantage in some GaAs processor environments.

If justified by frequency of use, complex instructions such as multiply, divide, and perhaps even multiply-accumulate may be added to the instruction set of a GaAs processor. Even if a transistor-scarce GaAs processor cannot support the hardware to directly execute these operations and must instead use the main datapath, there may be potential advantages to using complex instructions. For example, consider the implementation of the multiplication operation on a RISC, which can be performed in a number of ways.

A linear sequence of multiply-step instructions can be used for each multiply in the program. For a processor such as the Stanford MIPS, this may require nearly 20 instructions per multiply. If multiplies are 10 percent of all instructions executed, this technique nearly triples the program size.

Alternatively, a loop containing as few as one multiply-step instruction can be used. However, introducing loops into programs is not generally desirable both because of the time wasted on looping overhead and because of the large number of instructions required to perform branch fill-in, if the GaAs processor is highly pipelined, which is typical the case [Milut86].

A third technique is to include a linear sequence of multiply-step instructions into a system procedure that is callable from anywhere within the program. This technique, therefore, requires that a procedure call and return be executed for each multiply instruction. Beyond the normal overhead associated with procedure calls, this method degrades the execution locality, possibly decreasing memory hit ratios.

The implementation of a single multiply instruction entails none of the above disadvantages; however, complexity is introduced into the pipeline control mechanism. Single-cycle instruction execution is a feature of "true" RISCs because it leads to simple pipeline control. When a CISC-like multiply instruction is encountered, the processor will likely spend a long time executing it. Therefore, the instruction pipeline must be halted. If the instruction memory is also pipelined, a time delay will probably exist before the entire memory pipeline can be halted and buffering may be needed. Clearly, the benefits of CISC-like instructions must be weighted against their implementation complexity, and the decision to use (or not to use) CISC-like instructions should be considered in the context of the entire system.

1.3: Summary

We begin by explaining our motivation for performing the experiment, and then we present our choice of formats for examination. We describe the evaluation criteria and the theory and implementation of our instruction format evaluation methodology. We then discuss the procedure and results of our experiment, presented as three sub-experiments. We finish with a discussion of our results. As already indicated, our analysis is related to one specific RISC-type microprocessor—RCA's design of a 32-bit GaAs MIPS-style machine. However, the streamlined nature of the MIPS-style processor enables the results of this analysis to be more generally applicable.

2: Candidate Instruction Format Descriptions

The previous section indicated that considerable redundancy usually exists in the immediate field and address fields of silicon instruction formats. The constants located in immediate fields are usually small, and the higher order bits in such cases convey no essential information to the processor. Most computations do not require three addresses; therefore, three-address instruction formats often have address fields with no information content. We find redundancy elimination in these two particular areas to be deserving of further exploration in the context of a GaAs environment. Instruction format design to exploit common instruction sequences is also worthy of continued study but is not considered further in this paper.

We chose to study 10 instruction format candidates for incorporation into a GaAs processor. In addition to these, for comparison purposes, we also included the MIPS format. The instruction fields for the ten candidate formats are shown in Table 1, while the relevant instruction fields for the MIPS format are described in [GiGrH83] and briefly summarized in the Appendix.

Each of our candidate instruction formats has its structure encoded into its name. For example, the format "28(3210)" contains 28 bits and may use either 3, 2, 1, or 0 registers. In general, when a lower number of registers is used, the immediate field is increased accordingly. Since each format requires eight bits for its opcode and register specifications require four bits, the immediate field lengths for the 28(3210) format are 8, 12, 16, and 20 bits, corresponding to the cases with 3, 2, 1, and 0 registers, respectively.

The candidate instruction formats were chosen on the basis of their ability to be directly compared, so that a variety of sub-experiments are possible. Formats 28(3) and 24(2) allowed a direct tradeoff study between the higher number of register fields of 28(3) versus the reduced total number of bits in 24(2). Formats 28(3) and 24(32) allowed a direct tradeoff study between the higher immediate field length of 28(3) versus the reduced total number of bits in 24(32).

We compared the performance of the formats in each of the following pairs: 28(3) versus 28(3210), 24(2) versus 24(210), 24(32) versus 24(3210), 20(32) versus 20(3210), and 16(21) versus 16(210). In the comparisons, we were able to examine the result of shifting instruction bits from register fields to the immediate field, when a full set of register addresses is not required.

With formats 16(21) and 16(210), two instructions could be fetched concurrently using the same processor-memory bandwidth as a single 32-bit instruction. Therefore, packed versions of formats 16(21) and 16(210) could be compared to the packed MIPS format.

Table 1: Instruction Fields for Candidate Instruction Formats.

Format	Opcode (# bits)	Reg1 (# bits)	Reg2 (# bits)	Reg3 (# bits)	Imm1 (# bits)	Imm2 (# bits)	Total (# bits)
28(3)	8	4	4	4	8		28
28(3210)	8	4	4	4	8		28
	8	4	4		12		28
	8	4			16		28
	8				20		28
24(32)	8	4	4	4	4		24
	8	4	4		4	4	24
24(3210)	8	4	4	4	4		24
	8	4	4		4	4	24
	8	4	4		8		24
	8	4			12		24
	8				16		24
24(2)	8	4	4		8		24
24(210)	8	4	4		8		24
	8	4			12		24
	8				16		24
20(32)	8	4	4	4			20
	8	4	4		4		20
20(3210)	8	4	4	4			20
	8	4	4		4		20
	8	4			8		20
	8				12		20
16(21)	8	4	4				16
	8	4			4		16
16(210)	8	4	4				16
	8	4			4		16
	8				8		16

3: Evaluation Criteria, Methodology, and Implementation

In this study of compact instruction formats, there are three types of information that formed our basis for comparison.

First, we examined the magnitude of the effect of short instruction formats on the overall program size. Second, we examined how the use of short instructions affects the number of instructions that must be executed. Finally, we examined the effect of short instructions on execution time.

Impact of various instruction formats on cycle time was implicitly built into our simulator and is not explicitly visible.

We utilized simulation as our primary evaluation technique. We chose this approach because of its advantages over other evaluation methodologies [Myers82] and because the appropriate tools are readily available to us. Analytical models are also sometimes used, but these are generally not as representative as simulation models.

Our primary evaluation criterion is the time required to execute compiled HLL programs. In order to obtain HLL program execution times, a simulation system requires three principal components. First, an application environment in the form of HLL programs is necessary. Second, a simulation program that implements the architecture description is needed. Finally, a method of translating the HLL programs to the architecture description is required.

Our application environment contained a broad mixture of programs written in the high-level language PASCAL (provided by the customer as representative for the intended application of the RCA's 32-bit GaAs microprocessor.)* These programs vary considerably in their use of iteration, recursion, arithmetic, and data structures. Considered collectively, they represent a general purpose programming environment, while the characteristics of selected individual programs may be used to enhance the responsiveness of execution time to particular architectural variations. Many of these programs are widely used for benchmarking purposes and appear frequently in the literature:

- Ack—a highly recursive program to compute Ackermann's function.
- Bubble—a program to perform a bubble sort of 500 integers.
- Fib—a highly recursive program to compute a Fibonacci number.
- Intmm—a computation-heavy program to multiply two 40x40-element integer arrays.
- Perm—a highly recursive program to calculate all permutations of the numbers 1 through 7.
- Puzzle—an iteration-heavy, computation-heavy program to solve a 3-dimensional cube packing problem.
- Queen—a program to solve the Eight Queens problem.
- Quick—a program to perform a quick sort of 5000 integers.
- Sieve—a program that calculates the number of primes between 0 and 8190.

---

*The benchmarks were selected to be representative of the application environment for the target microprocessor, using the approach of [Ferra78].

- Towers—a highly recursive program to solve the Towers of Hanoi problem with 18 discs.

Our architecture model is based on a simulation program written in the high-level language C for the Stanford MIPS processor. The output is the program execution time, in terms of the number of instructions executed. The MIPS simulator, supplied by RCA, was modified by us to incorporate a cache memory simulator. The MIPS simulator performs simulation at the instruction level; therefore, it requires MIPS instructions for its input. Therefore, we had to modify it to be able to accept different instruction formats of interest for our study.

The cache simulator was implemented as a procedure that is callable from within the MIPS simulator. It receives addresses and possibly data and returns the number of instruction cycles required for access, while updating the data and tag information. Modifications to the cache size, block size, prefetch strategy, cache hit delay, and cache miss delay allow for a flexible cache implementation.

Modifications related to various instruction formats were of the "in-line" type. The changes were made in a way that enables performance comparison among various formats and with the original MIPS format. Some formats need additional references to fetch the other part of the "long-immediate" instruction. These references are also a part of the "in-line" modifications.

We have identified three areas where our candidate instruction formats differ from the MIPS instruction format, and these areas provide the basis for our simulation program changes.

First, the MIPS instruction format is packed; therefore, some MIPS *instructions* contain two *operations*. Since none of the candidate formats use packing, a packed MIPS instruction requires two candidate instructions.

Second, some of the candidate formats only have two register address fields, while the MIPS operations within MIPS instructions can have two or three register addresses. Therefore, in some cases, a single MIPS operation will require two candidate instructions.

Third, the candidate formats all have shorter immediate fields than the MIPS format. Consequently, in some cases two candidate instructions may be required in order to execute a single MIPS operation, as indicated above.

Because of these differences between the MIPS and candidate formats, there will be differences in their static instruction counts and dynamic instruction counts. The static instruction count is the number of instructions contained within a program; it is a measure of program *size*. The dynamic count is the number of instructions executed when a program is run; it is a measure of program *execution time*.

Since we know the instruction field sizes for the MIPS format and for all the candidate formats, it is relatively straightforward to determine, for each of the candidate formats, which MIPS instructions require multiple candidate instructions. We show in the Appendix the 10 candidate instruction formats and the number of instructions that they require in order to execute MIPS instructions of given characteristics. Actually, the Appendix shows the "additional" number of candidate instructions that are needed. We did not change the normal execution of the MIPS program with our additions; we merely added code to implement our data gathering.

Our methodology implies the use of the MIPS-style compiler technology of [Gross83]. Therefore, our results are valid for only this type of compiler technology. This is important to underline because the impacts of different compiler technologies may be as pronounced as the impacts of different instruction formats.

4: Experiment

As already indicated, our experiment consisted of three subexperiments. These are described next. Note that all data presented here have been averaged** over the entire set of selected benchmarks.

4.1: Static Instruction Count Subexperiment

Obtaining the static instruction count is relatively straightforward. We added code to the section of the MIPS simulator that loads the MIPS instructions into memory. For each of the candidate formats, we examined each MIPS instruction as it was loaded and performed the analysis, as indicated in the Appendix. After the loading was completed, the total number of candidate instructions was then outputed to a file.

The results of this subexperiment are shown in Figure 2. The program size is shown in terms of instruction words and bytes. In this figure, the candidate instruction counts were normalized to 1000 MIPS instructions. These results are for the entire set* of benchmark programs (each benchmark receiving equal weight) described in Section 3. Note that (in Figure 2) the number of bytes is not equal to four times the number of words (except for the MIPS format). This is a side effect of the fact that the bit-length of candidate formats is less than 32-bits.

4.2: Dynamic Instruction Count Subexperiment

We can obtain the dynamic instruction count in much the same manner as we obtain the static instruction count.

---

*The benchmark "towers" is not included in this experiment because of its excessive computational requirements.

**Average benchmark size was calculated as the sum of all benchmark sizes divided by the number of benchmarks.

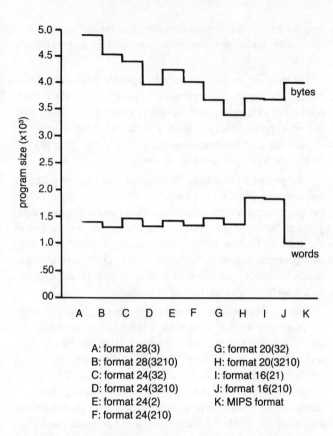

A: format 28(3)
B: format 28(3210)
C: format 24(32)
D: format 24(3210)
E: format 24(2)
F: format 24(210)
G: format 20(32)
H: format 20(3210)
I: format 16(21)
J: format 16(210)
K: MIPS format

Figure 2: Instruction Format Static Instruction Counts.

However, instead of adding code to examine MIPS instructions as they are *loaded* by the simulator, we add code to examine them as they are *executed*. The modified simulation program then outputs the total number of candidate instruction executions into a file.

The results are shown in Figure 3. Again, the dynamic instruction count for each candidate format was normalized to 1000 MIPS instruction executions. These results are for the same set of benchmarks that were used in the previous subexperiment, where each benchmark again received equal weight.

In Table 2 we show the breakdown of costs that cause the candidate formats to have higher dynamic instruction counts. The values in this table are the percentage increase in dynamic execution count, measured as a percentage of one MIPS instruction, caused by the associated cost. Most of the candidate formats show immediate costs of approximately 10 percent; only the 16-bit formats are significantly affected by address costs, and all the formats show a relatively high packing cost.

4.3: Execution Time Subexperiment

Determining the execution time for each of our candidate instruction formats was more difficult than calculating the

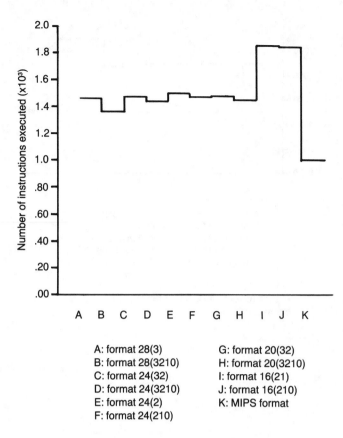

A: format 28(3) G: format 20(32)
B: format 28(3210) H: format 20(3210)
C: format 24(32) I: format 16(21)
D: format 24(3210) J: format 16(210)
E: format 24(2) K: MIPS format
F: format 24(210)

Figure 3: Instruction Format Dynamic Instruction Counts.

above static and dynamic instruction counts. Once again, the benefits derived from compact instructions are attributable to higher cache hit rates, main memory hit rates, and so forth. Therefore, for a fair instruction format comparison, we selected an instruction pipeline to be used by all the candidate formats. We used the pipeline indicated by Figure 1b, as it contains favorable properties for GaAs environment

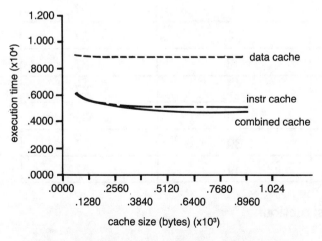

Figure 4: Instruction Format 28(3) Execution Time vs. Cache Size.

[MiFuH86]. Therefore, one instruction fetch corresponds to three datapath cycles. For this subexperiment, a cache hit results in a delay that is equivalent of three cycles, and a miss results in a six cycle delay. This is because the main memory is relatively fast and relatively small.

There are two parts to this subexperiment. First, we ran the MIPS simulator and cache simulator to obtain the execution time for each instruction format as a function of cache size. Then we used this information in order to obtain the execution time for each cache size as a function of instruction format.

In Figure 4, we show the results of the first part of this subexperiment. This figure plots execution time versus cache size for three cache configurations: instruction cache only, data cache only,* and combined instruction and data cache. In this figure, the execution time has been normalized to the number of instruction cycles necessary to execute 1000 MIPS instructions in its silicon environment, and with no cache miss penalties. We only present one plot because the results for the other candidate formats are nearly identical to this one.

In Figures 5 and 6, we show the second set of plots for this subexperiment. These figures show execution time versus instruction format for a particularly small cache size (64 and 128 bytes) and two different cache configurations (instruction-only and data-only). Again, the execution times have been normalized to the number of instruction cycles necessary to execute 1000 MIPS instructions in its silicon environment, and with no cache miss penalties. These two plots indicate a relatively large cache miss ratio. Therefore, although the caches of these sizes are sometimes the only caches feasible in GaAs systems, their incorporation is questionable due to the low efficiency.

5: Discussion

Here we discuss the conclusions related to six areas of possible impact of different instruction formats considered here. We have noticed a number of important differences between the E/D-MESFET GaAs study presented here and the recent CMOS silicon experiments [Chow 86].

5.1: The Effect of Instruction Format on Instruction Counts

From Figure 2, the number of words required to implement the benchmark programs, as expected, is seen to increase as the format lengths are decreased. All of the

---

*Although the "data-cache-only" approach is never (or almost never) used, for consistency reasons we present data for that case as well.

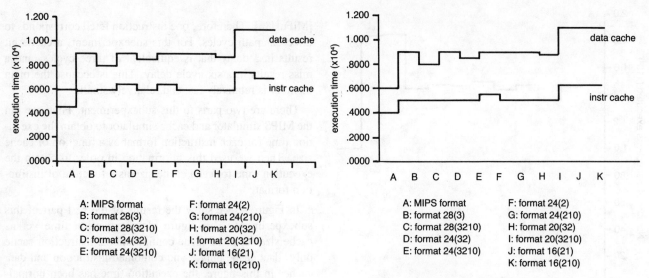

Figure 5: Execution Time for Each Instruction Format with Cache.

A: MIPS format
B: format 28(3)
C: format 28(3210)
D: format 24(32)
E: format 24(3210)
F: format 24(2)
G: format 24(210)
H: format 20(32)
I: format 20(3210)
J: format 16(21)
K: format 16(210)

Figure 6: Execution Time for Each Instruction Format with Cache.

A: MIPS format
B: format 28(3)
C: format 28(3210)
D: format 24(32)
E: format 24(3210)
F: format 24(2)
G: format 24(210)
H: format 20(32)
I: format 20(3210)
J: format 16(21)
K: format 16(210)

Table 2: Breakdown of Dynamic Costs for the Candidate Fomats.

Format	Immediate Cost*	Address Cost*	Packing Cost*
28(3)	10	0	37
28(3210)	0	0	37
24(32)	11	0	37
24(3210)	7	0	37
24(2)	10	3	37
24(210)	7	3	37
20(32)	11	0	37
20(3210)	8	0	37
16(21)	11	39	37
16(210)	11	39	37

* Measured as a percentage of one MIPS instruction.

308

formats have static instruction counts within 50 percent of the instruction count of the MIPS format, except for the two 16-bit formats: 16(21) and 16(210). These 16-bit formats have instruction counts almost 100 percent greater than the MIPS instruction count. Clearly, the transition from a 20-bit format to a 16-bit format can be damaging.

The number of bytes required to implement the benchmark programs, or equivalently, the program size, generally shows a decline as the format length is decreased, until the 16-bit formats are reached. The 20-bit formats generate the most compact programs, but the 16-bit formats achieve code sizes smaller than the MIPS format as well.

From Figure 3, the dynamic instruction count is seen to follow the same trend as the static instruction count. The 16-bit formats are again severely penalized. Tables 1 and 2 can help explain this phenomenon. From Table 1, we observe that the 8-bit opcode requirement only leaves eight bits for addressing, enough for two addresses. The extremely large address cost for these two formats (indicated in Table 2) allows us to conclude that two addresses are very frequently not enough. From Table 2, we see that three addresses are required 28 percent of the time (39/137). This is much higher than we anticipated, in light of the 13 percent figure for 3-address assignment statements presented in [Myers82].

5.2: The Effect of Cache Size on Execution Time

From Figures 4 and 5, we can observe some general trends. For these formats, execution time generally decreases as cache size is increased. We obviously expected this. However, the small memory capacity at which the execution time decrease levels off clearly demonstrates two facts: (a) that all benchmarks are relatively small and (b) that our benchmarks were written to obey strictly the basic rules of the top-down, structured, and modular programming.

We also observe that a data cache alone does a much poorer job than either an instruction cache alone or a combined cache. The reason for this is the much higher frequency of instruction fetches than data loads, in an environment that penalizes a noncache access. We see a small advantage for the combined cache at increasing cache sizes, but no significant difference between the performance of the instruction cache and the combined cache.

5.3: The Effect of Fewer Register Fields

Looking back at Table 1, we observe that the only difference between instruction formats 28(3) and 24(2) is the lower total number of bits in format 24(2) due to the removal of one register field. We now discuss the relative performance of these two instruction formats.

Figure 2 shows that the total program size for format 24(2) is approximately 10 percent lower than the program size for format 28(3). From Figure 3, we see that the number of format 24(2) instructions executed is only a few percentages higher than the number of format 28(3) instructions executed.

The execution times for these two instruction formats (shown in Figures 4 and 5) generally indicate a slightly inferior performance of the 24(2) instruction format. In memory configurations consisting of an instruction cache the 24(2) format execution time is generally a few percentages higher (approaching five percent) than the 28(3) format execution time. In the data-cache-only configurations, where we expect the relative performances to match their relative number of instruction executions, the performance of both formats is nearly the same.

This subexperiment indicates a slight degradation in performance when reducing instruction format size through the elimination of one register field.

5.4: The Effect of Smaller Immediate Field Lengths

Again looking at Table 1, we observe that the only difference between instruction formats 28(3) and 24(32) is the lower total number of bits in format 24(32), due to its smaller immediate field. We now discuss the relative performance of these two instruction formats.

Figure 2 shows that the program size for format 24(32) is nearly 10 percent lower than the program size for format 28(3). Again, Figure 3 shows the relative number of instructions executed, where it is seen that format 24(32) requires slightly more instruction executions than format 28(3).

The execution times shown in Figures 4 and 5 show little difference in performance between these two instruction formats, although the slight differences that do appear favor format 28(3). In general, the relative performance of these two instruction formats corresponds to their relative number of instructions executed.

In this experiment, we conclude that reducing instruction format size by reducing immediate field size has very little impact on performance.

5.5: The Effect of Variable Immediate Field Sizes

From Table 1, the difference between instruction formats 28(3), 24(32), 24(2), 20(32), 16(21) and 28(3210), 24(3210), 24(210), 20(3210), 16(210), respectively, is the greater flexibility in immediate field size allowed in the second set of formats. The formats in the first set maintain a rigid immediate field, while formats in the second set increase their immediate field size to consume all the bits not needed by register addresses. We now discuss the relative performance of these two methods of implementing immediate fields.

From Figure 2, we observe that the program sizes of the

variable-immediate-field formats are smaller, with the differences ranging from approximately 10 percent in formats 28(3210) and 24(3210) to almost no change in format 16(210). The same trend is evident in the number of instruction executions, shown in Figure 3. We can explain the lower improvement of the shorter instruction formats by viewing again Table 1, where we observe that the shorter formats do not have enough bits to substantially lengthen their immediate fields.

The execution times in Figures 4 and 5 consistently show that the formats with variable length immediate fields perform better, albeit only by a small margin, than the formats with fixed length immediate fields.

In this experiment, we have observed that varying immediate field lengths to use the instruction bits not needed by register addresses does indeed lead to smaller program size, fewer instruction executions, and lower execution time.

5.6: The Use of Compact Formats for Instruction Packing

Instruction formats 16(21) and 16(210) are both only one half as long as a single MIPS instruction; therefore, two such instructions may be fetched in parallel and require no more processor-memory bandwidth than required by the MIPS format. We find it interesting to examine the performance of such a form of instruction packing.*

From Figure 2, we observe that the program size of both 16-bit formats is nearly 10 percent lower than the program size of MIPS format. However, Figure 3 shows that the number of 16-bit instructions executed is nearly 90 percent higher.

If two instructions of the 16(21) format are concatenated to form a single 32-bit packed instruction, then this compact, packed instruction format would actually require five percent fewer instruction executions than the MIPS format. This is also true for the 16(210) format. It is apparent that this type of packed format is more successful in eliminating redundancy than is the MIPS format.

From Table 1, we see that much of the performance degradation in the 16(21) and 16(210) formats is due to addressing cost. Again, this cost results from the 2-address limit imposed by the short instruction length and from the 8-bit opcode. If 4-bit opcodes were used for some frequent operations, the number of instruction executions could be significantly reduced at the cost of additional decoding and control logic. Alternatively, 18-bit or 20-bit operations may instead be packed to provide much better performance with

reasonable instruction sizes. If two 20(3210)-format instructions were packed, as Figure 2 indicates, approximately 30 percent fewer of these 40-bit instructions would be required than the 32-bit MIPS instructions.

It is quite apparent that the successful elimination of redundancy from instructions makes instruction packing increasingly attractive. In an environment with long effective off-chip memory latency, the use of compact formats for instruction packing is an attractive approach.

6: Summary

In general, given our system implementation assumptions, this experiment has shown that reducing redundancy in immediate fields and address fields of instructions leads to programs that are more compact, programs that do not necessarily execute faster, and instruction formats that may be concatenated to form packed formats, which can be expected to perform better than the packed MIPS format.

In given conditions (relatively small cache memory and one specific compiler technology), the impacts of instruction format are relatively small—only about 10 percent (in terms of improving the execution time of compiled HLL code). Is this improvement good enough and worth the effort? This question should be answered in consideration of the fact that improvements to come from compiler technology may be higher than 10 percent.

Note that all of our system implementation assumptions directly affect our results. These include our particular choice of the pipeline structure, our choice of a two-level memory hierarchy, our memory access to datapath delay ratio choices, and so forth. In addition to these, the characteristics of our simulation system also affect our results.

7: Acknowledgment

The authors are thankful to Bill Heagerty of RCA Corporation for his help. Thanks are also due to the unknown reviewer who made a number of important comments and suggestions.

8: References

[AleWo75] Alexander, W.G. and Wortman, D.B., "Static and Dynamic Characteristics of XPL Programs," *IEEE Computer*, Vol. 8, No. 11, November 1975, pp. 41-46.

[Barne85] Barney, C., "DARPA Eyes 100-mips GaAs Chip for Star Wars," *ElectronicsWeek*, Vol. 58, No. 20, May 20, 1985, pp. 22-23.

[Chow 86] Chow, P., "Architectural Issues in Designing a Silicon CMOS Microprocessor," *Purdue University MSEE Thesis*, December 1986.

[EdWeL83] Eden, R.C., Welch, B.M., and Lee, F.S., "Implications and Projections of Gallium Arsenide Tech-

---

*Note that it is not always possible to execute every pair of consecutive instructions in parallel because the result of one instruction may be used by the next.

nology in High Speed Computing," *Proceedings of the IEEE International Conference on Computer Design; VLSI in Computers,* Computer Society of the IEEE, Washington, D.C., 1983, pp. 30-33.

[Ferra78] Ferrari, D., *Computer Systems Performance Evaluation,* Wiley, New York, 1978.

[FlyHo72] Flynn, M. J., Hoevel, L. W., "Execution Architecture: The DELTRAN Experiment," *IEEE Transactions on Computers,* Vol. C-32, No. 2, February 1983, pp. 156-175.

[FlyHe63] Flynn, J. J., Henderson, D. S., "Variable Field-Length Data Manipulation in a Fixed Word-Length Memory," *IEEE Transactions on Electronic Computers,* Vol. EC-12, October 1963, pp. 512-517.

[Fura85] Fura, D., "Architectural Approaches for GaAs Exploitation in High-Speed Computer Design," *Purdue University Technical Report, TR-EE 85-17,* West Lafayette, Ind., December 1985.

[GiGrH83] Gill, J., Gross, T., Hennessy, J., Jouppi, N., Przybylski, S., and Rowen, C., "Summary of MIPS Instructions," *Technical Note No. 83-237,* Stanford University, Stanford, Calif., November 1983.

[Gross83] Gross, T., "Code Optimization of Pipeline Constraints," *Technical Report No. 83-255,* Stanford University, Stanford, Calif., December 1983.

[Hehne76] Hehner, E.C.R., "Computer Design to Minimize Memory Requirements," *IEEE Computer,* Vol. 9, No. 8, August 1976, pp. 65-70.

[HeScZ85] Helbig, W.A., Schellack, R.H., and Zieger, R.M., "The Design and Construction of a GaAs Technology Demonstration Microprocessor," *Proceedings of Midcon/85,* IEEE, New York, 1985, pp. 23/1.1-23/1.6.

[HeJoG82] Hennessy, J., Jouppi, N., Gill, J., Baskett, F., Strong, A., Gross, T., Rowen, C., and Leonard, J., "The MIPS Machine," *Digest of Papers, Spring COMPCON 82,* Computer Society of the IEEE, Washington, D.C., 2-7.

[Huffm52] Huffman, D.A., "A Method for the Construction of Minimum Redundancy Codes," *Proceedings of the I.R.E.,* Vol. 40, No. 9, September 1952, pp. 1098-1101.

[Katev83] Katevenis, M.G.H., "Reduced Instruction Set Computer Architectures for VLSI," *Report No. UCB/CSD 83/141,* University of California at Berkeley, Berkeley, Calif., October 1983.

[MiFuH86] Milutinović, V., Fura, D., and Helbig, W., "An Introduction to GaAs Microprocessor Architecture for VLSI," *IEEE Computer,* Vol. 19, No. 3, March 1986, pp. 30-42.

[MiFuH87] Milutinović, V., Fura, D., Helbig, W., and Linn, J., "Architecture/Compiler Synergism in Galium

Arsenide Computer Systems," *IEEE Computer,* Vol. 20, No. 5, May 1987, pp. 72-93.

[Milut86] Milutinović, V., Editor, "GaAs Microprocessor Technology," *IEEE Computer,* Special Issue, Vol. 19, No. 10, October 1986.

[MiSiF86] Milutinović, V., Silbey, A., Fura, D., Bettinger, M., Keirn, K., Helbig, W., Heagerty, W., Zieger, R., and Curtice, W., "Important Issues in Designing GaAs Computer Systems," *IEEE Computer,* Vol. 19, No. 10, October 1986, pp. 45-57.

[Myers82] Myers, G.J., *Advances in Computer Architecture-Second Edition,* John Wiley & Sons, New York, 1982.

[PatPi82] Patterson, D.A., Piepho, R.S., "Assessing RISCs in High-Level Language Support," *IEEE MICRO,* November 1982, pp. 9-19.

[Patte85] Patterson, D.A., "Reduced Instruction Set Computers," *Communications of the ACM,* Vol. 28, No. 1, January 1985, pp. 8-21.

[SmiGo83] Smith, J.E., Goodman, J.R., "A Study of Instruction Cache Organizations and Replacement Policies," *Proceedings of the Tenth Annual Symposium on Computer Architecture,* Association for Computing Machinery, Inc., New York, 1983, pp. 132-137.

[Smith85] Smith, A.J., "Cache Evaluation and the Impact of Workload Choice," *Proceedings of the 12th Annual Symposium on Computer Architecture,* Computer Society of the IEEE, Washington, D.C., 1985, pp. 64-73.

[Whitb85] Whitby-Stevens, C., "The Transputer," *Proceedings of the 12th Annual International Symposium on Computer Architecture,* Computer Society of the IEEE, Washington, D.C., 1985, pp. 292-300.

[Wilne72] Wilner, W. T., "Burroughs B1700 Memory Utilization," *Proceedings of the Fall Joint Computer Conference,* AFIPS Press, Reston, Va., November 1972, pp. 579-586.

Appendix: Determination of Candidate Instruction Format Costs

In this appendix we present the costs associated with each candidate instruction format, and describe our methodology for determining these costs. Once again, the three costs which a candidate format may experience are:

(1) *Packing cost.* Some MIPS instructions are successfully packed and hence, contain two operations. None of the candidate formats can execute two operations from a single instruction fetch.

(2) *Address cost.* MIPS instructions contain operations with as many as three address specifications. Some of the candidate formats have only two register address

fields, while some have only two address fields, one of which may be an immediate field.

(3) *Immediate cost*. MIPS instructions have immediate fields containing as many as 24 bits. None of the candidate formats have immediate fields that long, and most immediate fields are much shorter.

A: Cost Determination

Packing costs are determined simply by examining MIPS instructions which are packable, and determining if the packed operation is a NOOP or not. The cost penalty is one instruction if the packed operation is not a NOOP. Because only 12 bits of a MIPS instruction are allocated to the packed operation, it must be a 2-address ALU operation. For our candidate formats, the packed operation cannot yield an address or immediate cost.

Address costs are determined by examining the address (register or immediate) needs of MIPS instructions and determining if the candidate format has enough of the right kind of address fields. The cost penalty is one instruction if the candidate format lacks the necessary fields.

Immediate costs are determined by examining the immediate values of MIPS instructions and determining if the candidate format has enough bits to represent them. The cost penalty is one instruction if the candidate format lacks the necessary immediate field length. We assume that the entire second word may be used for immediate field if necessary.** For some candidate formats, this yields a maximum immediate field size of 20 bits while some MIPS instructions contain 24-bit immediate fields. However, the

---

**Implemented in the RCA's 32-bit GaAs microprocessor.

MIPS 24-bit immediate fields are mainly used for addressing, and since the MIPS instructions and data are all loaded into memory addresses below 32,000, we should not see immediate fields of over 20 bits for addressing in this study. The only other MIPS instruction which uses over 20 bits of immediate field is the "load immediate" instruction; but we found this instruction to represent well below one percent of all instruction executions, so we can safely ignore it. Therefore, a maximum penalty of one is sufficient.

B: Presentation of Costs

In Table 1 we listed the fields for the candidate instruction formats. Based upon this table, Sections 4, and [GiGrH83], we can derive the costs for each candidate format. We list these costs in Tables B.1 through B.10. In Table B.11 we summarize MIPS instructions from [GiGrH83]. We use several shorthand notations:

(1) We say " + 1 over x" to indicate a cost of one instruction if a MIPS immediate value requiring more than x is encountered.

(2) We say " + 1 if packed" to indicate a cost of one instruction if a packed MIPS instruction is encountered.

(3) We say " + 1 if xreg" to indicate a cost of one instruction if a MIPS instruction requires x or more *distinct* registers.

(4) We say " + 1 if xaddr" to indicate a cost of one instruction if a MIPS instruction requires x or more *distinct* addresses (register or immediate operands).

(5) We say " + 1" to indicate a cost of one instruction always.

Table B.1: Costs for Candidate Format 28(3).

MIPS Instr.	Cost	MIPS Instr.	Cost
AA	+1 if packed	LI	+1 over 8
BC	+1	LSD	+1 over 8
	+1 over 8	SPC	+1 over 8
BU	+1 over 8	SC	+0
JB	+1 over 8	SB	+1 over 8
JBI	+1 over 8	SBA	+1 if packed
JBIA	+1 if packed	SBIA	+1 if packed
JD	+1 over 8	SBSA	+1 if packed
JI	+1 over 8	SD	+1 over 8
JISS	+1 over 8	SPCB	+1 over 8
LB	+1 over 8	SPCBA	+1 if packed
LBA	+1 if packed	SPCD	+1 over 8
LBIA	+1 if packed	SSUD	+1 over 8
LBSA	+1 if packed	TC	+1
LD	+1 over 8		+1 over 8

Table B.2: Costs for Candidate Format 28(3210).

MIPS Instr.	Cost	MIPS Instr.	Cost
AA	+1 if packed	LI	+1 over 16
BC	+1	LSD	+1 over 20
BU	+1 over 20	SPC	+1 over 20
JB	+1 over 16	SC	+0
JBI	+1 over 16	SB	+1 over 12
JBIA	+1 if packed	SBA	+1 if packed
JD	+1 over 20	SBIA	+1 if packed
JI	+1 over 20	SBSA	+1 if packed
JISS	+1 over 20	SD	+1 over 16
LB	+1 over 12	SPCB	+1 over 16
LBA	+1 if packed	SPCBA	+1 if packed
LBIA	+1 if packed	SPCD	+1 over 20
LBSA	+1 if packed	SSUD	+1 over 20
LD	+1 over 16	TC	+1

Table B.3: Costs for Candidate Format 24(32).

MIPS Instr.	Cost	MIPS Instr.	Cost
AA	+1 if packed	LI	+1 over 4
BC	+1	LSD	+1 over 4
	+1 over 4	SPC	+1 over 4
BU	+1 over 4	SC	+0
JB	+1 over 4	SB	+1 over 4
JBI	+1 over 4	SBA	+1 over 4
JBIA	+1 if over 4		+1 if packed
	+1 if packed	SBIA	+1 if packed
JD	+1 over 4	SBSA	+1 if packed
JI	+1 over 4	SD	+1 over 4
JISS	+1 over 4	SPCB	+1 over 4
LB	+1 over 4	SPCBA	+1 over 4
LBA	+1 over 4		+1 if packed
	+1 if packed	SPCD	+1 over 4
LBIA	+1 if packed	SSUD	+1 over 4
LBSA	+1 if packed	TC	+1
LD	+1 over 4		+1 over 4

Table B.4: Costs for Candidate Format 24 (3210).

MIPS Instr.	Cost	MIPS Instr.	Cost
AA	+1 if packed	LI	+1 over 12
BC	+1	LSD	+1 over 16
BU	+1 over 16	SPC	+1 over 16
JB	+1 over 12	SC	+0
JBI	+1 over 12	SB	+1 over 8
JBIA	+1 if packed	SBA	+1 if packed
JD	+1 over 16	SBIA	+1 if packed
JI	+1 over 16	SBSA	+1 if packed
JISS	+1 over 16	SD	+1 over 12
LB	+1 over 8	SPCB	+1 over 12
LBA	+1 if packed	SPCBA	+1 if packed
LBIA	+1 if packed	SPCD	+1 over 16
LBSA	+1 if packed	SSUD	+1 over 16
LD	+1 over 12	TC	+1

Table B.5: Costs for Candidate Format 24(2).

MIPS Instr.	Cost	MIPS Instr.	Cost
AA	+1 if 3reg	LI	+1 over 8
	+1 if packed	LSD	+1 over 8
BC	+1	SPC	+1 over 8
	+1 over 8	SC	+0
BU	+1 over 8	SB	+1 over 8
JB	+1 over 8	SBA	+1 if packed
JBI	+1 over 8	SBIA	+1 if 3reg
JBIA	+1 if packed		+1 if packed
JD	+1 over 8	SBSA	+1 if packed
JI	+1 over 8	SD	+1 over 8
JISS	+1 over 8	SPCB	+1 over 8
LB	+1 over 8	SPCBA	+1 if packed
LBA	+1 if packed	SPCD	+1 over 8
LBIA	+1 if 3reg	SSUD	+1 over 8
	+1 if packed	TC	+1
LBSA	+1 if packed		+1 over 8
LD	+1 over 8		

Table B.6: Costs for Candidate Format 24(210).

MIPS Instr.	Cost	MIPS Instr.	Cost
AA	+1 if 3reg	LI	+1 over 12
	+1 if packed	LSD	+1 over 16
BC	+1	SPC	+1 over 16
BU	+1 over 16	SC	+0
JB	+1 over 12	SB	+1 over 8
JBI	+1 over 12	SBA	+1 if packed
JBIA	+1 if packed	SBIA	+1 if 3reg
JD	+1 over 16		+1 if packed
JI	+1 over 16	SBSA	+1 if packed
JISS	+1 over 16	SD	+1 over 12
LB	+1 over 8	SPCB	+1 over 12
LBA	+1 if packed	SPCBA	+1 if packed
LBIA	+1 if 3reg	SPCD	+1 over 16
	+1 if packed	SSUD	+1 over 16
LBSA	+1 if packed	TC	+1
LD	+1 over 12		

Table B.7: Costs for Candidate Format 20(32).

MIPS Instr.	Cost	MIPS Instr.	Cost
AA	+1 if packed	LI	+1 over 4
BC	+1	LSD	+1 over 4
	+1 over 4	SPC	+1 over 4
BU	+1 over 4	SC	+0
JB	+1 over 4	SB	+1 over 4
JBI	+1 over 4	SBA	+1 over 4
JBIA	+1 over 4		+1 if packed
	+1 if packed	SBIA	+1 if packed
JD	+1 over 4	SBSA	+1 if packed
JI	+1 over 4	SD	+1 over 4
JISS	+1 over 4	SPCB	+1 over 4
LB	+1 over 4	SPCBA	+1 over 4
LBA	+1 over 4		+1 if packed
	+1 if packed	SPCD	+1 over 4
LBIA	+1 if packed	SSUD	+1 over 4
LBSA	+1 if packed	TC	+1
LD	+1 over 4		+1 over 4

Table B.8: Costs for Candidate Format 20(3210).

MIPS Instr.	Cost	MIPS Instr.	Cost
AA	+1 if packed	LI	+1 over 8
BC	+1	LSD	+1 over 12
BU	+1 over 12	SPC	+1 over 12
JB	+1 over 8	SC	+0
JBI	+1 over 8	SB	+1 over 4
JBIA	+1 if packed	SBA.	+1 if (2reg and over 4)
JD	+1 over 12		+1 if packed
JI	+1 over 12		
JISS	+1 over 12	SBIA	+1 if packed
LB	+1 over 4	SBSA	+1 if packed
LBA	+1 if (2reg and over 4)	SD	+1 over 8
		SPCB	+1 over 8
	+1 if packed	SPCBA	+1 if packed
LBIA	+1 if packed	SPCD	+1 over 12
LBSA	+1 if packed	SSUD	+1 over 12
LD	+1 over 8	TC	+1

Table B.9: Costs for Candidate Format 16(21).

MIPS Instr.	Cost	MIPS Instr.	Cost
AA	+1 if 3addr	LI	+1 over 4
	+1 if packed	LSD	+1 over 4
BC	+1	SPC	+1 over 4
	+1 if 2addr	SC	+1 if 3addr
	+1 over 4	SB	+1 if (3addr or over 4)
BU	+1 over 4		
JB	+1 over 4	SBA	+1 if (3addr or over 4)
JBI	+1 over 4		
JBIA	+1 over 4		+1 if packed
	+1 if packed	SBIA	+1 if 3addr
JD	+1 over 4		+1 if packed
JI	+1 over 4	SBSA	+1 if 3addr
JISS	+1 over 4		+1 if packed
LB	+1 if (3addr or over 4)	SD	+1 over 4
		SPCB	+1 over 4
LBA	+1 if (3addr or over 4)	SPCBA	+1 over 4
			+1 if packed
	+1 if packed	SPCD	+1 over 4
LBIA	+1 if 3addr	SSUD	+1 over 4
	+1 if packed	TC	+1
LBSA	+1 if 3addr		+1 if 2addr
	+1 if packed		+1 over 4
LD	+1 over 4		

Table B.10: Costs for Candidate Format 16(210).

MIPS Instr.	Cost	MIPS Instr.	Cost
AA	+1 if 3addr	LI	+1 over 4
	+1 if packed	LSD	+1 over 8
BC	+1	SPC	+1 over 8
	+1 if 2addr	SC	+1
	+1 over 8	SB	+1 if (3addr
BU	+1 over 8		or over 4)
JB	+1 over 4	SBA	+1 if (3addr
JBI	+1 over 4		or over 4)
JBIA	+1 over 4		+1 if packed
	+1 if packed	SBIA	+1 if 3addr
JD	+1 over 8		+1 if packed
JI	+1 over 8	SBSA	+1 if 3addr
JISS	+1 over 8		+1 if packed
LB	+1 if (3addr	SD	+1 over 4
	or over 4)	SPCB	+1 over 4
LBA	+1 if (3addr	SPCBA	+1 over 4
	or over 4)		+1 if packed
	+1 if packed	SPCD	+1 over 8
LBIA	+1 if 3addr	SSUD	+1 over 8
	+1 if packed	TC	+1
LBSA	+1 if 3addr		+1 if 2addr
	+1 if packed		+1 if over 8
LD	+1 over 4		

Table B.11: MIPS Instructions.

(AA)   ALU3 + ALU2. Contains two registers, one register/4-bit immediate field, and one packed operation.

(BC)   Branch Conditionally. Contains one register, one register/4-bit immediate field, one 4-bit condition field, and one 12-bit immediate field.

(BU)   Branch Unconditionally. Contains one 24-bit immediate field.

(JB)   Jump Based. Contains one register and one 20-bit immediate field.

(JBI)   Jump Based Indirect. Contains one register and one 20-bit immediate field.

(JBIA)   Jump Based Indirect + ALU2. Contains one register, one 8-bit immediate field, and one packed operation.

(JD)   Jump Direct. Contains one 24-bit immediate field.

(JI)   Jump Indirect. Contains one 24-bit immediate field.

(JISS)   Jump Indirect and Setup Su-register. Contains one 24-bit immediate field.

(LB)   Load Based. Contains one register and one 20-bit immediate field.

(LBA)   Load Based + ALU2. Contains one register, one 8-bit immediate field, and one packed operation.

(LBIA)   Load Base-Indexed + ALU2. Contains three registers and one packed operation.

(LBSA)   Load Base-Shifted + ALU2. Contains two registers, one 4-bit immediate field, and one packed operation.

(LD)   Load Direct. Contains one register and one 24-bit immediate field.

(LI)   Load Immediate. Contains one register and one 24-bit immediate field.

(LSD)   LoadS Direct. Contains one 24-bit immediate field.

(SPC)   SavePC. Contains one 24-bit immediate field.

(SC)   Set Conditionally. Contains one register, one register/4-bit immediate field, and one 4-bit condition field.

(SB)   Store Based. Contains two registers and one 20-bit immediate field.

(SBA)   Store Based + ALU2. Contains two registers, one 8-bit immediate field, and one packed operation.

(SBIA)   Store Base-Indexed + ALU2. Contains three registers and one packed operation.

(SBSA)   Store Base-Shifted + ALU2. Contains two registers, one 4-bit immediate field, and one packed operation.

(SD)   Store Direct. Contains one register and one 24-bit immediate field.

(SPCB)   Store PC Based. Contains one register and one 20-bit immediate field.

(SPCBA)   StorePC Based + ALU2. Contains one register, one 8-bit immediate field, and one packed operation.

(SPCD)   StorePC Direct. Contains one 24-bit immediate field.

(SSUD)   StoreSU Direct. Contains one 24-bit immediate field.

(TC)   Trap Conditionally. Contains one register, one register/4-bit immediate field, one 4-bit condition field, and one 11-bit code field.

Multiplier/Shifter Design Tradeoffs in a 32-Bit GaAs Microprocessor[†]

Veljko Milutinović and Mark Bettinger
School of Electrical Engineering
Purdue University
West Lafayette, IN 47907
(317) 494-3530

Walter Helbig
Advanced Technology Laboratories
RCA Corporation
Moorestown, NJ 08057
(608) 866-6530

Abstract

Here we concentrate on design tradeoffs between the bit-serial multiplier and the full barrel shifter combined with a larger register file. We analyze and compare three alternatives, for a given set of technology related parameters, and a given set of HLL benchmarks. Although our basic concern here is the design of a 32-bit GaAs microprocessor on a single chip, the implications of our results are more general.

1: Introduction

This paper presents the results of a simulation study that compares the impacts of different internal configurations on the overall performance of RCA's 32-bit GaAs microprocessor ([Barne83]). For more details about the architecture and the design of that microprocessor see [HelMi88]. We have conducted this analysis in conditions typical of the DCFL E/D-MESFET GaAs technology. For more information on the DCFL E/D-MESFET GaAs technology and on its brief comparison with CMOS silicon technology, see [Milut86].

We analyzed three different internal configurations for possible implementation in the GaAs technology: baseline, alternative #1, and alternative 2. "Baseline" is the basic Stanford University MIPS configuration [HeJoP83], with 16 general purpose registers and a full-barrel shifter (with shifting capabilities of 0 to 31 bits). "Alternative #1" includes 14 general purpose registers (i.e., two registers less, compared to the baseline), a minimal shifter (with shifting capabilities of only 1, 2, and 3 bits),* and a low-transistor-count on-chip bit-serial multiplier [Hwang79]. "Alternative #2" includes 20 general purpose registers (i.e., four registers more, compared to the baseline), a minimal shifter (1, 2, and 3 bits), and an off-chip bit-serial multiplier (of the same type as in the case of the alternative #1).

For the chosen DCFL E/D-MESFET GaAs cell family, all three candidate configurations are of approximately the same VLSI area.** Therefore, the basic question was how to invest the available VLSI area, i.e., which of the three candidate configurations to choose for the implementation. Obviously, the answer is application dependent. A general discussion of these and related issues is given in [MiSiF86].

The advantages and disadvantages of different configurations are discussed in Section 2. Our methodology for comparison of different candidate configurations, as well as the implementation of that methodology, are discussed in Section 3. Our experiments and their results are given in Section 4. Discussion of the results is given in Section 5.

2: Advantages and Disadvantages of the Candidate Configurations

The basic difference between the baseline and the alternative #1 is that the full shifter was replaced by the minimal shifter and a bit-serial multiplier. The ratio of VLSI areas of the chosen bit-serial multiplier and the chosen full shifter was about 12 to 7 (approximately 1200 versus 700 gates). Therefore, an appropriate number of general purpose regis-

---

†This research was supported by RCA Corporation, and is related to the design of RCA's 32-bit GaAs microprocessor on a single chip.

*In the case of the chosen DCFL E/D-MESFET GaAs cell family, once the shifting by 1 and 2 were implemented, it was trivial to implement the shifting by 3.

**Actually, in the initial stages of our research, we were considering still another alternative—one based on a barrel shifter with shifting capabilities of 1, 2, 3, 8, 16, and 24 bits, plus a combination of other resources, to maintain the same VLSI area as in the other alternatives discussed here. The major potential advantage of this configuration was related to byte manipulation operations. However, we did not continue to look into this configuration, as we were discouraged by our research sponsor, and his application.

ters had to be excluded from alternative #1, to equalize the VLSI layout area.

The smaller general register file size of the alternative #1 has some negative effects. In RISC-style architectures, the increased number of general purpose registers increases the reusability of data. Consequently, the dynamic percentage of LOAD and STORE instructions is decreased. This is very important for technologies like GaAs, which are characterized by a relatively high ratio of off-chip to on-chip delays [MiFuH86]. These long off-chip delays are especially dangerous in the case of cache misses. Typically, GaAs caches are off the CPU chip but on the same hybrid package. However, the main memory (or the second level of the cache memory) is off the hybrid package. For our GaAs technology, the ratio of cache access delay to datapath delay (register fetch + ALU operation + register writeback) was about 3, and the ratio of memory access delay to datapath delay was from about 6 to about 9, depending on the physical location of the memory cell.

The reduced capabilities of the shifter in alternative #1 also have negative effects. The shifts of more than 3 bits have to be synthetized with more than one shift operation. This means an increase in the program code size, which decreases the effective cache size (a semantically identical segment of code, for the alternative with the larger code size requires a larger cache memory to maintain the same hit ratio [Smith82]). Generally, the shift counts other than 1 or 2 are relatively rare. However, byte manipulation operations heavily rely on shift counts of 8, 16, and 24. Also, many optimizing compilers are able to substitute selected multiplication operations with one or more long shifts. Still, the dynamic probability of long shifts is relatively low.

On the other hand, there are several positive effects of replacing the barrel shifter with the bit-serial multiplier, especially in the applications with a relatively high dynamic percentage of multiplication operations.

First, if any form of a hardware multiplier is existing, the program code size will decrease.*** For example, in the Stanford University MIPS machine, 9 instructions are needed to synthetize a 32-bit by 32-bit multiplication based on the two-bit-shift Booth algorithm [GiGrH83]. As discussed earlier, this factor has an important impact on the effective cache size, and the overall execution speed of programs.

Second, if a bit-serial hardware multiplier is used, then the internal multiplication-related clock may be several times faster than the system clock. Several steps of the bit-serial multiplication can be performed during a single system clock interval. Therefore, the low transistor count bit-serial hardware multiplier does not necessarily result in a longer multiplication time.

Third, only a low transistor count bit-serial hardware multiplier can be placed on the CPU chip. Having a multiplier on the CPU chip (versus having it off the CPU chip) has advantages in relation to the multiplication fill-in problems [MiFuH87]. Actually, after the bit-serial multiplier is loaded, the CPU will either idle until the multiplication is completed or execute other useful instructions if the code optimizer is capable of finding them. For the current code optimization technology, the entire set of multiplication fill-in slots is likely to be filled only for small set sizes. Therefore, the smaller the number of multiplication fill-in slots, the smaller the number of NOPs (assuming no hardware interlock). Further, the smaller the static code size, the larger the effective cache size. One can argue that the number of fill-in slots for a moderate-speed on-chip serial multiplier may be larger compared with the number for an ultra-high-speed off-chip parallel multiplier. However, this is definitely not the case in GaAs systems with relatively long off-chip communication delays.

Fourth, the DCFL E/D-MESFET GaAs technology, unlike some other GaAs technologies (e.g., bipolar), are relatively sensitive to large fan-in/fan-out requirements [MiFuH86]. Note that these requirements are larger for a full barrel shifter than for a bit-serial multiplier. The GaAs VLSI area ratio of 12 to 7 (discussed earlier in this section) would be more than 2 to 1 in a technology like silicon CMOS/SOS.

Finally, in the case of alternative #2, the VLSI area of the bit-serial multiplier and the difference in VLSI area between the full and the minimal shifter are invested into the general register file of the increased size. Note, however, that positive effects of the increased size register file could be fully exploited only if the code optimizer is equipped with a relatively sophisticated mechanisms for the register lifetime maximization.

Therefore, the problem is to determine what architectural constructs to "build" on the available VLSI "real estate." Microprocessor architectures have two interfaces, one toward the high-level languages and the application and the other toward the VLSI design and the technology. Consequently, the solution to the problem depends on both, the application and the technology. Before we started the research and experiments, we felt that the alternative #1 would dominate the other two. However, as will be shown here, this was true only in some of the cases.

3: Performance Evaluation Methodology

In this section, we present our empirical performance evaluation methodology.

***Good optimizing compilers can reduce the number of multiplications. The amount of this reduction is application dependent.

The model of our application was based on the set of benchmarks for the evaluation of computer systems in defense applications. We used the modified benchmarks from DARPA's package [Barne85]. The list of these benchmarks is given in Table 5, and their dynamic workload characteristics are given in Table 6. The details about the used benchmarks can be found in [Betti85] and [Fura85]. The major modifications, compared with the benchmarks from the initial package, were related to their lengthening, so that cache-related and register-file-related results are more accurate. (Our research sponsor insisted that statistics of the application are closely related to the statistics of this benchmark set.) We used both optimized and nonoptimized code.

The model of our architecture was built into the ISP' based simulator implemented with the ENDOT software package [RoOrD84]. For the experiments related to the alternative #1, this simulator had to be modified to incorporate a minimal shifter and a bit-serial hardware multiplier. Also, this simulator had to be modified to reflect the compile time actions related to the need for multiply fill-in and the compile time actions related to the decreased number of registers. For the experiments related to the alternative #2, in addition to shifter related modifications, we found it necessary to include the modifications that will reflect the increased size of the general register file.

The substitution of a full barrel shifter with a minimal shifter was incorporated into the simulator, as explained by code segment (1).

For all immediate shifts, the shift was replaced by the minimum number of 3-bit shifts, followed by a 1-bit, or 2-bit shift, to complete the operation. For example, using the Stanford University MIPS notation, the execution of:

$$\text{sll } \#11, R_{src}$$

would be converted****into:

$$\begin{aligned}&\text{sll } \#3, R_{src}\\&\text{sll } \#3, R_{src}\\&\text{sll } \#3, R_{src}\\&\text{sll } \#2, R_{src}\end{aligned} \tag{1}$$

All shifts using the Lo register [HeJoP83] were replaced by a sequence of test, branch, and shift instructions. Both unoptimized and optimized versions used a jump table since it takes the least code and the least time. The transformed instructions are as follows in code segment (2):

****This solution may encounter problems with ALU latency if no ALU bypass is incorporated.

$$\begin{aligned}&\text{and } \#1, R_{cnt}, R_{tmp}\\&\text{bne } \#1, R_{tmp}\\&\text{or } \#1, R_{cnt}, R_{tmp}\\&\text{xor } \#1, R_{tmp}\\&\text{subr } \#8, R_{tmp}\\&\text{bra L1}[R_{tmp}]\\&\text{nop}\end{aligned}$$

L1: $\qquad\qquad\qquad\qquad\qquad\qquad$ (2)

$$\begin{array}{ll}\text{sll } \#2, R_{src} & \text{sll } \#2, R_{src}\\\text{sll } \#2, R_{src} & \text{sll } \#2, R_{src}\\\text{sll } \#2, R_{src} & \text{sll } \#2, R_{src}\\\text{sll } \#2, R_{src} & \text{sll } \#2, R_{src}\\\text{and } \#3, R_{src}, R_{tmp}\\\text{beq } \#0, R_{tmp}, \text{LEND}\\\text{nop}\\\text{beq } \#1, R_{tmp}, \text{LEND}\\\text{sll } \#1, R_{src}\\\text{beq } \#2, R_{tmp}, \text{LEND}\\\text{sll } \#1, R_{src}\\\text{sll } \#1, R_{src}\end{array}$$

LEND:

However, the actual code was not inserted into the simulator. Instead, when relevant instruction (sll or rlc) was found, the count for the executed number of instructions was updated.

We incorporated the existence of the bit-serial multiplier into the simulator as follows. We assumed that it takes the same number of operations to load and unload the registers of the Booth-step multiplier and the bit-serial multiplier (two instructions each). Next, we assumed a multiply delay, along with a number of instructions that the code optimizer should be able to fill in. Considering the current state-of-the-art of compiler technology, we also assumed that the multiplier fill-in would be equal only to 1 or 2, regardless of the actual number of multiplier fill-in slots. The bit-serial multiplier clock was simulated with a clock rate of 2, 4, 6, 8, and 10 times the system clock rate. By varying the relevant parameters, like the number of multiplier slots filled in or the clock rate of the bit-serial multiplier, we were able to learn about the impact of these parameters on the overall execution speed. One possible instruction sequence might be as follows:

$$\begin{aligned}&\text{ld } \#1234, R_M\\&\text{ld } \#1234, R_Q\\&\text{mult}\\&\text{nop}\\&\dots\\&\text{nop}\\&\text{mov } R_M, R_{dest_{low}}\\&\text{mov } R_Q, R_{dest_{high}}\end{aligned} \tag{3}$$

Again, instead of the actual code changes, only the simulation count was modified.

For the alternative #2, we assumed that the bit-serial multiplier is located off-chip. Therefore, for each multiplication operation, the simulator count had to be further increased to reflect the long off-chip communication delays. Depending on the placement of this multiplier for our particular GaAs technology, this additional delay could be equal from 2 to 4 system cycles.

Simulating the smaller register file (for alternative #1) was simply done by increasing the simulator count to reflect the register spilling. However, simulating the larger register file (for alternative #2) required very complex changes in the compiler. To avoid this complication, we incorporated the mechanism that would modify the simulator clock count to reflect the fact that the increased register file size results in the lower dynamic frequency of LOAD/STORE operations. In other words, we assumed that a certain percentage of LOAD and STORE operations was related to register spilling. In our simulator, it was possible to vary that percentage (R) in a wide range in order to determine the impact on the overall execution speed.

It was a good idea to incorporate the above described mechanism. This is because later we got some ideas about further improvements of algorithms for the register life-time maximization. Our estimate (when analyzing these improvements ahead of their implementation) was that the decrease in the dynamic frequency of LOAD/STORE operations could be equal to about N percent, and our experiment (see Section 4) was able directly to tell if additional work on compiler improvements would be justified, from the practical point of view (since it was shown what is the execution time improvement when the reduction of LOAD/STORE operations is N percent).

As in most RISC architectures, the compiler is an inherent part of the architecture. Therefore, several compilation related parameters were built into the architecture model. To summarize, these include: (1) the multiplier fill-in capabilities (s = 0, 1, and 2), i.e., the number of multiplier slots that has been filled in, (2) the percentage of LOAD/STORE instructions to be eliminated by having a larger register file and a better code optimization algorithm (R = 51; l = 0,1,2..,10); and (3) the option of using or not using the code optimizer.

As indicated previously, the technology parameters were also built into the architecture model. To summarize, the technology related parameters that we could change in our simulator were: (1) the ratio of the multiplier clock rate to the system clock rate (i = 2,4,8, and 10), (2) the number of system clock cycles to compensate for the off-chip delays in communications with the off-chip multiplier (k = 2 and 4), and (3) the ratio of the memory access time to datapath time for cache hit/miss (3/6).

Of course, the major performance measure was the execution time of benchmarks. In all our experiments, it was expressed in terms of the number of system clock cycles. Our experiments and their basic results are presented in the following two sections.

4: Experiments and Results

For all three candidate configurations, the entire set of 9 benchmarks was run for all previously mentioned combinations of compiler related and technology related parameters.

The results are given in Tables 1 through 4. Execution times for unoptimized benchmarks are given in Tables 1 and 3. Execution times for optimized benchmarks are given in Tables 2 and 4. Tables 1 and 2 are related to the baseline and the alternative #1. Tables 3 and 4 are related to the baseline and the alternative #2. Tables 3 and 4 are for the case of shorter off-chip delays related to communications with the off-chip multiplier (k = 2). The case of longer off-chip delays (k = 4) can be found in [Betti85].

Note that data are presented separately for different benchmarks. Actually, the overall conclusions should best be based on the benchmark mix, as we did during the process of defining the structure to be implemented [HelMi86]. However, each benchmark has its own "personality," i.e., different benchmarks are characterized with different dynamic probabilities of various language constructs. By separately providing the results for various benchmarks, we were able to judge the suitability of the three different candidates to various language constructs. As already indicated, functions of various benchmarks are given in Table 5, and their workload characteristics are given in Table 6. For example, "intmm" is heavy in arithmetic-related operations, and "puzzle" is heavy in branch operations.

5: Discussion of Results

In this section, we discuss the major results, using Tables 1 to 4 and related plots in Figures 1 and 2.***** The tables give a better understanding about the absolute performance, and the figures give a better picture of the performance trends.

In analyzing Table 1, which compares the baseline and alternative #1 configurations for unoptimized benchmarks, we can draw the following conclusions. The baseline is equal to or better (faster) than the alternatives for all benchmarks and for all combinations of relevant parameters.

*****In figures 1 and 2, we present results only for benchmarks "intmm" and "puzzle." For other benchmarks, see [Betti85].

Table 1: Execution Time for Unoptimized Benchmarks. All parameters defined in the text.

bench	ack	bubble	fib	intmm	perm	puzzle	quick	queen	sieve
baseline	3186804	3148975	602121	3852427	431167	19313270	1925039	39286	397121
i=2,s=1	3186845	3214602	602121	5508450	431190	26223985	2554365	40047	397162
i=2,s=2	3186845	3214102	602121	5308450	431190	25456897	2549365	40047	397162
i=4,s=1	3186845	3212602	602121	4708450	431190	23155633	2534365	40047	397162
i=4,s=2	3186845	3212102	602121	4508450	431190	22388545	2529365	40047	397162
i=6,s=1	3186845	3212102	602121	4508450	431190	22388545	2529365	40047	397162
i=6,s=2	3186845	3211602	602121	4308450	431190	21621457	2524365	40047	397162
i=8,s=1	3186845	3211602	602121	4308450	431190	21621457	2524365	40047	397162
i=8,s=2	3186845	3211102	602121	4108450	431190	20854369	2519365	40047	397162
i=10,s=1	3186845	3211102	602121	4108450	431190	20854369	2519365	40047	397162
i=10,s=2	3186845	3211102	602121	4108450	431190	20854369	2519365	40047	397162

Therefore, the combination of a more powerful shifter and a larger register file is better than an on-chip bit-serial multiplier with a minimal shifter and a smaller register file. In the case of "fib," there was no difference in performance because "fib" does not use large shifts. Also, the decrease in the register file size did not cause any spilling. In the case of "quick," the difference was as large as 31 percent to 33 percent (the faster structure was from 31 percent to 33 percent faster over the entire range of relevant parameters). The multiply delay fill-in(s) made the maximum difference of only about five percent (for "intmm"); however, for the same benchmark ("intmm"), changing the internal clock cycle of the bit-serial multiplier caused the execution speed to improve up to about 34 percent when the parameter "i" is varied from i = 1 to i = 10.

If comparing the results presented in Table 1 with those presented in Table 2, which compares baseline and alternative #1 configurations for optimized benchmarks, we derive a number of interesting conclusions. For optimized code, the baseline system has a higher margin of performance over alternative #1 than it does for the unoptimized code. In the case of "quick," the margin ranges from 40 percent to 43 percent over the entire range of relevant parameters. The multiply delay fill-in, however, makes the maximal difference of less than 3 percent (for "intmm"). Again, changing the internal clock cycle of the bit-serial multiplier improves the execution speed for up to about 25 percent ("intmm"). We believe that all these changes are a result of the optimization process decreasing the overall number of multiplication operations [Henne84]. The less the number of multipli-

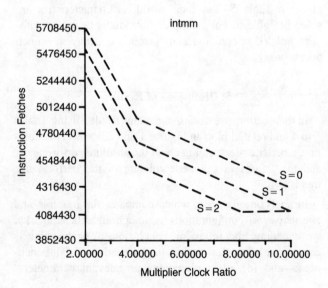

Figure 1: Execution Time of *Intmm* with an On-Chip Bit-Serial Multiplier. Parameter "s" refers to the number of multiplier slots which are filled in. This figure corresponds to Table 1.

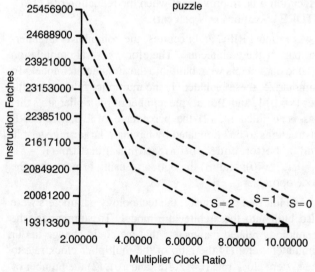

Figure 2: Execution Time of *Puzzle* with an On-Chip Bit-Serial Multiplier. Parameter "s" refers to the number of multiplier slots which were filled in. This figure corresponds to Table 1.

Table 2: Execution Time for Optimized Benchmarks. All parameters defined in the text.

bench	ack	bubble	fib	intmm	perm	puzzle	quick	queen	sieve
baseline	3101439	1191373	584330	1761026	337582	5040988	1101581	6529	166649
i=2,s=1	3101480	1240097	584330	2532249	337605	4985102	1582726	7290	166690
i=2,s=2	3101480	1239597	584330	2458649	337605	4985102	1577726	7290	166690
i=4,s=1	3101480	1238097	584330	2237849	337605	4985102	1562726	7290	166690
i=4,s=2	3101480	1237597	584330	2164249	337605	4985102	1557726	7290	166690
i=6,s=1	3101480	1237597	584330	2164249	337605	4985102	1557726	7290	166690
i=6,s=2	3101480	1237097	584330	2090649	337605	4985102	1552726	7290	166690
i=8,s=1	3101480	1237097	584330	2090649	337605	4985102	1552726	7290	166690
i=8,s=2	3101480	1236597	584330	2017049	337605	4985102	1547726	7290	166690
i=10,s=1	3101480	1236597	584330	2017049	337605	4985102	1547726	7290	166690
i=10,s=2	3101480	1236597	584330	2017049	337605	4985102	1547726	7290	166690

cation operations, the less effective the benefits of alternative #1. Also, the efficiency of optimization is always better for the baseline system than for the alternative #1. For "queen" (which is one extreme), optimization improves the code speed for the baseline system 6.02 times; while for alternative #1, the improvement is only 5.49 times. For "ack" (which is the other extreme) in both cases, the improvement by optimization is 1.03 times. In the middle is the case of "intmm," where the speed improvement after optimization is 2.19 times for the baseline system and 2.17 times for the alternative #1.

In conclusion, so far the baseline system has been shown to be superior in comparison with alternative #1. We believe this is partially because our application environment (defined by the given set of benchmarks) is related more to symbolic/data processing and less to numeric processing. Also, this type of application needs a larger register file and larger shifting capabilities than it needs multiplication, especially when strength reduction techniques are applied to decrease the number of multiplications in the optimized code.

From Table 3, which compares the baseline system and

Table 3: Execution Time for Unoptimized Benchmarks, and Off-Chip Delay Corresponding to k = 2. All parameters defined in the text.

bench	ack	bubble	fib	intmm	perm	puzzle	quick	queen	sieve
baseline	3186804	3148975	602121	3852427	431167	19313270	1925039	39286	397121
i=2,s=1,R=0	3186485	3217602	602121	6703450	431190	29292337	2584365	40047	397162
i=2,s=2,R=0	3186845	3217102	602121	6508450	431190	28525249	2579365	40047	397162
i=4,s=1,R=0	3186845	3215602	602121	5908450	431190	26223985	2564365	40047	397162
i=4,s=2,R=0	3186845	3215102	602121	5708450	431190	25456897	2559365	40047	397162
i=6,s=1,R=0	3186845	3215102	602121	5708450	431190	25456897	2559365	40047	397162
i=6,s=2,R=0	3186845	3214602	602121	5508450	431190	24689809	2554365	40047	397162
i=8,s=1,R=0	3186845	3214602	602121	5508450	431190	24689809	2554365	40047	397162
i=8,s=2,R=0	3186845	3214102	602121	5308450	431190	23922721	2549365	40047	397162
i=10,s=1,R=0	3186845	3214102	602121	5308450	431190	23922721	2549365	40047	397162
i=10,s=2,R=0	3186845	3214102	602121	5308450	431190	23922721	2549365	40047	397162
i=2,s=1,R=30	2618438	2907117	479951	6341229	348160	26470347	2258219	32516	368312
i=2,s=2,R=30	2618438	2906617	479951	6141229	348160	25703259	2253219	32516	368312
i=4,s=1,R=30	2618438	2905117	479951	5541229	348160	23401995	2238219	32516	368312
i=4,s=2,R=30	2618438	2904617	479951	5341229	348160	22634907	2233219	32516	368312
i=6,s=1,R=30	2618438	2904617	479951	5341229	348160	22634907	2232219	32516	368312
i=6,s=2,R=30	2618438	2904117	479951	5141229	348160	21867819	2228219	32516	368312
i=8,s=1,R=30	2618438	2904117	479951	5141229	348160	21867819	2228219	32516	368312
i=8,s=2,R=30	2618438	2903617	479951	4941229	383160	21100731	2223219	32516	368312
i=10,s=1,R=30	2618438	2903617	479951	4941229	348160	21100731	2223219	32516	368312
i=10,s=2,R=30	2618438	2903617	479951	4941229	348160	21100731	2223219	32516	368312

Table 4: Execution Time for Optimized Benchmarks, and Off-Chip Delay Corresponding to K = 2. All parameters defined in the text.

bench	ack	bubble	fib	intmm	perm	pussle	quick	queen	sieve
baseline	3101439	1196573	584330	1761026	337582	5040988	1101581	8529	166649
i=2,s=1,R=0	3101480	1242097	584330	2826649	337605	4985102	1602726	7290	166690
i=2,s=2,R=0	3101480	1241597	584330	2753049	337605	4985102	1597726	7290	166690
i=4,s=1,R=0	3101480	1240097	584330	2532249	337605	4985102	1582726	7290	166690
i=4,s=2,R=0	3101480	1239597	584330	2458649	337605	4985102	1577726	7290	166690
i=6,s=1,R=0	3101480	1239597	584330	2458649	337605	4985102	1577726	7290	166690
i=6,s=2,R=0	3101480	1239097	584330	2385049	337605	4985102	1572726	7290	166690
i=8,s=1,R=0	3101480	1239097	584330	2385049	337605	4985102	1572726	7290	166690
i=8,s=2,R=0	3101480	1238597	584330	2311449	337605	4985102	1567726	7290	166690
i=10,s=1,R=0	3101480	1238597	584330	2311449	337605	4985102	1567726	7290	166690
i=10,s=2,R=0	3101480	1238597	584330	2311449	337605	4985102	1567726	7290	166690
i=2,s=1,R=0.3	2429734	1124675	472780	2707588	271642	4398145	1510527	6462	142754
i=2,s=2,R=0.3	2429734	1124175	472780	2633988	271642	4398145	1505527	6462	142754
i=4,s=1,R=0.3	2429734	1122675	472780	2413188	271642	4398145	1490527	6462	142754
i=4,s=2,R=0.3	2429734	1122175	472780	2339588	271642	4398145	1485527	6462	142754
i=6,s=1,R=0.3	2429734	1122175	472780	2339588	271642	4398145	1485527	6462	142754
i=6,s=2,R=0.3	2429734	1121675	472780	2265988	271642	4398145	1480527	6462	142754
i=8,s=1,R=0.3	2429734	1121675	472780	2265988	271642	4398145	1480527	6462	142754
i=8,s=2,R=0.3	2429734	1121175	472780	2192388	271642	4398145	1475527	6462	142754
i=10,s=1,R=0.3	2429734	1121175	472780	2192388	271642	4398145	1475527	6462	142754
i=10,s=2,R=0.3	2429734	1121175	472780	2192388	271642	4398145	1475527	6462	142754

alternative #2 for unoptimized benchmarks, we see that the increased size of the register file may have a major positive effect on the execution speed of compiled HLL code. The case where R = 0 corresponds to the situation when there are no LOAD/STORE operations due to register spilling. The case where R = 30 corresponds to situations where 30 percent of the LOAD/STORE operations are due to register spilling (which would be avoided with a proper increase in the register file size). Of course, the higher the value of parameter R, the faster the alternative #2. For R = 0, the baseline system is as fast as or faster than both alternatives for all benchmarks. For R = 30, the baseline system is faster for multiplication-heavy benchmarks ("intmm" and "puzzle"). For R = 30, alternative #2 was faster than the baseline system in the extreme case of low multiplication count benchmarks for about 27 percent ("ack"). However, the baseline system was faster than alternative #2 in the other extreme ("intmm") and achieved a 28 percent advantage for large values of parameters "i" and "s" and a 64 percent advantage for small values of parameters "i" and "s".

We were not able to notice any correlation between the value of R and the amount of speed-up achieved when "s" increases from 0 to 2. In some cases, the amount of speed-up was higher for higher values of R. In other cases, it was just opposite. The same was the case with the correlation between the value of R and the amount of speed-up when "i" increases.

Based on the data from Tables 1 through 4, we made the following conclusions. (1) Alternative #1 is not worth considering for the application environment defined by the set of benchmarks from Table 5. (2) Alternative #2 would be worth considering only if the compiler would be able to decrease the occurrence of registers spilling by at least 30 percent. As such a decrease did not occur with the currently available compiler [MiFuH86], we decided to incorporate the full shifter and 16 general-purpose registers into the 32-bit GaAs CPU.

In the plots in Figures 1 and 2, notice the "segmented" shape of the related curves. This factor is because the number of NOP's inserted depends on the value of the internal multiplier clock. It appears that some "moderate" values of the internal multiplier clock represent a good design trade-off (e.g., the multiplier clock ratio of four, in conditions of Figures 1 and 2).

6: Design Decisions

Realizing that having a full shifter in the system rather than a multiplier is a must, our first design decision was to find the proper place in the arithmetic path for the shifter and to determine how to accomplish multiply operations with

Table 5: Functions of Selected Benchmarks [Fura85].

(1) Ack: A highly recursive program to compute Ackermann's function.

(2) Bubble: A program to perform a bubble sort of 500 integers.

(3) Fib: A highly recursive program to compute a Fibonacci number.

(4) Intmm: A computation-heavy program to multiply two 40-by-40-element integer arrays.

(5) Perm: A highly recursive program to calculate all permutations of the numbers 1 through 7.

(6) Puzzle: An iteration-heavy, computation-heavy program to solve a 3-dimensional cube packing problem.

(7) Queen: A program to solve the Eight Queens problem.

(8) Quick: A program to perform a quick sort of 5000 integers.

(9) Sieve: A program which calculates the number of primes between 0 and 8190.

the resources available. If the shifter were placed in series with the adder, then the traditional "shift and add" steps of multiply could be implemented with a single-pass, two-instruction "step" operation. That is, while this shift and add operation was taking place, the multiplier shift and multiplier control set-up functions would be interleaved with it in the pipelined execution. The third part of the operation, the fetching of the multiplicand from the register stack, would take place in parallel with the partial product fetch, shift, and add operations.

Two problems were encountered with this approach. First, with the shifter in series with the adder, all arithmetic operands would have to pass through the shifter, resulting in a slow-down of all operations. Simulations showed this slow-down to be almost two to one. The only way found to achieve the same machine cycle time as before was to add another stage to the pipeline. However, we reasoned that adding a stage was unacceptable because the code reorganizer was not able to totally compensate for the latencies in the original version of the pipeline. Increasing the pipeline length would only result in a further inefficiency in the latency fill operations.

The second problem was that the pipeline already had more stages in it than the number of steps required in each of the multiply's operations [HelMi88]. Thus, the pipeline would not be full during the execution of multiplication-related instructions and would result in slower than desired performance of all "multiply" operations. The solution used in the Stanford MIPS design [GiGrH83] was to add extra registers to shorten the pipeline length for multiply and divide operations. This procedure kept the shifting and adder units operate at full capacity but added to the device count of the system—something of no real concern to the MIPS designers because their implementation was in silicon. However, since we were to implement this design in GaAs, adding to the device count was of great concern.

Therefore, we decided to put the adder in parallel with the arithmetic unit and to use the registers of the General Register Stack to hold the operands and results of the multiply (and divide) operations [HelMi88]. Further, we decided that the multiplicand should be shifted rather than the partial product, as is traditional. This step provided four very desirable features. First, it achieved the same results. Second, it provided a multiply (divide) algorithm where no operand was subjected to more than one arithmetic operation for each step. Third, it permitted the construction of the algorithm such that the latency of the pipeline could be used to advantage in these repetitive operations. Fourth, if there was ever a chance that the result would overflow (possible since all operands [multiplier, multiplicand, and product] are single word length integers), this would be detected easily by an overflow in the multiplicand shift operation.

The final design selected closely followed the "suggestions" of the experiments. First, a full hardware shifter was included in the architecture to provide fast operations for those functions required the most. Second, the architecture was arranged so that the maximum speed of all operations was possible by keeping the pipeline path through the arithmetic unit as short as possible. Third, this arrangement enabled us to build into the design a Booth-type (two bits at a time) multiply algorithm that would use only three operations per step. This Booth-type algorithm is about 50 percent slower than the minimum obtainable with extra, non-shifting hardware registers that we could not afford, but it is about 25 percent faster than would be achieved with the shifter in series with the adder. Fourth, with this design, all single and multiple word length multiply and divide operations are achievable with code sequences that contain no latency-compensating NOP instructions. Finally, fifth, all of these results were obtained with a design that can be implemented with a gate count that is within today's limit for implementation on a single GaAs integrated circuit.

Table 6: Dynamic Workload Characteristics of Selected Benchmarks [Fura85].

Benchmark	ni	nb	nl	np	pbf0	plf0
ack	1000	216	270	189	0.62	0.90
bubble	1000	217	211	350	0.51	1.00
fib	1000	212	303	212	0.71	1.00
intmm	1000	63	134	637	1.00	1.00
perm	1000	143	304	230	0.75	0.88
puzzle	1000	316	263	489	0.95	0.92
queen	1000	151	299	252	0.63	0.65
quick	1000	208	156	633	0.56	0.97
sieve	1000	249	50	449	1.00	1.00
average	1000	190	235	364	0.72	0.91

ni = number of instructions (normalized data)
nb = number of branch instructions
nl = number of load instructions
np = number of packed instructions
pbf0 = probability of branch fill
plf0 = probability of load fill

7: Summary

Although the research results presented here were related to the design and implementation of RCA's 32-bit single-chip microprocessor for GaAs technology, they are more general. We concentrated on design tradeoffs between the bit-serial multiplier and the full barrel shifter combined with a larger register file. We analyzed and compared three alternatives for a given set of technology- and application-related parameters. The major contribution of our research is in providing an answer, under given conditions, to a question that is frequently asked among the designers of RISC-type microprocessors: "How do we incorporate the multiplication and shifting capabilities into a newly designed microprocessor?" Under given conditions, it was more advantageous to incorporate a full shifter and a larger register file, than a bit-serial multiplier and a smaller register file.

8: Acknowledgment

The authors are thankful to Bill Heagerty of RCA for his help.

9: References

[Barne85] Barney, C., "DARPA Eyes 100-MIPS GaAs Chip for Star Wars," *Electronics Week,* Vol. 58, No. 20, May 20, 1985, pp. 22-23.

[Betti85] Bettinger, M., "Comparison of E/D-MESFET GaAs and CMOS Silicon for VLSI Processor Design," *Purdue University Technical Report, TR-EE 85-18,* West Lafayette, Ind., December 1985.

[Fura85] Fura, D., "Architectural Approaches for GaAs Exploitation in High-Speed Computer Design," *Purdue University Technical Report, TR-EE 85-17,* West Lafayette, Ind., December 1985.

[GiGrH83] Gill, J., Gross, T., Hennessy, J., Jouppi, N., Przybylski, S., and Rowen, C., "Summary of MIPS Instructions," *Technical Note No. 83-237,* Stanford University, Stanford, Calif., November 1983.

[HelMi88] Helbig, W. and Milutinović, V., "A DCFL E/D-MESFET GaAs Experimental RISC Machine," *IEEE Transactions on Computers,* 1988.

[HeJoP83] Hennessy, J., Jouppi, N., Przybylski, S., Rowen, C., and Gross, T., "Design of a High Performance VLSI Processor," *Technical Report No. 236,* Stanford University, Stanford, Calif., February 1983.

[Hwang79] Hwang, K., *Computer Arithmetic: Principles, Architecture, and Design,* John Wiley & Sons, New York, 1979.

[MiFuH86] Milutinović, V., Fura, D., and Helbig, W., "An Introduction to GaAs Microprocessor Architecture for VLSI," *IEEE Computer,* Vol. 19, No. 3, March 1986.

[MiSiF86] Milutinović, V., Silbey, A., Fura, D., Bettinger, M., Keirn, K., Helbig, W., Heagerty, W., Zieger, R., Schellack, B., and Curtice, W., "Design Issues in GaAs Microprocessor Systems," *IEEE Computer,* Vol. 19, No. 10, October 1986.

[MiFuH87] Milutinović, V., Fura, D., Helbig, W., and Linn, J., "Compiler/Architecture Synergism in GaAs Microprocessor Systems", *IEEE Computer,* Vol. 20, No. 5, May 1987.

[RoOrD84] Rose, C.W., Ordy, G.M., and Drongowski, P.J., "N.mPc: A Study in University-Industry Technology Transfer," *IEEE Design & Test,* February 1984, pp. 44-56.

[Smith82] Smith, A.J., "Cache Memories," *ACM Computing Surveys,* Vol. 14, No. 3, September 1982, pp. 473-530.

[Milut86] Milutinović, V., "GaAs Microprocessor Technology" (Guest Editor's Introduction), *IEEE Computer* (Special Issue on GaAs Microprocessor Technology), October 1986, pp. 9-13.

Adder Design Analysis for a 32-Bit GaAs Microprocessor [†]

Veljko Milutinović and Mark Bettinger
School of Electrical Engineering
Purdue University
West Lafayette, IN 47907
(317) 494-3530

Walt Helbig
Advanced Technology Laboratories
RCA Corporation
Moorestown, NJ 08057
(609) 866-6530

Abstract

Research results presented in this paper are related to the design and implementation of RCA's 32-bit single-chip microprocessor for GaAs technology. We analyze three important adder design approaches. We also compare two radiation-hard technologies—E/D-MESFET GaAs and SOS-CMOS silicon—from the point of view of both processing speed and VLSI layout area. The major conclusion of this research is that traditionally slow adders like ripple-carry or similar, although still slower than traditionally fast adders like carry-lookahead or similar, are better suited for incorporation into GaAs microprocessors of the word lengths up to 32 bits. This is because in GaAs the "crosspoints" between the two groups of adders (as far as the speed is concerned) have moved toward the larger word lengths. On the other hand, in GaAs, the complexity gap between the same two groups of adders (as far as the VLSI area is concerned) has increased. Consequently, if simpler adders are incorporated, the remaining VLSI area could be "invested" into resources that would speed up the execution of compiled HLL code, more than the incorporation of fast but area-consuming adders. Although conclusions related to GaAs technology are compared with those related to silicon technology, the overall results are more general. They show how the adder design tradeoffs change when the dependency of gate delays on fan-in and fan-out is changed.

1: Introduction

The differences between silicon and GaAs technologies require different solutions to many problems in the area of adder design. Silicon technologies typically require high-speed adders to achieve high performance, because of the relatively small ratio of the memory access time to the datapath time. (For example, the NMOS-silicon HP-FOCUS used a full carry look-ahead adder to satisfy its 55ns cycle time [BeDoF81].) When the switch from silicon to GaAs technology* is made, the design changes are the direct result of the major two silicon/GaAs differences, and the indirect result of the other references [MiSiF86]. We examine the differences (as they apply to adder design) because the adder is an integral part of the CPU, and directly affects the datapath time and performance. This study presents findings on adder design concerning RCA's 32-bit microprocessor [Barne85] [HelMi87]. Our goal was to suggest the adder type to use.

The difference in transistor count limits the complexity of any adder to be implemented. For example, if the chip is limited to about 30K transistors, a frequently mentioned upper bound for near-term GaAs designs, then any adder that requires too many transistors is unacceptable.

The limited fan-in and fan-out* of GaAs gates affect both the VLSI area needed and the adder delay incurred. Single gates with high fan-in and fan-out must be implemented as a series of gates with low fan-in and fan-out, which increases transistor count. Because delay is highly dependent on load capacitance, high fan-out devices have a relatively large delay. If a tree is built in a random fashion, this dependence may cause the delay through N levels of high fan-out gates to exceed the delay through $N+1$ levels of low fan-out gates. This phenomenon also exists in some silicon technol-

---

*In this paper we concentrate on GaAs DCFL E/D-MESFET and silicon CMOS/SOS used by RCA. Note that detailed characteristics of these two technologies differ from detailed characteristics of other GaAs and silicon technologies [Milut86].

---

†This research was supported by RCA Corporation.

ogies; however, it is present much more in GaAs. For the basic gate data of the two technologies presented here, see [Milut87].

1.1: Pipeline Depth

The ratio of off-chip memory access time to on-chip memory access time indirectly creates additional GaAs/silicon differences. When this ratio is large, a memory pipeline is often used and is several levels deep. This depth increases the number of branch delay fill-in slots, and, in systems with software interlock, a larger number of NOOPs must be inserted to fill the pipeline until execution of the branch instruction is completed [HeJoP83].

The memory pipeline depth is determined by the ratio of the memory fetch time to the datapath time. If the datapath time is lengthened by allowing the addition to take longer, then the pipeline depth decreases and fewer NOOPs must be inserted into the instruction stream. On the other hand, lengthening the datapath typically means a longer clock cycle. However, a longer clock cycle does not necessarily mean a longer execution time for compiled HLL programs. This is because the version with a longer cycle will be characterized with a lower percentage of NOOPs, both before and after the code optimization [HeJoP83]. Actually, the version with a longer clock cycle may even be faster. This is because the lengthening of the adder time can be done by replacing a high-transistor count adder (e.g., a full carry look-ahead adder) with a ripple-carry adder or another adder type with a lower transistor count. The saved transistor count could be invested into the resources that will improve the speed of the compiled HLL code (e.g., larger register file). Note, however, that unless the initial pipeline is relatively deep, increasing the datapath time will increase the execution time of the compiled HLL code. Therefore, the above presented reasoning is valid for only technologies like GaAs (small on-chip transistor count and large ratio of off-chip to on-chip delays). In addition, as will be seen later, the difference between the two extremes, the ripple-carry adder delay and the full carry look-ahead adder delay, is smaller for GaAs technology than for silicon technology.

1.2: Adder Types

There is a large variety of adder designs available for GaAs technology, ranging from the high-speed, large area full-carry-lookahead adder to the low-speed, small area ripple-carry adder. Other designs having speed and resource requirements between these two extremes include (among the others) conditional-sum and carry-select adders [Hwang79]. In this paper, we have selected only three different adder types for presentation. These three types include the two extremes (full-carry-lookahead and ripple-carry) plus the adder type that was used in the most successful RISC machines (carry-select). Results for many other adder types can be easily derived or extrapolated from our results presented here.

As mentioned above, GaAs/silicon differences (transistor count per chip, the ratio of off-chip to on-chip memory access time, plus gate fan-in and fan-out) affect the choice of adders in many ways. Traditionally, the full-carry-lookahead adder has been preferred for high-speed applications, and the simplest adders like ripple-carry adders have been discounted for all but the shortest word length.

As will be seen later, reevaluation of the adders may show that the fastest adder in silicon is not the fastest in GaAs technology (i.e., because the fastest silicon adder is based on high fan-in and fan-out capability, and GaAs technology may be intolerant to high fan-in and fan-out [MiFuH86]). Of course, this depends on the adder word length. However, we want (once more) to underline that fan-in/fan-out problems are present also in silicon; but in GaAs those problems are present on a much larger scale and, therefore, considerably different solutions are required.

2: Evaluation Methodology

Our choice of adder structures to compare was influenced by previous research [BreKu82] [MiFuH86]. As already indicated, to cover the range of possibilities for our analysis, we chose an adder with a low number of stages but with high fan-in and fan-out requirements the full carry-lookahead adder and another adder with a large number of stages but low fan-in and fan-out requirements (the ripple-carry adder). To make the list complete, we also chose an adder that was a compromise between the two extremes. This choice was the carry-select adder presented in [Sherb84] [Katev83], which ran stages in parallel rather than serially while still keeping the fan-in and fan-out requirements relatively low.

To complete the list of adder parameters for various applications, each adder type was examined for word lengths from four to 32 bits. To determine the effect of technology changes, designs with the following fan-in and fan-out limitations were examined:

(1) fan-in = two and fan-out = two,
(2) fan-in = two and fan-out = five, and
(3) fan-in = five and fan-out = five.

To show the effects of different technologies when determining gate delays, we varied the delay per fan-in and fan-out and the base delay for each gate. These parameters were then used to generate delay information for each adder (test #1). However, adder delays give no information about implementation complexity. Therefore, we generated a hardware description and the VLSI layout for different adder lengths and for each adder type (test #2).

The first of the two tests was to determine the delay for each adder type, by using the delay formulas based on fan-in, fan-out, and word length. The formulas were based on [Hwang79] and implemented in C language for each of the three adder types.

The second of the two tests was to determine the VLSI area requirements of candidate adders. This was achieved empirically by entering the gate-level descriptions into the automatic layout tool, MP2D of RCA [FeNoS83], which then calculated VLSI areas for each adder type. This tool provides a cell-oriented custom VLSI layout.

3: Adder Delays

The first step of the analysis was to derive delay equations for a simple NOR gate which reflect different delays for different gate fan-in and fan-out, as well as for different gate inputs (some are faster than the others). Each NOR gate in the Triquint E/D-MESFET process (the process is intolerant to NAND gates) used by RCA has the following parameters:

slow — the rise and fall delay of the slowest input, per unit of capacitance,

fast — the rise and fall delay of the fastest input, per unit of capacitance,

C_{slow} — the load capacitance of the slowest input,

C_{fast} — the load capacitance of the fastest input,

C_{out} — the output capacitance,

slow*C_{slow} — the delay due to the loading on the gate which drives the slowest input,

fast*C_{fast} — the delay due to the loading on the gate which drives the fastest input,

fanin — the fanin of the circuit to be synthesized (may be longer than maxfanin),

fanout — the fanout of the circuit to be synthesized (may be longer than maxfanout),

maxfanin — the maximum fan-in allowed in the cell family, and

maxfanout — the maximum fan-out allowed in the cell family.

After applying the delay analysis techniques of Hwang [Hwang79], we get** the following delay formula:

**Our goal here is not to demonstrate the obvious derivation of adder delay formulas based on [Hwang79] but to demonstrate the impacts of GaAs technology on the adder choice for inclusion into a GaAs CPU.

$$delay = (\left\lceil \log_{maxfanin}(fanin) \right\rceil^\dagger - 1)*(base_{slow}(maxfanin) + slow*C_{fast})$$
$$+ (2 * \left\lfloor (\left\lceil \log_{maxfanout}(fanout) \right\rceil^\ddagger + 1)/2 \right\rfloor^\ddagger - 1)*(base_{fast}(1) + fast*C_{fast}) \quad (1)$$

where:

$$base_{slow}(maxfanin) = delay_{slowbase} + fan\text{-}in*(delay\ per\ fanin)$$
$$base_{fast}(maxfanin) = delay_{fastbase} + fanin*(delay\ per\ fanin)$$

and:

$$delay_{slowbase} = base\ delay\ of\ the\ slowest\ input$$
$$delay_{fastbase} = base\ delay\ of\ the\ fastest\ input$$

Formula (1) assumes that the two extremes of the delay (the slowest and the fastest) remain the same, independent of the number of inputs to the individual NOR gate. That is, if the slowest input to a two-input NOR gate has a delay equal to A and the fastest input to the NOR gate has a delay equal to Z, then additional inputs to make up three- or more-input NOR gates must have delays that fall between A and Z, and A and Z are independent of the number of inputs to the NOR gate.

The delay of the gate should then be equal to the largest of the delays of the input (base delay for each input + incremental increase of this delay per unit of capacitance * capacitance of that input line), plus the delay due to the gate fan-out (incremental increase in the delay per fan-out * fan-out). Note that there is no base delay for the output; this is taken care of by the base delay for the input.

The first term in Formula (1) reflects the number of NOR-inverter pairs (GaAs cell family members) that had to be cascaded in order to synthesize the desired input structure (desired fan-in and fan-out). The second term in Formula (1) reflects the number of inverting gate pairs (GaAs cell family members) that had to be cascaded (in the tree-like and/or the chain-like fashion) in order to synthesize the desired structure [Hwang79].

An important question is whether the delay caused by the conductors is significant compared with the delay of each gate. Given information on the chosen GaAs E/D-MESFET process and information from the GaAs standard cell library, we were able to determine that the capacitance of the longest expected conductor was less than one-fourth of the lowest input capacitance of any device in the entire GaAs standard cell library. This is due to the usage of special air bridges and makes it unnecessary to include the effect of wiring in the calculation of the adder delays. (This is convenient and leads to the final results of better accuracy because

---

$\dagger \left\lceil X \right\rceil$, the ceiling function, picks the smallest integer equal to or greater than X.

$\ddagger \left\lfloor X \right\rfloor$, the floor function, picks the largest integer equal to or smaller than X.

it makes the VLSI area studies linearly dependent on the delay study and the delay study independent of the VLSI area study, since no restriction was placed on the area an adder design could have.)

The delay for each adder depends on several parameters:

D - the delay of the critical path for an adder,
N - the number of bits in the adder,
Cf - the capacitance per additional fan-in,
Cfi_{fast} - Cfi for the fastest input,
Cfi_{slow} - Cfi for the slowest input,
Cfo - the capacitance per additional fan-out,
Nfi - the number of fan-ins,
Nfo - the number of fan-outs,
T - adder type.

The overall formula for delays always considers the varying delays associated with different gate inputs. The formulas also take into account all fan-in and fan-out limitations. However, our main concern here is the adder delay formula. The general adder delay formula is given as $D = f(N, T, Cfi, Cfo, Nfi, Nfo)$. For D(N), given T = ripple-carry, as shown in Figure 1, using the same methodology as above [Hwang79], we get the following formula:

$$D(N) = xor(Cfi_{fast}, Cfi_{slow}) + carry(Cfi_{fast})*N + xor(Cfi_{fast}) \qquad (2)$$

The first term in formula (2) refers to the delay of the first (left) propagate/generate box chain in Figure 1, the second term refers to the delay of the carry box in Figure 1, and the third term refers to the delay of the last (right) sum box in Figure 1. The same analogy with Figures 2 and 3 was used for formulas (3) and (4). Based on [Hwang79], the elements of the formula (2) are defined as:

$$
\begin{aligned}
xor(Cfi_{fast}, Cfi_{slow}) = \max(\ &base_{fast}(2) + fast*Cfi_{fast}*2 + \\
&base_{fast}(2) + fast*Cfi_{slow} + base_{slow}(2) + slow*C_{out}), \\
&base_{slow}(2) + slow*Cfi_{fast}*2 + \\
&base_{fast}(2) + fast*Cfi_{fast} + base_{fast}(2) + fast*C_{out}),
\end{aligned}
$$

$$carry(Cfi_{fast}) = base_{fast}(2) + fast*Cfi_{fast} + base_{fast}(2) + fast*C_{out},$$

Here, the meanings of the key terms are as follows:

Cfi_{slow} the capacitance per additional fan-in, for the slowest input.

Cfi_{fast} the capacitance per additional fan-in, for the fastest input.

$fast*Cfi_{fast}$ the delay due to the load of the next gate, in the xor subbox inside the propagate/generate box of Figure 1.

For D(N), given T = carry-select, as shown in Figure 2 [Hwang79], when $m = \left\lfloor \sqrt{N} \right\rfloor$, we have the following formula**:

Ripple-Carry Adder (RC)

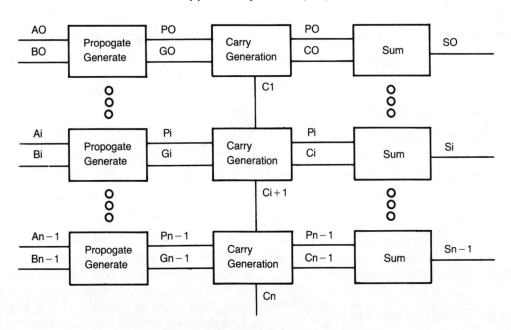

Figure 1: Block Diagram of Ripple-Carry Adder

Carry-Select Adder (CS)

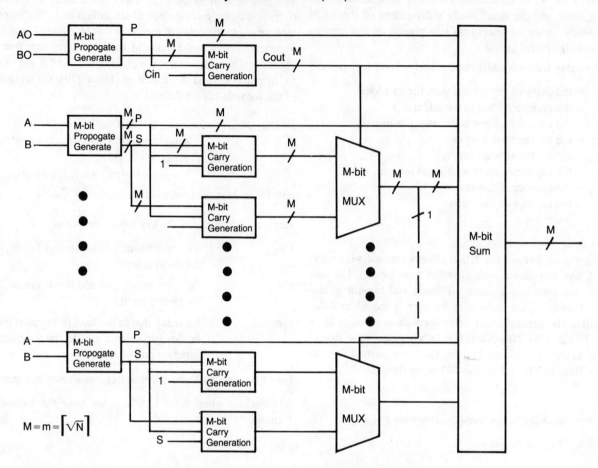

Figure 2: Block Diagram of Carry-Select Adder

$$D(N) = xor(Cfi_{fast}, Cfi_{slow}) + carry(Cfi_{fast})*m + xor_{fast}(Cfi_{fast}) +$$

$$mux(m, Cfi_{fast})* \left\lfloor N/m \right\rfloor + mux(N\%m, Cfi_{fast})*** \qquad (3)$$

where:

$$mux(m, C_{out}) = outtree(m, Cfi_{fast}) + base_{fast}(1) + fast*Cfi_{fast} +$$
$$base_{fast}(2) + fast*Cfi_{fast}$$
$$+ base_{fast}(\overline{2}) + Fast*C_{out,}$$

and:

$$outtree(m,C_{out}) = (\left\lceil \log_{maxfanout}(m) \right\rceil - 1)* (base_{fast}(1) + fast*Cfi_{fast}*maxfanout)$$
$$+ base_{fast}(1) + fast*C_{out}*maxfanout$$

See Figure 2 for the details of formula (3) and for the functions of different blocks (M-bit mux, etc.). For D(N), given T = full-carry-lookahead, as shown in Figure 3 [Hwang 79], we have the following formula**:

***"N%m" means "N modulo m," and m is here defined as

$$m = \left\lceil \sqrt{N} \right\rceil.$$

$$D(N) = xor(Cfi_{fast} + Cfi_{slow}) + carrytree(N, Cfi_{fast}) + xor_{fast} Cfi_{fast}. \qquad (4)$$

where:

$$carrytree(m,C_{out}) = outtree(+1,Cfi_{fast}) + intree(m,Cfi_{fast})$$
$$+ intree(m,C_{out}),$$

and:

$$intree(m,C_{out}) = (\left\lceil \log_{maxfanin}(m) \right\rceil * ((base_{slow}(maxfanin) + slow*Cfi_{fast})$$
$$+ base_{fast}(1) + fast + Cfi_{slow})$$
$$+ base_{slow}(maxfanin) + slow*C_{out}.$$

See Figure 3 for the details of formula (4) and for the functions of different blocks.

As already indicated, these equations were implemented in C language, for each adder separately. The base gate delays and delays per additional fan-in and fan-out were implemented as variables that were set at compile time. This information was plotted to show the difference between the

Full Carry-Look-Ahead Adder (FL)

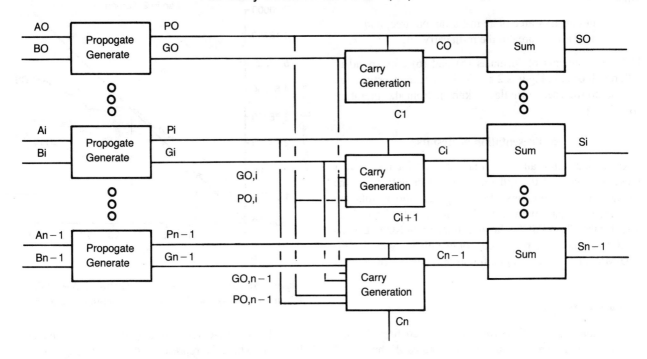

Figure 3: Block Diagram of Full-Carry-Look-Ahead Adder

adders, as the technology related parameters vary. The accuracy estimation for the above formulas is known from the literature [Hwang79].

4: Adder Area

So far only the delays of the individual adders have been discussed. To evaluate each adder, the delays should be used in conjunction with the VLSI layout area. We determined the VLSI layout area adder by using the TI's VHSIC HDL (hardware description language) software package [Betti85]. The resulting description was run through a translation program that extracted and formatted the data for RCA's MP2D software package [Betti85]. The MP2D, a multi-port 2-dimensional placement and routing program, takes the translated HDL information and generates cell-oriented custom layouts for portions of the adders and for complete adders. Included with this information was the actual VLSI layout and the VLSI layout area that each design required. This data was used to build general equations to determine the overall VLSI area of the adders considered in this paper. These equations allowed us to compare the adders from the VLSI layout area point of view.

The area of the ripple-carry adder was calculated by interpolation along a straight line between known points. This was relatively accurate since the structure is fairly linear.

The area of the carry-select adder of bit length N was approximated [BreKu82] by the following formula** related to Figure 2 [Hwang79]:

$$A(N) = area_{pg(m)} + area_{pg(N\%m)} \qquad (5)$$
$$+ (m-1)*2*(area_{cg(m)} + area_{cg(N\%m)} + area_{cg(m)})$$
$$+ (m-1)*(area_{mux(m)} + area_{mux(N\%m)})$$
$$+ m*(area_{sum(m)} + area_{sum(N\%m)})$$

where:

$$m = \lceil \sqrt{N} \rceil .$$

$area_{pg(m)}$ = area of an m-bit propagate generate box,
$area_{cg(m)}$ = area of an m-bit carry generation box,
$area_{mux(m)}$ = area of an m-bit mux, and
$area_{sum(m)}$ = area of an m-bit summation box.

The area for a full-carry-lookahead adder of the bit length N was approximated [BreKu82] by the following formula** related to Figure 3 [Hwang79]:

$$A(N) = area_{pg(N)} + area_{sum(N)} + fan\text{-}out_{carryin}$$

$$+ \sum_{i=0}^{i=N-1} (maxfanout_{cg}(N-i)$$
$$+ fanout_{pg}((i+1)*(N-i)+1) + area_{carryin}(i+1))$$

333

where:

> fan-out(m) = area of an m-bit fan-out tree, and
> carry(m) = area of the m-th carry bit.

Different elements of formulas (5) and (6) correspond to different blocks in Figures 2 and 3. The accuracy estimation for the above used formulas is known from the literature [BreKu82].

5: Presentation of Results

Using the delay and the area formulas for each adder type, we analyzed the differences in adder design for the chosen GaAs technology. In this paper, the results are presented comparatively with the analogously derived results for the CMOS/SOS silicon technology of RCA. Details of this technology, presented comparatively with DCFL E/D-MESPET GaAs, can be found in a number of sources [e.g., Milut86].

5.1: Adder Delays

The plottings for all above delays-related formulas are presented in Figures 4 through 9. Figures 1 through 3 display the delay of each adder in GaAs technology for three different fan-in and fan-out configurations. For comparison purposes, figures 4 through 6 display the delay of the adders in silicon technology for the same three fan-in and fan-out configurations. As already indicated, here we used the data for RCA's CMOS/SOS silicon technology. Each figure presents the delay in picoseconds versus word length in bits.

Simplified adder equations show that the delay of the ripple-carry adder increases by order N, i.e. $O(N)$, the delay of the carry-select adder increases by $O(\log(N)N^{1/2})$, and the

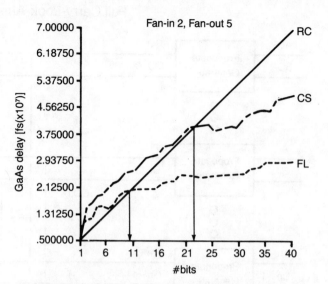

Figure 5: Adder Delays with GaAs E/D-MESFET Parameters, Maximum Fan-in = 2, Maximum Fan-out = 5

delay of the full-carry-lookahead adder increases by $O(\log(N))$, where N represents the word length of each adder, which matches ideally the existing theoretical results and proves the correctness of our approach. For large N, the comparison shows that the full-carry-lookahead adder will always be faster than the carry-select adder and that both will be faster than the ripple-carry adder. However, the technology related parameters determine the magnitude of the difference and the positions of "crosspoints."

For the word length of interest (N = 32 bits), the carry-select adder is slower than the full carry look-ahead adder, but this difference can be tolerated in GaAs CPU designs

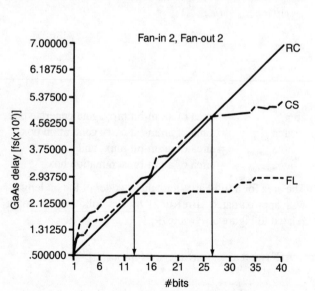

Figure 4: Adder Delays with GaAs E/D-MESFET Parameters, Maximum Fan-in = 2, Maximum Fan-out = 2

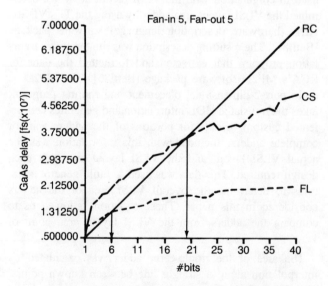

Figure 6: Adder Delays with GaAs E/D-MESFET Parameters, Maximum Fan-in = 5, Maximum Fan-out = 5

334

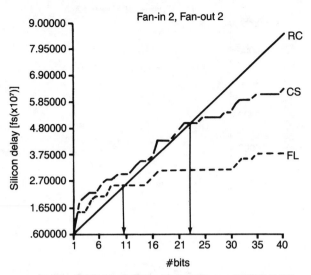

Figure 7: Adder Delays with Silicon CMOS/SOS Parameters, Maximum Fan-in = 2, Maximum Fan-out = 2

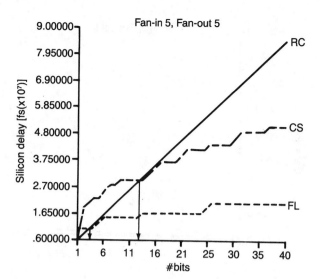

Figure 9: Adder Delays with Silicon CMOS/SOS Parameters, Maximum Fan-in = 5, Maximum Fan-out = 5

because of the facts explained in Section 1.1. A similar argument applies for the ripple-carry adder. For GaAs and larger N, the ripple-carry adder is slower than the carry-select adder, but less than for silicon. The crosspoint between these two adders has moved towards the higher values of N. The differences in the delays are caused by the relatively slow "rise" time of the GaAs E/D-MESFET gates and the relatively long "base delay" of the silicon CMOS/SOS gates (note the impact of various fan-in/fan-out limitations on the overall delay of different adders).

The relatively slow "rise" time severely degrades performance when fan-in and fan-out increase, as shown by the differences in propagation times for Figures 4 and 6, versus Figures 7 and 9. When only the "rise" time is changed, the speed of the individual adders increases dramatically.

Although a combination of the ripple-carry and the carry-select adder was chosen for incorporation into RCA's 32-bit GaAs microprocessor, we believe that if the designer wants to avoid an excessively deep memory pipeline, he should also consider the complete ripple-carry adder. Since the ripple-carry design is characterized by low fan-in/fan-out, the related GaAs/silicon differences would have almost no effect. In addition, the delay is only about twice that of the full carry look-ahead adder, and could increase the total datapath time of a processor such as SU-MIPS [HeJoP83]

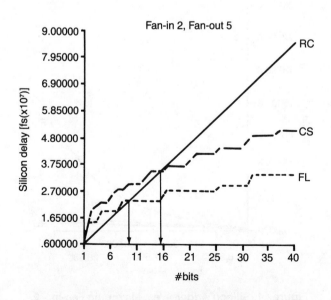

Figure 8: Adder Delays with Silicon CMOS/SOS Parameters, Maximum Fan-in = 2, Maximum Fan-out = 5

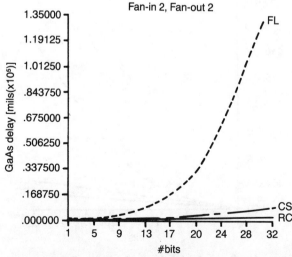

Figure 10: GaAs Adder Area, Maximum Fan-in = 2, Maximum Fan-out = 2

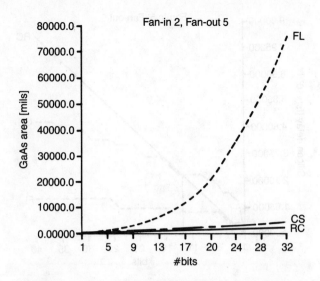

Figure 11: GaAs Adder Area, Maximum Fan-in = 2, Maximum Fan-out = 5

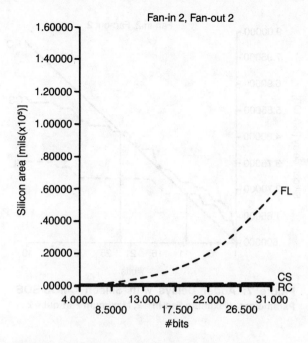

Figure 13: Silicon Adder Area, Maximum Fan-in = 2, Maximum Fan-out = 2

by about 30 percent. This increase would allow the designer to reduce the memory pipeline depth by approximately the same amount.

To point out how the speed of different adders changes when maximal allowed fan-in and fan-out change, we have indicated (on Figures 4 to 9) the crosspoints between the RC curve and the other two curves (FL and CS). The higher the maximal allowed fan-in and fan-out, the higher these crosspoints, which means that the ripple-carry adder becomes more attractive. The same conclusion applies for both GaAs and silicon, except that the crosspoints in GaAs are at higher word lengths.

In conclusion, speed differences between carry-looka-

head adder and other adder types (carry-select adder and ripple-carry adder) are generally smaller in GaAs than in silicon.

5.2: Adder Area

As mentioned before, comparisons solely on the basis of adder delays are deficient. Therefore, we plotted the VLSI

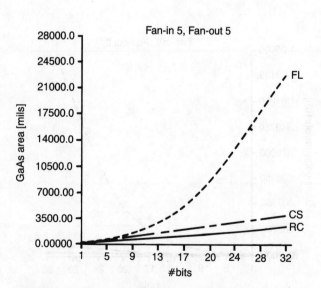

Figure 12: GaAs Adder Area, Maximum Fan-in = 5, Maximum Fan-out = 5

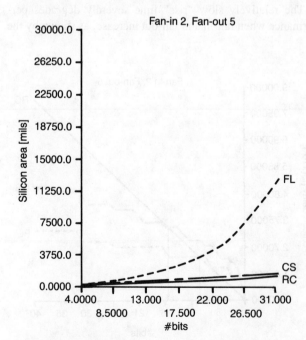

Figure 14: Silicon Adder Area, Maximum Fan-in = 2, Maximum Fan-out = 5

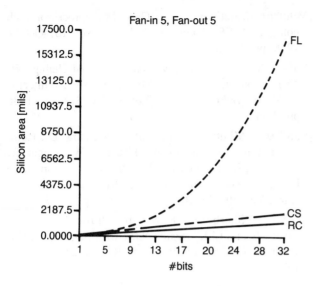

Figure 15: Silicon Adder Area,
Maximum Fan-in = 5,
Maximum Fan-out = 5

layout area consumed by each of the adders. The plots are presented in Figures 10 through 15. The area of each adder is shown in terms of mils squared and is plotted against the word length of each adder.

The area required by the ripple-carry adder increases linearly with the bit length and rises at the slowest rate of the three adders. The area of the carry-select adder is growing a little faster: $O(N)$, plus an $N^{1/2}$ component. The fastest adder, the full-carry-lookahead adder, consumes area at a much higher rate, $O(N^3)$. Although this finding is not surprising, the cubic growth rate quickly uses up the available area on a chip. In principle, if a "grouping" strategy is applied to the design of a carry-lookahead adder [Hwang79], its design complexity would decrease, but the overall conclusions of our study would not change.

The analysis of the graphs shows that even for large maximum fan-in and fan-out, the area consumed by the full-carry-lookahead adder is unreasonable for large bit length adders. Note, however, the impact of the limited fan-in/fan-out and the technology choice on the overall VLSI area of different adders. Only the carry-select adder and the ripple-carry adder conserve enough area to allow other important architectural structures to be placed on the same chip.

In conclusion, area differences between carry-lookahead adder and other adder types (carry-select adder and ripple-carry adder) are even greater in GaAs than in silicon.

6: Conclusion

In summary, the GaAs environment quickly challenges long-standing conventions. Unlike the silicon environment, ripple-carry adders are capable of performing the job with-out severe degradation of performance and can help reduce memory pipeline depth and improve performance. This supports using serial operations in GaAs, particularly when such operations have low fan-in and fan-out requirements. For adders such as full-carry-lookahead adders, their parallel nature uses area in such large quantities that they cannot be considered in a near term GaAs design environment. Those adders that serialize operations with high fan-in and fan-out requirements make a good compromise.

We definitely suggest a ripple-carry adder for technologies like GaAs (that are characterized with small on-chip transistor count, high ratio of off-chip and on-chip communication delays, and high intolerance to fan-in and fan-out), and for word lengths of up to about 24 bits. For word lengths from approximately 24 bits to 32 bits, we suggest either a ripple-carry approach (if the remaining transistor count could help to increase the register file size to above 16* or a combination of the ripple-carry adder and the carry-select adder (if the extra adder complexity will not drive the register file size below 16). For RCA's, 32-bit microprocessor, a combination of the ripple-carry and the carry-select adder was chosen.

Actually, the results of our analysis are more *general* and applicable to any technology with the above specified set of characteristics. Also, this is a *real-world* study, with all implementational constraints taken into account through an empirical analysis. Therefore, the results reflect both the theoretical aspects of the adder design and implementational aspects of a cell-oriented custom VLSI layout.

7: Acknowledgments

The authors are thankful to David Fura of Purdue University, and Bill Heagerty of RCA Corporation, for their help.

8: References

[Barne85]   Barney, C., "DARPA Eyes 100-mips GaAs Chip for Star Wars," *Electronics Week,* Vol. 58, No. 20, May 20, 1985, pp. 22-23.

[BeDoF81]   Beyers, J.W., Dohse, L.J., Fucetola, J.P., Kochis, R.L., Taylor, G.L., and Zeller, E.R., "A 32-Bit VLSI CPU Chip," *IEEE Journal of Solid-State Circuits,* Vol. SC-16, No. 10, October 1981, pp. 537-541.

[Betti85]   Bettinger, M., "Comparison of E/D-MESFET GaAs and CMOS Silicon for VLSI Processor Design," *Purdue University Technical Report,* TR-EE 85-18, Purdue University, West Lafayette, Ind., December 1985.

[BreKi82]   Brent, R.P. and Kung, H.T., "A Regular Layout for Parallel Adder," *IEEE Transactions on Computers,* Vol. C-31, No. 3, March 1982, pp. 260-263.

FeNoS83]   Feller, A., Noto, R., Smith, D.C., Wagner, B.S., and Putatunda, R., "CAD System Coordinates Complete Semicustom Chip Design," *Electronics,* June 16, 1983.

[HeJoP83]   Hennessy, J., Jouppi, N., Przybylski, S., Rowen, C., and Gross, T., "Design of a High Performance VLSI Processor," *Technical Report No. 236,* Stanford University, Stanford, Calif., February 1983.

[HelMi87]   Helbig, W. and Milutinović, V., "The RCA's DCFL E/D-MESFET GaAs Experimental RISC Machine," *High-Level Language Computer Architecture,* Computer Science Press, Rockville, Md., 1988.

[Hwang79]   Hwang, K., *Computer Arithmetic: Principles, Architecture, and Design,* John Wiley & Sons, New York, N.Y., 1979.

[Katev83]   Katevenis, M.G.H., "Reduced Instruction Set Computer Architectures for VLSI," *Report No. UCB/CSD 83/141,* University of California at Berkeley, Berkeley, Calif., October 1983.

[Milut86]   Milutinović, V., "GaAs Microprocessor Technology," *IEEE Computer,* Vol. 19, No. 10, October 1986, pp. 10-15.

[MiFuH86]   Milutinović, V., Fura, D., and Helbig, W., "An Introduction to GaAs Microprocessor Architecture for VLSI," *IEEE Computer,* Vol. 19, No. 3, March 1986, pp. 30-42.

[MiSiF86]   Milutinović, V., Silbey, A., Fura, D., Keirn, K., Bettinger, M. Helbig, W., Heagerty, W., Zieger, R., Schellack, B., and Curtice, W., "Issues of Importance in Designing GaAs Microcomputer System," *IEEE Computer,* Vol. 19, No. 10, October 1986, pp. 45-57.

[Sherb84]   Sherburne, R.W., Jr., "Processor Design Tradeoffs in VLSI," *Report No. UCB/CSD 84/173,* University of California at Berkeley, Berkeley, Calif., April 1984.

A DCFL E/D-MESFET GaAs Experimental RISC Machine†

Walt Helbig
Advanced Technology Laboratories
RCA Corporation
Moorestown, NJ 08057
(609) 866-6530

Veljko Milutinović
School of Electrical Engineering
Purdue University
West Lafayette, IN 47907
(317) 494-3530

Abstract

Architecture and design of RCA's 32-bit GaAs microprocessor are presented. To place the design in perspective, technology limitations and influences of the software environment are discussed. Details of the ISA (instruction set architecture) and of the IES (instruction execution sequence) are described.

Index Terms

32-Bit GaAs Microprocessor; DCFL E/D-MESFET GaAs; RISC Processor Architecture; RISC Processor Design; and ASIC.

I: Introduction

In this paper, we describe architecture and design of a 32-bit microprocessor intended for implementation using GaAs VLSI. The architecture of the microprocessor was patterned along the lines of the basic RISC philosophy. It was designed to include the fundamental operations (to support all functions needed for the intended applications) but was limited in the VLSI area for the implementation period was to be 1987, to what can be put onto a practical size GaAs VLSI chip. As will be seen later, design decisions that we had to make are different enough from typical silicon design decisions.

GaAs has definitely reached the VLSI level of complexity [1], and this work is a part of the effort to show that implementation of a 32-bit microprocessor on a GaAs chip is feasible. Still, GaAs chip densities are relatively small, and GaAs designs have a number of problems not present in silicon designs.

When using silicon VLSI, even the newest 1.25 μm technology, the on-chip gate delays are measured in nanoseconds, and the machine clock cycle time is most often 20 or more times longer. Delays on the board are of the order of one percent of the machine clock cycle time per inch of conductor path and result in board transmission times that are insignificant for design planning. In a GaAs design, this percentage is an order of magnitude higher and must be factored into the architecture. This factor usually necessitates pipelined interchip communications. Further, it means that the board layout must be critically controlled, both at the design level and the architecture level.

II: Impacts of the Technology

One problem with GaAs as an integration medium is the limitation on the logic functions that can be created with its devices. RCA chose to work with TriQuint, Inc.'s DCFL E/D-MESFET.* In the DCFL family, NOR gates of two to five inputs are present, but NAND gates do not exist. Further, on each input to a NOR gate, a two-input AND gate may be included.

This limitation is the result of the circuit construction technique and the inherent properties of GaAs, one of these being that the voltage swing of the signal in a logic gate is relatively small ($\pm$ 220 mV) and centered around the intermediate value of the reference voltage (+ 320 mV).

The important factor for the logic designer is that this characteristic causes the power dissipation in a given circuit to be high (since it is always drawing current), thus severely limiting the number of logic elements that can be put on a chip before its internal power consumption becomes prohibitive.

Of course, designing all of the circuits' internal impedances so that they are high (by using small-sized devices) results in circuits that have a small fan-out (but a large fan-in), use a small area on the chip, and require only a small amount of power. On the other hand, circuits with larger fan-out tend to permit a smaller number of inputs (smaller fan-in), use a larger area on the chip, and dissipate more power internally.

†This research was supported by RCA Corporation in 1984, 1985, and 1986.

*Only DCFL E/D-MESFET GaAs is treated in this paper.

Even more severe is the penalty that the logic designer pays by being unable to tie the outputs of two circuits together [2]. That is, phantom functions cannot be designed into logic. With no "off state" in the circuit, tying outputs together does not change the amount of power dissipated but does decrease the operating noise margin of the resulting logic tree. For the logic designer, this translates into a need to design a system bus, with its many inputs and outputs, as a single entity with only one active load circuit. In the system bus design, allowances should be made for the function of "bus pre-charge" and for time in each operating cycle to accomplish this pre-charge. The related loss of time could be substantial and, in the case of the DCFL E/D-MESFET GaAs logic family, is not justified. The reason is that the natural, and easily implemented, logic function AND-NOR is just what is needed to create a multiplexer—a perfect replacement for a bus.

With the above in mind, the choice that was used in the design of RCA's 32-bit microprocessor was as follows. In those areas where the design was to be handcrafted anyway and where the speed of operation was not penalized to the point of slowing the system, buses were used. (This occurred in two areas, the general register file and the barrel shifter.) In the remainder of the architecture, multiplexers were used. The multiplexers frequently resulted in including additional functional capabilities in the machine, simply because it was cheaper to keep them than to exclude them.

Another technology-dependent choice made for this design was to use circuits of three different power levels. One set of logic gates had a low power consumption, a low fan-out, and a small chip area requirement. One set had a high power consumption, a high fan-out, and a large (relatively speaking, of course) chip area requirement. In the third set of logic gates, everything was somewhere between the two extremes.

Interchip communications required a very special attention. Because of the circuit limitations, buses could not be used. This decision was reaffirmed later, when it became obvious that the state of the "packaging art" would not allow control signals to be passed freely throughout the system. Further, we determined that passing signals from one IC to another would be done only with signal delays that are equal to a significant fraction of the CPU cycle time. With a required minimum CPU clock frequency of 200 mHz and stripline construction on alumina substrates for controlled impedance and high power handling capability, the delays are approximately equal to 5 percent to 10 percent of the clock period, per inch of conductor path length. Thus, with any significant amount of conductor length, which is almost a foregone conclusion for paths that go from one board to another, the IC at the sending end could easily become involved in the clock cycle $n+1$ before the signals sent during the clock cycle n reach the IC at the receiving end. Further, by the time the second IC reacts to the signals sent by the first IC to perform the requested operation and to send the results of its operation back to the first IC, several clock cycles can have passed.

So severe is this problem that the designer must consider all of the latencies that might occur in order to construct a design that will operate no matter how the ICs are placed on the board. Delays will occur in instruction fetch, data store and fetch, and control and address signal distribution. Delays will occur in the distribution of the clock so that ICs will not necessarily be operating in phase with each other. The result may be that the latency in an operation may not be an integer number of clock periods. This phenomenon may also appear in fast silicon designs; however, its impact is much greater in GaAs designs.

On the other hand, the entire system may be designed to be pipelined, wherein the clock is distributed with the data, and at every junction point all signals are reclocked to remove any variations in delay they might have undergone in making their transit. Next, by having signals distributed out from the CPU through a series of these junction points to wherever they are destined to go and then going back through the same junction points to the CPU, the information will always arrive at the CPU in phase with its clock. Such an approach was chosen for the design of RCA's 32-bit microprocessor system.

III: Impacts of the Support Software

RISC architecture philosophy is allowing the support software to, as much as it can, compensate for decisions made in designing the hardware [3].

The most notable examples of RISC-type solutions are the "branch latency fill-in" and the "load delay fill-in" operations, performed by code optimizer, to give the CPU something useful to do while waiting for its pipeline to complete the operations needed to perform a branch or a load. With respect to these issues, an important difference between silicon and GaAs is that GaAs designs have much deeper pipelines, and the fill-in algorithms have to be modified [4,5].

Sometimes, however, features can be added to the hardware to eliminate, from the required support software operation, a function that the hardware can only perform crudely at best. Two such features were added to the design of the RCA's 32-bit microprocessor.

One feature allows the system to handle immediate values efficiently. Immediate values typically have the same range of values as addresses and data — equal to the word length of the machine. This means that the machine must have the ability to express or create immediate values of length equal to the data word length, or in this case 32 bits. Creating full word length immediate operands can be achieved by loading partial length operands and assembling them by instruction execution (requiring the allocation of at least two general registers for this function). They may also be handled by having an instruction format that includes, for some instructions, a field for an immediate value equal to the word length. Several problems arise here that the architect must handle. First, not all immediate values need to be the full 32 bits in width. In fact, most of the time 8 bits are sufficient [2]. Only a few percent of the time does one need the long immediate field.

The Stanford MIPS machine [6] gets around the problem by including some instructions that have 16-bit immediate fields and some with 24-bit immediate fields, but none with 32-bit immediate fields. This leaves the programmer/compiler with the problem of building, at run time, the full word length immediates or storing all needed immediates in memory and fetching them at run time. An alternative approach was used in the RCA ATMAC [7], where the instruction word was longer (24 bits) than the data word length (16 bits). It worked quite efficiently for this 16-bit machine because the nonimmediate instructions also required 24-bits to control the ATMAC's horizontal architecture. Other approaches include sequences of load and shift instructions or the special read-shift-OR-replace instruction.

RCA's 32-bit GaAs machine handles the problem in a way unusual for early RISC machines [8,9,10]. However, we had good reasons for such an approach (see below), and we have noticed that some recent (independently generated) designs have used a similar solution [11].

The instruction format chosen uses one- and two-word instructions. The first part of all instructions is of the same format, specifying the operation code of three general register file addresses (an unsigned 8-bit immediate value) called SIMM in Figures 1 and 2 (to take care of 95 percent of the cases where immediate data is needed). The first part also has a single bit to designate whether or not there is a second part to the instruction (see Figure 1). The optional second part of the instruction carries only the 24 most significant (MS) bits of the immediate value, where the 8 bits in the first part of the instruction are the least significant (LS) bits. This arrangement greatly simplifies the instruction decoding logic (see Figure 2), achieving very efficiently one of the principle goals of RISC machines: improved execution time for compiled HLL code [8,9,10]. As already indicated, a similar approach was used in AT&T's CRISP microprocessor [11].

While AT&T's motivations behind choosing this solution are as given in [11], our motivations were somewhat different. In designing this microprocessor to fit within the technology limits of a GaAs VLSI circuit, we were looking for simplicity and speed — the two basic demands of a RISC system. We used simplicity in the design wherever possible to accomplish as great a gain in performance as possible, while leaving as many as we could of the available devices for other functions. With our approach, we were able to inexpensively obtain the full word length immediate operand that we needed for logic- and arithmetic-oriented applications.

The *second* feature added to the architecture of the machine was a way to decrease the time between two executions of two load instructions. Normally, when a load instruction is executed, the data memory address is sent from the CPU, data is read from the memory, and sent back to the CPU. Then the value is put into the general register file during the course of execution of the instruction. In a RISC machine, however, especially one made using GaAs ICs, the time available for these operations is too short for any practical memory system. Further, with the interchip communication latency included, several of the machine's clock cycles can have passed between sending the address from the CPU and getting the result back to the CPU (storing the result into the general register file). Each of these clock cycles corresponds to another instruction execution period.

In order to keep straight where the data is to go when it gets back to the CPU, the normal approach is to hold the general register (GR) file address in the CPU and to have the

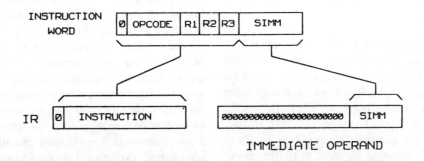

Figure 1: One-Word Format (SIMM: 8-Bit Short Immediate Operand).

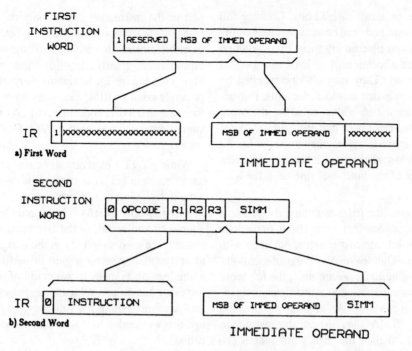

Figure 2: Two-Word Format.

program not execute another load operation until the first one is completed. The time elapsed is equal to the load latency.

An alternate approach, one that is built into this machine, is to send the destination address (the general register file address) out from the CPU, along with the memory address, to the memory and then have the destination address sent back with the data. When the data finally reaches the CPU, the destination register address is with the data, and the data may be properly stored. Therefore, no matter what the interchip communication and the memory system latencies are and no matter how may load requests are active (initiated but not completed, for we deal here with a relatively deep memory pipeline, as explained in a later section of this paper), at any time everything is kept straight. Consequently, requests for memory load may be issued at every instruction cycle, which would not be possible with standard pipeline organizations.

IV: CPU Architecture

Having established what the technology and support software guidelines are, the CPU architecture had to be created so as to fit within these guidelines [12,13]. We created the architecture by including in the design those features needed to make the system execute programs efficiently, in the conditions typical of the GaAs technology [12,13]. Instruction format details are given in Figures 3 to 6. Block diagram of the CPU is shown in Figures 7 to 10, for various execution phases of a typical instruction.

In our pipelined architecture, a stack of registers was required to be connected to the PC, so that the last N values of the instruction memory address can be remembered. These values will be used to restart those instructions that did not finish executing, when an interrupt occurred. Even though these N instructions were fetched, they may not have finished execution when they were stopped, in order for the CPU to execute the called sequence, that is, the interrupt response program. We have found that the traditional approach to this problem will work well in the GaAs environment, except for differences due to the fact that the value of N is larger [14-16].

As each instruction address is generated, it is simultaneously sent to the instruction memory to fetch the instruction and is pushed onto the register stack containing the last N values. When an interrupt occurs, that is, when the execution of the interrupt instruction begins, the operation of the stack ceases, while the PC continues to function. The PC first branches to the called routine and then goes through the execution of the called routine. When the interrupt service routine is fully executed, execution of the interrupted routine is restarted by retrieving the instruction memory addresses from the stack and refetching the instructions from memory. By the time the execution of the Nth instruction has begun, the CPU will have recovered from the interrupt and will be back to the point in the interrupted routine where it was interrupted. The PC stack operation is then restarted, and program execution is allowed to proceed normally until another interrupt is received. In this machine, the PC stack

ALU CLASS

| 31 | 30 | 29 28 | 23 22 | 18 17 | 13 12 | 8 7 | 0 |

LIMM	CLASS = 00	OPCODE	DST	SRC1	SRC2	IMMED

LOAD/STORE CLASS

| 31 | 30 | 29 28 | 23 22 | 18 17 | 13 12 | 8 7 | 0 |

LIMM	CLASS = 01	OPCODE	REUSE	DST/SRC	BASE	IMMED

BRANCH CLASS

| 31 | 30 | 29 28 | 23 22 | 18 17 | 13 12 | 8 7 | 0 |

LIMM	CLASS = 10	OPCODE	COND	SRC1	SRC2	IMMED

COPROCESSOR CLASS

| 31 | 29 | 28 27 | 23 22 | 18 17 | 13 12 | 8 7 | 0 |

0	CLASS = 11	OPCODE	DST	SRC1	SRC2	UNUSED

Figure 3: Instruction Format.

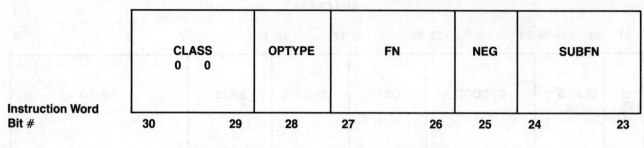

CLASS 0 0	OPTYPE	FN	NEG	SUBFN

Instruction Word Bit #

| 30 | 29 | 28 | 27 | 26 | 25 | 24 | 23 |

Figure 4:   ALU Class Op-Code Field Assignments.

CLASS 1 0	OPTYPE	SIGNED	ADDRMD	TF

Instruction Word bit #

| 30 | 29 | 28 | 27 | 26 | 25 | 24 | 23 |

a) OPcode field

Branch on Greater Than	Branch on Less Than	Branch on Equal	Branch on Overflow	Branch on EXT

Instruction Word bit #

| 22 | 21 | 20 | 19 | 18 |

b) Cond field (for all eaxcept INT & IGN)

*Note: If all bits = 0, then branch/ jump   i s unconditional

Figure 5:   Branch/Jump Class Opcode Field Asignments.

CLASS 0 1	OPTYPE	UNUSED	ADDRMD	DTTYPE

Instruction Word Bit #

| 30 | 29 | 28 | 27 | 26 | 25 | 24 | 23 |

Figure 6:   Load/Store Class Op-Code Field Assignments.

is located in the memory controller system rather than in the CPU. This decreased the number of devices to be put on the CPU chip and improved the speed of the recovery process. It allowed the stack to be built with a depth equal to the largest expected N and still operate efficiently with a smaller value for N.

One of the major design problems with GaAs microprocessors is the relatively high ratio of off-chip memory access time to on-chip datapath time. With the target execution rate being one instruction per CPU clock cycle, we have defined the system such that more than one instruction is in the process of being fetched.

The first phase of each instruction execution is instruction fetch (MAR loaded with the instruction's address from the PC). In this machine, a series of partial instruction decoders are included between a series of registers that hold the unused portions of the instruction at each stage of the execution cycle. The first of these registers is called the Instruction Register (IR) and holds the entire instruction. Its output is connected to multiplexers that sequentially use the general register file addresses to access the file and fetch the two operands to be used in the course of the execution of the instruction. Input logic recognizes whether the incoming instruction is the MS bits of the immediate operand or the following instruction. If the former is the case, then the transfer path (to copy the contents of the appropriate bits of the instruction to the immediate operand register for the ALU) is activated (see Figure 7).

When the next clock cycle of the CPU is completed, the next instruction is ready to be placed into the instruction register, so the present contents must be moved to the "next instruction register." This action occurs at the same time that the operands from the general register file are put into two registers at the input of the ALU, and the immediate operand is put into a third register at the ALU's input (see Figure 8). At this time the immediate operand is assembled (using 8 bits from the "second instruction register" and 24-bits from the input to the first instruction register, if the continuation bit is set) and put into the third ALU input register. If the continuation bit is not set (in the word at the input to the first instruction register), then the 8 bits from the "second instruction register" are put into the third ALU input register, with the 24 most significant bits of this register set to zero. Note the essential difference between this scheme and the "shifted control" scheme used in some other machines.

To accomplish all of this successfully, with the logic family available, this machine was designed with a two-phase CPU clock system and two levels of registers for each stage. It also uses a general register file that has one read port and one write port [17] but is fast enough that two pairs of read and write operations may be accomplished during a single CPU clock cycle. In reality, then, the system, on the first clock phase after the instruction is put into the instruction register, reads the first operand out of the general register file, puts it into a temporary holding register, and puts all of the remaining bits of the instruction into another instruction register. On the second clock phase, the first operand is put into the first ALU input register, and the second operand is fetched from the general register file, and put into the second ALU input register. Here, two decisions had to be made.

First, the ALU will only accept two operands, but we have assembled three. So two must be selected from the three. In many machines, the selection is based on the op-code, with some instructions being designed for immediate operands only and others designed to use two variables only. Other machines include an extra bit in the instruction format to specify which operands are to be used: the first and second operands fetched from the register file, or the first operand fetched from the register file, plus the immediate operand. This machine, instead, uses an arrangement to achieve more flexibility (without adding any bits to the instruction format) and to achieve a convenience that is needed later on in the instruction execution cycle. It does this through the implementation of the general register file so that "register zero" does not exist and the file, when register zero is addressed, always puts out a value of zero. Further, the ALU operand selection logic is designed to select the immediate operand if the second source register address is zero and to select the content read from the general register file if this address is nonzero. This solution adds a little to the overall complexity of the decoding circuitry but improves the code density, which is especially important in GaAs machines with a relatively small instruction cache (located off-CPU-chip/on-CPU-package).

Second, for ALU operations, the first operand is always sent to the ALU unmodified, and the second one may be sent unmodified or complemented, depending on the instruction op-code. However, destinations of operands are determined by the type of operation to be performed. For example, for arithmetic, logic, and shift instructions, the appropriate contents of the ALU input registers are sent to the adder, the logic unit, or the shifter. For coprocessor instructions, the CPU operation is meaningless; therefore, any operation is allowed as long as the result does not disturb a register whose content is to be kept valid from one instruction to the next. For branch instructions, the selected operands are sent to the ALU, but the value in the R1 field is used as an extension to the op-code in order to specify the test to be

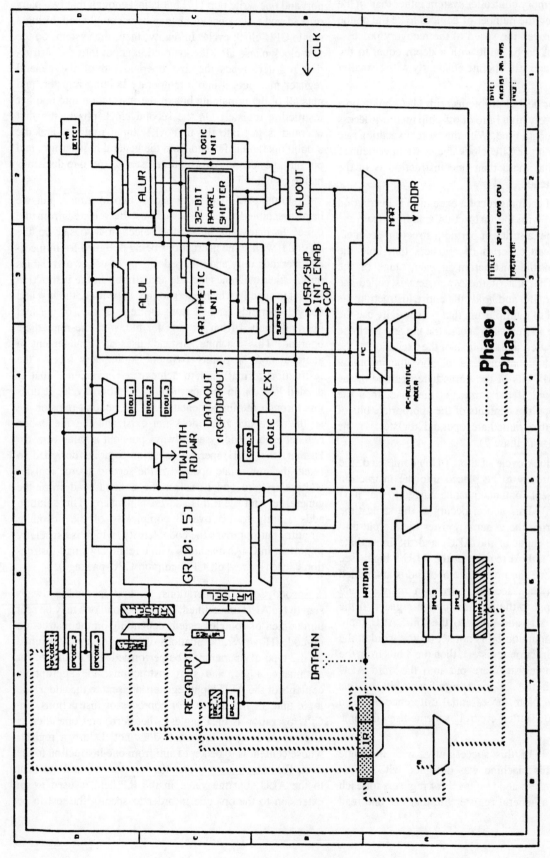

Figure 7: Instruction Read Phase.

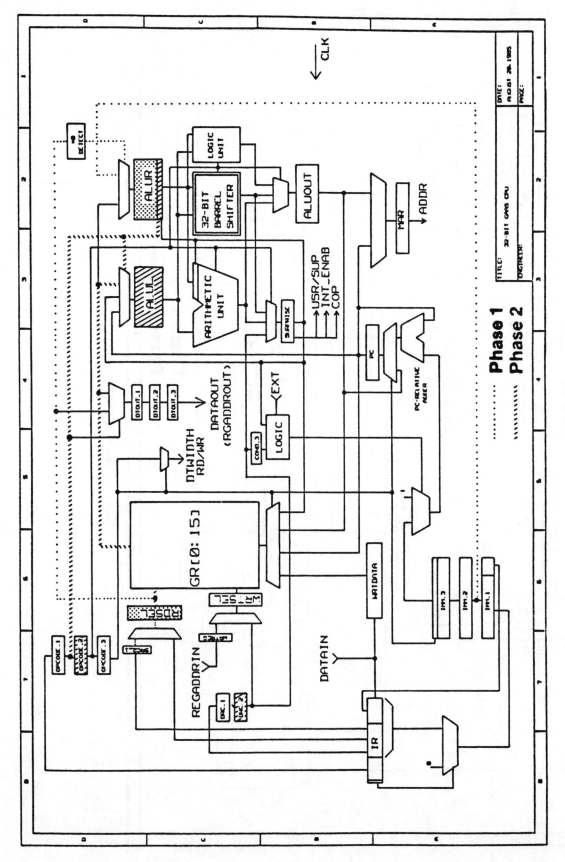

Figure 8: Register Read Phase.

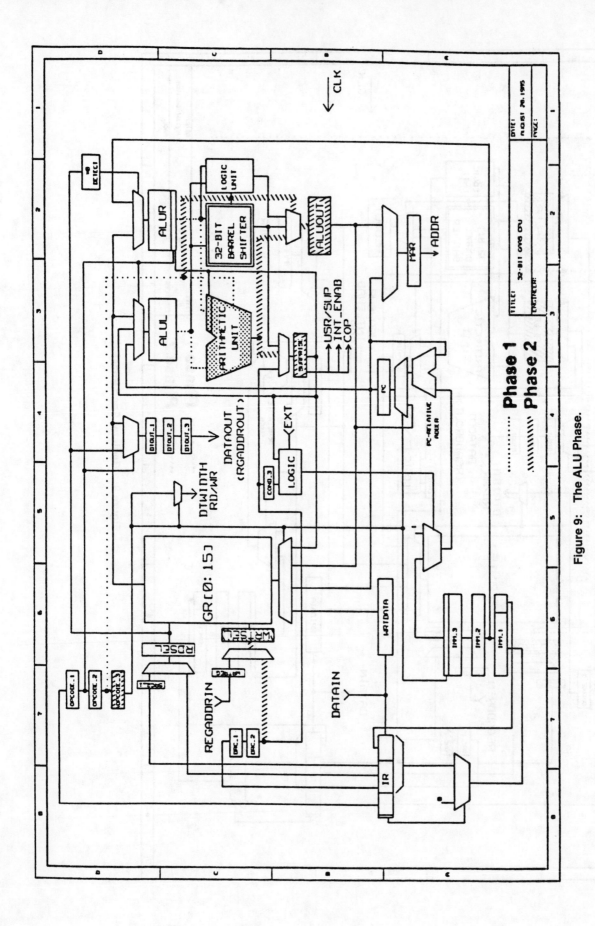

Figure 9: The ALU Phase.

348

performed on the result of the adder operation (to determine if the branch should be taken). In this case, the value in the "immediate operand register" is sent to the PC adder, so that it may be conditionally added to, or subtracted from, the present PC value for a PC-relative branch. For jump instructions, the values normally selected for the ALU input are sent to the adder, and the adder output is sent later on to the PC to execute the jump.

In Figure 9, we illustrate the execution of the subtract operation for the interval when the operands are sent to the ALU during the next two phases of the CPU clock. During this cycle, the inputs to the ALU are available at the beginning of the first phase of the clock and the selected output of the ALU goes into the ALU "output register" and the "surprise register" at the end of the second phase of the clock. Figure 11a illustrates the phases of the instruction execution sequence through the ALU operation stage.

The last stage of the execution of an instruction in the CPU is the stage in which the output of the ALU is sent to its ultimate destination: either to the data memory system as an address, or to the general register file as the result of the computation. In the case of the memory reference, the address goes out, but the result is not sent back immediately, so the information requested by load operation cannot be put into the general register file during the next cycle of the CPU clock. This value will come back later and then will be put into the file.

In the case of the ALU operation, the result is written into the general register file on the first of the two clock phases of this last instruction execution stage (see Figure 10). The alternate phase of operation is used to handle the storage of any data that comes from the data memory (from some previously executed load operation). This part of the operation of the machine is illustrated in Figure 11b, which shows how the destination address has been delayed during the instruction execution, so that it arrives at the general register file at the same time when the result arrives. The complete instruction execution cycle is shown in Figure 11c. Shown also are the two latency periods, one related to the instruction fetch and one related to the operand fetch for a load operation.

Several other unique features were added to solve problems caused by the operation of the architecture at a rate of 200 mips, a cycle time so short that any interchip communication would use up much of this time (about 0.5 ns per inch of conductor length). This fact mandates the use of memory pipelines, in conjunction with the small number of devices on each related GaAs chip. The first of these added features is the "ignore instruction" to help reclaim some of the instruction memory space lost due to the long branch latency.

What happens in a pipelined machine is that following a branch instruction, there are several instructions that will have entered the pipeline and will be executed, whether the branch is taken or not. For these types of machines it is the job of the code optimizer to find things for the CPU to do, either those that need to be done all the time, or those that are useful sometimes (say when the branch is taken) and harmless the other times (when the branch is not taken). Unfortunately, for the current state of the art of compiler technology, code optimizer efficiency is not very high for relatively deep pipelines. Consequently, branch fill-in of one or two instructions is about all that can be accomplished [3]. Therefore, the remainder of the instruction slots in the branch latency area have to be filled in with NoOp instructions. This results in wasting a relatively large part of the memory space.

Through the use of the ignore instruction, this space can be reclaimed. This is accomplished by having the code optimizer place the ignore instruction following the last useful instruction migrated into the branch latency area. The count in the ignore instruction is then set to cause the CPU to ignore execution of the number of instructions specified, no matter what they are. The memory space following the ignore instruction can be used to hold other instructions.

Most of the decisions made for this processor's design were verified by simulating the execution of compiler generated code sequences on the alternative architectures and by choosing the best [14-16]. In our design, the ignore count was integrated with the branch instruction, putting a count and a control bit in an unused portion of the instruction word. The control bit specified whether the execution of the following N instructions (count field value) should be performed, if the branch is taken or not.

This version of the design, quite similar to the branch squashing technique (for example, [18]), was simulated for several programs (see Table 1). Two types of statistics were gathered to evaluate the usefulness of this approach. The first statistic showed that, through the use of this technique, the amount of filling of the branch latency area with useful instructions increased on the average about 10 percent (with the best being an improvement from about 17 percent to about 66 percent). It also showed that the number of NoOp instructions in the program memory decreased by an average of about 5 percent (see Table 1).

Another place where this technique showed its usefulness was in the area of the elimination of NoOp instructions in the CPU's instruction memory following a coprocessor instruction and in the execution of NoOp instructions by the CPU while it is waiting for the coprocessor to finish the execution of its instruction. In this case, an average of about three percent of the NoOps were eliminated in both the static and the dynamic count. These figures could be improved if the count field were larger. Further, the separate instruction

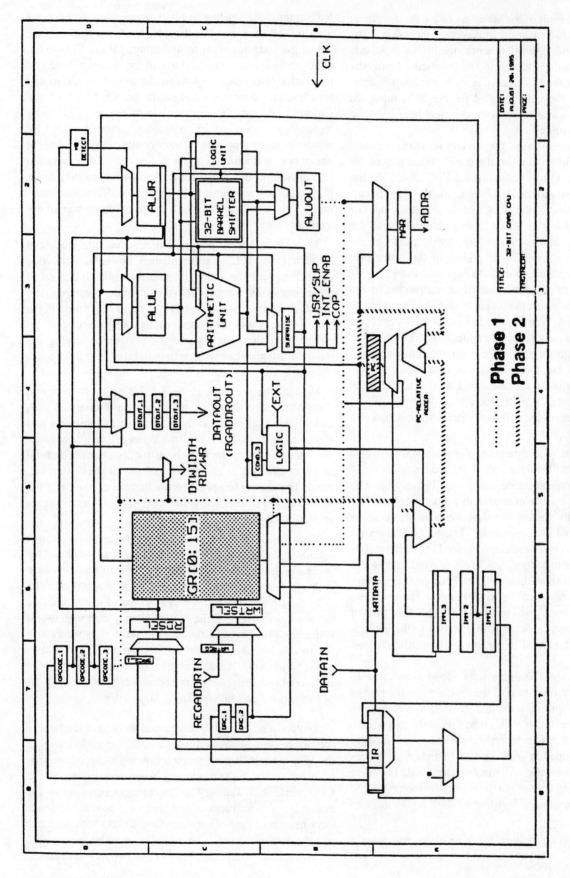

Figure 10: The Write-Back Phase.

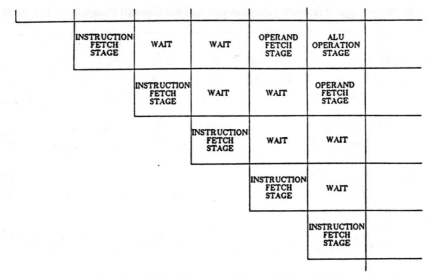

Figure 11a: **Instruction Execution Sequence Through the ALU Operation Phase.**

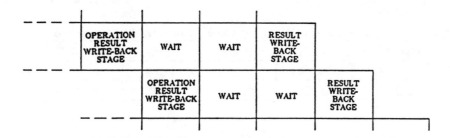

Figure 11b: **The Operation Result Write-Back Phase of Instruction Execution.**

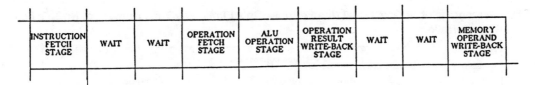

Figure 11c: **Complete Instruction Execution Cycle.**

is less expensive in terms of device count than the branch squashing approach (see Table 1).

Another important problem in a pipelined machine is that of interrupts. These may be handled totally by hardware on the CPU chip, if there is no external memory pipeline. If a memory pipeline exists in the system, however, no hardware control on the CPU alone can solve the problem conveniently for the same reason that necessitated the presence of the memory pipeline in the first place. The problem was solved in this machine by having the interrupt handler logic insert an "interrupt instruction" in the instruction stream (when an interrupt request is placed by the external logic) in place of one of the instructions already fetched from memory. The INT was to be used by the hardware with the base register specified as zero. An appropriate ignore field count is also included with this instruction, so that the proper number of instructions already in the memory pipeline (ones that immediately follow the interrupt instruction) are ignored. Note that the PC stack contents mentioned earlier will be used to refetch the instructions that were fetched but not executed, when the interrupt occurred. This will permit their execution upon return from the interrupt.

Table 1a: Percentage of Branch Fills with/without the Squash Mechanism (Static Numbers)

benchmarks	total branches	% 3-fills	% 2-fills	% 1-fills	% 0-fills	% fills
REALMM (without)	29	31.0%	20.7%	13.8%	34.5%
(with)		42.9%	35.7%	3.6%	17.9%	67.9%
PUZZLE (without)	84	8.3%	9.5%	8.3%	73.8%	17.5%
(with)		33.7%	44.2%	9.3%	12.8%	66.3%
BUBBLE (without)	23	26.1%	17.4%	13.4%	43.5%	42.0%
(with)		29.2%	16.7%	1.3%	41.7%	44.4%
WEIGHT (without)	131	37.4%	17.6%	25.2%	19.1%	57.5%
(with)		40.8%	21.5%	23.1%	14.6%	62.8%

Table 1b: Percentage of NoOp's (Total Number of NoOp's/Total Number of Instructions)

	without coprocessor			
benchmarks	static		dynamic	
	non-reorg'd	reorganized	non-reorg'd	reorganized
REALMM	66.6%	16.8%	54.2%	17.0%
PUZZLE	39.4%	18.9%	40.0%	10.7%
BUBBLE	48.3%	23.4%	47.4%	20.3%
WEIGHT				
with coprocessor				
REALMM	48.5%	29.1%	44.2%	26.5%

Table 1c: Percentage of NoOp's (Total Number of NoOp's Eliminated/Total Number of NoOp's before Reorganization)

	without coprocessor							
	static				dynamic			
	by intrablock reorganztn	by branch optimiztn	by squash	total	by intrablock reorganztn	by branch optimiztn	by squash	total
REALMM	83.3%	5.1%	1.6%	90.0%	68.3%	11.2%	4.5%	84.0%
PUZZLE	68.7%	2.9%	7.4%	79.0%	65.3%	7.9%	11.2%	84.4%
BUBBLE	56.8%	11.1%	1.3%	69.2%	65.2%	5.2%	1.9%	72.3%
WEIGHT								
with coprocessor								
REALMM	44.4%	9.0%	2.9%	56.3%	43.5%	7.8%	3.1%	54.5%

without coprocessor		
	static	dynamic
REALMM	60.2%	49.1%
PUZZLE	45.6%	46.3%
BUBBLE	36.3%	35.3%
WEIGHT		
with coprocessor		
REALMM	30.5%	24.0%

The two other problem areas found in machines of this type are associated with the implementation of the multiply and divide operations. In the Stanford MIPS computer, these operations were augmented by the inclusion (in the hardware) of special shift registers, called the Hi and Lo registers, and by putting the barrel shifter in series with the adder. This allowed the MIPS to process two multiplier bits and one quotient bit per instruction cycle.

For this GaAs machine, that solution was not viable. First, the barrel shifter could not be put in series with the adder. Unlike the MIPS that executed instructions at the rate of one every other machine cycle, this machine was designed to execute instructions at the rate of one every clock cycle, requiring that the critical path be very short. Second, the cost of the Hi and Lo registers was too large for what gain could be achieved in the throughput. Since GaAs chips must be small, the Hi-Lo register was felt to be one thing that could be omitted. And finally, the machine was designed to support double precision arithmetic (on a coprocessor), including multiply and divide, and these would make the Hi-Lo register approach even more expensive.

As a result, the machine was designed to perform the multiply and divide operations by reading the operands from the general register file, operating on them, and putting them back into the same file. This resulted in a very inexpensive approach that permitted the system to handle single, double, or higher precision operations, without having any ALU or branch latency problems. The result is that multiply is executed at the rate of two multiplier bits for every three machine cycles for single precision and every six machine cycles for double precision. Divide is executed at the rate of one quotient bit for every three machine cycles for single precision and every six machine cycles for double precision.

When it came time to decide how to do multiply in this machine, we were faced with several ground rules and a difficult choice to make. Without a multiply operation or a barrel shifter, the computer implementaion took up all but about 700 of the allowable active devices that could be put on a GaAs VLSI (to assure a "non-zero" fabrication yield). The question that faced us was what to use these remaining devices for. We needed an extendable length multiply and divide operation because the processor had to perform the same operations without the floating point coprocessor as it did with the floating point coprocessor. Thus, we had to be able to program both 24×24 bit multiplies and 53×53 bit multiplies to provide both the short and the long floating point operations.

We did not want the shifter in series with the adder because this would double the critical path delay time and, therefore, cut the throughput. We have also performed some preliminary designs and have found out that we could add either the barrel shifter, or the single-length Hi-Lo register combination [10], or a series multiplier in parallel with the adder, but we couldn't have more than one of these items without exceeding the device count limit.

To find out which one was the most valuable [15], simulations were run on designs of machines that had one of these three items but not the others. The barrel shifter was by far the best choice. Combining it with the designs for the multiplier and divide operation explained before, the average throughput for the machine design was clearly better in almost all benchmark programs tested.

Additionally, we found that the long divide operations, while simple to program with the chosen approach, would have been costly to implement with the Hi-Lo register approach [10]. Not only did the design permit long divide to be achieved, but multiword multiplies were easy to get as well.

V: Conclusions

No project is ever undertaken properly if all that is accomplished is that something is built. For any project to be truly successful something should be learned. In this project (to design a computer for construction in GaAs VLSI that would be patterned after the Stanford MIPS architecture, and thus, would have a support software system to make optimum use of the architecture) several lessons were learned in each of the three major areas: technology, architecture, and software.

One was that any significant differences in the lengths of conductors among the lines of parallel paths to carry the bits of a single word would necessitate the use of deskewing buffers at the receiving end. This approach is very inconvenient because of the small amount of logic that can be put on a GaAs VLSI chip today.

Another was that handling one instruction per machine clock cycle increases the problems related to designing the logic for the CPU. All critical paths between registers (such as through the adder and the shifter) must be very short, and typically no more than 20 gate delays long.

Further, it was found that the faster the machine operates, the longer the memory pipeline will be. The increasing pipeline length increases the latency that the code optimizer must compensate for: the branch latency, the load latency, and perhaps even the ALU latency. It lengthens the stack that must accompany the program counter to enable the handling of interrupts. It also increases the number of CPU resources that must be "shut down" and then "restarted" properly during the process of interrupt handling.

Finally, it was proven that in GaAs RISC systems, more than in any silicon RISC systems, the compiler should be considered as an integral part of the architecture. (This is partially due to the deeper memory pipelines of GaAs systems and partially due to the fact that designers tend to move many traditional hardware functions into the compiler.) However, compiler technology (code optimization technology) not being ready for code optimization in the presence of deep pipelines, caused the execution rate for many benchmarks to be well below the peak execution rate of 200 mips.

VII: Acknowledgement.

The authors are thankful to Bill Heagerty, Thomas Geige' and Nancy Chen for their help.

VIII: References

[1] Karp, S. and Roosilv, S., "DARPA, SDI, and GaAs," *IEEE Computer*, October 1986, pp. 17-19.

[2] Wedig, R. and Lehr, T., "The GaAs Realization of a Production System Machine," *Proceedings of the HICSS-19*, Honolulu, Hawaii, January 1986.

[3] Gross, T., "Code Optimization of Pipeline Constraints," *Stanford University Technical Report*, No. 83-255, December 1983.

[4] Milutinović, V., Fura, D., Helbig, W., and Linn, J., "Architecture/Compiler Synergism in GaAs Computer Systems," *IEEE Computer*, May 1987.

[5] Linn, J., "Horizontal Microcode Compaction," *Handbook of Microprogramming*, edited by Habib, S. and Dasgupta, S., Van Nostrand, New York, 1987.

[6] Gill, J., et al., "Summary of MIPS Instructions," *Stanford University Technical Report*, No. 83-237, November 1983.

[7] Helbig, W. and Stringer, J., "A VLSI Microprocessor: The RCA ATMAC," *IEEE Computer*, Vol. 10, No. 9, September 1977, pp. 22-29.

[8] Colwell, R., et al., "Computers, Complexity, and Controversy," *IEEE Computer*, September 1985, pp. 8-20.

[9] Patterson, D. and Sequin, C., "A VLSI RISC," *IEEE Computer*, September 1982, pp. 39-47.

[10] Hennessy, J., et al., "The MIPS Machine," *Digest of Papers, Spring COMPCON 82*, San Francisco, Calif., February 1982, pp. 2-7.

[11] Ditzel, D.R., McLellan, H.R., and Berenbaum, A.D., "The Hardware Architecture of the CRISP Microprocessor," *Proceedings of the ACM/IEEE International Symposium on Computer Architecture*, Pittsburgh, Penn., June 1987, pp. 309-319.

[12] Milutinović, V., et al., "An Introduction to GaAs Microprocessor Architecture for VLSI," *IEEE Computer*, March 1986, pp. 30-42.

[13] Milutinović, V., et al., "Issues of Importance in Designing GaAs Computer Systems," *IEEE Computer*, October 1986, pp. 45-57.

[14] Fura, D., "Architectural Approaches for GaAs Exploitation in High-Speed Computer Design," *Purdue University Technical Report*, TR-EE 85-17, December 1985.

[15] Bettinger, M., "Comparison of CMOS Silicon and E/D-MESFET GaAs for VLSI Processor Design," *Purdue University Technical Report*, TR-EE 85-18, December 1985.

[16] Milutinović, V., "Microprocessor Design for GaAs Technology," *Purdue University Technical Report*, TR-EE 86-22, December 1986.

[17] Helbig, W., Schellack, R., and Zieger, R., "The Design and Construction of a GaAs Technology Demonstration Microprocessor," *Proceedings of the MIDCON 85*, Chicago, Ill., September 1985, pp. 1-6.

[18] Chow, P. and Horowitz, M., "Architectural Trade-offs in the Design of MIPS-X," *Proceedings of the 14th Annual International Symposium on Computer Architecture*, Pittsburgh, Penn., June 1987.

[19] Rose, C.W., Ordy, G.M., and Drongowski, P.J., "M.mPc: A Study in University–Industry Technology Transfer," *IEEE Design & Test*, February 1982, pp. 44-56.

[20] Milutinović, V. (Editor), "GaAs Microprocessor Technology (Special Issue)," *IEEE Computer*, October 1986.